Bribery and Corruption

Bribery and Corruption

How to Be an Impeccable and
Profitable Corporate Citizen

MICHAEL J. COMER and
TIMOTHY E. STEPHENS

Routledge
Taylor & Francis Group

LONDON AND NEW YORK

First published in paperback 2024

First published 2013 by Gower Publishing

Published 2016 by Routledge
4 Park Square, Milton Park, Abingdon, Oxon OX14 4RN

and by Routledge
605 Third Avenue, New York, NY 10158

Routledge is an imprint of the Taylor & Francis Group, an informa business

Publisher's Note
The publisher has gone to great lengths to ensure the quality of this reprint but points out that some imperfections in the original copies may be apparent.

British Library Cataloguing in Publication Data
Comer, Michael J.
    Bribery and corruption : how to be an impeccable and profitable corporate citizen.
    1. Corporations – Corrupt practices – Prevention. 2. Corporation law – Criminal provisions.
    3. Corporate internal investigations.
    I. Title II. Stephens, Timothy E.
    658.4'73 – dc23

The Library of Congress has cataloged the printed edition as follows:
Comer, Michael J.
    Bribery and corruption : how to be an impeccable and profitable corporate citizen / by Michael J. Comer and Timothy E. Stephens.
        p. cm.
    Includes bibliographical references and index.
    ISBN 978-1-4094-5357-4 (hardback : alk. paper) – ISBN 978-1-4094-5358-1 (ebook)
    1. Corruption. 2. Corruption – Prevention. 3. Bribery – Prevention. I. Stephens, Timothy E.
II. Title.

    HV6768.C6496 2013
    658.4'73 – dc23

2012031299

ISBN: 978-1-4094-5357-4 (hbk)
ISBN: 978-1-03-283739-0 (pbk)
ISBN: 978-1-315-56991-8 (ebk)

DOI: 10.4324/9781315569918

Contents

List of Figures

List of Tables

'OK. Technically the orders I gave were illegal, but I expected my subordinates
were honest and would refuse to carry them out'

The royalties from this book are dedicated to 'Save the Children Fund' in memory of Tim Stephens.

Originals of the cartoons are available from http://www.mikewilliamscartoons.co.uk/

Foreword

THE HONOURABLE KENNETH MUTT KC[1] (THE DOG)

A Sad Case

For readers of Mike Comer's previous eight books – or, more accurately, the same book regorged eight times: now nine – it is with sorrow that I report that my father Spot the Dog has expired and his spirit levitated to the great kennel in the sky. If you have dodged Mr Comer's previous rants, my father's name will mean nothing to you. That is a pity, because he was a good dog, wrote brilliant forewords to Mr Comer's falderalish books and was the canine referred to by auditors when exculpating that they were watchdogs and not bloodhounds every time they failed to spot skul<u>dog</u>gery, which was pretty often. In fact, Spot was a poodle, so it is not surprising that auditors bonded with him. I am a bit of a crossbreed; part poodle (obviously) but more Rottweiler with a tad of Alsatian, husky, Dalmatian, spaniel and pit bull terrier thrown in.

Corruption is Wicked

Spot kept Mr Comer – more or less – on track and talked him out of publishing some of his more extreme views. I apologise that I don't have the same influence on the geriatric, pipe-smoking, politically scandalous ex-guru. He has got it into his head that corruption is wicked; that it is kicked off at the highest political and academic levels and that commercial bribery is a reaction. He has little confidence in the enforcement of anti-bribery laws and the fixation on overseas bribery while much worse corruption takes place under British noses but is ignored.

Cutting Out the Doggerel

On his death dog basket my father promised me the ex-guru would never again put pen to paper or, in his case, hairy fingers to a tobacco-stained keyboard and that I would be safe. But it seems that the old man has become so maddened over the Bribery Act, political, media and academic corruption that he's struggled onto his Zimmer, bought himself the latest version of Dragon NaturallySpeaking voice recognition software and is now dictating 100,000 words a day – albeit mostly incomprehensible, especially since he had his new National Health teeth fitted. So, in his favour – and there is not much of that

---

1   Kennel Club.

around – you can put any typos in this book down to his new gnashers, which are far too small and keep falling out.

Another ameliorating[2] factor on the ex-guru's bluster came from Tim Stephens, who was vaguely sensible in human terms. How on earth Mr Comer ever convinced Tim to associate his name with his is a mystery. The same is true of the long-suffering Mike Williams, whose cartoons are the highlight of the book, and Gower, which has yet again been conned into publishing something that is so far removed from good taste that it makes me think that bribes have been paid. The only counterfactual is that the ex-guru is so tight, that it is against his nature to pay for anything, even to get his books published. So, for once, I don't know.

Keeping it Short

I will keep this Foreword short. My father always told me this: 'always keep it short, Kenneth Mutt', he said and 'if you can do it in one bite, do it'. I was never exactly sure what he meant, but in doggy circles I am known for concision, lack of foreplay and premature termination. For these reasons my friends say I could have Scottish blood in me and it is true that I do have gingerish, spiky, hair, don't wear underpants and flatulate a lot, especially after meals, when I get excited, watch football or see my hero Nicholas Peter William Clegg on TV. So that is all I have to say: well except for four things.

Corruption and Bribery Are Not the Same

The first is that this book is about corruption, which is a far wider and worse wickedness than bribery. Bribery is largely a commercial phenomenon, whereas corruption is primarily the preserve of politicians, academics, the media and others ungainfully employed in a monoculture that is as keen to stop skulduggery as Dracula is to illegalise blood-sucking. This is why the new Act (of 2010) – which supposedly replaces those on corruption – is called the Bribery Act. It has been reframed to avoid dealing with the stratospheric corruption discussed in Chapter 10.

The guileful change of framing tells you all you need to know: corruption and bribery are not the same thing and by cunningly avoiding the C-word politicians and fellow travellers can carry on as before but collect lots of lovely taxes from technical infringements that are only identified as crimes after prosecutorial discretion has been exercised. This is really cunning and allows betting on the race after it has been run.

Less than voluntary penalties from companies subject to prosecutorial discretion can then be remitted to China, India, Brazil and Russia, among others, to save our planet from global warming or, now it has been shown that for the past 14 years it has been stable, to prevent climate change. No doubt when further evidence emerges that it is all a scam, we will be faced with the problem of climate stagnation or some other reframing. It doesn't matter what it's called, so long as the Milibands, Gores and Huhnes support it as a noble cause, much as they do with anti-bribery initiatives, and so long as it can be taxed.

---

2   A great word for a dog: don't you think?

Scandals to Come in the Carbon World

The ex-guru was the one of the first to recognise the corruptive nature of global warming and emissions abatement. This noble cause is awash with corruption to maximise free allocation of carbon credits and to falsify baseline emissions; and bribes to get offset projects in foreign lands, trading exchanges, OTC (over-the-counter) transactions, green investments and corporate social responsibility programmes. The only benefit is that the green initiative raises yet more taxes. But the Carbon World creates entirely new financial systems that are perfection for paying and concealing bribes. There is no such thing as Suspicious Activity Reporting (SAR) in the Carbon World and virtually no regulatory oversight. In fact it would be much easier if rules came in that compelled reporting of carbon transactions that were ***not*** suspicious. It really is that bad but no one seems to care or even think. All they say to me is 'It's global warming, innit? Saving the planet; know what I mean, John?'

The word 'innit' appears to be the justification for everything along with Human Rights, health and safety, equality, privacy or multiculturalism:[3] all noble causes that herd the UK towards the cliff's edge. True: innit?

Not All Bribery is Equal

I suggested that the title of this book should be *The Corruption of Bribery*, which everyone except Gower and the Guru's wife thought was extremely clever and insightful. It exposes the fact that the word 'bribery' has been cynically perverted in the Act to imply that it is a replacement for previous legislation on 'corruption': which it is not. The Act makes a clear distinction between bribes paid and bribes received,[4] with the former being excoriated as much wickeder than the latter and therefore justifying the Section 7 corporate, essentially strict liability offence of failing to prevent bribery. This is dreadful spinning of the truth and another corruption of the word 'bribery', because Section 7 only relates to failure to prevent bribes being paid by corporates,[5] not to extortion or bribery generically.

The Dreaded Section 7

Section 7 of the Bribery Act 2010 is the equivalent – in the world of unwanted teenage pregnancies – of holding a boy's parents absolutely, corporately liable for their son's wanton fornication while absolving the girl's mother and father of all responsibility. Bribery, like more fulfilling forms of sex, involves two or more people, but the Act is far more concerned with giving than receiving, or supply rather than demand: of active rather than passive. You should ask yourself why this is.[6]

---

3   I never voted for this: did you?

4   Although both are referred to as 'bribery'.

5   I was taught that using an adjective as a noun is bad form and akin to flatulating in church.

6   It is because it is a serious revenue earner for the Government and a less-than-transparent source of funding for the Serious Fraud Office, which pockets a third of all recoveries and penalties.

Not All Animals Are Equal

The clever corruption of language – or, even more, reframing – results in governmental organisations, whose controls are so appalling that they are magnets for incoming bribery, not being held corporately liable unless the involvement of a senior manager can be proven, but even then absolution comes to the rescue under the Crown Body exclusion. It is one rule for corporates and another for officialdom, or as Kenneth Clarke,[7] the ex-Justice Secretary, ex-Anti-bribery Champion and Hush Puppies' shuffling advert explains it, the initiative is 'business-led'. You can always tell something is utter bunkum when politicians describe it as an 'initiative'.

'Business-led' means that politicians and government departments need to do nothing except collect the cash and condemn evil corporates who pay their wages and, of course, unlimited Parliamentary expenses. Also, since government departments are not 'relevant commercial organisations' they are absolved from Section 7 corporate liability even if they **pay** bribes ... and please don't tell me that local and state government officials don't pay bribes or share them with their colluders, because they do. Have you noticed that under the old Corruption Acts, once an advantage was shown to have been given to, or received by, an official, the burden of proving that it was not corrupt shifted to the parties involved? The new Act removes this in yet another Animal Farm scam.

British politicians struggled long and hard, late into mid-mornings, sometimes at their second, third or fourth heavily subsidised and fortified homes, in the houses of other men's wives or, more likely, civil partners, in bingo halls, steam baths and at the Pink Pussy Cat Lap Dancing Club,[8] to resolve the vile threat to parliamentary privilege which if removed by the new laws would make their prosecution for corruption much more likely.

After urgent agonising over some 20 years, Parliament decided not to decide but to defer the matter for further review: you guessed it, by yet another committee. And by cleverly framing the Act as 'bribery' they hoped no one would notice.

Bribery of Luigi Foreigner

In justifying the extraterritoriality of the Act, the Ministry of Justice claims that the provisions relating to bribery of foreign public officials (FPOs) harmonises international and domestic laws. This, I'm sorry to say, is another corruption of both the word 'bribery' and the truth. Prosecution for facilitation payments made to a UK official requires proof that the payer's intention was to get the official to perform improperly, whereas for Ahmed or Luigi Foreigner, FPO, simply proving influence is enough. The obvious presumption is that British officials can be trusted with being influenced without being corrupted, while those to the east of Dover and south of Land's End can't. How bloody superior and patronising is that? And might I ask what happens when our tartan-wearing, caber-tossing colleagues gain independence and become FPOs?

Section 6 of the Bribery Act makes it an offence, punishable in the UK, to pay bribes to an FPO, yet it absolves the sneaky no-goods, who extort them, of all responsibility

---

7   I have never liked him since I heard he wears Hush Puppies and is a Europhile.

8   The significance of this club will become clear later.

because there is little chance they will be prosecuted in their home countries. If politicians really wanted to stop FPOs being corrupted they could start by extending Section 6 to the receipt of bribes: extradite FPOs to the UK and incarcerate them here or, more seriously still, force them to take on British citizenship, pay our taxes and put up with unending political and other skulduggery. What is also amazing – in most if not all of the regulatory actions by the Department of Justice (DOJ), Securities & Exchange Commission (SEC) and the Serious Fraud Office (SFO) against companies- is that the names of official and other bribe extorters are never mentioned. In the Siemens case there must have been hundreds of extorters. But who were they? Are most still in position to extort bribes from others? I suspect they are. So much for the fight against global corruption and due diligence.

Now for another thing! Payments to foreign political parties, opposition politicians or candidates are permissible under the Act. The conspicuous opportunity for evil corporates and aid agencies is, of course, to corrupt foreign politicians before they get into power. This is a really smart ploy because it encourages democratic change, which is clearly another noble cause except for those whose change is outwardly directed, have to bribe their way back in, or pass through revolving doors into meaningful employment. But the good news for them is that when they are in opposition they can be bunged without limit to help get back into power. Isn't that a neat little political circuit: jobs for the boys and democracy at its very best?

The UK Leads the Way

The UK is the only country I can find that has extraterritorial laws to punish bribe payment and receipt in the overseas private sector. This supposedly gives UK firms a competitive advantage, although I must say I fail to follow the logic. UK politicians seem fixated on the view that if UK citizens self-flagellate and suffer enough – with draconian laws over such things as emission reduction, waste recycling, plastic bags, obesity, smoking, salt, sugar, alcohol, meat, fish, mushrooms, sunbeds, Polish potatoes and other noble cause initiatives – oinks of the world will be so inspired that they will follow suit and change their loathsome ways.

The informed opinion in the canine community is that this is crass stupidity. There is no way I am cutting back on my consumption of bones unless Chinese, Indian, Korean and Russian dogs do the same. And if they unilaterally cut back, that means more bones for me. That's how things are in real life, but politicians *bent* on noble causes don't want to understand this. The UK leads the way, they say, and it, matters not that it is over a cliff.

The End Game

If British companies decide they just cannot cope with the Act and pull out of supposedly corrupt markets, the Chinese and companies from other countries which don't have draconian laws will be in there like legs up a lamp post. They will be able to charge whatever prices they like and bribe without limitation. They will also cement relationships that secure and monopolise strategic resources like oil, copper, tin and, of course, bones and cement. So, rather than help the long-suffering poor in Less Developed Countries, the Bribery Act will make things far worse, as is already the case with overseas development aid, much of which is trousered by the same kleptocrats who extort bribes and rob their citizens blind.

I sometimes say that humans are destined for extinction through a mix of stupidity, apathy and noble causes but without the excuse of dinosaurs. They, at least, were hit by a meteorite. Now that's what you call an adequate defence.

The Dangers of Perception

Preventing corruption demands paying attention to detail based on facts; not perception, anecdotes, crystal balls, phases of the moon or patterns of tea leaves in cups. Recommending silly controls that don't work just encourages box-ticking and jobsworths. Branding entire countries as corrupt is another nonsense which is self-fulfilling and much like advertising that 'Bribes'R'Us' setting an expectation that skulduggery is the norm, if not positively encouraged. I agree with Mr Comer that corruption takes place in discrete contexts and that generalisation is a bad thing. It results in guards being dropped only because a country is 'perceived' to be safe.

Unquestionably, the Act will raise lots of taxes disguised as penalties, deflect corporates' attention from the supposedly export-led financial recovery, let politicians and government agencies off the hook and create lots of non-productive jobs for civil servants, NGOs, lawyers, consultants and investigators,[9] all in pursuit of the noble cause.

The way the Act is to be enforced with 'civil disposals' and Deferred Prosecution Agreements – allowing crooks to pay their way out of trouble at a cost to honest competitors – subverts the criminal justice and economic systems. Where will it all stop? If the Yorkshire Ripper Version II were to make a self-disclosure and retain Price-Slaughterhouse-Coopers to investigate him on behalf of the police, would he be offered a 'civil disposal'?

So please do not fall for the spin that the Act will forestall or even reduce gross corruption. IT IS A STEALTH TAX on businesses and another Animal Farm initiative. That said, prevention of fraud, and incoming, outgoing, internal and competitive corruption is vital, so that economies can survive, companies flourish, and families have enough money to afford lots of juicy bones. To me, that's what corruption is all about; but for humans it could be even more important.

Finally, a humanoid that Mr Comer foolishly invited to review my Foreword asked me – with a sort of condescending smirk – 'If you are so clever how would you stop corruption?' The answer I gave was very simple: 'For a limited period, I would offer absolute immunity to every extorter who comes forward with evidence that convicts a coercer. When everything is done and dusted I would contrive a technical locution, apologise and then prosecute everyone'.

Yours aye
Kenneth Mutt KC

PS I started this Foreword with some sad news and I close in the same vein. Tim Stephens died on 7 April 2012 and will be sadly missed. He was the sensible one.

---

9   Bless!

PPS I have just realised that despite their extensive verbiage, the authors have forgotten to define two important terms. So I will try to do so.[10]

COTTAGE INDUSTRY

This term was coined by Mike Koehler, known as the 'FCPA Professor' and one of Mr Comer's heroes. In this book it refers to a collection of politicians, regulators, academics, researchers, lawyers, consultants, journalists and even investigators who make lots of money and exert excessive influence by terrifying others into believing that the anti-bribery laws are even more important than bones. A great deal of reciprocation – 'scratch my back and I'll scratch yours' – takes place within the Cottage Industry.[11] This is not to suggest that there is anything dodgy going on, merely that companies should note when dealing with the Cottage Industry that the rule is: 'Never ask a barber if you need a haircut'.

ANIMAL FARM

This term – based on George Orwell's excellent, but almost canine-free book – is used when a member of the Cottage Industry insists on someone else doing something he has no intention of doing himself. It is the equivalent of 'do as I say, not as I do' and there is a lot of it about.

A LEGAL TERM

'Civil Disposal' is a term that is frequently used in cases involving corruption. It refers to the process where allegations of corruption are resolved by acceptance by the alleged bribe payer of a Civil Recover Order – under the Proceeds of Crime Act (POCA) – rather than a prosecution through the criminal courts. UK judges have generally not been in favour of civil disposals.

A FINAL WORD AND THANKS

When the authors locked themselves away in the coal shed to write this book, no one in their right minds could have imagined it resulting in the monster it now is. To be honest, I thought the two old boys were hiding from their wives to sniff Philosan. Gower was stunned at the book's length, but found it easier to capitulate – and publish something that is bigger than my first kennel – than to argue.

Despite its length, the reader will appreciate the excellent layout: organised by Emily Ruskell and Helen Varley for Gower and the great cartoons by Mike Williams. I don't expect anyone to read the entire book, but rather pick out bits that could be useful. I can't guarantee usefulness because I have not read it. However, I plan to see the film.

---

10   E&OE.

11   It should be noted, however, that not all politicians, regulators, academics, etc., or even lawyers and investigators are in the Cottage Industry, nor is any impropriety alleged. However, 'never ask a Barber if you need a haircut'.

'I'm telling you Comer, that dog is performing services on your behalf'

'He's so pleased it's qualified as an offset project'

'Typical of the bloody Brits. Always have to make it more difficult than it is, hoping that others will follow. Which of course they don't'

1 *Noble Cause Corruption*

Introduction

This book, which is about corruption rather than just bribery, is unavoidably long, detailed and possibly disputatious because it takes an assertive, managerial – rather than a timorous legalistic – approach to both. It is based on the principle that regulators do not run businesses and is intended mainly for commercial managers who do. It contains more detail than ordinarily would be the case, to explain some of the things not emphasised by the Cottage Industry (see Foreword), but which are very important from a managerial perspective.

It is based on the principle that companies have both the right and the obligation to manage their affairs, effectively and honestly, while putting compliance in context.

The balance – if not conflict – between compliance and entrepreneurship is typically represented in Figure 1.1.

Figure 1.1   Typical Representation of the Balance between Entrepreneurship and Compliance

In fact, there is no conflict and the objectives of entrepreneurship and compliance should be fully aligned, as represented in Figure 1.2:

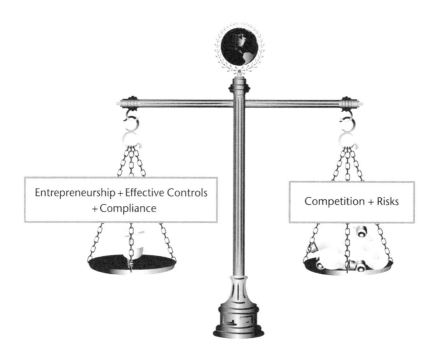

Figure 1.2   The True Relationship between Entrepreneurship and Compliance

Effective controls are not a brake on a company's performance but rather the essential equipment that empowers it to go faster and further in safety and to participate assuredly in markets perceived by others as too difficult. Effective controls provide opportunities and competitive advantages.

This book suggests more effective and realistic solutions based on four axioms:

1. **Concentrate on discrete contexts** in which corrupt decisions are taken.
2. **'Perform on principle'**, assert the right to take decisions and defend them with determination. Aim for 'Inspired Integrity' and not just compliance,
3. **'Be the first to know'** that things might be going wrong and deal with them.
4. **'Be an impeccable and profitable corporate citizen'** and a very hard target.

The emphasis is on 'profitable'. It is central to the recommendations in this book and so is creating happy working environments in which prudent trust is nurtured.

Against this background, despite all of its limitations and associated political posturing, the Bribery Act 2010[1] should be manageable for good companies. That is, providing they do not sit frozen in the headlights waiting for honest decisions to be second-guessed.

---

1   Available at: http://www.legislation.gov.uk/ukpga/2010/23/contents (accessed 7 November 2012).

Proving that intent was demonstrably innocent and decisions were honestly taken is one of the most important concepts in this book. It is the most solid and fail-safe defence to all offences under the Act and even more importantly it saves serious money.

The Importance of Frames and Framing

Communication between people involves framing. Frames embody the social, ethical and other parameters in which dialogue takes place. In 2009 Jim A. Kuypers[2] published research which concluded 'framing is a process whereby communicators, consciously or unconsciously, act to construct a point of view that encourages the facts of a given situation to be interpreted by others in a particular manner'.

The War On Terror

The attacks on the New York, Twin Towers of 11 September 2001 were initially framed as crimes against humanity. This framing was quickly replaced and the reaction classified as a 'war on terror', thereby justifying a military response.

Global Warming

The hypothetical catastrophic deterioration of the planet's climate was framed as 'global warming' until it became obvious that there has been no increase in temperatures since 1995. Then the framing had to be switched[3] to 'climate change' so that citizens would support emissions reductions measures and not question escalating energy costs.

Cash For Access

Regulators have made it clear that if a business pays to arrange a meeting with a foreign government official, it will be regarded as 'bribery'. Paying £50,000 for a dinner place with the Prime Minister at Conservative Central Office is framed as 'lobbying' and is therefore acceptable.

False framing is an essential element of both deception and politics. People tend to accept the frames presented to, or imposed upon them and this is certainly true of

---

2   Associate Professor in the Department of Communications at Virginia Tech, Blacksburg, VA.

3   This should provoke the question: 'if global warming is not the cause of climate change: what is?' If you get a sensible answer, please contact www.info@cobasco.com.

corruption and bribery. One of the most serious framing mistakes is the classification of countries based on Transparency International's Corruption Perceptions Index.[4] It leads to inaccurate risk assessment, unjustified relaxation in contexts that are unsafe and, worse still, sets up an expectation that skulduggery is inevitable.

Framing of the UK Bribery Act

The Bribery Act 2010 was framed as essential to bring the UK's 'antiquated laws' (from 1889, 1906 and 1916) up to date, to comply with pressure from the Organisation for Economic Cooperation and Development (OECD) and to show that Britain – with its stereotypical stiff upper lip – sets an example for others to follow.

Digging the Same Hole Deeper

Political and regulatory posturing over the Act is at best dubious. Both the present and current Attorney Generals confirmed that the UK has always been compliant with its OECD obligations.

The reality is:

- UK anti-corruption laws were updated by the Anti-Terrorism Crime and Security Act 2001 and were thus not 'antiquated'. These complied with the OECD Convention on the Bribery of Foreign Public Officials in International Business Transactions.[5]
- Although the UK ratified the OECD Convention it was never incorporated into its statutes, meaning that there was, and still is, no obligation to comply.

Too Close for Comfort

In fact the UK specifically opted out of Article 15 of the Council of Europe Convention on Corruption because politicians did not like the idea of legislating against trading in influence, which would have severely constrained political skulduggery.

The fact that the new laws are framed around the word 'bribery' (when all previous legislation was about corruption) shows how the undoubted evil has been narrowed to

---

4   For a discussion of Transparency International see pages 229–32; for the Corruptions Perceptions Index, see http://www.transparency.org/research/cpi/overview (accessed 6 November 2012).

5   Routinely extended and reframed to become The OECD Convention on Corruption: which it is NOT.

avoid dealing with controversies such as trading in influence, political funding, granting of honours and privileges and, of course, the old chestnut of parliamentary privilege.

Politicians Were the Laughing Stock

The way the Blair and Brown governments reacted to the British Aerospace (BAE) investigation and the release of the Lockerbie bomber (most likely in exchange for Libyan oil concessions) made the UK a laughing stock.

Most exclusions under the Bribery Act favour politicians and civil servants. This bias is referred to in this book as 'Animal Farm'.

Letting Civil Servants Off The Hook

Under the old Prevention of Corruption Act the burden fell on public officials to prove that any potentially questionable benefit they received was not corrupt. This very important tool in the fight against public corruption has disappeared from the Bribery Act.

The Blair–Brown Labour government in its last days before losing power rushed through the Bribery Act 2010 based on false framing.[6] The offences were then narrowed even further so that the corporate bribe payer is to be punished far more severely than the organisation that did nothing to prevent extortion. Yet extortion is the driving force in most cases.

Just Like Unwanted Teenage Pregnancies

In the field of unwanted teenage pregnancies, the lopsided Section 7 offence of the UK Bribery Act is like holding the boy's parents corporately and absolutely liable for their son's bunga bunga while absolving the girl's mother and father entirely.

---

6   The government had the habit of 'burying the bad news' on corruption reform. ATCSA was buried in the post 9/11 horrors and framed an an anti-terrorism measure. The Bribery Act was buried in the clamour of MPs to get back to their constituencies to fight the General Election.

The outcome is that government agencies – which are magnets for incoming corruption – are absolved from corporate liability even if their procedures are woefully inadequate and they condone or consent in bribe receipt.[7]

Another interesting point on the George Orwell[8] front is the apparent lack of interest by the Serious Fraud Office (SFO) and other agencies in using their powers under the Proceeds of Crime Act (see page 185) to expose politicians, government and business extorters whose excessive personal wealth is a good indication of bribes receipt (see page 463) or other skulduggery. This is a great opportunity missed by regulators because each extorter who is exposed could identify multiple corporate bribe payers, leading to nifty Section 7 settlements. So why don't they do it?[9]

The Nature of Corruption

Bribe payment can be concealed in the books of the coercer in thousands of ways (see pages 299–300) but extorters hold two very visible and ugly babies. The first are the perverted decisions leading to improper performance; the second are signs of excessive wealth. If the SFO were to focus on these, using its powers under Part 5 of the Proceeds of Crime Act 2008, it would quickly expose extorters and thereby coercers. The rule in fraud and corruption is to 'follow the money'.

A really positive aspect of the Bribery Act, which has escaped the attention deserved, is that it potentially[10] criminalises what is referred to in this book as 'internal corruption', in addition to the more conventional outgoing and incoming variety. The typical collusive relationship is between a coercer and an extorter, as shown in Figure 1.3.

From the coercer's position, the corruption is 'outgoing'. In return for an advantage he provides the extorter takes a perverted decision and thereby acts improperly. From the position of the organisation associated with the extorter, the corruption is 'incoming'. With 'internal corruption' (Figure 1.4), the financial or other advantage, as well as the perverted decision and improper performance, are within the same organisation.

The following hypothetical case illustrates the nature of internal corruption and the possible offences against the Bribery Act:

---

7   However, if a directing mind is an active participant the organisation could be corporately liable under Section 2. But it is unlikely ever to be corporately prosecuted.

8   Author of *Animal Farm* for ignoramuses.

9   Because they do not want to chase after extorters, especially if they are politicians or government officials.

10   Whether it will be enforced is a different matter.

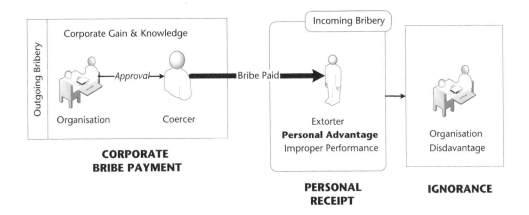

Figure 1.3   Typical Corrupt Relationship

In a typical corrupt transaction the bribe payer (or coercer) acts on behalf of an organisation, intending that it should gain. His dishonesty is usually organisationally condoned. The receiver (or extorter) is induced by a financial or other advantage to perform improperly. His dishonesty typically results in a disadvantage for the organisation he represents and is organisationally concealed.

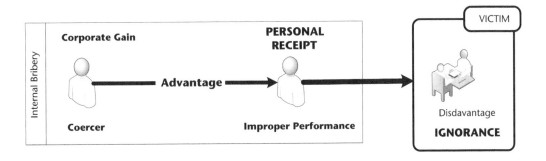

Figure 1.4   The Effect of Internal Corruption

In internal corruption one associate of an organisation offers an advantage to a decision-making or outward-facing colleague to perform improperly. This results in an innocent party (normally external but also possibly internal) being disadvantaged.

Leery Bank Inc.

Sam Slime is a Senior Vice President of Leery Bank Inc. He instructs his salesmen to mislead clients into buying shares in XYZ plc. which the bank knows are heading south and are being sold short by its investment arm. Gerald Good, one of the better salesmen, asks Sam whether doing this is ethical and Sam responds: 'If you want your bonus, get on with it and don't ask too many questions. If you sell this junk to pensioners they will be dead before they find out'. Gerald, laughs out loud and sells like there is no tomorrow.

Although it is unlikely that the skulduggery would amount to a criminal offence under the Fraud Act, there are potential breaches of the Bribery Act: Section 1 (by Sam: offering an advantage to induce Gerald's improper performance), Section 2 (by Gerald: performing improperly) and Section 7 (by the company: inadequate procedures to prevent a Section 1 offence).

Solutions to bribery[11] have been framed almost entirely in a legal context, especially the requirement to prove adequate procedures to defend a charge under Section 7 of the Act. The *legal* emphasis is on box-ticking paper trails to prove – after the event – that procedures should have been adequate to prevent bribe payment, rather than optimising *management* controls to anticipate and eliminate all forms of corruption. Figure 1.5 represents the difference:

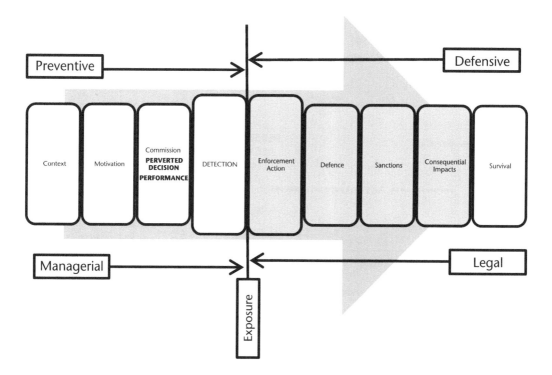

Figure 1.5   Reaction to the Bribery Act
The usual legal approach to the Bribery Act starts with the assumption that controls have failed and aims at constructing a defence of adequate procedures: it is essentially backward-looking. Managerial solutions should be inspirational and persuasive, preventative and forward-looking. There is a big difference.

---

11   But not corruption.

Companies should plan for 'Inspired Integrity' involving controls that maximise profitability by eliminating or reducing fraud and incoming, internal, outgoing and competitive corruption. This is achieved through management and psychological tools rather than only through legal diktats and box-ticking, as discussed in Chapters 23–33.

The Blind Leading the Sighted

Compliance is a demeaning word, implying that someone has to be led by the nose by another who believes he knows better into doing something he would otherwise not do. It makes the false assumption that those doing the leading know more than those being led.

Putting Politicians in Charge

It is difficult to identify a single example of politicians having been put in charge of a commercially inclined project that has not failed through rampant fraud, corruption and abuse. Examples include the administration of the European Union (EU), the United Nations (UN) – including such projects as Oil for Food or the United Nations Framework Convention on Climate Change (UNFCCC) – and overseas development aid.

Few political leaders, regulators and commentators have ever had to manage a Balance Sheet and, as a consequence, they misunderstand the nature of business. Please consider how many of the immediate past Labour Government or the current coalition has ever held down a job in the real world. How many have ever had to confront extortion by a foreign public official (FPO) or try and sell into a market where bribes are demanded? It is no different from Trappist monks advising on better orgasms: it is all theoretical and up in the air.

About This Book

OBJECTIVES

The recommendations made in this book should help companies:

- Maximise their profitability and entrepreneurial flexibility while surpassing compliance standards through a campaign of inspired integrity;
- Maintain effective controls, based on more accurate risk evaluation, empowering them to operate safely in high-risk contexts and thereby gain a competitive advantage;

- Prevent and recover losses and minimise regulatory exposures from outgoing, incoming, internal and competitive corruption;
- Enjoy life and be happy.[12]

The word 'compliance' is used sparingly throughout. It is replaced by 'integrity' and 'assurance': two alternatives that reflect the principle that most managers do not need to be led, treated like idiots or coerced into submission. Similarly, the word 'corruption' is used to frame real-world problems, while the word 'bribery' is used to refer to the much narrower political and regulatory focus. Watch how often politicians use the two words interchangeably. They are not the same, as Kenneth Mutt explained in the Foreword, but are confused to allow the laws to be expansively interpreted.

A Convention That Doesn't Exist

At a conference in the spring of 2012 the author asked delegates who were aware of the 'OECD Convention on Corruption' to put up their hands and virtually all did. It was a trick question, because there is no such thing. The OECD Convention is on the 'Prevention of Bribery of Foreign Public Officials in International Business Transactions', which is a much narrower frame. Yet people repeatedly run ahead of a noble cause and expansively interpret.

This book frames controls as they should be, positively.

STRUCTURE OF THE BOOK

Chapters 2–4 attempt to set out the background to the Act and what it means in working terms. It is based on a chronological forensic linguistic analysis – indexing and lemmatising – of around two million words in the Act itself, official and other guidance, Law Commission and Joint Parliamentary reports, speeches by the SFO, Ministry of Justice and others.[13]

Chapters 10–13 analyse the taxonomy of corruption in mature and developing economies. Recommendations in Chapters 21–37 are intended to help companies deal with incoming, outgoing and competitive corruption, based on what happens in the real world rather than on political dogma, academic perceptions or reframing of corruption as bribery to suit the narrow political agenda of throwing the entire burden on businesses.

Most chapters include a number of principles, surrounded by practitioner level detail. For convenience, the masculine pronouns 'he', 'him' and 'his' have been used throughout. Hopefully this will not shock too many people, but if it does an electronic version can be made available so that those offended by such things can globally replace politically horrifying pronouns with alternatives that give them more pleasure.

---

12   Not words normally associated with compliance, but a valid objective and achievable (see Chapter 23).

13   A CD containing this analysis is available from www.info@cobasco.com.

Misconceptions

AN EARLY POINT

The book discusses – and gives examples of – many contexts where politicians and regulators have misunderstood the taxonomy of corruption and the consequences of their doing so. There is one that is so fundamental that it should be mentioned at an early stage, to set the frame. It is the fixation on bribery by companies from developed countries in foreign lands.

This problem has been hyperbolised as rapacious companies from developed nations exploiting innocent – if not near-saintly – indigens and has been overstated well beyond its importance. This results in risks that are much closer to home being ignored, box-ticking on due diligence based on perceived country risks, unwarranted stigmatisation and genuine commercial opportunities being disregarded.

Political Skills

One of the greatest political skills is to be able to claim credit for a noble cause while making sure someone else has to do the work. This is one reason why foreign corruption is a British political priority and why Kenneth Clarke was the Anti-bribery champion, but only for overseas.

Repeatedly in the corruption field, politicians and regulators endorse generalisations, stereotypes, not to mention red flags, that on one hand oversimplify the problem and on the other allow sweeping conclusions to be drawn over controls that are supposedly effective, but which are mostly cosmetic. The outcome is that country or sectorial risks, culture and tone from the top are all officially promoted as determinative, which they are not. Corruption appears in specific contexts: one size does not fit all and it takes place right under our noses What's more, the division between public and private sector corruption is meaningless and the greatest risks arise when their interests collide.

NOT JUST LESS DEVELOPED COUNTRIES

Corruption is not confined to those Less Developed Countries (LDCs) that are perceived to be the most crooked; and there are no such things as 'demand-side' or 'supply-side' countries, nor is there active and passive bribery. The reality is that every country is both the victim and perpetrator of corruption and extorters and coercers are equally at fault.

It is highly unlikely that corruption in the UK, France, the USA, Italy and the EU is any less than in countries such as Nigeria, Indonesia or Mexico. It is just different.

Is the UK a Supply-side Country?

The UK is classified by Transparency International (see pages 2–9 and 58–9) and its followers as a supply-side country. But the fact is that, like all other countries, it is both demand and supply. The misclassification results in extortion of British politicians, academics, and businessmen dropping off the regulatory radar.

Political and Official Corruption

Entrepreneurial leaders in LDCs generally want their cash immediately or even up front, whereas their more sophisticated brethren delay collecting their rewards until they revolve out. It is the difference between President Mubarak and Prime Minister Blair or Al Gore.

The higher the level politicians can reach and the longer they can stay in power, the more marketable they become in the afterlife. For some, preparation means grabbing and retaining power at all costs, forming alliances and taking decisions with longer-term personal objectives in mind. It is difficult to see any significant difference between the more blatant shenanigans by leaders in LDCs and the subtlety in developed nations. Both pervert the governmental process and enrich politicians. The only real difference is in timing.

Similarly, an official's importance in service as well as his revolving door marketability depends on how significant his portfolio is perceived to be. The more dramatic and important he can make it, the more funding is allocated and the more attractive he becomes when he passes through the revolving door. These are powerful incentives for politicians and officials to empire-build and – as Ali G would say – to 'big it up' and to build relationships that can be rewarded later.[14]

Some, if not many, readers will dispute the suggestion of equality of corruption levels in developed countries and LDCs and this is understandable because it conflicts with accepted framing. But the suggestion may prompt fresh thinking and the conclusion that:

- Corruption in LDCs is principally internal (Figure 1.6) and is one of a number of other much more serious evils.

---

14   In fairness, it must be said that there are also many (maybe even the majority) of officials and regulators who behave impeccably and to whom the above comments do not apply.

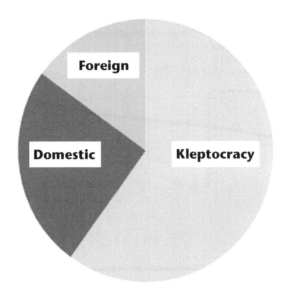

Figure 1.6   Putting Supply-side Corruption into Context[15]
The most devastating problem in LDCs is not corruption by companies from developed nations. The risks discussed on pages 247 et seq are far more withering, but are not dealt with because they cannot be 'punished' by a stealth tax on businesses.

- If companies from developed countries were to withdraw from markets perceived to be corrupt the floodgates would open for even more skulduggery; corrupt local companies, as well as those from countries that don't give a hoot about ethics, would have a free run.
- Corruption is a minor contributor to financial and social devastation in LDCs. It vaporises into insignificance against the evils of overpopulation, kleptocracy, looting, expropriation, rent-seeking, civil wars, tribal and religious conflict, natural disasters, ethnic cleansing, electoral fraud, extortion and theft of foreign aid. Of course, none of these can be blamed on rapacious Western companies and thus fall off the regulatory radar.
- Corruption in developed economies as just as bad; just more subtle.

Figure 1.7 represents the position suggested. A senior marketing manager commented on the difference between LDC and the UK as follows:

In some countries you may succeed with a few transactions by being – let's say – flexible. In the UK it is almost impossible to break into the closed shop because relationships are permanent. What with cronyism, patronage, freemasonry, old boy's networks, revolving doors, referral fees, political influence and whatever we have no chance. If you are not part of the 'in crowd', you are in the 'out crowd'. In most cases, now, we don't even bother bidding for business with UK government or large companies and the EU is even worse.

---

15   Based on the authors' best guess but with 40 years of experience!

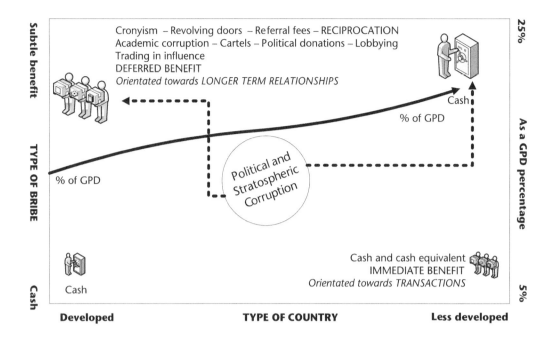

Figure 1.7   Corruption in Developed and Less Developed Countries

Figure 1.7 suggests that losses from corruption (and the difficulty for honest companies to break into a market) is not significantly different between developed and less developed countries, except for the way that bribes are paid and their timing. In developed countries bribes tend to pervert *relationships* and *transactions* in those that are less developed.

A number of political leaders in LDCs support this view.

The International Dimension of African Struggles Against Corruption

This excellent publication by John Mukum Mbaku[16] states: 'the internal causes of poverty in the African continent, which significantly outweigh external ones, include excessive state control of the economy, massive and pervasive corruption, merciless exploitation of the peasantry and ethical violence verging on genocide'. He adds that total incompetence of 'political leaders who are ill-equipped to manage modern and complex economies' is also a significant contributing factor.

---

16   Mbaku, J.M. 2010, The International Dimension of Africa's Struggle Against Corruption. Asper Review of International Business and Trade Law, 35 (available online at LexisNexis). John Mukum Mbaku is Willard L. Eccles Professor of Economics and John S. Hinckley Fellow at Weber State University, Ogden, UT, and former (1986–2007) Associate Editor (Africa), *Journal of Third World Studies*. He received his PhD in economics from the University of Georgia in 1985.

Africa's Bane: Tax Havens, Capital Flight and The Corruption Interface[17]

This brilliant 2009 report by John Christensen, for Real Insituto Elcano, continues in a similar vein: 'it is disturbing, to put it mildly, that the prevailing corruption discourse remains largely focused on pointing fingers at petty officials and ruling kleptomaniacs':

> Regrettably, Transparency International, despite its commendable role in putting corruption on the political agenda, has undermined the efforts of reformers through its publication of the Corruption Perception Index, which reinforces stereotypical perceptions about the geography of corruption…. A more critical examination of the index reveals that over half of the countries identified by the CPI in 2007 as 'least corrupt' are tax havens, including major centres such as Singapore, The Netherlands, Switzerland, the UK Luxembourg and Hong Kong.

CORRUPTION IS A COMPLEX WEB

Corruption is a complex web involving primarily:

- International politicians and organisations such as the UN, the EU, the World Bank and its correspondents;
- National politicians in developed and LDCs;
- Civil servants;
- Non-governmental organisations and charities;
- Academics and research establishments;
- Businesses.

Each group has its own agenda and, within specific contexts, may be an extorter or a coercer. Table 1.1 is the authors' best guess[18] of the relative seriousness of the web of *corruption* on the baseline of 100 for *bribery* by companies from developed countries into foreign markets.

---

17   Available online at: http://www.realinstitutoelcano.org/wps/portal/rielcano_eng/Content?WCM_GLOBAL_CONTEXT=/Elcano_in/Zonas_in/Sub-Saharan+Africa/DT1-2009 (accessed 14 October 2012).

18   Abridged to fit into one table.

Table 1.1   Best Guess of the Web of International Corruption

COERCERS Bribe Payers ↓↓↓↓↓↓	International organisations	Politicians developed countries	Politicians LDC	Officials in developed countries	Officials in LDCs	NGOs and charities	Academic and research	Businesses in developed countries	Businesses in LDCs
International organisations, etc.		80	100	80	100	80	120	50	100
Politicians in developed countries	80	80	120	120	120	100	120	50	50
Politicians in LDCs	120	80	120	50	150	150	100	100	150
Officials in developed countries		**50**	**60**	**80**	**100**	**100**	**120**	**100**	**100**
Officials in LDCs	60	80	100	100	150	120	100	200	200
NGOs and charities	80	80	120	80	120		100		
Academics and research	80	100	100	120	120	100	150	80	80
Businesses in developed countries →	80	**150**	**100§**	120	**100§**	**50**	100	120	**100§**
Businesses in LDCs	100	80	200	100	300	20	50	200	300

(The leftmost table axis is labelled **COERCERS**, and the top axis is labelled **EXTORTERS**.)

Table 1.1 is based on over 40 years' experience of working inside government agencies and companies in developed countries and LDCs, but is not proposed other than as a best guess. It highlights the complex web,[19] suggesting that corruption in LDCs is largely indigenous. It also suggests that for some companies, corruption in their home markets is no better than overseas. Finally, it indicates that government officials are the most prevalent extorters, both in developed countries and LDCs.

CULTURE AND TONE FROM THE TOP

There should be no serious dispute that different historical, cultural, ethical and other factors are influential (though far from determinative) in the levels of corruption in a country, region or, more accurately, a context, but it is quite wrong to attach – as Transparency International does – supposedly precise indices to them.[20]

---

19   And the over-simplification of demand and supply sides or active and passive bribery.

20   As is the case with Transparency International's Corruption Perceptions Index (see Note 3).

Different Ethical Standards

Countries in some Gulf states take a more relaxed position to commissions and conflicts of interest than in the West. They are also usually against investigations, litigation and prosecution. That is their tradition and who are we to say it is wrong? The problem crystallises when Western companies open businesses there, because cultures conflict and must be reconciled internally – and in specific contexts – to ensure that controls are maintained.[21]

Stereotyping is also unfair and probably self-fulfilling, because expectations may be created that corruption is the norm.

Bribes'R'Us

Some countries might consider putting a positive spin on the Corruption Perceptions Index by advertising that 'Bribes'R'Us' because that is what the index implies.

Corruption usually takes place at a personal, secret level and is negotiated through a one-to-one dialogue, often initiated by the extorter or endemic in the specific context concerned.

Examples of Extortion and Innocent Indigens

As soon as an expat manager arrived to take up a position in a foreign country, the priority of local subordinates was to, as they laughed, 'bed him in'. This meant compromising him sexually, financially or otherwise, so that he was malleable. So much for corruption being an evil imported into LDCs!

In developed countries blatant extortion is accepted as the norm. For example, what is the difference between the London Underground drivers threatening to go on strike – for contrived reasons – during the Olympics (unless they are paid a bonus) and a corrupt FPO extorting a bribe? Extortion is also a factor in many Employment Tribunal cases, based on concocted allegations of racial or other discrimination. In developed countries extortion is decriminalised, if not the norm, and what's more, we accept it.

---

21   Chapter 23 makes suggestions on this point.

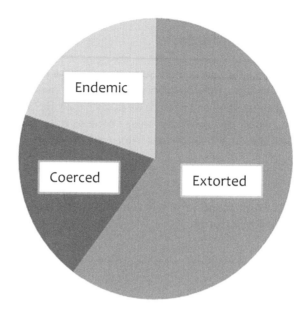

Figure 1.8   Initiation of Corrupt Relationships

Figure 1.8 represents the authors' best guess and suggests that extortion is the most important driver of corruption.

The examples confirm that extortion is the driving force in most perverted decisions, but there are subtle differences between the way the wickedness appears in developed countries and LDCs. In the latter, extortion seems to be more individualistic: such as the bent customs officer wanting cash for himself to remove an obstacle he has contrived to detain a cargo. In fact, as explained in Chapter 31, this is seldom the case but it is essentially institutional, possibly backed by organised crime, but covert. In developed countries the extortion is more often overt and justified by a 'Dodgy Dossier'[22] or some other plausible justification. It is organisational, with payment being made to a collective.

It is also usual[23] that in cases of *gross bribery*, the extorter's share of the spoils in LDCs is proportionately higher and in the case of kleptocratic politicians may be 80–95 per cent of the loss–gain in the transaction concerned. In developed countries the extorter's share tends to be proportionately less and is typically in the range of 5 per cent to 15 per cent.

In any event, corruption is context-dependent rather than nationally dependent. At the specific point of collusion, cultural, traditional and other factors do not enter into the equation, although one of two conditions may apply. The first is deep personal integrity, inner values and principles. Because of these values, corruption is rejected by one or both parties. It is the perfect solution and occurs far more often than regulators might imagine. However, honesty cannot be taken for granted and is situational: meaning it depends on the context.

---

22   More about these on page 244.

23   In the authors' experience of working inside and outside overseas revenue and other agencies.

> ## Values and Principles
>
> These mean that honest behaviour is assured even when no one is looking,[24] or where there is no chance of exposure. It is the difference between stroking Granny's cat when she is watching and kicking its ass when her back is turned.

The second condition is where a person refuses to participate in a corrupt transaction, usually because he:

- Does not trust the potential collaborator: possibly because he fears he is walking into a trap;[25]
- Wants a larger share of the benefits;
- Fears the dishonesty will be exposed.

Experience suggests that fraudsters and corrupters – at the point of colluding – are not normally deterred by thoughts of punishment.[26] There is virtually no deterrent for extorters or their associated organisations (usually government agencies) whose controls are so poor and managers so disconnected that corruption is encouraged. But again, it is all about context.

Things That Are KNOWN about Corruption

NO ONE REALLY KNOWS

No one knows how bad corruption is today; although the authors' best guess is that in the UK and equivalent economies it costs at least 10 per cent of Gross National Product (GNP), primarily through procurement overcharged or dishonestly diverted in pursuit of a noble cause.

Some things are known about corruption with reasonable certainty:

- The majority of corruption cases are not reported and are therefore excluded from official statistics.
- It is not the large spectacular cases that are the problem, but rather the relentless erosion of profits and integrity on a daily basis.
- There is no correlation between the size of an improper advantage given and the resulting profit and loss. Small bribes may result in massive losses and vice versa.

---

24   Known as the 'Hawthorne bias'.

25   This is one reason why pretext and undercover investigations (see Chapter 9) are important.

26   However, fear of detection should be emphasised and is one reason why audit and similar programmes should be given a high profile (see Chapter 18 et seq).

- Corruption is most often originated by extorters. They are honeypots to multiple coercers.[27]
- The most persistent and costly extorters are politicians and officials.
- Some companies are much more submissive in the face of extortion than others and are equally as corrupt in their home markets as they are overseas: for this reason the mandatory and permanent debarment of offenders should be enforced; subject only to the precondition that the extorter is also brought to justice.[28] Offenders should not be able to buy their way out of trouble.
- Gross corruption is normally associated with a noble cause, with skulduggery extending from top to bottom.
- For every corrupt gain there is an equal loss: for every winner there is a loser and for every coercer an extorter. To this extent corruption is a zero sum game.
- In every case of corruption there is a perverted decision.
- Perverted decisions result from misunderstanding, error, fraud or corruption: best guessed as shown in Figure 1.9.

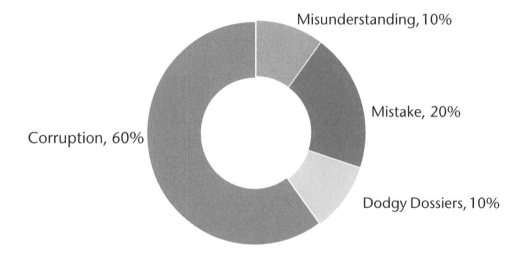

Figure 1.9   Causes of Perverted Decisions

Figure 1.9 suggests that the main cause of perverted decisions (that result in obscene profits or exceptional losses) is corruption and that around 10 per cent of cases are supported by a dodgy dossier, which may itself have been improperly influenced or financed.

- The more bureaucratic a decision-making process is, the more likely it is to be attacked by corruption: thus excessive bureaucracy incites collusion.
- Perverted decisions in sophisticated contexts are usually supported by supposedly convincing evidence; such as dodgy dossiers on a noble cause.

---

27   This is another reason why more attention should be paid to supply-side countries.

28   This approach would be a powerful deterrent and a powerful incentive for the SFO to ensure that extorters were prosecuted.

Given the above, it is possible to get a fair idea of the scale of corruption in developed countries from:

- Exceptional losses;
- Obscene profits;
- Pursuit of a noble cause.

In LDCs, also, exceptional losses and obscene profits are also a common indicator of corruption and are often further reinforced by displays of excessive personal wealth by political and governmental leaders. Leaders in developed countries are usually more careful.[29]

SOURCES OF ADDITIONAL AND RELIABLE INFORMATION

Reports by Transparency International, the US Department of Justice (DOJ) and the Securities and Exchange Commission (SEC) are useful background but they are limited because they only relate to overseas bribery of FPOs. There are no consolidated references on corruption in the private sector.

However, one of the most reliable and extensive sources of corporate skulduggery[30] in developed economies is the Tax Payers Against Fraud (TAF) website[31] which collates all DOJ sanctions under the Fair Claims Act (FCA). This Act is meant to deter and punish overcharging on US Government procurement contracts and has been very successful, mainly because it pays whistle-blowers (called 'relators') an average of 17 per cent of all recoveries made and penalties paid. The largest single reward – paid to an individual and his lawyers – is believed to be in excess of $100 million![32] Unsurprisingly such bounties have prompted law firms to pursue claims on contingency fees, thereby making the FCA probably the most powerfully enforced anti-fraud law in the world. Its limitation is that it applies only to skulduggery against the US Federal Government by public companies.

Another very important source of information is the Federal Contractor Misconduct Database,[33] which sets out massive procurement overcharging, again by federal contractors.

EXCEPTIONAL LOSSES IN THE USA

The TAF website sets out details of hundreds of cases over the past years and in 2011 alone 105 separate enforcement actions were concluded, including the blue-chip companies named in Table 1.2.

---

29   Although few can resist spiffy shoes (see page 426, footnote 20).

30   But not referenced by corruption academics.

31   See http://www.taf.org (accessed 6 November 2012).

32   So much for whistle-blowers having a hard time.

33   See POGO (Project on Government Oversight; available at: http://www.contractormisconduct.org/ (accessed 14 October 2012)).

Table 1.2   FCA Penalties in 2011. These are all leading companies!!

No.	Company	Penalty US$	Nature of Fraud
1	GlaxoSmithKline	600,000,000	Adulterated drugs: quality
2	Abbot Laboratories Inc.	421,000,000	Price inflation
4	Quest Diagnostics	241,000,00	Price inflation
9	Verizon Communications	93,525,411	Overcharge on voice and data services
11	Fresnius Medical Care	82,600,000	Fraudulent overbilling
14	AstraZeneca Pharmaceuticals	68,500,000	Off-label marketing
15	Sandoz Inc.	66,000,000	Over charges to Medicaid
17	Accenture LLP	63,675,000	Overcharging on IT contracts
21	Oracle America Inc.	46,000,000	Violations of the Anti-kickback Act on referral fees
24	GlaxoSmithKline	40,750,000	Failure to comply with manufacturing guidelines
30	Blue Cross Blue Shield (Illinois)	25,000,000	Fraudulently accounted for Medicaid programmes
36	BP Amoco (ex-Amoco)	20,500,000	And the payment of royalties on gas extractions
42	Hewlett Packard Corp.	16,250,000	Violated competitive bidding rules
54	Securitas GmbH	9,100,000	Charged for guarding hours not worked
57	Fed Ex	8,000,000	Misused security delay codes
74	Flour Hanford Inc.	4,000,000	False claims and kickbacks (radioactive waste)
91	Shell Oil Company	2,200,000	Underpaid royalties on natural gas extractions

Almost all of the pharmaceutical cases related to overcharging Medicare and Medicaid.[34]

By March 2012 there was a further $9 billion worth of claims in the pipeline, including one of $70 million against New York City for overcharging the US Federal Government; an $830 million claim against Allied Home Mortgage Capital Corporation in relation to false insurance claims and defaulting home loans; $1 billion against Bank of America; and another of $2 million against Oracle for alleged price-gauging.

The five largest claims over the past few years are shown in Table 1.3.

---

34   Medicare is a national social insurance programme, federally administered, that guarantees access to health insurance for citizens over 65 years of age and to younger people with disabilities. The budget for Medicare was reported at $523 billion in 2010. Medicaid is a means-tested programme for low-income families and is jointly funded by federal and state authorities.

Table 1.3   Top Five Claims Under Fair Claims Act

No.	Company	Penalty US$	Nature of Fraud
1	Pfizer	2,300,000,000	Off-label marketing
2	Tenet Healthcare	900,000,000	Kickbacks and overcharging
3	The Healthcare Company	731,400,000	Unlawful billing practices
4	Merck	650,000,000	Kickbacks and pricing
5	The Healthcare Company	631,000,000	False claims to Medicare

There are some important points to note about all of the above cases:

- The companies are regarded as ethical, with impressive business integrity policies, heavyweight compliance and legal departments: most were regulated by the SEC.
- The number of repeat offenders suggests that lessons are not quickly learned and that dishonesty is deeply ingrained.
- Every case involved collusion and internal corruption.
- The companies were clearly willing to defraud the federal government in one of the most regulated economies in the world.

The above raises two questions. The first is to ask what the offenders might do in commercial markets that are not so well regulated. The second is why none of the employees in the government organisations who were involved in or condoned fraud or who were negligent were as far as is known not prosecuted.

EXCEPTIONAL LOSSES IN DEVELOPED COUNTRIES

Procurement overcharging

The UK has no similar process to the US False Claims Act. The Metropolitan Police apparently keep a central record of 'official corruption', although it should be noted that in the past ten years there has[35] not been one prosecution of a civil servant for corruption. This is incredible given the following background of overcharging:

- A report by the National Audit Office estimated waste in the Civil Service between 2009 and 2011 at £31 billion.
- Fifteen of the largest Ministry of Defence contracts are currently £6.1 billion over budget.
- The massively expensive IT system for the National Health Service (around £12 billion) was abandoned as a failure.[36]
- The starting budget for the Scottish Parliament building was estimated at between £10 and £40 million. The final cost exceeded £440 million.

---

35   Apparently.

36   Although the consultants are still being paid.

- A new passport system, estimated at £80 million, was finally delivered at a cost of £365 million.
- The National Health Service, which has a budget of £100 billion (around a third of Medicare), has detected comparatively few cases of large-scale corruption.
- There are an estimated 700 projects under the Private Finance Initiative (PFI) worth £60 billion, but they have liabilities of £130 billion.[37] Under PFI there are examples of hospitals being charged £150 to fit a light bulb and £3,500 for a basic laptop computer.
- The Department of Work and Pensions outsourced £180 million worth of contracts, which were intended to get people back to work, to a private company, A4e (Action for Employment). In March 2012 A4e came under investigation[38] for serious fraud and overcharging.

It is, of course, possible that some or all of these cases can be attributed to misunderstanding or negligence although corruption is the most likely explanation. It is hard to believe that innocent people could be that careless or so stupid.

Media, Police and Political Corruption

Operations Elveden and Weeting – the so-called 'Hackingate' investigation by the Metropolitan Police – have exposed a viper's nest of collusion in the UK between the media, politicians and police that would put even the most corrupt nation to shame. The cases are classic examples of stratospheric corruption and the corroding effects of reciprocity.

Table 1.4   Examples of Potential Reciprocation

		Advantages Taken by		
		Media	**Police**	**Politicians**
Given By	**Media**	**Key Drivers** Competitive pressures for scoop stories and circulation figures	Cash Personal and corporate publicity	Donations Positive corporate and personal publicity Voter influence
	Police	Inside information Access	**Key Drivers** Crime statistics Disciplinary investigations Public relations	Political endorsement Voter influence
	Politicians	Inside information PR and other contracts Revolving door appointments Honours	Budgets Appointments Honours	**Key Drivers** Grabbing and retaining power Public relations

Table 1.4 suggests the key drivers of reciprocity in the contexts concerned. An interesting side note is that many participants generally considered themselves above the law.

---

37   Suggesting gross price inflation: albeit in the noble cause of keeping the debt off the Government's Balance Sheet.

38   The director paid herself an annual dividend of £8.5 million.

Reciprocation, nepotism, fraternalism and their like are common characteristics of corruption in developed countries and range from informal links through to established cartels. They destroy fair competition and are difficult to expose.

Other Dodgy Dealing

Comparatively few cases of entirely private-sector corruption are prosecuted in either developed countries or LDCs, although a significant number are settled through the civil courts. A number of these are discussed on pages 182 and 802.

Formula One

In January 1997 Bernie Ecclestone, the head of Formula One, generously donated £1 million to Mr Blair's New Labour Party, but this was not disclosed at the time. In May 1997 the Labour Government came into power and announced that it would ban tobacco advertising at all sporting events. A few weeks later Labour fundraisers entered into secret talks with Mr Ecclestone and in October 1997 there was a personal meeting between him and Prime Minister Blair.

On 5 November 1997, the government announced it had exempted Formula One from the tobacco advertising ban. The shenanigans that followed are too numerous to describe here, although in November 1997 the Labour Party returned £1 million to Mr Ecclestone and the tobacco ban was enforced.

***

In 2001–2002 a 75 per cent interest in Formula One Racing was bought by the German company EM TV. Subsequently, as a result of bankruptcies and other manoeuvres, the interest was acquired by Bayern LB, JP Morgan and Lehman Brothers at a cost of $1.6 billion. The investment was subsequently written down to a book value of $650 million.

In 2006, with Mr Ecclestone's help, the banks' interest was sold to CVC Capital Partner's Fund for $1.2 billion, ostensibly showing a profit over book value of $328 million and a loss of $400 million on acquisition costs. Then out of the blue, Gerhard Gribkowsky, Bayern's Risk Manager, was arrested by the German police for allegedly receiving a $44 million bribe from Mr Ecclestone as a reward for undervaluing the bank's interest.

Mr Ecclestone was called to give evidence in a German civil action and admitted giving Mr Gribkowsky the $44 million, but claimed he had done so only to suppress false allegations – involving the Ecclestone family trust – the German had threatened to make about him to HM Revenue and Customs.

There is no information in the public domain that throws further light on where the $44 million came from or how it was paid. However, the case illustrates the point made on page 318 of the possibility that bribes may be funded from a wealthy owner's personal funds.

Political Funding (More of)

Political funding is probably the most corrupting force in developed countries. It perverts society from top to bottom.

French Scandals

It is alleged that Colonel Gaddafi gave Nicholas Sarkozy £42 million to fund his 2007 election campaign. Enquiries are continuing, as they are into the affairs of Dominic Strauss Kahn (DSK), the ex-Managing Director of the International Monetary Fund, one of the most powerful politicians in the world and a candidate for the French presidency. DSK (as well as the head of police and government officials) is said to have repeatedly participated in bacchanals where prostitutes were provided free of charge by a French construction group. DSK said he had not realised they were prostitutes because everyone had been naked at the time.

Another noteworthy thing about political corruption is the persistence of some to wilfully circumvent the rules. When outright donations were tightened up, the way round was to mis-describe contributions as loans. When this ruse was censured, donations continued but were reclassified as contributions to the 'Private Office of Mr X'.

Kleptocrats versus Greedy Bankers

The total plundered by kleptocrats[39] in LDCs – estimated to be around $450 billion over the past 40 years – pales into insignificance against the $11.9 trillion lost in the 2006–2010 banking crisis. Although the catastrophe has been attributed to incompetence, the real cause is more likely to have been fraud, internal and external corruption. This possibility was never comprehensively investigated and the scandal was simply explained as 'greedy bankers'. The fact is that many were crooks and that they escaped unpunished. In the stratosphere some people are too important to touch and some companies too big to fail.

---

39   Ranging from President Marcus through to Colonel Gaddafi.

Internal Corruption and External Scams

Many other cases have come to light showing the level of corruption within supposedly reputable organisations. Payment Protection Insurance (PPI)[40] was a massive scam that cost the poorest in society many millions of pounds and largely succeeded because of internal collusion between senior managers and sales forces which were coerced into selling policies they knew to be worthless. The Lloyds Banking Group initially put aside £3.2 billion to cover PPI claims and then, in November 2012, a further £1 billion.

Other cases of internal corruption involved bankers urging customers to buy investment products such as subprime mortgage derivatives which they knew were worthless. Not only that, but bankers simultaneously short-sold the derivatives in their own portfolios.

European Union And United Nations Scams

International government agencies such as the UN and the EU, supposedly sophisticated representatives of developed societies, are riddled with inefficiency fraud and corruption. The evidence comes from such failings as the Oil-for-Food programme, the Reconstruction of Iraq and Afghanistan, and overseas development aid programmes. They also show a remarkable unwillingness by international officials to confront corruption when it takes place under their own noses.

European Union Skulduggery

A report titled 'Fight against Fraud'[41] stated that irregular payments and fraud in the EU amounted to €1.3 billion a year and that 20 per cent of revenues were 'siphoned off by corrupt officials'.

Cash for Amendments

In 2011, four Members of the European Parliament were found to have taken cash to ensure that laws that that could disadvantage their sponsors were not enacted as intended. Parliamentary President Jerzy Buzek was unwilling to have the case investigated for suspected bribery stating: 'I cannot allow OLAF[42] to enter into MEPs' offices and I urge the agency to fully respect the immunity of members...'.

---

40   Sold to protect borrowers against the risks of unemployment. More than 80 per cent of claims were rejected mainly for technical reasons, making the policies worthless from the outset.

41   See the Europa website, available at: http://europa.eu/pol/fraud/index_en.htm (accessed 14 October 2012).

42   Office de Lutte Anti-Fraude – the EU's anti-fraud 'force'.

Over the years – stretching back to the days when Neil Kinnock was important – the EU has had an appalling record of dealing with whistle-blowers, although this has not prevented its leaders and officials pronouncing on the imperative for effective controls in companies. Such attitudes are referred to throughout this book as 'Animal Farm', meaning there is one standard for politicians and officials and another for businesses. There are far too many examples of this.

Obscene Profits

Obscene profits – by a commercial sector, company, or project – are another indicator of corruption in both developed countries and LDCs. The sectors normally singled out for comment (some unjustifiably) include:

- Aerospace and defence
- Alcohol
- Banking and financial services
- Computer hardware and software
- Construction
- Consultancy
- Drugs and biotechnology
- Health care
- Hedge funds
- Insurance
- Media
- Mining and Minerals
- Oil and gas
- Professional services
- Retail stores
- Telecommunications
- Tobacco
- Utilities.

Sectorial targeting is usually a meaningless generalisation because corruption takes place in specific contexts. There are contexts in what are regarded as ethical sectors where corruption is rampant, including religion and academia.

Specific, contextual indicators are much more significant, including:

- Disproportionate profits to those of competitors or to similar internal operations;[43]
- Windfall profits on a specific project or transaction;
- Massive increases on year-to-year results;
- Ability to operate in a market closed to others;
- Consistently achieving or outperforming key performance targets.

---

43   For example, one subsidiary or affiliate of a company outperforms its peers.

All of these outliers can be detected by the Critical Point Auditing (CPA) techniques discussed in Chapters 18–20.

Noble Cause Corruption

Among the most relentless drivers of fraud and corruption, especially in developed countries, are supposed noble causes, including:

- Corporate Social Responsibility programmes and environmental programmes;
- Deregulation and privatization;
- Equality;
- Foreign aid;
- Global warming;
- Health and safety;
- Human rights;
- Immigration and multiculturalism;
- Job creation;
- National Health Service;
- Private Finance Initiative;
- Welfare.

The characteristic of a noble cause is that it is framed as overwhelmingly for the public good: like saving humanity from the effects of global warming or making sure a golfer does not get his toes trapped in a hole on a putting green.[44] A noble cause seizes the moral high ground, discourages dissent and is often driven by a messianic zeal bordering on the maniacal. Most end up enriching bankers, hedge funds, other speculators or tax collectors and few serve any useful purpose.

There are many ways that companies can become involved in a noble cause: as winners, losers, unavoidable participants, observers or opponents. They can be providers or receivers of advantages or initiators or victims of improper performance. The combinations are too numerous to enumerate here,[45] but the common pattern is that most are riddled with corruption from top to bottom, are distorted by political and academic skulduggery and fraudulent metrics and infiltrated by organised crime. Thus, companies[46] should take the greatest care whenever a noble cause appears on their radar and THINK:

- Is the framing of the noble cause valid?
- Is it supported by legitimate independent research, that is, is it genuinely peer and dissenter group reviewed?
- Is the supporting research independently funded or sponsored by organisations with a vested interest?

---

44   See page 237.

45   The original 20 drafts of this book included a very long chapter on the Carbon World. When Gower ran short of paper it was withdrawn but is available on http://www.cobasco.com It is not for the timid!

46   And individual investors.

- Are performance targets and key performance metrics valid?
- Does the cause distort economic markets and if so why, how and where?
- Are the supporters of the cause open about its limitations (or, as in the case of global warming, insist that the 'debate is closed' and vilify dissenters)?
- Who benefits[47] the most?

Finally, companies should consider all of the decisions that are involved (both outside and within the organisation), catalogue how they might be perverted and then decide to what extent the cause should be supported, while still remaining on the lookout for indicators of skulduggery.

Conclusions

Readers are urged not to be misled by the framing of the Bribery Act and its supporting research, and to accept the possibility – if not probability – that corruption and fraud are taking place under their own noses and possibly in ways framed as the norm. Equally, they should not write off entire countries as corrupt and refuse to deal with them, or jump onto a noble cause bandwagon without very careful thought.

Finally, from today onwards, if they don't already do it, readers are advised to think carefully about the frames in which everything is presented to them and what they really mean. The following chapters try to put the anti-bribery legislation (and all that goes with it) into a real-world frame of corruption. It is all about C-O-N-T-E-X-T and decision-centricity.

---

47   By applying the rule 'Follow the money'.

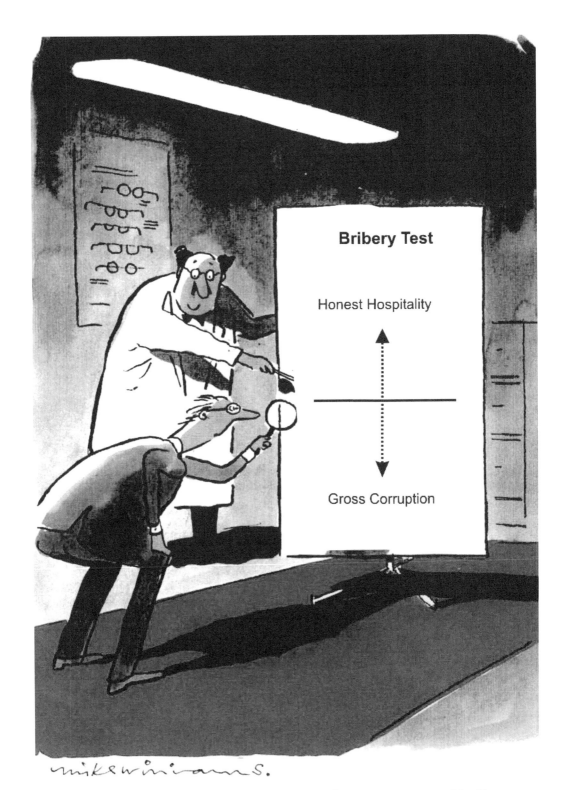

'I know you think it's a fine line Mr Jones, but can you see anything?'

'It's disgusting and they are not even on fees'

I
Background on Corruption Laws

Introduction

The UK is believed to be the first country to pass anti-corruption legislation in 1215 in the Magna Carta,[1] and by the late 1890s was still ahead of the game. What happened between 1890 and 2010 may not appear immediately relevant and **readers who are not worried about the context or framing of the recent legislation can happily skip Chapter 2 and scoot off to the Pink Pussycat Lap Dancing Club[2] providing they note that the Bribery Act is not all that it seems.**

However, Part 1 says a lot about the political shenanigans behind the current Act – the Bribery Act 2010 – the organisations that have driven it and its framing and motivation. It explains the corruption of the word 'bribery' and all that goes with it and the things politicians should have done but, because it would constrain their own flexibility, did not.

The laws in existence prior to 2010 are relevant because for the next few years they still apply, as will the Companies Acts, the Proceeds of Crime Act, the Fraud Act and the money-laundering regulations. It is also important – because of the promised cooperation between international agencies – to recognise the part played by American laws and regulators in the corruption field, as well as other bodies such as the Organisation for Economic Cooperation and Development (OECD), the United Nations and Transparency International, to name but a few. Their roles and the conventions they promote are explained in Part I.

PUTTING THE BRIBERY ACT IN CONTEXT

Some members of the Cottage Industry, not to mention politicians and the media, have hyperbolised bribe payment (but not bribe extortion or stratospheric corruption) as the evil of all evils and fighting it a noble – if not Godly – cause ranking alongside ~~global warming~~ climate change, multi-culturism, England's independence from Scotland or, in Kenneth's case, sustainability of bones. **In fact, bribery is just one of many priorities faced every day by business managers.** Unlike members of the Cottage Industry, bribery comes low on the managerial radar behind more important things like

---

1   'We will sell to no man ... either justice or right'.

2   The significance of which will become clear later. (Readers who cannot stand the suspense should read the Law Commissioner's comments on page 110. They kicked off the authors' childish humour.)

ensuring that their businesses survive in the face of a worldwide economic crisis, political dishonesty, ever burgeoning bureaucracy, misplaced social engineering initiatives and taxation.

Unquestionably, effective control is very important for all organisations. Firstly, to ensure that they run profitably with true integrity, can be sustained economically and otherwise, to avoid throwing hard earned income down the drain through incompetence or skulduggery and then to tick all compliance boxes in multiple silos. **But readers should note that proof of adequate procedures or, in America, effective compliance and ethics programs (EPECs) to stave off prosecution or to mitigate penalties is usually a chimera** (see pages 73 and 613).

Even in the narrow field of compliance, chasing down bribery comes near the bottom of the regulatory priority list. This is confirmed in an excellent paper by Brandon L Garrett, Professor of Law, University of Virginia School of Law, published in the Virginia Law Review in December 2011, of which more later. He notes that in over 95 per cent of federal prosecutions defendants plead guilty. Some commentators view this as a sign of investigative excellence: others consider it little more than the result of coercion. The paper estimates that 72.4 per cent of FCPA actions are against foreign firms and that penalties imposed on them are 22 times larger than for their domestic counterparts. **It sometimes appears that American regulators are primarily interested in protecting national interests.**

Another problem is that laws and regulatory requirements are issued in silos with each agency promoting its own interests above all others. Where guidelines are issued, they are seldom if ever co-ordinated leaving it for companies to decide on priorities. The silo mentality is even more acute when international regulations are taken into account and it is more a case of multiple than simply double jeopardy (see page 146) and of trying to resolve direct conflict.

The Silo Mentality

In January 2013 the Danish company Novo Nordisk was fined $3 million by the Russian authorities for anti-competition violations based on the argument that its requirement that potential agents must submit to due diligence reviews and other measures necessary to comply with the FCPA were restrictive and were not fair under Russian law. The claim was that the compliance program disqualified suitable candidates and that Novo's practice of carrying out due diligence, especially when based Internet searches, was unreliable, unfair and unacceptable. **The Russians, effectively, demanded that Novo abandon its anti-bribery compliance program.** The Ministry of Justice repeatedly recommends Internet searching.

Although Novo's may appear an exceptional case, potential conflicts arise between regulatory silos in other fields. Therefore companies should not view the Bribery Act in isolation but ensure that their integrity programmes achieve all business objectives and deal with disparate regulatory silos. This is the approach recommended in Chapter 23.

2 *A Bit of Dodgy History*

Introduction

Prior to the Bribery Act, British anti-corruption[1] enforcement was based on a mixture of statute and common law, differentiating between the private and public sectors and supported by a raft of other legislation relating to fraud and Companies Act violations. The main problem, so the prosecutors said, was that the laws, as they stood, made it difficult for them to convict companies whose representatives paid bribes, unless responsibility could be pinned to a 'directing mind'. The Bribery Act 2010 overcomes this problem with the draconian Section 7 corporate offence, which comes into play simply if any associated person – no matter how junior – is or **would be** guilty of an offence.

The old legislation was mainly based on the principal–agent relationship,[2] whereas the new Act centres on improper performance and, in the case of foreign public officials (FPOs), mere 'influence'. These changes may not appear striking, but they are. The old legislation (that applies to offences committed before 30 June 2010) is as detailed below.

The Public Bodies Corrupt Practices Act 1889

This Act made corruption of a member, officer or servant of a **public body** a criminal offence. The definition of a public body was amended by a 1916 Act to include: 'local and public authorities of all descriptions with statutory or public duties to perform'. Unsurprisingly the definition does not include MPs, judges or certain other elected officials.

The Act prohibited a public officer, whether by himself or in conjunction with any other person, 'from corruptly soliciting or receiving, or agreeing to receive, etc., for himself, or for any other person, any gift, loan, fee, reward or advantage whatever as an inducement to, or reward for, doing or forbearing to do anything in respect of any matter or transaction whatsoever, actual or proposed, in which the public body is concerned'. (This is erroneously called 'passive corruption'.)

It was also illegal for a person to corruptly promise, or offer, etc. (erroneously called 'active corruption'), 'any gift, loan, fee, reward, or advantage whatsoever, to any person, whether for the benefit of that person, or of another person, as an inducement to, or reward for, doing or forbearing to do anything in respect of any matter or transaction whatsoever, actual or proposed, in which the public body is concerned'.

The maximum penalties were:

---

1   Note that it was always 'corruption'.

2   The Bribery Act is quite different and is structured on an 'improper performance' model. So, more or less, is the civil law.

- On summary conviction, six months' imprisonment, or a fine not exceeding the statutory maximum, or both;
- On conviction on indictment, seven years' imprisonment, or an unlimited fine, or both;
- In addition, conviction could result in:
  - Liability to pay to the public body in question the amount or value of any gift, loan, fee or reward received, or any part thereof;
  - Prevention from being elected or appointed to any public office for five years from the date of conviction, and forfeiture of any office held at the time of the conviction;
  - On a second conviction for a like offence, prevention for ever from holding any public office, and prevention, for five years, from being registered as an elector, or voter, for elections to Parliament or any public body;
  - Forfeiture of any right or claim to compensation or pension to which the person might otherwise be entitled.

The consent of the Attorney General or the Solicitor General was necessary to start a prosecution. Although there is no suggestion that political influence had ever prevailed (ho hum!), political involvement in prosecutorial decision-making did not comply with the conventions of the Organisation for Economic Cooperation and Development (OECD) or the Council of Europe, which require a totally independent prosecuting authority.[3]

The Prevention of Corruption Act 1906

BASIC OFFENCES

This Act dealt with the corruption of agents who, in simple terms, are people entrusted to act on behalf of a principal. All employees, in both the private and commercial sectors, were regarded as agents. They were prohibited from 'corruptly accepting or obtaining, or agreeing to accept or attempting to obtain, from any person, for themselves, or for any other person, any gift or consideration as an inducement or reward for doing or forbearing to do any act, or for showing or forbearing to show favour or disfavour to any person', in relation to their principal's affairs or business.

It was an offence for any person 'corruptly to give or agree to give, or offer, any gift or consideration to any agent as an inducement or reward for doing or forbearing to do, or for having done or forborne to do, any act, or for showing or forbearing to show favour, or disfavour, to any person in relation to his principal's affairs or business'.

ACCOUNTING OFFENCES

It was also an offence for any person 'knowingly to give to any agent, or for any agent knowingly to use, with intent to deceive his principal, any receipt, account or other document, in respect of which his principal was interested, and which contains any

---

3   Ironically, the American system, which has been greatly applauded, relies on judges who are political appointees!

statement which was false or erroneous or defective in any material particular, and which to his knowledge was intended to mislead the principal'.

The maximum penalties were:

- On summary conviction, six months' imprisonment, or a fine not exceeding the statutory maximum, or both;
- On conviction on indictment, seven years' imprisonment, or an unlimited fine, or both.

Although this Act was promoted as the UK's primary law against corruption, it had been used very rarely and prosecutions were more often run as a common law conspiracy or under the Theft Acts, which did not require the permission of the Attorney General or Solicitor General.

The Prevention of Corruption Act 1916

This Act effectively extended and clarified its predecessors but created a presumption of corruption where it was proved 'that any money, gift or other consideration had been paid, or given to or received by a person in the employment of Her Majesty, or any Government Department or public body, by or from a person, or agent of a person, holding or seeking to obtain a contract from Her Majesty, or any Government Department or public body'. Any money, gift, or consideration was deemed to have been paid or given and received corruptly, unless the contrary could be proven. It was a rare example of the burden of proof being shifted to the defendant to prove his innocence. It is noteworthy that the Bribery Act makes it far harder to prosecute public officials (a bit more 'Animal Farm'[4]) **because it no longer requires the person giving an advantage to a UK official, as well as the official himself, to prove that it was not corrupt.**

Comment on the Statutes 1998

In March 1998 the Law Commission made a stinging criticism of the three Acts, stating that they were: 'obscure, complex, in spectacular disarray, inconsistent and insufficiently comprehensive'.

Notwithstanding this view, as we shall see in a moment, the defective legislation was incorporated, warts and all, into the Anti-terrorism Crime and Security Act and, to make matters worse, given extraterritorial coverage.

In 2004, the Home Office told the authors:

The three Acts have provided the United Kingdom with generally effective legislation to combat corruption and have, to a certain extent,[5] stood the test of time. Nonetheless, there are concerns about the scope and overlap of the existing legislation, about the difficulty of interpreting language and concepts used in the statutes and about procedural difficulties.

---

4   Explained in the Foreword.

5   Is this mealy mouthed, or what?

This claim is not borne out by the facts, because there had been only one successful prosecution for corruption of a public official in Britain in the previous 100 years and none involving a company. This raw statistic hides the reality that a number of public officials were prosecuted under the Theft Act, or for conspiracy, for what was effectively corruption.

Political Corruption in the UK

AN ARCHAIC PRIVILEGE

Members of Parliament have from time immemorial been in a privileged and influential position and are obvious candidates for corruption, not least of all because of the system of party political funding and cronyism. Cases exposing all of the leading parties (except the Raving Monster Loony Party) are all cause for concern and there are too many to list here.

More recent scandals such as 'cash for questions', 'cash for honours' and, of course, the incredible British Aerospace (BAE) settlement, reinforced the grounds for concern about the integrity of British politicians. Even more recently cases involving alleged corruption by senior police officers and the press confirm that corruption in the UK prospers.

All three Corruption Acts failed to tackle corruption by MPs, who were not defined as public officers[6] or agents and, in any event, were supposedly not accountable to the courts because of ancient (if not archaic) laws on parliamentary privilege under the Bill of Rights Act 1689. No member of the House of Commons or House of Lords had ever been prosecuted for corruption, or seriously threatened with prosecution for such an offence.

PUBLIC COMMITTEES AND REVIEWS 1994

There were multiple studies, committees and reviews of political corruption, starting with the Redcliffe–Maude report into local government in 1973 through to the Salmon Report in 1974 and the Committee of Standards in Public Life and to Codes of Conduct for MPs in 1974 and 1975.

In 1994 and 1995 the Committee on Standards in Public Life, chaired by Lord Nolan, recommended that: 'the Government should now take steps to clarify the law relating to bribery'[7]. The Government accepted Nolan's recommendations and in June 1997 the Home Office made a statement on the Consolidation and Amendment of the Prevention of Corruption Acts, 1889 to 1916.

It stated:

> *The question of the law relating to the bribery of Members of Parliament, however, touches on constitutional issues involving parliamentary privilege, the application of the Bill of Rights and the Claim of Right and the sovereignty of Parliament. It was therefore considered that this was*

---

6   The position is quite different in other countries and, for example, Hungary has recently passed laws explicitly exposing elected politicians to prosecution for corruption.

7   See http://www.public-standards.gov.uk/Library/OurWork/First7Reports_ProgressReview.pdf (accessed 7 November 2012).

not simply a question of law for the Law Commission but a question of policy which should be considered by Parliament itself.

To assist this consideration the Home Office published a discussion paper, 'Clarification of the Law relating to the Bribery of Members of Parliament' in December 1996.[8] This was formally submitted to the House of Commons Select Committee on Standards and Privileges and to the House of Lords Committee on Privilege. The government – in a typical 'Sir Humphrey' non-comment said it 'would wish to reflect carefully on ... that paper before it reached a view on whether and how the law on corruption needs amendment'. It did not actually say it would reflect, merely that it 'would wish to reflect'. The two phrases do not mean the same and what actually happened, as far as can be seen, was nothing.

LAW COMMISSION REPORT 1998

In March 1998, the Law Commission published a nearly excellent report on corruption (based on the consultation paper issued around two years earlier and referred to above) and included a draft Bill. However it avoided the question of corruption of MPs and stated that

> the report does not deal with that issue. This is because the issue is currently under consideration by the Home Office and Joint Committee on Parliamentary Privilege. In these circumstances we have decided that it would be a wasteful duplication of effort for us to examine it as well.[9]

It appears, yet again, that the question of MPs and their corruption was simply too difficult to handle.

Thus the regulation of MPs remained with the Committees on Standards and Privileges and a Parliamentary Commissioner for Standards, who was responsible for ensuring that elected politicians complied with a Code of Conduct, including the registration of potentially conflicting interests. It should be noted, however, that the Commissioner had no statutory power to compel witnesses to give evidence or to produce records and that no declaration was necessary of conflicting interests by an MP's spouse, or close family members.

JOINT COMMITTEE 1999

In March 1999, the Joint Committee on Parliamentary Privilege submitted its report and concluded that corruption (of MPs) could only be dealt with effectively by using the police and the courts. It continued: 'The proposed bribery legislation will expose

---

8   See Home Office Discussion Paper, December 1996, available at: http://www.publications.parliament.uk/pa/jt199899/jtselect/jtpriv/43/8012002.htm (accessed 7 November 2012).

9   See 'Legislating the Criminal Code: Corruption' (Executive Summary) [Report Law Com No. 248], 3 March 1998: paragraph 2. Available at: http://www.lgcplus.com/lgc-news/legislating-the-criminal-code-corruption-executive-summary/1477470.article (accessed 7 November 2012).

MPs and prosecution should require the consent of the Attorney General or the Lord Advocate'.[10]

The Committee recognised that the definition of 'proceedings in Parliament' needed to be clarified and supported an earlier recommendation that the term should cover 'everything done by an MP or Peer as part of his or her duties', obviously including a trip to a lap dancing club if it took place the day before a debate or with a constituent.

Although the Government again promised to change the law, it did nothing, even though suspicions and hard cases of political corruption continued to surface.

COMMITTEE ON STANDARDS AND PRIVILEGES 2001

In December 2001, Elizabeth Filkin, then Commissioner for Committees on Standards and Privileges, left, or was pushed out of, her job, claiming that some Government Ministers had briefed (which means spun and lied) against her and had obstructed her. Still, British citizens could sleep peacefully in their beds knowing that the report of the Joint Committee on Parliamentary Privilege was being vigorously pursued and that a review of the law was imminent. Ten years later it is still awaited!

MORE HANKY-PANKY BY POLITICIANS

Besides the high-profile cases of political corruption that come readily to mind, there are others which are quickly forgotten but illustrate the appalling 'tone from the top':

Political Donations

In March 2006, Angus MacNeil, a Scottish Nationalist MP, made an allegation to the police that the rules on party political funding had been evaded by mis-describing what were effectively donations as loans. If any UK company had been involved in the same sort of shenanigans they could have expected a knock on their door by the Old Bill. Mr MacNeil also suggested that these 'loans' had been made in anticipation of the donors being rewarded by elevation to the House of Lords.

During a 14-month investigation by the Metropolitan Police, costing more than £800,000, four people were arrested, including Lord Levy, Tony Blair's personal envoy to the Middle East and fund-raiser extraordinaire, Ruth Turner, Director of Government Relations, Christopher Evans, a biotech multimillionaire and 'lender' and Des Smith, a headmaster involved in setting up Mr Blair's Inner City Academies. Mr Blair, who was then serving Prime Minister, was questioned three times by the Metropolitan Police; allegations of perverting the course of justice were raised but Lord Goldsmith, then Attorney General, took out an injunction against the BBC preventing it from reporting the story.

---

10   See http://www.parliament.the-stationery-office.co.uk/pa/jt199899/jtselect/jtpriv/43/4303.htm (accessed 7 November 2012).

Although the police repeatedly expressed confidence that there was sufficient evidence to prosecute, in July 2007 the Crown Prosecution Service decided not to do so by exercising 'prosecutorial discretion', and all charges were dropped against everyone. Prosecutors were quick – if not too quick – to volunteer that their decision had not been influenced by political pressure. This is known in skulduggery circles as an 'unprovoked denial', and is therefore questionable.

On 25 January 2009, The reported a sting operation against five Labour Party peers, three Conservative lords, one Liberal Democrat and one Ulster Unionist. Four of the Labour peers fell into the trap and offered lobbying and political services in return for heavy fees. None of the others rose to the bait, possibly because they all had prior engagements at the Pink Pussycat Lap Dancing Club or the local Turkish Baths.

House of Lords

The Code of Conduct of the House of Lords requires that members must never accept a financial inducement for exercising influence in Parliament, nor vote on any bill or motion, or ask any question in the House or a committee, or promote any matter in return for payment or other material benefit. The rules are very clear. Notwithstanding this the four Peers had offered to have laws changed or new ones introduced to help their fee-paying clients, to lobby ministers on their behalf and to persuade senior civil servants and committee members to assist.

Lord Taylor of Blackburn was asked by undercover reporters how he could get dodgy amendments through Parliament and whether he would do it himself. Lord Taylor responded: 'No, no, no. You don't do things like that. What you do is to talk to the Parliamentary team who drafts the statutes … You meet the Minister, you meet the various people'.

On 11 February 2009, after one of the shortest investigations ever, the Metropolitan Police concluded that no action would be taken, stating that: 'application of the criminal law to members of the House of Lords in the circumstances that have arisen here is far from clear. In addition there are very clear difficulties in gathering and adducing evidence in these circumstances in the context of parliamentary privilege'.

The case was dropped, faster than a hooker's bloomers.

Parliamentary privilege is very important in the corruption context – given the unhealthy interplay between some large commercial organisations, which sponsor scientific surveys or other research to justify changes in the law or to gain some other advantage for their business. Funding of far too many scientific, academic or research organisations is conditional on reports ('dodgy dossiers') that support the funder's commercial agenda. If academics and researchers fail to produce the right result, money quickly dries up.

RELIANCE ON 'DODGY DOSSIERS'

'Dodgy dossiers' have become the justification for politicians to introduce dodgy legislation or drive through other decisions that benefit research funders and their sponsors. The circle is inherently corrupt and ultimately funded by the taxpayer.

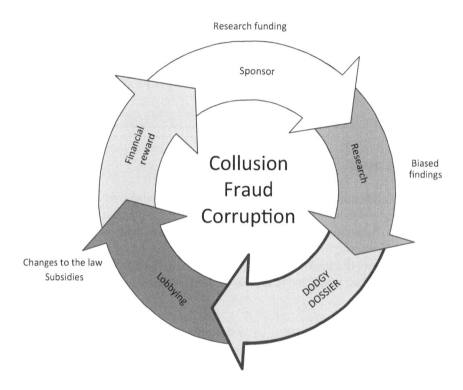

Figure 2.1   Circle of 'Dodgy Dossiers' and Corruption

Figure 2.1 suggests that the spiral often starts with a commercial, social or political interest, which sponsors research (possibly 'dodgy dossiers') leading to political intervention that benefits the sponsors. Corruption can be involved at any stage in the spiral.

Misleading, false or perjured evidence may be given in Parliament, either before the assembled House or in committee, but nothing that is said or submitted, by anyone, can be adduced in evidence against anyone. This is one of the problems with parliamentary privilege: trading in influence and lobbying. The fact that all of these levers of stratospheric corruption were deliberately and cynically excluded from the Bribery Act 2010 says all that needs to be said about political commitment to the fight against corruption. As Kenneth Clarke, the ex-Justice Secretary and supposed 'anti-bribery'[11] champion has said – the initiative must be 'business-led'. This means, in the words of Samuel Goldwyn 'include me out'.

---

11   Note: Not the 'anti-corruption champion'.

UK Ratifies the OECD Convention February 1999

The British Government accepted that the three existing domestic acts were defective and undertook to pass new legislation when Parliamentary time became available. The Government also promised to remove what was effectively immunity for MPs against prosecution for corruption and to bring them under the criminal law.[12]

On 15 February 1999 the UK ratified the OECD Convention but continued to argue that the UK's domestic laws complied with every condition. A point which is often overlooked or not understood is that the UK did not adopt the Convention into British law and is therefore not bound by it. In fact, the UK specifically opted out of the Council of Europe's provisions concerning 'trading in influence' (for example, political lobbying, 'cash for questions' and 'cash for honours' type skulduggery) as compliance would – supposedly – constrain the legitimate work of Members of Parliament! This is yet another example of the UK government cherry-picking the OECD and other conventions to protect the political status quo.

The UK Government's Intentions June 2000

In June 2000, Jack Straw, then Home Secretary, at long last responded to the Law Commission recommendations (March 1998!) and reported ('Raising Standards and Upholding Integrity: The Prevention of Corruption')[13] that 'corruption is like a deadly virus'. He stated his commitment to fighting corruption 'wherever it is found'.[14] As well as reforming the corruption offences, the Government proposed two major changes:

- UK citizens will be triable in the UK for corruption offences committed abroad;
- Citizens of any country to be prosecuted in the UK, even for offences that did not occur wholly within the UK.

Jack Straw stated: 'our overriding consideration is to clarify and codify the law in line with developments both in this country and internationally'.

If he had stuck to his word and dealt with MPs, as he had promised, no one could have had any reasonable objection; but he did not. Part 6 of the Report sets out a summary of the Government's proposals:

- The Government proposes replacing the existing principal statutes of corruption in England and Wales by a single statute, modelled on that published by the Law Commission. Its provisions will reflect:[15]
    - Acceptance of the Law Commission's recommendation that there should be a single offence of corruption to cover both public and private sectors;

---

12   By removing Parliamentary Privilege.

13   TSO, 22 June 2000; available at: http://www.archive.official-documents.co.uk/document/cm47/4759/4759.htm (accessed 7 November 2012).

14   But not in politics.

15   Note provisions that are quite different from the Bribery Act 2010.

- Abolition of the current presumption of corruption for public servants in the Prevention of Corruption Act 1916;
- A statutory definition of what is meant by 'acting corruptly', and a definition of the concept of 'agent';
- The inclusion in the offence of corruption of 'trading in influence', where the decision-making of public officials by intermediaries is targeted;
- That the corruption of, or by, a public official is not confined to the public of the UK;
- Extending jurisdiction over offences of corruption to cover both offences committed in whole or in part within the jurisdiction and those committed by UK nationals abroad;
- Evidence relating to an offence committed or alleged to have been committed by a Member of either House of Parliament to be admissible notwithstanding Article 9 of the Bill of Rights;
- The Law Commission's recommendations that the new offence of corruption should continue to be triable either in the Magistrates' Court or in the Crown Court, and the Government view that the current maximum penalty of seven years' imprisonment should be unchanged;
- Retention of the requirement for the consent of the Law Officers for prosecution.

The report seems to have sat on the shelf for another year, with a complacent government believing that nothing had to be done to comply with the OECD Convention. They had a shock coming.

Council of Europe: Civil Law Convention

On 8 June 2000, with testosterone levels at breaking point in the 'fight against corruption wherever it happens', Jack Straw signed the Civil Law Convention. It required Member States to provide in its internal laws effective remedies for persons who had suffered damage as a result of corruption, including the possibility of obtaining compensation from the state for hanky-panky by officials.

However, the UK never ratified the Treaty, although 34 other countries did. Other notable 'non-rats' include Denmark, Germany, Ireland, Italy, Russia, Sweden and Switzerland, which corroborates just how prepared politicians are to fight corruption on a political or official level.

International Development Select Committee, April 2001

In April 2001, the International Development Select Committee of the House of Commons reported:[16]

---

16   Select Committee on International Development, Fourth Report, available at: http://www.publications.parliament. uk/pa/cm200001/cmselect/cmintdev/39/3912.htm

- The Committee criticises the fact that the Government has yet to introduce legislation to implement the OECD Convention.
- Simple and clear legislation should be brought forward as a matter of urgency.
- The Committee concluded:
  - Corruption undermines development, hampers growth and has to be tackled. We must continue to help developing countries build an environment that will eliminate corruption. The impact of petty corruption must not be overlooked, for it is petty corruption that will have the most direct impact on the poor.
  - The Government cannot continue to make improvements in governance a condition for development assistance when it has failed to implement the OECD Convention.
  - A lack of focus and coordination is hampering efforts to tackle corruption and money-laundering in the UK. There is a need for one department or body to take a lead and provide a focus for current activity. We urge the UK Government to act on these issues swiftly.
  - We must equip companies with the necessary legislative backing to resist extortion and bribery. The law should provide companies with a shield that protects them from those who solicit bribes by giving the argument that a company and the individuals concerned would face the stiffest penalties (including prison) in the UK if they were to engage in corruption of any sort.
  - We believe that the DTI should work with companies to help them address issues of corporate governance and ethics and through Trade Partners should provide help and support on the ground to companies working in countries where corruption is endemic.

Transparency International said: 'To delay enacting this offence could severely damage the future success of the Convention, which rests on the basic assumption that the same rules will apply to all major exporters'.

A common thread of the OECD's influence has been to penalise what are quaintly classified as 'demand-side' countries while making little headway with controlling countries whose nationals routinely extort bribes. This appears to reflect the current trend of controlling those who are amenable to it while letting blatant skulduggers escape unpunished. It happens in every aspect of law enforcement from parking to violence, tax and benefits fraud.

The Anti-terrorism Crime and Security Act 2001

THE SUPPOSED JUSTIFICATION

By April 2001 the UK government was faced with increasing pressure to keep its promises to do something about corruption and to comply with the OECD Convention:

- The Law Commission had made strong recommendations to revise Britain's anti-corruption laws and in June 2000 the Government had agreed to do so.
- The public was concerned about corruption by MPs and Government Ministers.

- Various committees had suggested that the laws on corruption, including those relating to MPs, should be changed.
- Parliament had undertaken to review the question of political corruption and privileges.
- The Parliamentary Commissioner of Standards was creating mayhem by chasing after Ministers.
- The UK's partners in the OECD and the USA were pressing for action.

Notwithstanding this, the Government did nothing until the tragic events of 11 September 2001 appeared to have provided a golden opportunity to 'bury the bad news'.

It subsequently emerged that Jo Moores, the aide to Stephen Byers, then Transport Minister, used this phrase and worked on this principle when consigning other bad news to the back pages, so it is not going too far to believe that the same happened with corruption legislation. Otherwise it is difficult to see how or why anti-corruption measures were submerged in a law on terrorism. It should be noted that in none of the research, nor in any of the conventions, is any convincing connection made between corporate corruption and terrorism. The Anti-Terrorism, Crime and Security Act (ATCSA) was a convenient way of getting the OECD off Britain' s back without causing too much public scrutiny over the new corruption laws. But politicians had no will to enforce it.

SUPPOSED LINKS BETWEEN CORRUPTION AND TERRORISM

The Home Office summary of the ATCSA[17] states:

> *Part 12 brings in provisions to strengthen the law on international corruption, which is linked to conditions which cause terrorism.*

There is absolutely no support for this preposterous statement, but no one seemed to challenge it at the time and probably would have accepted any restrictions that countered terrorism in the light of 9/11.

ATSCA came into force on 14 February 2002 and ranks as one of the strangest pieces of legislation ever passed. It is arranged in 14 parts with 8 schedules. Its purpose was supposedly to enhance the UK's anti-terrorist and security capability. It does this via measures tackling terrorist finance; streamlining relevant immigration procedures;[18] provisions against inciting religious hatred or violence; new offences on Weapons of Mass Destruction; better security in dealing with pathogens and toxins; improving civil nuclear security; better security at airports and nuclear sites; extension of police powers; extension of the jurisdiction of the British Transport Police and Ministry of Defence Police; intelligence measures, including on-data retention and data gateways; an enabling power to implement by secondary legislation a small number of terrorism-related European Union (EU) agreements on Justice and Home Affairs; and amendments to the Terrorism Act 2000.

---

17   A summary is available at: http://image.guardian.co.uk/sys-files/Politics/documents/2001/11/20/Anti-terrorism_bill.pdf (accessed 7 November 2012).

18   Yes: that's what it says!

ANTI-CORRUPTION PROVISIONS

Part 12, sections 108 and 109, in simple terms, applied extraterritorial provisions to the three existing corruption acts – accepted by anyone with any sense as hopeless – criminalising and making punishable in the UK:

• Facilitation payments made to FPOs (which are permitted under the Foreign Corrupt Practices Act (FCPA), and the OECD and Council of Europe Conventions);
• Persuasive payments to members of the private sector in foreign countries (which are not replicated under the FCPA or the OECD Convention and are only included in the Council of Europe Convention when a breach of trust is involved).

No other OECD member had passed equivalent legislation criminalising corruption in the overseas public *and* private sectors; no other country had mixed corporate corruption with anti-terrorism; no other country has got itself into such a mess.

On 29 January 2002, Baroness Symons, Minister for Trade and Investment, told a DTI-sponsored conference that the new measures will 'outlaw acts of bribery by UK nationals and companies abroad in the same circumstances as they are outlawed here'.

This was not so. The Law Commission and others had already recognised that the three UK Acts were unworkable, so giving them extraterritorial scope was hardly sensible.

BUT DON'T WORRY ... WE WON'T PROSECUTE

At the same DTI-sponsored conference, Mr Martin Polaine representing the Crown Prosecution Service (CPS), said that neither the Attorney General nor the CPS would be likely to take action in respect of facilitation payments. He said that even if the evidence was sufficient to bring a prosecution, the CPS would consider the circumstances in which the payment was made and whether coercion was involved in deciding whether to prosecute. It was the strongest 'wink, wink, nudge-nudge' possible that the ATSCA was a sham.

PROSECUTIONS UNDER SECTION 12 OF ATSCA

This paragraph can be kept very short because there were no prosecutions under ATSCA and all went quiet after a very successful 'burying of the bad news'. But the objective of placating the OECD had been achieved. It was also a double whammy because the absolution afforded to MPs under the Bill of Rights remained unmolested.

The Law Commission Report, October 2008

In October 2008 (believed to be in response to public outrage over the Blair-induced collapse of the BAE case) the Law Commission was charged with, yet again, reviewing the UK laws on 'bribery'.[19] The reframing of the old laws on corruption to those planned on bribery was no coincidence and effectively enabled the thorny problems of political

---

19   Not corruption.

corruption to be averted. The Commission's report was produced in one month, indicating the urgency with which the government felt obliged to react.

The Commissioners' proposed Bribery Bill was subsequently reworded by the Ministry of Justice (MOJ) to become the Bribery Act 2010. Although there are some significant differences between the draft Bill and the final Act, the Commissioners' thought processes throw light on the way judges might interpret the new legislation.

Such interpretations are important for three reasons. The first is because there is not a single precedent that companies can refer to when deciding what to do, or not to do, in relation to the Bribery Act. The second is that the Serious Fraud Office (SFO) has already made moves to expansively interpret the Act on such definitions as what constitutes a bribe and what is a relevant commercial organisation, or to obtain or retain business or other advantage (see pages 80 to 105). The third reason is that judges have not been impressed with the SFO's approach to civil disposals[20] and are expected to overturn settlement agreements and lenient sentences for cooperating witnesses. Judges have implied that they want blood on the carpet for serious corruption offences and they are right. It is morally wrong and an abuse of process that Section 2 orders, intended to assist the SFO (and now other prosecutors) convict serous fraud, should be used for pre-investigation fishing trips with a view only to grabbing money from alleged perpetrators.

The Commissioners' comments on facilitation payments, hospitality and other difficult and uncertain areas are incorporated in Chapters 28–33. To what extent their views will be followed by judges is uncertain.

The Impact Assessments

OBLIGATION TO PREPARE AND FILE

The UK Government undertakes to prepare a formal 'Impact Assessment' (IA) of all proposed legislation to 'provide transparency for all significant government interventions'. An unattributed,[21] and undated, document titled 'Impact Assessment Guidance' states that assessments are a continuous process linked to five important stages in the following chronological order:

1. Development
2. Consultation
3. Final proposal
4. Implementation
5. Post-implementation review.

The guidance continues that one of the purposes of publishing assessments is 'to ensure affected parties are given the opportunity to identify potential unintended consequences,

---

20   'Civil Disposal' is defined in the Foreword.

21   No mention of the department or author, but probably the Department for Business, Enterprise and Regulatory Reform (BERR), the predecessor of the Department for Business Innovation and Skills (BIS).

primarily through a consultation process' and that the Impact Assessment's minimum requirements include:

- The rationale for the proposal;
- Details of the costs and benefits of the policy change;
- Consideration of the options;
- The consultation summary.

If the procedure is followed, interested parties can see for themselves what effect consultation has had in the development of the law. The assessments are also critical for Parliament in deciding whether or not new laws are justified and proportionate.

In August 2011, more detailed guidance was published by the Department for Business Innovation and Skills (BIS),[22] titled 'Impact Assessment Overview' and 'IA Toolkit. How to do an Impact Assessment'. Both sets of guidance require detailed calculations of the financial impacts of new laws, their effect on UK competitiveness, social, equality and other considerations.[23] According to the overview, every assessment should be signed off by a minister, who is required to certify:

> *I have read the Impact Assessment and I am satisfied that the assessment (i) represents a fair and reasonable view of the expected costs, benefits and impact of the policy and (ii) the benefits justify the costs.*

The guides do not say anything about the need for honesty, accuracy or integrity, although the earlier unattributed version states:[24]

> *[S]purious accuracy in the presentation of the with ranges used where appropriate. (Emphasis added)*

The avoidance of spuriousness – in aspects other than costs and benefits – does not appear to be a priority, although if a proposal goes beyond the minimum requirements of a related EU directive (known as 'gold-plating'),the overview requires that this is made clear:

> *It is critically important that the evidence base should show how the headline costs and benefits have been generated, by clear and transparent disaggregation of figures. This information must stand up to external scrutiny – that is, it should be accessible to the lay reader, and external parties with an interest must be able to contest the data.*

Since April 2008, all central departments are required to archive copies of their assessments in a web-based library managed by BIS.[25]

---

22   BERR's successor (see Note 20 above). The 'Impact Assessment Overview' is available at: http://www.bis.gov.uk/feeds/~/media/2B4A9F36CFA64DF3A9F354505C0CDCDC.ashx; and the 'IA Toolkit. How to do an Impact Assessment' is available at: http://www.bis.gov.uk/assets/biscore/better-regulation/docs/i/11-1112-impact-assessment-toolkit.pdf (both accessed 7 November 2012).

23   Inevitably including 'climate change', with no mention of 'global warming'.

24   Omitted from the later, more polished, versions.

25   Available at: http://ialibrary.bis.gov.uk/search/index.cfm (accessed 7 November 2012).

THE ARCHIVED IMPACT ASSESSMENTS

The BIS archive has no references, whatsoever, to any Impact Assessment on the Bribery Act. This is both amazing and unacceptable given its importance. The Ministry of Justice (MOJ) website[26] refers to two assessments:

- Impact Assessment – Guidance about commercial organisations preventing bribery (Section 9 of the Bribery Act 2010 (filed on 13 September 2010));
- Bribery Bill Impact Assessment – 'Version 2' (filed on 20 November 2009, but undated).

When the authors asked the MOJ about the missing assessments, its Bribery Bill Team was helpful and provided another document,[27] dated 20 February 2009, titled: 'Version 1: Draft Implementation Stage'. The significance of this document is discussed later.[28]

THE MISSING ASSESSMENT

The first mention of any Impact Assessment in relation to the proposed bribery law was a 'draft implementation stage document',[29] referred to in paragraph 96 of the 'Bribery – Draft Legislation – Explanatory Notes' on 25 March 2009 (Cm 7570). Although the document is not annexed to that report,[30] it is hyperlinked to the MOJ website where it can – supposedly – be found. The problem is, it has vanished.

However, the Explanatory Notes extract from the missing assessment are as follows:

- [F]or the most part, the provisions in the draft Bill represent a *reformulation of existing*[31] bribery offences. *Due to low levels of offending,*[32] the increase in the maximum sentence of imprisonment for those offences should have a negligible impact in terms of prison places.
- **[W]e believe that the draft Bill will not impose any significant additional administrative burden on business.**
- [T]he corporate offence[33] is not regulatory in nature and there will be no monitoring of compliance.
- [T]he offence will have a beneficial effect for corporate governance by encouraging those companies which have not already done so to adopt adequate systems to prevent bribery.
- [T]he benefits of the new corporate offence include enhanced ability on the part of business organisations to assess the suitability of their systems due to increased clarity

---

26 Available at http://www.justice.gov.uk (accessed 7 November 2012).

27 Which had been scanned rather than being in a direct PDF format, which is normal on the MOJ website.

28 The MOJ subsequently claimed that there were no other assessments of the Bribery Act.

29 With no mention of its date.

30 When it would have been prudent to do so.

31 (Emphasis added.) Misleading.

32 (Emphasis added.) How does this align with the doom and gloom scenarios?

33 Section 7 – strict liability.

in the law and in efficiency savings through, for example, reducing the cost of risk assessment.[34]

- In addition, the enhancement of the UK's reputation as a consequence of our reforms should allow UK business to compete more successfully in international markets.[35]

Anyone reading the Explanatory Notes could be forgiven for concluding that the proposed law was pro-business and that its implementation would incur negligible costs and administrative burdens. How unrealistic is this – but where is the actual document?

ASSESSMENT REVIEWED BY THE JOINT COMMITTEE

The next mention of an Impact Assessment appears in the Joint Parliamentary Committee Report dated 28 July 2009.[36] Again the document referred to is not annexed[37] but the Committee was scathing, stating that: 'further explanation is required as to why it[38] is not complete'. The Committee did not think it necessary to record the date of the Impact Assessment it had cited, its version number or any other identifying details. It is clear, however, that what the Committee did review is not among the documents on any government website.

It now appears that the scanned 'Version 1', dated 20 February 2009, provided by the MOJ to the authors, was the document referred to by the Joint Committee; it states – among other things – that:

- The average annual cost of the provisions of the draft Bill is estimated at £4.1 million, including £2.1 million to fund additional enforcement activities by the SFO[39] (and others) and £2 million for additional private sector defence costs.
- It is based on an additional 1.3 criminal prosecutions and three extra civil recovery actions per year. The Committee was critical that the calculation of these estimates was 'insufficiently explained'.
- **There is no detailed explanation for the cost–benefit impact on the private sector**.
- **The proposals go beyond the minimum EU requirements** (that is, they are 'gold plated').
- The new discrete corporate offence is 'intended particularly to combat the use of bribery in high-value transactions in international markets'.
- Given the fact that the new proposed general offences and the new discrete offence of bribing a FPO are a reformulation[40] of existing criminality, we do not expect any significant additional burden on the Criminal Justice System.

---

34   Nonsense.

35   On what basis?

36   Available at: http://www.publications.parliament.uk/pa/jt/jtbribe.htm (accessed 7 November 2012). The assessment was reviewed by the House of Commons Scrutiny Committee in April 2009 and its analysis is at Annex 1 of the Joint Report. Again the date of the Impact Assessment reviewed is not recorded!!

37   Nor is its date recorded!!

38   That is, the Impact Assessment.

39   A supposed further £6 million of funding for the City of London Police is not discussed.

40   This is not correct.

- The House of Commons Scrutiny Committee[41] commented that: '**[there is no] formal competition assessment and no evidence is provided to support the assertion that the draft Bill will have a positive effect on UK companies' international competitiveness**'.
- 'Therefore, the Joint Committee may wish to recommend that the formal Competition Assessment is undertaken as part of a primary legislation resulting from the draft Bill'.[42]
- 'In a memorandum to the Committee, the Ministry of Justice explained that there was only a limited opportunity for the government to prepare a detailed Impact Assessment and that the decision had been taken to publish the proposals as draft legislation and to develop the Impact Assessment [later]'.
- 'While a consultation summary is not provided, the structure of the assessment conforms […]' (Footnote 372 states 'because the range of consultations previously carried out in relation to the reform of the law on bribery, no further formal consultation process on the impact of the draft Bill is anticipated').
- It '"Applauded"[43] [that] the Government's suggestion that a review of the impact of the legislation would be conducted after three to five years of its enactment, but recommended that any revised Impact Assessment generated by the Government should set out a comprehensive set of performance indicators so that the criteria against which the legislation is being assessed are clearly understood'.[44]

Notwithstanding what should have been regarded as fatal defects, the Joint Committee passed the Bill through pre-legislative scrutiny. It would not be unreasonable to expect that incomplete and misleading though it was, the Impact Assessment might have caused a few feathers to fly in Parliament. But this was not the case. In fact, the debates were described by some Honourable Members as 'love fests' and although there was some mandatory and token pouting, debates lacked enthusiasm, mainly because the Labour Party was determined to drive through the Act and the Conservatives were not prepared stir up the wrath of Luvvie-leaning voters by raising objections to such a 'noble cause' immediately before an election. So just to get thoughts absolutely clear about the two most important laws on corruption: ATCSA was buried with the bad news of 9/11 and the Bribery Act was coerced through in pre-election euphoria.

THE BOTTOM LINE?

The bottom line of all of the shenanigans related above is that it is impossible from publicly available records to track how many Impact Assessments there were, their dates, the minister who signed them off, the stage concerned or the supposed benefits and costs. Whether the mess is deliberate or just inefficiency is impossible to say.

Anyway the MOJ (finally) estimated that the Act would result in:

---

41   Which assisted the Joint Committee.

42   The Joint Committee made no such recommendation.

43   Pure 'Luvvie'.

44   This recommendation was not followed. The undated 'Version 2' referred to in the Government's response is far from complete.

- Just 1.3 additional contested prosecutions a year;
- Three additional civil disposals;
- No additional burdens on the criminal justice system or prison accommodation;
- Additional enforcement cost of £2.1 million for the SFO and £2 million of defence costs.

It did not calculate the extra compliance costs for British businesses and, as far as can be seen, made no attempt to do so. On the contrary, it implied that the Act would have a beneficial effect by improving the reputation of UK companies and making them more assured in overseas markets. Ho, hum!

So what is the alternative and likely more realistic estimate? The following are working assumptions which readers are invited to adjust or recalculate:

- There are around 2 million businesses registered in the UK, of which 2,300 are listed.
- They mostly have parents, subsidiaries, siblings, associates, customers, suppliers, most of whom – for purposes of prosecutorial prudence – will be assumed to be 'associated persons'.
- The top 1,000 companies in the UK will take the Bribery Act seriously and will fully deploy legal, compliance and other internal and external teams to make sure their compliance systems are sound. Their initial legal and other costs are unlikely to be less than £400,000.
- The next 49,000 ranked companies will spend, say, an average of £25,000 a year.
- Companies outside the top 50,000 will not incur additional compliance costs.
- Based on the above, the estimated annual costs of compliance with the Bribery Act can be estimated at no less than £1,625 million per annum excluding allocations of management time or lost opportunity costs.

Whatever *realistic alternative* figures are chosen, the results demonstrate the complete codswallop of the MOJ's claims that the impact on British business will be negligible or manageable. It is a lot of money to spend for 1.3 additional prosecutions! But it is a noble cause, although one the UK can ill afford in the present economic climate.

The Broken Silence: January 2007 to 2009

Everything remained nice and quiet, with possibly a few rumblings by the OECD, but nothing that could not be batted away with a few 'Sir Humphreyisms'.[45] Things were about to change. The six-year investigation by the SFO into scandalous worldwide corruption by BAE was, in January 2007, brought to an abrupt end by Mr Blair, who argued that prosecution would result in Saudi Arabia flouncing away and refusing to assist in the fight against Al Qaeda, thus causing British deaths on the streets. This explanation was nonsense but allowed the BAE directors to escape imprisonment and the problem to be buried.

Mr Blair's decision clearly outraged OECD countries and, especially, America, and all of a sudden pressure came back on the UK to get its anticorruption house in order.

---

45   The phrase refers to Sir Humphrey Appleby, the fictional character from the British TV series, 'Yes, Prime Minister'.

In April 2008, morale in the SFO hit rock bottom and Robert Wardle, the director and other senior officials left for pastures new. And who could blame them?

House of Lords and Commons Joint Committee Report, July 2009

In July 2009 a Joint Committee of the House of Lords and the House of Commons reported on their deliberations into what was then the Bribery Bill, and started off by expressing their disappointment that the government had given them so little time to carry out their task. This is another indication of the unhealthy rush to get the law onto the statute books.

There are some significant points in the report:[46]

- **'At no stage has the government accepted that the UK is non-compliant with any of its international obligations'**, but it has acknowledged that failure to implement law reform could 'bring into question the UK's commitment to the OECD convention'.[47]
- The committee believed that in making the 'reasonable expectation test' all of the circumstances should be taken into account. This qualification was not adopted in the Bribery Act and it makes a significant difference.
- The committee concluded that 'improper performance' would include the case where a senior banker, being asked by a rival bank to induce his or her trading team to join it in return for increased remuneration, would be in breach of expectation of good faith and could fall within the provisions of the Act.
- The committee struggled with the offence relating to bribery of FPO, believing that the advantage should be 'improper' or 'not legitimately due'. These conditions were removed from the Act.
- On offset projects, the OECD Secretariat acknowledged that those payments that incidentally benefited an official alongside other members of the public were unlikely to amount to bribery.
- It is hard to imagine any circumstances in which the procedures could be regarded as adequate where a senior officer was at fault.
- It is generally accepted that corporate hospitality is a legitimate part of doing business at home and abroad, provided it remains within appropriate limits. The committee concluded that 'we [...] call upon the government to reassure the business community that it does not risk facing prosecution for providing proportionate levels of hospitality as part of competing fairly in the international arena'.
- The committee seriously struggled with the role of the Attorney General in establishing a balance between prosecutorial independence and Parliamentary accountability.
- Unsurprisingly the committee struggled with the question of Parliamentary privilege and Article IX of the Bill of Rights 1689, which states that: 'freedom of speech and debates or proceedings in Parliament ought not to be impeached or questioned in any court or place out of Parliament'. The committee pointed out that it is not intended

---

46   Joint Committee on the Draft Bribery Bill. First Report, 28 July 2009. Available at: http://www.publications. parliament.uk/pa/jt/jtbribe.htm (accessed 7 November 2012).

47   This conflicts with the justification given for the 'draconian act'.

to protect members from the criminal law but as a result of a 'historical accident' this is currently the case as neither House is considered for the purposes of the Public Bodies Corrupt Practices Act 1889 or the Prevention of Corruption Act 1906 to be a public body. The committee concluded that reform is best left to a separate review of the Parliamentary Standards Bill (or other legislation) and should not be addressed in the Bribery Act.

The committee was critical of the MOJ's Impact Assessment questioning whether the estimated £50,000 promotional costs would be adequate to bring the Act to the attention of business: that 1.3 additional prosecutions for bribery per year was almost laughable and that the cost of enforcement to British businesses was likely to far exceed the estimate of £3 million per year.

Government Response to the Joint Committee Report, November 2009

In August 2009, the 'Lockerbie Bomber' was released from prison, supposedly because he had only weeks to live but more likely in exchange for an oil deal with Libya. The UK's international reputation had again suffered because of skulduggery by its political leaders, so there was an increasing need to get things moving on the corruption front.

The MOJ's patronising response was published in November 2009 and concludes:[48]

- '[T]he draft Bill provides a modern and comprehensive scheme of bribery offences, in **order to allow investigators, prosecutors and courts to tackle bribery effectively**'. This Freudian slip reveals the real purpose of the Act, whose main public justification was to help British businesses succeed in corrupt international markets!
- The government considers that relying on prosecutorial discretion is the proper way to proceed and that 'an important element of the government's policy in this area is to encourage a changing culture in emerging markets away from the cynical and pragmatic acceptance of bribery as the only effective way of doing business'.
- The government intends to review the Honours (Prevention of Abuses) Act 1925 once the Bribery Act is established.[49]
- The government agrees that guidance should be available to commercial organisations (but clearly not government departments). However, in our view, it would not be appropriate to add a clause to the Bill giving the government power to approve guidance prepared by others
- We confirm that the government does not intend that this legislation should be used to penalise the legitimate and proportionate use of corporate hospitality to establish or maintain good relationships with prospective customers.
- The exercise of confiscation powers is directed towards the recovery of all the proceeds of crime. It is not intended to be punitive in effect.

---

48   See 'Government Response to the conclusions and recommendations of the Joint Committee Report on the Draft Bribery Bill', November 2009. Available at: http://www.official-documents.gov.uk/document/cm77/7748/7748.pdf (accessed 7 November 2012).

49   If you believe in Father Christmas.

• The EU procurement directive introducing mandatory debarment of suppliers convicted of specific offences including corruption (actually this means only paying bribes) represented a strengthening of earlier rules. Bribery is a serious offence and the government considers it important that we work with our European partners to identify good practice in the application of exclusion procedures. We are considering whether a conviction for the proposed new corporate offence of failure to prevent bribery would trigger the conditions of automatic debarment.

The above response (mainly composed by the Bribery Bill Team in the MOJ) reveals a remarkable misunderstanding of the nature of corruption and the ways in which it might be controlled.

World Bank, December 2010

In December 2010, the World Bank sponsored the modestly named 'International Corruption Hunters' Alliance' meeting in Washington, admitting that there was a long way to go in achieving the OECD's objectives and that only 9 out of the 39[50] signatory countries had taken *any* enforcement action relating to facilitation payments to FPOs (see page 243). The fact is that 'demand-side' countries have done virtually nothing to implement the Convention.

Passing of the Act, April 2011

The Act was passed through Parliament on the day before it prorogued pending the General Election. It was the Labour Government's final present to British industry. Chapter 5 continues with the sorry tale.

---

50   As of November 2012.

CHAPTER **3** *The Main Conventions*

Overview

The main international conventions on corruption rather than bribery are as follows:

Table 3.1   Main Conventions on 'Corruption'

Sponsor name and Convention	Deals with	Extent and current position
European Union: May 1997 Convention on the Fight Against Corruption Involving Officials of the European Communities and Member States	Corruption of foreign and domestic public officials of EU Member States (extraterritorial)	15 Member states plus candidates. Not ratified Not in effect A very limited convention applying only to the EU
OECD: December 1997 Convention on Combating Bribery of Foreign Public Officials in International Business Transactions	Corruption of foreign public officials (FPOs) (extraterritorial)	30 Member States 5 Non-Member States Now effective Effectively applies only to 'supply-side' states
Council of Europe: November 1998 Criminal Law Convention on Corruption	Corruption of domestic public officials Corruption of Parliamentarians Corruption in the private sector Trading in influence Money-laundering and proceeds of corruption offences Accounting offences relating to corruption (extraterritorial and domestic)	43 Member States Ratified by 8 Member States Needs 14 ratifications to become effective Not in effect, but signed by the UK A very good convention
United Nations: January 2002 Convention against Corruption	As Council of Europe only even wider (extraterritorial and domestic)	140 signatories A good convention that has been overtaken by the much narrower OECD edition possibly because it does not tackle political corruption. For these reasons it is not fully analysed in this book

To keep this book to the indecently short length it now is, other conventions – which regionalise or tinker with the above – have not been included.

The UK has signed (or will sign) all four conventions and has ratified the first two. Followers of committees and conventions will already know that signature means that the terms are generally agreed and ratification that domestic laws comply or will be put in place. The third stage is that the convention is taken onto a country's statute books. If a country which ratifies a convention fails to observe its obligations, it may come under pressure from other members and in the case of the European Union (EU), political, legal and financial sanctions. In most cases this is akin to being mauled by a dead sheep.

However, it should be noted – despite all of the political posturing on Britain leading the way – it has cynically avoided incorporating the Organisation for Economic Cooperation and Development (OECD) Convention into its statutes and can therefore ignore it. It has done precisely this with the Council of Europe Convention, relating to 'trading in influence', thereby further protecting skulduggery by politicians.

Organisations Concerned With Corruption

INTRODUCTION

There are a number of organisations that are leading the way in the supposed fight against corruption, including those described in detail below and:

- The World Economic Forum
- International Chamber of Commerce
- United Nations Global Compact
- Extractive Industries Transparency Initiative.

All of these issue guidelines that are of limited value to companies, but the most significant players[1] are described below.

TRANSPARENCY INTERNATIONAL (TI)

TI is an international non-governmental organisation devoted to combating corruption and its publicity[2] claims that

> it brings civil society, business, and governments together in a powerful global coalition. TI, through its International Secretariat and more than 80 independent national chapters around the world, works at both the national and international level.

TI is funded by donations from chapter contributions, foundations and business organisations, some of which (such as Enron), have had less than impeccable track records. That said, TI has done some good work and has been among the most effective pressure groups in the anti-bribery field.

TI's publicity continues:

---

1   There are many others, including the World Bank.

2   See http://www.transparency.org/ (accessed 7 November 2012).

In the international arena, TI raises awareness about the damaging effects of corruption, advocates policy reform, works towards the implementation of multilateral conventions and subsequently monitors compliance by governments, corporations and banks. At the national level, chapters work to increase levels of accountability and transparency, monitoring the performance of key institutions and pressing for necessary reforms in a non-party political manner.

TI also produces the Perceptions of Corruption Index and Bribe Payers' Index (which are discussed in Chapter 4) and some other interesting papers. One, by Paul Lashmar, in the organisation's 'Global Corruption Report of 2001', notes the corrupt influence of political party funding and massive corruption of politicians in, among other places, Germany, Italy, Ireland, Spain, France, Greece, Portugal, Belgium and, of course, the grand EU headquarters itself.

Mr Lashmar comments that:[3]

- In 1998 the US Intelligence Community found that some 60 major international contracts valued at US$30 billion went to the biggest briber. In 2002, *The Economist* reported that 'the US government learned of significant allegations of bribery by foreign firms in over 400 competitions for international contracts valued at $200 billion. The practice is global in scope, with firms from over 50 countries implicated in offering bribes for contracts in over 100 buyer countries over the past seven years'.
- The OECD Convention contains a major loophole: 'It does not bar multinational companies from making contributions to foreign political party officials[4] and that may prove to be a key means to gain influence'.

Some spectators believe that any criticism of TI is beyond the pale and that its image – which is akin to that of the Red Cross or Mother Theresa – should be protected at all costs. There is no doubt that TI has done some very good work, but criticism is justified because:

- It concentrates too heavily on the so-called 'supply side' of corruption (around 22 countries) while paying little regard (or at least, not emphasising the results) to approximately 160 countries on the so-called 'demand side'. In fact, corruption is an equal transaction between an extorter and coercer and very often initiated by the former.
- It should publish a summary of the internal laws against corruption in so-called 'demand-side' countries and promote these widely to the international business community.
- It should abandon the misleading terms 'active' and 'passive' corruption.

But most of all it should coordinate and think again about its perceptions (and what they entail) and concentrate much more on tackling extortion, kleptocracy, political corruption and the plundering of foreign aid.

---

3   See http://archive.transparency.org/publications/gcr/gcr_2001 – Regional Reports: West Europe and North America (accessed 7 November 2012).

4   The Foreign Corrupt Practices Act (FCPA) has such a provision but the UK Bribery Act does not.

TRACE INTERNATIONAL

TRACE International Inc. is an America-based, non-profit membership association that pools resources to provide practical and cost-effective anti-corruption compliance solutions for multinational companies and their commercial intermediaries (sales agents and representatives, consultants, distributors, suppliers, etc.). It is funded, primarily, by subscriptions.

TRACE provides several core services and products, including: due diligence reports on commercial intermediaries; model compliance policies; an online Resource Center with foreign local law summaries, including guidelines on gifts and hospitality; in-person and online anti-corruption training; and research on corporate best practices. It also produces the excellent 'Trace compendium' of enforcement actions taken throughout the world.

EUROPEAN UNION

The EU was set up after the Second World War, and the drive towards European integration was launched on 9 May 1950 when France officially proposed the creation of 'the first concrete foundation of a European federation'. Six countries (Belgium, Germany, France, Italy, Luxembourg and The Netherlands) were the founder members. Today, after four waves of accessions (1973: Denmark, Ireland and the United Kingdom; 1981: Greece; 1986: Spain and Portugal; 1995: Austria, Finland and Sweden) the EU has 15 Member States and is preparing for the accession of 13 eastern and southern European countries.

An early version of the EU website stated:

> The European Union is based on the rule of law and democracy. It is neither a new State replacing existing ones nor is it comparable to other international organisations. Its Member States delegate sovereignty to common institutions representing the interests of the Union as a whole on questions of joint interest. All decisions and procedures are derived from the basic treaties ratified by the Member States.

The principal objectives of the Union are to:

- Establish European citizenship (fundamental rights; freedom of movement; civil and political rights);
- Ensure freedom, security and justice (cooperation in the field of justice and home affairs);
- Promote economic and social progress (the single market; the Euro, the common currency; job creation; regional development; environmental protection);
- Assert Europe's role in the world (common foreign and security policies; the EU in the world);
- The EU is run by five institutions, each playing a specific role:
  - The European Parliament (elected by the peoples of the Member States)
  - The Council of the Union (composed of the governments of the Member States)
  - The European Commission (the driving force and executive body)
  - The Court of Justice (compliance with the law)
  - The Court of Auditors (sound and lawful management of the EU budget).

- Five further bodies are part of the institutional system:
  - The European Economic and Social Committee (expresses the opinions of organised civil society on economic and social issues)
  - The Committee of the Regions (expresses the opinions of regional and local authorities on regional policy, environment, and education)
  - The European Ombudsman (deals with complaints from citizens concerning maladministration by an EU institution or body)
  - The European Investment Bank (contributes to EU objectives by financing public and private long-term investments)
  - The European Central Bank (responsible for monetary policy and foreign exchange operations).

A number of agencies and bodies complete the system.

On 26 May 1997, the EU enacted the 'Convention on the Fight Against Corruption Involving Officials of the European Communities or Officials of Member States'.[5] The Convention comes into force 90 days after the Secretary-General of the Council of the European Union has been notified by the last Member State to ratify.

The Convention states: 'For the purposes of this Convention, the deliberate action of an official, who, directly or through an intermediary, requests or receives advantages of any kind whatsoever, for himself or for a third party, or accepts a promise of an advantage, to act or refrain from acting in accordance with his duty or in the exercise of his functions in breach of his official duties constitutes passive corruption' (i.e. excludes facilitation payments).

There is a parallel offence of active corruption and Member States will be required to take the necessary measures to ensure that both are made a criminal offence. The definition of 'official' and 'Community Official' are vague and would seem to exclude MPs and certain other elected representatives like Members of the European Parliament (MEPs). At the present time, it is not a convention worth worrying about.

COUNCIL OF EUROPE

The Council of Europe is a non-statutory body, not backed by the compulsion of law. Any European state can become a member of the Council provided it accepts the principle of the rule of law and guarantees human rights and fundamental freedoms to everyone under its jurisdiction. The Council should not be confused with the EU. The two organisations are quite distinct. It has 43 members including the 15 EU states.

The Criminal Law Convention on Corruption was adopted by the Committee of Ministers of the Council of Europe on 4 November 1998 and opened for signature on 27 January 1999. The website explains: 'The Convention is an ambitious instrument aiming at the co-ordinated criminalisation of a large number of corrupt practices'. It also provides for complementary civil law measures and for improved international cooperation in the prosecution of corruption offences.[6]

---

5   Available at: http://eur-lex.europa.eu/LexUriServ/LexUriServ.do?uri=CELEX:41997A0625(01):EN:NOT (accessed 7 November 2012).

6   For the Council of Europe website see http://hub.coe.int/ (accessed 7 November 2012). Full details of the Convention are available on http://conventions.coe.int/treaty (accessed 7 November 2012).

The Convention is open to the accession of non-member States. Its implementation will be monitored by the Group of States against Corruption (GRECO), which started work on 1 May 1999. To date, the Convention has been ratified by 8 countries and signed by 31, including the UK. It provides for enhanced international cooperation (mutual assistance, extradition and the provision of information) in the investigation and prosecution of corruption offences and will come into force when it has been ratified by 14 states.

States are required to provide effective and dissuasive sanctions and measures, including deprivation of liberty, which can lead to extradition. Legal entities will also be liable for offences committed to benefit them, and will be subject to effective criminal or non-criminal sanctions, including monetary sanctions.

The Convention also incorporates provisions concerning aiding and abetting, immunity, criteria for determining the jurisdiction of states, liability of legal persons, the setting up of specialised anti-corruption bodies, protection of persons collaborating with investigating or prosecuting authorities, gathering of evidence and confiscation of proceeds. It is a good convention and far better than the OECD's.

The Council also supported a civil law convention (see page 44), which has not been ratified by the UK.

THE ORGANISATION FOR ECONOMIC COOPERATION AND DEVELOPMENT

The OECD has been called a think tank, a monitoring agency, a rich man's club, an un-academic university and a load of hot air. Its publicity explains that its 34 member states,[7] grouped in a unique and supposedly economic forum,

> discuss, develop and refine economic and social policies. They compare experiences, seek answers to common problems and work to co-ordinate domestic and international policies to help members and non-members deal with an increasingly globalised world. Their exchanges may lead to agreements to act in a formal way – for example by establishing legally binding agreements to crack down on bribery, or codes for free flow of capital and services.

The OECD is also known for soft law – non-binding instruments on difficult issues such as guidelines for multinational enterprises. Beyond agreements, the discussions at the OECD are said to make for better-informed work within member states' own governments across the broad spectrum of public policy and help clarify the impact of national policies on the international community.

The publicity also states:

> The OECD is a group of like-minded countries. Essentially membership is limited only by a country's commitment to a market economy and a pluralistic democracy. It is rich, in that its [...] members produce two thirds of the world's goods and services, but it is by no means exclusive and now involves in its work some 70 non-member states from Brazil, China and Russia to less developed countries in Africa and elsewhere.[8]

---

7   A list of member states and other information about the organisation is available on the OECD website at http://www.oecd.org/ (accessed 7 November 2012).

8   Whiteford, Peter, 'Anticipating Population Ageing – Challenges and Responses', available at: http://www.oecd.org/social/socialpoliciesanddata/31639461.pdf (accessed 7 November 2012).

Over the years there has been a considerable amount of international pressure – mainly from the USA – to standardise anti-bribery laws. TI and the OECD took up the challenge, resulting in the Convention on Combating Bribery of Foreign Public Officials in International Business Transactions.

On 21 November 1997, negotiators from 29 OECD member states and five other countries adopted the convention. A signing ceremony took place in Paris on 17 December 1997.[9] The Convention makes it a crime to offer, promise or give a bribe to an FPO in order to obtain or retain international business deals. A related text effectively puts an end to the practice of affording tax deductibility for bribe payments made to foreign officials. It is concerned only with 'active bribery' of FPOs.

The Convention commits the 35 signatory countries to adopting common laws to punish companies and individuals who engage in bribery transactions. So far, 28 countries have been subjected to close monitoring to determine the adequacy of their implementing legislation.

Article 1 states:

Each Party shall take such measures as may be necessary to establish that it is a criminal offence under its law for any person intentionally to offer, promise or give any undue pecuniary or other advantage, whether directly or through intermediaries, to a foreign public official, for that official or for a third party, in order that the official act or refrain from acting in relation to the performance of official duties, in order to obtain or retain business or other improper advantage in the conduct of international business.[10]

Further, Article 2 states that

each Party shall take any measures necessary to establish that complicity in, including incitement, aiding and abetting, or authorisation of an act of bribery of a foreign public official shall be a criminal offence. Attempt and conspiracy to bribe a foreign public official shall be criminal offences to the same extent ....

And Article 5 forbids considerations of international relations or economic interest to influence the investigation of or prosecution for bribery of an FPO.[11]

For the purpose of this Convention a 'foreign public official' means any person holding a legislative, administrative or judicial office of a foreign country, whether appointed or elected; any person exercising a public function for a foreign country, including for a public agency or public enterprise; and any official or agent of a public international organisation. This is usually interpreted to include elected politicians.[12]

---

9   Not at le Rose Chatte Boîte de Nuit.

10   The Convention is available at: http://www.oecd.org/investment/briberyininternationalbusiness/anti-briberyconvention/38028044.pdf (accessed 7 November 2012).

11   This was why Mr Blair's initial attempts to scupper the British Aerospace case had to be 'reframed' in the context of Saudi withdrawal in the fight against terrorism.

12   But not in the UK.

FPO Anomaly

Thus a Belgian businessman who bribes a British MP could be prosecuted in his home country whereas the MP could not.

After ratifying the Convention on 15 February 1999, the UK argued that its existing laws (and especially its Common Law provisions) were in compliance and that nothing had to be done. It maintained this stance until April 2001 when, facing severe criticism from the International Development Select Committee of the House of Commons, and pressure from the USA and its OECD partners, the Government agreed to act. Although the Anti-terrorism Crime and Security Act (ATSCA) complied with the OECD Convention, the British Aerospace scandal put the UK under even more pressure to put its house in order and this ultimately led to the Bribery Act 2010.

THE GROUP OF STATES AGAINST CORRUPTION

GRECO came into being on 1 May 1999 and 49 states are now members, including the UK. GRECO is responsible for monitoring not only the OECD Convention but also the application of the Guiding Principles for the Fight against Corruption and other conventions or legal instruments drawn up by the Council of Europe under its Programme of Action against Corruption.

4 UK and US Regulatory Agencies

UK Regulatory and Law Enforcement

OVERVIEW

The Business Anti-Corruption Portal maintained by the British Government[1] (note: rather than being comprehensive and 'anti-corruption', its concern is business and 'anti-bribery', relating only to 'emerging markets and developing countries') states that it is 'a comprehensive and practical tool tailored to meet the corruption risk management needs of small and medium sized companies (SMEs) operating in or considering doing business in emerging markets and developing countries'.

The website[2] provides 17 'country profiles',[3] sample policies, codes of conduct, guides on such things as a one-page 'risk assessment procedure',[4] and notes on control tools and training. It lists some of the UK government agencies concerned with 'corruption' as detailed in Table 4.1 and more detail on page 66.

Table 4.1   UK Government Departments Involved in 'Corruption' (or is it 'Bribery'?)

Department	Activities
Anti-corruption Champion	On 10 June 2010 the Prime Minister appointed the Lord Chancellor (Kenneth Clarke) as 'Anti-corruption Champion'. The role seems to have been passed on to Chris Grayling after the reshuffle in 2012.
Business Innovation & Skills (BIS)	Coordinates government work to support ethical business overseas. It represents the UK at the OECD Working Group on **Bribery** and provides the contact point for the OECD Guidelines for multinational enterprises.
Department for International Development (DFID)	The department is committed to tackling corruption and ensuring that foreign aid is used for its intended purpose.
Export Credits Guarantee Department (ECGD)	Takes corruption risks into account when asked to support export transactions.
UK Trade and Investment (UKTI)	Provides advice and support on how to trade internationally 'but does not make commercial judgements for a company'.

---

1   Supported by Austria, Denmark, Germany, The Netherlands and Sweden (only).

2   At http://www.business-anti-corruption.com/ (accessed 7 November 2012).

3   But not aligned with Transparency International (TI) perceptions.

4   Based almost entirely on 'country risk'.

The site does not mention the very important Crown Agents, which is 'an international development company that helps raise revenue, manage debt and plan expenditure,[5] and provides procurement and supply chain services'. It is intimately involved in many, if not most, UK overseas aid projects and 'disburses £3 billion per annum', including £151,000,000 of European Union (EU) aid.

The involvement (or lack of) by the following departments is also important.

MINISTRY OF JUSTICE

This ministry (headed, as we write, by Chris Grayling),[6] is responsible for administering criminal and civil courts, 135 prisons, the probation service and attendance centres. It is also concerned with reforming the justice system, making new laws and modernising the constitution,[7] and 'support[ing] the victims' of crime. It employs 95,000 people and has a budget of around £9 billion per annum. In recent times its key performance drivers have been set on cutting costs rather than upholding justice.

HOME OFFICE

This office, after much reformation, is now the lead government agency for immigration, drugs policy, crime, counter-terrorism and police.

ATTORNEY GENERAL, CROWN PROSECUTION SERVICE AND DIRECTOR OF PUBLIC PROSECUTIONS

The Attorney General is Chief Legal Adviser to the Crown, a government minister with responsibility for the prosecuting departments such as the Crown Prosecution Service and SFO and has a number of independent public-interest functions.

The Crown Prosecution Service (CPS), headed by the Director of Public Prosecutions (DPP), is the government department responsible for prosecuting criminal cases investigated by the police in England and Wales. It is responsible for:

- Advising the police on cases for possible prosecution;
- Reviewing cases submitted by the police;
- Determining any charges in all but minor cases;
- Preparing cases for court;
- Presenting cases at court.

The CPS is organised on a regional basis throughout England and Wales.

---

5   For less developed countries. More information on Crown Agents is available at: http://www.crownagents.com/Home.aspx (accessed 7 November 2012).

6   Supposedly the anti-bribery 'champion' – but only the 'overseas bribery champion' – there is no such animal for the UK.

7   But not the Bill of Rights or Parliamentary Privilege.

THE SERIOUS FRAUD OFFICE

A brief history

The Serious Fraud Office (SFO) was established under the Criminal Justice Act of 1987, as a result of the Roskill Report, with the primary objective of investigating and prosecuting serious fraud. Its terms of reference and methods of operation are described in Chapter 36. It was the first to be awarded powers under Section 2 of the Criminal Justice Act[8] (see page 196) which remove the principle against self-incrimination and constitute one of the most powerful law enforcement tools anywhere in the world.

After the British Aerospace (BAE) case collapsed following the intervention of Prime Minister Blair, Robert Wardle, the Director, retired, and it is alleged that over 60 per cent of senior officers left. Morale in the SFO reached rock bottom and it is far from clear that recovery will ever be possible. When Richard Alderman was appointed Director,[9] he announced that he wanted to move away from prosecuting complex cases[10] and more towards an advisory role that would help prevent consumer and other public fraud. Then, when the Bribery Act appeared in 2010, there was a further change of emphasis.[11]

The emphasis changed yet again when David Green, CB CQ took over as the SFO's Director in June 2012. He has stated that the agency will concentrate on serious strategic targets and serious frauds. He continued:

> the perception has emerged over the past few years that perhaps there is more a willingness to compromise than to prosecute. I would like to rebalance the relationship between prosecution and civil settlement. We are primarily a crime-fighting agency, and we've got to remember that .... a company might say 'if we come and self-report we might not get prosecuted'. Well, they might get prosecuted![12]

Mr Green dismissed rumours that the SFO might be abandoned, although he was clearly displeased with its shrinking budget. In 2010–2011 this was £39.5 million, although the agency will – in addition – collect around a third of all civil recoveries. Whether this perverse incentive will influence 'prosecutorial discretion' remains an open question.

SFO acceptance criteria

The SFO's guidance indicates that it will normally only accept cases for investigation that satisfy the following conditions:

- The value of the alleged fraud should exceed £1 million and concern a 'serious issue'.

---

8   Although these have been extended to other prosecuting authorities.

9   Appointments are made by the Attorney General.

10   In 2008 the SFO brought 18 cases involving 18 guilty pleas, 9 convictions and 24 acquittals.

11   Mr Alderman's title as Director of the SFO is used throughout this book even though to be technically correct he should be described as the 'Ex-director'. He retired in April 2012 and was replaced by David Green, CB, QC. Post retirement, Mr Alderman has worked for the World Bank trying to sort out corruption problems in India.

12   Cited in The *Financial Times*, 26 April 2010 'New SFO Director pledges tougher stance', by Caroline Binham.

- It has a significant international dimension and is of 'widespread public concern'.[13]
- Investigation requires highly specialised knowledge.
- There is a need to use the SFO's special powers (such as Section 2 CJA Orders).

In addition, other factors are to be considered, including:

- Seriousness;
- Complexity;
- Whether the case requires complex accounting analysis;
- The suspected fraud is such that the direction of the investigation should be in the hands of those responsible for the prosecution.

Many cases of alleged bribery (especially involving facilitation payments and hospitality) are unlikely to satisfy the above criteria. But this does not mean the SFO will refuse to accept them.

Cases can be referred to the SFO by anyone, any company or government agency and it can initiate its own enquiries. Referrals are usually vetted by the Referral Evaluation Team (RET) and a 'vetting note' (with supporting evidence) prepared for the Chief Operating Officer, to include details of:

- The nature of the allegations made;
- The evidence submitted in support of the referral;
- Any potential difficulties in pursuing the investigation or a prosecution that the evidence discloses;
- A consideration of the alleged facts by reference to the SFO acceptance criteria;
- A recommendation as to whether the case should be accepted or rejected;
- The reasons for that recommendation.

The SFO mandate continues that if the case is rejected it may be passed to another agency for investigation, regulatory action or other disposition. Alternatively, the case may be accepted or retained pending receipt or development of further information and extended vetting.

At the point of making a self-disclosure, companies do not know whether the case will be handled by the SFO (thus providing the opportunity of a 'civil disposal') or passed to another law enforcement agency that has no such option. Thus companies that believe in the value or ethicality of 'civil disposals' (see page 450) should be absolutely sure that their cases qualify for SFO acceptance.

Civil disposals

Companies should never forget that information is shared between UK and international enforcement agencies, with the result that cooperation with one means knowledge by all. Once one agency becomes involved, experience shows – as in the Oil for Food Programme –

---

13   It can be inferred (although probably incorrectly) that the SFO will not accept bribery offences that are entirely domestic.

that it is a case of bees round the honeypot and a stinging frenzy. Thus companies should take UK and US guidelines on civil settlement into account, if not treat them as one.

The SFO's guideline on overseas corruption were published on 21 July 2009[14] and directed towards encouraging 'corporates'[15] to self-disclose offences of *overseas corruption*;[16] and it recognises that 'a corporate will not want to approach us unless it has decided, following advice and a degree of investigation by its professional advisers, that there is a real issue and that remedial action is necessary…'.

The Department of Justice also encourages internal investigations before self-disclosure, but the Financial Services Authority (FSA) does not. This is another uncertainty.[17]

The SFO guidelines state that when considering civil disposals they will be looking for the following:[18]

- A clear statement of the anticorruption culture, visibly supported at the highest levels in the corporate;[19]
- A code of ethics with a commitment making it explicit that the anti-bribery code applies to business partners;
- Principles that are applicable regardless of local laws or culture;
- Individual accountability;
- Policies on
  - gifts
  - hospitality
  - facilitation payments
  - outside advisers/third parties including vetting, due diligence and appropriate risk assessments
  - political contributions and lobbying activities;
- Training to ensure dissemination of the anticorruption culture to all staff at all levels within the corporate;
- Regular checks and auditing in a proportionate manner;
- A helpline within the corporate which enables employees to report concerns;
- Appropriate and consistent disciplinary processes.

In simple terms the above means that the SFO might take a different view if a company has 'adequate procedures' in place, yet these are not at all relevant to defending a charge of 'influencing' a foreign public official (FPO)[20] under Section 6.

The guidance discusses the procedures after a case has been self-disclosed as follows, stating that very soon after the self-report the SFO will want to establish the following:

---

14   Based on David Green's realignment of the SFO as a prosecutorial agency, these guidelines were removed from its website and are unlikely to apply in the future.

15   But not government departments.

16   There are no equivalent guidelines on domestic corruption.

17   This is an unsubtle way for the SFO to maximise its budgets by passing its responsibilities to 'corporates'.

18   Here the SFO Guidelines are paraphrased.

19   SFO-speak for a company or business, but does not include government departments.

20   Again reflecting a fixation with Section 7.

- Is the board of the corporate genuinely committed to resolving the issue?[21]
- Is the board of the corporate prepared to work with us on the scope and handling of any additional investigation *we* consider to be necessary?
- At the end of the investigation,[22] will the corporate be prepared to discuss resolution on the basis of a civil recovery, as well as:
  - a programme of training and culture change
  - appropriate action when necessary against individuals
  - and at least in some cases external monitoring in a proportionate manner?
- Does the corporate understand that any resolution must satisfy the public interest and be transparent?
- Will the corporate want us, where possible, to work with regulators and criminal enforcement authorities both in the UK and abroad in order to reach a global settlement?

The guidance continues, stating that the SFO can give no unconditional guarantee that it will not prosecute, although it states that 'it would want to settle self-referral cases civilly, unless a board member had been personally involved in corrupt activities'.

Finally, and again menacingly, the document repeats the warning that

> if a 'corporate' chooses not to self-report, the SFO would regard this failure as a negative factor, increasing the prospect of a criminal investigation followed by prosecution and a confiscation order ... [a] corporate will need to be aware of the expense of an SFO investigation, the considerable publicity and destruction to the business.

If this did not smack of a shakedown it is difficult to know what does! And what is to be made of the framing of these guidelines, which are at best one-sided? Would a helpful regulatory agency not have made some commitment that it would assist UK companies to deal with competitive corruption and try to level the playing field? Why are the guidelines restricted to overseas corruption? What are the procedures for entirely domestic cases? What is the position if a case fails to pass the SFO acceptance test and gets transferred to a prosecutorial agency that does not, or is unable to, handle civil disposals? How can the SFO offer civil disposals when it knows its ability to deliver is uncertain? What precisely will be the position on civil disposals when American or other regulators are involved in parallel actions? All of the above add to the Act's uncertainty.

It should be noted that David Green has taken a much more conventional – and most would say realistic prosecutor's – approach to self disclosure and has made it clear that compliance with earlier SFO guidance is a factor that might be considered but is not a guarantee that prosecution will be avoided.

CITY OF LONDON OVERSEAS CORRUPTION UNIT

The City of London Police[23] has a dedicated unit (part of the Economic Crime Directorate) of around 40 officers who focus on overseas corruption. It works closely with and often

---

21   This presupposes that there is an 'issue' after the investigation has been completed.

22   Assumes guilt.

23   Supported by the Metropolitan Police.

provide investigative resources for the Serious Fraud Office. Is it generally regarded as an effective team which works closely with the SFO.

SERIOUS ORGANISED CRIME AGENCY

The Serious Organised Crime Agency (SOCA) is an Executive Non-Departmental Public Body of the Home Office led by a board with a majority of non-executive members. SOCA tackles serious organised crime, including Class A drugs, people-smuggling and human trafficking, major gun crime, fraud, computer crime, money-laundering and Politically Exposed Persons.

It acts as the coordinating body for around 220,000 Suspicious Activity Reports submitted each year in compliance with the Proceeds of Crime Act and other money-laundering legislation.

NATIONAL CRIME AGENCY

This new agency – under the Home Office – is planned to come into existence sometime before 2013 and will confront serious and organised crime. It will work 'with police and crime commissioners, chief constables, devolved administrations and others, genuinely connecting activity from the local to the international – in the country, at the border and overseas'. It is hoped that it will become the UK equivalent of the Federal Bureau of Investigation (FBI) in the USA.

FINANCIAL SERVICES AUTHORITY

The FSA, an independent non-governmental body established in 1985, acts under the Financial Services and Markets Act 2000, of which it is the sole regulator. It is a company limited by guarantee and financed by the financial services industry.

The FSA regulates most financial services markets,[24] involving 29,000 firms and 165,000 individuals and can impose heavy financial penalties and civil sanctions, recent cases include actions against large insurance brokers for failing to keep records of payments that could have been bribes. It issues guidelines including, possibly the most important, 'Senior Management Arrangements, Systems and Controls'.[25]

In 2013, its supervision of the banking sector is expected to revert to the Bank of England, with its remaining functions divided between the Prudential Regulatory Authority and the Financial Conduct Authority.

US Regulatory Agencies

SECURITIES AND EXCHANGE COMMISSION

The Securities and Exchange Commission (SEC) is an agency responsible for defining, interpreting and enforcing US securities laws and regulations through five main divisions,

---

24   But only in very limited ways for the 'Carbon World'.

25   This has not been included in the Concordance analysis discussed in pages 79 and 620 et seq.

headquartered with a staff of 3,500 in Washington, DC and with 11 regional offices. The Commission's website states:

> The Division of Enforcement assists the Commission in executing its law enforcement function by recommending the commencement of investigations of securities law violations, by recommending that the Commission bring civil actions in federal court or before an administrative law judge, and by prosecuting these cases on behalf of the Commission. As an adjunct to the SEC's civil enforcement authority, the Division works closely with law enforcement agencies in the U.S. and around the world to bring criminal cases when appropriate.
>
> The Division obtains evidence of possible violations of the securities laws from many sources, including market surveillance activities, investor tips and complaints, other Divisions and Offices of the SEC, the self-regulatory organizations and other securities industry sources, and media reports.
>
> **All SEC investigations** are conducted privately. Facts are developed to the fullest extent possible through informal inquiry, interviewing witnesses, examining brokerage records, reviewing trading data, and other methods. With a formal order of investigation, the Division's staff may compel witnesses by subpoena to testify and produce books, records, and other relevant documents. Following an investigation, SEC staff present their findings to the Commission for its review. The Commission can authorize the staff to file a case in federal court or bring an administrative action. In many cases, the Commission and the party charged decide to settle a matter without trial.
>
> Whether the Commission decides to bring a case in federal court or within the SEC before an administrative law judge may depend upon the type of sanction or relief that is being sought. For example, the Commission may bar someone from the brokerage industry in an administrative proceeding, but an order barring someone from acting as a corporate officer or director must be obtained in federal court. Often, when the misconduct warrants it, the Commission will bring both proceedings.
>
> **Civil action:** The Commission files a complaint with a U.S. District Court and asks the court for a sanction or remedy. Often the Commission asks for a court order, called an injunction, that prohibits any further acts or practices that violate the law or Commission rules. An injunction can also require audits, accounting for frauds, or special supervisory arrangements. In addition, the SEC can seek civil monetary penalties, or the return of illegal profits (called disgorgement). The court may also bar or suspend an individual from serving as a corporate officer or director. A person who violates the court's order may be found in contempt and be subject to additional fines or imprisonment.
>
> **Administrative action:** The Commission can seek a variety of sanctions through the administrative proceeding process. Administrative proceedings differ from civil court actions in that they are heard by an administrative law judge (ALJ), who is independent of the Commission. The administrative law judge presides over a hearing and considers the evidence presented by the Division staff, as well as any evidence submitted by the subject of the proceeding. Following the hearing the ALJ issues an initial decision that includes findings of fact and legal conclusions. The initial decision also contains a recommended sanction. Both the Division staff and the defendant may appeal all or any portion of the initial decision to the Commission. The Commission may affirm the decision of the ALJ, reverse the decision, or remand it for additional hearings. Administrative sanctions include cease and desist orders,

suspension or revocation of broker–dealer and investment advisor registrations, censures, bars from association with the securities industry, civil monetary penalties, and disgorgement.[26]

The SEC primarily focuses on civil enforcement, including the accounting provisions of the Foreign Corrupt Practices Act (FCPA) and works in close cooperation with the Justice Department.[27]

There are less than 200 UK companies with SEC registration and reporting obligations, which are thus bound by the FCPA international accounting provisions.

DEPARTMENT OF JUSTICE

The aims of the Department of Justice (DOJ) are stated to be:

To enforce the law and defend the interests of the United States according to the law; to ensure public safety against threats foreign and domestic; to provide federal leadership in preventing and controlling crime; to seek just punishment for those guilty of unlawful behaviour; and to ensure fair and impartial administration of justice for all Americans.[28]

It has administrative responsibility for a number of agencies, including the FBI, Drugs Enforcement Administration (DEA) and Alcohol, Tobacco and Firearms Explosives (AFT) and thus integrates investigative and prosecutorial resources.

The DOJ has become the world's largest law offices and the primary agency for the enforcement of federal laws. It has recently formed a Kleptocracy Unit.

International Record of Prosecutions

Despite political, media and regulatory bombast over corruption, there have been very few enforcement actions, virtually no contested trials or judicial approval of the expansive interpretations arrogated by regulators. The Department of Justice has flounced away with a bloody nose in spectacular cases (such as the 'Shot Show' trial and Lindsey Manufacturing: see page 839). Moreover, American judges have been reluctant to approve penalties sought by regulators: sometimes reducing them from recommendations of life imprisonment to 42 months. UK judges have been more than critical of the SFO's civil disposal manoeuvrings (see page 170). **Unsurprisingly, these setbacks are seldom mentioned by the Cottage Industry because they do not help the noble cause.**

The delusion is created that if companies who discover the most trivial suspicions of bribe payment don't immediately self-disclose they will be hammered by omnipotent regulators. The other side of the coin is that self-disclosure and effective compliance programs will result in sympathy, reduced penalties and avoidance of mandatory debarment from future government contracts, etc, etc. It is the ultimate stick and carrot, but it is a cynical fantasy to scare people and companies into flagellating when there is no legal requirement that they should do so. Let's have a closer look at *some* of the facts:

---

26   See http://www.sec.gov/about/whatwedo.shtml (accessed 7 November 2012).

27   Responsible for enforcement of the criminal laws.

28   See http://www.justice.gov/about/about.html (accessed 7 November 2012).

- Between 2004 and 2011, the SEC and the DOJ were involved in between 269 and 285 enforcement actions for outbound bribery.[29] **This is an average of 40 a year!**
- The UK statistics for domestic bribery are shown in Table 4.2: **there was not a single prosecution for overseas corruption, including facilitation payments.**
- **Negotiated penalties for companies that self-disclosed were 42 per cent higher than those whose skulduggery emerged by other means** (see the paper by Bruce Hinchey http://papers.ssrn.com/sol3/papers.cfm?abstract_id=1650925).
- The probability of a non-American company being nabbed in the USA by the DOJ or SEC is estimated as **7 times greater than for a domestic equivalent**. What's more penalties imposed on foreign companies were 22 times greater than for their domestic counterparts.
- **THE SUSPICION IS THAT FEDERAL PROSECUTIONS DELIBERATELY PROTECT AMERICAN COMMERCIAL INTERESTS (see page 218).**
- The US Sentencing Commision reported that of 3,433 organisations that were sentenced only 5 received any credit for their compliance programs.
- It has been impossible to confirm a single case of a genuine declination in a bribery case (which is where there is sufficient evidence to prosecute).

Table 4.2   Prosecutions

Law	2004		2005		2006		2007	
	Cases	Guilty	Cases	Guilty	Cases	Guilty	Cases	Guilty
1906 Act Principal–Agent	3	4	1	1	6	10	5	12
1889 Act Public Bodies	1	0	0	0	4	3	5	0
ATSCA 2001	0	0	0	0	0	0	0	0
Totals	**4**	**4**	**1**	**1**	**10**	**13**	**10**	**12**

Companies should recognise the important differences between the proposed adequate procedures defence in the UK and the effective compliance and ethics programs (EPEC) that theoretically justify mitigation under the FSG. Both should be influential in persuading regulators not to prosecute but there the similarity ends. Adequate procedures will be considered by a UK jury for the purposes of establishing corporate guilt under section 7. They play no part in computing sentences. ECEPs are of no interest to an American jury but are merely an optional guide for sentencing judges. This difference means that UK companies should be much more interested in assessing the way their procedures will be evaluated by a jury.

Conclusions

So against this background we will now be able to see what is right and wrong with the Bribery Act and what honest companies might do about it.

---

29   See http://www.traceinternational.org/ as an example of statistical reporting.

The SFO was fairly confident it would meet its targets

'He's been like this since he joined Compliance'

The Bribery Act 2010 and Friends

CHAPTER **5** *Objective and Limitations*

Digging into Detail

The objective of this chapter is to attempt a managerial–practical (rather than just a timorous legalistic) analysis of the Bribery Act 2010 and related legislation and their significance for honest companies. ***For busy managers who don't have time to get into the detail, they can cut to the chase by accepting just two points:***

1. Don't even think of trying to weasel word your way around the Act.
2. Manage on principle.

This chapter draws together the applicable laws and guidelines mainly in the UK and tangentially in the USA[1] to provide an overview and then detail to support the controls discussed in Chapters 21–7 and investigation procedures in Chapters 34–7. It discusses points and problems that some people might believe are best left unmentioned.

The chapter is based on a forensic linguistic analysis[2] of a corpus around 2,000,000 words extracted from the Ministry of Justice (MOJ) Guidance, Law Commission reports, Joint Committee deliberations, guidelines, Acts of Parliament, Explanatory Notes, Transparency International (TI) proposals and transcripts of around 50 speeches by the Serious Fraud Office (SFO), and all relevant Parliamentary debates. Every word in the corpus was indexed in date order and lemmatised[3] using Concordance software[4] and hyperlinked to source.[5] It has therefore been possible to examine how official views, opinions and guidelines have changed over time. It also exposes inconsistencies, and more than a little official weaseling.

---

1   Because many companies will be bound by both.

2   See Comer, Michael J. and Stepens, Timothy E., *Deception at Work* (Gower, 2004) for more details of this linguistic analysis system, which analyses the structure, syntax and lexicons of writing to find their deep – sometimes subconscious – meaning.

3   Lemmatisation (or lemmatization) is, in conventional linguistics, the process of grouping together the different inflected forms of a word so they can be analysed as a single item. In forensic linguistics the grouping is arranged by topic or by words that are indicative of truth or deception.

4   See http://www.concordancesoftware.co.uk/ (accessed 7 November 2012).

5   A CD containing this analysis is available from www.info@cobasco.com.

Shifting Sands on Facilitation Payments

The MOJ and the SFO kicked off by taking the toughest line possible over facilitation payments, saying that any company making them would be regarded – for this reason alone – of not having adequate procedures. Even tipping a foreign doctor $5 to avoid being injected with an infected needle (Alderman's Needle[6]) could be prosecuted. Then, a little common sense prevailed and the last known SFO pronouncement on facilitation payments – the six-step nuanced approach (see page 125) is much more sensible. However, in the light of David Green's repositioning of the SFO, it is possible that the 'nuanced approach' has been abandoned. Only time will tell!

A powerful conclusion of the Concordance analysis is that the MOJ on one side and the SFO and the Crime Prosecution on the other are not exactly as one over their interpretations of the Act. The former appears to have backed away from its opening draconian enthusiasm, while the latter is still in full bloodsucking mode.[7]

The Consultation Paper on Deferred Prosecution Agreements

Over the past decade, the Department of Justice has recognised the potentially harmful effects that prosecuting a commercial organisation can have on investors, employees, pensioners, suppliers and customers and [this] has prompted the use of alternatives to prosecution including Non-Prosecution Agreements (NPAs) and Deferred Prosecution Agreements (DPAs).

In May 2012, David Green CB QC, the newly appointed SFO Director, said: 'Corporates cannot be seen[8] to be allowed some special kid glove treatment. In any case where there is a reasonable prospect of conviction and it is in the public interest to prosecute,[9] the SFO will prosecute, whether individuals or corporates'.

So, what is the story? The Consultation Paper states that DPAs can only be negotiated when a case passes the Full Code Test. The SFO Director says that if a case meets this standard it will be prosecuted.

---

6   See page 80.

7   Which may be subject to change following the appointment of David Green, CB, QC as its Director.

8   This is very interesting phrasing: it does not say corporates 'should not be allowed', only that they should not 'be seen to be allowed'.

9   That is the Full Code Test.

No Judicial Interpretations

One of the problems with the Bribery Act, since it is on a different basis from previous laws, is that there are no precedents or judicial interpretations that might clarify its many uncertainties. The SFO and MOJ have avoided committing themselves on important points, leaving doubts that will, supposedly, be resolved by prosecutorial discretion. Case examples described by the various parties involved, such as the Law Commissioners and Joint Committee, are mainly based on drafts before the Act was finalised and are only limited indicators of the way courts *might* decide.

Examples extracted from speeches by the SFO – again analysed with Concordance – contain uncertainties that will only be resolved by prosecutorial discretion. Also, the Foreign Corrupt Practices Act (FCPA; see pages 202 et seq) has been expansively interpreted by regulators mainly without judicial backing. So on both sides of the Atlantic there is much uncertainty over what the laws really mean in practice, with far too much emphasis on constructing legalistic defences and not enough on true prevention and managerial control.

A Progressive Discourse and a Few Rules

This chapter is written on a more or less progressive basis,[10] starting with general explanations and drilling down into specific detail later. Senior managers who are dedicated enough to read the first few pages, to get the general drift, can probably ignore the rest of what is an interminably long chapter, but may like to consider the following points:

- Corruption is evil but will not be rooted out by existing laws and threats of punishment: no matter how draconian. The solution is in 'inspirational integrity' rather than 'coerced compliance'. The law can only go so far and that is not far enough or in the right direction.
- The justice system should be driven by J-U-S-T-I-C-E and not by money or prosecutorial whims.
- Everyone should be assumed innocent until proven otherwise through a fair trial.
- No one should rely on being able to weasel out of trouble on a technicality or by paying over money.
- Judges are far more sensible than ordinary humans and courts more just than regulators.
- Managers have the right and obligation to manage and take decisions; it is implicit that they should do so honestly and in the best interests of those to whom they owe obligations of good faith.
- It is much easier and far more effective to take decisions based on principle than by trying to weasel around esoteric points in the law.
- Regulators do not run businesses.
- The creative ability of prosecutors is unbounded and sometimes beyond bounds.

---

10   Digging deeper as it goes along. This results in some duplications to save the need for readers to constantly refer back.

- Regulators should be much more attentive to conflicts of interest within their own ranks.
- There is every incentive for members of the 'Cottage Industry' (see Foreword) to amplify the importance of anti-bribery and other laws.
- Criminal charges can always be found for anything that is remotely illegal and for lots of things that aren't.
- If criminal charges cannot be sustained, civil alternatives of punishment can always be found.
- Regulators are not always right and do not necessarily hold the moral high ground.
- For multinational companies, the United States of America should be regarded as a British Colony,[11] or, alternatively, the United Kingdom should be regarded as a US State or, more likely, county. **For most bribery offences their laws are inseparable.**
- Decisions to self-disclose are three-dimensional. Is it right to do so on principle? Is it essential to comply with laws? Is it justified commercially?
- Effective controls are essential to maximise profits and to achieve objectives: box-ticking compliance should never be a driving force.
- Once an individual or a company appears in a regulatory rifle sight, it is too late.
- Prevention is much better than cure.

The most important principle is that prevention is much better than cure.

A Common-sense Approach

For once, the words of Kenneth Clarke, ex-Justice Secretary, to the effect that companies should take a common sense approach to the Act – ring out loud and sensible. So do the admonitions of Richard Alderman, the ex-Director of the Serious Fraud Office, that people who think they can weasel their way around the Act on technicalities are in for a shock. For this reason, answers to the seven questions on pages 97–8 are a key to making day-to-day management decisions safely. Decisions that could lead to accusations of corruption should be taken on principle, without worrying too much about the fine detail – or lack of it – in the laws and guidance.

For honest companies the new law gives them the opportunity to improve controls, to optimise performance by dealing with incoming, outgoing, internal and competitive corruption and fraud. Compliance should not be a problem unless the companies become the target of regulatory attention and then all hell can break loose. The mere rumour of regulatory interest can be devastating for a company's reputation, morale, relationships and business. So the lesson is to keep off the regulatory radar by performing on principle and by being an exemplary corporate citizen and an extremely hard target when under attack.

Words of Caution

While the authors' opinions have been reviewed by top lawyers (working *pro-bono*[12]) **this book is not a substitute for legal advice**. In fact, the lawyers who were kind enough to

---

11   Meaning that the Bribery Act is more comprehensive than the FCPA.

12   This is not a typo.

help insisted on remaining anonymous, have taken to wearing false glasses, artificial moustaches and to abandoning their wigs. They are no longer to be seen in public. Other lawyers[13] with whom the geriatric duo have worked for years and years, and are members of the 'Cottage Industry', ran for cover when they were asked to review the manuscript and who can blame them for not wishing to rock the boat?

The book is not intended to be a manifesto for circumventing the law or frustrating political or regulatory initiatives, although some might see it in that light. It does, however, widen the narrow horizons of adequate procedures by embracing incoming, internal, outgoing and competitive corruption and suggests ways that companies can remove much of the Act's uncertainty and run their businesses more assuredly (see Chapters 21–32).

Supposed Justification for Yet Another Act

The Bribery Act was the last to be passed by Gordon Brown's government in April 2010 prior to the proroguing of Parliament and the General Election on 6 May 2010. To say it was rushed through at the last moment – after some 20 years of stymying – would be an understatement. The most important justification for such pressing action was that UK laws made life too difficult for prosecutors to nail companies unless they could prove that offences were committed by their directing minds. As we will see, this is simply not true and the Concordance-based suspicion is that the Act's main role is not to eradicate corruption[14] at all but rather to make life easier for prosecutors by empowering them to impose heavy financial penalties for technical or trivial infractions.

The UK has laws coming out of its ears and if it is able, as it is, to prosecute a blind and crippled old-age pensioner[15] for putting recyclable orange peel in the red rather than the blue dustbin, or kids for fishing in the Lower River Esk rather than the Upper flow, or selling grey squirrels or Polish potatoes (see page 236 et seq), it can prosecute anyone for anything: as it does. A shortage of laws, lawyers, officials, jobsworths and regulators has never been a British failing. The truth is that there were plenty of bribery prosecutions, but made under the Theft and Fraud Acts and for common law conspiracy. So give us a break!

UK Prosecutions

UK prosecutions and settlements prior to the Bribery Act bear witness to the fact that:

- UK laws, whether antiquated or not, were quite sufficient to harvest an impressive number of cases.
- Companies and individuals were successfully prosecuted.
- Civil disposals were negotiated despite the fact that there is no defined process for judicial approval or DPAs.

---

13   They know who they are!

14   Or even 'bribery'.

15   Not the authors, just in case anyone suspects this is the case.

It is, however, notable that in the USA and to a lesser extent the UK:

- Foreign companies and individuals accounted for a disproportionate number of cases, as did the Oil for Food programme, which was a sitting duck for regulators worldwide.
- There is no mention of any extorter in any of the cases being sanctioned in his home country.

And, of course, no politicians or UK officials were prosecuted for corruption. The fixation is clearly on overseas skulduggery.

A second justification for rushing the Act through was that it was necessary to revise the UK's laws to comply with the Organisation for European Cooperation and Development (OECD) Convention: again this is a mis-speak. The Anti-terrorism Crime and Security Act 2002 (ATSCA) is far from antiquated. The UK had more than complied with OECD standards: not that it is bound by them in any case because they were intentionally not incorporated into UK statutes. It is far more likely that the true driving force behind ATSCA was international execration of the disgraceful conduct of politicians in the British Aerospace and Lockerbie bomber cases.

Some Immediate Points

A DIFFERENT MODEL AND AN IMPORTANT DISTINCTION

The UK Bribery Act 2010 came into force on 1 July 2011 – after considerable delay caused by the MOJ being unable to finalise the Section 9 guidelines which were required to enable the Section 7 strict liability corporate offence to take effect. It repealed the previous three acts on corruption, the Anti-terrorism Crime and Security Act and common law offences. The Act is based on an improper conduct model rather than the agent–principal relationship of earlier times. This is a very important difference, because conduct can be improper even if it is with the knowledge and consent of a principal.

An example was given by the Law Commissioners:[16]

Example of Internal Bribery

R[17] is employed by a normally reputable newspaper as a financial commentator. The newspaper's proprietor makes it clear to R that she does not mind if R supplements his low salary by taking payments from companies to promote their financial products. R receives a large payment from company P to praise their crappy life insurance products. R writes

---

16   In all of its examples, 'R' refers to the receiver or extorter and 'P' to the payer or coercer.

17   Receiver.

> an article comparing other life insurance products unfavourably with P's, but adding in conclusion that, 'of course anyone reading this would be crazy to trust my judgment!' In this case R could be guilty of an offence under Section 1.

It is also important to stress that corruption can be within the same organisation, when one employee provides an advantage to a colleague to induce his improper performance. This offence is not generally recognised, but it is very important. An example is given on page 7–8, showing that perversion that is entirely within a single organisation can give rise to sections 1, 2 and 7 offences.

APPLICATION OF THE ACT

The Act applies to 'persons', which includes humans and body corporates in England, Wales, Scotland and Northern Ireland. There is a difference between a body corporate and a 'relevant commercial organisation', which is another significant term used in the Act. A body corporate is a person but a separate legal entity consisting of any group of people acting together with a common purpose and includes companies, partnerships, joint ventures, charitable organisations and non-governmental organisations.

A relevant commercial organisation is defined in Section 7(5) as:

a)   A body which is incorporated under the law of any part of the United Kingdom and which carries on a business (whether there or elsewhere).
b)   Any other body corporate (wherever incorporated) which carries on a business, or part of the business, in any part of the United Kingdom.
c)   A partnership which is formed under the law of any part of the United Kingdom and which carries on a business (whether there or elsewhere).
d)   Any other partnership (whereever formed) which carries on a business, or part of a business in any part of the United Kingdom.

Trades and professions are classed as businesses and may be relevant commercial organisations.

Only relevant commercial organisations can be convicted of the new corporate offence under Section 7, but a body corporate is guilty of offences under sections 1, 2 and 6 when bribes are paid by a directing mind: meaning a director or other senior officer. The defence of 'adequate procedures' primarily applies to Section 7 offences. This means that a company can have adequate procedures in abundance and still be convicted under sections 1 and 2 and 6. However, if an organisation can prove it has effective procedures and has made every effort to be a good corporate citizen, this may tug at the heart strings of prosecutors, making them less nasty and positively influence juries and judges. But the primary reason for adequate procedures is not to weasel out of trouble after the event: it is to prevent problems, to optimise profits and make sure other management objectives are achieved (see page 581 et seq).

The MOJ has clarified what is meant by part of the business in a way that excludes foreign companies whose shares are listed on a UK stock exchange, those simply with banking arrangements or investments in the UK, and overseas parents and subsidiaries that do not provide services for a UK entity. As usual, the SFO takes a more assertive position[18] and says it will seek to expansively interpret the Act to include as relevant commercial organisations all UK issuers, parents and subsidiaries, and any company anywhere in the world that uses UK banking, settlement, or other facilities.[19]

THE NEW OFFENCES

The Act can be considered to consist of three primary offences, which can be committed by persons both individual and bodies corporate:

> **Section 1** makes it a criminal offence for any person to offer, promise or give a bribe (outgoing bribery or coercion) in the private or public sector, in the UK or overseas.[20] with the intention of inducing another person in a position of trust to perform improperly. It is not necessary for the SFO to prove that the purpose of the advantage was to obtain or retain business or a business advantage.

> **Section 2** is almost a mirror image of Section 1 and makes it an offence for any person in the UK and overseas private and public sectors to request or agree to receive or accept a bribe to perform improperly. It should be noted, however, that a person can be found guilty under Section 2 without an equivalent conviction or even a prosecution under Section 1 and vice versa. *A point that has somehow slipped into the Act – or, more precisely, slipped out – is the requirement under the 1916 Corruption Act for government officials and those connected with them to prove that benefits given were not corrupt. This is yet another example of the bias in the Act against the private sector and the misconception that bribe payment is more evil than extortion.*[21]

> **Section 6** makes it a criminal offence, directly or through a third party, to offer, promise or give any financial or other advantage to influence a foreign public official with the intention to obtain or retain business or other advantage in the conduct of business.

When a Section 1 or Section 6 offence (bribe payment) is committed by an associated person of a relevant commercial organisation ('C'), that organisation is liable for what can be regarded as a derived corporate – strict liability – offence under **Section 7** if the purpose of the skulduggery was to obtain or retain business etc. **for C.**

Section 7 has been the dominant focus of regulatory interest but, for reasons beaten to death later, in the wider corruption and risk management context it is not. Far more significant are losses through incoming, internal and competitive corruption that barely merit an official mention: possibly because their stealth tax benefits are not so attractive. Offences under sections 1, 2 and 6 committed by directing minds all incur corporate liability even when the purpose is not to obtain or retain business.

---

18   In fact, based on other cases and FSA interpretations, the SFO is probably correct. See FSA v Fradley & Woodward November 2005.

19   Thus some foreign companies might conclude that it is better to sever all ties with the UK rather than expose their worldwide operations to SFO prosecutorial discretion.

20   With limitations discussed later.

21   Referred to later as the 'Animal Farm' syndrome (see Foreword).

Table 5.1 summarises the main offences under the Act:[22]

Table 5.1   Main Sections of the Act

Section	Sector Public or Private	Elements of the Offence *All involve offering or giving, requesting or receiving, etc. a financial or other advantage*		
		Intention	Applies to	Distinguishing Features
1 Bribe **payment** in the UK	All	The advantage is intended to induce improper performance or the advantage itself constitutes improper performance and the payer knows this	Persons and body corporates (where the bribery is committed by a directing mind)	Act takes place in the UK
Bribe **payment** overseas	All			Part of the act takes place in the UK or the payer must be closely connected with the UK
2 Bribe **receipt** in the UK	All	Acceptance is intended to induce or reward improper performance or the acceptance etc. itself constitutes improper performance whether or not the receiver knows this	The person and a body corporate may both be convicted from the same facts	Act takes place in the UK
Bribe **receipt** overseas	All			Part of the act takes place in the UK or the receiver must be closely connected with the UK
6 Bribe **payment** to an Foreign Public Official (FPO)	Official Public	The advantage is intended to influence the FPO in his capacity AND when the payer's intention is to obtain or retain a business etc. or other advantage	Where a body corporate is convicted any senior manager who consented or connived in the offence may also be convicted	May be directly or through a third party. Some part of the offence must take place in the UK or the payer must be closely connected with the UK
7 Absolute corporate offence Relates only to bribe payment	All	Derived liability where the bribe payer is or would be guilty of an offence under sections 1 or 6 AND the payer's intention was to obtain or retain a business etc. or other advantage for the Relevant Commercial Organisation	Relevant Commercial Organisations[23] ONLY	For overseas bribe payment it is NOT necessary that any part of the offence took place in the UK or that the payer is closely connected with the UK

---

22   Progressive detail appears on page 107 et seq.

23   For the definition of this term in Section 7 of the Act, see http://www.legislation.gov.uk/ukpga/2010/23/section/7 (paragraphs (5) (a), (b), (c) and (d) (accessed 7 November 2012)).

It should be noted that only sections 6 and 7 require proof that the intention was to obtain or retain business or other advantage. For the prosecution to succeed with a Section 7 charge, no one needs to be convicted under sections 1 or 6 of bribe payment. The fact that he 'would be guilty' is enough. Furthermore, for overseas bribe payment, the person who would be guilty does not need to have a close connection with the UK, nor is it necessary (for Section 7) that any part of the offence took place in the UK.

All of the above means that a jury at the trial of a relevant commercial organisation for a Section 7 offence has to hypothesise that a person would have been found guilty of a predicate offence and then decide on corporate culpability. How a jury can honestly adjudicate on the first matter – when the defendant may not even be in the UK, does not present his defence and is unavailable for cross-examination – is difficult to see and, given the limitless ingenuity of defence lawyers, could lead to interesting Human Rights Act arguments.

EXTRATERRITORIAL JURISDICTION OF FOREIGN BRIBE PAYMENT AND RECEIPT

There are two conditions under which liability arises – for both natural persons and bodies corporate – under sections 1, 2 and 6 for overseas bribery. The first is when any part of the offence takes place in the UK. This may be as little as arranging for a payment, taking a decision or sending an email. The alternative condition is where the person paying or receiving the bribe has a close connection with the UK, such as being a British citizen or normally resident in the UK.

Liability for overseas bribe payment, for a relevant commercial organisation, under Section 7 derives from the theoretical[24] guilt of any individual for a section 1 or 6 offence, even if no part of the offence takes place in the UK and the bribe payer is not closely connected.

The extraterritorial reach of the Act – unlike the laws of every other country as well as the OECD Convention on the Bribery of Foreign Public Officials in International Transactions[25] – applies to bribe payment and receipt in overseas private markets and public sectors. Table 5.2 summarises the position.

Although extra-territoriality may seem a great wheeze for British and American regulators it does not necessarily sit comfortably with other countries some of whom regard it as a 'Big Brother' intervention. The case of Novo Nordisk (pages 33–4) is a good example, as is the unwillingness of the French to accept the FCPA requirement for anonymous whistleblowing lines.

Extra-territoriality appears to be based more on regulatory whim rather than on any deep resolve to eradicate corruption. Why is it that – in the light of the unwillingness some governments to take *any* action against corruption – the UK and USA does not extradite bent foreign public officials? Why don't people – like Jack Straw, who like Batman is pledged to fight the 'evil of corruption wherever and whenever it happens' – insist that lists are published of bent officials so that others can avoid them? **Why is it that we continue to pump foreign aid into countries that clearly don't give a hoot about the OECD or other conventions?**

---

24   Would be guilty.

25   Usually called 'The OECD Convention on Corruption', WHICH IT IS NOT!

Table 5.2   The Patchwork Quilt of International Bribery Laws

Type of Bribery Offence	In the UK		Foreign Bribery	
	Public Sector	**Private Sector**	**Public Sector**	**Private Sector**
BRIBES PAID (Coercion)				
By individuals				
Bribery Act	Section 1	Section 1	Section 1 or 6 *Influencing*	Section 1
FCPA (OECD)	UK officials are counted as FPOs	No	Yes but only by US citizens, etc. *Wrongfully influencing*	No
CORPORATE LIABILITY				
Bribery Act	Section 1 committed by a directing mind Section 7		Section 1 or 6 when committed by a directing mind Section 7	Section 1 when committed by a directing mind Section 7
FCPA (OECD)	Vicarious liability	No	Vicarious liability	No
BRIBES RECEIVED (Extortion)				
By individuals				
Bribery Act	Section 2	Section 2	Section 1	Section 2
FCPA (OECD)	No	No	No	No
CORPORATE LIABILITY				
Bribery Act	Section 2 when committed by a directing mind			
FCPA (OECD)	No	No	No	No
ACCOUNTING OFFENCES				
Bribery Act	Companies Acts			
FCPA (OECD)	Only if regulated by the Securities and Exchange Commission (SEC)			

Different Standards

For a company to be convicted of bribing a UK official, the prosecution must prove that there was an intention by the payer to induce improper performance of a relevant function or activity; whereas bribing a foreign public official requires only intent to influence him to obtain or retain a business or other advantage in the conduct of business. They are two entirely different standards.

Table 5.2 proposes that UK businesses are at a disadvantage in overseas private markets because of uncertainties created by the Act that legitimate hospitality, gratuities or donations might be interpreted as bribery (see Chapters 30–31).

EXAMPLES OF OFFENCES

The following are simple examples of how the Act *might* be interpreted:

Foreign Bribery by a British National

- P, who is a British national (closely connected person) working for a branch of a C, a British company in Ghana (relevant commercial organisation), pays a bribe to a buyer working in the private sector (not an FPO) with the intention of inducing him to perform improperly. P is liable under Section 1, making the company (C) liable under Section 7. The company may also be liable under Section 1 if P is a directing mind. If the buyer is in the public sector (that is, an FPO), there may be further offences under sections 6 and 7 if the purpose of the bribe is to obtain a business or other advantage for C.
- P, who is a British national (closely connected person), working for a branch of C, a Chinese company in Ghana (not a relevant commercial organisation), pays a bribe to a buyer working in the private sector (not an FPO) with the intention of inducing him to perform improperly. P is liable under Section 1. The company has no exposure under the Act unless it carries on part of its business in the UK and is classified as a relevant commercial organisation. If the bribe is paid to influence an FPO, P may additionally be liable under Section 6, although the company is not.
- P, who is a British National (closely connected person) working for an American company in Angola (not a relevant commercial organisation) accepts a bribe to perform improperly. He is guilty of an offence under Section 2.

Foreign National with a British Company

- P, who is a French national (not a closely connected person) working for a British company (a relevant commercial organisation) in Ghana (C), pays a bribe to a buyer working in the private sector (not an FPO) with the intention of inducing him to perform improperly. P is in breach of Section 1 but is unlikely to be prosecuted in the UK. If he is a directing mind the company commits an offence under Section 1 but would escape prosecution under that section in P's absence. However, the company (C) is liable under Section 7 but only if the purpose of the bribe was to obtain or retain business or another advantage for (C).
- P, who is a French national (not a closely connected person) working for a Korean company (not a relevant commercial organisation) in Ghana, pays a bribe to buyers working in the private (not FPOs) and public sectors (classified as FPOs) with the intention of inducing them to perform improperly or to be influenced. Neither P nor his company has any exposure under sections 1, 6 or 7.

A British Inspection Company

- ABC is a UK inspection company (a relevant commercial organisation) with offices throughout the world. It works for local Customs departments and as Designated Operational Entities under the UNFCCC. Tommy Tucker, one of its senior British managers and a director of ABC (a closely connected person and a directing mind), extorts bribes to give false certificates. He achieves this by inducing his Chinese subordinates to comply by giving them increased monthly bonuses.
- Mr Tucker would be guilty of an offence under Section 2 for bribe receipt and so would the company because of his directorship status. He and his employer would also be guilty under Section 1 for his coercion of subordinates. Adequate procedures would count for nothing. The company would also be guilty under Section 7, which could, technically, be defended by adequate procedures. ABC would be exposed to confiscation and recovery orders in the UK under the Proceeds of Crime Act. Finally, bear in mind that because of their official roles, Mr Tucker and his subordinates would all be classified as FPOs.

The examples are at the simple end of the scale. Liability can get extremely complicated depending on the nationality of the briber, his intention, the organisation he represents, its place of incorporation and the precise nature of its presence in the UK, whether or not the extorter is an FPO (and the briber must know this), his capacity and responsibilities, the countries in which elements of the offence take place and what their written laws say – or don't say – the nature of the transaction concerned and whether or not the purpose was to obtain or retain a business or other advantage and for whom.

If companies try to weasel-word their way around the sort of subtleties described above, they are headed for trouble. The key word is 'intent' and if an accused can prove his intent was honest, there should be no problem. This is why the decision-centricity model discussed later is so important (see page 571 et seq).

ASSOCIATED PERSONS

A relevant commercial organisation may be liable under Section 7 for bribes paid by its associated persons, including employees, agents, intermediaries, joint ventures, subsidiaries, parents, associates, siblings, customers, suppliers and other third parties who perform services on its behalf. What performing services means is not defined, other than in Section 8, which reads:

Whether a person performs services or not is to be determined by reference to all of the relevant circumstances and not merely by reference to the nature of the relationship.

However, the MOJ had stated that vendors and customers who simply supply or buy goods are not normally to be regarded as performing services and therefore relevant commercial organisations should not incur liability for their misbehaviour. The Ministry has also said that responsibility for bribe payment by parent companies, subsidiaries, joint ventures, etc. will be limited to cases where they were providing services explicitly on behalf of a relevant commercial organisation to provide it with business or other advantage (see more details on page 814).

The solution proposed by regulatory agencies to mitigate a relevant commercial organisation's responsibility for associated persons is due diligence, mainly based on country risks, red flags and their supposed reliability as reflected in public or trade records and on the Internet. For reasons explained later (Chapter 25) due diligence is a regulatory chimera founded on costly box-ticking and bureaucracy that gives virtually no assurance of *anything*.

MINISTRY OF JUSTICE GUIDANCE AND ADEQUATE PROCEDURES

These guidelines[26] – which discharge the government's statutory obligations – under Section 9 of the Act – are restricted to the very narrow objective of providing relevant commercial organisations with a defence to charges under Section 7. They are of absolutely no value in preventing incoming bribery or internal and competitive corruption and of little benefit in defending Section 1 or Section 6 charges: they are, in fact skewed.

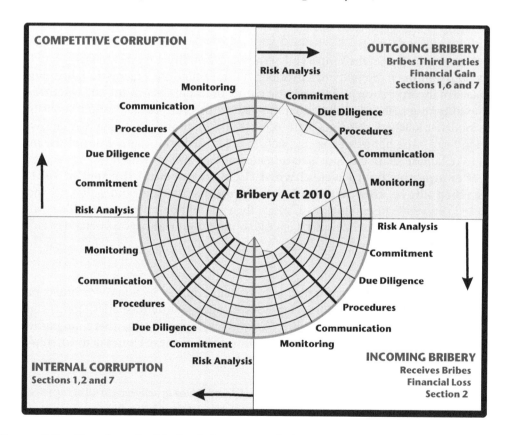

Figure 5.1   Showing the Limited Coverage of the Ministry Of Justice Guidance

Figure 5.1 indicates the bias towards outgoing bribery.

---

26   There are two sets of Guidance: the main publication ('Bribery Act 2010: Guidance about commercial organisations preventing bribery') and a Quick Start Guide for small companies. Both available at: http://www.justice.gov.uk/legislation/bribery (accessed 7 November 2012).

Legally Led

Many companies have reacted to the Act in only a legal frame, retaining external lawyers to draft paper policies and procedures that are primarily aimed at defending a Section 7 charge with only token efforts to evaluate risks and none to detect current problems, incoming, internal or competitive corruption. This is putting the cart before the horse and planning the autopsy of a patient while he is still alive and kicking.[27]

The Guidance suggests that adequate procedures should incorporate six main principles:

1. **Proportionate Procedures:** A commercial organisation's procedures to prevent bribery by persons associated with it are proportionate to the bribery risks it faces and to the nature, scale and complexity of the commercial organisation's activities. They are also clear, practical, accessible, effectively implemented and enforced.
2. **Top-level Commitment:** The top-level management of a commercial organisation (be it a board of directors, the owners, or any other equivalent body or person) are committed to preventing bribery by persons associated with it. They foster a culture within the organisation in which bribery is never acceptable.
3. **Risk Assessment:** The commercial organisation assesses the nature and extent of its exposure to potential external and internal risks of bribery on its behalf by persons associated with it. The assessment is periodic, informed and documented.
4. **Due Diligence:** The commercial organisation applies due diligence procedures, taking a proportionate and risk-based approach, in respect of persons who perform or will perform services for or on behalf of the organisation, in order to mitigate identified bribery risks.
5. **Communications (Including Training):** The commercial organisation seeks to ensure that its bribery prevention policies and procedures are embedded and understood throughout the organisation through internal and external communication, including training, that is proportionate to the risks it faces.
6. **Monitoring and Review:** The commercial organisation monitors and reviews procedures designed to prevent bribery by persons associated with it and makes improvements where necessary.

If a company were to rely on the principles and vague detail in the MOJ Guidance it would have little hope of evidencing that its procedures were adequate and none at all – in the real world – of preventing or detecting most types of bribery, let alone corruption. The Guidance has not been altogether blessed by the SFO, making it almost irrelevant. The problem is aggravated by the fact that unlike its American counterparts the SFO has refused to establish a system ('Opinion Letters') through which companies can obtain comfort that what they plan to do will not violate the laws. Merely speaking to the SFO is not without its dangers.

---

27   Mixing metaphors is the most endearing quality of most investigators.

Come into my Parlour Said the Spider to the Fly

On 13 January 2011, following an industry-wide webcast, Mr Vivian Robertson, QC, the then SFO's General Counsel[28] was asked: 'If a company goes to the SFO to get guidance on how to comply with the Act, does that company run the risk that it will subsequently be the subject of an investigation–prosecution based on the company's potential questions regarding its risk areas?'

Mr Robinson responded: 'We can't exclude that as a possibility, but the more likely approach would be to ask the company to conduct an internal enquiry and then provide a report to the SFO concerning the specific matter at issue. The SFO would then decide how to proceed based on that report'.

The response suggests it is best to keep off the regulatory radar. See page 133 for a further discussion on adequate procedures.

SELF-DISCLOSURE AND PROXY INVESTIGATIONS

The Act does not require companies to report (or self-disclose) suspected breaches, although mandatory reporting is expected under the Proceeds of Crime Act (POCA) when offences involving criminal property are associated with bribery. Further, companies regulated by the Financial Services Authority (FSA) and the SEC are subject to strict reporting obligations. All of these result in a potential dilemma: if POCA, FSA and SEC requirements are complied with, failing to report associated bribery offences (but not mere suspicions) would be inviting trouble. It is akin to an adulterer asking his mistress not to grass to his wife.

The SFO has made it clear that it expects everyone to self-disclose (known as 'Come to Jesus') and if they don't, to expect a thrashing. A detailed decision matrix for self-disclosure is at pages 451 et seq and in many circumstances it is not advised.

The official plan is that companies that self-disclose will be invited to work with the SFO in a collaborative (or proxy) investigation, at the end of which an agreement (civil disposal or in future a DPA) might be made that will avoid prosecution. It is important to emphasise the word 'might'.

The ethicality of the self-disclosure regime are at best questionable (see more at page 448) and are mainly attractive when:

- A company believes on principle it is the right thing to do;
- Mandatory reporting of other matters is likely to result in related bribery offences coming to the attention of any regulator anywhere in the world;
- A company believes it can minimise its punishment by cooperating with regulators.

---

28   Mr Robertson has revolved into the private sector.

An excellent report by His Honour Judge David Swift, Chairman of the Criminal Subcommittee of the Select Committee of Home Affairs, dated June 2008, notes that judges are fundamentally opposed to the 'undesirable descent into plea-bargaining in all types of cases' and are expected to increasingly insist that courts alone decide on penalties.[29] The lesson is that any civil disposal or DPA can be overturned by a court.

The criteria that a company should carefully consider before making any self-disclosure are set out in detail on page 448 et seq but a *few* are worth getting in quickly here:

- There is no requirement to self-disclose bribery offences, although lawyers of the more timorous nature will usually recommend doing so.
- If a company makes it known it might be amenable to civil settlements it is more likely to become a target of regulatory attention.
- The SFO is the only UK anti-bribery agency currently ready, willing and able to negotiate civil settlements: this will change (see page 159 et seq).
- If a case does not meet the SFO's acceptance criteria, it may be transferred to other regulators whose only option is to prosecute or to take no action.
- Self-disclosures will almost certainly result in publicity and derivative litigation.
- Companies that self-disclose are expected to fund a proxy investigation, jettison co-accused individuals and probably to give evidence against them.
- The standard of proof required for a civil disposal is far lower than that necessary for prosecution: if most negotiated cases were taken to trial, the prosecution would fail.
- Civil settlements are unlikely ever to be offered to individuals or to companies where a directing mind is involved.
- Civil disposals are overwhelmingly in the interests of prosecutors, who are keen to avoid contested trials.

Moreover, proxy or adversarial investigations (see page 883 et seq) are likely to identify other problems, transgressions and outright skulduggery that inflame the case initially reported. The bottom line is that self-disclosure is not a panacea[30] and companies should fully evaluate the consequences and collateral damage before doing anything.

PROSECUTORIAL DISCRETION

Prosecutorial discretion is discussed in detail on pages 95, 139, 147 and 597, but for immediate purposes can be limited to the decision as to whether prosecution will be ordered or a civil disposal or a DPA negotiated following self-disclosure.

Politicians, regulators and supporters of the Act have made great play of the fact that prosecutorial discretion amounts to an assurance of fairness. But the fact is that there is a perverse incentive[31] for the SFO to seek a settlement even when the evidence falls well short of that needed to prosecute. Besides that, the ethicality of allowing rich defendants

---

29   See also the excellent report by Nicholas Purnell QC and his colleagues at Cloth Fair Chambers titled 'The Risk of Abusing a Dominant Position' (2009). Available at: http://www.clothfairchambers.com/images/files/issue_8_dominant.pdf (accessed 7 November 2012).

30   But more likely a Pandora's box.

31   Because it trousers 33.33 per cent for its own budget.

to buy themselves out of trouble is highly questionable. Where should the line be drawn? Why stop at bribery? Why not murder? Why not multiple murder?

The SFO may exploit its powers to permanently debar companies from government contracts to leverage a civil settlement. This smacks of coercion, if not extortion. Why should a company that has deliberately engaged in bribery – knowing full well the potential risks to its government business – escape mandatory debarment?

A Model Case of Self-disclosure

Massive worldwide corruption by Siemens was spun as accounting offences (deliberately avoiding the word 'corruption'), so that it would not be debarred from European Union (EU) contracts. As a result of this prosecutorial magnanimity it subsequently won the contract to build the new railway carriages for Thameslink, resulting in the Bombardier Works in the UK at Derby being threatened with closure, with the loss of hundreds of British jobs.

Siemens has been more successful than it ever was and is being held out as a model of excellent regulatory cooperation. This overlooks the truth that the company only came forward after Munich prosecutors had raided its offices. Where is the justice in this? Where is the deterrent? What protection was given to Siemens' competitors?

Transparency International in its 2010 publication on the 2010 UK Bribery Act, 'Adequate Procedures Guidance'[32] criticised companies for failing to impose deterrents:

No Deterrent: Animal Farm

It is common for a company in dealing with an instance of bribery to feel it preferable to ask the employees to resign rather than to apply dismissal proceedings. This may be to avoid making public the violation, to avoid the risk of subsequent litigation .... because the company has struck a deal on the recovery of assets. The company should resist using (this) option as it sends out a distinct signal to employees that the company is not stringent in applying sanctions.

Ironically, this 'Animal Farm', do as I say, not as I do (DAISNAID) approach is precisely the signal that regulators emit when negotiating civil disposals or drafting indictments specifically to avoid permanent and mandatory debarment. The fact that the SFO can

---

32   See http://www.transparency.org.uk/our-work/bribery-act/adequate-procedures (accessed 7 November 2012).

choose not to use its most draconian deterrent[33] sort of confirms that the Bribery Act is primarily a stealth tax.

NEGOTIATING WITH DRACO

Companies usually delegate their external laws firms to negotiate settlements, but this is not advised for reasons explained on pages 158, 676, 831 and 848. Negotiation is a specialist commercial rather than a legal skill that must be driven from people outside the 'Cottage Industry'.[34]

FACING CRIMINAL PROSECUTION

The prospect of being dragged into court to face criminal charges is daunting, but it is not the end of the world. It is one thing for prosecutors to puff up a case in pre-trial discussions and quite another to convince a jury beyond reasonable doubt. A prosecutor's path from puffing to plaudits is jam-packed with dangers. One technical error and the case fails. **This is why regulators are probably so keen on civil disposals and DPAs.**

THE MANAGEMENT BOTTOM LINE

Throughout a long career – unexpectedly extended by Gordon Brown's purloining of pension funds and growing tribes of grandchildren – the authors have been privileged to work with some of the best companies, managers, lawyers, regulators and even a few striking HR types. Their dominant characteristic was that they took decisions honestly and on principle. They were not timorous, nor were they box-tickers.

Managers, when agonising whether to surrender to facilitation extortion, or to take clients to the Pink Pussycat Lap Dancing Club, to make a donation to charity, or to do any of the other things that could be interpreted with the benefit of prosecutorial imagination as a bribe, they should ask themselves four questions:

1. Is acceptance of the financial or other advantage improper in itself?
2. Is the intention of the advantage to induce improper performance (or to unduly[35] influence an FPO)?
3. Is the expenditure recorded (or to be recorded) fully and accurately?
4. Can all of the above be proven beyond reasonable doubt?

If the answer to the first two questions is unequivocally 'no' and to the second two unequivocally 'yes', managers should grab the nettle and get on with it. This is no guarantee that months, years or even decades later some regulator somewhere might not infer that what took place was inappropriate[36] and technically a bribe: but so what? It is impossible for managers to run a business by trying to weasel around every technical nook and cranny or to anticipate the inferences of second-guessers who have never tried to run a commercial operation.

---

33   As is the case in Singapore, where Siemens and all of its associates were banned for five years.

34   See Foreword for a clarification of this term.

35   This term is not used in the Act.

36   The most pathetic word in the English language.

In relation to acts that could be misconstrued as bribe receipt, the equivalent questions are:

- Is the acceptance of the financial or other advantage improper in itself?
- By accepting the advantage is it, or was it, the intention to perform improperly, to be rewarded for past improper performance or in anticipation of future skulduggery?
- Can it be proved beyond reasonable doubt that any decisions taken would unquestionably pass the expectation test?

If the answers to the first two questions are unequivocally in the negative and the last unequivocally positive, then managers should follow Nike's example and 'Just Do It'.

When trepids recover their composure after reading the above, let it be said that there is far more to the recommendations in Chapters 21–7 than just the seven answers given above, but they are a good starting point. The only hope that the UK has to escape from the dreadful financial, social, political and criminal justice mess it is in – created largely by too much regulatory intervention and otiose noble causes – managers must be brave enough to manage. It is implicit that they do so with honest intent and that they can prove it.

Definitions Applying to the Bribery Act

INTRODUCTION

A number of definitions are included in the Act but there are others, supposedly to be interpreted by common English usage, that are also relevant and they are discussed below.

INTENTION AND CAUSATION

Proof of a person's intention is a critical element of all bribery offences. The word and its derivatives (see Figure 5.2) are not defined in the Act, nor in any guidance, but they are frequently encountered in the criminal law and represent the highest degree of fault.[37] In layman's terms intent requires a desire to achieve a particular outcome and foresight to anticipate the result with a very high degree of probability.

It should be noted that the bribe payer may be proven to have the intent to induce improper performance – and is therefore guilty under Section 1 – even though the receiver has no equivalent intention and is judged innocent under Section 2. It is the state of mind of the individual that counts.

---

37   *Mens rea*, or guilty knowledge.

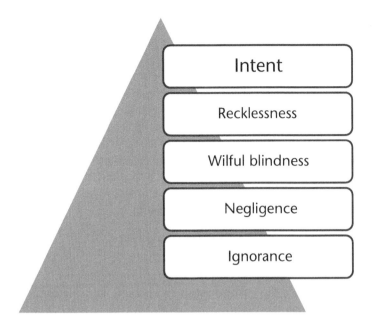

Figure 5.2   Intent, Desire and Foresight

Section 8 of the Criminal Justice Act 1967[38] states:

A court or jury, in determining whether a person has committed an offence (with intent),
    (a) shall not be bound in law to infer that he intended or foresaw the result of his actions
    by reasons only of its being a natural and probable consequence of those actions; but
    (b) shall decide whether he did intend or foresee that result by reference to all of the
    evidence, drawing such inferences [...] as appear proper in the circumstances.

In the case of R v Hancock & Shankland (1986) 1 ALL ER641 Lord Scarman stated that

the greater the probability of a consequence the more likely it is that the consequence was
foreseen and if that consequence was foreseen, the greater probability is that it was also
intended.

In 1978 the Law Commission published a report and proposed a revised definition of the
word 'intention':

A person should be regarded as intending a particular result of his conduct if, but only if either
he actually intends that result or he has no substantial doubt that the conduct will have that
result.

In 2006 the Law Commission suggested the jury in murder trials should be directed as
follows:

---

38   See http://www.legislation.gov.uk/ukpga/1967/80/pdfs/ukpga_19670080_en.pdf (accessed 7 November 2012).

[A]n intention to bring about a result may be found if it is shown that the defendant thought that the result was a virtual certain consequence of his or her action […].

Evidence of intention is pivotal both at the vetting stage, when a prosecutor (primarily the SFO in the UK) decides whether or not to pursue a case, and again at trial. The prosecutor is required to prove a direct connection (causal link) between a person's intention to induce an improper performance or, in the case of FPOs, influence. The bribe payer must know that the performance he intended to induce would be improper: such proof is not a requisite for a receiver[39] to be found guilty under Section 2.

The prosecution does not have to prove any wrongful act took place – the intent to induce it is enough. However, the fact that the performance complained of turned out to be honest is a factor that a jury would likely consider.

ASSOCIATED PERSON AND PERFORMING SERVICES

The role of an associated person is central to a charge under Section 7, but is less relevant to others. Section 8 defines the term to mean any person who performs services for or on behalf of a relevant commercial organisation. The capacity in which services are performed is unimportant but will be judged in all of the circumstances when the offence takes place in the UK. For overseas offences, under Section 5(2), any local custom or practice is to be disregarded unless it is permitted or required by the written law applicable to the country or territory concerned.

There are two points to note about this qualification. The first is that the exclusion of *local* custom or practice applies only to overseas bribery. Therefore a jury *should* be able to consider, for example, what level of hospitality is normal in a particular international market or sector, especially by competitors who are not subject to the UK Act. Secondly, 'permitted or required by the written law' means that the receipt of the advantage is specifically approved and not merely that there is no law prohibiting it.

Laws on Nose-scratching

In the UK citizens are allowed to scratch their noses.[40] This is not because there is a written law permitting it, but because there is no prohibition.[41] Thus nose-scratching is not 'permitted'.

In relation to Section 7, courts will be charged with a four-level test:

1. Is the person associated?
2. Did he provide services for or on behalf of the relevant commercial organisation?

---

39 Except when the advantage is given for performance already completed.

40 Although that luxury could change.

41 At least not yet.

3. Did he pay a bribe or would he be guilty of doing so?
4. Did he intend to obtain or retain business or to obtain or retain an advantage in the conduct of business for **that** organisation?

Only if the answer to all four questions is in the affirmative will the prosecution of a Section 7 charge succeed.

The MOJ Guidance indicates that:

- Routine **suppliers** will not be considered to be performing services for a commercial organisation ... but rather simply acting as sellers of goods.
- Bribes paid by a **joint venture**, which operates through a separate legal entity, will only create a liability for the participating relevant commercial organisation when the joint venture is performing services specifically on its behalf and specifically to provide it with a business or other advantage.
- A business advantage to the participating relevant commercial organisation will not arise simply because of its investment in or partial ownership of the joint venture.
- The situation may be different where the **joint venture** is conducted through a contractual arrangement and will depend on the degree of control the participating relevant commercial organisation has in deciding liability.
- Again, the fact that a participating relevant commercial organisation benefits indirectly from its interest in the joint venture is very unlikely, in itself, to incur liability.

Similarly a bribe paid by a subsidiary will not automatically incur liability for the parent if the prosecution cannot show the briber was also a directing mind of the parent (Section 1) or was a relevant commercial organisation for which the subsidiary was performing services. In the second case the prosecution must show that the purpose of the skulduggery was to obtain or retain business or a business advantage for the parent. This is so even though the parent company may benefit indirectly from shareholding or dividends.

IMPROPER PERFORMANCE: EXPECTATION TEST

The reasonable person test is applicable to charges under sections 1 and 2 when determining whether the intended or actual performance of a relevant function or activity was improper. It is implicit that the function or activity should be performed in good faith, impartially and while in a position of trust. Unlike the old laws the trust may be owed to other than a principal.

Carbon Fraud

Douggy Skuller was an Independent Financial Adviser. Mr Skuller agreed to promote what he knew were almost worthless carbon offset projects to elderly investors in return for massive personal commissions. Did he owe an obligation of good faith to the investors?

A reasonable person is defined in legal precedents as one who is

appropriately informed, capable, aware of the law and fair-minded, resulting in decisions being based on moral integrity in the context concerned. A reasonable person may do something extraordinary in certain circumstances, but whatever he thinks or does is always reasonable.

In other words the reasonable person is to take account of all the circumstances present in the particular context. Section 5(1) is consistent with this definition so far as the UK is concerned. However, section 5(2), which relates to performance in foreign countries, requires local custom and practice to be disregarded, unless it is permitted or required by the written law applicable to the country or territory concerned.

The MOJ Guidance appears to conflict with the point about disregarding local custom and practice. This may be the result of the dumbing down, following the outcry over the draft guidelines (see page 92).

For example paragraph 28, referring to foreign public officials, states:

[I]n many cases, however, the question [...] will depend on the totality of the evidence which **takes into account all the surrounding circumstances** *[...] such as the level of influence the particular foreign public official has over the awarding of business.*

Paragraph 29 states, again in relation to FPOs;

[T]he standards or norms applying in a particular sector may also be relevant here.

Paragraph 30 states that hospitality of FPOs

is commensurate with the reasonable and proportionate norms for the particular industry [...].

Again such apparent discrepancies suggest that coordination between the lawyers drafting the MOJ Guidance and the SFO leaves much to be desired. It is also important to note that the influence defined in the Guidance is the level of influence the particular foreign public official has over the awarding of business. This indicates (as discussed more fully later) that Section 6 was not intended to capture facilitation payments but simply to address corruption[42] in the area of public sector procurement and to make it easier to prosecute.

Section 5(3) states:

In subsection (2) written law means the law contained in:
(a) any written constitution, provision made by or under legislation in the country or territory concerned or
(b) any judicial decision which is so applicable and is evidenced in published written sources.

The Joint Prosecution Guidance of the Director of the SFO and the Director of Public Prosecutions, issued in March 2011, states that interpretation of the test is to be applied by a jury on the ordinary meaning of the words.

---

42   Meaning 'bribery'.

INFLUENCING AN FPO

Section 6 is triggered if the financial or other advantage is intended to influence an FPO with the objective of obtaining or retaining a business or other advantage in the conduct of business.

Although the word 'influence' is not defined in the Act, it is clearly a lesser evil than improper performance. The significance of influence would appear to be as shown in Table 5.3.

Table 5.3   Influencing a Foreign Public Official

The Provider of the Advantage's Intent is to ensure that the FPO	Not resulting in obtaining or retaining business or ...	Results in obtaining or retaining business or ...
OPTION 1 WITH SPEED Takes a routine decision he is required or duty bound to take: representing proper performance, but possibly to complete it more efficiently	Not amounting to influence No Section 6 offence	
BACK TO OPTION 1 Removes any artificial or dishonest impediments he has contrived to extort a bribe and takes the decision he is required or duty bound to take: amounting to proper performance		
OPTION 2 Takes a decision contrary to his obligations	Not amounting to influence No Section 6 offence	Section 6 offence
OPTION 3 Takes a decision amounting to improper performance	Section 1 offence	Section 6 offence
Knows that acceptance of the advantages amounts, in itself, to improper performance	Section 1 offence	

In all of hundreds of thousands of words analysed in Concordance (see page 620), the word 'influence' is mentioned 400 times and 50 times in SFO speeches often predicated by the word 'undue'. But in spite of this, what influencing an FPO, means will be left for a jury to decide, in all likelihood in the FPO's absence.

CONSENT, CONNIVANCE, AIDING AND ABETTING

Once a body corporate[43] is convicted of an offence under sections 1, 2 or 6 any senior officer who consents or connives in its commission is also guilty of the like offence. A manager or employee who consents or connives in a Section 7 offence cannot be charged personally, although they may face other allegations of aiding and abetting or conspiracy. The Law Commission clarified the term in the context of the Draft Bill:

> *We do not believe it is right to impose liability on an individual respecting a fraud offence, a fraud-like offence, or a bribery offence, if that individual has merely been careless. That is, in this context, a standard of liability that should be regarded as sufficient only to justify civil liability. Nothing short of proof of consent or connivance should be enough in this context to justify individual criminal liability.[44]*

In practical terms this probably means that once a company has been convicted, any senior officer who deliberately or wilfully closes his eyes to bribe payment or *receipt* will also be prosecuted. It also implies that if a senior officer is wilfully blind to bribery by or of a junior employee – and which therefore does not result in a corporate offence under sections 1, 2 and 6 – he will not be guilty.

Mr Alderman's Speech: St Petersburg, March 2011

There is an important new offence in the Bribery Act which is focused on senior members of companies. This will of course include directors. They will be guilty of an offence if they consent to or connive in bribery. This will be important to you both as executive directors and indeed as non-executive directors. If you are aware of bribery in a company of which you are a director and you do nothing about it, then in my view you are consenting to or conniving in the bribery.

I know that this is a particular concern to non-executive directors who are asking about their own exposure to this legislation, if they are aware that there is bribery somewhere within the company. The test is clear and there can be personal criminal liability if they do nothing about it.

Mr Alderman would have been more precise had he explained that before a director's derived liability comes into play it is first necessary for the prosecution to prove corporate guilt under sections 1, 2 or 6.

---

43   Because of participation by a directing mind.

44   The Law Commissioners Report 31 November 2008 paragraph 6.135.

CARRYING ON BUSINESS IN THE UK

This is an important term that results in the reclassification of a body corporate as a relevant commercial organisation. The MOJ Guidance suggests that to fall under this definition an overseas company must have a distinct physical presence in the UK. The SFO disagrees, arguing, for example, that listing on a British stock exchange makes a foreign company a relevant commercial organisation. US regulators interpret the FCPA to mean that any company that processes a transaction through the American banking or clearance systems comes under their jurisdiction. The SFO is likely to follow the American lead.

Going for the Difficult Cases: Ho Hum!

In July 2011 Jonathan Russell of The *Daily Telegraph* interviewed Mr Alderman, who stated: 'All companies listed in the UK potentially fall under the remit of the new Act'. He said, 'You bet we will go after foreign companies. This has been misunderstood. If there is an economic engagement with the UK then in my view they are carrying on business in the UK'.

The MOJ Guidance indicates that a common-sense approach should be taken and that ultimately a determination of whether or not a business is bound by the Act will be made by juries on a case-by-case basis.

OBTAINING OR RETAINING BUSINESS (AND MORE ON FPOS)

The term 'obtaining or retaining business', or an advantage in the conduct of business, is relevant only to sections 6 and 7, but it is critically important. A similar form of words was first used in connection with the FCPA and meant precisely what it said. It was to stop American companies bribing FPOs to win government contracts.

The term has since been subject to expansive interpretation by the American regulators (see pages 156, 172, 205 and 214), who have concluded that most facilitation payments inevitably provide a business advantage.

Rotten Apples

The argument is that bribing an FPO $40 to clear a cargo of apples that he has detained on a trumped-up problem so he can extort money does result in a business advantage. It stops the apples going rotten and allows them to be sold.

In fairness to the American regulators, they have only made such claims when an FPO has been bribed in connection with a significant commercial decision.

Other FPO Cases and Obtaining Business

- The freight forwarder Con-way paid a $300,000 penalty as a result of its making multiple small payments to Customs officials in the Philippines, which included inducements to violate tariffs, settle disputes and not to enforce legitimate fines and penalties.
- In 2009 Helmerich & Payne paid a penalty and disgorged $1.3 million resulting from facilitation payments of between $2,000 and $5,000 a time to secure customs clearances in Argentina and Venezuela for goods that could not lawfully be imported.
- DynCorp allegedly paid $300,000 via subcontractors to expedite visas and other documentation.
- Panalpina and six of its customers were fined $257 million for making payments to circumvent import tariffs and to obtain preferential treatment for shipments primarily into West Africa.

None of the above could be regarded as simple facilitation payments or routine decisions.

US regulators have also expansively interpreted the definition of an FPO to include any person involved in any organisation (government instrumentality or state-owned enterprise (SOE)) where a government has a directing or managerial influence. This would mean, for example, that the UK government's rescue of banks results in their employees becoming FPOs under the FCPA.

6 *Main Sections of the Bribery Act*

Introduction

The following paragraphs dig into more detail and study some of the features offences and interpretations of the Bribery Act 2010 given in the Ministry of Justice (MOJ) Guidance released on 30 March 2011 (see page 92) and in the various Law Commission and Parliamentary deliberations discussed in Chapter 2.

Section 1: Bribes Paid in the UK

MAIN PROVISIONS

The main provisions of what can be regarded as a primary (or predicate) offence are shown in Table 6.1.

Looking in the Wrong Direction?

The dominant focus of the UK Bribery Act and the Ministry of Justice guidance is on bribe payment by associated persons in the private sector at home and overseas. The guidance incorrectly implies that bribery in foreign markets – especially in countries perceived by Transparency International as the most corrupt – is by far the most dangerous.

In fact, as discussed in detail later, the reality is quite different. Much more emphasis should be placed on;

- extortion of bribes and skulduggery by UK politicians and officials;
- other stratospheric corruption that spills over into the commercial world.

The real problem of corruption and fraud is financial loss: throwing away hard earned revenues of between 2 per cent and 10 per cent of turnover for some organisations. Even in the narrow context of section 1 of the Act the potential for internal corruption-when one employee of a company provides an advantage to a colleague to perform improperly – is grossly understated as is skulduggery by blue collar workers (page 260).

Table 6.1   Section 1 Offences in the UK

Section 1 Offering or Payment of Bribes By a person or body corporate *in the UK wherever incorporated*		Bribery takes place in the UK **PERSONAL AND CORPORATE LIABILITY**
Person Paying the Bribe ☹[1]		**Person Receiving the Bribe** ☺
Offers, promises or gives	Directly or through a third party	It does not matter whether the person to whom the advantage is offered is the same person who is to perform or has performed the function or activity concerned
A financial or other advantage	Not defined	
And **intends** the advantage		***Improper performance (Section 4)*** *Performing or failing to perform in breach of a relevant expectation*
To induce the person to perform improperly	**Section 4** Improper Performance	
A relevant function or activity	**Section 3**	***Relevant function or activity (Section 3)*** • *Any function of a public nature* • *Any activity connected with a business, trade or profession* • *Any activity performed by or on behalf of a body of persons* • *Which the person is expected to perform in good faith and impartiality and is in a position of trust by virtue of performing it even if it has no connection with the UK or is performed outside the UK*
Or		
To reward the person for improper performance of such function or activity		***Relevant expectation (Section 5)*** *What a reasonable person in the United Kingdom would expect in relation to the performance of the type of function or activity concerned*
Or		*Only when the advantage rewards past performance is it necessary to prove that the recipient knew it was improper*
Where he knows or believes the acceptance of the advantage would itself constitute the improper performance		
CORPORATE LIABILITY **Section 14 (1)** If committed with the **consent or connivance** of a senior officer or person [he or she] is guilty of the offence as well as the body corporate or partnership *Section 14 (4) Senior Officer means in relation to a body corporate, a director, manager, secretary or other similar officer*		*Bribe acceptance with the consent or connivance of a senior manager or a directing mind may result in corporate liability under Section 1 except for Crown Bodies*

---

1   An early reviewer of the draft of this book did not like the smilies but they are meant to reflect the reality that most bribes are usually extorted.

SOME POINTS TO NOTE

The following points are relevant to a Section 1 charge:

- The offence can be committed by any person and body corporate while in the UK,[2] irrespective of nationality or place of incorporation and whether or not it carries on business in the UK as a 'relevant commercial organisation'.
- The offence can be committed entirely internally. For example, by one employee offering etc a financial or other advantage to a colleague to perform improperly.
- A sexual favour will be considered to be an advantage.
- Blue collar workers (for example delivery truck drivers) may be prosecuted under the Act if, they offer, give an advantage to a goods inwards employee to condone a 'short delivery' of goods.
- Government departments are excluded from corporate liability under the exclusion for Crown Bodies although individual officials can be convicted.
- Adequate procedures are no defence to a Section 1 charge.
- The bribe must be intended to induce improper performance.
- Proof of actual improper performance is not necessary (it is an inchoate offence).
- A person may be convicted under Section 1 even if his collaborator, charged under Section 2 for receiving or even extorting the advantage, is acquitted (or not even charged).
- Unlike Section 7 there is no requirement to prove the intent of the bribe was to obtain or retain business or an advantage in the conduct of business.
- When an individual associated with a relevant commercial organisation is convicted or would be guilty of a Section 1 offence, the organisation may be charged under Section 7, but only if the purpose was to obtain business or other business advantage.
- Any 'person' may be charged with or aiding or abetting any offence under the Act or conspiring in its commission even if he is outside the UK.

The most uncertain aspect of Section 1, when applied to acts in the UK, is how hospitality will be interpreted.

NOTES ON HOSPITALITY

Regulators are concerned that corporate hospitality is a primary inducement for improper performance improper performance and in some cases they are right.

The Law Commissioners deliberated as follows:[3]

- *Even in the private sector context, rare though this will be, the provision of hospitality may be of such a nature or extent that it amounts to an inducement to employees or agents of potential contractors to breach an expectation that they will act in good faith*

---

2   Or arguably while using any of the UK's banking or other facilities.

3   Extracts from The Law Commission, *Reforming Bribery* (Crown Copyright 2008), Appendix D, Special Cases: D.18, D.15 and D.17 (emphasis added). Available at: http://lawcommission.justice.gov.uk/docs/cp185_Reforming_Bribery_report.pdf (accessed 7 November 2012).

or impartially. In such circumstances, the provision and acceptance of the hospitality can amount to bribery.[4]

- *Where the entertainment was only one factor amongst a number in the employee's mind leaning in favour of doing business with the supplier, the placing of business [...] would not have been bribery. If however the entertainment was the main factor in the employee's mind, overwhelming all other considerations, it would have amounted to bribery [...].*

- *In run-of-the-mill cases in which people accept hospitality in a private sector context, there is simply no breach of a relevant expectation about the way that they will behave that is raised by that acceptance.* **So the ordinary giving and receiving of hospitality remains well outside the scope of the law of bribery under our recommendations.** *(Emphasis added)*

The Commissioners were obviously a little flustered about some aspects of hospitality and gave an example of where it may overstep the boundary and become bribery.

The Pink Pussycat Lap Dancing Club

An example might involve the covert entertainment of potential contractors' employees at a lap dancing club, where the company providing the entertainment intends the employees to feel obliged to favour the company in case the nature of the entertainment they received comes to the attention of their employer.

While conceding that the Commissioners may know much more about lap dancing clubs than the authors, who have never been to one – much preferring the Old People's Home Bingo Night – the example given is odd. Hairy-armed contractors (not to mention investigators and even lawyers) are much more likely to boast about their night out in the club, and cavorting with Flossie Flowfinger, than to hide it. What's more, when the boss hears about Flossie, he will expect an invitation; that's how things are in the real world. So Flossie may be corrupting but for a quite different reason from that hypothesised by the Commissioners.

The MOJ Guidance[5] gives detail about hospitality, gifts and sponsored travel only under the heading of Section 6 and related *exclusively to foreign public officials* (FPOs). **It does not clarify what the regulators think is permissible in the private sector either at home or overseas**.

The guidelines seem to take the view that although local custom and practice has to be disregarded in cases of foreign bribery, it is permissible for the reasonable person to consider the other circumstances such as what is normal in the international business sector concerned.

---

4   But still demands proof of intent.

5   There are two sets of Guidance: the main publication ('Bribery Act 2010: Guidance about Commercial Organisations Preventing Bribery') and a Quick Start Guide for small companies. Both available at: http://www.justice.gov.uk/legislation/bribery (accessed 7 November 2012).

More On Pussycat Clubs

If foreign competitors routinely take clients to the Red Pussycat Lap Dancing Club in downtown Mombasa and the Blue Pussycat Gentleman's Club in Singapore this could be held to set an international or sectorial norm that should be considered acceptable under the reasonable person test.

In relation to FPOs, the Guidance indicates that the following are acceptable and do not amount to bribery under either Section 1 or Section 6:

- An invitation to foreign clients to attend a Six Nations rugby match at Twickenham as part of a public relations exercise designed to cement good relations or enhance knowledge of the organisation is extremely unlikely to engage Section 1, as there is unlikely to be evidence of an intention to induce improper performance;
- A routine business courtesy;
- Reasonable travel and accommodation expenses to allow an FPO to visit and inspect an operation, product or premises.

The Guidance (paragraph 31) states that a 'five-star holiday for a foreign public official which is unrelated to the organisation's services is, all things being equal, far more likely to raise the necessary inference of bribery'. But note that the prosecution still has to prove that the intent of the hospitality was to induce improper performance under Section 1, to influence under Section 6 and to obtain or retain business, to succeed with a prosecution under sections 6 or 7. This will not be easy.

TRADING IN INFLUENCE

Trading in influence (usually a form of political skulduggery) was one crime too many and too close to home when the Act was finally drafted.

The Law Commission commented as follows:[6]

- *(5.59) [We] will not be recommending that the discrete offence covers this kind of case. There is too great a risk that all advantages conferred in order to secure influence with politicians on certain issues will be turned into bribes. The taking of such a large step, in a highly controversial area, is more appropriately considered as part of a review of standards in public life, and not as part of the reform of the law of bribery.*
- *(5.45) [T]he Government has exercised its right to opt out of a provision of The Council of Europe's Criminal Law Convention on Corruption that would have addressed trading in influence. Article 12 of that Convention covers the promising, giving or offering, directly or indirectly, of any undue advantage to anyone who asserts or confirms that he or she is able to exert an improper influence over the decision-making of any person referred to [in relation to the principal offence].*

---

6   The Law Commission (2008), *Reforming Bribery* (see Note 3 above).

- *(5.46) The Government has consistently maintained its intention not to extend the criminal law into this area, for fear that lobbyists might be caught by the expanded offence. In the CP, consultees were not asked specifically for their views about this situation […].*
- *(5.47) However, we do not now believe that it would be right to make recommendations at this juncture that would undermine the point and purpose of the Government's opt-out with respect to Article 12 of Europe's Criminal Law Convention on Corruption. It will always be the case that firms sometimes seek to use personal, business or other connections to secure contracts ahead of their competitors.*

Tackling political corruption, as explained in Chapters 10 and 11, is a step too far.

Section 1: Bribe Paid Overseas

MAIN PROVISIONS

The main provisions of what can be regarded as a primary offence are summarised in Table 6.2.

Table 6.2   Section 1 Offences Overseas

Section 1 Offering or Payment of Bribes OVERSEAS By a person or body corporate but only if there is a close connection with the UK		Bribery takes place Overseas PERSONAL LIABILITY
Person Paying the Bribe ☹		Person Receiving the Bribe ☺
If any part of the offence takes place in the UK OR by a closely connected person		
Section 12 (4) Close connection with the UK means: • A British citizen • An individual ordinarily resident in the United Kingdom • A body incorporated under the law of the UK • A Scottish partnership		
Offers, promises or gives	Directly or through a third party	It does not matter whether the person to whom the advantages is offered is the same person who is to perform or has performed the function or activity concerned
A financial or other advantage		***Improper performance (Section 4)***
And **intends** the advantage		*Performing or failing to perform in breach of a relevant expectation*
To induce the person to perform improperly		

A relevant function or activity		*Relevant function or activity (Section 3)*
Or		• *A function of a public nature* • *Any activity connected with a business trade or profession* • *Any activity performed by or on behalf of a body of persons* • *Which the person is expected to perform in good faith and impartiality and is in a position of trust by virtue of performing it even if it has no connection with the United Kingdom or is performed outside the United Kingdom*
To reward the person for improper performance of such function or activity		*Relevant expectation (Section 5)* *What a reasonable person in the United Kingdom would expect in relation to the performance of the type of function or activity concerned **disregarding any local custom or practice unless it is permitted or required by the written law applicable to the country or territory concerned***
Or		
Where he knows or believes the acceptance of the advantage would itself constitute the improper performance		
CORPORATE LIABILITY **Section 14 (1)** If committed with the **consent or connivance** of a senior officer or person [he or she] is guilty of the offence as well as the body corporate or partnership ***Section 14 (4) Senior Officer** in relation to a body corporate is a director, manager, secretary or other similar officer*		*Only when the advantage rewards past performance is it necessary to prove that the recipient knew it was improper* *Bribe acceptance with the consent or connivance of a senior manager – a directing mind – may result in corporate liability except for Crown Bodies*

SOME POINTS TO NOTE

The offences are similar to those shown in Table 6.1 (see page 108), except:

• Under Section 12 (1) liability for bribes paid overseas arises only if any act or omission which forms part of the offence takes place in part of the UK. Thus companies and individuals who have absolutely no connection with the UK may be prosecuted if they merely make the payment through UK banking channels. However, foreign nationals are unlikely to be extradited.
• If no act or omission takes place in the UK, liability for offences under sections 1,2, or 6 only applies if the person has a close connection with the UK (as defined in Section 12 (4)).
• Bribery of an FPO may be charged under Section 1 or Section 6 (see page 121).
• The UK is believed to be the only country in the world that applies extraterritorial liability to private sector bribery overseas.

In the case of overseas bribery local custom and practice has to be ignored for the purposes of the relevant expectation test. International custom and practice may be considered.

HOSPITALITY OF FOREIGN PUBLIC OFFICIALS

The Law Commissioners appeared to take a pragmatic approach to hospitality of FPOs and gave the following example:

> *(3.70) P (the Payor) invites officials from the Ministry of Commerce in Blueland to an evening of hospitality at P's company's expense. P's intention is that the officials should be impressed by the business opportunities that the company has to offer, and accordingly will offer P the chance to do business in Blueland.*
>
> *P realises that some of the officials may be so impressed by the hospitality that they would recommend that P be offered the chance to do business in Blueland irrespective of the real merits of the company. However, it is not P's intention that this should be the reason that the officials give him or her that chance (although, obviously, P may not especially mind why the officials do give it to him or her).*
>
> *P should not be guilty of bribery in this kind of case. As we have said, we now believe that the law would extend too far if it caught cases in which P merely realised that there was a serious risk that R would be motivated by the advantage to act improperly.[7]*

In the Bribery Bill and Joint Committee deliberations, the idea was that prosecution had to show that hospitality was the primary reason for a perverted decision being taken. This was not incorporated into the Act on the grounds of proving primacy was 'too onerous'.

FACILITATION PAYMENTS

The Law Commissioners commented as follows:[8]

- *(5.86) Facilitation payment is not a legal term of art. The law of England and Wales does not recognise facilitation payments as a distinct category. In the consultation process, we said it is generally accepted that a facilitation (or speed or grease) payment is a payment made with the purpose of expediting or facilitating the provision of services or routine government actions which an official is normally obliged to perform.*
- *(5.88)* **The** *[Organisation for Economic Cooperation and Development]* **(OECD)'s position on facilitation payments is not so straightforward, contending that they are not made to obtain or retain business or other improper advantage and, accordingly, are not an offence.** *(Emphasis added)*
- *(5.89) A number of Parties to the Convention have accordingly provided that payments made to a foreign public official in order to expedite, ensure or secure the performance of a routine government action are not prohibited. Some of those Parties expressly require that the payment is of a minor nature or small and some require that a record be kept of the payment.*

---

7   The Law Commission (2008), *Reforming Bribery* (see Note 3 above).

8   The Law Commission (2008), *Reforming Bribery* (see Note 3 above).

- *(5.108) We believe that facilitation payments are best handled through sensible use of the discretion not to prosecute.*
- *(5.109)* **Whilst it will clearly be a matter for the prosecution authorities, we suggest that it will rarely be in the public interest to prosecute individuals or organisations for the payment of small sums to secure the performance of routine tasks.** *(Emphasis added)*

The bottom line on facilitation payments was given[9] by Mr Alderman, the SFO Director. in July 2011 in the so-called 'nuanced approach' (see page 125).

DEFINITION OF A FOREIGN PUBLIC OFFICIAL

The Law Commission sounded a warning bell over recruiting officials under the 'revolving door' practice:[10]

- *3.26 It is important that whatever definition of public function, trade, employment or business etc. is adopted, the definition applies not only when R (the FPO) is currently involved in such activities, but also* **when he or she has been in the past.** *A simple example illustrates the point.*
  R has recently retired from an influential position in the civil service. He or she is approached by P who is seeking a lucrative contract with a Government department. P pays R a large sum of money to provide confidential information to P about the bidding processes. (Emphasis added)
- *In this example, a prosecution should not fail at the outset simply because R is not currently engaged in a profession or performing a public function.*
- *The position of regulators who have revolved out of the SFO into private sector jobs is interesting because they could be regarded under the Foreign Corrupt Practices Act (FCPA) as FPOs.*

EXTRADITION OF FOREIGN PUBLIC OFFICIALS

It is highly unlikely that FPOs who extort bribes would be extradited to the UK:[11]

- *(5.139) The Serious Fraud Office stated that it may be unrealistic to expect that the FPO will be prosecuted in their own country.[12] That country may lack the resources to undertake such a prosecution, or even if it has such resources it may care little about the official's conduct. There might also be litigation advantages in making the FPO subject to potential prosecution. If the FPO was immune from prosecution, he or she might readily give false evidence to support a defence offered by P.*

---

9   At the time although the current Director seems to have changed the position, dramatically.

10   The Law Commission (2008), *Reforming Bribery* (see Note 3 above).

11   The Law Commission (2008), *Reforming Bribery* (see Note 3 above).

12   So much for the power of the OECD Convention.

- *(5.140) The Crown Prosecution Service thought that it would be distasteful[13] for the FPO to face criminal sanctions in England and Wales for conduct that may have been perfectly in accordance with his or her own national law.*
- *(5.142) The OECD Convention is primarily concerned with active bribery (euphemistically bribery by the person who provides the advantage), and does not require states to grant themselves power to prosecute FPOs.*
- *(5.143) The objections or concerns raised by the Crown Prosecution Service and the Council of HM Circuit Judges have persuaded us that the case for extending the offence to cover the conduct of FPOs themselves is insufficiently compelling. As a representative of the International Chamber of Commerce (UK) pointed out to us, were the UK to depart in this instance from the territorial principle, other states including those where trials fail to meet basic standards of fairness would feel entitled to extend their criminal law to cover officials from the UK. We would not want to set such developments in train.*

PAYMENTS TO POLITICIANS IN OPPOSITION AND POLITICAL PARTIES

It is difficult not to look in shock and horror at the way politicians support each other, often in pursuit of the noble cause of spreading democracy.

The Law Commissioners commented:[14]

- *(5.129) There is thus no obligation on Parties (to the OECD Convention) to provide for the case in which P confers an advantage on a political party, or party official. We will not be recommending such an extension. It is true that the problems addressed in the Convention may well be engaged when people seek to do business with party officials in one-party states.*
- *However, it would in practice be difficult to distinguish between party officials in such states, who may or may not be able to put business someone's way in an official capacity on behalf of the state, and party officials in other states who may be perfectly entitled to accept advantages in exchange for (say) seeking greater influence within the party for the person providing the advantage. Further problems may lie in deciding when someone is, or is not, a member of a political party.*

A final point worth noting is that under the Bribery Act advantages provided to opposition political parties and candidates is permissible, whereas under the FCPA they are prohibited. Isn't that a nice little touch?

Section 2: Bribes Received in the UK

MAIN PROVISIONS

The main provisions of what can be regarded as a primary offence are summarised in Table 6.3.

---

13   Cripes! Distasteful? How very British!

14   The Law Commission (2008), 'Reforming Bribery' (see Note 3 above).

Table 6.3   Section 2: UK Offences Bribe Receipt

Section 2: Requesting or accepting a bribe – UK By a person or body corporate *in the UKwherever incorporated*		Bribery takes place in the UK **PERSONAL AND CORPORATE LIABILITY**
Person Receiving the Bribe (Extorter) ☹		**Person Paying the Bribe (Coercer)** ☺
Case 3 Requests, agrees to receive or accepts		*The recipient must know that the performance would be improper*
Intending in consequence		

A relevant function or activity
Relevant function or activity (Section 3)
•   *A function of a public nature*
•   *Any activity connected with a business trade or profession*
•   *Any activity performed by or on behalf of a body of persons*
•   *Which the person is expected to perform in good faith
   and impartially and is in a position of trust by virtue of
   performing it even if it has no connection with the United
   Kingdom or is performed outside the United Kingdom*		

Should be performed improperly	Whether by himself or another person	
Improper performance (Section 4) *Performing or failing to perform in breach of a relevant expectation*		
Relevant expectation (Section 5) *What a reasonable person in the United Kingdom would expect in relation to the performance of the type of function or activity concerned*		
Or		
Case 4 The request, agreement or acceptance itself constitutes improper performance by the receiver of a relevant function or activity		*The recipient need not know that the performance was improper*
Or		
Case 5 As a reward for improper performance by the receiver or another person of a relevant function or activity		
Case 6 in anticipation of or in consequence of the receiver requesting, agreeing to receive or accepting a financial or other advantage a relevant function or activity is performed improperly by himself or another person at his request or with his ascent or acquiescence		
In cases 3 to 6 does not matter whether the receiver requests etc. the advantage directly or through a third party or whether the advantage is (or is to be) for the benefit of himself or another person		

Section 2: Requesting or accepting a bribe – UK By a person or body corporate *in the UKwherever incorporated*	Bribery takes place in the UK **PERSONAL AND CORPORATE LIABILITY**
Person Receiving the Bribe (Extorter) ☹	**Person Paying the Bribe (Coercer)** ☺
In cases 4 to 6 it does not matter whether R knows or believes that the performance is improper	
Section 14 (1) If committed with the **consent or connivance** of a senior officer or person [he or she] is guilty of the offence as well as the body corporate or partnership *Section 14 (4) Senior Officer in relation to a body corporate is a director, manager, secretary or other similar officer*	
CORPORATE LIABILITY **Section 14 (1)** If committed with the **consent or connivance** of a senior officer or person [he or she] is guilty of the offence as well as the body corporate or partnership *Section 14 (4) Senior Officer in relation to a body corporate is a director, manager, secretary or other similar officer*	*Only when the advantage rewards past performance is it necessary to prove that the recipient knew it was improper* *Bribe acceptance with the consent or connivance of a senior manager, a directing mind, may result in corporate liability except for Crown Bodies*

SOME POINTS TO NOTE

The main thrust of the OECD, Transparency International (TI)'s pronouncements and the legislation is to penalise bribe payment, mainly in so-called supply-side countries, and to leave extorters – especially if they are politicians or civil servants – virtually undisturbed.

- Corporate liability (under Section 2) arises where bribes are extorted by a directing mind, although government departments are excused as Crown Bodies.
- In the UK, one of the most prevalent forms of bribery is payment by the private into the public sector.
- Since for every coercer there is an extorter, one of the most effective ways of exposing bribe payment (and Section 7 offences) would be to require government departments to detect incoming bribery and then expose collaborators: yet nothing seems to have been done about this.
- Similarly, why are organisations whose controls are so pathetic that they incite their employees to extort bribes not subject to an equivalent to a Section 7 offence?
- The provision under the Prevention of Corruption Act 1916, putting the burden on civil servants and their collaborators to prove that an advantage was not corrupt, has vanished, disappeared, no more: it is a dead parrot.[15] This will make it much more difficult to prosecute officials for extorting bribes.

---

15   Funny that!

Since the MOJ Guidance is limited to defending Section 7 charges involving bribe payment, there is not a word about incoming bribery. Equally, there is no evidence that TI, British and American regulators, commercial departments or embassies have taken the slightest interest in naming and shaming the FPOs who have colluded in known cases, let alone prosecuting them. It seems that the rule is to only sanction those amenable to it.

Section 2: Bribe Received Overseas

MAIN PROVISIONS

The main provisions of what can be regarded as a primary offence are as summarized in Table 6.4.

Table 6.4   Section 2: Bribe Receipt Overseas

Section 2: Requesting or accepting a bribe – OVERSEAS By a person or body corporate *in the UK wherever incorporated*		Bribery takes place Overseas PERSONAL AND CORPORATE LIABILITY
Person Receiving the Bribe ☹		Person Paying the Bribe ☺
If any part of the offence takes place in the UK OR by a closely connected person		
Section 12 (4) Close connection with the UK means: • *A British citizen* • *An individual ordinarily resident in the United Kingdom* • *A body incorporated under the law of the UK* • *A Scottish partnership*		
Case 3 Requests, agrees to receive or accepts		*See Table 6.3*
Intending in consequence		
A relevant function or activity		
Relevant function or activity (Section 3) • *A function of a public nature* • *Any activity connected with a business, trade or profession* • *Any activity performed by or on behalf of a body of persons* • *Which the person is expected to perform in good faith and impartiality and is in a position of trust by virtue of performing it even if it has no connection with the United Kingdom or is performed outside the United Kingdom*		
Should be performed improperly	Whether by himself or another person	
Improper performance (Section 4) *Performing or failing to perform in breach of a relevant expectation*		

Section 2: Requesting or accepting a bribe – OVERSEAS By a person or body corporate *in the UK wherever incorporated*	Bribery takes place Overseas PERSONAL AND CORPORATE LIABILITY
Person Receiving the Bribe ☹	**Person Paying the Bribe** ☺
Relevant expectation (Section 5) *What a reasonable person in the United Kingdom would expect in relation to the performance of the type of function or activity concerned* **disregarding any local custom or practice unless it is permitted or required by the written law applicable to the country or territory concerned**	*See Table 6.3*
Or	
Case 4 The request, agreement or acceptance itself constitute improper performance by the receiver of a relevant function or activity	
or	
Case 5 As a reward for improper performance by the receiver or another person of a relevant function or activity	
Case 6 in anticipation of or in consequence of the receiver requesting, agreeing to receive or accepting a financial or other advantage a relevant function or activity is performed improperly by himself or another person at his request or with his assent or acquiescence	
In cases 3 to 6 does not matter whether the receiver requests etc. the advantage directly or through a third party or whether the advantage is (or is to be) for the benefit himself or another person	
Section 14 (1) If committed with the **consent or connivance** of a senior officer or person [he or she] is guilty of the offence as well as the body corporate or partnership *Section 14 (4) Senior Officer in relation to a body corporate is a director, manager, secretary or other similar officer*	
CORPORATE LIABILITY **Section 14 (1)** If committed with the **consent or connivance** of a senior officer or person [he or she] is guilty of the offence as well as the body corporate or partnership *Section 14 (4) Senior Officer in relation to a body corporate is a director, manager, secretary or other similar officer*	*Only when the advantage rewards past performance is it necessary to prove that the recipient knew it was improper* *Bribe acceptance with the consent or connivance of a senior manager a directing mind may result in corporate liability except for Crown Bodies*

SOME POINTS TO NOTE

The offences are exactly the same as Table 6.3 except:

- A person working overseas for a company not bound by the Bribery Act can be convicted under Section 2 if any part of an offence took place in the UK or if he is closely connected. However, the SFO has no intention of extraditing skulduggers unless they happen to be British citizens.
- If the foreign extorter is British and classed as a directing mind, the associated body corporate would be guilty of an offence under Section 2.[16]

Section 6: Bribery of a Foreign Public Official

MAIN PROVISIONS

The main provisions of what can be regarded as a primary offence are as follows:

Table 6.5   Bribery of FPOs

Section 6: Bribery of Foreign Public Officials OVERSEAS		Bribery takes place Overseas PERSONAL AND CORPORATE LIABILITY
Person Paying the Bribe ☹		**Person Receiving the Bribe Foreign Public Official** ☺
A person is guilty of an offence		*Section 6 (5)*
If any part of the offence takes place in the UK or by a closely connected person		*Foreign public official means:*
Section 12 (4) Close connection with the UK means: • *A British citizen* • *An individual ordinarily resident in the United Kingdom* • *A body incorporated under the law of the UK* • *A Scottish partnership*		• *An individual wholholds a legislative, administrative or judicial position, whether appointed or elected of a country or territory outside the UK and:* – *exercises a public function* – *for and on behalf of the country outside the UK* – *for any public agency of that country or territory or* – *is an official or agent of a public international organisation*
If his intention		
Is to influence the FPO	*Section 6 (4)* **Influencing in the performance** *of his functions includes any omission to exercise those functions any use of his position even if not within his authority*	
In the FPO's capacity as a foreign public official		

---

16   If it a foreign company it is unlikely to be charged but any of its assets in the UK could be confiscated under the Proceeds of Crime Act.

Section 6: Bribery of Foreign Public Officials OVERSEAS		Bribery takes place Overseas PERSONAL AND CORPORATE LIABILITY
Person Paying the Bribe ☹		Person Receiving the Bribe Foreign Public Official ☺
P must also intend to obtain or retain a business or other advantage in the conduct of business		*Section 6 (6)* *Public international organisation* *means* • *an organisation whose members are any of the following:* – *countries or territories* – *governments of countries or territories* – *other public international organisations* – *any mixture of the above*
		Section 6 (3) *P bribes FPO if and only if directly or through a third party offers, promises or gives any financial or other advantage to the FPO or to another person at the FPO's request, assent or acquiescence*
		Section 6 (3)(b) *And is neither permitted nor required by the written law[17] applicable to be influenced by the offer, promise or gift*
Section 14 If committed with the **consent or connivance** of a senior officer or person [he or she] is guilty of the offence as well as the **body corporate or partnership** *Section 14 (4) Senior Officer in relation to a body corporate is a director, manager, secretary or other similar officer*		

SOME POINTS TO NOTE

This is possibly one of the most contentious sections of the Act and for reasons explained on page 751 will not be helped by nonsense such as 'Alderman's Needle'. Bribery of an FPO may be charged under section 1 or 6. They capture the same conduct with differences, shown in Table 6.6.

---

17   Hong Kong is one of the few jurisdictions to have a written law allowing FPOs to accept gifts, but only to celebrate special occasions.

Table 6.6   Differences Between Section 1 and Section 6

Section	Intent of the Advantage	Purpose of Making
1	To induce improper performance	To reward the person for improper performance of such function or activity. Does not have to be to obtain or retain business
6	To influence *Applies to publicly funded business* *Is very likely to amount to improper* *performance but does not require proof of it* *The offence is formulated to overcome* *evidential difficulties (see below for* *clarification of the italicised comments)*	**To obtain or retain a business or other advantage in the conduct of business**

- An FPO[18] does not include politicians in opposition or members of political parties, members of royal families, a candidate for appointment to a FPO position, nor an FPO's union representative or some others defined in the FCPA.[19]
- The FPO does not have to be a serving officer: the laws apply post-employment.
- The standards are different from those in the FCPA (see page 204).

COMMENTS BY THE MINISTRY OF JUSTICE

Section 6, paragraphs 21 to 32 of the MOJ Guidance,[20] WHICH ARE VERY IMPORTANT, relate exclusively to bribery of an FPO, but there is not a single mention in the section of facilitation payments. On the contrary it relates entirely to government-funded contracts or public procurement.

Paragraph 23 states that:

- Sections 1 and 6 may capture the **same conduct**.
- The policy that founds the offence at Section 6 is the need to prohibit the influencing of decision-making in the context of ***publicly funded business opportunities*** by the inducement of personal enrichment of FPOs or others at the official's request, assent or acquiescence.
- Such activity *(that is, influencing a decision in relation to a publicly funded business opportunity)* is very likely to involve conduct which amounts to improper performance of a relevant function to which Section 1 applies.
- But unlike Section 1, Section 6 does not require proof of it *(that is, improper performance)* or an intention to induce it. This is because the exact nature of functions of FPOs is often very difficult to ascertain with any accuracy and securing evidence will often be reliant on cooperation of the state any such officials serve *(implying that the SFO does not expect to receive assistance from the FPO's employer).*

---

18   Under the Bribery Act. However, they are regarded as FPOs under the FCPA.

19   Since there is so much drum-banging about international cooperation, it would not have been unreasonable to expect definitions to be consistent. This is another example of regulatory silos.

20   See Note 4 above.

- To require the prosecution to rely entirely on Section 1 would amount to a very significant deficiency in the ability of the legislation to address this particular mischief *(which is influencing a decision in relation to a **publicly funded business opportunity**): but not facilitation payments.*
- That said, it is not the government's intention to criminalise behaviour when no such mischief *(i.e. corruption relating to publicly funded business opportunities)* occurs, but merely to formulate the offence to take account of the **evidential difficulties** referred to above.

Paragraph 25 continues under the same section and again relates to publicly funded contracts and offset projects.

So here we have it, in words of black and white, from the horse's mouth, so to speak. Section 6 is concerned – as is Section 1 – with bribery of FPOs in relation to publicly funded business. It is included in the Act only to get over evidential difficulties in proving Section 1 offences.

PRONOUNCEMENTS BY THE SERIOUS FRAUD OFFICE

Mr Alderman and his colleagues at the SFO have not been slow in coming forward with their draconian views on facilitation payments and at various times have said:[21]

- *I **have made it clear**[22] that facilitation payments are already bribes under the current UK law[23] and that the position will remain under the Bribery Act. (Emphasis added)*
- *I **have also made it clear** that US corporations that are FCPA compliant need to look at their anti-bribery programmes because there is no exemption for facilitation payments under our law. The SFO will reserve the right to prosecute in appropriate circumstances, particularly where corporates make facilitation payments as a way of disadvantaging ethical corporates. (Emphasis added)*
- *The SFO **has made it clear** that the aspiration has to be zero tolerance for these payments, although it will be sympathetic to the difficulties that companies have in getting to that standard. (Emphasis added)*
- *The SFO requires organisations to impose a blanket ban on facilitation payments and to work on stamping them out as a top priority.*
- *[Facilitation payments] are not something that can be solved on an individual national basis. Nor is it something that can be solved just by one company (however large) acting alone. What is needed here is international involvement between countries and including institutions such as the World Bank and others. It can also mean companies working together to share their experiences of working in other countries and bringing those experiences to us.*

---

21   See http://thebriberyact.com/2011/03/02/richard-alderman-facilitation-payments-us-ok-uk-no-kay/ and http://thebriberyact.com/2010/12/18/facilitation-payments-sfo-help-to-ethical-companies-to-prevent-them/ (accessed 7 November 2012).

22   The forensic linguistic analysis of SFO speeches is very interesting. Such introductory phrases (known as 'referral softeners') are normally indicative of uncertainty, deception, or that the speaker is a shy retiring type. This is not alleged of Mr Alderman, who is a lawyer.

23   This could be regarded as a porky. The Anti-terrorism Crime and Security Act 2002 (ATSCA) makes facilitation payments a criminal offence when any part of such a payment is committed in the UK or, if overseas, by a UK national. A company would only be liable if a directing mind was involved. Thus the Bribery Act dramatically extends the law.

SFO Meeting With Gibson, Dunn & Crutcher, July 2010[24]

Mr Alderman said:

- The SFO does not approve of any company that fails to adopt a zero tolerance policy regarding facilitation payments. **If a policy allows for facilitation payments it will be regarded as failing the adequate procedures** test even if the company concerned is allowed such payments because it is predominantly US-based. (Emphasis added)
- The SFO takes a sympathetic approach towards emergency facilitation payments and offered an example:
  - A visitor to a foreign country requires an inoculation and is offered the choice of paying $5 to be inoculated with a clean needle, or not paying and being inoculated with a used needle. They stated that in this case, prosecution is unlikely if the payment is made.[25]
  - If a company's failure to report an offence is later revealed to the SFO, the company will have to justify its failure to report earlier and the SFO is likely to draw negative inferences on the basis of a 'report now or expect worse consequences later' standard.

The good news was that Mr Alderman's thoughts appeared to have become more realistic over time and his last known pronouncement on facilitation payments was to the law firm Pinsent Masons on 21 June 2011, when he said:

The Six Step Or Nuanced Approach

When considering the activities of a company which continues to make small facilitation payments after 1 July 2011, the SFO will be looking to see:

1. Whether the company has a clear issued policy regarding such payments.
2. Whether written guidance is available to relevant employees as to the procedure they should follow when asked to make such payments.
3. Whether such procedures are being followed by employees.
4. If there is evidence that all such payments are being recorded by the company.
5. If there is evidence that proper action (collective or otherwise) is being taken to inform the appropriate authorities in the countries concerned that such payments are being demanded.

---

24   http://www.gibsondunn.com/publications/pages/UKSeriousFraudOfficeDiscussion-RecentlyEnactedUKBriberyAct. aspx, with not a word of it mentioned on the SFO website.

25   This is simply ridiculous!

> 6. Whether the company is taking what practical steps it can to curtail the making of such payments.
>
> If the answers to these questions are satisfactory then the corporate should be shielded from prosecution.

As a result of this detonation of pragmatism, 'Cottage Industry' players (see Foreword) – believing their revenues threatened – gathered on rooftops preparing to jump. Then they realised that the 'shielded from prosecution' did not mean there would be no action taken and thus there was no real threat to fees. Phew!! However, when David Green took over at the SFO, most of Mr Alderman's warm and cuddly stuff went out of the window (see pages 70–80 and 718) so it is far from clear what rules now apply.

WILL FACILITATION PAYMENTS BE PROSECUTED?

Despite Mr Green's refocusing of the SFO on its intended role as a prosecutor, there are a good reasons for believing that facilitation payments will **rarely** be prosecuted[26] for the following reasons:

- The OECD Convention does not impose a prohibition on facilitation payments.
- A number of countries, including the USA, Canada, Australia and New Zealand allow facilitation payments, without any complaint from the OECD. In fact, the FCPA, which specifically allows them, has been held out by the international community as a model.
- When the Anti-terrorism Crime and Security Act was passed in 2002, the Crown Prosecution Service and the Home Office gave strong assurances that facilitation payments would not be prosecuted.
- In the last eight years there has not been a single prosecution under the Anti-Terrorism Crime and Security Act 2002 (ATSCA) for facilitation payments.
- The MOJ has gone as far as its mettle will allow to confirm that facilitation payments will not be prosecuted and recognises the long-term commitment involving both governmental and private sector support.
- The Law Commission report made it very clear that it did not believe facilitation payments should be prosecuted, but was prepared to rely on prosecutorial discretion to ensure this.
- There is no public interest, either in the UK or overseas, to be served in prosecuting companies for making facilitation payments.

Finally, and most importantly, the nuanced approach appears fair and workable (see page 755).

---

26   But no breath should be held over Civil Recovery Orders and Deferred Prosecution Agreements.

Section 7: Corporate Offence

MAIN PROVISIONS

This can be regarded as a derived – strict liability – offence which only comes into play when a person has been convicted or would be found guilty of an offence under section 1 or 6. *Note: there is no equivalent absolute corporate liability offence for organisations whose controls are so wretched that they invite incoming bribery.*

Table 6.7   Section 7 Corporate Liability

Section 7; Failure of Commercial Organisations to Prevent Bribery	Bribery takes place anywhere ABSOLUTE CORPORATE LIABILITY
Relevant Commercial Organisation	**Act of an Associated Person**
Section 7 (5) *Relevant commercial organisation means:* • A body which is incorporated under the law of any part of the UK and which carries on business (whether there or elsewhere)	
• Any other body corporate (wherever incorporated) which carries on a business or part of a business in any part of the United Kingdom	
• A partnership which is formed under the law of any part of the UK and which carries on a business (whether there or elsewhere)	
• A partnership (wherever formed) which carries on business or part of the business in any part of the United Kingdom	
Section 12 (5) An offence committed under Section 7 irrespective of whether the acts or omissions which form part of the offence take place in the United Kingdom or elsewhere	
A relevant commercial organisation is guilty of an offence under this section if a person (A) associated with it bribes another person intending:	***Section 8 Associated Person*** *A is associated with C if A is a person who performs services for or on behalf of C* • *The capacity in which A performs does not matter* • *Accordingly A may be C's employee, agent or subsidiary* • *Whether or not A is a person who performs services for or on behalf of C is to be determined by reference to all the relevant circumstances* • *But if A is an employee of C, it is to be presumed, unless the contrary is shown, that A is a person who performs services for or on behalf of C* • *Whether a person performs services or not is to be determined by reference to all the relevant circumstances and not merely by reference to the nature of the relationship*

Section 7; Failure of Commercial Organisations to Prevent Bribery	Bribery takes place anywhere ABSOLUTE CORPORATE LIABILITY
Relevant Commercial Organisation	Act of an Associated Person
To obtain or retain business for C	*Section 7(3)* *A bribes another person if and only if A is, or would be, guilty of an offence under section 1 or 6 (With the closely connected conditions in Section 12 removed)*
To obtain or retain an advantage in the conduct of business	
Section 7(2) But it is a defence for C to prove that it had adequate procedures in place to prevent such conduct	

SOME POINTS TO NOTE

Section 7 offences have been the main focus of regulatory attention, prioritised well ahead of preventing losses from incoming, internal and competitive corruption. Developing adequate procedures to defend Section 7 has been a goldmine for lawyers, consultants and even elderly investigators (Yum Yum!).

The Only Defence

A distinguished lawyer, addressing an audience of eager seminar delegates, said: 'Adequate procedures are the ONLY defence to a Section 7 charge'. This is not so. The most effective defence is to disprove the predicate section 1 or 6 offence. Only if this fails do adequate procedures become important.

- To succeed with a Section 7 charge, the prosecution must show a breach of section 1 or 6 and an intention to obtain or retain business an advantage in the conduct of business.
- The adequate procedures defence may apply.

An unresolved question is whether or not a Section 7 conviction amounts to a bribery offence, leading to debarment from government contracts.

LAW COMMISSIONERS' VIEWS

The Law Commissioners commented on the fact that a company can be convicted under Section 7 even if no one has been convicted of a predicate offence under section 1 or 6:

- *If a company is charged with a failure to prevent bribery, should there be a need to show [...] failing adequately to supervise [...]? We believe that this would be too onerous and too restrictive a requirement. In a case where the individual was an agent living overseas, such a person might never be prosecuted. It should be enough that, in the proceedings against the company for a failure to prevent bribery, the tribunal of fact is satisfied that [...] the bribery offence was committed by someone on behalf of the company.[27]*

Too onerous? More intelligent observers believe – in the worldwide clamour to coerce people to plead guilty – a little bit more onerousness on prosecutors would not be a bad thing.

LIABILITY FOR THE PERFORMANCE OF THIRD PARTIES

Section 7 makes a relevant commercial organisation responsible for others performing services on its behalf with the purpose of obtaining or retaining business (see page 105 et seq). The Law Commissioners commented on this liability but its requirement for proof of negligence was again regarded as too onerous and expunged from the record, never to be mentioned again.

LIABILITY FOR SUBSIDIARIES

A relevant commercial organisation is vicariously liable (under Section 7) for bribes paid by anyone performing services on its behalf anywhere in the world. Thus parent companies may be liable for bribes paid by subsidiaries and vice versa.

The Commissioners considered this point:

- *Under our scheme, a company may be held liable (subject to a due diligence defence) for a negligent failure to prevent bribery being committed by anyone who is proved to have acted on behalf of the company. It would be anomalous if subsidiary companies were specifically to be excluded from the range of persons who may be considered to be acting on behalf of the company, for the purpose of establishing the company's liability in this respect.*
- *(6.120) [T]he test of whether a subsidiary company is providing services on behalf of a main company should be a substantive rather than a formal test. In other words, the question of whether the test has been satisfied will depend on all the circumstances. It should not depend simply on whether, for example, the subsidiary company does business with foreign officials using papers that all say, 'None of the (subsidiary) company's actions are done on behalf of the main company'.*
- *(6.121) This kind of situation is different from the situation in which a question arises whether liability should be imposed on a company for a failure adequately to supervise a subsidiary, when that subsidiary has committed bribery on its own account, and not specifically on behalf of the main company. It is this difficult question that we believe is best left to the general review of corporate liability.*

The position was adequately covered in the MOJ Guidance but will the SFO go along with its suggestions or try to expansively interpret? As Mr Alderman might say; You bet!

---

27   The Law Commission, 'Reforming Bribery' (Crown Copyright 2008), 6.122. Available at: http://lawcommission. justice.gov.uk/docs/cp185_Reforming_Bribery_report.pdf (accessed 7 November 2012).

SUCCESSOR LIABILITY

A preponderance of cases within the self-disclosure regime were first uncovered by companies during the course of pre-acquisition due diligence, Initial Public Offerings (IPOs) or management buyouts, structural, management or regime changes, commercial litigation or disciplinary actions. They are different from the normal types of self-disclosure because those coming forward are unlikely to be involved in the skulduggery concerned, and:

- Can stand on the sidelines throwing rocks at everyone else;
- Can accuse and thus retaliate against managers they didn't like;
- Can negotiate lower acquisition prices (whether the allegations turn out to be true or not);
- Leverage other concessions.

If skulduggery is not uncovered prior to completion,[28] the successor takes on liability and this is clearly bad news. But a ruling in a case involving Haliburton grants a reasonable time after a deal has been completed for the acquirer to make more thorough checks. If they then expose earlier bribery and it is self-disclosed, successor liability may be reduced or avoided.

EQUITY INVESTMENTS

Mr Alderman's energy, enthusiasm and opportunism has genuinely to be admired. In June 2011 he addressed a meeting sponsored by the leading law firm of Debevoise & Plimpton LLP which no doubt frightened daylights out of its private equity clients. The Director's drift was:

> *Owners should not stand aside and say this is nothing to do with them but is an operational issue for the company. It is not. As owners of companies, private equity (as well as the big institutional shareholders) have a responsibility to society to ensure that the companies in which they have a shareholding operate to the right standards. It may even be that it is a condition of investment by fund managers allocating funds to you to invest that you invest only in companies that are FCPA and Bribery Act compliant.*[29]

You might reasonably ask how on earth this is possible and what does 'FCPA and Bribery Act compliant' mean? How can you tell? Do compliant companies have a special neon sign outside their offices? Does it mean that before Granny Jones puts fifty quid into BT shares she should carry out her own due diligence by interrogating the CEO?

OK, agreed, this is flippant, but it is important to repeat the point that compliance can only go so far, after which it becomes ridiculous. Compliance is all about balance and not just perpetual self-flagellation.

---

28   But note that successor liability applies only to acquired companies that were obligated to UK laws.

29   Richard Alderman 21 June 2011, available at: http://www.sfo.gov.uk/about-us/our-views/director's-speeches/speeches-2011/private-equity-and-the-uk-bribery-act,-hosted-by-debevoise--plimpton-llp.aspx (accessed 7 November 2012).

WHAT ARE ADEQUATE PROCEDURES?

There is no specification of what are and are not adequate procedures. But don't worry, the SFO has addressed the position in a lot of its speeches:

Ninth Corporate Accountability Conference, December 2010

What I am concerned about is a system of principle that is part of an overall approach to business ethics on the part of the corporate. It is all about the ethical standards that underline the creation of sustainable businesses. We look for a set of principles that are essential in this area and the MOJ draft guidance has set those out.[30]

Bottom Line: Companies should perform on principle and not just box tick in respect of bribe payment as the MOJ Guidance suggests

---

Herbert Smith Conference, February 2011

The Guidance is designed to be of general application and is formulated around guiding principles. The question of whether an organisation had adequate procedures in place to prevent bribery in the context of a particular prosecution is a matter that can only be resolved by the Courts taking into account the particular facts and circumstances of the case.[31]

Bottom Line: Adequate procedures can only be resolved by a court.

Breakfast Briefing, Moscow, March 2011

Some people have said that the very fact that corruption occurs means that the procedures must by definition have been inadequate. I do not agree with this. It is quite possible in the context of a major global corporation that an instance of bribery can happen somewhere in the world despite the very best procedures.[32]

---

30 Speech by Richard Alderman, available at: http://www.sfo.gov.uk/about-us/our-views/director's-speeches/speeches-2010/ninth-corporate-accountability-conference.aspx (accessed 16 October 2012). The guidance does not even get off the ground in terms of adequacy.

31 Available at: http://www.sfo.gov.uk/about-us/our-views/other-speeches/speeches-2011/icc-conference-hosted-by-herbert-smith.aspx (accessed 16 October 2012).

32 Available at: http://www.sfo.gov.uk/about-us/our-views/director's-speeches/speeches-2011/the-implications-of-the-uk-bribery-act-for-russian-business.aspx (accessed 16 October 2012).

Bottom Line: If a major corporation has one incidence of bribery, it does not mean its procedures were inadequate.

Russia Legal Seminar, June 2011

We hear as well that the company is not prepared to pay very much for [compliance] and expects a certificate of adequate procedures for its worldwide enterprise under, say, £25,000. This will not impress us very much. This does not mean that we expect companies to spend millions of pounds on this. What we do expect, though, is a proportionate approach by companies focussing on the key risks and on what they are doing in order to be able to combat those risks. This is what companies should be doing anyway.[33]

Bottom Line: The SFO does not expect companies to spend millions on adequate procedures but will not be impressed with just £25,000.

Anti-Corruption Summit, Washington DC, October 2011

Please take it from me that simply handing us a large pile of documents with lots of boxes ticked on checklists will not be enough to satisfy us that you have adequate procedures. That is a paper exercise. It is part of what is needed but only part. We shall want to know what lies behind this and what the real issues are.[34]

Bottom Line: The SFO would be happy to see large piles of documents with lots of boxes ticked but also wants to know what lies behind them. Mr Alderman continued:

You may find this surprising[35] but we do have a regular succession of corporations coming to the SFO to seek our views on their procedures and what they are doing. We stress that we can give no guarantee and certainly, no certificate to the effect that their procedures are adequate, but we are able to give them helpful advice. The feedback we get is that these are positive and pragmatic discussions.

Bottom Line: The SFO can give no guarantee that procedures are adequate.

---

33   Available at: http://www.sfo.gov.uk/about-us/our-views/director's-speeches/speeches-2011/russia-legal-seminar-2011,-london.aspx (accessed 16 October 2012).

34   Available at: http://www.sfo.gov.uk/about-us/our-views/director's-speeches/speeches-2011/anti-corruption-summit-2011,-washington-dc.aspx (accessed 16 October 2012).

35   Permission phrase!

So now all becomes clear. The SFO may or may not recognise adequate procedures when it sees them, but can give no guarantee to that effect. So what chance does a company have? Then to make matters worse the OECD Phase III Report[36] – in March 2012 – into the UK's compliance with the Convention came up with some gems to the effect that the MOJ Guidance was of comparable authority to an academic text, was not prescriptive, was not liked by judges and was not a safe harbour defence.

There is one further point to cheer everyone up.[37] It is – since Section 7 is effectively a strict liability offence – even if companies follow policies or procedures drafted by their lawyers to the letter they may be of little value. This is because the 'advice of counsel defence' is unlikely to help for strict liability offences. Then, even to try it, privilege may have to be waived on all related correspondence, work sheets and attendance notes. This may not be such a good idea.

So what is the point of fixating on adequate procedures, which in no way achieve the benefits of an Inspired Integrity campaign, discussed in Chapter 23. Probably the only justification is that they may persuade the SFO – at the vetting stage – not to launch a prosecution. This means that potential defendants must get their case across quickly and powerfully before minds are made up. An Adequate Procedures Dossier can do this (see page 722).

Comments on Other Sections of the Act

INTRODUCTION

Other sections of the Act include important definitions and interpretations. They are not always consistent with the MOJ Guidance or with the SFO interpretations. The most important which have not been discussed earlier are as follows.

SECTION 9: GUIDANCE

The Act required the MOJ to issue guidelines to help companies with the adequate procedures defence to Section 7 charges. In November 2010 the MOJ issued consultant draft which turned out to be worse than hopeless, but wondrously draconian. The consultees persuaded the minister that reconsideration was necessary. While this was taking place, the popular media, as well as the usual horde of altruistic groups, complained, moaned and protested that delay was causing the deaths of thousands of starving children in Africa and that the Act should be implemented immediately – if not even quicker – without softening any of its terms. It was a noble cause demanding immediate attention: or so they claimed.

The MOJ succumbed to the pressure and rushed through the Guidance, which it issued on 31 March 2011. The publication was supported by words of wisdom from the Justice Minister – Kenneth Clarke – and a Ministerial Statement, which contained verbiage that was neither included in the Act nor the Guidance itself. On the same day – and possibly with the intention of scooping the MOJ – the SFO and the Crown Prosecution Service

36 http://www.oecd.org/daf/briberyininternationalbusiness/50026751.pdf.

37 Definitely in the USA for strict liability offences and probably in the UK.

issued an undated document titled 'Bribery Act 2010: Joint Prosecution Guidance' (see page 145). This, again, differs from both the MOJ Guidance and from the Ministerial Statement.

Because of its statutory authority, the MOJ Guidance is potentially important, but it is of very little use because it is so basic and vague. It is also at variance with instructions and pronouncements by the SFO, which continues to claim the position of lead agency in the Act's enforcement.

SECTION 10: CONSENT TO PROSECUTION

This section introduces changes so that proceedings can now be commenced in England and Wales by the:

- Director of Public Prosecutions;
- Director of the SFO;
- Director of Revenue and Customs Prosecutions.

This removes the absolute power of the (politically appointed) Attorney General, although he or she can still override a decision to prosecute. Since he has the authority to appoint the Director of the SFO, he presumably has some influence on day-to-day operations. The OECD fretted over the intervention of UK politicians in the judicial process,[38] but, ironically, seemed unconcerned that in America judges are political appointees.

SECTION 12: TERRITORIAL APPLICATION

If any part of a foreign offence is committed in the UK, there is no question about jurisdiction and the nationality of the payor does not matter. Bribery that occurs entirely outside the UK is governed by the close connection rule for an offence under sections 1, 2 and 6. A close connection, as defined in section 12 (4), includes British citizens, people ordinarily resident in the UK and citizens of British Dependent Territories. It also includes bodies incorporated under the laws of the UK but not those established in British Overseas Territories. To laymen this is a strange omission because it leaves the British Virgin Islands, Cayman, etc. outside the anti-bribery net. Yet these are often central players in money-laundering and related offences.

SECTION 13: PROVISIONS RELATING TO THE INTELLIGENCE SERVICES

The Bribery Bill exempted serious criminal investigations by the police and activities of the intelligence services (MI5 and MI6) and army. The rationale behind this is that paying bribes may be necessary to protect UK citizens against terrorism, acts of war and organised crime. In the final drafting, the exemption for the police was removed, but still remains for the Intelligence Services. The UK is believed to be the only country in the world to have such an exclusion and it could be exploited again to protect bent defence contractors.

---

38   Which is not surprising following the British Aerospace (BAE) investigation.

SECTION 14: OFFENCES BY BODIES CORPORATE

If an offence is proved against a body corporate – by showing participation by a directing mind – any other senior officer who consented or connived may be liable under sections 1, 2 or 6. A directing mind may be superior to a senior officer, at the same level, or may be the same person.

SECTION 16: APPLICATION TO CROWN

This section applies the Act to individuals in the public service. It should be noted, however, that as Crown Bodies, government departments cannot be held corporately liable for incoming or outgoing bribery, even when it is committed with the consent or connivance of a senior officer or minister. This is so even if the department is filling a commercial role, such as under the Private Finance Initiative or by the police when selling its services into the private sector.

SECTION 19: TRANSITIONAL ARRANGEMENTS

The Act is not retrospective, thus offences committed before 1 July 2011 may – technically – still only be prosecuted under the superseded legislation, which has no equivalent to a Section 7 offence. Given that most cases of bribery do not emerge until a year or more after their commission, it is unlikely that Section 7 will be immediately relevant. However, there is little doubt that reference to absolute corporate liability will be raised in negotiations with the SFO, regardless of the time periods in which offences took place.

An Unwelcome Postscript

To prove that some people are never satisfied; in March 2012 the OECD produced its Phase III report on the UK's implementation of the Convention on the Bribery of Foreign Public Officials in International Business Transactions.

The report did not like:

- The six step (or 'nuanced') approach[39] to facilitation payments and went banging on about 'zero tolerance' policies even though these are not required;
- Civil Recovery Orders and Deferred Prosecution Agreements;
- That the SFO failed to insist upon maximum possible confiscations;
- That cases handled by the Financial Services Authority (FSA) (AON and WILLIS) were not also prosecuted by the SFO;
- Failure to insist on debarment;
- The SFO's self-appointed advisory role.

If this were not bad enough, the final blow were the comments that the Ministry of Justice Guidance on adequate procedures has no 'legal standing or force of law' and carries no more weight than an 'academic text', and is not binding on prosecutors or courts.

---

39   Which as explained earlier may have been abandoned by the new SFO Director.

Some judges told the OECD that government statements about legislation are 'normally not of great relevance'. Thus even total adherence to the Guidance is not a safe harbour defence. So, dear reader, what is the freaking point of adequate procedures?

7 *Enforcement, Penalties and Sentencing*

Introduction

Enforcement troubles start as soon as a suspected violation is internally detected (as represented in Figure 7.1) and continues until the case is resolved. Based on experience with the Foreign Corrupt Practices Act, resolution even after a voluntary disclosure can take up to 7 years! Given that adequate procedures and effective compliance ethics programs are likely to count for little when things have gone wrong, the lesson is to GET INTEGRITY RIGHT FIRST TIME and keep off the regulatory radar.

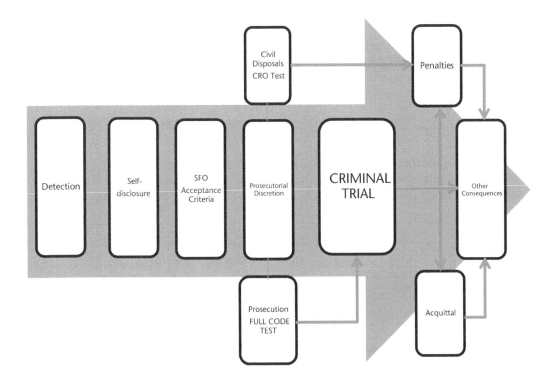

Figure 7.1   Flow from Detection to Resolution

The first critical decision is to self-disclose if:

* The suspicions are founded; or
* There is a requirement to report associated money laundering or other actual breaches of Securities and Exchange Commission (SEC) or Financial Services Authority (FSA) rules.

This decision is analysed on page 451 et seq, 596 and 635.

Detection By Regulators and Self-disclosure

Regulators have been consistently unsuccessful at detecting acts of bribery and despite their braggadocio the position is unlikely to improve. This is one reason they are so keen to encourage self-disclosure.

The Bribery Act 2010 does not require companies to self-disclose any form of bribery, although the Serious Fraud Office (SFO) makes it clear that failure to do so will result in a merciless public flogging.[1] In speeches in March 2011 and October 2011, the SFO Director said:

What the SFO Thinks Society Expects

Society expects senior members of a corporation to be responsible for ensuring that there is a true ethical culture. They have a key responsibility here. My view is that if they find that their efforts to do this meet with resistance or no success then they should consider[2] resigning and telling us about their concerns. Expressing doubts about the company's culture but remaining a highly paid officer would not be sensible because this would seem to be a model case of conniving in bribery for the purposes of the legislation […].[3]

This will be important to you both as executive directors and indeed as non-executive directors. If you are aware of bribery in a company of which you are a director and you do nothing about it, then in my view you are consenting to or conniving in the bribery.[4]

This more than slight over-egging of the cake is a repeated ingredient of regulatory pronouncements, mostly to terrify companies into self-disclosing, but it borders on the unethical. If society really 'expected' what the SFO Director said it does, why was a mandatory requirement to report offences not incorporated into the Act?[5]

---

1   Although there is no statutory guarantee that compassion will be exercised or that any settlement will be endorsed by a court.

2   Known in forensic linguistic circles as a 'non-verb', because nothing tangible results.

3   Speech by Richard Alderman, October 2011, quoted in http://thebriberyact.com/2011/10/13/beware-partners-directors-managers-company-secretaries-of-corporates-in-the-cross-hairs/ (accessed 16 October 2012).

4   Speech by Richard Alderman, March 2011, available at: http://www.sfo.gov.uk/about-us/our-views/director's-speeches/speeches-2011/joint-rbccchadbourne--park-llp-seminar,-st-petersburg.aspx (accessed 16 October 2012).

5   As is the case with Road Traffic Act and the few other offences.

Serious Fraud Office Acceptance Criteria

The SFO powers – of negotiating civil disposals in lieu of criminal prosecution – are at present exceptional in the UK bribery enforcement network.[6] This position may change and the FSA has some common and civil law opportunities which were used in the cases of AON and WILLIS to negotiate financial penalties for control deficiencies.[7]

Most companies, when contemplating whether they should buy their way out of criminal prosecution, would be well advised to be certain that their case passes the SFO acceptance criteria (see pages 67–8). Self-disclosing in the absence of such assurance would be unwise because the case could be referred to another agency (such as the City of London Police); this would have no alternative but to prosecute,[8] or drop the case, which goes against the grain.

Prosecutorial Discretion

A LONG ROPE

Prosecutorial discretion means what the term implies and includes, among other things, the decision to charge criminal offences or not. Discretion results in the SFO, the Crown Prosecution Service (CPS), Her Majesty's Revenue and Customs (HMRC) and other agencies being among the most powerful officials in the UK. They are required to maintain the highest ethical and professional standards and, in fairness, they try hard although sometimes with just a little too much bluster.

The chain of prosecutorial discretion does not start and end with the SFO and other agencies but is evident throughout the entire criminal justice chain: sometimes driven by questionable key performance metrics,[9] political, professional or personal biases.

POLICE AND INVESTIGATORY DISCRETION

When a case is reported to or detected by the police, a decision will be made by a senior officer whether or not to investigate. The *News of the World* hacking case is an example, as is the so-called banking crisis. Many reported crimes are not recorded as such and, to use an old police expression, are 'cuffed'.

---

6   And have not been adopted by the Crown Prosecution Service (CPS).

7   What is surprising in both these cases is that no one was prosecuted or, as far as we know, even personally investigated. The SFO was not involved.

8   Although in future the CPS and other agencies may be purveyors of Deferred Prosecution Agreements (DPAs).

9   The Review of the Serious Fraud Office (2008) by Jessica de Grazia (available at: http://www.sfo.gov.uk/media/34318/ de%20grazia%20review%20of%20sfo.pdf (accessed 16 October 2012)) was primarily driven by statistical analysis.

An Example of Cuffing[10]

In July 2011, in response to a Freedom of Information Act request by The Times, the Home Office admitted that 1 in 3 of the 2 million crimes reported to the police (especially burglary, theft and criminal damage) are written off at an early stage as unsolvable.

In January 2012, the HM Inspectorate of Constabulary found that 1 in 7 crimes (14 per cent) reported to police were not recorded as such. This was an improvement on the 19 per cent under-recorded in 2009.

The great news that under-recording has dropped to 14 per cent gives you a warm, fuzzy feeling: doesn't it, especially if someone has broken into your home and stolen your new Scottie Cameron putter which the local police fail to investigate?

TESTS BY PROSECUTORS

Summary of guidelines

UK prosecutors have issued a number of guidelines (some would say far too many, which are not coordinated, indexed or cross referenced) that are relevant to Bribery Act enforcement:

- CPS 'Code for Crown Prosecutors' issued in February 2010.
- 'Approach of the SFO for Dealing With Overseas Corruption' issued on 21 July 2009.[11]
- 'Guidance on Corporate Prosecutions' issued on 21 April 2010.
- 'CPS and SFO Joint Guidance' issued on 31 March 2011.
- 'Attorney General's Guidelines on Plea Discussions' issued on 5 May 2009 (see page 173).

They are discussed below more or less in date order. The 'Approach of the SFO for Dealing with Overseas Corruption' appears to have been withdrawn, following the appointment of David Green as the SFO Director.

'The CPS Code for Crown Prosecutors' and 'The Full Code Test'

Normally at the end of a police investigation a report will be submitted to a prosecution authority (such as the CPS or internally within the SFO), who will take a decision whether or not to prosecute based on two factors called the 'Full Code Test':

---

10   Cuffing is an ancient term used by police to refer to the practice of writing down criminal complaints on the cuffs of their shirts rather than official records. Once away from the complainant the cuffed note was erased.

11   Now appears to have been withdrawn.

- Is there a reasonable chance of obtaining a conviction?
- Is prosecution in the public interest?

In February 2010, the Crown Prosecution Service published 'The Code for Crown Prosecutors',[12] in Bengali, Punjabi, Gujarati, Welsh, Tamil, traditional Chinese, Somali, French, Polish, Arabic and Urdu: but notably not in Yiddish or Scottish.[13]

Its purpose was to guide prosecutors on the general principles to be applied when making decisions about prosecution. It is, actually, a very well written and clear document.

It states:

- '[A]lthough the prosecution service works closely with the police and other investigators, it is independent of them. The independence of prosecutors is of fundamental constitutional importance'.[14]
- Prosecutors must always act in the interests of justice and not solely for the purpose of obtaining a conviction.
- Prosecutors should swiftly stop cases which do not meet the evidential stage of the Full Code Test and which cannot be strengthened by further investigation, or where the public interest clearly does not require a prosecution.
- Prosecutors must make sure that they do not allow prosecution to start or continue where to do so would be seen by the courts as oppressive or unfair so as to amount to abuse of the process of the court.
- A realistic prospect of conviction is an objective test based solely on the prosecutor's assessment of the evidence and any information that he or she has about the defence that might be put forward [...] and is more likely than not to convict the defendant of the charges alleged.
- Where there is sufficient evidence to justify a prosecution or an out-of-court disposal, prosecutors must go on to consider whether a prosecution is required in the public interest.
- A prosecution will usually take place unless the prosecutor is sure that there are public interest factors tending against prosecution which outweigh those tending in favour.
- In deciding whether a prosecution is required in the public interest, prosecutors should take into account any views expressed by the victim regarding the impact the offences had.
- The prosecution service is responsible for deciding whether to offer an offender a conditional caution in certain cases. In such cases, the Full Code Test must be met. Prosecutors will offer a conditional caution where it is a proportionate response to the seriousness and consequence of the offending.
- The offer of a conditional caution, which is accepted and complied with, takes the place of a prosecution.
- **Prosecutors should select charges which reflect the seriousness of the offending** supported by the evidence, to give the Court adequate powers to sentence and impose appropriate post-conviction orders, and enable the case to be presented in a clear and

---

12   Available at: http://www.cps.gov.uk/publications/code_for_crown_prosecutors/ (accessed 16 October 2012).

13   Racial discrimination: innit?

14   This makes something of a mockery of the SFO's ambition to become a compassionate advisory agency, an investigatory body, a prosecutorial agency and, of course, a judicial authority.

simple way. This means that prosecutors may not always choose or continue with the most serious charge where there is a choice.

- **Prosecutors should never go ahead with more charges than are necessary just to encourage a defendant to plead guilty to a few.** In the same way, they should never go ahead with a more serious charge just to encourage a defendant to plead guilty to a less serious one.
- Prosecutors must be satisfied that the Full Code Test is met and that there is a clear admission of guilt by the offender in any case in which they authorise or direct a simple caution to be offered by the police.
- Prosecutors should only accept the defendant's plea if they think the court is able to pass a sentence that matches the seriousness of the offending. **Prosecutors must never accept a guilty plea just because it is convenient.**
- Particular care must be taken when considering pleas which would enable the defendant to avoid the imposition of a mandatory minimum sentence.
- It is the duty of the prosecutor to apply for compensation and ancillary orders, such as antisocial behaviour orders and confiscation orders, in appropriate cases.

These instructions suggest that Non-Prosecution Agreements (NPAs) and Deferred Prosecution Agreements (DPAs) should only be entered into when the evidence and public interest surpass the Full Code Test.

SFO Test for Civil Disposals for Overseas Corruption

On 21 July 2009 the SFO published a document 'The Serious Fraud Office's Approach to Dealing with Overseas Corruption',[15] which suggests that it will be favourably[16] disposed when the organisation has:

- A clear statement of the anticorruption culture, visibly supported at the highest levels in the corporate;[17]
- A code of ethics with a commitment making it explicit that the anti-bribery code applies to business partners;
- Principles that are applicable regardless of local laws or culture;
- Individual accountability;
- Policies on:
  - gifts
  - hospitality
  - facilitation payments
  - outside advisers/third parties including vetting, due diligence and appropriate risk assessments
  - political contributions and lobbying activities
- Training to ensure dissemination of the anticorruption culture to all staff at all levels within the corporate;

---

15   Available at: http://www.pwc.co.uk/fraud-academy/publications/sfo-guidance-approach-of-the-serious-fraud-office-to-dealing-with-overseas-corruption.jhtml (accessed October 2012).

16   That is not to prosecute. It does not mean it will not seek a civil settlement or other sanctions.

17   SFO-speak for a company or business but does not include government departments.

- Regular checks and auditing in a proportionate manner;
- A helpline within the corporate which enables employees to report concerns;
- Appropriate and consistent disciplinary processes.

It should be noted (carefully) that the new SFO Director has withdrawn all of the above and that has stated that he intends to prosecute when a case passes the Full Code Test.

The criteria do not precisely align with the Ministry of Justice (MOJ) Guidance or similar tests used by American Regulators.

The guidance continues:

We appreciate that a corporate will not want to approach us unless it had decided, following advice and a degree of investigation by its professional advisers, that there is a real issue and that remedial action is necessary.

The idea of a pre-disclosure investigation conflicts with the FSA's implied requirement to report without any delay and with the UK Sentencing Guidelines Council (see page 179), which condemns the idea that wealthy defendants should be able buy their way out of trouble.

The SFO approach continues by explaining the procedures after a case has been disclosed as follows:

Very soon after the self-report we will want to establish the following

- *Is the board of the corporate genuinely committed to resolving the issue?*
- *Is it prepared to work with us on the scope and handling of any additional investigation we consider to be necessary?*
- *At the end of the investigation will the corporate be prepared to discuss resolution on the basis of a civil recovery as well as:*
  – a programme of training and culture change
  – appropriate action when necessary against individuals
  – and at least in some cases external monitoring in a proportionate manner;
- *Does the corporate understand that any resolution must satisfy the public interest and be transparent?*
- *Will the corporate want us, where possible, to work with regulators and criminal enforcement authorities both in the UK and abroad in order to reach a global settlement?*

It therefore seems implicit that by indicating possible acceptance of a civil disposal the SFO expects the corporate to participate in and pay for a collaborative[18] investigation and to make all sorts of other disclosures. For reasons explained fully on pages 48 and 169 (and particularly having fully flagellated, a judge may say 'no way') this may not be such a good idea. It is also noteworthy that the SFO – in the cases of Macmillan and Oxford University Press (see page 148) – applied completely different criteria when negotiating civil disposals! The bottom line is that few people have any idea how the SFO will react in anything!

---

18   Or 'proxy'.

The CPS Guidance on Corporate Prosecutions

This guidance,[19] issued in April 2010, states, among other things, that:

- *A company is a legal person, capable of being prosecuted, and should not be treated differently from an individual because of its artificial personality.*
- *Prosecution of a company should not be seen as a substitute for the prosecution of criminally culpable individuals such as directors, officers, employees, or shareholders.*
- *It is usually best to have all connected offenders prosecuted together at the same time.[20]*
- *In the absence of legislation which expressly creates criminal liability for companies it may be established in the following ways:*
    - *by vicarious liability[21] for the acts of a company's employee/agents, which in the corporate world will normally arise, and offences of strict liability*
    - *in cases requiring proof of guilty knowledge being attributable to a directing mind and will of a senior manager in the company;*
- *A company can be party to a criminal conspiracy but only when it involves at least two human beings (for example a company cannot conspire with its own directors);*
- *Where a number of officers in the company have been concerned in the act or omission giving rise to the offence but none individually has the required guilty knowledge it is not permissible to aggregate all states of mind.*

Indicators of seriousness include not just the value of any gain or loss but also the risk of harm to the public, to identified and unidentified victims in the UK and internationally, shareholders, employees and creditors and to the stability of financial markets and international trade.[22]

Where the evidence provides a realistic prospect of conviction, the prosecutor must consider whether or not it is in the public interest to pursue the case.

The factors that a prosecutor should consider in favour of a corporate prosecution include:

- A history of similar conduct and flagrant breaches of the law;
- If the conduct is part of an established business practice;
- If the company had an ineffective compliance programme;
- If the company has previously been subject to warnings, sanctions or criminal charges and has nonetheless failed to take adequate action to prevent future unlawful conduct;
- Failure to report the wrongdoing within a reasonable time of the offending coming to light or concealing its full extent.

Factors that should be considered against prosecuting include:

---

19   Available at: http://www.cps.gov.uk/legal/a_to_c/corporate_prosecutions/ (accessed 7 November 2012).

20   Although the SFO prefers to reach a civil disposal with the corporate first and to whack individuals later.

21   In layman's terms, vicarious liability means that a company is corporately liable for skulduggery by its employees and agents when they are acting within the general scope of their employment, and intend to obtain an organisational benefit.

22   Article 5 of the OECD Convention does not allow economic and relational considerations in relation to bribery of foreign public officials (FPOs).

- A genuine proactive approach adopted by the management team when the offending was brought to notice, including self-reporting and remedial actions, including compensation of victims;
- Absence of a history of similar conduct;
- The existence of a *genuinely* proactive and effective corporate compliance programme;
- The availability of civil or regulatory remedies that are likely to be effective and more proportionate;
- The offending represented isolated actions of an individual;
- The offending is not recent and the company in its current form is effectively a different body to that which committed the offences;
- The conviction is likely to have adverse consequences for the company under European law *(for example, debarment, but please note that this is not in accordance with Article 5 of the Organisation or Economic Cooperation and Development (OECD) Convention);*
- The company is in the process of being wound up.

Alternatives to prosecution may include Civil Recovery Orders combined with a range of agreed regulatory measures.

Crown Prosecution Service and Serious Fraud Office Joint Guidance

Another publication titled: 'Bribery Act 2010: Joint Prosecution Guidance of The Director of the Serious Fraud Office and The Director of Public Prosecutions'[23] miraculously appeared on 31 March 2011, coinciding with the MOJ's Guidance. The timing of the joint release could be viewed, not as prosecutorial discretion but rather as prosecutorial disrespect to scoop the Justice Secretary's media appearances. This is, of course, pure speculation, but inside information indicates that prosecutors considered that politicians had caved in to pressure from the business community to dumb down their original stance on facilitation payments and were more than a little miffed.

The Joint CPS–SGO Guidance is considerably tougher than the MOJ's efforts and states:[24] that the **Bribery Act – Section 7 – does not apply to Crown Bodies.**[25]

In relation to facilitation payments, the factors in favour of prosecution are:

- Large or repeated payments are more likely to attract a significant sentence;
- Payments are planned for or accepted as part of the standard way of conducting business, which may indicate that the offence was premeditated;
- Payments may indicate an element of active corruption of the official in the way the offence was committed;
- The commercial organisation has a clear policy setting out procedures and these have not been correctly followed.

Factors tending against prosecution for facilitation payments:

23   Available at: http://www.cps.gov.uk/legal/a_to_c/bribery_act_2010/index.html (accessed 7 November 2012).

24   Among other things.

25   None of the other guidelines state this.

- A single small payment is likely to result in only a nominal penalty;
- The payments came to light as a genuinely proactive approach involving self-reporting and remedial action;
- The commercial organisation had clear and appropriate policies which had been correctly followed;
- The payer was in a vulnerable position arising from the circumstances in which payment was demanded.

The publication was followed by speeches talking about zero tolerance for facilitation payments, including the notorious Alderman's Needle (see pages 80 and 125).

DOUBLE JEOPARDY

For over 800 years the English common law has prevented citizens being tried more than once for criminal offences arising from a single set of circumstances. This is still true unless, following an acquittal, new and compelling material comes to light.

It is less clear what the double jeopardy[26] rules are for cases pursued by both UK and USA regulators, although fair play would suggest that prosecution should be in one or the other of the jurisdictions. In evidence to the International Development Committee Financial Crime and Development in July 2011, Mr Alderman said (paraphrasing his detailed evidence):

SFO on Double Jeopardy

We are now dealing with a range of cases, particularly involving very large global corporations, where there are parallel investigations in other jurisdictions. The question arises: how are these cases to be brought to an end, given the particular issue of double jeopardy? [...]

Once there is an agreement in another jurisdiction relating to the facts which gave rise to an SFO or other UK investigation that **would bring an end to any *potential prosecution in the UK***, because if an individual or company has been acquitted or convicted in another country in relation to a certain state of affairs they cannot be ***prosecuted again*** in this jurisdiction in relation to the same affairs. [...].

It is a complete waste of resources for the UK criminal investigative process to be trumped by the criminal process of another jurisdiction which offers effective plea-bargaining and certainty.[27]

---

26   In November 2012 the Director of Prosecutions issued "Interim Guidelines on the Handling of Cases Where the Jurisdiction to Prosecute is Shared with Prosecuting Authorities Overseas" See http://www.cps.gov.uk/consultations/concurrent_jurisdiction_consultation.pdf.

27   Cited at: http://www.publications.parliament.uk/pa/cm201012/cmselect/cmintdev/uc847-i/uc84701.htm (accessed 13 November 2010).

No one seemed bothered to ask the Director, if this were the case, how come British Aerospace (BAE), Innospec and some other companies were sanctioned in both the UK and the USA on essentially the same facts? The answer is that Mr Alderman was only talking about double jeopardy in *prosecutions* and not civil disposals. The second is there was some very fancy footwork in settling the charges to avoid claims of double jeopardy.[28] However, the SFO is clearly worried that if companies make their initial self-disclosures in the USA it will be unable to prosecute in the UK: but if the order is reversed it can take action and without preventing American regulators from doing the same.

CONCLUDING ON PROSECUTORIAL DISCRETION

It is obvious from the above discussion that the SFO and other prosecutors can cherry-pick – from a vast array of guidelines – the criteria they will use when deciding 'not to prosecute': whatever that term means.

Humpty Dumpty Land

'When I use a word', Humpty Dumpty said, in rather a scornful tone, 'it means just what I choose it to mean – neither more nor less'.

Stating that there will be no prosecution does not mean that there will be no civil disposal or civil recovery order, or that other sanctions, possibly in other jurisdictions, will be abandoned. The shifting sands of prosecutorial discretion are obvious from the press releases issued in July 2011 (under Director Richard Alderman's rule) in relation to Macmillan Publishers Limited and in July 2012 – under the new Director, Richard Green, announcing the settlement with Oxford University Press, as summarised in Table 7.1.

---

28   See the Trace International Compendium for more details. Available at: https://secure.traceinternational.org/Knowledge/Compendium.html (accessed 16 October 2012).

Table 7.1 **Macmillan Publishers Ltd and Oxford University Press: Factors For and Against Prosecution**

Factors Against Prosecution	
Macmillan July 2011 (MLP)	**Oxford University Press July 2012 (OUP)**
Agreed to pay £11,263,852 and SFO costs of £27,000 as a result of corrupt operations in East and West Africa. It was impossible to be sure that tenders were not awarded through corrupt relationships. An aggressive approach was taken to calculating the revenue received	Agreed to pay £1,895,435 in recognition of sums it received by its subsidiaries in Tanzania and Kenya (which was more than its actual profits) and SFO costs of £12,500
No monitor	Appointment of a monitor
MPL approached the SFO with a view to cooperation	OUP has conducted itself in a manner which fully meets the criteria set out in the SFO guidance on self-reporting matters of overseas corruption
MPL had fully cooperated with the SFO throughout the process and complied with an agreed timetable	
MPL had fully complied with other authorities including the World Bank Group;	
The Company had, in response to learning of the allegations of bribery and corruption, reacted appropriately in firstly, reviewing its internal anti-bribery and corruption policies and procedures, and appointing external consultants to recommend and help implement an internal, appropriate anti-bribery and corruption compliance regime	
As a result of the parallel World Bank process the company has been debarred from participating in World Bank Funded tender business for a minimum period of three years. In addition, the ompany has taken the decision to cease all live and prospective public tenders in its Education Division business, in East and West Africa regardless of the source of funds	
The Company, as a result of withdrawing from the sector, lost significant revenue including surrendered bid securities	
The actual products supplied were of a good quality; and	The products supplied were of a good standard and provided at 'open market' values. This means that the jurisdictions involved have not been victims as a result of overpaying for the goods or as a result of being supplied goods which were unsuitable or not required
There was no material identified to support a conclusion that the products supplied were overpriced.	

MPL will be subject to review by a monitor who will report to the Director of the SFO within 12 months and to the World Bank. The monitor must meet strict criteria including clear independence from the company.	
	The test under the Code for Crown Prosecutors in relation to the case meeting the criteria to prosecute has not been met at this point and there is no likelihood that such a standard would be met in the future. This view is based on a number of factors including, but not limited to (i) key material obtained through the investigation is not in an evidentially admissible format for a criminal prosecution; and (ii) witnesses in any such prosecution would be in overseas jurisdictions and are considered unlikely to assist or cooperate with a criminal investigation in the UK
	Difficulties in relation to obtaining evidence from the jurisdictions involved and potential risks to the personal welfare of affected persons
	There is no evidence of board level (or the equivalent) knowledge or connivance within OUP in relation to the business practices which led to the case being referred to the SFO
	The resources needed to facilitate an investigation into this matter are considerable, e.g. 12 terabytes of data collected as part of the investigation, and a civil recovery disposal allows a better strategic deployment of resources to other investigations which have a higher probability of leading to a criminal prosecution
	The settlement terms ensure all gross profit from any tainted contract will be disgorged.
	OUP East Africa and OUP Tanzania will be subject to parallel World Bank procedures which will result in them being debarred from participating in future World Bank funded tenders for a number of years
	In addition to the property recovered under the civil recovery order, OUP unilaterally offered to contribute £2 million to not-for-profit organisations for teacher-training and other educational purposes in sub-Saharan Africa

Factors Against Prosecution	
Macmillan July 2011 (MLP)	**Oxford University Press July 2012 (OUP)**
	SFO decided that the offer should not be included in the terms of the court order as the SFO considers it is not its function to become involved in voluntary payments of this kind. However, the SFO welcomes OUP's commitment to make this contribution and to work with a range of not-for-profit organisations in sub-Saharan Africa to achieve the above objectives.
	The SFO has previously been subject to criticism in relation to the transparency of the processes and proceedings in civil recovery matters. As a result the Consent Order and Claim (which sets out the basis for the proceedings) have been made public
	SFO Director David Green CB QC said: 'This settlement demonstrates that there are, in appropriate cases, clear and sensible solutions available to those who self-report issues of this kind to the authorities. The use of Civil Recovery powers has been exercised in accordance with the Attorney General's guidelines. The company will be adopting new business practices to prevent a recurrence of these issues and these new procedures will be subject to an extensive and detailed review'

The differences were first spotted by TheBriberyAct.com blog with the question 'Spot the difference?' Good question, but an even better one is 'why and how?'

Regulatory Fixation on Corporate Liability

Politicians and regulators, throughout the world, fixate on pinning liability for bribery and other offences on companies, but apparently only if they are from developed countries, erroneously classified as 'demand-side'. In the USA establishing corporate criminal responsibility is relatively straightforward based on vicarious liability:[29] meaning that skulduggery by employees,[30] when acting within the scope of their employment, can be attributed to the body corporate where the intended result would be to its benefit.

---

29 *Respondeat superior.*

30 And 'associated persons'.

In the UK corporate criminal liability only arises in cases where the skuldugger is a 'directing mind'.[31]

Hounding companies is more attractive to regulators than just prosecuting individuals,[32] because:

- Companies are more likely to yield on the basis that doing so is the easiest and cheapest solution, irrespective of guilt; it is a depersonalised problem solved by surrendering a small percentage of profits.
- Companies are more likely have the money to pay fines and compensation.
- Managers who take corporate decisions to self-disclose and then capitulate are unlikely to be involved – themselves – in skulduggery: they are bystanders rather than defendants[33] and less emotionally entangled.
- Companies may be persuaded to incriminate individuals to downplay their own culpability.
- Individuals, potentially facing long terms of imprisonment, are more likely to contest trials.

The Ethicality of Corporate Guilty Pleas

In some UK and US cases boards of directors have entered corporate guilty pleas when none of them were employed by the company at the time the alleged offences were committed. By doing so they effectively set themselves up as jury and judge over their forerunners. Further, by entering into cooperative agreements with prosecutors – including waiving of privilege (see page 804) – there is a significant danger that previous directors are denied the right to a fair trial. The process is not unlike Nick Clegg's entering a corporate guilty plea on behalf of the government to Mr Blair's decision to invade Iraq.

The bottom line is that companies are softer and more lucrative regulatory targets. Prosecuting them also generates revenue, whereas pursuing individuals, who may qualify for legal aid, is not.

Unethical Practices by Prosecutors

In 2012 Professor Monroe H. Freedman from Hofstra University published a paper titled 'The Persistence of Unethical and Unconstitutional Practices and Policies by Prosecutors'

---

31   The Bribery Act is one of a few exceptions because Section 7 effectively imposes vicarious liability on relevant commercial organisations for bribe payment.

32   Although, funnily enough, US regulators who have more than enough powers to whack companies are now much more concerned about doing the same to individuals. Can you ever win?

33   The Mabey & Johnson case is an example of this. In fact, the current management or new owners of a company may have strong personal reasons for reporting malpractice by their predecessors.

Offices'[34] which is recommended reading for anyone engaging with regulatory agencies. The report refers to Professor Abe Smith from Georgetown University who stated that 'being a prosecutor is inherently corrupting'.[35]

In the USA corporate liability is easier to prove and it is obvious that UK politicians and prosecutors would like a move in that direction, despite the fact it goes against hundreds of years of tradition. But vicarious liability is not universally supported and the fact is that the laws of most countries align with the CPS rather than the USA.[36]

In the UK, where there is clear evidence of participation by a directing mind in a bribery offence,[37] it is more likely than not that prosecution will follow. Where such evidence is lacking and a prosecution would fail, the CPS Code for Prosecutors (see page 140) requires that the case should be abandoned.[38] Dropping cases that are potentially money-making does not flow naturally through the regulatory DNA and in 2008 the SFO realised that it could use the Proceeds of Crime Act to negotiate Civil Recovery Orders (CROs) when the evidence did not satisfy the Full Code Test.

Civil Disposals and Civil Recovery Orders

The essence of CROs is that they deprive offenders of their criminal gains from 'illegal conduct'. CROs are not regarded as 'punishment' and even when contested are judged to a civil standard. The money recovered goes into central funds and is shared with the investigatory and prosecutorial agencies concerned (see pages 178–9). This is a powerful incentive for the SFO to pursue CROs.

The Attorney General's Guidance under the Proceeds of Crime Act states that CROs are appropriate when:

- It is not feasible to secure a criminal conviction;
- A conviction is obtained but a Confiscation Order is not made;
- A relevant authority is of the view that the public interest will be better served by using CRO powers than by seeking a criminal disposal.

For a while CROs, which do not raise problems with Human Rights or the UK's double jeopardy rules, became the flavour of the month. But the SFO was not satiated because the orders:

- Do not allow for the imposition of monitors (see page 167);
- Do not raise European Union (EU) debarment opportunities;
- Do not demand publicity and therefore lack transparency and the ability for regulators to grandstand.

---

34 http://papers.ssrn.com/sol3/papers.cfm?abstract_id=2017178.

35 'Can You Be A Good Person and a Good Prosecutor' 14 *Georgetown Journal*. Legal Ethics 355 (2001).

36 It is also notable that Germany opposes corporate criminal liability in virtually any shape or form.

37 Or a strict liability offence under Section 7.

38 Although this does not preclude a civil recovery under the Proceeds of Crime Act.

Nor do CROs require victims to be compensated.[39] But the real problem was that judges did not like them,[40] primarily because they only came before them for rubber-stamping.

The present position is that the MOJ Consultation Paper (see below), recognises the judiciary's distaste of CROs, suggesting that in future they will be used sparingly and will be supplanted by DPAs. These give the illusion of judicial direction and validation, but this is not always the case.

There are differences between CROs and DPAs, shown in Table 7.2, but they are not mutually exclusive.[41]

Table 7.2 Civil Recovery Orders and Deferred Prosecution Agreements

Civil Recovery Order (Against Property)	Deferred Prosecution Agreement (Against Persons)
Freestanding civil action taken in the High Court (or more often negotiated) based on a 'balance of probabilities'. This is a much lower standard than the Full Code Test	Should satisfy the Full Code Test to a criminal standard of 'beyond reasonable doubt'
Directed against the recovery of criminal property obtained by 'unlawful conduct' and in the possession of anyone whether or not they were complicit	Directed against individuals and companies who are complicit in offences
Recovery is possible even if the respondent did not know or suspect that the property was the proceeds of crime	Most DPAs require victim compensation (see page 183)
Companies in control of or benefiting from criminal property may be subject to a CRO. The orders do not require proof of involvement by a directing mind	Corporate liability is established on the identification principle and only when a 'directing mind' is involved
Does not require proof of intent	Requires proof of intent

To what extent DPAs will satisfy the SFO and other prosecutorial agencies remains to be seen, but they are unlikely to result in the low fruit and soft pickings of CROs.[42]

Victim Compensation

The SFO, under its Director Richard Alderman, showed commendable enthusiasm for compensating the supposed victims of bribery. People who know the ex-director say his views on compensation were honourably held and well intentioned. However, they lead to anomalies and injustice.[43]

---

39 Although there is nothing to stop the UK government or the SFO allocating part of the recovery to victims.

40 Anyone with experience of the justice system knows that you should never upset a judge.

41 Meaning that a DPA may incorporate a CRO.

42 Full versions of all American DPAs are available on the website for the University of Virginia Law Library.

43 Akin to compensating a mugger for losing his mask.

British Aerospace and Tanzania

In the BAE case, on the insistence of the SFO, the value of the £39 million unnecessary radar contract with Tanzania was reimbursed[44] to the tune of £29.5 million, notwithstanding that its own nationals, who had extorted bribes, were as culpable – if not more so, than those who had paid them. Where is the justice in that? What's more, none of the Tanzanian extorters have been prosecuted. BAE was criticised[45] for holding funds until it was certain that they would not be snaffled by the original extorters.[46]

The real victims of corruption are ordinary citizens (in both developed and less developed countries) and the honest companies who lose business to skulduggery. Yet nowhere in any official documentation, Transparency International (TI), OECD reports or pre-indictment disposition agreements is there any evidence that the interests of honest businesses are ever considered. So much for the regulatory promises to 'level the playing field!' So much for the political and regulatory bombast to stamp out corruption 'wherever and whenever it occurs'.[47]

Deferred and Non-Prosecution Agreements (DPAs and NPAs)

AN AMERICAN GIZMO

DPAs and NPAs[48] have been around in America since the 1960s,[49] initially for SEC, racketeering and labour union offences and later adopted by the Independent Private Sector Inspectors General (IPSIG) model that took on construction overbilling in New York. DPAs, described by one prosecutor as 'a stroke of genius', are substitutes for conventional prosecutions, but delayed for a period to give the alleged offender the chance to rehabilitate. If it does, the prosecution is dropped: otherwise it starts afresh. DPAs are not new, do not have any statutory backing, nor have they always been effective.[50] Some people say they are no more than a chimera to get companies to self-disclose. Then having fallen for the story, they get whacked.

In May 2012, the MOJ issued a Consultation Paper, recommending that DPAs (but not NPAs) should be adopted by the UK (see pages 80, 152 and 159).

---

44   Eventually after much soul-searching to ensure that those Tanzanians who had extorted bribes did not also pocket compensation.

45   For once unfairly.

46   Compensation was ultimately handled with the assistance of the Department for International Development, thus suggesting it was no more than an unsubtle way of increasing the UK's overseas aid budget ....

47   Jack Straw in full flow.

48   Both classed as 'pre-indictment dispositions'.

49   See the excellent summary by Cristie Ford and David Hess: 'Can Corporate Monitorships Improve Compliance', *Journal of Corporate Law*, 670 (2008–2009). Available online at: http://webuser.bus.umich.edu/dwhess/Ford%20and%20Hess%20JCL%202009_PDF.pdf (accessed 16 October 2012).

50   Such as the case of Consolidated Edison, which, a few months after its monitorship ended was back to its old ways; and, more recently, the cases of Aibel Group and AIG.

DPAs and NPAs, classified as 'pre-indictment dispositions' were given new life by the US Department of Justice (DOJ) and the SEC, supposedly to incentivise and reward companies who recant, self-disclose and capitulate. The characterisation of DPAs and NPAs as being primarily to help companies, their employees and shareholders survive isolated instances of skulduggery is misplaced for two main reasons. The first is that Article 5 of the OECD Convention on Combating Bribery of Foreign Public Officials in International Business Transactions specifically prohibits any commercial considerations in prosecutorial decisions. **The fact is that regulators – in ostensibly compliant countries[51] – flagrantly disregard this principle.** American regulators talk openly about avoiding 'collateral consequences'. Such words expose the falsity of arguments that compliance with the OECD Convention is essential. The reality is that politicians and regulators comply only when it is their interest to do so.[52]

Secondly, the guidelines of most countries (particularly the USA and the UK) specifically state that prosecutors must pursue charges which reflect the seriousness and extent of the offending and which enable the court to impose adequate sentences and post-conviction orders. What, in fact, happens with many DPAs, NPAs and plea bargains is that prosecutors skirt around reality, contriving far less serious charges to encourage pre-trial dispositions that avoid debarment.

Dual Standards

The BAE, Siemens, Daimler and other headline cases – where there was rampant, endemic corruption (charged usually as accounting or technical violations so as to avoid permanent and mandatory debarment from government contracts) – are examples of regulatory pussyfooting and it is plain wrong. Debarment should be a powerful deterrent, but it is not.

US prosecutors have been repeatedly critical of the SFO's treatment of BAE but conveniently overlook their own shenanigans. An excellent essay on the 'Beyond Conformity' website discusses Pfizer Inc. and its painkilling drug Bextra.[53] The drug was approved – in 2001 – by the US Food and Drug Administration (FDA) with maximum allowable dosages of 20mg.

Pfizer ignored these restrictions and 'off-label marketed' the drug for dosages of up to 40mg, which could have been fatal for patients with heart disease.[54] The company also used a multi-million dollar educational budget to pay hundreds of doctors for speaking and supporting Bextra at professional and other conferences 'and to serve as public relations salespeople'.[55]

In 2009, the FDA launched a prosecution in the certain knowledge that conviction would debar Pfizer from government-funded health programs such as Medicare and Medicaid.

---

51   Who claim that they lead the way.

52   See also the UK's reaction to complying with the Council of Europe's Convention (page 44).

53   See http://www.beyondconformity.co.nz/_blog/Hilary's_Desk/post/Big_Pharma_systemic_corruption/ (accessed 13 November 2012).

54   When Bextra was taken off the market in April 2005, more than half of its $1.7 billion in profits had come from prescriptions written for off-label applications.

55   If the doctors had been FPOs, each instance would have been a breach of the FCPA.

But all was not lost. Two years earlier a dummy company had been created – called Pharmacia & Upjohn Co. Inc. (PUCI) – which on the date of its incorporation had pleaded guilty to bribery offences involving a company Pfizer had earlier acquired. Although PUCI had never sold a single pill, it became the sacrificial lamb for the Bextra case, and accepted token debarment from Medicare programs. This dodge allowed Pfizer to continue as normal.

In 2009 PUCI reappeared and pleaded guilty to the Bextra skulduggery. It was fined $1.2 billion, which was the largest the federal government had ever collected at that point. It also paid billions of dollars more to settle civil lawsuits.[56]

Kevin Perkins, Assistant Director of the FBI's Criminal Investigative Division, touted the prosecution as a model for tough and effective enforcement, continuing that it 'sends a clear message to the pharmaceutical industry'.[57]

Mike Loucks, the federal prosecutor concerned, supported the settlement, stating: 'if we were to prosecute Pfizer, they get excluded [...] and a lot of people who work for the company who haven't engaged in criminal activity would get hurt'. In July 2010, Mr Loucks joined the staff of Skadden, Arps, Slate, Meagher & Flom LLP: one of whose major clients was (you guessed it) Pfizer!! And, of course, there was no need for a DPA or monitor.

The US DOJ has issued a series of memos on the way pre-trial dispositions will be handled.[58] The SEC follows guidance[59] of the 'Seaboard Report'. All of these publications – which have barely any statutory authority – require almost total capitulation to the whims and wishes of regulatory agencies if a DPA or an NPA is to have any prospect of success.

Mike Koehler, the 'FCPA Professor', commented:[60]

The SEC policy, like the DOJ's principles of prosecution, often cause companies to disclose ambiguous conduct – including that if subjected to judicial scrutiny may not be a violation – and to agree to whatever settlement terms the SEC views proper in the hopes of receiving lenient treatment and avoiding a long protracted legal dispute ... The common thread of these resolution vehicles is the practical absence of judicial scrutiny. Thus the untested and dubious legal theories leading to .... them ... are never questioned or examined in any meaningful way.[61]

This position, unfortunately, is one for which the UK seems to be heading. It is one where regulators expansively interpret the law and usurp the powers of the courts supposedly in the interests of overcoming 'inadequacies in the justice system' (see Table 7.3). It is, more often, a naked power grab.

---

56   The total penalties across all fronts were the equivalent of three months of Pfizer's profits, but its government contracts remained intact.

57   Which planet does this person live on?

58   Their main points are discussed later in connection with the proposed English and Welsh versions.

59   http://www.sec.gov/litigation/investreport/34-44969.htm#P16_499

60   http://www.questia.com/library/1G1-242668635/the-facade-of-fcpa-enforcement

61   See http://fcpaprofessor.blogspot.co.uk/ (accessed November 2012).

BENEFITS AND ETHICALITY OF PRE-TRIAL DISPOSALS

Self-disclosure and pre-trial disposals are not without their detractors: their supposed benefits (Relative Advantages = 'RA' in columns (1) and (3) in Table 7.3 below) can be summarised as follows:

Table 7.3   Benefits of a Deferred Prosecution Agreement

Benefits to Companies		Benefits to Regulators and Prosecutors	
RA	**Details**	**RA**	**Details**
(1)	*Column (2)*	*(3)*	*Column (4)*
2	The company avoids criminal prosecution and possible conviction but only if a court agrees. Such approval is uncertain	10	A DPA provides the opportunity for intervention in cases regulators would not otherwise detect
2	Creates a good relationship with regulators and peace of mind that offences have been dealt with	10	Eradicates investigative, disclosure, procedural and other problems which frequently result in failure to convict. Passes all responsibility to the alleged offender and creates fees for members of the 'Cottage Industry' (see Foreword)
3	Results in reduced fines *(but only very slightly and probably no greater than would be available through an early plea of guilty)*	4	Preserves resources to devote to other cases
0	Avoids debarment from government contracts *(which, based on the prosecutorial track record, is very unlikely)*	8	Minimises costs and optimises income for the government, regulatory and prosecutorial agencies
1	Minimises adverse publicity, investigatory and legal costs *(a DPA will be published, leading to further third-party litigation and regulatory action)*	7	Provides positive publicity of regulatory successes
1	Public disclosure provides the company with a fresh start. *(It is not necessary for public self-flagellation to achieve effective remedial action)*	10	Ensures that expansive interpretations are not challenged
1	Results in a quicker solution and back to business *(The MOJ figures suggest that a DPA will reduce the time involved from nine to four years)*	5	Increases the importance and standing of individual regulators, enhancing their marketability through the revolving doors and along the yellow brick road to private practice
-4	*To achieve a DPA a company may make admissions in the Statement of Facts it would never make if prosecution was in prospect. These admissions can be produced as irrefutable if – in the regulator's view – a DPA has not been honoured*	5	Overcomes the UK double jeopardy problem

Benefits to Companies		Benefits to Regulators and Prosecutors	
RA	Details	RA	Details
		5	Creates jobs and income for the 'Cottage Industry'
6	TOTAL RELATIVE ADVANTAGE	64	TOTAL RELATIVE ADVANTAGE

Suggesting that DPAs are 10 times more advantageous to prosecutors than to defendants.[62]

DPAs and NPAs are far more beneficial to prosecutors than they ever could be to alleged corporate and individual offenders. Negotiated settlements raise (or should raise) questions of deep integrity such as whether it is ethical:

- For companies to buy their way out of trouble;
- For prosecutors to demand or coerce self-disclosure of bribery offences when, in most cases, there is no legal requirement to do so;
- For companies to be required or permitted to conduct proxy investigations into their own skulduggery;
- For prosecutors to demand that companies provide incriminating evidence against their own employees to save their own skins;
- For prosecutors to ignore their own guides and minimise charges simply to allow companies to avoid debarment;
- For prosecutors to ignore the OECD's Convention by taking commercial factors or collateral consequences into account when deciding whether or not to prosecute;
- To demand full reparation for countries that are the supposed victims of corruption when their own officials are at least equally culpable;
- Not to identify and compensate – or even consider the interests of – honest companies which are the real victims of bribery;
- To put the interests of shareholders, employees and others who benefit from their participation in corrupt companies ahead of those of shareholders, employees and others involved in honest competitive businesses, which suffer;
- Not to ensure – as part of the settlement agreement – that those who extort bribes are brought to justice;
- To permit prosecutors to demand that their associates are appointed as monitors (see page 167) or to make other important decisions that could result in reciprocal benefits for compliant players in the 'Cottage Industry' (see Foreword);
- For the regulatory agencies to expansively interpret their powers, when they have no statutory authority to do so, and to usurp the role of the courts.

The conclusions in this book are that the entire self-disclosure, proxy investigation, pre-trial disposition circus is so riddled with potentials for injustice, skulduggery, conflicts of interest and covert reciprocity that honest organisation should think very carefully before jumping into the ring. Yet UK politicians are hell bent on joining the circus.

---

62   A similar comparative table – summarising the benefits of self-disclosure to companies in one column and to their legal advisers in another – has been resisted on the grounds that it would be too provocative. But companies should recognise that they and their advisers may not have the same objectives when confronted by regulators.

THE MINISTRY OF JUSTICE CONSULTATION PAPER

The arguments supposedly in favour

The MOJ Consultation Paper[63] is wildly over-enthusiastic, if not disingenuous, in promoting the UK case for self-disclosure and DPAs. Some of the more questionable points in the paper and in an associated Impact Assessment are summarised in Table 7.4.

Table 7.4   Propositions in the Consultation Paper

Proposition in the Consultation Paper and Impact Assessment	Comment
ECONOMIC HARM Corporate economic crime causes serious harm. In 2012 the National Fraud Authority (NFA) estimated that fraud committed by 'all types of offenders' costs the UK £73 billion per annum	*The Consultation Paper cannot make up its mind whether it is talking about 'economic crime committed by commercial organisations', 'corporate economic crime', 'all types of offenders', or 'white collar crime'* *In the confusion it gives the impression that fraud committed by companies amounts to £73 billion per annum; this is not so. The NFA report's total includes £20.3 billion of public sector crime and £6.1 billion by individuals. The overstatement of commercial sector misbehaviour– by 35% – is unlikely to be accidental*
INADEQUACY OF THE JUSTICE SYSTEM 'The present justice system in England and Wales is inadequate for dealing effectively with criminal enforcement against commercial organisations in the field of complex and serious economic crime' 'Investigations and trials are forebodingly long, particularly where offences are in multiple jurisdictions'	*The failure to successfully prosecute complex fraud is not limited to companies and the SFO's record against individual skulduggers has been less than impressive. See the recent case of Robert and Vincent Tchenguiz (pages 606 and 835) as an example of gross prosecutorial incompetence* *Whether regulators like it or not UK laws are based on the 'identification principle' for corporate offences and require proof of involvement by a directing mind. If this cannot be proven beyond reasonable doubt, the company is innocent* *The real problem, for all fraud cases, is that juries do not understand the complexities and through uncertainty acquit.* ***The obvious answer – which is a red rag to Luvvies – is to abandon jury trials for complex* fraud cases**

---

63   Which is arguably a 'dodgy dossier'. See http://lawcommission.justice.gov.uk/docs/cp185_Reforming_Bribery_consultation.pdf

Proposition in the Consultation Paper and Impact Assessment	Comment
DIFFICULT TO PROVE CORPORATE LIABILITY In modern corporations, where responsibility for decision-making is distributed quite widely, it is very difficult to prove criminal liability	*This is a myth as evidenced from the 'domino theory' in cases from Enron through to Sainsbury*
SERIOUS TREATMENT OF CRIME AND PUBLIC CONFIDENCE Treating economic crime as seriously as other crimes and taking steps to combat it effectively are key commitments in the coalition government	*The Ministry of Justice seems to believe that its efforts to control crime in the UK are lauded. In fact, the UK justice system would be a sick joke were the consequences not so serious. The UK legal system is now more about money, media and political posturing than justice*
LIMITED TOOLS Law enforcement agencies complain that they have a relatively narrow range of tools available to identify and bring corporate offenders to justice	*The SFO has the widest choice of tools conceivable, ranging from the draconian Section 2 CJA powers, Suspicious Activity Reports, access to every imaginable official and unofficial database, to interception and other facilities allowed under the Regulation of Investigatory Powers Act. Short of permitting 'waterboarding' or other forms of torture it is difficult to see what other tools are possible, especially with Section 7 strict liability offences in play*
FRAUD IS INREASINGLY SOPHISTICATED Corporate economic crime has become increasingly sophisticated and international, making it much more difficult to detect and investigate	*This again is not borne out by the facts, including the NFA report. There are very few entirely new methods of fraud, and bribery cases are simple: they always involve a perverted decision*
INTERNATIONAL COOPERATION The lack of equivalent enforcement tools for the UK makes negotiations between UK and US prosecutors, and ultimately resolution of the case, difficult	*The SFO has repeatedly blustered about the brilliant levels of international cooperation: especially the USA. The problem-based prosecutorial fear of 'forum-shopping' – is that if a case is first reported to overseas regulators (and especially those in the USA), no action can be taken in the UK because of double jeopardy rules* *The Consultation Paper is to ensure that the UK shares in the spoils of self-disclosure*
DPAs WILL PROTECT INNOCENT SHAREHOLDERS ETC The suggestion is that DPAs will ensure that innocent shareholders, etc. will not suffer as a result of a company's permanent debarment from contracts, etc.	***Taking 'Collateral Consequences' into account is a breach of Article 5 of the OECD Convention*** *Every contortion has been used by both US and UK regulators to ensure that indictments and agreements are framed to allow even the most corrupt organisations (such as BAE, Siemens and Daimler) to evade supposedly mandatory debarment*
The Consultation Paper quotes the case of Arthur Anderson as 'a graphic illustration of the problem', suggesting that an unjustified indictment in 2002, which was reversed by the	*Shareholders and others involved in corrupt or fraudulent companies have generally benefited from skulduggery, whereas employees and shareholders in honest competitors have*

US Supreme Court in 2005, was the cause of the firm's collapse *and the loss of 28,000 jobs*	*consistently suffered. It is totally unfair to shareholders and employees in honest companies that dishonest competitors avoid debarment*
In some cases the impact of criminal prosecution [...] can be disproportionate to the culpability of the conduct involved	*The evidence is overwhelming that Anderson was doomed long before the indictment was issued. Besides that, the Supreme Court's overruling was based on a technicality. Anderson deserved what it got. Few, if any, jobs were lost*
[A] conviction may also make the possibility of civil claims against the organisation more likely to succeed	*In fact a DPA, supported by a statement of facts which cannot be disputed, is more likely to provoke third-party litigation*
DPAs WILL GIVE CERTAINTY OF OUTCOME Removing uncertainty from business operations is a vital factor influencing behaviour	*The proposed process does not resolve uncertainty. An agreement may be drafted and rejected – at any time prior to finalisation – by a judge*

Arthur Anderson and the Myth of the Corporate Death Penalty

An excellent article by Gabriel Markoff, a graduate of the University of Texas Law School and currently law clerk at the Southern District of Texas, in the FCPA Professor's blog, debunked the idea that the prosecution of major companies for fraud and corruption would result in their collapse.

Mr Markoff found that:

- between 2001 and 2010, 51 American or US-based public companies were found or pleaded guilty to serious criminal offences;
- 36 continued to be successful on the stock exchanges on which they had previously been active;
- 11 merged with other companies under favourable conditions;
- 4 failed, but for reasons that were not connected to the prosecution;
- only one company – Japan Airlines – failed within three years of conviction.

Mr Markoff concluded: 'reasonable caveats such as the possibility of selective prosecution aside, the fact remains that, if the threat of collateral consequences is as terribly dire as it is made out to be, at least some of the convicted public companies should have gone out of business as a result of their convictions. But they did not ...'.[64]

The two main justifications usually cited for preferring DPAs over convictions appear groundless. But the nearly indiscriminate use of DPAs with large corporations – in contrast to the DOJ's continued tendency to prosecute and convict small companies – that predominates today is not supportable.

---

64   See http://www.fcpaprofessor.com/category/collateral-effects (accessed 7 November 2012).

The repeated over-egging in the MOJ's Consultation Paper raises suspicions that its purpose is different from that stated and is simply a wheeze to get companies to self-disclose and cough up cash in cases that prosecutors would otherwise never detect.

Not Expected To Have An Impact

The Consultation Paper states: 'the introduction of this new tool is not expected to have an impact on the level of economic crime committed by commercial organisations – primarily it would have an impact on how it is tackled'. This is an amazing admission.

The Impact Assessment which accompanied the Consultation Paper is unclear on the financial and other benefits of DPAs: partly because **it admits that the SFO retains insufficient statistics to make meaningful calculations**. However the impression is given that the 'new tool' will produce a positive economic gain for the government of around £52 million per annum. Time will tell.

The Impact Assessment sets out some interesting statistics (Table 7.5).[65]

Table 7.5   Statistics Relating to Prosecutions and Deferred Prosecution Agreements

Factor	UK	USA
PENALTIES		
Average penalties for SFO prosecutions (excluding not guilty verdicts and abandoned cases)	£2.8 million	
Average DOJ DPA settlement		£25 million +
Average Civil Recovery Order	£6.2 million	
Average term of imprisonment for bribery offences	2 years	9 years
Average Financial Services Authority penalty	£2.5 million	
Average penalty for the Office of Fair Trading (Cartels)	£13 million	
Suggested discounts for self-disclosure	30%	25% +
Debarment from government contracts	Mandatory	Discretionary
TIME TO COMPLETE CASES		
Time from case opening to closure	9.2 years	
Estimated time to complete a DPA from opening to closure	4.8 years	
COSTS		
SFO costs for a contested trial	£2.5 million	

---

65   Some are clearly stated and others implied or derived.

Estimated SFO costs for a DPA	£600,000	
Court Costs for a contested trial	£193,000	
Estimated Court costs for a DPA	£4,000 to £6,000	
MISCELLANEOUS		
SFO case load	88 cases per annum	40
Estimated CROs per annum	17–20	
Estimated DPAs per annum	10	

The table reinforces two points discussed more fully later. The first is that DPAs in America are more attractive to offenders than their UK counterparts because the penalties on conviction are so much more severe. The second is that corporate liability in the USA is easier to prove.[66]

When will Deferred Prosecution Agreements be offered?

The Consultation Paper does not discuss the position that will apply to many international companies – even relatively small ones – of having to evaluate their American exposures in addition to English and Welsh laws. At the last count there were at least ten UK and American prosecutorial and other guidelines (see Chapters 8 and 9) which could have an impact on whether or not a DPA might be offered in one or both jurisdictions. The guidelines are not coordinated but are issued in the usual blinkered 'regulatory silos' (not even cross-referenced and in some cases undated) and are far from consistent.[67]

Companies should assume that it is entirely within the creative ability of prosecutors to justify any decision in relation to DPAs or CROs, but there are four points to note:

1. Once a case is identified as having the flimsiest connection to a particular jurisdiction (i.e. the UK or the USA), the regulators concerned will want to share in the spoils; self-disclosures to any one regulator are gold dust for all.
2. Although the UK has ostensibly strict rules on double jeopardy, ways around them can always be found.[68]
3. There is little point in entering into a DPA with the Serious Fraud Office that is not mirrored by the Securities and Exchange Commission and the Department of Justice and vice versa.

Finally, UK and US laws in relation to bribery are different. **Companies should work on the assumption that suspected offences under the Foreign Corrupt Practices Act** (FCPA) are inevitably sanctionable under the Bribery Act. However the reverse is not true and

---

66   Ironically, USA regulators are more concerned with establishing personal liability!

67   There is an interesting and useful diagram in the GAO report purporting to show whether it is likely that a DPA will be offered in the USA. But the conditions are quite different from those that appear to apply in the UK.

68   This is one important reason for promoting UK DPAs.

there will be many international and domestic cases of bribe payment, bribe receipt and internal corruption, of interest to the SFO, that are outside the scope of the FCPA.

What the Consultation Paper fails to cover

The Consultation Paper starts from the point where a DPA is in play. This is much like defining the rules of engagement after the war has been won and then limiting guidance on how to torture the survivors. Procedures[69] should start from the day a company discovers the first suspicions of skulduggery, and also cover subsequent stages: internal investigation, identifying reporting requirements, considering self-disclosure, making an initial approach to the regulators, guiding through a proxy or joint investigation and then appearing at the negotiating table.

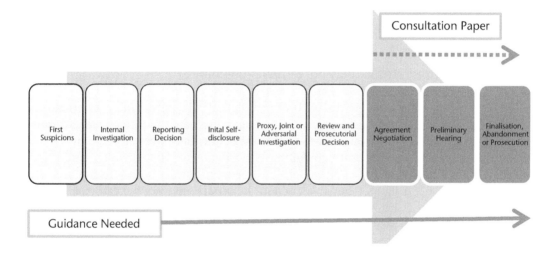

Figure 7.2   Start to End Process
It is in the early stages – before a DPA is even in prospect – that guidance should start. The regulatory agencies should also be required to publish details of all self-disclosures that result in no action being taken.

HOW ENGLISH AND WELSH DEFERRED PROSECUTION AGREEMENTS ARE EXPECTED TO WORK

Fundamentals

Although the Consultation Paper lacks detail,[70] English and Welsh DPAs are likely to be incorporated in a new Criminal Justice Act in 2014 or 2105 and to follow the US model:

---

69   For both companies and prosecutors.

70   Which is understandable and will supposedly be clarified by codes of practice, but only for prosecutors, not companies.

- The SFO is more likely to prosecute where offenders were in a position of authority or were 'directing minds', or where the company did not self-disclose or cooperate.
- DPAs will not be limited to the SFO and the CPS but will be available to other bodies from 2014 or early 2015.[71]
- **DPAs should only be pursued when a case passes the Full Code Test of evidential strength and public interest.**
- DPAs will be available for certain cases of 'economic crime', including fraud and bribery in England and Wales, and are expected to be limited to first-time offenders.
- The UK will not introduce Non-Prosecution Agreements, primarily because they lack judicial oversight and public scrutiny.
- DPAs will only apply to companies and not individuals.
- DPAs do not count as criminal convictions, although for double jeopardy purposes they are prosecutions.
- DPAs as well as the Statement of Facts are public documents and may be used by third parties in civil proceedings (possibly introduced under the hearsay rule), in other criminal prosecutions and regulatory actions. What is more the alleged offender cannot later question or correct anything in the statement of facts and this become sitting ducks for regulatory action or litigation anywhere in the world.[72]
- DPAs will normally involve a financial penalty, confiscation and reparation: in around 30 per cent of cases the SFO is likely to require a period of monitoring.
- The offending company will be obliged to use 'all reasonable efforts to make available to prosecutors all relevant non-privileged information and material, to provide access to witnesses', to replace culpable management and possibly withdraw from the marketplace in which violations took place.
- A DPA will normally discount the *financial penalty* that could be expected from contested conviction by 33.33 per cent. No discount will be offered on confiscation or reparation payments.
- An offender's willingness to enter into DPA negotiations is entirely voluntary and may be withdrawn at any point prior to finalisation. However, once a Statement of Facts has been agreed it is irrevocable.
- If a DPA is not concluded and not subsequently prosecuted, any admissions made during negotiations are protected: but investigative leads can be pursued.
- An independent body[73] will prepare DPA guidelines for prosecutors but it is 'not necessary to issue guidance for commercial organisations'.[74]
- The procedure for DPAs will apply retrospectively to the settlement of offences which took place prior to enabling legislation coming into force.
- If a DPA is issued and fails, 'it does not follow that penalties already paid would be offset' in any subsequent prosecution.

The expected process, which will normally stem from self-disclosure, will be along the following lines and will normally precede the prosecution of individuals:

---

71   And possibly prosecutors working for local authorities.

72   It is worth noting that under Sections 260–264 of the Companies Act 2006 shareholders may take action against any past or present director following an actual or proposed act or omission involving negligence, default or breach of duty.

73   Probably the Sentencing Commission.

74   When in fact such commercial guidelines are critical and should be integrated with US existing procedures.

- The offending company and the SFO will discuss the possibilities of a DPA in confidence and without prejudice. Such discussions will not be in the presence of a judge because 'judicial involvement at this stage would be premature and inappropriate'.[75]
- Outline proposals will be heard in camera at a 'preliminary hearing' before a judge, who will give a non-binding[76] opinion on the suitability of a DPA in 'the interests of justice'.
- Prosecutors will explain to the judge 'any international aspects of the offending and how multiple jurisdictions plan to split any identified criminality'.[77]
- The judge may give a non-binding indication of the potential sanctions which should be 'fair, reasonable, proportionate and in the public interest'.
- A draft agreement will be prepared, including some or all of:
  - A Statement of Facts drafted by the prosecutor and irrevocably accepted by the company. Admissions made in the statement cannot be used against individuals, nor against the company if the DPA does not conclude. However, evidence in existence prior to a DPA remains admissible and prosecutors can pursue all leads that emerge during negotiations;
  - Relevant considerations which set out the level of cooperation given by the offending company;
  - The company's undertaking to assist prosecutors in all countries to sanction individuals and third parties;
  - Draft indictment or outline of charges;
  - Calculations of losses and gains;
  - The suggested sanctions, including the duration of the agreement,[78] financial penalties, disgorgement of profits, compensation, reparation, recovery of costs, etc., and whether or not a monitor is to be appointed;
  - Proposed actions in other jurisdictions;
  - Penalties for breach of the agreement;
  - Waiving of the statute of limitations;
  - Resolution of the board of directors to accept the agreement.
- The draft agreement will be returned to the judge in a public hearing. He or she may accept, amend or reject it.
- If the judge agrees, an indictment will be prepared and held on file.
- The company must fully comply with the agreement. Any disputes – such as failing to comply with recommendations made by a monitor – will be referred to the court and the SFO.
- Breaches of a DPA will not be regarded as separate criminal offences, but may result in a reinstatement of the indictment.
- If at the end of the term the agreement has been honoured, the indictment will be withdrawn.[79]
- The period of the agreement may be extended with permission of the court.

---

75   In fact judicial oversight at this point would be extremely useful to avoid the suggestion of a 'cosy deal', or companies being coerced into settlement when the evidence does not satisfy the Full Code Test.

76   Which makes a mockery of the Consultation Paper's suggestion that the proposed procedures provide certainty.

77   With the intention of persuading the judge over problems of double jeopardy.

78   Normally three years.

79   See a typical American DPA with Panalpina (http://lib.law.virginia.edu/Garrett/prosecution_agreements/pdf/panalpina.pdf (accessed October 2012).

If the judge rejects the draft agreement, the prosecutor is free to proceed with a prosecution or CRO.

The role of monitors

Regulators like the idea of appointing colleagues from the 'Cottage Industry' to monitor the ongoing activities of the companies caught in skulduggery. However, there is little in the Consultation Paper to clarify their roles in the UK.[80] A monitor is paid for by the offending company, is primarily responsible to the court, but also reports directly to the regulatory agency.[81]

No single factor seems to be determinative in whether or not a monitor might be imposed, although there are two common characteristics:

1. The degree of ingrained corruption prior to the offending, including its widespread nature and collusion of top management.
2. The existence of an effective corporate compliance programme and resources.

The first critical point in monitorships is how selection is made.

Jobs for the Boys

In 2006–2007 US regulators – under the direction of Chris Christie, US Attorney for New Jersey (and later its State Governor), made an FCPA industry sweep, culminating in five suppliers of orthopaedic equipment and prosthetic limbs entering into four DPAs and one NPA. Mr Christie selected all five monitors without specific Department of Justice approval,[82] which, given his potential conflicting interests, would have been prudent:

- John Ashchroft – Attorney General under President Bush and Mr Christie's old boss – was appointed in September 2007, without any pre-qualification or competitive bidding – for an 18-month assignment monitoring Zimmer Holdings Inc. for fees estimated at $52 million. Mr Ashcroft said he knew nothing about the assignment until the possibility had been raised by Mr Christie. Zimmer said Mr Christie had specifically directed it to hire Mr Ashcroft. There was no publication of the appointment and it only came to light as a result of the company's SEC filings some time later. Mr Ashcroft said there were no public funds involved in the deal: 'it does not cost the taxpayers one thin dime'.
- David N. Kelley, the former United States Attorney in Manhattan and at the time a Partner in the Cahill law firm, was appointed monitor for Biomed. Mr Kelley had previously investigated a fraud involving Mr Christie's younger brother Todd, but had not prosecuted him. The monitoring contract was worth US$10–12 million.

---

80 Based on American experience, monitors are likely to be appointed in around 30–40 per cent of all DPAs.

81 Which is hardly surprising given that in most cases he was appointed on their insistence.

82 He probably did not need to advise head office.

- Debra Wong Yang, who had been Mr Christie's counterpart in Los Angeles, was appointed monitor for another orthopaedic company.
- David Sampson, the former Republican Attorney General in New Jersey, was appointed monitor for Smith & Nephew. Mr Sampson is a founding member of Wolf & Sampson and was previously Counsel to Mr Christie's governorship election campaign and served as Chairman of his Transition Committee.
- John Carley, a former vice president of Cendant Corporation and Federal Trade Commission lawyer, was appointed to monitor Stryker Orthopaedics.

In total, Mr Christie recommended or approved at least seven DPAs while serving as US Attorney for New Jersey, including:

- one where the offending company was required to endow a professorship at Seton Hall Law School, his alma mater;[83]
- appointing Herbert Stern, his mentor and long-time colleague, to monitor the University of Medicine and Dentistry, New Jersey. Mr Stern's fees came to over $10 million. Subsequently Mr Stern and his colleagues contributed $23,800 to Mr Christie's election campaign.

When the facts emerged, the then Attorney General Michael B. Mukasey ordered an internal enquiry, although he made no public announcement that he had done so. He was later careful to point out that there were no accusations of wrongdoing on the part of anyone. Draft Bills were introduced into the House of Representatives and a report produced by the Government Accountability Office in December 2009 succinctly titled 'Corporate Crime: DOJ Has Taken Steps to Better Track Its Use of Deferred and Non-Prosecution Agreements, But Should Evaluate Effectiveness'.

The results of this flurry of activity[84] was a memorandum issued in March 2008 by Craig S. Morford, Acting Deputy Attorney General ('the Morford Memorandum') for DOJ and US Attorneys' Offices (criminal cases).[85] The memo stated:

- A monitor's primary responsibility is to assess and monitor a corporation's compliance with the terms of the agreement specifically designed to address and **reduce the risks of recurrence** of a corporation's misconduct and not to further punitive goals.
- In negotiating agreements [...] prosecutors should be mindful of both the potential benefits that employing a monitor may have for the corporation and the public and the cost and its impact on [...] operations.

The memo included nine principles, which UK DPAs may follow:

1. The monitor should be **selected by agreement** between the company and the regulator.

---

83   Soon afterwards Mr Christie issued guidelines banning such endowments.

84   Which resulted in absolutely no legislation being passed.

85   Available at: http://www.justice.gov/dag/morford-useofmonitorsmemo-03072008.pdf (accessed 7 November 2012).

2. The monitor is **an independent third party**, not an employee or agent of the Corporation or of the government.

3. The monitor's **primary role and responsibility** should be to assess and monitor a corporation's compliance with the terms of the agreement that are specifically addressed of recurrence.

4. The monitor will need to **understand the scope of the corporation's misconduct** and should be no broader than necessary to address and reduce the risk of recurrence.

5. **Good communication** is in the interest of all parties.

6. If a corporation chooses **not to adopt recommendations** made by the monitor, either or both should report that fact to the government.

7. The agreement should clearly identify any types of previously undisclosed or new misconduct that the monitor will be required to report upon.

8. The duration of the agreement should be tethered to the problems that have been found to exist and the types of remedial measures needed.

9. In most cases an agreement should provide for an extension of the monitor provisions at the discretion of the government, as well as a provision for early termination.

In May 2010, Acting Deputy Attorney General Gary G. Grindler issued an additional guidance, adding a tenth principle that 'an agreement should explain what role the Department should play in resolving disputes that may arise between the monitor and the corporation, given the facts and circumstances of the case'. In fact, the revision empowers the DOJ as the arbiter of all disputes.

Sometimes, in cases where the SEC and the DOJ are involved in the same or related cases, each will appoint its own monitor, under separate agreements, with distinct work plans and objectives. It is not inconceivable that the SFO and the FSA would do the same and that some companies could have up to four monitors in their midst.

There has been continuing and lively debate in the US over whether ex-federal prosecutors or even lawyers are best qualified (or even suitable) to serve as monitors. The argument against is that they are inclined to view life in a narrow legalistic way and few have little understanding of commercial matters. Monitors are very expensive and their intervention can be traumatic. Further, a company's communications with them are not privileged.

INNOSPEC

The appointment of monitors in the Innospec case was criticised by Lord Justice Thomas, who stated 'imposing an expensive form of probation order seems to me unnecessary for a company which will also be audited by auditors well aware of the past conduct'.

It seems that all judges are not committed to the worth of monitors.

Approval of Deferred Prosecution Agreements by courts

The Consultation Paper assumes that courts will formalise DPAs, yet experience shows this is far from certain: judges do not like being usurped.

Judges Are In Charge

On 14 April 2010, Robert John Dougall, the ex-Marketing Manager of DePuy International Limited, pleaded guilty at Southwark Crown Court to being involved in the corruption of Greek doctors. To everyone's astonishment, Mr Dougall – who had become the SFO's first cooperating witness – was sentenced to 12 months' imprisonment and carted off to jail. The surprise was more so because the SFO had previously joined with Mr Dougall's lawyers to make a submission to the judge that a jail sentence was not warranted.

On 29 April 2010, Mr Dougall appeared before the Court of Appeal and in another joint submission the SFO urged suspension of his sentence. The judges were scathing of the SFO and stated that:

- It was not within the SFO's power to suggest a specific sentence and doing so was contrary to principle;
- In the course of plea discussions, the prosecutor must make it clear to the defence that any joint submission as to sentence (including confiscation) is not binding on the court;
- Recommendations as to sentence from the Director of the SFO carry no greater weight than if they had come from the defendant's own advocate;
- A defendant who cooperates on the basis of being first through the door cannot expect treatment any more favourable than other defendants who also plead guilty at an early stage;
- Principles of transparent and open justice require a court sitting in public to itself first determine by a hearing in open court the extent of the criminal conduct ....

The Court of Appeal reviewed the sentence in the light of the above, noting that terms of imprisonment of more than 12 months could not be suspended. The judges explained how Mr Dougall's sentence should have been computed and concluded that, after making allowances for his cooperation under Section 73 of the Serious Organised Crime and Police Act 2005, it would be appropriate to suspend the jail sentence.

In the Innospec case, Lord Justice Thomas was scathing about the agreement between the SFO and the DOJ to share in the spoils and stated: 'I have concluded that the Director of the SFO had no power to enter into the arrangements made and no such arrangement should be made again'.

The lesson for companies who are considering entering into pre-trial dispositions is that they engage in a game of Russian roulette with a judge holding the gun. He or she may decide to whack the defendants, the prosecution, or both. So approval of a DPA is not as certain as the Consultation Paper implies.

How successful will UK Deferred Prosecution Agreements be?

American DPAs have not been the overwhelming success that is usually suggested. In fact they create a noxious odour and bad taste, ranging from conflict of interest to extortion.

Professor Ellen Podgor wrote in her paper, 'White Collar Innocence; Irrelevant in the High Stakes Risk Game':

> [O]ur existing legal system places the risk of going to trial, and in some cases even being charged with a crime, so high that innocence and guilt no longer become the real considerations [...] maneuvring the system to receive the least onerous consequences may ensure the best result for the accused party, regardless of innocence.[86]

Professor Podgor detailed several cases involving disparate criminal sanctions and stated that

> the real moral of these stories is not whether the punishment was warranted, but rather the appropriateness of the level of risk that one has to take to proceed to trial, and the chilling effect of the high risk caused by the trial penalty [...] innocence becomes irrelevant as the real question becomes whether it is worth the risk of testing an innocence claim.

There are four main reasons why DPAs are unlikely to be successful in the UK:

1. If the involvement of a 'directing mind' is so difficult to prove, there will be few cases resulting in corporate liability. So why should any company volunteer to concede liability in a DPA,[87] when culpability cannot be proven?
2. Punishment following conviction in the UK is significantly less than in the USA. Thus the attractiveness of penalty discounts is questionable and may be less than would be granted by a judge for an early guilty plea.
3. The collateral consequences of self-disclosure far outweigh the possible benefits, especially since a court may decide to withhold its approval.
4. Penalty discounts under a DPA may be no more (and possibly less) than those granted by a judge for an early plea of guilty.

Section 7 of the Bribery Act 2010 – effectively involving vicarious liability – may at first appear to be uniquely amenable to DPAs. However, when the exact wording of potential indictments is analysed, it is possible that courts will apply a two-step process:

---

86   Chicago–Kent Law Review: Stetson University College of Law Research Paper 2009–30.

87   Except for Section 7 offences.

1. Was a directing mind involved?
2. Is there proof beyond reasonable doubt of the *company's intention*[88] to obtain or retain business, etc.?

If the company is able to show that the directing mind was working ultra vires or that it had procedures in place that demonstrate that its intent was to function honestly, the chance of a conviction even under Section 7 is far from certain.

From a risk management, pure utility theory point of view, what a company gains on reducing criticality it more than loses on probability. **For this reason it will normally be overwhelmingly in a company's best interest[89] not to self-disclose or to consider entering into DPAs.** The practical implications of this view – which is unlikely to be endorsed by the 'Cottage Industry' – are examined later on page 171 et seq.

Prosecutions, Trials and Plea-bargaining

If a case passes the Full Code Test and is not settled, defendants can expect a knock on their doors by a hominid with a broken nose, large feet and halitosis, armed with a summons or arrest warrant. But companies should understand that the probability of such an occurrence is remote, given that the SFO expects to handle only 80 to 100 cases per annum and that there are over 1 million businesses in the UK, all of which could be potential targets.

The prosecution has to prove its case beyond reasonable doubt to the satisfaction of a jury of 12 ordinary folk who will decide – based on common sense – such matters as:

*   Intent;
*   Influence or improper performance;
*   The definition of an FPO;
*   Obtaining or retaining business;
*   Adequate procedures.

In reaching its verdict it matters little to the jury what expansive interpretations have been conjured by the regulator: courts, judges, juries and trials are real-time. Regulators understand this and have generally performed badly in court.

A jury must normally follow the judge's instructions on points of law, but in the UK and the USA a jury can exercise a long-established – but legally repugnant and never-mentioned[90] – power known as 'jury equity' or 'jury nullification'. This comes into play if a jury believes a law is unjust.

---

88   Rather than the individual's.

89   Where the Company does not have mandatory reporting requirements under SEC, FSA rules or the Proceeds of Crime Act.

90   American jurors can be dismissed by the judge if he believes a juror is even aware of the possibility of nullification. A trial judge said: not only do we not tell jurors that they have this right, but we tell them they are to take the law as it is explained to them, the strong implication being that there is no right of nullification. Isn't that nice to know?

Jury Equity

In the Official Secrets Act prosecution of Clive Pointing the trial judge instructed that the public interest is 'what the government of the day says it is', which was tantamount to directing a conviction. The jury did not agree and decided in Mr Pointing's favour.

It is not beyond belief that juries would give the Bribery Act similar treatment in cases such as Alderman's Needle (see page 125), and there is always the chance that prosecutors will make one fatal mistake that will result in acquittal. Just check the web for the Tchenguiz case in the UK or the 'Africa Sting' fiasco in the USA.

Of course, a defendant may plead guilty and by doing so at an early stage, qualify for a discount equal to that of a DPA or better. And in the period between considering self-disclosure and trial, there is a possibility that prosecutors will make one fatal mistake or lose their enthusiasm.

The Attorney General's Guidelines on Plea Discussions[91] came into effect on 5 May 2009 and apply mainly to prosecutions of serious and complex fraud. They state that prosecutors:

- Should not file excessive or exaggerated charges to encourage defendants to plead guilty to something less;
- Must not pressurise defendants into making admissions or false guilty pleas.

Prosecutors may discuss sentencing with a defendant, but settlements must be fair and subject to final approval by a judge.

The guidelines do not address the problem of a corporate defendant being required to give evidence against employees and other co-accuseds, and whether or not it is required to waive privilege over interviews conducted during internal investigations.[92] However, a press release issued by the Attorney General stated that no request should be made of corporate suspects to waive privilege over internal interviews, continuing that:

The plea negotiation framework [...] is not about offering discounts, immunity or incentives to fraudsters. It doesn't require a defendant to assist the prosecution and is careful to avoid the perception of plea 'bargaining' associated with the US. (Attorney General's Office News Centre, 18 March 2009)[93]

In response, the SFO Director somewhat ruefully commented:

---

91   Available at: http://www.attorneygeneral.gov.uk/Publications/Documents/AG's%20Guidelines%20on%20Plea%20Discussions%20in%20Cases%20of%20Serious%20or%20Complex%20Fraud.pdf (accessed 7 November 2012).

92   See the Upjohn Warning, page 843.

93   Available at: http://www.attorneygeneral.gov.uk/NewsCentre/Pages/CriminalJusticeMeasuresToEnhanceFraudProsecutionsToBeIntroduced.aspx

Since I arrived at the SFO, I have been looking at ways in which we can sharpen up the tools available to us [...] early plea negotiations are not the same as plea bargains in the United States although I am keen to take what we usefully can from the American experience. (Attorney General's Office News Centre, 18 March 2009)

So here we have another example of uncertainty. The Attorney General wants to keep well away from the nasty American system of plea-bargaining and the SFO would like to adopt it: or at least part of it.

Other Consequences of Regulatory Attention

THE DAMAGE COMES EARLY

Companies that are targeted by regulators are likely to suffer badly whether the allegations are justified or not.

The Deferred Prosecution Racket

In 2006, Richard Epstein, at that time a Professor at the University of Chicago Law School, published a paper in *The Wall Street Journal* titled 'The Deferred Prosecution Racket'. He stated that: 'a conviction carries at most a million-dollar fine, but [the] simple indictment, which lies wholly within the prosecutor's discretion, imposes multi-billion dollar losses. Faced with that kind of pressure, the indictment is all that matters'.

Professor Epstein continued 'yet given these weird incentives, DPAs no longer serve the public interest. The agreements often read like the confessions of a Stalinist purge trial, as battered corporations recant their past sins and submit to punishments wildly in excess of any underlying offense'. (*The Wall Street Journal*, November 28, 2006)

The SFO believes that all cases, including CROs, should be made public, ostensibly on the grounds that justice should be transparent, or words to that effect. In reality it is well within the SFO's authority to settle CROs without any publicity and it has, apparently, considered the option of going down an entirely civil route to avoid settlements being overturned by courts.

Memories of massive collapses such as Enron, or horrendous fraud such as the Madoff Ponzi scheme, remain for a long time but the majority of scandals are quickly forgotten and it is possible that the public relations impact of skulduggery in good firms, such as Daimler, Siemens or even British Aerospace, KPMG, PWC et al. do not remain in the public consciousness for very long. In fact, Siemens and Mabey & Johnson put a positive spin on their convictions and their current ethical superiority.

This is not to say that companies should be relaxed about skulduggery or the effects of adverse publicity. But headlines in tabloids rarely bring about the end of the world, although they may result in ribbing at the Wimmins' Institute, Masonic Lodge or Pink Pussycat Lap Dancing Club.

DEBARMENT FROM GOVERNMENT CONTRACTS

The European Procurement Rules were codified in EU Directive 2004/18/EEC and 2004/17/EEC and enacted in the UK as Regulation 23 Public Contracts Regulations 2006. Both supposedly enforce the mandatory and permanent debarment of companies *convicted* of serious fraud, including participation in a criminal organisation, bribery and money-laundering. Bidders on all public procurement contracts in the EU and within Member States are **required to confirm** that they have no convictions that would debar them. Where adequate assurance is not forthcoming the agencies involved are expected to carry out their own enquiries[94] and to take action if they are aware of a relevant conviction. It is a sloppy and inconsistent process with no teeth.

The United States has debarment rules which are set out in Part 9.406 of the Federal Acquisition Regulations (FAR), although debarment is neither mandatory nor permanent and requires the active intervention of a federal official.[95] The European laws are intended to be both preventive and punitive while those in the USA are primarily to protect future government expenditure.

The Project On Government Oversight (POGO) reported[96] that only one of the top ten recidivist companies has ever been debarred which had 63 instances of misconduct leading to fines, restitution and settlements, and clean-up costs (note: these are listed under the heading 'Scale' in Table 7.6) totalling $982,859,555.

Table 7.6   Companies that Avoided Debarment

Name of Company	Instances of Skulduggery	Scale
Lockheed Martin	63	$231,872,404
Boeing	36	$357,973,000
Raytheon	24	$128,652,919
Northrop Grumman	21	$87,876,581
Flour	19	$70,016,614
United Technologies	18	$214,836,860
TRW	16	$389,484,000
AT & T	14	$16,090,000
Unysis	12	$182,245,692

---

94   But there is no index available to help them!! It is estimated that there are over 500 different debarment lists currently in existence, none of which are officially coordinated.

95   Whatever that means.

96   The report has recently been updated with slightly different figures.

It is not clear whether the conviction of a relevant commercial organisation for its failure to prevent bribery under Section 7 of the Bribery Act 2010 would lead to mandatory debarment, although the MOJ has implied it would not.

Debarment and Section 7

On 30 March 2011 in a written Ministerial Statement from the Ministry of Justice entitled 'Implementation of the Bribery Act 2010', the Justice Secretary – Kenneth Clarke – stated: 'the Government has also decided that a conviction of a commercial organisation under Section 7 of the Act in respect of failure to prevent bribery will attract discretionary[97] rather than mandatory[98] exclusion from public procurement under the UK's implementation[99] of the EU procurement directive (Directive 2004/18). The relevant regulations will be amended to reflect this'.

The SFO, true to form, has threatened a much tougher line. Therefore it is difficult to guess how debarment in a particular case may progress.

Politicians and regulators are more than aware of the public outcry that would result if punishment resulted in losses of thousands or tens of thousands of British jobs. Prosecutors may bluster and threaten but it is doubtful that they are willing to accept the blame when British companies fail. The likely outcome is a game of bluff and counter-bluff, with UK regulators having no real intention of seeing large British companies being debarred, especially if they are too big to fail, or politically well connected.

When regulators claim that they will support honest companies, they usually do precisely the opposite when it comes to debarment, letting even the most obnoxious skulduggers off the hook, supposedly in the interests of their shareholders and employees. This can never be in the public interest.

The bottom line is that debarment is mainly a hollow contrivance to coerce supposedly offending companies to agree a pre-indictment disposal or to enter an early plea of guilty. Similarly, although the World Bank extols its draconian debarment regime, most disqualified businesses are one-man bands operating from sheds[100] in the boondocks.

NULLIFICATION OF COMMERCIAL CONTRACTS

A party whose associated person was paid bribes to make perverted decisions can rescind or nullify the commercial contracts concerned and obtain compensation through the civil courts. This may be the most serious of all sanctions for bribe payment.

---

97   The procurement rules do not allow for such discretion.

98   What a joke!

99   Weasel words that do not suggest the EU would do the same.

100   There are a couple of notable exceptions, but they are exceptions.

Nullification of Commercial Contracts

The precedent was set on 4 October 2006 at the International Centre for Settlements of Investment Disputes, Washington DC, involving the World Duty Free Company and The Republic of Kenya (ICSID Case ARB/00/7).

Publicity of intended or actual regulatory action may provoke third parties – such as suppliers, customers, competitors and shareholders – to file suits for compensation. Actions may be supported by contingency-fee lawyers, resulting in consequences that far outweigh any discount for self-disclosure.

DISGORGEMENT AND VICTIM COMPENSATION

Laws, guidelines and the regulatory agencies use varying terms for civil and criminal sanctions that require payment to the government or compensation for victims. For the purpose of this book, 'disgorgement' includes all of the methods listed in Table 7.7 on page 180.

Disgorgement is not Punishment

Disgorgement is not viewed as a punishment. The SEC routinely insists on disgorgement even for technical breaches of the FCPA's books, records and internal control provisions, although it has little – if any – statutory authority to do so.

Politicians and regulators have consistently shown a lack of interest in compensating honest companies which have been disadvantaged by corrupt competitors and of levelling the playing field, despite promises that they would do so.[101] Hopefully this position will change and compensation for honest companies will be given priority over countries whose citizens had extorted bribes.

EXTRADITION AND RENDITION

It appears from the Joint Committee deliberations (see Chapter 2) that the SFO – unlike its American counterparts – is not keen to extradite foreign nationals accused of bribery to

---

101 A recommendation made later in this book is that DPAs should identify transactions influenced by **corruption**, thereby giving honest companies the chance to take remedial action.

stand trial in the UK. There is, however, a fair possibility that UK citizens based overseas will be returned for punishment.[102]

COSTS AND TAX

The costs of proxy investigations and of then defending regulatory action should not be underestimated; Siemens' costs were estimated at over $1 billion; and in the case of Mabey & Johnson the costs exceeded £30 million when the total of all penalties was £6.5 million.

COMMERCIAL IMPACTS OF UNCERTAINTY

An interesting paper by Drury D. Stevenson and Nicholas J. Waggoner, Professor of Law at the South Texas College of Law, titled: 'FCPA Sanctions: Too Big to Debar?' stated:

> One of the central tenets of law and economics holds that punishment of borderline corporate misconduct with severe penalties may unintentionally lead to over-deterrence. In other words, (honest) conduct might be shunned by businessmen who choose to be excessively cautious in the face of uncertainty regarding possible exposure to criminal punishment for even good-faith error of judgement.[103]

This is precisely the problem identified earlier in this book. It is impossible to quantify the impact of uncertainty especially for honest UK companies operating in overseas private-sector markets, but it has to be a serious impediment to the development of export markets.

The Bottom Line on Penalties

INDICATORS AND POSSIBILITIES

There are very few cases in the USA and none in the UK where a court has started with a clean sheet in determining the penalties for a bribery offence because they have already been carved out between the alleged offenders and regulators, or more correctly their legal advisers. Experience shows that prosecutors – unsurprisingly – push for the highest penalties imaginable. They may discount these as a result of an offender's cooperation or for other factors that are largely undefined and subject to good old prosecutorial discretion.

The division between fines, confiscation and other orders is of particular significance to regulators. In the UK, for example, under the Asset Recovery Incentive Scheme, a bounty of over 36 per cent based on confiscations[104] is payable to investigatory and

---

102 Three cheers for the USA, which has no hesitation in extraditing skulduggers of any nationality (as the cases of Lappin, McKinnon and the Nat West five, et al. demonstrate).

103 *Fordham Law Review*, 80(2), Article 13, 2011.

104 But not fines or victim compensation.

prosecutorial agencies. The temptation, therefore, is for the SFO and the CPS to be more interested in confiscation, whereas courts tend to be more concerned over fines.

The aggregate of sanctions should be fair, in the interests of justice and of the public. These noble ideals are all subject to prosecutorial and judicial discretion and are particularly complicated when regulatory agencies from more than one country are involved. In neither the USA nor the UK are there sufficient precedents to predict sentences or trends. Companies should assume that everything is up for grabs and that even if they self-disclose they will be whacked.

CALCULATION OF BENEFITS, PROFITS AND CONFISCATION

Confiscation and Civil Recovery Orders in the UK and their equivalents, including DPAs, in the USA – for bribery offences – are based on the alleged benefits (or 'gains') resulting from unlawful conduct. They may be calculated on specific charges or, in the UK, based on proof of a 'criminal lifestyle'.[105] Although criminal lifestyle is normally applicable to individuals, it can also be alleged against companies where offending is repetitive.

In both pre-trial dispositions and criminal trials, prosecutors usually submit calculations of alleged benefits ('recoverable amount') and leave it to the defendant to disprove.[106] In cases where an offender submits that it, he or she does not have the funds to satisfy a Confiscation or Civil Recovery Order, a court may determine and substitute an 'available amount' for the recoverable amount (see also page 183 et seq).

SENTENCING GUIDELINES COUNCIL

The UK has no direct equivalent of the Federal Sentencing Guidelines (see page 207) but judges (unlike regulators) cannot just impose punishment willy-nilly simply because they are having a bad wig day or don't like the defendant's rakish shoes. Prosecutors may suggest a range of penalties which the court may accept or reject. A court must ensure that the overall sentence remains commensurate with the seriousness of the offence and that the **size of the fine does not enable wealthier offenders to buy themselves out of jail**.[107]

The Sentencing Council for England and Wales is an independent, non-departmental public body of the MOJ and replaced the Sentencing Guidelines Council and the Sentencing Advisory Panel. It aims to 'promote greater consistency in sentencing, whilst maintaining the independence of the judiciary'.

A publication titled 'Sentencing for Fraud – Statutory Offences' (Sentencing Guidelines Council, 2009) sets out factors judges should consider:

- **Assessing the seriousness** of the offence, including culpability and harm, planning, determination, number of offenders and the extent of collusion, the loss to victims and society at large, the impact on the victim, whether there was a higher

---

105   Proceeds of Crime Act, Section 75.

106   See Chapter 9, which discusses the importance of retaining experienced forensic accountants.

107   This again questions the integrity of the SFO's enthusiasm to persuade accuseds to agree civil disposals.

level of profit from the offence, the attempt to conceal or dispose of the evidence, the targeting of vulnerable victims and an abuse of a position of trust;

- **Mitigating factors,** including illness or disability of the perpetrators, youth or age, the offender's role, involuntary participation at the outset, voluntary cessation of the offending, complete and unprompted disclosure of the offence, providing information against others, the early point at which disclosure is made, voluntary restitution or genuine financial pressure.

Judges take a very serious view of bribery and generally want to see blood on the carpet. Although this may appear to be a strong argument in favour of DPAs, a judge's cannibalistic tendencies only become relevant after guilt has been proven. So it all comes back again to probability theory, and if the evidence is overwhelming and there are no technical or procedural disasters in the prosecutor's case an early plea may be better than or equal to anything in a DPA.

PENALTIES UNDER THE BRIBERY ACT

The Act imposes a maximum term of imprisonment – on indictment before a Crown Court – of ten years and unlimited fines. Companies may be prosecuted for incoming (sections 1 and 6) or outgoing (Section 2) bribery only when committed by a directing mind. Section 7 is much wider. It is unlikely (and possibly adding grief to the already bereft) that a company will be prosecuted for incoming bribery (Section 2) when it has lost its shirt through improper performance by one of its senior officials; but a corporate charge is possible![108]

Table 7.7 summarises the UK position, showing sanctions applicable to companies and individuals.

Table 7.7   Penalties under the Bribery Act

Potential Penalty	For Individuals	For Companies
Punishment *To punish the defendant and to serve as a deterrent to others*		
Imprisonment for up to ten years on each offence	☹	
Unlimited fines *Each corrupt transaction may be charged as a separate offence* *Imposed by a judge or negotiated by the SFO*	☹	☹
Disgorgement: Forfeiture of Property and Proceeds *To deprive the defendant of the benefits of criminal conduct*		
Restraint Order To preserve assets that may later be subject to a Confiscation Order	☹	☹

---

108 Not only is it possible but it should also be relentless, because stamping out bribery demands dealing with the coercer and the extorter: equally.

Confiscation Order (Part 2 Proceeds of Crime Act – applies to offences committed after 23 March 2003) following a conviction *Paid into central funds and is normally considered part of the penalty*	☹	☹
Forfeiture Order To deprive the offender of his assets *Usually issued in lieu of rather than additional to a Confiscation Order*	☹	☹
Civil Recovery Order (Part 5 Proceeds of Crime Act): civil recovery of criminal property and proceeds. Does not require a criminal conviction and is judged on a balance of probabilities in the High Court *Paid into central funds*	☹	☹
Compensation Order (Powers of Criminal Courts (Sentencing) Act 2000) May be part of a separate Confiscation or Civil Recovery Order. The amount of the order is unlimited subject to the offender's means and should only be made in 'simple straightforward cases' *To the benefit of a victim of crime*	☹	☹
Restitution Orders (Powers of Criminal Courts (Sentencing) Act 2000) Primarily relates to the return of stolen goods	☹	☹
Deprivation Order (Powers of Criminal Courts (Sentencing) Act 2000) *Where property has been used for the commission of an offence and following conviction*	☹	☹
Pre-judgement Interest Notional interest benefits between the commission of the offence and trial	☹	☹
Debarment and Contract Termination *Minimising future problems*		
Debarment from government contracts (Directive 2004/18)	☹	☹
Revocation of commercial and employment contracts	☹	☹
Disqualification as a director (including FSA approval)	☹	
Professional disqualification *(or equivalent for a business: such as the CBI)*	☹	☹
Other Costs and Impacts		
Legal fees and investigation costs	☹	☹
Orders to pay prosecution costs	☹	☹
Loss of shareholder value	☹	☹
Adverse credit and other ratings	☹	☹
Ongoing Monitoring and Restrictions *Minimising future problems*		
Deferred Prosecution Agreements and Monitoring	☹	☹
Serious Crime Prevention Order (Serious Crime Act 2007)	☹	☹
Financial Reporting Order	☹	☹

Potential Penalty	For Individuals	For Companies
EXTRADITION AND RENDITION *Bringing offenders to justice*		
Especially for UK citizens back to act trial in the UK and for everyone to the USA	☹	
Extradition of FPOs to face trial in the UK or USA	Remote	
Deportation (UK Borders Act 2007) Automatic deportation of any person who is not a British citizen, sentenced to imprisonment for 12 months or more	☹	
Other and Third Party Litigation *Obtaining compensation*		
Third-party civil actions (including RICO actions) in the USA	☹	☹
Compensation claims by disadvantaged competitors	☹	☹
Reputational damage and market value	☹	☹

It is impossible to guess from the available statistics what terms of imprisonment might be imposed, but the trend is for the US courts to be much more severe than their UK counterparts. UK fines appear to be in the range of 4 to 15 times the profits attributable to bribery. These may be in addition to confiscation, deprivation and other orders.

POINTS ON COMPENSATION AND CONFISCATION

Both American and British regulators claim to make victim compensation a priority and the Federal Sentencing Guidelines impose fines on that assumption. The problem with bribery cases is that nowhere is it *fairly* stated how victims are identified and their losses assessed or gains from bribe payment calculated.

In most cases regulators have taken an overly simplistic view that:

- the organisation represented by the recipient of the bribe (the extorter) is the victim even when one of its own employees was the initiator;
- the victim's loss is equivalent to the gains by the bribe payer.

In most cases none of the above is true nor fair. The principle seems to be that the gains of the bribe payer are first assessed. We will call this 'A'. The victim is then handed back an amount equivalent to A which may or may not be purloined by the extorter or his colleagues. Under the FSG, A is used to determine the offence level and it can make a massive difference to the maximum and minimum penalties. **Estimated gains are much more influential on sentencing than any deduction for self-disclosure or effective compliance and ethics programs.**

The SFO – as a first or independent step – may confiscate A (and any other assets associated with it) under the Proceeds of Crime Act as criminal property. This does not, necessarily, reduce the requirement to compensate the victim.

Regulators appear wholly disinterested in compensating the real victims – who are the honest competitors of the corporate bribe payer – but may argue that it is a commercial matter between the parties. This would be great if full details of the bent contracts were published, but they seldom are. **The result is that most honest competitors usually don't realise what has hit them.** So much for levelling the playing field!

Often the alternative transaction that was available to the victim was less advantageous than the deal accepted; even though it was tainted by bribery. In fact, the assumed victim organisation may lose only by the amount of bribe extorted by its employees. When its controls were so appalling that they encouraged skulduggery, there is a good case for saying that there should be no compensation.

Usually the corporate gain is calculated as the profit before tax – (A) – from the perverted transactions, but again this is over-simplistic and should be subject to the strict 'but for' test. This means examining closely what other options were available to the bribe payer at the time. If it had a full order book and could have deployed its resources elsewhere with an income of say 'B', its 'but for gain' is A minus B. **Unadjusted gross profit is irrelevant.** There are lots of other points that could be made on compensation etc, but to maintain this book's indecent brevity, they cannot be mentioned.

The lesson is that companies accused of skulduggery should not simply accept the loss calculations proposed by regulators, nor should they concede that losses are necessarily equivalent to gains. Also before making any self-disclosure they might consider negotiating with the supposed victim to agree losses (if any) taking into account the culpability of its own employees and the possibility of charges under Section 2 of the Bribery Act. Armed with such an agreement it is much more likely that fanciful figures produced by regulators can be rebutted. **But even more importantly and ethically significant, honest companies should have intelligence and monitoring systems in place to alert them to competitive skulduggery.**

Have a Nice Day

The reaction to anti-bribery legislation has been framed almost entirely in a legal context and driven primarily by regulators and lawyers, with very little involvement by the courts or businesses. The taxonomy of corruption[109] has been delineated primarily by TI, the OECD, academics and large legal and accounting firms in a way that is over-simplistic and biased towards punishing bribe payment (mis-described 'active bribery'), and by rapacious companies in supposedly supply-side countries. Corruption is not that simple: neither is it the main reason why poor countries (including the UK) suffer (see pages 13, 14 and 59).

The discussions and recommendations that follow in subsequent chapters are unlikely to be supported by players in the 'Cottage Industry'. For many the idea of taking self-disclosure and other decisions on a risk probability, commercial basis will be worse than obnoxious. In the final analysis it falls to each company to decide how it will respond to anti-bribery and other legislation, but it should not be a case of capitulating in the face of every regulatory diktat or cry of 'Boo!'

This book is deliberately agitative and intended to get people thinking about the wider aspects of corruption and how honest companies can best survive in less than helpful commercial and regulatory environments. So let's continue and for those who want to self-flagellate: have a nice day.

---

109 But more often limited to bribery.

CHAPTER 8

Other Relevant UK Legislation and Guidelines

Introduction

There are many other criminal laws and civil rules that are relevant in the bribery area. The most significant are described below.

The Proceeds of Crime Act 2002

OFFENCES

This Act is highly relevant because it creates:

- Money-laundering offences that apply to anyone who has criminal property in the UK or which has passed through the UK;[1]
- Reporting obligations mainly applicable to members of the regulated sector;
- Civil recovery and seizure possibilities against all criminal property in the UK.

The Proceeds of Crime Act (POCA) 2002[2] came into force on 24 February 2003 and replaced an array of money-laundering laws and regulations. The main offences created by the Act are as follows in Table 8.1.

---

1   To this extent the Act is extraterritorial.

2   Available at: http://www.legislation.gov.uk/ukpga/2002/29/contents (accessed 7 November 2012).

Table 8.1   Summary of Primary Offences Under the Proceeds of Crime Act 2002

	Part 7 Section	A person commits an offence if he	A person does not commit such an offence if he
			• Makes an authorised disclosure under section 338 *– or was given consent to proceed*[3] • Intended to make such a disclosure but had a reasonable excuse for not doing so • The acts he carries out relate to the enforcement of any provision of this Act or other enactment relating to criminal conduct • *He did not know or suspect the property was criminal property*
	328	**ARRANGEMENTS** Enters into or becomes concerned in an arrangement which he **knows or suspects** facilitates by whatever means the acquisition, retention, use or control of criminal property by or on behalf of another person	• Makes an authorised disclosure under section 338 *– or was given consent to proceed*[4] • Intended to make such a disclosure but had a reasonable excuse for not doing so • The acts he does relate to the enforcement of any provision of this Act or other enactment relating to criminal conduct • *He did not know or suspect the property was criminal property*
	329	**ACQUISITION USE OR POSSESSION** Acquires, uses or has in his possession criminal property	• Makes an authorised disclosure under section 338 *– or was given consent to proceed*[5] • Intended to make such a disclosure but had a reasonable excuse for not doing so • The acts he does relate to the enforcement of any provision of this act or other enactment relating to criminal conduct • Acquired or used or had possession of the property for adequate consideration • *He did not know or suspect the property was criminal property*
	PENALTIES for sections 327, 328 and 329 on indictment to imprisonment for a term not exceeding 14 years or to a fine or to both		

3   This is not the strict wording of the Act, but covers cases where consent of regulators has been given to a specific transaction.

4   This is not the strict wording of the Act, but covers cases where consent of regulators has been given to a specific transaction.

5   This is not the strict wording of the Act, but covers cases where consent of regulators has been given to a specific transaction.

REPORTING	330	**FAILURE TO DISCLOSE REGULATED SECTOR** (Schedule 9 defines the regulated sector) Knows or suspects or has **reasonable grounds for knowing** or suspecting that another person is engaged in money-laundering	• Has reasonable excuse for not disclosing the information • He is a professional legal adviser and the information came to him in privileged circumstances • He did not know or suspect that another person is engaged in money-laundering and he has not been provided by his employer with such training as specified • *Did not have grounds for knowing or suspecting engagement in money-laundering*
		That the information on which knowledge or suspicion etc. is based came to him in the course of a business in the regulated sector	
		Does not make the required disclosure (to a nominated officer etc.) as soon as is practicable	
	331	**FAILURE TO DISCLOSE BY A NOMINATED OFFICER IN THE REGULATED SECTOR** *A person nominated to receive disclosures under Section 330 commits an offence if he:* knows or suspects or has reasonable grounds for knowing or suspecting another person is engaged in money-laundering	• Has reasonable excuse for not disclosing the information or other matter • Followed any relevant guidance by a supervisory authority • *Did not have grounds for knowing or suspecting or reasonable grounds for knowing or suspecting engagement in money-laundering*
		That the information on which knowledge or suspicion etc. is based came to him in the course of a disclosure made under Section 330	
		He does not make the required disclosure as soon as is practicable	
	332	**FAILURE TO DISCLOSE BY OTHER NOMINATED OFFICERS** **Knows or suspects** that another person is engaged in money-laundering, that the information came to him in consequence of a disclosure made under Section 337 or 338, and he did not make the required disclosure as soon as was practicable	• Has a reasonable excuse for not disclosing the information or other matter • *Did not have grounds for **knowing or suspecting** engagement in money-laundering*

	Part 7 Section	A person commits an offence if he	A person does not commit such an offence if he
TIPPING OFF	333	**TIPPING OFF** Knows or suspects that a disclosure under Section 337 or Section 338 has been made and makes a disclosure that is likely to prejudice an investigation	• He did not know or suspect that disclosure was likely to be prejudicial • The disclosure is made in carrying out a function he has relating to the enforcement of any provision of this Act or of any other enactment relating to criminal conduct or benefit from criminal conduct • He is a professional legal adviser and the disclosure falls within subsection (3) • *To seek legal advice*
OTHER	340 (11)	**ATTEMPT, CONSPIRACY OR INCITEMENT** To commit an offence under sections 327 to 329	• As for the substantive offences
OTHER	342	**PREJUDICING AN INVESTIGATION** Makes a disclosure that is likely to prejudice an investigation or falsifies, conceals, destroys or disposes of (any evidence) which are relevant to an investigation	• He does not know or suspect disclosure etc. will prejudice an investigation • The disclosure is made in carrying out a function he has relating to the enforcement of any provision of this Act or of any other enactment relating to criminal conduct or benefit from criminal conduct • He is a professional legal adviser and the disclosure falls within subsection (4)
		PENALTIES for sections 330,331,332, 333 and 342 on indictment to imprisonment for a term not exceeding five years or to a fine or to both	

In addition the Money Laundering Regulations 2007 (MLR2007) require firms in the regulated sector to specify and maintain effective controls (including due diligence). Regulation 42 gives Supervisory Authorities the power to impose unlimited civil penalties for, among other things, failure to register, to keep adequate records or to train employees. Regulation 45 creates the offence of failing to comply with MLR2007 and Regulation 14 of the Transfer of Funds (Information on the Payer) contains similar provisions, with both incurring maximum penalties of two years' imprisonment and unlimited fines.

A body corporate or relevant commercial organisation is only liable under POCA when money-laundering offences are committed by a directing mind.

The Act is not extraterritorial but the Crown Prosecution Service (CPS) Guidance for Prosecutors[6] states that

> *offences which were committed abroad are relevant predicate crimes if laundering acts are committed within our jurisdiction.*

Thus if the proceeds of overseas bribery are laundered through the UK the provisions of POCA are triggered.

---

6   Available at: http://www.cps.gov.uk/legal (accessed 13 November 2012).

Offences under POCA may be prosecuted in addition to a predicate crime: for example misbehaviour that leads to a charge under the Fraud Act (the predicate offence) may be reinforced by prosecution under sections 327 to 329.

The CPS Guidance states:

*Money-laundering and the underlying criminality are separate offences but money-laundering should not be seen as simply part and parcel of the underlying criminality. [...] A money-laundering charge ought to be considered where the proceeds are more than de minimus. [...] A careful judgement will need to be made as to whether it is in the public interest to proceed with money-laundering offences in the event of a plea to the underlying criminality by the defendant who was also indicted for laundering his **own** proceeds.[7]*

The above could be regarded as a subtle hint that money-laundering offences should be charged to convince defendants to plead guilty to predicated offences.

DEFINITIONS UNDER POCA

Section 340 sets out a number of important definitions:

Criminal conduct is conduct which:

a) constitutes an offence in any part of the United Kingdom; or
b) would constitute an offence in any part of the United Kingdom if it occurred there.

It should be noted that any crime is a potential predicate offence to charges under POCA, including illegal parking to draw money from a bank.

Property is **criminal property** (Section 340(3)) if:

a) it constitutes a person's benefit from criminal conduct or it represents such a benefit (in whole or part and whether directly or indirectly); and
b) the alleged offender knows or suspects that it constitutes or represents such a benefit

It is immaterial –

a) who carried out the conduct;
b) who benefited from it;
c) whether the conduct occurred before or after the passing of the Act.

It should be noted that the prosecution must prove that the proceeds were criminal AND that the accused knew or suspected this was the case.

Property is all property wherever situated and includes –

a) money;
b) all forms of property, real or personal, heritable or moveable;
c) things in action and other intangible or incorporeal property.

---

7   Proceeds of Crime Act 2002 Part 7 – Money Laundering Offences.

Examples Of Bribery and Criminal Property

Where A bribes B, resulting in B's employer being induced to give an advantage to A:

- at the time the bribe is paid from A to B it is criminal property because it arises from criminal conduct and represents a benefit to B;
- when A receives the advantage from company B it is receiving criminal property.

Therefore if evidence of the arrangement comes to the notice of either company A or company B or to any of their advisers in the regulated sector a Suspicious Activity Report must be filed. Any contract obtained directly or indirectly as a result of a bribe will qualify as criminal property as well as any value later derived from it.

Money-laundering is an act which:

a) constitutes an offence under sections 327, 328 or 329;

b) constitutes an attempt, conspiracy or incitement to commit an offence specified in paragraph (a);

c) constitutes aiding, abetting, counselling or procuring the commission of an offence specified in paragraph (a); or

d) would constitute an offence specified in paragraph (a), (b) or (c) if done in the United Kingdom.

Regulated Sector: Schedule 9 states that

1. *A business is in the regulated sector to the extent that it engages in any of the following activities:*[8]

   (a) *accepting deposits by a person with permission under Part 4 of the Financial Services and Markets Act 2000 (c. 8) to accept deposits (including, in the case of a building society, the raising of money from members of the society by the issue of shares);*

   (b) *the business of the National Savings Bank;*

   (c) *business carried on by a credit union;*

   (d) *any home-regulated activity carried on by a European institution in respect of which the establishment conditions in paragraph 13 of Schedule 3 to the Financial Services and Markets Act 2000, or the service conditions in paragraph 14 of that Schedule, are satisfied;*

   (e) *any activity carried on for the purpose of raising money authorised to be raised under the National Loans Act 1968 (c. 13) under the auspices of the Director of Savings;*

   (f) *the activity of operating a bureau de change, transmitting money (or any representation of monetary value) by any means or cashing cheques which are made payable to customers;*

---

8 Note: a business may be in the regulated sector and can conduct activities outside it; similarly a business may not be registered with a regulator and yet may conduct regulated activities.

(g) *any activity falling within sub-paragraph (2);*

(h) *any of the activities in points 1 to 12 or 14 of Annex 1 to the Banking Consolidation Directive, ignoring an activity described in any of sub-paragraphs (a) to (g) above;*

(i) *business which consists of effecting or carrying out contracts of long-term insurance by a person who has received official authorisation pursuant to Article 6 or 27 of the First Life Directive.*

2. *An activity falls within this sub-paragraph if it constitutes any of the following kinds of regulated activity in the United Kingdom:*

(a) *dealing in investments as principal or as agent;*

(b) *arranging deals in investments;*

(c) *managing investments;*

(d) *safeguarding and administering investments;*

(e) *sending dematerialised instructions;*

(f) *establishing (and taking other steps in relation to) collective investment schemes;*

(g) *advising on investments.*

It should be noted that an activity – including an occasional one – determines whether a transaction falls within the regulated sector.

Other important interpretations come from other laws and decisions:

- 'Knowing or believing' implies a conscious, deliberate certainty that a fact exists.
- 'Suspecting' means that there is a possibility, which is more than fanciful, that the relevant facts exist. A vague feeling of unease is not sufficient;
- 'Reasonable grounds for knowing or suspecting' is not defined in the Act, but the Secretary of State has issued a code in relation to the reasonable grounds for search powers conferred on law enforcement officers to search for cash as follows:

Whether there are reasonable grounds for suspicion will depend on the circumstances in each case. There must be some objective basis for that suspicion based on facts, information and/or intelligence. Reasonable suspicion can never be supported on the basis of personal factors alone without reliable supporting intelligence or information.[9]

In practice, it is likely that the test will be at the higher level of negligence or wilful blindness.

UK SUPERVISING AUTHORITIES

The main supervising authorities in the UK are:

- Her Majesty's Revenue and Customs (HMRC)
- The Financial Services Authority (FSA)
- The Office of Fair Trading (OFT)
- The Gambling Commission
- The Department for Business Innovation and Skills (BIS)
- The Department of Enterprise, Trade and Investment in Northern Ireland.

---

9   Police and Criminal Evidence Act 1984 Code A.

Some professional bodies are designated as supervisory authorities, the most notable of which are the law societies that regulate solicitors.

The HMRC Money Laundering Regulations Central Intervention Team provides advice to businesses on whether or not they should be supervised and, if so, the relevant authority.

DEFENCES TO POCA CHARGES

Evidential

The initial reaction of sensible people over the linkage between POCA and the Bribery Act 2010 is that they would be best advised to leave the country and take up breeding parrots in Argentina. But the underlying spirit of POCA is fair enough: it is only the default to extreme safety interpretation taken by some practitioners,[10] plus an over-reliance on box-ticking that leads to problems.

More Fear and Panic from the Serious Fraud Office

Fear and panic have been inflamed by the SFO to encourage people to self-disclose potential bribery offences. At a conference for General Counsel an SFO representative said:

> Which of you would like to go and visit your CEO and CFO in a police station where they are being held following arrest on money-laundering charges? Those charges will be based upon decisions by the CEO and CFO on your advice that disclosure will not be made to the SFO and that any benefit of the corruption will therefore be retained within the corporate. I can imagine some difficult discussions.

This is persuasion of a particularly nasty kind and hopefully was seen as such by the senior lawyers in attendance. POCA is an attractive prop for the SFO for three reasons. First, it can be used to scare companies into reporting bribery offences. Secondly, money-laundering offences can be added to an indictment – possibly with no intention of pursuing them – to give weight to the attractiveness of a civil disposal or plea bargain. Thirdly they may be charged as a standalone offence when bribery evidence is non-existent. The CPS Guidance to Prosecutors[11] states:

> *Prosecutors are not required to prove that the property in question is the benefit of a particular or a specific act of criminal conduct, as such an interpretation would restrict the operation of the legislation. The prosecution need to be in a position, as a minimum, to be able to produce sufficient circumstantial evidence or other evidence from which inferences can be drawn to the required criminal standard that the property in question has a criminal origin.*

---

10   To cover their own backsides.

11   http://www.cps.gov.uk/legal/p_to_r/proceeds_of_crime_money_laundering/.

The fact is that putting offences on the statute book is easy but proving a specific case beyond reasonable doubt is an entirely different matter and may fall into the dust for three main failures:

1. To prove a predicate charge;
2. To prove the proceeds are connected to unlawful conduct;
3. To prove that the accused knew or suspected (or, for members of the regulated sector, did not have reasonable grounds for knowing or suspecting) that criminal property was involved.

Home Office, Ministry of Justice, FSA and Serious Organised Crime Agency (SOCA) statistics are silent on how many people and companies have been successfully prosecuted for money-laundering offences, but circumstantial evidence suggests the results are far from impressive and that yet another noble cause has – to use the words of the distinguished Jamaican philosopher, Ali G – been 'bigged up'.

Suspicious Activity Reports

A defence to all POCA offences is that a consent was given or a Suspicious Activity Report (SAR) was submitted to SOCA. Suspicious Activity Reporting has been portrayed as a major weapon in the fight against crime, yet the truth is counterfactual.

SOCA reported that between October 2009 and September 2010 it received 240,582 SARS, with over 78 per cent from banks and mainly from four firms. As a result of interventions arising from refused consent requests, £353,929 was seized and a total of 17 arrests made, while interventions arising from granted consents resulted in seizures of £1,385,797 and 22 arrests. **Thus, if the figures are accurate, on average each SAR involves criminal proceeds of £5.70.**

SOCA's website claims that in 2009–2010 it:

> Denied criminals access[12] to assets worth £317 million and recovered 205 properties, 37 vehicles, 190 bank accounts, 17 financial products, 56 cash payments and numerous other assets including paintings, licence plates, cattle and jewellery.
>
> However figures on their own are of limited use in measuring the impact of asset recovery.[13] Some people have attempted to value SOCA's assets recovery work by dividing the entire budget by what's in the recovery pot. This oversimplification has led to the statistic that it costs £15 every £1 recovered.[14]

SOCA received 7,156 SARS indicating corrupt politically exposed persons (PEPs) and disseminated 240 intelligence packages as a result, many[15] of which have initiated or supported successful intervention activity against corrupt foreign officials. The report

---

12   Whatever that means.

13   Note the clever framing of this statement.

14   See http://www.soca.gov.uk/about-soca/how-we-work/asset-recovery (accessed 7 November 2012).

15   But no mention of how many.

does not clarify the outcome of these packages or intervention activity, but had they been spectacular no doubt we would have been told.

Asset Recovery Agency

The short-lived Asset Recovery Agency was abandoned because it was ineffectual. During its short life it cost £60 million but stopped criminal assets of only £8.3 million.

From October 2009 to September 2010, SOCA processed 14,334 consent requests[16] 90 per cent of which were unsubstantiated. UK government statistics (with the usual confusion of percentages, trends and absolutes worthy of the Carbon World) throw little light on the effectiveness of suspicious activity-reporting or the precise outcomes of the cases involved.

Sitting on the Loot

The clearest demonstration of this is that until the Arab Spring, Western banks were happy to sit on billions of dollars in assets stolen by despots and kleptocrats without saying a word. Only when they fell from power was the whistle blown. If the Financial Action Task Force and others wanted to be really effective, why has so little attention been paid to the Carbon World and its new financial systems, which are unregulated and in which there is no such thing as a SAR? Or why do alternative systems – such as Hawala – not come under the spotlight? Why did the SFO and other agencies not use their extensive powers under Part 5 of the Proceeds of Crime Act to put British and other extorters – who are often in government jobs – under pressure?

Would it be too cynical to say that the SAR regime is primarily a box-ticking exercise whose main benefit is that it collects taxes and keeps lots of people busy chasing their tails with lovely conferences in exotic locations?[17]

BOTTOM LINE: POLICY ON SUSPICIOUS ACTIVITY REPORTS

Companies should be concerned about money-laundering to:

---

16   Consent requests are submitted before a transaction is completed, whereas convention SARs are after the event.

17   There are much more effective ways of catching money launderers, corrupt PEPs and kleptocrats if regulators would think afresh and stop digging the same hole deeper.

- Help stamp out crime, especially involving kleptocracy, narcotic drugs, terrorism, organised gangs and frauds in the Carbon World;
- Make sure their policies on SAR reporting, especially in the light of its impact on the Bribery Act, are sensible.

The effect of POCA on a company's decision whether or not to self-disclose potential bribery offences is discussed later and on page 451.

CONFISCATION AND RECOVERY ORDERS

The Act, as amended by the Serious Organised Crime and Police Act 2005, contains important provisions to deprive criminals of illicit profits[18] via two types of orders: neither is regarded as part of the punishment, as summarized in Table 8.2:

Table 8.2   Confiscation and Recovery Orders under POCA

Type of Order	Standards of Proof	Applicability
Confiscation Against Individuals Criminal Law Crown Court **Part 2**	Proof beyond reasonable doubt of a predicate offence *Criminal law evidential standards*	Can be issued to recover assets but only AFTER CONVICTION of a criminal offence. Orders may be founded on a 'criminal lifestyle'[19]
Recovery Against Property Civil Law High Court **Part 5**[20]§ 242 et al.	On a balance of probabilities *Civil Law standards, including hearsay evidence* *20-year time limit* *Described cheerfully as 'the most draconian tool available to prosecutors'*	Can be applied for ex-parte[21] where any enforcement agency has suspicions that any recoverable property has been obtained through any unlawful conduct anywhere in the world. Can be applied for even when a defendant has been acquitted of an associated criminal offence, not even prosecuted, when he is outside UK jurisdiction or is dead

Note: For all practical purposes, 'unlawful conduct' and 'criminal conduct' are one and the same.

Although the above orders may appear straightforward, they are, in fact, complex both in terms of applicability and quantification (discussed earlier, see pages 152–3).

---

18   i.e., Which is he equivalent of 'criminal property'.

19   Per Section 75 and Schedule 2 of the Act.

20   Had been restricted to the Assets Recovery Agency until it was closed, when its powers were granted to other enforcement agencies, including the SFO.

21   Without the accused's knowledge but subject to the enforcement authority making a full and true disclosure of all relevant facts. Assets may be frozen pending a hearing.

Other Acts

The acts (in date order) in Table 8.3 may also be relevant to prosecuting bribery offences:

Table 8.3   Other Relevant Legislation

Act	Year	Importance
Criminal Law Act	1967	This removed the obligation to report all crimes in the UK and abolished the offence of Misprision of a Felony except for treason and under Section 19 of the Terrorism Act 2000. The only other mandatory reporting offences are under the Road Traffic Acts and Proceeds of Crime for regulated sectors
Criminal Law Act	1977	Relating to conspiracy outside the United Kingdom. Currently used by the SFO for offences committed before July 2011
Companies Act	1985	Accounting offences in relation to bribery
Criminal Justice Act	1987	Established the SFO and Section 2 orders including pre-investigation discovery in cases of overseas bribery. Removes a suspect's right against self-incrimination. Punishes false information given to the SFO in response to an order Makes it an offence to falsify, destroy or tamper with evidence when it is known or suspected that an SFO investigation is in process
Criminal Justice and Public Order Act	1994	Qualified a suspect's right to remain silent and allowing an adverse inference to be drawn against defendants who chose not to answer questions in interviews
Enterprise Act	2002	This act is the main sources of the UK's competition regulation – in line with articles 81 and 82 of the Treaty of Amsterdam (articles 85 and 86 of the Treaty of Rome) and deals primarily with restrictive business practices, such as cartels, and exploitation of dominant market positions
Public Contracts Regulations	2006	A company found guilty of a corruption offence[22] will be mandatorily and perpetually debarred from competing for public contracts, throughout the European Union and possibly worldwide. Unlike in the USA where, under Presidential Direction (Executive Order number 12549 and 12689), there is no scope for self-cleansing and a corporate offender might be punished for acts that took place many years ago and under directors and officers who have long since ceased to be employed. However clause 23 (2) of the regulation can be used to repeal a debarment where a relevant public body considers there to be overriding requirements in the general interest.
Companies Act	2006	Over 100 offences created. The 1980 Act sanctions insider dealing

---

22   As well as other offences such as fraud, cheating HMRC, fraudulent trading and money-laundering.

Fraud Act	2006	Offences: • fraud by misrepresentation • failure to disclose information that he is under a legal duty to disclose • fraud by abuse of position[23] • possession of articles for use in fraud • making or supplying articles for use in frauds • participating in a fraudulent business • obtaining services dishonestly Penalties of up to 10 years' imprisonment may be imposed for offences under the Fraud Act
Serious Crime Act	2007	Came into force in October 2008. UK nationals and registered companies encouraging or assisting bribery committed wholly overseas by foreign nationals or companies will also be liable to prosecution for committing bribery • abolition of the Assets Recovery Agency • civil recovery orders that do not require a conviction • serious crime prevention orders • powers of forfeiture of anything the court considers to have been involved in the offence
Money Laundering Regulations	2007	Comprehensive AML regulations and reporting

Most of the above laws should be considered as part of a regulatory risk evaluation, discussed in Chapters 14–17.

The UK Civil Law on Bribery

The UK civil law is still primarily based on the agent–principal relationship providing extensive rights of action for damages, nullification of contracts negotiated by the agent and other penalties. The plaintiff needs only to prove that an undisclosed benefit was given to an agent who had fiduciary obligations to him. The principal does not have to prove any causal link to improper performance, nor corrupt intent by any of the parties involved, all presumptions being in his favour. It is only necessary to show that the coercer knew he was dealing with an agent and that payment was offered.

Even More UK and other Guidelines[24]

INTRODUCTION AND THE PROBLEM OF REGULATORY SILOS

The problem with guidance and guidelines is that there are far too many of them: they are often superficial and issued in silos by the agencies and bodies, prioritising their own

---

23 Section 4 is basically the old agent–principal offence.

24 Whenever possible reviewed in date order.

interests. Some are not dated and none are indexed. This makes what could be good advice difficult to consolidate into practical working procedures and to eliminate duplication.

UK GOVERNANCE CODES AND OTHER STUFF

The Institute of Chartered Accountants in England and Wales issued in September 1999 (and updated in 2005) a very useful document: 'Internal Control Guidance for Directors on the Combined Code',[25] which contains advice on the standards expected of companies listed in the UK.

The rules require boards to maintain a sound system of internal control to safeguard shareholders' investment and company assets. These should include:

- An assessment of the nature and extent of the risks facing the company, identifying those which it regards as tolerable;
- The cost of operating particular controls relative to the benefits;
- The system of internal control includes policies, processes, tasks, behaviours and other aspects that together facilitate effective and efficient operation of the business in compliance with laws;
- The internal control system should reflect the organisation's control environment and will include:
  - control activities
  - information and communications processes
  - processes for monitoring the continuing effectiveness of controls
  - maintaining an ethical culture
  - being capable of responding quickly to evolving risks
  - procedures for reporting immediately to the appropriate levels of management any significant control failings together with details of corrective action being taken.

The directors should, at least annually, conduct a review of the effectiveness of all internal controls and should report to shareholders that they have done so.

The London Stock Exchange Listing Rules state that annual reports and accounts of companies should include a narrative statement of how and to what extent it has applied the principles set out in the combined code. Companies should consider extending this narrative to compliance with the Bribery Act and the Foreign Corrupt Practices Act.

THE WOOLF REPORT INTO BRITISH AEROSPACE, MARCH 2008

In May 2008 Baron Woolf, the ex-Lord Chief Justice of England and Wales, produced a very weighty report for British Aerospace following settlement of criminal charges involving corruption in Saudi Arabia, Tanzania and South Africa. It sets out 23 main recommendations, most of which can be regarded as standard and in line with Committee of Sponsoring Organisations of the Treadway Commission (COSO).

---

25   Available at: http://www.icaew.com/en/library/subject-gateways/corporate-governance/codes-and-reports/turnbull-report (accessed 7 November 2012).

The recommendations relating to the company's obligations are prefaced by the word 'should', implying an almost mandatory requirement. However, when addressing actions that should be taken by government, the word is replaced with 'could' or 'would'. This is consistent with the perception that responsibility for anti-bribery measures rests entirely in the private sector.

Lord Woolf has an apparent soft spot for committees and his recommendations include:

* Setting up a Corporate Responsibility Committee for primary oversight for the company's compliance programme;
* Giving special training to heads of business units on anticorruption measures;
* Carrying out an impact assessment on the integrity of all significant business decisions;
* Preparing routine reports aggregating expenditure on hospitality;
* Paying particular attention to the activities of lobbyists;
* Investigating and disclosing material findings of suspected bribery to the relevant authorities.

Lord Woolf's recommendations on facilitation payments are especially interesting:

Recommendation 13

The company should continue to forbid facilitation payments as a matter of global policy. While it may not be possible to eliminate such payments immediately in some countries, management and employees need to be supported to ensure all such payments are reported to senior executives and to the board, and the means developed to *eliminate them completely over time*. (Where practical this should be done in conjunction with other companies, non-governmental organisations, and the countries' governments and if necessary with the assistance of the UK government).[26]

It is refreshing that the ex-Lord Chief Justice of England and Wales admits that BAE has *no option but to* continue making facilitation payments. This truth is explained fully on pages 31 and 751.

TRANSPARENCY INTERNATIONAL, MAY 2009

In May 2009 Transparency International (TI) issued a useful, but somewhat dishevelled, publication, 'Business Principles for Countering Bribery Self-Evaluation Tool' which contains 241 core indicators. It has also produced a number of other guidelines which all follow the same mantra of zero tolerance. The problem is that if any company tried to implement TI's recommendations, it would grind to a halt.

---

26   Woolf Committee Report, 'Business ethics, global companies and the defence industry', May 2008, page 48. Available at: http://ir.baesystems.com/investors/storage/woolf_report_recommendations.pdf (accessed 7 November 2012).

FINANCIAL SERVICES AUTHORITY, 2010

In 2010, following the AON Insurance corruption case, the Financial Services Authority issued an important report titled 'Anti-Bribery and Corruption in Commercial Insurance Broking'. Its recommendations include:

* Risk-based approach and gap analysis to identify optimum controls;
* Due diligence before appointing agents and monitoring thereafter;
* Detection and investigation procedures;
* Regular reviews of relationships with approved third parties.

The report commented that many firms were not currently in a position to demonstrate adequate procedures to prevent bribery and was critical of the practice used by one, which relied almost entirely on Transparency International's Corruption Perceptions Index (see page 229 et seq) in deciding what level of due diligence should be applied. This is another example of regulatory silos and inconsistency.

FINANCIAL ACTION TASK FORCE 2010

The Financial Action Task Force (FATF) is an important sponsor of anti-money laundering regulation which is often associated with corruption. It has achieved some good results. It is therefore extremely disappointing that its guidelines on corruption are so limited and are directed almost exclusively at cosmetic controls in the private sector while ignoring political and governmental crime. They add very little to the debate.

TRANSPARENCY INTERNATIONAL 'ADEQUATE PROCEDURES', JULY 2011

This 100-page guide – erroneously dated July 2010 – sets out 231 points that it considers best practice and that surpass adequate procedures. It again focuses on establishing a defence rather than covering all aspects of corruption, preventing competitive bribery and seizing commercial opportunities.

It is also framed around the misconception of supply–demand, active and passive, and on a zero-tolerance policy to facilitation payments.[27] It says little on risk assessment and even less on detection, conducting investigations, self-disclosure, plea negotiations, risk-management strategy, payments control or emerging problems in the Carbon World.

---

27   The SFO's 'Nuanced Approach' (see page 125) was released after publication of this guide.

9 US and Worldwide Legislation and Guidelines

Introduction

All companies with even the slightest connection to the USA must take great care over their control and compliance programmes in what is an extremely comprehensive, complex and ever-changing regulatory environment. There are 52 separate judicial systems in the USA[1] concerned with fraud and bribery,[2] each with its own State and local enforcement arms. In addition the US Attorney General has offices in over 90 districts with heavyweight investigatory teams: all bristling with lawyers turbocharged with testosterone.

Although the main focus, internationally, is on the Foreign Corrupt Practices Act (FCPA), companies with US connections must also evaluate their risks and compliance exposures for incoming and internal bribery as well as anti-competition and export control. The FCPA is part of a much wider picture. However, for companies operating internationally, compliance with the Bribery Act 2010 and the UK Companies Acts is likely[3] to satisfy most of the provisions of the FCPA: but not vice versa.

Responsibility of Directors and Employees

Many States have adopted laws which require a director to discharge his duties in good faith, with the care an ordinarily prudent person in a like position would exercise in similar circumstances and in a manner he believes to be in the best interests of the corporation.[4] A director is allowed to rely on the expertise of professional advisers.[5] Under American laws, companies may be held vicariously liable for the acts of omission of all employees and agents and not, as in the UK, only if they are directing minds.

---

1   In addition to Federal laws agencies.
2   Although none of the State laws seem to apply to overseas bribery.
3   This cannot be guaranteed because of the unlimited creativity of regulators and changing laws.
4   This is a higher standard than in the UK.
5   Except the 'advice of counsel' in strict liability offences.

Foreign Corrupt Practices Act

HISTORY

In 1976, Congress was concerned with the Watergate scandal and over the collapse of Equity Funding Corporation and Penn Central, following which 300 leading companies, including Lockheed, Bendix and ITT, admitted to wholesale bribery of Japanese and European officials *to obtain government contracts*. The Foreign Corrupt Practices Act 1977[6] was the result and it attempted to juggle the very fine balance between the damage that was supposedly being inflicted on less developed countries by corruption, on one side, with the ability of American companies to remain competitive, on the other.

American businesses argued that the Act went too far and put them at a disadvantage in international markets where their foreign competitors were not constrained by similar rules. Thus in 1988 the facilitation payment ('grease payment') exclusion came into effect and at around the same time the United States put serious pressure on the Organisation for Economic Cooperation and Development (OECD) to insist on equal standards, worldwide. The OECD Convention on the Bribery of Foreign Public Officials in International Business Transactions was the result. There were further amendments in 1998.

BASIC ELEMENTS AND DOMESTIC CONCERNS

The FCPA consists of two main parts, which impose both criminal and civil sanctions on bribery of foreign public officials:

1. Anti-bribery provisions, which apply to all 'domestic concerns' and to acts taking place in or involving the USA.
2. Accounting provisions (usually referred to as the 'books and records' and 'internal controls' provisions, which apply to publicly held corporations and their subsidiaries which issue securities in the USA ('Issuers').

Any company that does anything within the borders of the USA is considered to be a domestic concern. Thus any foreign businesses with offices, subsidiaries or associates in America, as well as those that use its wire transfer, banking, or other systems, are likely to be pulled into the FCPA's anti-bribery provisions in their worldwide operations. Companies that have any doubt over this should assume they are domestic concerns.

EXTRATERRITORIALITY

American regulators have claimed jurisdiction over all companies which have any connection with the USA ('domestic concerns') and have been forceful in asserting rights to discover evidence from overseas, demanding the attendance of witnesses and in some cases extraditing offenders, including foreign public officials (FPOs).

---

6   Detailed information about the FCPA is available at: http://www.justice.gov/criminal/fraud/fcpa/ (accessed 7 November 2012).

The courts have also claimed extraterritorial jurisdiction (see the case of Leasco v Maxwell 2nd Cir 1972) over companies operating entirely outside the USA where their conduct has a significant effect in the domestic market or where it causes injury within America (see Laker Airways v SABENA (DC Cir.1984)). Bills are currently in play that would add statutory weight to this precedent.

ANTI-BRIBERY PROVISIONS

The anti-bribery provisions make it an offence for any person in the USA, a domestic concern (as well as any officer, director, employee, or agent of a firm or any stockholder acting on behalf of the firm) to:

- pay, offer to pay or authorise the payment or any gift or promise anything of value
- to any foreign official (including private persons acting for the foreign government, usually called 'State Owned Enterprises') any **foreign political party or candidate**
- for the purpose of **wrongfully influencing**[7] any act or decision in order to assist the domestic concern in directing business to itself or another, including obtaining favourable tax treatment.

It is also unlawful to make a payment[8] to any person, while *knowing* that all or a portion of it will be offered, given, or promised, directly or indirectly, to any foreign official for the purposes of assisting the firm in obtaining or retaining business. 'Knowing' includes 'conscious disregard' or 'wilful blindness'.

The anti-bribery provisions have one exception (facilitation payments, discussed later) and two affirmative defences. These are:

1. That the thing of value, etc., was permitted under the written laws of the country concerned; and/or
2. Was directly related to the promotion, marketing, etc. of goods or services.

It should be noted that the FCPA's anti-bribery provisions do not apply to incoming, internal or outgoing bribery or to skulduggery in the private sector. However, other federal and state laws do. It is also noteworthy that the anti-bribery provisions are not 'securities laws' and therefore do not qualify whistle-blowers to rewards under the Dodd Frank Act (see pages 215 and 665).

FACILITATION PAYMENTS

Facilitation payments are not normally considered illegal under the FCPA provided they are solely to encourage an official to carry out a function that he or she is already duty bound to perform. Such functions include routine stuff: granting permits and licences, issuing visas or work orders, obtaining police protection, unloading or loading cargo, or providing utility services. The American regulators have expansively interpreted what constitutes 'obtaining or retaining business' and the few cases that have been clarified

---

7   Much more sensible than the Bribery Act.

8   That is, 'anything of value'.

by the courts have concluded that the definition will be 'case factual'. The FPO's lack of authority to award business may be taken as a factor in differentiating between a bribe and a grease payment.

An FPO is defined as 'employees, officers, or representatives of any civilian or military government agency, instrumentality of a government agency, government-controlled commercial enterprise or public international organisation, or has an *officer position in a political party or as a candidate for political office or otherwise holds any royal family, official, ceremonial, or other positions* with a government or any of its agencies'. The word 'instrumentality' is not defined, but has been expansively interpreted to cover any entity in which a foreign government has a 'dominant influence'.[9] Definitions of who is, and who is not an FPO can cause problems:

A Really Mixed Bag

C, a UK company (relevant commercial organisation), has shares listed in the USA (an issuer bound by the accounting provisions) and a small representative office in Houston (a domestic concern). It pays cash to a British Member of Parliament (Gerry Greedy – an FPO under the FCPA) and a Member of the European Parliament (MEP) (Pascal Plunder – an FPO under the FCPA but not the Bribery Act) to influence their licensing decisions. The influence concerned does not extend to improper performance.

C's main competitor, ABC, which is based in but never ventures outside Bristol, also bribes Messrs Greedy and Plunder. The question is: what are the likely offences?

Table 9.1   FCPA and Bribery Act Offences

Name	Probable Violations	
	FCPA	**Bribery Act**
C Company	Classified as a domestic concern and an issuer **Bribery and Accounting offences**	Classified as a relevant commercial organisation **No offence under sections 1 or 6**
ABC Company	Not applicable Not a domestic concern or an issuer	Classified as a relevant commercial organisation **No offence under sections 1 or 6**
Greedy **Plunder**	**CLASSIFIED AS FPOs** Aiding, abetting, conspiring etc. May be extradited to the USA	**NOT CLASSIFIED AS FPOS** No Section 2 offence

Table 9.1 indicates that even though C and ABC are both British companies, if C influences a UK Member of Parliament (MP) or a European MEP it could be punishment for all of them. ABC has no troubles.

---

9   The interpretation was subject to considerable speculation and objection but seems to have been resolved in February 2012. In the case of Control Components Inc., Judge James V. Selna, of the US District Court for the Southern District of California, ruled that the determination of who was and was not an FPO was one for a jury to decide based on all of the facts.

Complicated though the above is, things may be even more confused when members of a foreign royal family, politicians in opposition, FPOs before or after appointment and members of political parties are involved. Most of these would not be regarded as FPOs under the Bribery Act. **The point from the above hypothetical is that companies should not try to weasel their way around the law.** If they act on principle and can demonstrate honest intent, there should be few problems with either the Bribery Act or the FCPA.

ACCOUNTING PROVISIONS

The accounting provisions[10] apply to any company that has securities registered pursuant to Section 12 of the Securities Exchange Act 1934 or that is required to file reports with the Securities and Exchange Commission pursuant to Section 15 (d) of the Exchange Act. An issuer that controls more than 50 per cent[11] of a foreign subsidiary's stock must make its best efforts to ensure that the subsidiary adheres to the books and records provisions, which are to:

- Ensure that books, records[12] and accounts are kept in reasonable detail to accurately and fairly reflect transactions and the dispositions of assets;
- Maintain a system of internal accounting controls devised in order to provide reasonable assurances that transactions are executed in accordance with management authorisations;
- Ensure that assets are recorded as necessary and to limit access to management authorisations;
- To make certain that recorded accountability for assets is compared with the existing assets at reasonable intervals and appropriate actions taken in respect of any differences.

The Act does not give detail on what is, or is not, accurate record-keeping other than:

- It applies a reasonableness (but not materiality) test.[13]
- 'Reasonable detail' means 'such level of detail and degree of assurance that would satisfy prudent officials in the conduct of their own affairs'.

There are two further Securities and Exchange Commission (SEC) rules that are relevant to the FCPA. Rule 13b2-1 states that 'no person shall [...] falsify or cause to falsify any record' (that is subject to FCPA accounting provisions). This applies to any person and not just issuers. Rule 13b2-2 prohibits false (oral or written) statements by directors and officers in connection with an audit or an SEC filing. There is also a requirement for effective internal and external auditing.

The accounting provisions have been expansively interpreted to apply to bribery in the overseas private sector, but this was not their original intent. In practice,

---

10   Sometimes called 'Bookkeeping and Internal Controls'.

11   If it owns less than 50 per cent it must use its best efforts and SHOULD DOCUMENT THESE.

12   This has been interpreted as applying to all documents (such as legal agreements and contracts) and not just financial or transactional records.

13   In fact any accounting entry – no matter how insignificant – has been argued to be material if it conceals a criminal offence.

the accounting provisions are more powerful than those relating to anti-bribery but only apply to 'Issuers' and there subsidiaries.

Violations of the accounting provisions are enforced by the SEC under the civil law. However, where the offence involves 'wilful conduct', Section 32 (d) of the Exchange Act adds a criminal element. This is enforced by the Department of Justice and criminal charges may be in addition to SEC administrative or other action.

The Sarbanes–Oxley Act, passed in 2002, adds even further weight to the accounting provisions and sections 302 and 404 pin responsibility firmly on senior managers, making them personally liable. Also under Section 906 of Sarbanes–Oxley a manager who wilfully certifies a false periodic report filed with the SEC faces criminal prosecution, up to 20 years' imprisonment and fines of up to $5 million.[14]

PROPOSED CHANGES TO THE FCPA

The US Chamber Institute for Legal Reform has proposed changes to the FCPA, including:

- Adding a compliance defence along the lines of adequate procedures in the UK Bribery Act *(yet there is no equivalent Section 7 absolute offence in the US laws) provided:*
  - The persons with operational responsibility for the company's compliance programme had a direct reporting obligation to the board of directors or to an appropriate committee of the board.
  - The company's compliance programme must have detected the offence before external discovery or before such discovery was reasonably likely.
  - The company must have promptly reported the offence to the appropriate governmental authorities.
  - No person with operational responsibility for the company's compliance programme participated in, condoned or had been wilfully ignorant of the offence.
- Limiting successor liability;
- Adding a wilfulness requirement;
- Limiting the parent's liability for the acts of a subsidiary;
- Clarifying the definition of 'foreign official'.

It is unclear whether some or all of these will be implemented, but the point is that the law is dynamic and amendments carefully monitored.

PENALTIES

Basic stuff under the FCPA

Under the anti-bribery provisions offenders may be subject to a fine of up to $2 million per offence or the amount of the pecuniary gain, whichever is the greater. Officers, directors and stockholders are subject to similar level fines and substantial terms of imprisonment: seven to ten years is not exceptional but neither is a short period of home confinement. Fines imposed on individuals may not be paid by the company.

---

14   The Dodd-Frank Act also adds further personal grief for directing minds.

In addition, the Attorney General or the SEC may bring a civil action for anti-bribery violations which could result in a fine of up to $10,000 against any firm as well as any officer, director, employee, or agent of a firm, or stockholder acting on its behalf. Civil and criminal sanctions are not mutually exclusive. Conduct that violates the anti-bribery provisions may also give rise to a private cause of action[15] for treble damages under the Racketeer Influenced and Corrupt Organizations Act (RICO), or to prosecution under other federal or state laws.

Criminal fines of up to $25 million may be imposed against companies for wilful breaches of the accounting provisions and up to $5 million and 20 years' imprisonment against natural persons. In addition, orders may be made for the disgorgement of profits and offenders may be banned from doing business with any or all US government agencies.

Federal Sentencing Guidelines

The Federal Sentencing Guidelines (FSG) came into effect on 1 November 1991 and are intended to provide just punishment, adequate deterrents and incentives for organisations to maintain internal mechanisms for preventing, detecting and reporting criminal conduct.[16]

The Act takes a base penalty for an offence[17] and, in layman's terms, modifies it by two factors: a culpability score and a mitigation score. The culpability score increases the base penalty, according to various formulae, and takes into account such factors as:

- The size of the organisation;
- Aggravating circumstances;
- The seniority of management involved in the offences;
- The offender's record of previous offences;
- Any obstruction of justice.

Regulators take a dim view of wilful or deliberate ignorance, conscious disregard or unwarranted obliviousness and companies that fail to investigate their suspicions can expect little sympathy.

Mitigating factors, which reduce the culpability score, include:

- Whether or not the offences were voluntarily disclosed;
- The level of cooperation afforded the regulators;
- Acceptance of responsibility;
- Whether the company had an effective programme to detect and prevent violations.

An effective compliance programme should include the following seven principles:

---

15   It should be stressed that there is no private right of action under the Bribery Act.

16   The Federal Sentencing Guidelines 2012 Manual is available at: http://www.ussc.gov/Guidelines/2012_Guidelines/index.cfm (accessed 7 November 2012).

17   And bribery is considered very serious.

1. Having compliance standards and procedures that are reasonably capable of reducing criminal conduct;
2. Specifically designating high-level officials to oversee the programme;
3. Exercising due care not to delegate major authority to a person known to have criminal tendencies;
4. Developing a method of communicating the policies and procedures to all employees and other agents, either with ethics training or practical publications which explain the programme;
5. Taking reasonable steps to achieve compliance, by using auditing and monitoring systems designed to detect criminal conduct by employees and having in place and publicising a reporting system through which employees can report criminal conduct by others without fear of retribution;
6. Consistently enforcing the standards through appropriate disciplinary mechanisms;
7. Taking steps to prevent any similar occurrences in the future.

The precise standards that are required in a particular case depend on a number of factors, including:

- The size of the company and the degree of formality necessary;
- The risks that arise because of the nature of the company's business and the countries in which it operates;
- The company's history of previous problems.

The failure of a company to follow normal industry standards or professional guidelines will act to its disfavour, as will failure to report suspected violations.

Negotiated settlements, DPAs and NPAs

US regulators lead the way in reaching negotiated settlements, including Deferred Prosecution Agreements (DPAs), Non-Prosecution Agreements (NPAs), and plea bargains. The main provisions of these were discussed in a UK Bribery Act context in Chapters 5 and 6.

Precedents and examples

The track record of bribery prosecutions in the USA is far better established than in the UK, but even so it is difficult to identify norms and trends other than that suspected offenders must anticipate being whacked. Most actions are settled, but when they go to a full trial they are as likely to fail as to succeed (see pages 33–4).

The US Department of Justice's Principles of Prosecution

The US Department of Justice (DOJ) is primarily responsible for prosecuting criminal offences under the anti-bribery and accounting provision of the FCPA and the SEC for administrative and civil actions. Many cases will involve both agencies and they work closely together.

The DOJ considers a range of factors in deciding whether or not to prosecute.[18] They are:

- The nature and seriousness of the offence, including the risk of harm to the public;
- The pervasiveness of the wrongdoing within the corporation, including the complicity in, or the condoning of, the wrongdoing by corporate management;
- The corporation's history of similar misconduct, including prior civil to criminal and regulatory actions against it;
- The corporation's timely and voluntary disclosure of wrongdoing and its willingness to cooperate in an investigation;
- The existence and effectiveness of the corporation's pre-existing compliance programme;
- The corporation's remedial actions, including efforts to implement an effective corporate compliance programme or to improve an existing one, to replace responsible management, to discipline or terminate[19] wrongdoers, to pay restitution, and to cooperate with relevant government agencies;
- *The collateral consequences, including whether there is a disproportionate harm to the shareholders, pension holders, employees, and other persons not proven personally culpable, as well as the impact on the public arising from the prosecution;*
- The adequacy of the prosecution of individuals responsible for the corporation's malfeasance;
- The adequacy of remedies such as civil regulatory enforcement actions.

It is interesting to note that American prosecutors ignore the OECD Convention requirement[20] that economic and other consequences ('collateral consequences') must be disregarded when deciding whether or not to prosecute. They are also creative in citing violations so that they avoid a company being debarred.

US Principles of Federal Prosecution of Business Organisations

This guidance, as the title suggests, is about the prosecution of corporations under American federal law.[21] Important points include:

- Prosecution of a corporation is not a substitute for the prosecution of criminally culpable individuals and only rarely should provable individual culpability not be pursued.

---

18   Which are different from the Federal Sentencing Guidelines!! Available at: http://www.justice.gov/usao/eousa/foia_reading_room/usam/title9/27mcrm.htm (accessed 7 December 2012).

19   This presumably means terminate a relationship rather than the Al Capone meaning of terminate.

20   Article 5. The OECD Convention is available at: http://www.oecd.org/daf/briberyininternationalbusiness/anti-briberyconvention/oecdconventiononcombatingbriberyofforeignpublicofficialsininternationalbusinesstransactions.htm (accessed 13 November 2012).

21   Available at: http://www.justice.gov/dag/cftf/corporate_guidelines.htm (accessed 13 November 2012).

- It is entirely proper for a prosecutor to consider the corporation's pre-indictment conduct, for example voluntary disclosure, cooperation, mediation or restitution, in deciding whether to seek an indictment.
- The prosecution must establish that the actions were within the scope of the individual's duties and were intended, at least in part, to benefit the corporation.
- The Anti-trust Division has established a firm policy that credit should not be given at the charging stage for a compliance programme and that amnesty is available only to the first corporation to make full disclosure (first through the door rule[22]).
- Waiving of privilege has never been a prerequisite under the department's prosecution guidelines for the corporation to be viewed as a cooperative (although the prosecutor may require the production of relevant factual information acquired through privileged interviews).
- In evaluating cooperation, prosecutors should not take into account whether a corporation is advancing or reimbursing attorney's fees or providing counsel to employees, officers or directors under investigation on the same or other indictment.
- Similarly, the mere participation by a corporation in a joint defence agreement does not render it ineligible to receive credit.
- A corporation should not be able to escape liability merely by offering up its directors, officers, employees and agents.
- In conjunction with other regulatory agencies the Department encourages corporations […] to conduct internal investigations and disclose the relevant facts to the appropriate authorities.
- Prosecutors should determine whether a corporation's compliance programme is merely a paper pretence or designed, implemented, reviewed and revised in an effective manner.
- The decision whether or not to prosecute will not depend upon the target's ability to pay restitution. A corporation's effort to pay restitution even in advance of any court order is, however, evidence of its acceptance of responsibility and […] may be considered in determining whether to bring criminal charges.
- Prosecutors may consider the collateral consequences of the corporate criminal conviction and the effect on its employees, investors, pensioners and customers, many of whom may, depending on the size and nature of the corporation and their role in its operations, have played no part in the criminal conduct, have been unaware of it, or have been unable to prevent it.
- Where collateral consequences of the corporate conviction for innocent third parties would be significant, it may be appropriate to consider a DPA.
- In negotiating plea agreements prosecutors should generally seek a plea to the most serious, readily provable offence. Pleas should be structured so that the corporation may not later proclaim lack of culpability or even complete innocence.

It is clear from the above – if not already so from earlier discussions – that a company exposed to simultaneous American and UK regulatory action faces enormous difficulties, partly because of the differences in the laws and prosecutorial procedures. **The simple rule is 'if the buzzards don't get you, the vultures will, but more likely both'.**

---

22   So quite different from the UK.

Special Problems of Multi-jurisdictional Cases

Many offenders fall under American and UK laws and may be prosecuted in either or both countries. America's laws on double jeopardy are more relaxed that those in the UK, but multi-jurisdictional cases are problematic:

Marine Hose Case (R v Whittle) ... 2008

The defendants were arrested in the USA in the process of committing a cartel offence and proceedings were started by the Department of Justice and in the UK by the Office of Fair Trading. The agreement between the prosecutors was that the defendants would be sentenced in the USA and returned for a further trial in the UK. If the UK courts imposed a lesser sentence than that already set by the US, the defendants would be sent back to the US to serve their sentence there. The defendants were sentenced in the US and returned, as agreed, to face trial in the UK.

The UK judge imposed a higher sentence than the US courts, and thus the question of the defendants returning to the USA was irrelevant. But the defendants appealed against the UK sentence (at some risk because if it had been reduced below the US level they would have been returned for imprisonment there). In the event the UK appeal judges set the sentence to exactly match that imposed in the USA.

The Court of Appeal noted that it 'had considerable misgivings about disposing of these applications in the way in which we intend but, if we are to avoid injustice we feel we have no alternative'.

In practice, through close cooperation between regulatory agencies and careful structuring of sanctions, the UK's laws on double jeopardy are not a serious obstruction to combined or even duplicated regulatory action.

The Resource Guide to the US Foreign Corrupt Practices Act

In November 2012, the DOJ and SEC published the Resource Guide,[23] which Assistant Attorney General Lanny Breuer described as 'the boldest manifestation of the DOJ's transparent approach to enforcement'. However, this is more than a slight exaggeration, given the opening caveat, the way it has spun the only case ever where details of a 'declination of prosecution'[24] have been given. It completely omits to mention dreadful regulatory failures, such as the prosecutions of the Lindsey Manufacturing Company and the Gun Show sting (see pages 213, 827 and 839). The guide is akin to a publicity brochure for the DOJ and SEC.

---

23   Available at: http://www.sec.gov/spotlight/fcpa/fcpa-resource-guide.pdf (accessed 7 December 2012).

24   Morgan Stanley (see supra).

The guide's opening states:

[It is] non-binding, informal, and summary in nature and the information contained therein does not constitute rules or regulations. As such, it is not intended to, does not, and may not be relied upon to create any rights, substantive or procedural, that are enforceable and any law by any party, in any criminal, civil or administrative matter. It is not intended to substitute for the advice of legal Counsel on specific issues related to the FCPA. It does not in any way, limit the enforcement intentions or mitigating positions of the US Department of Justice, the US Securities and Exchange Commission, or any other US government agency.

Thus the Guide can be viewed as the ultimate manifesto for prosecutors to keep every option open and is therefore of very limited value to companies. It contains very little that is new and everything described earlier in this chapter seems still to apply, although it does reinforce a few important points:

- To convict a company under the FCPA, prosecutors must prove that it acted 'corruptly' with intent or desire to 'wrongfully influence' whereas for individuals the test is that they acted 'wilfully'.[25]
- An amendment to the Act in 1998 was made to conform with the 'anti-bribery convention'[26] and expanded its scope to include (1) payments made to secure 'any improper advantage', (2) reach certain foreign persons who commit an act in furtherance of a foreign bribe while in the United States, (3), public international organisations in the definition of 'foreign official', (4) add an alternative basis for jurisdiction founded on nationality,[27] (5) apply criminal penalties to foreign nationals employed by or acting as agents of US companies.
- The Department of Commerce and State both maintain good governance initiatives globally and regularly assist US companies doing business in overseas markets. The Department of Commerce has published a new anticorruption section in its country commercial guides
- Gives a few useful clarifications and hypothetical cases, on gifts and entertaining and reasonable, promotional expenditures and successor liability.[28] It is less clear on facilitation payments, possibly indicating a prosecutorial intent for future expansive interpretations.
- Emphasises the risks of prosecution for aiding and abetting a crime. Individuals and companies, including foreign nationals, may be liable for conspiring to violate the FCPA even if they are not, or could not be, independently charged with substantive offences.
- Does not specify a particular set of controls that issuers are required to implement to satisfy the accounting conditions.[29] The DOJ and SEC have no formulaic requirements

---

25   Proof of wilfulness by a corporation is not required: the test is of a corrupt intent.

26   The OECD Convention.

27   That is US nationality.

28   Action has only been taken against successor companies in limited circumstances; generally in cases involving egregious and sustained violations or where the successor company directly participated in the violations or failed to stop the misconduct after acquisition.

29   Note that these only apply to 'issuers'.

regarding the credit they may give for compliance programs but rather apply common sense approach based on three questions:
- Is the company's compliance program well designed?
- Is it being applied in good faith?
- Does it work?

- If an issuer owns less than 50 per cent and subsidiary or affiliate, it is only required to *use its best efforts* to cause the minority owned entity to devise and maintain a system of internal accounting controls consistent with its own obligations
- Under section 10A of the Exchange Act, independent auditors who discover impropriety including the payment of bribes to domestic or foreign government officials are required to report to an 'appropriate level within the company' and only if it fails to take appropriate action to notify the SEC.
- On risk assessment the guide states 'devoting a disproportionate amount of time to policing modest entertainment and gift giving instead of focusing on large government bids, questionable payments third-party consultants, or excessive discounts to resellers and distributors, may indicate that the company's compliance program is ineffective'.
- A company's code of conduct is often the foundation upon which effective compliance programs is built (see Chapters 23–4). Codes must be relevant and regularly updated.

The reaction of the Cottage Industry to the guide has been mixed. Jan Hanzlik, a defence counsel in the DOJ's failed fiasco with the Lindsey Manufacturing Company stated[30]

... the new guidance amounts to much sound and fury, signifying very little. Instead of responding to widespread concerns about the Act's lack of clarity, [it] for the most part simply reiterates positions taken by the DOJ and SEC in past enforcement actions. The DOJ now cites as settled law its own interpretations of the Act and the 'principles' developed over the years through deferred prosecution agreements. It is doubtful that US companies and individuals trying to understand the consequences of their actions when doing business abroad will find much real guidance here.

Ryan McConnell (Baker & McKenzie and a former DOJ prosecutor) stated that 'notably missing from the DOJ's collection of sources are cases where FCPA enforcement actions have fallen flat'.

Mike Koehler, FCPA Professor stated

... my interpretation is that the DOJ-SEC was saying that part of the reason why companies have such a high level of FCPA anxiety is not necessarily because of its enforcement, but rather the marketing and commentary by certain segments of FCPA Inc (the Cottage Industry). If that was their intent and purpose, I agree.

But there are others who have seized upon the declination to prosecute Morgan Stanley – supposedly because of its excellent procedures, self-disclosure and co-operation – as a new dawn (see page 615).

---

30 All references from www.fcpaprofessor.com. The Guidance: The FCPA Bar Reacts, November 2012.

One Cottage Industry blog[31] stated

You have to give the Justice Department credit – they are crafty and can be very politically astute…. It played a very subtle political game with the Morgan Stanley settlement. You have to give them credit for how they used the case to make a point.

The Justice Department wanted to show everyone that they can be reasonable, credit a corporate compliance program, and exercise discretion not to charge a company even though it could have easily done so. DOJ will cite Morgan Stanley as a case in which they did not inflexibly rely on the doctrine of respondeat superior to hold every company liable for the acts of a single, rogue employee.

More importantly, Morgan Stanley is a precedent that will be limited to the facts of the case, which were unusual. The case gave DOJ the opportunity to show reasonableness without creating a precedent that would seriously hamper the FCPA enforcement program. It is unusual to have the facts play out in such a clean way.

The question is, should a prosecutorial agency be 'crafty' or 'politically astute', permitted to sit on the fence, expansively interpret the law and investigate in the disgraceful ways exposed in the Lindsey and Gun Show cases and in the UK involving the Technguiz brothers?

Other US Laws

INTRODUCTION

There are many other federal and state corruption laws which companies need to consider depending on the areas, sectors and contexts in which they operate. The following federal acts, in addition to those on money-laundering, the Travel Act and those on foreign assets control, are important.

PUBLIC ACCOUNTING REFORM AND INVESTOR PROTECTION ACT 2002 (SARBANES-OXLEY)

In July 2002, in an effort to restore public confidence in financial markets following the Enron and WorldCom collapses, President Bush signed a law (often referred to as the Sarbanes-Oxley Act) which imposes tough penalties on frauds by publicly listed companies.

The Act:[32]

- Improves the quality and transparency of financial reporting which is its primary focus;
- Creates a Public Accounting Oversight Board to monitor auditing standards and enforce the independence of auditors;

---

31   http://corruptioncrimecompliance.com/2012/05/morgan-stanley-did-the-justice-department-rollover.html.

32   Available at: http://www.govtrack.us/congress/bills/107/hr5070 (accessed 13 November 2012).

- Forbids auditing firms from providing consulting services to the companies they audit;
- Ensures the objectivity of security analysts who work for banks;
- Increases the resources of the SEC.

One of the most important aspects of the Act is the requirement for CEOs of publicly listed companies to personally vouch for the accuracy and fairness of their companies' disclosures. The Act is supported by a set of excellent guidelines of the Committee of Sponsoring Organisations (COSO) – which, surprisingly, have been virtually ignored by the anti-bribery regulatory community.

DODD-FRANK WALL STREET REFORM AND CONSUMER PROTECTION ACT

This Act,[33] signed by President Obama in July 2010, is a sweeping review of the financial services market and includes provisions that impact on the Foreign Corrupt Practices Act and indirectly on the UK Bribery Act.

Section 922 authorises the payment of rewards to whistle-blowers (called 'relators') who voluntarily provide original information leading to successful enforcement actions by the SEC and Commodities Futures Trading Commission (CFTC) –against regulated firms:[34]

- Rewards may be up to 30 per cent of the penalties collected.
- Relators who have been convicted of criminal violations in relation to the offences concerned cannot be rewarded.
- Additional protection is provided for relators throughout the financial and commodities sectors.
- Companies must maintain rigorous control systems and thoroughly investigate suspicions.
- Firms commercially involved in the extractive industries must include in their annual reports information relating to royalty, licensing, taxes, fees, production entitlements, bonuses and other material benefits.

It is possible that people – and especially employees – who have information about corruption will choose to report directly to the SEC simply to claim rewards. Thus, as discussed in Chapter 25, companies should consider paying rewards for information. However, there is an important point not usually emphasised. It is that rewards only apply to violations of the securities laws. The FCPA's anti-bribery provisions do not come within this category.

Under Section 954 (which is controversial and may not be implemented), a company that is required to restate its accounts must claw back all incentive compensation paid within the past three years to any former or current executive officer.

---

33   Which runs to an estimated 16,000 pages!! (Available at: http://www.sec.gov/about/laws/wallstreetreform-cpa.pdf (accessed 13 November 2012)).

34   That is 'Issuers'.

THE FALSE CLAIMS ACT 1986

This was originally enacted during the Civil War to combat overcharging by corrupt defence contractors and was amended in 1986[35] to encourage private *qui tam* lawsuits, thereby assisting the federal government stamp out overcharging. The Act prohibits the knowing submission of false or fraudulent claims to the government, provides for triple damages and allows whistle-blowers to bring an action on behalf of the federal government. The government can then decide whether or not to intervene and take over from the whistle-blower, who may be rewarded with up to 30 per cent of *worldwide* penalties and recoveries.

Bribery Laws Worldwide

Multinational companies are confronted with a significant and costly problem of researching what corruption laws apply to countries in which they are considering investing or in which they have done so already and there is a remarkable lack of information provided by government agencies. However, an excellent source is a book and CD titled *Anti-bribery Risk Assessment*, edited by Thomas Gruetzner, Ulf Hommel and Klaus Moosmayer.[36] It gives details of the applicable laws in over 200 countries. Another very useful publication – which is reserved for clients – is the *International Agency and Distribution Handbook* by Baker and McKenzie.

Legislative and Enforcement Trends

ONE FOR ALL AND ALL FOR ONE

The International trend is towards more and more regulation, extension of the criminal law into the commercial sector and holding individuals (other than politicians, civil servants, academics and the media: see Chapter 2) responsible for the acts of organisations for which they work. There is also massive enthusiasm in the opposite direction to hold companies liable for the acts and omissions of everyone; even those they pass in the street. This is clever stuff from a regulatory perspective because companies have the money to pay up: individuals less so and whacking both for the same offence is efficient.

Increasingly regulators work together – internationally – on joint prosecutions, sharing information and evidence. Once a cadaver is in the jaws of one agency it will be mauled and chewed by the worldwide regulatory pack. Whatever remains will be mangled further by commercial lawyers working on contingency fees. It is a daunting prospect that can only be managed on principle.

Regulators will continue to be driven by key performance indicators – such as case numbers, turnaround times, conviction rates, etc. and will manage these by going for low

---

35   For more information about the Act see: http://www.justice.gov/jmd/ls/legislative_histories/pl99-562/pl99-562.html (accessed 13 November 2012).

36   (Beck/Hart, 2011) – this publication is available on the Internet for about £200. The suspicion is the authors' real names are Smith, Jones and Black!

fruit and refusing to accept difficult cases at the vetting stage. They will push submissive organisations for financial settlements even when the evidence falls short of the Full Code Test. They will try to avoid difficult investigations and long and contested trials. While all this is happening they will apply relentless pressure to self-disclose. DPAs are part of this process.

NOT IN MY BACK YARD (NIMBY)

Regulators are highly sensitive to the criticism they would face if their draconic enthusiasm were to lead to the loss of jobs in their own countries. It is probably no accident that a disproportionate number of cases pursued by the Justice Department, the SEC and State agencies has involved other than American companies. This has the quadruple whammy of making the agencies appear effective, collecting what are effectively taxes, protecting American jobs and avoiding public indignation.

Mr Alderman, ex-Director of the Serious Fraud Office (SFO), has also 'made it clear' that he intended to focus on foreign companies even when they have only tenuous connections to the UK.

Helping Honest Companies

On 9 June 2011 at a presentation to the US–Russia Business Council, Mr Alderman said:

'Our view is that if a foreign group has a subsidiary in the UK and in another country and the bribery occurs in that other country, then that bribery is within the remit of the SFO. The sort of case that we will be interested in is one where the bribe paid disadvantages an ethical UK corporation. In such a case there is a strong UK public interest in bringing that foreign group before the UK courts. This will be a high priority for us'.

On 21 June 2011, Mr Alderman spoke at a breakfast seminar run by Kingsley Napley and Carmichael Fisher, and said: 'Again, I have made it very public[37] that foreign companies within my jurisdiction that use corruption anywhere in the world to the disadvantage of UK ethical companies will be a target of SFO activity'.

No Weaseling

'What I have said to corporates is that it would be very dangerous for them to use a highly technical interpretation of the law to persuade themselves that they are not within the Bribery Act and that it is permissible for them to carry on using bribery. I have said that they can have a very unpleasant shock in a few years' time and that the best and least risky way of doing business is to avoid bribery'.[38]

---

37 But not, as usual, 'clear'.

38 Speeches made by Richard Alderman are available on the SFO website at: http://www.sfo.gov.uk/about-us/our-views/director's-speeches.aspx (accessed 7 November 2012).

All of the above would be much more reassuring for honest companies if the SFO and other agencies were to chase after bent UK and foreign officials, compensate them as the real victims (rather than dodgy governments), and enforce the debarment provisions: which, of course, they won't. But they will continue to use menaces to blag civil disposals and DPAs. **That said, Mr Alderman is dead right; the only way for companies to perform is on principle, and if they do, there should be few problems.**

The bottom line is that regulators are expected to increasingly chase after foreign companies that make any sort of show in their jurisdiction. The Brits will bash the Americans, the Americans the Limeys and both will wallop the French.[39] This will lead to a retaliatory spiral of enforcements that are selected primarily because they produce lots of funding, and are politically, publicly and electorally palatable and career-enhancing for the officials concerned.

The pure elegance of this approach is that American regulators can be blamed for the failure of British companies; British regulators for American collapses and the French for whatever comes to mind.[40] Then, when regulators chillax at International Corruption Hunters' Alliance conferences and garden parties, or let it all hang out at the Pink Pussycat Lap Dancing Club, they can high five and buy each other drinks: provided doing so is accurately recorded and 'proportionate'.

---

39   Proving there is some justice, after all.

40   Which is as it should be.

'If you're really sure, Officer, you must have a little gift of $50 and you don't give a hoot about the OECD Convention on Corruption, or UNAC, Transparency International or the UK Bribery Act or Trace International or GRECO or the Serious Fraud Office, Mr Alderman, or the SEC, Vivian Robertson QC or Kenneth Clarke, even Vince Cable and Nicholas Clegg or Tony Blair, Richard Branson, Gordon Brown, Jack Straw, Peter Mandelson, six British Bishops, the Pope, the British Ambassador, President Obama, Kofi Annan, Lenny Henry and Premier Inns, or that I have a wife and two kids, a mortgage with Northern Rock, a dog called Daisy who has just had pups – one with an ingrowing toenail – drive a carbon neutral Toyota, pay all my taxes, go to Church, voted for the LibDems and have severe gout ...'

'I suppose I better pay up ..... but I want a receipt for $400'

'Can I just get this right? You took a bung of £100,000 and spent it all on Viagra and that is the result'

The Taxonomy of Corruption

CHAPTER 10 *Introduction to a Universal Problem*

A Universal Problem

Every person and every organisation in every country pays for corruption. It is an international disgrace[1] that permits an evil minority to prosper at the expense of the majority. But for many politicians, gross corruption is a problem that is too close for comfort, too hot to handle, resulting in the UK Bribery Act being framed in a way that blames businesses for what is a much nastier stratospheric problem. Attention is therefore diverted to cosmetic legislation primarily confined to bribes *paid* by the private sector.

The Tone From the Very Top

The genesis of corruption in developed societies is political: driven by the rewards from obtaining and retaining power at all costs. This corruption flows down to all levels of society, setting a tone in which outright deception becomes merely spin and blatant lying, facetiously framed as 'sexing up a dodgy dossier'. And do you know what? We have all become conditioned to accept it as the norm.

The Bribery Act 2010 and related legislation gives the illusion of international political commitment that in reality does not exist. It allows politicians to carry on as normal, to collect the penalties they impose on others and to gloat. The false framing of the Act results in citizens and some honest businessmen, sitting frozen like rabbits in the headlights or following guidance like sheep when they should be holding politicians and regulators to account to deliver the level playing fields they know are needed if British businesses are to survive.

It is Still Happening and Moving Forward

Some people assume that cases that are now emerging in the media are all in the past, that skulduggery has declined and society moved forward to better times. This is not true.

---

1   Unfortunately one of many.

The reality is that corruption has not decreased one iota – despite extensive huffing and puffing – over the past ten years to the effect that it has.

Rather than declining, corruption has become more sophisticated and better concealed and it starts at the very top of society with our political leaders.

The Arab Spring

It is amazing that even in recent cases – like President Mubarak – that Western politicians remained silent for 30 years when they knew he and his family had pillaged billions of dollars from Egyptian citizens. Within days of his fall from power, politicians, regulators and others circled like vultures to seize his funds.

Publication by regulators and others of historic red flags and profiles have educated persistent corrupters to change their tactics just as they did when agents were introduced to circumvent the Foreign Corrupt Practices Act (FCPA). Thus, regulators who continue to rely on red flags and focus on intermediaries operating in the perceived most corrupt countries are hunting the dodo. Life moves on, but corruption moves faster: it is far more determined and much more widespread than officially portrayed. It is not about facilitation payments and corporate hospitality.

Who Says the UK and the USA Lead the Way?

There is a congenital arrogance that the UK and other developed countries are more honest than those below the equator or in less developed regions. British politicians and regulators repeatedly bombast about the UK's superiority and that it is leading the way in the fight against international corruption.[2] This is a joke when they know only too well that the draconian UK laws came about by accident (see Chapter 2), were never intended in the way they now appear and that corruption in the UK flourishes at every level.

The World Bank statistics on banned companies[3] shows the truth of the lie that the UK (and the USA) are leading from the front. It may be true that corruption in developed countries is more subtle and sophisticated than handing over suitcases full of cash. But it is equally as pervasive, although concealed by official spin.

---

2   In the same way as global warming.

3   Which ironically omits crooked companies that have supplied the Bank directly: see, for example, the Satyam scandal.

Do As I Say Not As I Do

Transparency International (TI) complains that by not prosecuting fraudsters, companies send out the wrong signal, yet it stays silent when regulators allow companies guilty of gross corruption to avoid mandatory debarment under European Union rules and then go on to win massive government contracts at the expense of honest competitors.

The Oil for Food Programme, which was one of the greatest scandals of this generation, raised suspicions of corruption involving two Secretary Generals of the United Nations (UN), a number of Undersecretary Generals, more than 2,300 companies, inspection organisations and officials scattered throughout the globe. More than 100 companies were pursued, but no meaningful investigation of senior UN officials took place. The impression is given, as in the British Aerospace (BAE) case, that some cases are too hot to handle and too big to fail and that political leaders are above the law.

And the idea that if the UK self-flagellates enough it will embarrass other nations – such as China, Korea and Russia – to adopt near sainthood is madness. Many international competitors believe Britain is nuts[4] to introduce the Bribery Act as well as the Climate Change Act and so much other stultifying legislation because it creates uncertainty, endless bureaucracy and unaffordable costs – at a time when businesses should be dragging the country out of recession.

Putting Things in Context

The political and other backgrounds[5] discussed in this book is important because they define the frame in which solutions to corruption have to be found:

- The background puts in context the obligation demanded of companies, with little government support, for stopping gross corruption and the foolishness of believing that attention to trivia – such as facilitation payments and hospitality – will make any difference.
- Based on the Oil for Food Programme and other UN fiascos, the background serves as a warning to investors in the Carbon World that they might not only they lose their shirts but also be criminally liable for corruption committed by those who supply services or run projects on their behalf.
- The background can encourage companies to challenge everything related to the regulation of corruption and to reframe compliance as a support to commercial operations and not as an end in itself.

---

4   The actual term used.

5   Which might not always accord with the reader's (note by Kenneth the Dog) but true.

This chapter's first objective is to provoke thought, challenge established views and, by exposing the misconceptions about corruption and by penetrating the smoke and mirrors, assist businesses to become more profitable, while complying with all laws (and not just the Bribery Act).

Definitions of Corruption and Bribery

Corruption is defined as the improper influencing or abuse of entrusted discretion; and bribery as a subset in which money or money's worth is the persuasive lever used. Someone pays a bribe or uses improper influence to corrupt a decision entrusted to another and gains as a result. The critical point of all bribery and corruption is a perverted decision. For this reason, risk assessment should be based on decision centricity (see pages 276 and 568).

In this book the word 'coercer' refers to the person or organisation offering a financial or other advantage; and 'extorter' to the person demanding or accepting it and whose decisions are to be, or have been, corrupted. These terms are deliberately starker and more emotive, than those used by TI, the OECD and their supporters, who talk about 'supply' and 'demand' sides or 'active', or 'passive', and 'givers' and 'receivers'. These mealy-mouthed terms conceal the evil of corruption, giving it an air of normality, if not respectability, that sets a false frame. There is no such thing as passive corruption, but the framing excuses the lack of interest in making Less Developed Countries (LDCs) put their affairs in order: it is a cop-out.

Similarly, the idea that some countries are 'demand' and others 'supply' is an over simplification bordering on the nonsensical. All countries are a mixture of demand and supply, of coercers and extorters. Nations which are supposedly led from the straight and narrow path by evil Western corporates are packed, crammed full of local citizens and companies that both pay and extort bribes, steal, rob and plunder their own citizens, and most corruption is driven or condoned by political leaders. It is stratospheric.

Five Types of Corruption

There are five main types of corruption viewed from the position of organisation A:

1. **Incoming corruption** is where an extorter acting for A receives an undue personal advantage from a third-party coercer to influence an internal decision entrusted to him or her, resulting in a breach of trust and **financial loss to A** (in this case the extorter's organisation).
2. **Internal corruption is** where one representative of A bribes a colleague to perform improperly. When A's organisation is a relevant commercial organisation it may be corporately liable under Section 7 when the intention of the bribe was to provide it with a financial or other advantage.
3. **Outgoing corruption** refers to those cases in which a coercer acting for A offers or gives an advantage to a third-party extorter to influence an external decision entrusted to him or her with the intention of **A receiving an advantage**.
4. **Competitive corruption** relates to those cases where A is disadvantaged as a result of external collusion between third-party coercers and extorters.

5. **Conflict of interest** does not necessarily involve collusion; person can in effect a corrupt himself.

Regulators are primarily interested in outgoing bribery, less so with the incoming variety and not at all with supporting honest companies to maintain a level playing field, especially against international competitors who are not bound by the UK's draconian laws. Virtually nothing has been said about internal corruption, but it could have very serious regulatory and other consequences. The Serious Fraud Office (SFO) has commented that it may be prepared to help British businesses deal with competitive bribery: how reassuring is this?

The challenge for companies – besides complying with the laws on incoming, internal and outgoing corruption – is to identify and respond to improper behaviour by competitors so that they are able to participate on equal terms. Effective controls against these three evils are discussed in Chapters 21–7 and 33.

Misconceptions

BACKGROUND

Transparency International, the OECD, the United Nations, the World Bank, academics and research and charitable bodies have framed corruption in a way that is not supported by reality. Much like the Intergovernmental Panel for Climate Change (IPCC), which has inflamed an obsession with global warming, the most vocal organisations in the anti-corruption field are similarly driven by a noble cause based on a misunderstanding of the problems concerned.

This is not to allege that work of such bodies does not have value. The problem is that the academic – rather sterile, politically biased and formalised approach – taken towards what is a random, irregular and complex relational crime of corruption – involving an equality of evils by coercer and extorter – has resulted in simplified solutions that are worthless in the real world. The academic slant is that corruption is a white-collar crime, or Western, but this again is rarely true. Corruption is indigenous, often linked to organised crime, violence, murder, narcotics-smuggling, people-trafficking and money-laundering. The lives of people who seriously challenge it are at risk.

Another problem with the research and legislation based upon it is the displacement from dealing with gross corruption to an obsession with trivia such as whether it is permissible for a UK company to entertain a client at a lap dancing club, give away mouse mats at Christmas or submit to making small facilitation payments to foreign public officials (FPOs) who extort them. The belief, apparently, is that by prioritising minor transgressions in developed countries, kleptocracy and gross corruption in less developed nations will be eradicated. If this is not the height of naivety, nothing is.

Distorted Focus

An excellent report by The Corner House entitled 'Exporting Corruption: Privatisation, Multinationals and Bribery, stated:

'Most commentators on corruption [...] dwell on developing countries, not on industrialised ones. Most scrutinise politically lax cultures in the South, not the North. Most call attention to the petty corruption of low-paid civil servants, not to grand corruption [...]. Most focus on symptoms such as missing resources, not causes such as deregulation of state enterprises. Most talk about bribe-takers not bribe-givers'. (Briefing Paper 19, 30 June 2000)

Corner House is absolutely right, but the distortions are unlikely to be by accident and are almost entirely framed as a noble cause.

THE SCALE OF CORRUPTION AND BRIBERY

The World Bank speculates that more than US$1 trillion in bribes is paid annually; this amounts to around 5 per cent of the world's Gross National Product (GNP) and is likely to be an underestimate of at least 100 per cent, especially when the impact of other forms of related skulduggery is taken into account.

Dwindling Turnover

If any company with more than 1,000 employees loses less than 10 per cent of turnover through corruption it would be a miracle.

No one has produced an accurate measurement of corruption, nor is such a metric possible. Surveys come and go, bandying about and dissecting different figures and trends that occasionally make interesting reading but have no underlying factual base.

Corruption's effect is not purely financial: it comes well behind civil and religious wars, kleptocracy and overpopulation in driving citizens into starvation and premature deaths. It eats into foreign aid, with funds being plundered in such disasters as New Orleans, Haiti, Thailand and, no doubt, more recently in Japan and Ethiopia. Aid and charity organisations repeatedly complain that they have to bribe officials – whose citizens they are trying to help – to get visas and work permits.

Helping Others Help Themselves

One charity organisation donated wheelchairs to Liberia to help war invalids. The chairs turned up in Monrovian streets modified into ice cream carts and mobile shops. Vendors who had nothing wrong with their legs were using the chairs, while amputees dragged themselves on their hands and knees through the filthy streets. Local government officials had distributed the wheelchairs among their own kith and kin who in turn had rented them out to small-time entrepreneurs.

If politicians and regulators were simply to speak to charity workers they would find that the populist view that corruption is driven entirely by businesses in developed countries is badly mistaken: corruption is more often the result of extortion. The academic view is that companies volunteer bribes to get business, but the truth is that advantages are extorted to avoid a company being disadvantaged. As we shall see later this involves quite different motivations and risk dynamics.

PERCEPTIONS OF CORRUPTION

Country league tables

Many organisations produce indices or league tables supposedly classifying countries as the most or least corrupt. Most are a collection of other surveys, often sharing or mixing sources. The rankings across the various reports are not consistent and deviate from the real-world enforcement actions taken by the US Department of Justice, the Securities and Exchange Commission (SEC), the SFO and other agencies.

The UK Does Lead the Way

For example, of the 171 corrupt companies banned, at one time, from business by the World Bank 38 were from the UK, revealing it to be far worse than countries such as Bangladesh, Indonesia, China and Russia!

The league tables purport to measure the immeasurable.

TRANSPARENCY INTERNATIONAL AND THE CORRUPTION PERCEPTIONS INDEX

TI's Corruption Perceptions Index (CPI) leads the way in the league table section of the 'Cottage Industry' (see Foreword) and allocates scores for 182[6] countries, ranging from 10 for near sainthood to 0 for hideousness, but:

---

6   In the 2011 Index.

- Countries are not corrupt: people are but only in some contexts;
- It is cockeyed and unfair[7] to brand entire nations as corrupt;
- The rankings discourage foreign investment in countries perceived to be corrupt, thereby opening the doors to international and indigenous competitors who don't give a hoot about anti-bribery legislation or depriving poor citizens;
- The CPI was only intended to raise awareness of the risks of corruption; or, more particularly, bribery of FPOs.
- Many companies now rely on the CPI to determine how controls can be applied 'proportionately'. This is bunkum for two reasons. First: most controls cannot be applied proportionately: they are either on or off. Even if proportionality were possible, the cost of maintaining different systems – for example, levels of due diligence – would far outweigh any supposed cost savings. Second, how and by whom should the dividing line be drawn between countries perceived to be at different risk levels?

An excellent report on the insurance industry by the Financial Services Authority (FSA) stated:

Good Sense from the FSA

'Some firms had very unsophisticated methods of using the CPI index to assess country risk. One simply regarded the top 60 countries as low risk, countries 61 to 120 as medium risk and those placed lower than 121 as high risk. The firms did not consider the score attached to each country. Only 2 out of the 17 firms inspected demonstrated risk assessment processes which took account of factors other than country risk'.

There are many other examples where the CPI has led to problems:

HSBC and Mexico

In the more recent scandal involving the Hong Kong and Shanghai Bank (HSBC) for alleged money-laundering offences, the US Senate Subcommittee on Investigations under Senator Carl Levin[8] was scathing about the bank's country risk classification of Mexico – and thus all its Mexican customers – in a lower risk band. This resulted in around $7 billion laundered for drugs barons and other skulduggers not being effectively monitored and, according to the Senate report, put the USA at risk.

---

7   And arguably racist.

8   See 'US Vulnerabilities to Money Laundering, Drugs and Terrorist Financing: HSBC Case History', U.S. Senate Permanent Subcommittee on Investigations, 17 July 2012. Available at: http://www.levin.senate.gov/newsroom/speeches/speech/levin-opening-statement-us-vulnerabilities-to-money-laundering-drugs-and-terrorist-financing-hsbc-case-history (accessed 13 November 2012).

Respected members of the 'Cottage Industry' seem unclear over the way the CPI should be interpreted.

The SFO Boardroom Guide on Serious Economic Crime

This influential report – published in September 2011 by the Serious Fraud Office and supported by Transparency International – emphasises the importance of proportionate controls based upon the CPI:

- TI[9] recommended that – based on positions on the Index – countries ranking between 1 and 39 could be regarded as 'low risk'; those positioned between 40 and 133 as 'medium risk' and the remainder as 'high risk'.
- In the same report PriceWaterhouseCoopers (PWC) recommended[10] that countries should be classified based on their score. It recommended that those with 6 or more points should be classified as high risk and between 3 and 6 as medium risk. PWC seems to have misdirected itself because the higher the score on the Index, the LESS corrupt a country is perceived to be.[11]

It may appear that these differences are unimportant but – even after correcting the PWC error – they are extremely significant and could result in companies badly misclassifying risks as summarised on Table 10.1 overleaf.[12]

OTHER CONFLICTING PERCEPTIONS

At the last count there were at least eight *different* indices suggesting *different* levels of international corruption. An interesting report-by Global Financial Integrity, entitled 'Illicit Financial Flows from Developing Countries: 2001 to 2010' list countries with the most missing money and slush funds. It is significantly different from the CPI and places the People's Republic of China as the worst, followed by Mexico and Malaysia. If HSBC (see page 230) had seen this report would it still have categorised all of its Mexican customers as low risk?

---

9   Based on the CPI for 2010.

10   See Serious Fraud Office, *Serious Economic Crime: A boardroom guide to prevention and compliance* (White Page Ltd., 2011), page 265, Table 2.

11   PWC did not respond to our suggestion that it might like to correct the figures in what is supposed to be an authoritative report backed by the SFO. It is also amazing that none of the other contributors noticed the error. Does this show the seriousness with which the 'Cottage Industry' treats perceptions?

12   Based on the 2011 CPI.

Table 10.1 Transparency International's Corruption Perceptions Index

Perceived Country Risk	Transparency International – Ranks on position does not mention scores		PriceWaterHouseCoopers – Ranks on scores does not mention position	
	Position	Score	Score	Position
High Risk	133–182	1 to 2.4	1 to 2.9	101–182
Medium Risk	40–133	5.6[13] to 2.5	3 to 6	33–100
Low Risk	1–39	5.6 to 10	6.1 to 10	1–32

Table 10.1 shows that according to TI's interpretation, Malta (with a score of 5.6) would be low risk and Cape Verde with a score of 5.5, would be classed as medium risk. This means that Malta is perceived to be 1.8181818181 per cent less corrupt than Cape Verde and would therefore justify more proportionate and, of course, relaxed controls.[14]

The CPI implies far more accuracy than all other perceptions such as that every Frenchman is a brilliant cook (but a poor investigator), every Italian a passionate lover and every Scot a miserable caber tosser. Applying the Index's elaborate statistical system to this we could report that: Frenchmen are 1.818181818 per cent better cooks than Italians and Scots 0.00000001 per cent more miserable than Cornishmen. Such levels of accuracy based on perceptions are impossible.

Pickled Fish

It may simply be coincidence that most countries that regularly top the CPI are in the northern hemisphere, have small populations of healthy, fair-haired, beautiful women and well-favoured men, who spend most of their time in the dark eating buckets of pickled fish. The same countries come out on top of virtually every perception index from happiness, sexual power through to freedom and political stability. Is it that they are consistently exceptional or that they just tell better lies?

The enforcement actions, taken worldwide (see the excellent reports in Trace International's Compendium (see pages 490 and 845)) confirm the differences between reality and perceptions of corruption. Over the past 12 years countries perceived to be the most corrupt have not improved one iota:[15] they are as corrupt now, if not worse, than they ever were. But even this is difficult to assess because TI's source of perceptions has not remained constant.

---

13   Malta and Puerto Rico both score 5.6. But Malta is at 139 and therefore low risk and Puerto Rico at 140 and thus medium risk.

14   PS Has anyone ever seen the Vatican on any list?

15   Even if it were possible to make such measurements.

Probably the most important point about the CPI is this. Repeatedly denigrating countries as being the most corrupt becomes a self-fulfilling prophecy. It sets a level of expectation that Bribes'R'Us – for both citizens and business partners – thereby attracting skulduggers who cannot compete in fair markets while deterring honest investors. It also demoralises honest citizens.

The bottom line is that perceived country corruption is one of the factors that should be considered in risk assessment, but it is by no means determinative. Context is much more important and if country divisions have to be made they should be:

a) High Risk (cash in suitcases and hookers)
b) High Risk (subtle methods and hookers).

It is unlikely that this idea will be adopted anytime soon.

COMPARISON OF CORRUPTION

Corruption in developed countries – such as the UK – is as damaging for honest citizens and companies as it is for those perceived to be the most corrupt. True, the impact may not be so obviously one of life, death or starvation,[16] but it is still debilitating.

Table 10.2 Some Differences in Corruption in Developed and Less Developed Countries

The Nature and Effects of Corruption	
Less Developed Countries	**Mature, Sophisticated and Developed Countries**
The tone from the top is one of kleptocracy driven by sectorial, religious or tribal conflict and greed	The tone from the top is primarily driven by the intention of political leaders to gain and retain power
'Animal Farm' mentality by political and commercial leaders who put themselves above the law	
Bribes paid primarily in cash or its equivalent	Corruption is more subtle, involving reciprocation, nepotism, trading in influence and revolving doors
Backed by violence	Backed by political power, social and commercial exclusion
Blatantly corrupt decisions	Corrupt decision justified by 'dodgy dossiers', distorted academic and other research resulting in blame avoidance
Contrived bureaucracy	Actual bureaucracy (see the UK's 3,000 new laws and red tape)
Ineffective law enforcement and judiciary	Selective law enforcement driven by distorting key performance indicators with cost dominating justice
Absence of a deterrent to fraud and corruption because of inefficiency and dishonesty	Absence of a deterrent to fraud and bribery because of cost-cutting, and noble cause laws prioritising the rights of criminals over their victims

16   Which, although blamed by altruists on corruption, results from kleptocracy, civil and religious conflict and overpopulation.

The Nature and Effects of Corruption	
Less Developed Countries	**Mature, Sophisticated and Developed Countries**
Results in poverty and deprivation	Results in increased costs, reduced public services, such as health, policing, social benefits
15% cost to GNP	10% to GNP
Marginalisation of honesty, resulting in commercial and social disadvantages	

Table 10.2 suggests three main conclusions. The first is the importance of context and decision-centricity in assessing risks (see Chapters 14–17). The second is the fact that political leaders and their acolytes put themselves in a super-class above the law. This is why the failure to tackle corruption in the Bribery Act is so unacceptable. The third is that the poorest in society suffer the most.

SUPPLY- AND DEMAND-SIDE COUNTRIES

TI's Corruption Perceptions Index, as well as much of the information provided by the OECD and regulatory agencies, is based on the peculiar notion that corruption is formalised in two sides. The theory is that the supply side consists predominantly of rapacious, Western corporates that entice poor, gullible but honest oinks in developing or demand-side countries into skulduggery. This is repudiated by honest managers who know that bribes are routinely extorted by greedy and unregulated FPOs and commercial employees – quite often backed by organised crime – and that if they do not submit they have no chance of obtaining business or of even getting routine tasks performed. They may also be killed.

Besides that in LDCs, overpopulation, internal corruption, kleptocracy and other indigenous plundering is far more damaging than coercion by supply-side companies:

A 2012 report by the Population Reference Bureau illustrates the dangers to developing countries of overpopulation. For example, in 2012 Spain and Tanzania each had a population of around 48 million. By 2050, Tanzania's head count is forecast to rise to 138 million, while Spain's is expected to remain stable.

Figure 10.1 overleaf, which is based on an amalgam of official and NGO reports indicates that the main problems for developing countries are overpopulation, kleptocracy, civil wars, oppressive taxation, terrorism and the plundering of foreign aid. It also suggests that domestic – or entirely internal – corruption is a more significant problem than bribery by foreign companies.

Even accepting that there may be significant errors in the sectorial division in the figure, the lesson is clear. It that is unless the international political and regulatory community gets away from the false notions of supply and demand side countries and of active and passive bribery – and insist that all countries deal with fraud and corruption problems – meaningful progress will be impossible. At present such co-ordinated international political will does not exist. The bad guys need to do nothing, except to trouser lots of foreign aid. After all, it's 'business led' innit?

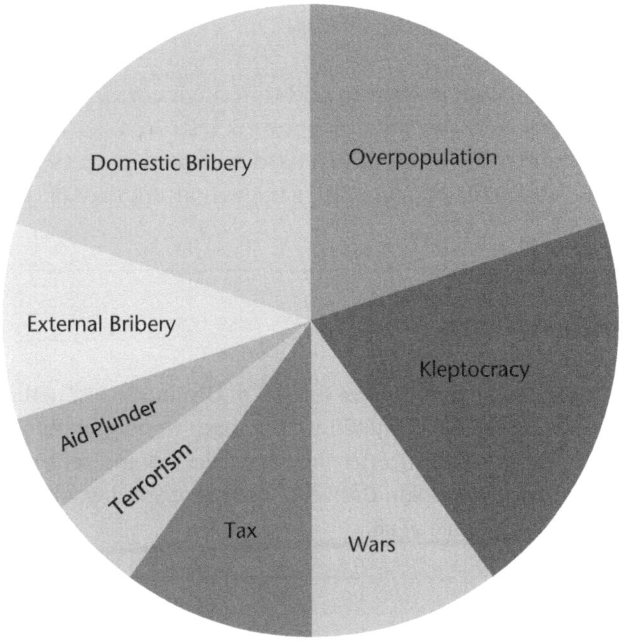

Figure 10.1 Putting Supply-side Bribery In Context

Figure 10.1 indicates that bribery is a small part of a much greater problem in LDCs.

CORRUPTION AND RESTRICTED GROWTH

Another argument for prioritising control over supply-side companies is that corruption restricts development and market growth in LDCs. Again the evidence is counterfactual. China, India, Indonesia and Brazil, which are unquestionably among the most corrupt countries on the planet, have far outstripped their international competitors in virtually every metric possible. On the other hand countries that are perceived to be equally corrupt, such as Zimbabwe and Angola, have struggled. The difference between success and failure appears to be a matter of whether corruption is centralised or decentralised, formalised or random and whether or not the country has sufficient natural resources to absorb the impacts.

PUBLIC AND PRIVATE SECTOR CORRUPTION

The official approach usually makes an artificial distinction between public and private sector corruption which is, of course, consistent with the fixation on punishing the corporate bribe payer, while leaving the extorter untouched. In reality the worst skulduggery takes place at the interfaces between private and public sectors and it is usually initiated by extorters in official positions (see page 296).

THE MYTH OF VICTIMLESS CORRUPTION

A few years ago a distinguished academic said that most corruption was victimless in the sense that the bribe giver and the bribe payer took part in a zero sum game where both were satisfied. Fortunately the academic retired to breed parrots and parakeets so her ideas are seldom repeated. The example she gave was along the following lines:

Referral Commissions

Police officers who attend car crashes have the job of clearing roads, getting rid of the dead bodies, collecting missing limbs and getting traffic back to normal. As part of this process they have to contact local garages to get the cars collected and repaired. So what if they happen to get a backhander for doing this very unpleasant job. I would not want to do it. It is a victimless crime: if it is a crime at all.

The victims in this case included the garages that refused (or were not given the chance) to pay bribes and therefore lost business, the insurance companies who effectively had to cover the cost of bribes before passing them on in increased premiums to consumers and the people involved in accidents, who were plagued with contingency fee lawyers offering injury compensation.

The fact is that every case of corruption has victims; there is no such thing as a victimless crime.

The Nanny State and Over-regulation

Lord Judge, the Lord Chief Justice for England and Wales,[17] joined in the criticism of the last Labour government's 'frenzied law making', which between 1997 and 2010 introduced 3,500, mostly new, criminal offences. This was more than double the rate of any previous administration.

The laws, besides the Bribery Act, criminalised:

- Selling grey squirrels, ruddy ducks or Japanese knotweed without permission;
- Importing Polish potatoes;
- Wilfully pretending to be a barrister;[18]
- Attaching an ear tag to an animal when it has previously been used to identify another animal;
- Using non-approved techniques for weighing herring and mackerel;
- Holding another person in slavery or servitude;
- Allowing an unlicensed concert in a church hall;

---

17   But obviously not Scotland because he wears pants

18   These would be great cases to listen to.

- Disturbing a pack of eggs without permission;
- Impersonating a traffic warden;
- Offering to provide air traffic control services without a licence;
- Entering the hull of the Titanic without permission.

Finally, the mother of all crimes is that of causing a nuclear explosion! Unsurprisingly, many of these offences involve heavy financial penalties, thus helping politicians' insatiable need for more money rather than the ethical satisfaction of saving ruddy ducks, grey squirrels or Polish potatoes.

The political lead on ridiculous law-making was quickly followed by Luvvies who;

- Prohibited golf clubs from putting flags on putting greens because they were a safety hazard. Another public course filled in the holes on practice greens for the same reason;[19]
- Stopped members of a Suffolk bowls club from giving their groundskeeper a monetary gift at Christmas, alleging that it would contravene the Bribery Act;
- Banned Father Christmas from wearing a beard because it was a fire hazard.

These pettifogging rules, usually dreamed up by jobsworths, are typical of regulatory creep, also known as 'expansive interpretation', which means that the scope of even marginally sensible laws gets extended on iteration. In the case of corruption legislation, the expansive interpretation has been kicked off by the regulatory agencies themselves and has created a virtual industry for policy and procedure-writing, with increasing levels of draconianism.

Timorous Advice

One firm of chartered accountants produced a list of items that could be given away as Christmas presents and suggested that anything more than a cheap bottle of wine would lead to incarceration. It is little wonder, with advice such as this, that companies are immobilised.

A survey by The Economist Intelligence Unit into strategies for regulatory risk reported that:

- 36 per cent of executives said regulation stifled innovation;
- Only 17 per cent of companies said they were very confident over their compliance with regulations in the overseas markets;
- 57 per cent said that their perception of a country's regulatory burden had an important or very important impact on the decisions to invest compared to 4 per cent that believed it was of no importance;

---

19 It took Mr Comer three weeks to discover that the reason he could not hole out was because the holes had gone (Kenneth).

- 33 per cent of companies said they had been deterred from investing in a new market because of regulatory restrictions.

The report concluded that executives were keenly aware that a breach of regulations could result in severe consequences that stretch far beyond any direct penalty involved and that regulatory excesses made their firms risk-averse and uncompetitive.

Roy Snell, Chief Executive of the Society of Corporate Compliance and Ethics, wrote a very interesting chapter for the SFO's *Serious Economic Crime: A boardroom guide to prevention and compliance*.[20] He said:

> Some of us are tired of the bureaucracy because it is onerous, expensive, complicated, vague and generally very frustrating. But if we want to stop the onslaught of regulations we do have to prevent, find and fix our own problems. We have to take away society's reasons for adding more rules. (Chapter 9, page 77).

He correctly suggested that proactive compliance and ethics programmes (rather than more rules and regulations) are the future, and concluded that to 'Deny and defend is passé'. Mr Snell did not comment on the fact that bureaucratic laws and regulations tend not to get retired.

The book, *The Strange Laws of Old England* by Nigel Cawthorne[21] lists the following unrepealed offences:

- Dying or wearing a suit of armour in the House of Commons;
- Eating mince pies on Christmas Day;
- The possibility of being charged with treason for placing a postage stamp bearing a British monarch's image upside down;
- Stealing the head of a dead whale found on the British coast.

Although the accuracy of some of Mr Cawthorne's research has been challenged,[22] there is little doubt that once laws are passed and rules made they are likely to stick forever and in the compliance area to remain and expand, no matter how effective a company's internal procedures are.

Ruling the Innocent

Ayn Rand[23] commented: 'There is no way to rule innocent men. The only power government has is the power to crack down on criminals. When there aren't enough criminals, one makes them. One declares so many things to be a crime that it becomes impossible for men to live without breaking laws'.

---

20   See Note 10 above.

21   (Portrait/Piatkus Books, 2004).

22   Possibly by Kenneth Clarke, whose extended naps in the House of Commons are little different from death.

23   Ms Rand was a Russian–American philosopher, novelist, screenwriter and playwright. She rejected ethical altruism and advocated reason as the only means of acquiring knowledge.

So the bottom line is that UK companies should not expect any relaxation of red tape, anytime soon.

Not a Slippery Slope

Another academic–regulatory misconception is that small facilitation payments (which are in truth facilitation extortions) are at the top of a slippery slope and that by criminalising them despots, kleptocrats, politicians and seriously bent businessmen will reform. This is ridiculous. Regulators should realise that the psychology involved in extorting and submitting to facilitation payments is entirely distinct from gross corruption. They operate at entirely different levels and for different reasons.

On the contrary, suddenly criminalising minor technical infringements, such as facilitation or hospitality payments, especially in contexts where they have been traditionally extorted, may lead those involved into believing they have nothing further to lose by far more serious misbehaviour. Once a line has been overstepped, the floodgates open. Also, passing laws when there is no intention to enforce them clears the way for regulatory partiality and corruption.

Another fallacy – regarding the draconian treatment of facilitation and hospitality payments – is that corruption spirals upwards with no limit. According to this idea, the company prepared to pay the largest bribes always wins. This is not so, as believers in efficient markets will affirm. Corruption reaches a natural ceiling as soon as its benefits become economically unviable. And there is the clearest evidence that the motivational factors that drive corruption to avoid a loss are quite different from those involved in seeking gains (see page 291).

The Tone from the Top

A central feature in TI's and other control guidelines is that organisations are urged to set the tone from the top through such things as policies, procedures, training, memos, supervision, example and leadership. The expectation is that an ethical culture will cascade down from the CEO through the management line, like magic fairy dust, alighting on the heads of subordinates, immediately converting them to near sainthood. There are at least eight serious problems with this.

The first problem is the assumption that at the very top of organisations people are honest and packed full of ethical DNA. In reality, to get to the top of many organisations (and especially politics) a high degree of ruthlessness and an unerring ability to dissemble the truth are necessary. The chairman of a large organisation commented:

> Don't talk to me about ethics. I got where I am today by clambering over the dead bodies of my colleagues. If I thought I could avoid losing $100 by poisoning my Granny and getting away with it, I would give it careful consideration. It's a very cutthroat world out there and my priority is not f****** compliance but competing with the Chinese that don't give a hoot about the law.

The conclusion from this – even though the Chairman may have been jesting – is that the tone from the very top might not be exactly what altruists would like to think it is.

The BAE Chairman's Letter

On 16 November 2000 the then Chairman of British Aerospace wrote to the US Secretary of Defense stating that:

'I am pleased to reaffirm BAE Systems Plc's commitment to adhering to the highest ethical standards in the conduct of its business throughout the world […]. I commit that the company and its affiliate will not knowingly offer, pay, promise to pay etc. […] directly or indirectly […] anything of value to obtain or retain business'.

This statement was manifestly untrue and the subsequent Sentencing Memorandum, in suggesting a penalty of $400 million for what must be ranked as one of the most expensive letters ever written, stated:

- 'corporate leadership knowingly and wilfully failed to adopt any anti-corruption compliance system after making representations to the US government that such mechanisms would be or had been created,
- made undisclosed payments (for corrupt purposes in Saudi Arabia etc.) which were tolerated or condoned up to the highest corporate levels'.

And corporate leadership created the structures for the payment of undisclosed commissions in order to frustrate investigations and avoid identification of those payments through market advisers.

It is also very difficult to reconcile the attitude of some business leaders who use sophisticated offshore tax avoidance schemes for themselves while penny-pinching with junior employees, customers and suppliers.

There is no doubt that relying on the tone from the top appears to be a slick solution, but it has little value or resilience in practice, although oft repeated by Luvvies as a soundbite. Far more important, as discussed later, are: the culture in the discreet contexts in which decisions may be corrupted, peer group pressure, and social proof.

The second point is that the tone from the top is not determined within the organisation but to a large degree is provoked by external factors such as political leadership, regulatory interference, competition, media pressure, employment and laws, as well as a raft of factors which combine together to influence distinct contexts in which commercial corruption and fraud take place. The notion that companies operate inside an ethical vacuum is naïve.

The third point is that culture is determined more by the expectation of shareholders, analysts, bankers and key performance drivers than ever it is by the genetic make-up of top executives. The relentless pressure to achieve short-term results, and the fear that any admission of even minor mistakes will be inflamed in the media and in any other way possible, can negatively influence even the most honest executive.

The fourth point is that the ethical performance of middle- and lower-level employees is often higher than – or certainly equal to – those at the top. It is notable, even in today's cynical world, how often ordinary people do the right thing. The trouble is that they are seldom consulted or empowered. Over-regulation leads to companies being unwilling to delegate authority but to insist that even the most routine decisions are approved at the highest levels. Decisions may be driven entirely by the fear of incurring a personal liability rather than what is right on principle. This disenfranchises lower levels, diverts the attention of directors towards trivia, constipates the organisation and destroys trust and entrepreneurship.

The fifth point is that the tone radiating from many top teams is far from cohesive, with disagreeing factions pulling and pushing to outmanoeuvre each other. In fact the condition at the top is often more of turmoil or tension than tone, with mixed signals being passed down the line.

The Tone(Y) From the Top

The Blair and Brown Cabinets are perfect examples of this, with senior factions pulling in every conceivable direction, causing confusion and lack of cohesion at levels below.

The sixth point is that regulations and guidelines are separately issued by the agencies responsible for enforcing them and in the belief that the world revolves around them. Guidelines flow down to companies in fragmented silos and result in multiple and duplicated policies or procedures when they should be integrated.

Integrated Integrity

A company's policy on business ethics should consolidate in one document to include such things as relationships with customers and suppliers, fair accounting, standards of honesty, political contributions, conflict of interest, health and safety, and anticorruption controls. Separate policy documents for each subset – although they mirror the silos on which they were based – lead to duplication and ambiguity and are counter-productive. In fact one of the clearest indications of paper policies is that they are precisely segregated into the regulatory silos.

The seventh point is that policies that are supposed to set the tone are usually not written by – or even discussed in detail among – top managers. They are initiated and then drafted by lower-level compliance, legal, audit or security specialists who cut and paste the work of others to cover every eventuality and often more. Policies are prepared that go far beyond the law, each iteration outdoing the other and, being unworkable, legalistic and turgid, are rejected or ignored. In fact, cosmetic policies and procedures are counter-productive and rather than support an ethical culture, they destroy it.

The eighth point is that tone from the top is promoted as primarily necessary to achieve compliance, but in fact – to the extent that it is relevant at all – is much more important than that. It should define the ethos of the organisation, upbeat and imaginatively. It should inspire integrity and make it clear that management asserts the right to manage, to responsibly delegate authority, to empower employees and others, to make profits, create wealth, to succeed, to respect employees, customers and suppliers and to be recognised as an exemplary corporate citizen. There is no reason why companies should not be happy, creative places: instead they are suffocated by red tape.

Finally, the tone from the top is not a one-way channel. These days it is even more imperative – as demonstrated by the Bob Diamond and Barclays LIBOR problem – that senior managers are aware of significant developments that take place below them, especially if they relate to compliance. Yet experience shows that bad news does not travel upwards and top managers may be kept deliberately in the dark. For this reason, companies should insist upon letters of representation and make sure that continuous monitoring processes are in place. These are discussed on pages 18–20 and 21–6. Managers should do everything possible to make their organisations enjoyable and satisfying places in which to work.

Chapters 21 and 22, which deal with baseline controls, support the need to maintain a culture of integrity, but takes a radical approach to it, driven on a cellular 'tipping point' basis rather than being simply top-down.

The Inadequacy of Due Diligence

Due diligence on agents, other intermediaries and counterparties is again recommended by all regulatory agencies as a basic control against corruption. But all due diligence does is give a one-time historical black and white snapshot, essentially from public sources, that the subject has no record as a bad apple. It does not mean he or she is not rotten to the core: only that he has not been exposed in the contexts in which he has previously worked. Besides that, a person's record of misbehaviour is determined more by a victim's willingness to prosecute or to expose chicanery than it is by the dispositional honesty of the individuals concerned (see page 651).

Limitations of Public Records

Even the most disgraceful crook may escape with an unblemished record if his victim chooses to keep quiet or is blackmailed into silence. This happens a lot.

Suppressed Information

The fact that the majority of extorters involved in cases in which companies have been sanctioned over the past ten years have escaped unpunished is clearly unacceptable and confirms the emphasis of enforcement in only the private sector. It is even worse when extorters are not 'named and shamed' and therefore pass through even the most stringent due diligence enquiries.

Not one of the guidelines specifies what derogatory information, such as red flags, would debar a job candidate or intermediary from consideration. The decision to appoint a candidate or not is left until after due diligence checks have been made and then taken on a subjective basis with a finger held high in the air to test wind direction: the so-called 'smell test'. This results in inconsistency and sometimes unfairness. Companies should specify as a standard what is acceptable and what is not in agreed and auditable decision matrices (see page 568).

Another problem is with red flags, because each one – whether valuable–questionable– anecdotal or frivolous – is given the same weight. Thus, if even one red flag is ignored it leaves the door open for regulators to claim that procedures were not adequate. For this reason, page 692 recommends that any relevant red flags should be incorporated in an integrated decision matrix and weighted so that a consolidated, supportable and auditable evaluation is produced.[24]

Official guidance also stresses the importance of carrying out proportionate due diligence on the appointment and management of intermediaries. Although this is a control recommended in page 766 et seq, it is far from being the end of the story when a decision-centric approach is used. The greatest risks of corruption do not centre on the appointment of the intermediary but on decisions that are later agreed between it and end parties: such as customers or suppliers. Due diligence should extend to end party decisions and whether they might involve improper performance.

The Altruism of Whistle-blowers

The popular view that whistle-blowers are agreeable people who report for altruistic reasons is a fallacy. In fact the most effective relators[25] were, at some point, active colluders and report only because it suits their immediate purpose to do so.

The strongest motivation, for previously active colluders, is financial reward, the possibility of becoming a cooperating witness or of being granted absolution for their own crimes. In other cases, allegations only surface when the whistle-blower claims for unfair dismissal, discrimination or becomes a party to litigation against the company.

---

24 This approach means that one red flag cannot be isolated as a means of proving that procedures were inadequate and also fully justify decisions made.

25 The title 'whistle-blower' has negative connotations and is little different from 'grass', 'stool pigeon' or 'snitch'.

244 Bribery and Corruption

Altruistic Whistle-blowers

Harry Markopolos has been eulogised for blowing the whistle on Bernard Madoff. However, if the report by the US Congressional Committees is read carefully – and especially the appendices – a different picture emerges. Mr Markopolos apparently derived most of his income from exposing overcharges by suppliers to the US government under the Fair Claims Act, from which he was able to claim a percentage reward. When it was clear that the SEC would not pay him a reward in the Madoff case, Mr Markopolos's interest waned. It was not until the case imploded of its own accord that he came forward publicly and claimed credit. He is a good man, but whistle-blows for money.

Until established otherwise, whistle-blowers should always be treated with extreme caution (see Chapter 2). The most productive are seldom altruists.

Why Competitors do not Report Corruption

The majority of cases handled by American and British regulators were self-disclosed and there is little evidence to suggest that even businesses that are seriously disadvantaged by competitive corruption or malpractice are prepared to complain. The possible reasons for this include that they were not aware of the facts or do not care or, more likely, that they do not want to get involved in what could become a litigious battle or have no confidence that law enforcement agencies will take any action. The position might change as a result of the Dodd–Frank Act (see pages 215 and 665), but don't hold your breath.

The Importance of 'Dodgy Dossiers'

The term 'dodgy dossiers' is an accepted euphemism for blatant lying.[26] In the corruption field 'dodgy dossiers' are increasingly important props used to support or explain corrupt political and commercial decisions.

The deceptive input typically involves:

- Fraudulent or misleading research or academic reports;
- Corrupt media reporting;
- False statistics and key performance outputs;
- False or inaccurate accounting and financial analyses and especially spreadsheets.

The real problem is that false reports are often the direct cause of improper performance by innocent or gullible decision-makers.

---

26   And often framed as something to be admired or not serious.

The credibility of false reports may be enhanced by so-called Peer Group[27] reviews and other superficially independent support, but it is very rare for those responsible to be held to account.[28]

'Dodgy Dossiers'

An Analyst working for a major oil company was promised a bribe by a small independent operator if he would help him negotiate a reduced price for its disinvestment of three service stations in a popular holiday resort. The Analyst prepared detailed – but grossly understated – spreadsheets summarising the stations' performance and discounted rates of return going forward. The oil company's managers disinvested for less than 50 per cent of the proper price. The Analyst's claim that he had made a genuine mistake was disproven when he was found to have bought a £50,000 Porsche from his windfall.

Dodgy dossiers can be very difficult to identify and when they do come to light there is nearly always a plausible excuse.

Virgin on the Ridiculous

In October 2012 the £5.5 billion franchise to run the West Coast rail line came up for review and a fresh round of competitive bidding. Virgin Rail, which had run the contract for 15 years (not without criticism, it should be said), lost out to First Group PLC but complained that critical figures in a spread sheet used to calculate forward passenger and inflation rates were wrong and that the tender should be rebid.

Justine Greening, the then Minister of Transport, retained her ex-employer PWC to look into the figures and concluded that Sir Richard's concerns were not valid. His application for a judicial review coincided with Ms Greening's transfer and the appointment of a more amenable successor. His advisers discovered that the spread sheet was riddled with 'deeply regrettable and completely unacceptable mistakes' that would have made the winning bid untenable. Coincidentally, the incorrect figures also reduced First Group's £600 million up-front payment guarantee by £400 million. What a nice mistake to make!

Three officials were suspended but at the time of writing the investigation has not been concluded. The words 'fraud and corruption' have not appeared anywhere on the radar. The 'mistake' was reviewed by the European Spread sheet Risk Special-Interest Group one of whose members commented 'when there is a financial incentive to put in assumptions that

---

27   Such as are used by the global warming community.

28   Even though such cases breach the Fraud Act.

may get past the scrutiny of those with less insight than the proposers, bad data sometimes does get in'. Too true, old bean. So was it a dodgy dossier?

11 *Sectoral Corruption*

Regulatory Focus

The official guidelines on corruption highlight some or all of the following sectors as being the most corrupt:

- Armaments
- Aviation
- Banking and Financial Services
- Carbon World
- Chemicals
- Commodities
- Computer software
- Construction
- Defence and military
- Emerging markets
- Energy
- Extractive industries
- Financial products
- Insurance
- Logistics
- Maintenance and service
- Pharmaceuticals
- Property development
- Retail
- Telecoms

To an extent this is good advice, but why do the guidelines completely avoid political and official corruption, foreign aid and other aspects in which the most powerful have their noses in the trough? And why is it that information technology (IT) is not on the list?

Information Technology is Far from Safe

A chapter by PriceWaterhouseCoopers (PWC) on due diligence[1] in the Serious Fraud Office (SFO)'s publication, *Serious Economic Crime – A Boardroom Guide to Prevention Compliance,*

---

1   White Page Ltd., 2011, Chapter 35.

suggests that IT falls into a low-risk band. But what about PWC's own role – as auditors – in the $1 billion collapse of Satyam Computer Services: described as 'India's Enron'. Among other things, Satyam was banned for eight years from World Bank business for bribing one of its senior managers with preference shares and other goodies.[2]

The chapter also fails to mention other IT cases involving Department of Justice action against Accenture, CISCO, Sun, Hewlett-Packard, EMC and CSC for paying referral fees to systems integrators contrary to government regulations.

Although most of the IT companies denied misbehaviour, they all agreed to substantial financial settlements. A representative of Hewlett-Packard, which coughed up $55 million, stated that settlement was 'in the best interests of our stakeholders to resolve the matter'.

An interesting point from the above is whether or not companies – when conducting their due diligence – should debar and disqualify these major corporations because of their 'red flags'.[3]

Corruption in the UK

In December 2010 Transparency International (TI) published yet another survey: this time revealing what citizens believed were the most corrupt organisations or activities in the UK. The results were as follows:

Area or Sector	Most corrupt
• Political parties	65.5 per cent
• Professional sport	56.9 per cent
• Parliament	55.7 per cent
• Local government	47.4 per cent
• Business and private sector	43.8 per cent
• Public official civil servants	41.3 per cent
• Immigration Services	40.8 per cent
• Media	39.8 per cent
• Prison services	28.2 per cent
• Religious bodies	28.1 per cent
• Police	28.1 per cent
• Non-governmental organizations	19.5 per cent
• Judiciary	19.3 per cent
• National health service	14.4 per cent
• Ministry of Justice	13.3 per cent
• Educational system	10.8 per cent

---

2   However, the company is not on the Bank's list of banned businesses.

3   The fairly obvious answer is that they shouldn't. This confirms that not all 'red flags' are equal and that it is permissible to ignore some.

If the survey[4] has any validity at all, it confirms that an appalling tone from the top is set by political leaders, but we accept it as the norm.

Political Corruption

The tone from the top starts with political corruption and with cases such as cash for questions, cash for honours, the first Bernie Ecclestone – tobacco advertising – affair, the fall and rise of Lord Mandelson, David Blunkett et al. and the release of the Lockerbie bomber, to name just a few. The ultimate motivation is the unquenchable hunger to seize and retain political power.

Many corrupt political decisions are justified or supported by 'dodgy dossiers',[5] whose authors – although equally culpable – invariably escape censure. This is one reason why anti-corruption and Sarbanes–Oxley type standards should be extended into academic, research, media and civil service organisations (see Chapters 10 and 13).

Cab for Hire

In March 2010, as part of an exposé by The *Sunday Times* and Channel 4's 'Dispatches' programme, Stephen Byers, former Trade and Transport Secretary, was secretly recorded offering himself – as he said – 'like a sort of cab for hire' for £5,000 a day to influence law-making. Mr Byers boasted of having negotiated a secret deal with Lord (Andrew) Adonis, the Transport Secretary, enabling National Express to jettison a loss-making rail franchise without penalty. Mr Byers boasted: 'we agreed with Andrew [...] he would be publicly very critical of National Express as long as he agreed terms which were favourable to it'.

The decision is said to have cost UK taxpayers hundreds of millions of pounds.

The Last Straw

When the revelations appeared about the ex-ministers, Jack Straw, then Home Secretary, said: 'There is such anger in the Parliamentary Labour Party as well as, I may say, incredulity about their stupidity in allowing themselves to be suckered in a sting like this'.

So what is most unsavoury about this case? It is not just that senior politicians tried to trade on their influence, because that must happen all the time. What is startling is

---

4   Which indicates that three times as many people believe politicians are more corrupt than the police.

5   Such as that which 'justified' the invasion of Iraq.

that the Home Secretary's reaction was not to harshly condemn the greed, conflict of interest and duplicity of his ex-colleagues but simply to comment about their stupidity in getting caught. This reaction says everything necessary about political morality and the tone from the top.

A few months later, when introducing the UK Bribery Act to Parliament, the same Jack Straw eulogised the UK's reputation in leading the fight against corruption; but the fact is that successive British Governments – from Thatcher to Brown – were at the heart of the British Aerospace (BAE) affair and related skulduggery: which was the real reason for killing the SFO investigation.

Keys to the Door

BAE was rightly punished in the UK and the USA for bribery in Saudi Arabia, Tanzania and South Africa and at the same time escaped with a multitude of further bribes in other countries.

The British government – and especially Tony Blair – was involved in the negotiation of the corrupt contracts (as Mrs Thatcher had been on earlier rounds) and was interested in generating revenues for UK companies. He overruled his other ministers and allowed BAE's chairman such unrestricted access to 10 Downing Street that Robin Cook – then Foreign Secretary – commented that he must have the keys to the door.

But who took the rap?

Trading in influence[6] is defined by the United Nations Convention against Corruption[7] as:

The promise, offering or giving to a public official or any other person, directly or indirectly, of an undue advantage [...] in order that the public official or the person abuse his or her real or supposed influence with a view to obtaining from an administration or public authority of the State Party an undue advantage for the original instigator of the act or for any other person.[8]

There is the reciprocal offence involving receipt of an advantage by public official and the recommendation is that they should result in criminal prosecution.

Conformance with the above recommendation was considered in the discussions leading to the Bribery Act but rejected by politicians because, they said, it would restrict their ability to represent their constituents and would lead to false accusations, making them less effective! In the light of the case of Mr Byers, referred to earlier, not to mention other scandals, a limiting of MPs' freedoms would appear more than justified.[9]

---

6   There are said to be 15,000 active lobbyists in the European Union (EU).

7   Available at: http://www.unodc.org/documents/treaties/UNCAC/Publications/Convention/08-50026_E.pdf (accessed 13 November 2012).

8   Article 18 (a).

9   For a comprehensive discussion of political corruption cases, see http://www.U4.no/themes/political-corruption/cases.cfm (accessed 16 October 2012).

Getting Round the Principles

The Liam Fox affair relating to what was effectively a cash for access scheme seems to have opened up a new can of worms involving political corruption. In this case the financial or other advantages appear to have been paid to fund his private office. It remains to be seen how many other politicians have been influenced in the same way.

Is it any wonder that politicians are so keen not to interfere with the arrangements on lobbying, trading in influence and other skulduggery. What is also interesting is the dogged determination of politicians to evade restrictions and visibility.

A Real Pickle

The generously upholstered Eric Pickles, appointed Secretary of State for Communities and Local Government to the Coalition Government in May 2010, was challenged that he had not declared in the Gifts Register a lavish dinner with a lobbying and PR firm. He exculpated himself on the grounds that reporting was not required because he had attended in a private capacity.

The names of visitors to the White House are recorded and reviewed, which is not to everyone's liking. Cafés, restaurants (and maybe even lap-dancing clubs) in the area around Pennsylvania Avenue are reported to be doing a booming business in off-site meetings.

Organised Crime

Organised criminal gangs – traditionally ranging from the Italian and American Mafia to the more recent groups of Jamaican, Mexican and Colombian drug cartels, and including Eastern European and Chinese people-traffickers – are heavily engaged in corruption and protection rackets that extort money from white-collar criminals, trades unions and companies. Organised crime is also often involved in foreign public official (FPO) corruption, linked to narcotics-smuggling, money-laundering and share and investment scams.

The point to note about this is that sitting behind what may appear to be innocuous petty corruption may be violent organised criminals who would not hesitate to use extreme violence to achieve their goals or the goals of those whom they protect.

Organised Grime

In a UK case, organised South London criminals repeated a scam in which they would corrupt employees of reputable companies to sell them redundant stocks and scrap inventory. Other members of the syndicate would approach other, innocent, employees of the same company and finalise contracts to purchase the same goods. The sales would be completed and the criminal group would then sue the company for breach of contract, producing evidence that goods they had agreed to buy for say £50,000 had been resold through a number of fictitious intermediaries for £2 million to £3 million. Working through reputable lawyers and supported by evidence from the corrupted employees, the crooks would settle their claims.

In one case a corrupted employee expressed second thoughts and woke up to find two heavies in his bedroom, who attacked his knees with axes and shovels, crippling him for life. Unsurprisingly, his colleagues gave evidence to support the breach of contract claim.

Corruption in Government Departments

ANIMAL FARM[10]

The Bribery Act is very tolerant of UK and other government departments who are unquestionably prime targets (or, more often, lodestones) for incoming and internal bribery. Although extorting officials may be liable under Section 2 of the Act, even the most negligent department escapes corporate responsibility. Worse still, when a government department operates in the commercial sector – possibly through Private Finance Initiative (PFI) projects – and is effectively a relevant commercial organisation – as a Crown Body it is immune from a Section 7 charge.

Under the old corruption laws (and still the same under UK civil law) once a benefit was proven to have been given to an official the burden of proof shifted with a presumption that it was corrupt. In yet another 'Animal Farm' realignment, the Bribery Act removes this burden, making it much harder to convict bent officials and those who bribe them.

IMPLEMENTING POLICIES

The tone, strategies, policies, not to mention whims, foibles, noble causes and perversions of British politicians cascade down to 24 Ministries, 57 Executive Agencies, 10 Offices for the Regions and 22 Non-ministerial Departments,[11] and then to local authorities, thousands of quangos, NGOs and a host of other partly government-funded operations. There are believed[12] to be:

---

10   See George Orwell's magnificent book, *Animal Farm*, about all animals not being equal: such as politicians and civil servants versus businesses.

11   This heading includes the SFO, The Crown Prosecution Service, HM Revenue and Customs, and the Office of Fair Trading.

12   Statistics vary dramatically, according to source.

- 6 million   civil servants[13] and local government officials
- 6 million   people are dependent on the state for benefits

The result is that something like 30 per cent of the UK population is dependent on the State and thus more likely to vote Labour. So to a large extent the Blair–Brown policies on immigration and multi-culturalism, benefits and social re-engineering worked very much to their political advantage because they bought votes.

TONE FROM THE TOP IN GOVERNMENT DEPARTMENTS

No one could say, despite the most emphatic denials at the time, that New Labour's tone from the top was inspiring with the Blair faction pulling one way and Brown's another. Unfortunately, the tone from the current Coalition government is not a great deal better, with so many mixed signals on such things as how society can be protected against terrorism, civil unrest, hooliganism or bribery, and how offenders should be treated and, ideally, rehabilitated.

Mixed signals trickle down to the civil servants, who have to implement political diktats and noble causes, mostly driven by perverted or key performance drivers.

CIVIL SERVICE MORALE AND OPERATIONS

In days gone by, the senior departmental civil servants (of the Sir Humphrey variety) would take barmy political ideas and kill or delay them so that they never saw the light of day. These days, there are layers of unelected political advisers or spin doctors and private offices which have no departmental loyalty or real-world experience sandwiched between top politicians and the Civil Service that cannot, and do not want to, filter out nonsense if it might be popular with their masters. The outcome is a dissembling of the Civil Service (including the police and to an extent the SFO), loss of moral and poor performance.[14] There are many good, honest and hardworking state employees, but there are many who are not.

Other things that add to the state enterprise problem include:

- Decentralisation (often transferring massive departments to the constituencies of Cabinet ministers in danger of losing votes);
- Privatisation (including the dreadful and corrupt PFI);
- Ridiculous key performance drivers and distorted or dishonest reporting;
- Social engineering of the Civil Service, resulting in some offices and contexts being packed with what are officials who have arrived in the UK from other countries: many of them supposedly very corrupt.

---

13   Using the wide definition.

14   In June 2012 The *Daily Telegraph* was scathing about 'the exodus of top mandarins'.

Immigration and Nationality

In 2004–2005 there were 703 cases reported of alleged corruption – involving demands for sex and cash – in the Immigration and Nationality Directorate,[15] resulting in 31 employees being referred for prosecution and 79 for disciplinary action, with the majority of case still pending.

The reasons for the collapse of standards in the directorate and departments more generally include:

- A watering down of entry standards to achieve the Labour Government's ethnicity and equality targets with minorities making up more than 38 per cent of the workforce.
- The minority groups have not performed well, despite extensive additional training by the Home Office Network specifically created to support them.
- The Home Office brought in consultants to advise on how minority performance might be improved, and recommended reducing the number of skills to be assessed and allowing minority candidates more time to complete the tests.

Distorting Equality Targets

Many civil servants are said to have watched in stunned disbelief as recruitment and promotion on merit has been discarded to meet equality and other key performance measurements. They quickly learnt that it was best to keep quiet because staff who spoke out in favour of fair procedures found themselves in trouble for 'inappropriate behaviour'.

THE POTENTIAL FOR CORRUPTION

The purpose of this background is to put official expenditure – all of which has the potential for corruption, into context:

Official government expenditure

- Central Government: £99,389,430,852.30
- Local Government: £15,682,819,570.67
- Emergency Services: £78,629,500.56
- Non-departmental Bodies: £3,114,832,048.07

---

15 A subset of the Home Office. The directorate has a total of around 16,000 employees.

- National Health Service: £27,738,042,538.57
- Foreign Aid: £10,000,000,000.00

Payroll and other costs are in addition to the above.

The risks of corruption within UK government[16] departments – on the procurement side alone – is a serious problem, despite repeated chest-thumping on integrity and supposedly best-in-class procedures. In addition, every item of wasteful public expenditure is the result of a mistaken, politically biased or perverted decision, including the wasted billions on computer systems that are unworkable, the human form of mad cow disease (Variant Creutzfeldt-Jakob disease), swine flu and, of course, carbon reduction and green technologies. It is also notable that most wasteful expenditure is based on, or justified by, research reports ('dodgy dossiers': see Figure 2.1, page 42) often promoted by the organisations[17] that benefit most from the resulting perverted decisions.

Rarely in any of the reports by the Organisation for Economic Cooperation and Development (OECD), TI, or other academic reports are the problems of bribery by (outgoing or internal corruption) government departments ever mentioned or effectively risk-assessed. Yet increasingly, departments and civil servants are involved in contexts where they are motivated to pay bribes to individuals, companies and other government agencies. Typically, payments are made to enable departments (or their managers) conceal problems, avoid litigation or adverse publicity, to achieve targets and to increase their powers. Time after time inefficient, negligent or dishonest state employees are given massive payouts to walk away, sometimes being re-employed by other government-backed enterprises at equivalent or higher salaries.

Bribe payment may be through accounts payable, by agreeing reciprocal benefits or giving favours in other areas. But possibly the most worrying aspect in the UK is corruption, fraud and waste in the PFI and the provision of commercial services by central and local authorities.[18]

THE BOTTOM LINE

The bottom line – although this book is not primarily concerned with controlling corruption in the public sector[19] – is that companies should very carefully risk-assess their dealings with any government agency, whether in the UK or overseas, and not drop their guard simply because the UK is perceived to be less corrupt, because it is NOT. And as a final word of caution, even greater care – bordering on mild paranoia – should be used when dealing with any EU or UN agency.

---

16   And the EU is too bad to contemplate.

17   Including companies, NGOs, charities and pressure groups.

18   They are not classified as relevant commercial organisations; and further, as Crown Bodies they have exemption from corporate liability.

19   Both national and local authorities.

Green Corruption

Over the next few years sustainable and other energy, green technology, projects under the Clean Development Mechanism (CDM), other greenhouse gas reduction projects, cap and trade schemes and the Carbon World generally will surpass – in terms of corruption and skulduggery – anything that has gone before. Fraud and corruption in the Carbon World will outstrip by multiple factors everything seen in the Oil for Food Programme (see page 265 and 312) and that was dreadful enough.

The biggest beneficiaries of carbon's unrestrained wealth redistribution will be not just the countries that are perceived to be the most corrupt, but in fact are; political and other supporters of the green initiative will also continue to make millions for themselves on what is, in truth, a conflict of interest.

The Carbon World has created new currencies, new financial instruments, backed by nothing but hot air, and exchange and trading mechanisms that are demonstrably insecure. The way that carbon credits are valued by their holders creates massive hidden financial reserves that can be misused to pay bribes with minimal chances of detection. There is no such thing as a Suspicious Activity Report in carbon trading and virtually no enforcement.[20]

Profits from Carbon Credits

A European company, which is a massive project developer and investor in the CDM, values[21] its carbon credits at the lower end of cost and net realisable value. However as soon as the carbon credits are sold, income is booked at the prevailing price. This, in effect, creates reserves running into tens of millions of pounds. These can be pulled in and out of accounts to adjust profits.

Corruption in Overseas Aid Programmes

The United Kingdom donates a higher percentage of its gross national product (GNP) to foreign aid than any other country on the planet and although the current government is slashing costs in every other direction, it has decided to increase its overseas aid budget by 34 per cent. Current contributions are seven times greater than the deficit in the National Health Service. Not only that, because of the deliberate and possibly corrupt over-allocation of AAUs to Central European and other Less

---

20   The early drafts of this book included a long chapter on corruption in the Carbon World. It can be found on http://www.cobasco.com

21   As is currently required by accounting standards.

Developed Countries (LDC), the UK's aid programme is actually billions of pounds in excess of that acknowledged.

Eighty-five per cent of Aid is Purloined

Prime Minister Rajiv Gandhi estimated that only 15 per cent of aid money got through to its intended beneficiaries. Please think about this. It means that 85 per cent is wasted or stolen!

This generosity might be justifiable if the monies were allocated to specific projects that were effectively implemented and monitored. But this is not the case and increasingly contributions go towards a country's general budget to be used in whatever way its rulers decide; in most cases it is for their personal benefit, with expenditure on massive palaces and fleets of private jets.

Kleptocracy and Bribery

Nigeria is said to lose $25 million a day as a result of kleptocracy and corruption. A $100 million aid package to Uganda was used to buy a $55 million private jet for the President. The President of Nigeria went a stage further and bought three private jets, costing $155 million; Malawi lashed out $13.26 million and the President of Uganda had urgent need for a new Gulfstream 550 costing $48 million.

A number of political leaders demanded that their countries' central banks guarantee commercial loans made to their acolytes. In the case of President Marcos, the Philippines picked up the tab of $2.54 billion.

Tanzanian Corruption

Export credit agencies routinely close their eyes to additional advances to cover corruption. When the Department for International Development (DFID) objected to guaranteeing a loan to Tanzania to buy a military radar system from BAE that was unwanted,[22] Tony Blair overruled and insisted on the sale going ahead, financed by Barclays Bank and guaranteed by the Export Credits Guarantee Department (ECGDP)! Nothing apparently happened to the corrupt Tanzanians, although the British Government thought it proper that the country should be compensated.

---

22   Because it had no military aircraft!!

Blood Diamonds

Blood diamond smuggling from African countries is far more corrupting than skulduggery by Western companies. Privatisation, urged by the World Bank and other bodies, has led to massive corruption and deprivation of poor citizens. Civil wars are estimated to have killed 20 million people since 1945 and displaced a further 67 million.

And the SFO frets about giving an FPO a Homer Simpson mouse mat or paying to have a new needle used for an injection!

Foreign Aid is not Helping

In June 2011 Mike Kendrick, the founder of the highly respected Mineseeker Foundation, commented (views shared by Nelson Mandela) that aid was turning Africa into a spoilt child and that:

> It is completely pointless and totally detrimental to spend endless billions on projects that are well intentioned but badly thought out and poorly implemented [...]. International financial aid, unless specifically targeted towards practical and ongoing projects, is of little use and should be stopped immediately to prevent yet more suffering. The problem is that aid when badly directed, actually kills people and this is a matter of fact – not opinion. In the past few decades the West has provided several trillion dollars of aid, yet the average African is now twice as poor as he was before all that started.

It is also a sad fact that international aid agencies are among the greatest victims of extorted bribes, primarily from political and governmental representatives, in the countries they are seeking to help.

Excessive Bureaucracy: European Union

$1.4 billion of EU aid is passed on to other multinational donors such as the UN and The World Bank, with $243 million circled back to the national donor governments to eventually distribute. This gives a total of $1.65 billion and is subject to recycling up to three times before it ever reaches a recipient country – and all subject to unnecessary administration transaction costs.

Although the EU claims to demonstrate commendable transparency, the European Court of Auditors reported that the European Commission has not developed a sound risk-management framework for corruption and bribery in its programmes. However, because budget support is less bureaucratic it is considered a good way of getting money out of the door faster.[23]

UK Overseas Aid

In June 2011 the highest-ranking civil servant in the DFID admitted that his department had no idea about the amount of aid stolen or diverted to corrupt purposes. Margaret Hodge, Chairman of the Public Accounts Committee, accused the department of being daft and of outrageously bad planning when it was revealed that, from aid of over £7 billion, it had recovered only £199,000 from misappropriations.

LDC Leaders' Profligate Lifestyles

In 2009, French Customs intercepted an aircraft chartered for Teodorin Nguema Mangue, son of Equatorial Guinea's President, containing 26 new supercars, including seven Ferraris, five Bentleys, four Rolls-Royces and two Bugattis, as well as five Harley-Davidson motorcycles.

If politicians are really committed to cutting back corruption they should first live up to their own responsibilities. However, there is a remarkable reluctance on the part of donors and political leaders to demand that recipients do not steal or waste aid. A few robust souls have said that they would stop all payments unless countries changed their homophobic ways, which is yet another noble cause *(bless)*. So it seems, through political eyes, that homophobia is a far greater sin than genocide and klepocracy: funny old world, innit?

Money Better Spent at Home

The Anti-corruption Resource Centre[24] states: 'Using corruption as an excuse, donors are able to appease tired publics who would rather see money spent at home. Why are donors so confident that they can fight corruption in recipient countries when they can't even control corruption at home? The questions continue when conditionality is brought to the table. How dare the donors put conditions on us when they are in such a mess themselves?'

---

23   An EU quotation.

24   A sort of TI clone.

The answer is very simple Old Bean: It is our bloody money you are stealing!

Corruption in Banking and Financial Services

The 2008–2009 economic collapse was framed as poor decision-making by banks and greed by their senior, bonus-driven, managers, yet realism suggests that many of the appalling decisions taken must have been improperly influenced by bribery or corruption.[25] If there was ever any serious investigation of the possibility, it has never been made public. This is an amazing omission and still multi-million-pound dodgy loans and derivatives transactions are being written off at the taxpayers' expense: again with little investigation.

Internal Corruption

A UK bank was heavily criticised for refusing to ring fence cash invested by members of the public – to pay for Christmas hampers –and continued to collect deposits when it knew the company was facing irrecoverable problems. Immediately before Farepak's collapse the bank transferred customers' funds to reduce its own exposure. Did this incredible decision involve internal corruption?

Another remarkable thing about the banking collapse is that the ratings agencies, which had taken some incredible decisions, walked away unscathed.

Blue-collar Corruption

It is easy to overlook corruption by blue-collar or operational workers, some of whom are empowered to take decisions that could have serious financial, regulatory and other consequences. The 'Green Sausage Case', referred to on page 543, is a good example. A principle suggested in this book is that every context in which a decision is given or received is a potential candidate for corruption, and this definitely includes blue-collar contexts.

Field Service Scams

Field Service Engineers were rewarded in cash by their employer for 'discovering additional problems' when they were called out by customers to fix defective machinery. The incentive motivated them to contrive problems with properly functioning equipment or, worse still, to sabotage good machines. The scam resulted in one customer being overcharged by $500,000 in a 24-month period.

---

25   If not cash in the briefcase, then excessive incentive packages.

The types of blue collar jobs and their exposure levels to corruption are suggested below in Table 11.1.

Table 11.1 Categories of Blue Collar Corruption

Type of Job	Examples of Jobs	
	Travelling or Mobile	**Static**
Outward-facing or 'wet jobs' *Deals directly with third parties*	**VERY HIGH RISKS**	
	Delivery drivers *(incoming and outgoing)* Van salesmen Service engineers	Goods inwards and warehouse employees Maintenance staff Manufacturing supervisors
Internally-facing or 'dry jobs' *No contact with third parties*	Not applicable	**MEDIUM TO HIGH RISK**
		Route-planning and vehicle-scheduling Equipment and building maintenance staff Waste disposal employees Inventory supervisors Labour supervisors Trades union representatives Control equipment[26] supervisors Computer maintenance Vehicle maintenance Building maintenance[27]

A Director's Perks

A director of a medium-sized engineering company was a veteran car enthusiast with an impressive collection of pre-1940 private and commercial vehicles. He coerced the company's Transport Manager to retain third-party mechanics to refurbish and maintain his fleet and to build a 12-bay, air-conditioned garage at his home. All the material and labour costs were billed to the company. Although the case would normally be regarded as one of fraud, these days it could result in Bribery Act offences, including corporate liability under Section 7.[28]

Chapter 14 emphasises the importance of including blue-collar corruption in risk evaluations. It is, as is associated fraud, a prime candidate for Critical Point Auditing.

---

26 Such as weighbridges and flow-metres.

27 Often internally corrupted by senior managers to work on their homes.

28 The director was asked to resign but was not prosecuted. The Transport Manager was promoted in return for his silence.

Corruption in the Law

Over the past few years the legal profession has become more commercial, more fee-conscious and more willing – like its American counterparts – to work on contingency fees. One outcome has been an overburdening of the courts with frivolous litigation, whose results are based more on which party has the largest funding than on justice. A second outcome is that far too many managerial and personal decisions are influenced by (if not based on) their potential for hostile litigation rather than on principle. The threat of litigation, coupled by a constipating regulatory regime, has made it even more difficult for UK businesses to survive.

A third outcome – and the one of greatest concern in the corruption area – is the practice of some law firms to pay and require referral fees to and from third parties such as claim handlers and insurance companies and to collect fees from specialists (including some barristers), and other advisers they appoint on behalf of their clients. If the fees are openly declared to and approved by the clients concerned there is no reason for deep concern: but is this always the case? And doesn't the practice open the door for personal deals to be made behind the backs of the principals, companies and clients concerned?

Legal Referral Fees

Christopher Kinch, QC, Chairman of the Criminal Bar Association, stated that any system in which the representation of the defendant is effectively sold to the lowest bidder is corrosive and leads to the selection of advocates based on cost, not on quality.

John Cooper, QC, writing in *The Times* on 9 June 2011 stated: 'There are some who argue that outlawing referral fees will cause them to go underground: there may be some truth in this because the practice by Chambers of entertaining potential solicitors has become increasingly imaginative as well as routine'.

The problem of referral fees is discussed in more detail on pages 236, 248, 262 and 318.

Crooked Judges

Two Pennsylvanian Judges conditionally agreed to plead guilty and serve up to seven years in prison for receiving $2.6 million in bribes from the owners of a juvenile detention centre. The judges, allegedly, used their prosecutorial discretion to unnecessarily incarcerate junior offenders in return for a per capita incentive. The privately owned centre generated additional revenues of some $58 million as a result of the judges' activities.

Corruption in Sport

It is no exaggeration to say that corruption in sport is endemic. The risks can be viewed in the following main categories:

- Administration at an international, national and club level;
- Infrastructure and finance, including stadium construction, franchising and advertising;
- The game: involving players, equipment and referees;
- Marketing, including club sponsorship, product endorsements and appearance fees;
- Betting on results, spreads and individual incidents;
- Player transfers involving managers, agents and players.

Clubs are relevant commercial organisations for the purposes of the Bribery Act.

FIFA Scandals

In the Spring of 2011 (having successfully negotiated the 2022 World Cup for Qatar) Mohammed bin Hammam challenged the existing incumbent – Seb Blatter – for the Presidency of FIFA and arranged a meeting though Jack Warner, FIFA's local Vice President, at the Hyatt Regency in Trinidad to lobby representatives of the Caribbean football organisations CONCACAF and CFU. Some 50 delegates attended (all expenses paid by Mr bin Hammam through a travel agency (Simpaul Travel), in which Mr Warner had an interest).

In the morning of May 11 2011 Mr Warner told the delegates that he had instructed Mr bin Hammam to bring the cash equivalent of any gift he had intended for the people attending the meeting; and that the money could be used for any purpose the individuals saw fit. He told them that a present was waiting for them in a separate conference room.

In that room there were envelopes marked with the names of each delegate country containing $40,000 in $100 bills. Mr Fred Lunn, FIFA Vice President for the Bahamas, photographed the envelope intended for him, reported the matter to his association and returned it to the conference room. It appears that no other delegates followed his example.

The above case is even more remarkable because at the time FIFA was under close scrutiny, with allegations being investigated that Russia's bid for the 2018 World Cup, as well as Qatar's in 2022, had been obtained by corruption of FIFA officials, a number of whom had already been suspended.

Other Sporting Scams

In 2008 the Argentine FIFA representative, Julio Grondona, is alleged to have told the UK representatives that he would vote in favour of England holding the next World Cup if it gave up all claims to the Falklands Islands.

In July 2011, The *Sunday Times* Insight Team reported that a director of West Ham Football Club paid £20,000 to an employee of the Olympic Park Legacy Company (OPLC) before and after it accepted the club's bid for the £470 million stadium against strong competition from Tottenham Hotspur Football Club.

The *Sunday Times* claimed that the West Ham director and the female OPLC employee were involved in a relationship, which the OPLC employee had disclosed on joining the company. But she had said nothing of allegedly moonlighting for the club on a procurement project.

The OPLC said the woman was not involved in the bidding process and that the team handling it was entirely independent and based in the offices of its London solicitors. However, the West Ham director and the OPLC were both suspended.

The article stated that Tottenham Hotspur had retained private investigators who had obtained copies of the woman's bank accounts showing the West Ham payments and claimed that the Information Commissioner had expressed the view that such access did not contravene the Data Protection Act because it was in the public interest.[29]

Possibly the most disgraceful aspect of corruption in sport involves the rigging of a result or elements of it, such as a few members of the Pakistani cricket team and spread betting on such things as the number of no balls, run rates etc.

Corruption in the Media

Media corruption is dangerous and includes:

- Corruptive influences by media owners on politicians and others;
- Distortion or omission of facts by journalists and competitors to support a commercial interest or privately held view (another 'dodgy dossier');
- Infiltration and improper influence of websites and forums (misleading the Commentariat).

The 2011 case of News International and the power wielded by its owner over British politicians and officials is an example of the subtle ways in which corruption operates in developed countries, illustrating the importance of reciprocation and cronyism.

---

29   This is a strange interpretation!

The News International case is believed to be the tip of an iceberg inhabited by other media barons. This sort of corruption, which is far more serious than facilitation payments or corporate hospitality, is unlikely ever to come on the SFO's radar or be considered by TI. It, and misreporting, are seldom challenged.

The UK media has been very reluctant to publish anything that might throw doubt on the noble cause of global warming For example, who has read about the defection in June 2011 of David Evans,[30] a leading protagonist of global warming in the Australian Department of Climate Change and a contributor to the Intergovernmental Panel on Climate Change (IPCC) classics, that led him to announce the following.

Global Warming 'Dodgy Dossiers'

The debate about global warming has reached ridiculous proportions and is full of micro-thin half-truths and misunderstandings. I am a scientist who was on the gravy train, understands the evidence, was once an alarmist but am now a sceptic. The whole idea of carbon dioxide as the main cause of the recent global warming is based on a guess that was proved false by empirical evidence during the 1990s. The gravy train was too big, with too many jobs, industries, trading profits, political careers and the possibility of world government and total control riding on the outcome. So rather than admit they were wrong, the governments, and their tame climate scientist, now outrageously maintain the fiction that carbon dioxide is a dangerous pollutant.

This news was only mentioned in one UK newspaper and not at all on television.

Corruption in NGOs and Independent Surveys and Research

Almost any jobsworth can get governmental or charitable support to set up a body that has non-governmental status and publish surveys or supposedly scientific findings on any noble or not so noble cause, free of any responsibility or accountability. We would never know if the organisation or its backers had conflicting interests because they are never required to make any declarations of independence. They simply produce reports, studies or surveys that are accepted without question.

Supposedly authoritative reports ('dodgy dossiers') – that are biased or financially corrupt – are relied upon by investors, consumers and by politicians to formulate public policies and the authors are rarely sanctioned, even if they can be located.

---

30   Who has subsequently come under attack by the believers, with claims that he has been corrupted by the big oil companies.

Sensa-Stiffy

In June 2011, the Australian Competition and Consumer Commission obtained an order freezing the assets of SensaSlim, a supposedly brilliant company that produced a £26 aerosol spray that enabled fatties to lose weight by suppressing appetite. The company's website claimed that the miracle ingredient had been accidentally discovered by an Italian dentist and had been perfected by Swiss scientists through over 20 years of diligent research. It also claimed that the (impressive-sounding but untraceable) Institut de Recherche Intercontinental (IRI) of Geneva – had carried out clinical trials involving of 11,453 users in 100 countries who collectively had shed 146,040 kilos.[31]

Prior to the Freezing Order SensaSlim had been in the process of selling worldwide franchises (at £60,000 a pop) and was poised, so it boasted, for sales of $369 million, through 1,405 distributors in 17 countries.

Its website also contained an impressive cameo appearance of Dr Matthew Capehorn, the Rotherham UK-based Clinical Director of the National Obesity Forum, an NGO supported by medical practitioners from the UK's National Health Service, Anne Diamond, the TV presenter, and Dr Hilary Jones, the famous TV health pundit. Dr Capehorn's video shows him eulogising the benefits of SensaSlim and the worldwide clinical trials that validated it: no doubt about it. It was good stuff.

The only problem was that the research was fabricated and the product did not work as claimed. Photographs on the website showing IRI's Swiss scientists were in fact cut and pasted from the St Paul Lung Clinic, in Minnesota, USA, which had absolutely no connection with the product. If this was not enough, the same photographs had been used on another website for the Mountebank Clinic in the New South Wales town of Bargo. Names of scientists supposedly working on Mountebank's behalf – such as Dr Joseph Balsamo – were falsified. The photograph used was that of Alberto Balsamo, a singer listed with the Florida Talent Corporation in Fort Lauderdale. Dr Balsamo's biography was word for word identical to that of a South Australian academic, Dr Mary Harris.[32]

When the bubble burst in early July 2011, Dr Capehorn admitted being paid privately by SensaSlim (he said £10,000: they said £25,000 plus £675 a day in expenses, with a further demand for £450,000 for his continued support). He admitted: 'I'm a little embarrassed. Quite frankly. I have been very naïve. I have no idea whether the product works or not […]. They have never shown me any clinical data'. This is not what he said in his cameo TV appearance.

David Haslam, Chairman of the National Obesity Foundation, told reporters that SensaSlim had offered him £250,000 to become a sponsor but that this had been rejected because it had all been a facade. It is far from clear whether this opinion was communicated to Dr Capehorn.

---

31   This would be true if 1,826 users had died.

32   A connection can be made between the legal advisers for Mountebank and Peter Foster, Cherie Blaire's friend and buyer of property on her behalf and, before his exposure, a promoter of an aerosol slimming product called SLIMist.

However, as has been exclusively revealed elsewhere in this book, no bad deed goes unrewarded and a report in the Gay and Lesbian Review Worldwide states that a Norwegian man is suing SensaSlim for $1 million after he had experienced acute sexual arousal for over *30 days* after spraying the product on his todger. The company is denying liability, maintaining that the plaintiff wilfully misused the product.

There are two things to note from this report. The first is not to spray SensaSlim on your genitals. The second is to be very careful before relying on any report or survey as justification for a difficult decision.

Academic and Research Corruption

Seldom a day goes by without some academic, research, scientific body or non-governmental organisation producing a mind-boggling scare story whose ultimate result curtails freedoms, raises taxes, heaps untold benefits on its sponsors or advises against eating, drinking, smoking or sex.

Research financing usually depends on results being found that support the funder's objectives. If the findings are adverse, funding dries up; thereby creating a perverse incentive to spin supposedly independent research.

Finance Driving Research and Dossiers

There is perhaps no better example of the finding–funding–political interest–let's raise taxes relationship than in the reports from the University of East Anglia's Climate Research Unit and the Goddard Space Center in the US. Their research was, among others, consolidated by the IPCC in its Assessment Reports and especially in the summary sections for policymakers. These were highly influential in justifying draconian laws to cut carbon dioxide emissions. Over the next few years these will cost European taxpayers billions of pounds and will make no difference to the planet, even if a difference is possible.

What started off as global warming had to be rebranded as climate change when independent researchers proved that man-made rises in global temperatures were barely detectable. However, such contrarian research was ignored, with the scientists involved being secretly banned from peer-reviewed journals, thereby removing their influence.

It is against this background that Stephen Schneider, a leading IPCC author, wrote the following.

We Are Human Beings

On one hand, as scientists we are ethically bound to the scientific method – in effect promising to tell the truth, the whole truth and nothing but – which means that we must include all doubts, the caveats, the ifs ands and buts. On the other hand, we're not just scientists but human beings as well. And like most people we would like to see the world a better place, which in this context translates into our working to reduce the risk of potentially disastrous climate change [...]. Each of us has to decide what the right balance is between being effective and being honest. I hope that means being both.

Swine Flu Windfalls

The Swine Flu scare – promoted jointly by the World Health Organisation and pharmaceutical companies – was that up to 150 million people would die from the disease. The research and the estimates based upon it proved hopelessly wrong, with total deaths worldwide being no more than a few thousand people, no worse than from common or garden flu. However the result was that over $1 billion's worth of medicines and vaccines had to be scrapped. In the meantime the suppliers booked windfall profits.

This is not to say that any or part of the scheme was corrupt, but in all windfall profit-making decisions corruption should be viewed as a possibility and the principle of 'follow the money' applied.

The relationship between questionable research, the funding of it and government intervention to raise taxes and sometimes to impose criminal penalties is a worrying trend. It raises the question of why academics, researchers, scientists, government officials and politicians should not be required to comply with standards equal to Sarbanes–Oxley and to put their own wealth and freedom at risk when they deliberately deceive the public or make reckless conclusions that coincidentally happen to help their commercial backers. Other forms of academic corruption are instanced by the recent cases of UK education boards releasing details (at expensive seminars attended by teachers) of their proposed questions for upcoming GCSE examinations. The motivation for this was to encourage schools to enter their pupils for a particular board's examinations, on the basis that they would achieve better grades.

In another case, a school scheduled for an official inspection paid for disruptive students to take a few days off and temporarily drafted in better teachers from other, unconnected schools to impress inspectors.

But one of the saddest trends is for overseas schools and universities to charge premium fees for poor students, guaranteeing them jobs after qualification in the UAE, the UK or the USA. Most are empty promises, but others are engineered by the schools bribing HR representatives to approve short-term appointments. The schools charge the students full fees, but the jobs only last for a few weeks or even days.

Corruption in Religion

After the tragic attacks on the World Trade Center in New York, Jerry Falwell, a high-profile American evangelist said the following.

God Speaking

I really believe that the pagans, anti-abortionists, the feminists, and the gays and lesbians who are actively trying to make an alternative lifestyle, the ACLU, People for the American Way, all of them who have tried to secularise America will stop. I point the finger in their face and say you helped this happen.

Following the earthquake in Haiti, another evangelist, and once a candidate for the US presidency, Pat Robertson, stated that the people were paying for a pact with the devil made in the nineteenth century to get rid of the island's French colonists.

HOW DO THEY KNOW, or are they just making it up?

Bringing things more up to date, so-called Shock Jock religious devotee and conspiracy fantasist, Glenn Beck of Fox TV, suggested that the Japanese earthquake, tsunami and possible nuclear meltdown were the wrath of God. He suggested that lack of compliance with the Ten Commandments was the sin that resulted in the slaughter of 14,000 men, women and children. But how would he know this? Did he just make it up?

True enough, these pronouncements are not necessarily supported by the more conventional religions, but they do illustrate the power of naked fear and the threat of eternal damnation, based on contrived reasons, to force populations to conform and pay over money. This, to the more perceptive is not entirely unlike global warming a.k.a. climate change or even the Bribery Act.

Conclusions

If you have had the patience to read the above, does not it give you a warm feeling that you are saving the world by refusing to pay $5 to avoid being jabbed with an infected needle; turning off a 60W light bulb or not printing out an email from your Granny? **But please don't despair, bribery and other skulduggery should be prevented and doing so is well worth the effort. But it is not just about compliance.**

12 *The Mechanics of Corruption*

Different Worlds of Corruption

Corruption rarely appears in the simple and predictable ('red flag' – 'country risk' – 'active and passive') form suggested by Transparency International (TI) and regulatory agencies, and it certainly does not start and end with bribe payment by companies from developed countries in foreign lands. Much more evil is an entirely different genre – called in this book 'stratospheric corruption' – involving international political leaders,[1] kleptocrats, government agencies, high-level officials, academics, law enforcement, media barons, the judiciary and, to an extent, the regulatory agencies themselves.

Stratospheric corruption is motivated by an insatiable quest for power to achieve both sectarian and global political goals and for control. If, in the process, a few billion dollars can be tucked away in secret accounts or hidden assets – while in power or after surrendering it – so much the better. The term also applies to continuing grand corruption by countries whose ambitions are to secure strategic resources or political domination: at almost all cost and regardless of international conventions.

The OECD Convention

Less than 10 of the current 39 signatories to the OECD Convention[2] take more than a passing interest in enforcement. It is rare for extorters to be prosecuted or even 'named and shamed'.

There is little enthusiasm – at the highest political levels – to deal with stratospheric corruption, except when there is no alternative, such as when a kleptocrat falls from power or when not taking action against an outrage that has already leaked into public consciousness cannot be excused. Even then, there may be a closing of ranks, as in the resurrection of Peter Mandelson, David Blunkett et al.

From this point on Stratospheric corruption is outside the scope of this book, except when it collides with bribery in the commercial sector, but it is unremittingly in the background and sets

---

1   Including the Vatican.

2   The Organisation of Economic Cooperation and Development Convention on the Prevention of Bribery of Foreign Public Officials in International Business Transactions – see page 57.

the frame in which honest companies and people have to live. It is, in fact, the true tone from the top and all of the official guidelines avoid this fact.

Commercial Corruption or Is It Only Bribery?

The options for commercial corruption are infinitely variable and evolving, depending on, among other things:

- The precise characteristics of the contexts concerned, their traditions, internal cultures and the decisions exposed to perversion;
- The personal circumstances of the extorter and coercer and their motivation.

The following analysis proposes that corruption in the commercial world, rather than being primarily a problem of country risk, cash payments, facilitation payments or transfers through agents, is far more complex and involves at least 2,000 combinations, mostly with deeply concealed symptoms. Corruption is always context-dependant, decision-centric, with constantly evolving mechanics. Red Flags are simply the footprints of dodos.[3]

A Refresher of Terms and Characteristics

The relationship between a coercer and an extorter and their roles can be summarised, as in Table 12.1.

Table 12.1 Different Roles Involved in Corruption

Factor	Outgoing Corruption Bribes Paid	Incoming Corruption Bribes Received
Corruption	Improper influence on a decision with the intent to induce improper performance	
Bribery	Corruption where the improper influence is primarily financial	
Bribery Types and *Examples*	**Corporate** payments of bribes ('Outgoing')	**Individual** receipt of bribes ('Incoming')
	To sell goods *To obtain a licence* *To become a distributor*	*To buy goods* *To issue a licence* *To appoint a distributor*
Internal Corruption	The coercer induces an associate (usually a co-employee) to make a perverted decision to benefit him or a third party. *Examples include pension mis-selling or attempts to influence the LIBOR rates*	
Participant	Coercer or bribe payer	Extorter or bribe receiver

---

3   But the principle suggested in this book is to get and stay one step ahead.

Transparency International's Terms	Supply side or active	Demand side or passive
Essentials of the relationship	The coercer enters into a corrupt agreement to influence the extorter to make a decision prompting improper performance usually resulting in the **coercing company making a financial gain**	The extorter enters into a corrupt agreement with the coercer, receiving a **personal benefit** in return for making or influencing a decision that results in a **corporate loss**
Organisational knowledge and consent	Usually involves internal collusion and consent	Seldom involves internal collusion with no consent

It is important to recognise that bribe payment (by a coercer) is usually condoned by the organisation he represents whereas the demand (by the extorter) is individualistic, for personal gain, rarely organisationally profitable or corporately condoned. **One obvious outcome of this difference is that suspected bribery is much more likely to be reported by the extorter's principal or organisational victim than by the body corporate represented by the bribe payer.** Regulators should pay more attention to this fact and understand that if *any* progress is to be made much more attention has to be paid to taking extorters out of circulation whether they are foreign public officials (FPOs), civil servants, politicians, academics or commercial wheeler-dealers.[4]

Public Sector Procurement

Over 18 per cent of the UK's Gross Domestic Product (GDP) is consumed in public sector projects (excluding the Private Finance Initiative), mostly placed by competitive bidding, but still resulting in massive overruns. Although government procurement is seriously exposed to incoming and internal corruption it is barely on the UK regulatory radar. In fact one of the most important weapons against official corruption – in the old Prevention of Corruption Acts – that shifted the burden of proof onto the skulduggers has been abandoned in the Bribery Act.[5]

---

4   Dealing with extorters is not an international regulatory priority and there are a number of reasons for this. First, they are generally individuals who have no money to enter into deferred prosecution agreements or to agree civil settlements. Second. if they are prosecuted they are likely to contest prosecution to the limit to avoid jail (possibly claiming legal aid in the process). Third, many are national or local civil servants or elected representatives whose prosecution would reflect badly on stratospheric operators. Fourth, many are in foreign countries which have no intention of enforcing anti-corruption laws. Fifth, if foreign exporters – many of whom are major and minor kleptocrats – were prosecuted, a rat's nest of foreign aid diversion (in which many are also involved) would be exposed. Finally, pursuing extorters is not revenue-generative, whereas coercing companies into commercial settlements is.

5   Although there is no evidence that anyone in the Ministry of Justice or the 'Cottage Industry' has commented on this remarkable change.

The Criticality of Context

DEFINITIONS

A context (for our purposes) is defined as 'a unique combination of factors and circumstances that create the environment in which decisions are made, opinions formed and actions taken'. Risks are shaped within a specific context, by, among other things:

- Its financial or other significance and the nature of the assets, processes and transactions with which those working in it are entrusted;
- Its level of accountability, supervision and reporting standards;
- The skills, honesty and commitment of its employees and third parties with whom they interact;
- Corporate, personal, internal and external pressures often determined by key performance drivers, including the expectations of shareholders and analysts;
- Its location and level of integration within the extended enterprise;
- Its connection – if any – with stratospheric corruption;
- The effectiveness of controls and regulatory demands;
- Its current performance;
- The position and authority of the potential coercer or extorter, their motivation and the nature of their relationship.

Although it is commonly assumed that some contexts are exposed only to bribe payment (for example, sales and marketing) and others such as procurement to bribe receipt, this is not the case. The reality is that contexts in which extortion is tolerated are far more likely to be equally involved in bribe payment and internal corruption. In addition there are scores of contexts that are not usually considered vulnerable to corruption, but are:

- Advertising, sales and promotion
- Bankruptcy and liquidation recoveries
- Business development
- 'C-suite' (top executive) activities
- Corporate planning
- Corporate social responsibility
- Credit control
- Equity and other investments
- Hedge funds
- Human resources
- Information technology
- Legal, compliance and audit
- Logistics and transportation
- Manufacturing and blue-collar corruption
- Payment processing
- Research and development
- Security
- Treasury and finance.

The fact is that every context in which decisions are given or received is a potential target for incoming, outgoing and internal corruption, fraud and conflicts of interest.

Products in Short Supply

Certain components required by Company A for manufacturing electronic goods were in short supply, worldwide. A purchasing officer (who was extorting bribes from A's other suppliers) bribed three salesmen to obtain priority allocations. The scam became so successful that the purchasing agent and the salesmen set up their own company (using the maiden names of their wives) to route scarce products to Company A and to other consumers at premium prices.

The characteristics of a context are transient and risks may reduce or increase following a change of personnel or processes. Some become more exposed towards year end (when there is immediate pressure to meet targets) or, especially, when they are confronted with financial difficulties or other adverse events. A methodology for identifying high-risk contexts is suggested in Chapters 14–17.

CHARACTERISTICS OF VULNERABLE PROCESSES

Some accounting and other processes are more exposed to corruption, fraud and bribe concealment and typically involve:

- High-value transactions and especially acquisitions, capital investments, disinvestments and other strategic activities;
- Noble causes;
- Interfaces between stratospheric players and commercial organisations;[6]
- Transactions based on competitive bidding;
- Excessive complexity or bureaucracy, especially when it is artificial or contrived;
- Unreconciled gateways between apparently related systems;
- Uncontrolled changes to standing data (such as vendors' bank accounts);
- Poorly controlled exceptions, error adjustment and systems failures.

Fraud and corruption thrive in contexts and processes that are performing badly, suffering from low morale, unjustified optimism, arrogance, or are ineffectively controlled. It is usually much easier to uncover these characteristics by talking to people and observation than by simply reviewing documents.

---

6   Particularly with strategically important industries such as weapons sales and aviation.

The Importance of Decisions

DEFINITIONS AND PROBLEMS

Decision-making may be defined as 'the cognitive processes that result in the selection of a choice of action or formation of an opinion'. Perverted decisions[7] are at the heart of all corruption and bribery. Despite this, most organisations are woefully unaware of both the contexts and decisions most exposed to incoming, internal, outgoing or competitive corruption. The importance of decision-centricity is also ignored by regulators, who much prefer more simple[8] 'solutions', supposedly provided by country risks or red flags, but only then when they touch on bribe payment.

The reality is that corruption and its control are usually set in a legal frame and decisions evaluated on their short-term financial outcomes. Little attempt is made to understand the psychology of corruption and instead generalised, high-level 'solutions'[9] are substituted when there is a need to drive into the finest detail. Also, judging the effectiveness of decisions purely on their immediate financial results, while ignoring the consequential or long-term impacts and the integrity of the processes used, is a recipe for disaster.

Rejecting an Agent

You reject an application from an agent because he is based in a country perceived to be corrupt and requires a higher than normal commission. Do you ever follow up how and for whom he has performed since your rejection? How would this affect your decision criteria if you found he had worked impeccably for a competitor and had produced multi-million dollar results?

Repeated regulatory and compliance failures – and not just in the anti-bribery domain – show that the current almost entirely post facto approach, based on box-ticking to contrive a defence of adequate procedures, simply does not work. Much greater emphasis has to be placed on psychological, motivational and management processes and effective prevention.

The Wrong Trousers[10]

Analysis of four recent conference brochures, supposedly on anticorruption, revealed that 94 per cent of the topics related to *post facto* legal defences. There was not one presentation by a commercial manager, psychologist, general manager or control specialist.

---

7   Usually resulting in improper performance.
8   But ineffective.
9   Country risks and red flags, etc.
10 With apologies to Wallace and Gromit.

HOW DECISIONS ARE MADE

The outstanding book *Thinking Fast and Slow*, by Daniel Kahneman[11] is recommended reading for every manager, lawyer and compliance specialist. Professor Kahneman proposes that there are two ways in which decisions are made. The first[12] (which he calls 'System 1') is mainly unconscious, instinctive, intuitive and fast ('heuristic') and subject to cognitive bias. Cognitive bias is the way that humans unconsciously distort reality and make irrational decisions in replicable situations.[13] Most biases are believed to be relic of evolution; driven by the need for rapid reactions to survive.

A test of cognitive bias

Figure 12.1 below presents a test of cognitive bias. Please write down the number of the dotted line you calculate is longer than the others.

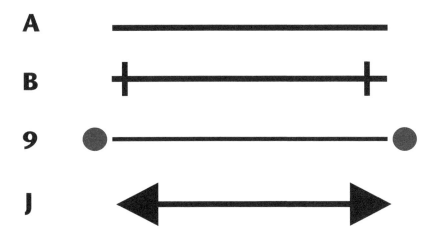

Figure 12.1 Cognitive Bias

Did you notice that they were all the same length?[14]

When System 1 heuristics do not result in an acceptable or quick solution, a second, more considered and rational process ('System 2') kicks in.

It is usually assumed that decisions to engage in corruption are consciously made (effectively under System 2), are rational and are therefore driven or declined, among other things, by corporate ethical standards, fear of punishment and the tone from the top.

---

11   Penguin Books, 2011. Senior Scholar at Princeton University and Emeritus Professor of Public Affairs, Woodrow Wilson School of Public and International Affairs, Professor Kahneman was awarded the Nobel Prize in Economics in 2002.

12   In simple terms!

13   Please see the excellent explanation on Wikipedia.

14   In fact, they were not. If you thought they were it is most likely because you have seen a similar diagram before and made an incorrect heuristic decision.

For this reason most training programmes simply explain the legal essentials, instil dollops of fear that the Serious Fraud Office (SFO) is hiding behind every tree and tick a few boxes, all in the hope that if things go wrong procedures will be judged adequate. This, as explained later, puts the cart before the horse and prepares for a post mortem on a healthy patient.[15]

Examples of Cognitive Bias[16]

There are more than 200 recognised cognitive biases, which are not always consistently described. Those of immediate interest are as follows:

'**Availability bias**' is the human tendency to judge probabilities based on the ease or fluency of recalling associated information. Availability is normally skewed towards events that are emotionally charged, vivid, unusual or most often repeated.[17] The result is that low probability events are grossly overestimated simply because of an 'availability cascade' – they are at the front of the mind.

'**Base rate fallacy**' is the disposition to ignore statistical data in favour of an 'availability cascade'.

'**Confirmation bias**' is the tendency to search for and accept information that confirms preconceptions while rejecting conflicting views.

'**Fear of failure**' suggests that a perception of the consequences of failure affect perceptions of the probability of occurrence.[18]

'**Fundamental attribution error**' occurs when people overweigh character- or personality-based perceptions of others while discounting the power of situational influences.

'**Herd Instinct**' is the trend to adopt the opinions of others and to follow the majority so as to feel safe and avoid argument.

'**Pseudo-certainty**' bias is the tendency to make risk-averse choices if the outcome is positive, but to make risk-seeking choices to avoid negative outcomes.

'**Stereotyping**' is the expectation that all members of a group have common characteristics.

Sunk cost fallacy refers to the unwillingness to write off a loss. This bias is often the driver of corruption.

---

15   Mixing metaphors is a characteristic of all good investigators.

16   If you thought the lines in Figure 12.1 were all the same, you were wrong. Line A is longer but that was not the question you were asked and there is no correct answer because no lines are dotted. But, you have probably seem the test before and were suffering from the 'curse of knowledge bias'.

17   The 'availability cascade'.

18   See page 566 for notes on 'raising the pavement'.

The significance of cognitive bias in controlling corruption is discussed in pages 277–8 and 382 but centres on bringing decisions into consciousness.

Asymmetric Relationships

The decisions taken and received by a coercer and an extorter are asymmetric, as are their motivations (see page 291 et seq). Typically, one will be the initiator of a corrupt arrangement and may take the lead thereafter. One will remain more confident than the other. Even in cases of grand corruption, the relationship between a coercer and an extorter is frail and subject to constant pressure.

Professor Kahneman's research supports real-world experience to the effect that the vast majority of corruption is initiated through instinctive (System 1) reactions.

It Happens in the Moment

A coercer or extorter may have already made up his mind to act corruptly but he has to collude. His grooming, offer, or extortive demand will probably come as a surprise to the other, whose autonomic reaction is critical. If within the moment and specific context an understanding is reached,[19] a course is set which is unlikely to be rejected by System 2. Further, the instinctive response is unlikely to be influenced by the tone from the top or threats of imprisonment. Rejection of a corrupt offer or demand must come instinctively and from within, as is the case with honest people.

If this view is correct, which experience suggests it is, training programmes and procedures should be reoriented and extended along the lines suggested in Chapters 21 and 32. They should not just be box-ticking, cover-your-rear-end sort of stuff, but should be really useful in the moment. It is at such points that corruption is best stopped dead in its tracks. However, really smart (or well-trained) people can do this – and avoid corruption – while maintaining the business relationship (see page 732).[20]

GOOD, BAD AND CORRUPT DECISIONS

Organisations cannot survive without taking decisions involving risks. 'Zero risk' and 'zero tolerance' are illusions. A problem in the corruption domain is that decisions that are taken honestly for commercial reasons that are considered sound at the time they are

---

19   Sometimes unconsciously.

20   Any dummy can say 'Buzz off' and lose the business.

made (such as hospitality or sponsorship) may be misinterpreted years later – and with the benefit of hindsight and prosecutorial discretion – as corrupt. This leads to risk aversion and over-compliance at a cost to entrepreneurship, competitiveness and profitability. It is therefore essential that companies employ processes that empower and train managers to take entrepreneurial decisions in real time and to prove after the event that they were sound. Such processes are described on pages 568 et seq.

Decision Bottlenecks

If you want to find corruption identify contexts and processes that involve decision bottlenecks.

Theories on Risk-taking

THE DRIVERS TOWARDS RISK AVERSION

It is axiomatic that every company needs people who are willing to take risks: doing so honestly and sensibly is the essence of entrepreneurship and should be encouraged. A problem with the current regulatory and 'Nanny State' mentality is that honest people are afraid to take decisions that involve the slightest shade of risk. A monstrosity of risk aversion has been constructed, in which honest people are terrified of making or admitting genuine mistakes lest a testosterone-packed regulator or litigator somewhere on the planet launches an attack. This has to change and companies must assert the right to manage: politicians and regulators do not run businesses and decisions cannot be deferred to await prosecutorial sanctification.

IMPORTANT PSYCHOLOGICAL THEORIES

Professor Kahneman explains the psychological essentials of risk-taking. He gives the example that if people are offered the choice between a gamble and a fixed amount approximately equal to its expected value,[21] they will usually choose the sure thing. In effect they are prepared to pay a premium to avoid uncertainty, but in doing so often abandon genuine opportunities.

Example: Options

If a salesman has the following options:

Option A is a 30 per cent chance of closing a $1 million contract. This is represented by an expected value of $300,000 (0.3 × $1,000,000).

---

21   This is a simple calculation of probability of success multiplied by financial outcome.

Option B is to pay a bribe of $100,000 resulting in a 100 per cent chance of success. Here the expected value is $900,000 ($1 million less the bribe of $100,000).

In choosing Option B the salesman may not factor in the chances of being exposed to regulatory or other penalties. This exposes an important point about the way risks are perceived by different people and how the cognitive bias of 'Déformation professionelle'[22] slips in.

Members of the 'Cottage Industry' (see Foreword), compliance specialists, auditors and the like are submerged in an 'availability cascade' where the evils of corruption, draconian penalties and the omnipresent fear of regulatory agencies is fluently recalled, repeated and reinforced. Commercial managers are seldom immersed to the same extent and this can result in risk perceptions and attitudes being seriously misaligned.[23]

People who are inherently risk-averse will pay a higher premium to eliminate uncertainty:[24]

Example 1

If an instinctively risk-averse decision-maker is invited to gamble on the toss of a coin:

Option A: he wins $100 if he guesses correctly and loses $20 if he is wrong. (The expected value is $40.[25])

Option B: he accepts $20 for certainty. (The expected value is $20.)

He is likely to accept Option B. A natural risk-taker would either take the gamble or negotiate a higher fixed amount.

Let's consider another example.

---

22   Meaning 'professional bias'. But, for some reason, it is usually expressed in French!

23   Which is a problem that is not difficult to resolve if managers and their advisers recognise their cognitive biases and different frames.

24   This is why companies are so willing to accept Deferred Prosecution Agreements.

25   Calculated as (0.5*100) − (0.5*40).

Example 2

A person is faced with the following decisions:

Decision A: Get $900 for sure or accept a 90 per cent chance to receive $1,000 or nothing.

Decision B: Lose $900 without doubt or accept a 90 per cent chance to lose nothing or $1,000.

The majority of people would accept the safe bet in Decision A and gamble with Decision B because a near-certain loss is risk-aversive.

An important lesson in the corruption field is that people become more risk-seeking when they perceive that all of the options are bad. This suggests that people are more likely to gamble (and bribe) to avoid losses or admit that they were wrong than to exploit opportunities.

The simple expected value calculation (or 'rational model') is not what usually happens in practice and decision-makers are shaped by emotional and other biases. The Expected Utility Theory[26] proposed by the Swiss scientist Daniel Bernoulli, refines the rational model to take account of psychological responses[27] to the outcomes of good and bad decisions. It is based on the fact that the 'decision weight' or psychological response to a gain of $1 by a person who only has $1 is much greater than the same benefit would be to someone whose existing wealth is $10.

In other words, the psychological response[28] to a change in wealth (for example, a bribe) is inversely proportional to a person's existing wealth.

No one Said It Was Rocket Science

A juicy Big Mac at MacDonald's might be enough to influence an FPO but is unlikely to impress Bernie Ecclestone or even Nick Clegg. This suggests that the dividing line between genuine hospitality and corruption cannot be judged only by its cost. It has to be commensurate within the context.

Monsieur Bernoulli's table of decision weights is as follows:

---

26 Also known as the 'Rational Model'.
27 'Expected utility' or 'moral expectation'.
28 Or 'Utility Units'.

Table 12.2 Expected Utility Theory: Psychological Values or Decision Weights

Existing Wealth of Recipient $	1	2	3	4	5	6	7	8	9	10
Gain		1	1	1	1	1	1	1	1	1
Utility Units of Gain: Existing	10	30	48	60	70	78	84	90	96	100
Increment		20	18	12	10	8	6	6	6	4

Table 12.2 indicates that the utility of a gain of $1 to someone with $1 has an increment of 20 points, whereas the same gain to someone who already has $9 is only 4 points.

The St Petersburg Paradox

The situation was that five out of every 100 cargo ships sailing between St Petersburg and Amsterdam sank with an average loss of $1 million.[29] For a trader with assets of $3 million – according to Bernoulli's theory – his loss would be 18 utility points. But for an underwriter with an existing wealth of $10 million the loss would be 4 points.

Monsieur Bernoulli's theory stood the test of time for over 300 years and was believed to help explain risk appetite and why people would tolerate excessive premiums to achieve certainty.

Professor Kahneman and his colleague Amos Tversky recognised an error in Bernoulli's work and in 1972 published their 'Prospect Theory' which, for current purposes and in simple terms, suggests that risk appetite is also influenced by 'reference points'.[30]

Jack and Jill and Reference Points

Jack and Jill each has $5 million and according to Bernoulli's theory should accept or reject a gamble in the same way. But: yesterday Jack had $1 million and Jill had $9 million. Professor Kahneman asks whether they would be equally happy and whether their risk appetite would be the same? What do you think and how does this translate into the bribery field?

---

29   The estimated value of the loss would have been calculated as .05 × 1 million = $50,000. Therefore everyone would treat the loss equally.

30   Also through loss aversion, anchoring bias and availability heuristics.

Let's consider another example of reference points, more relevant to the corruption scene:

Success is a Motivator for Good

A $5 billion company with successful worldwide operations, a full order book and highly valued shares, confronted with demands for bribes in a new market, is likely to take a completely different approach than a similarly sized or smaller company which is making redundancies and struggling. Again, it comes back to context in which reference points are an important part.

While it is true that the research described above never mentions the word 'corruption' it suggests betters ways to prevent skulduggery by applying psychological as well as conventional principles. These are discussed in Chapters 21–32.

Finally, there is a good example that emphasises the heighted cognitive awareness when a loss is in prospect and it comes from the world of golf.[31]

People Try Harder to Avoid Adverse Outcomes

Professional golfers putting to save a par are 5 per cent more effective than when aiming for birdies (meaning one better than par). In fact it has been suggested that if Tiger Woods had putted for birdies with the same efficiency as he did to save par he would have won at least 5 more major championships.

If Tiger Woods is loss-averse, what hope is there for the rest of us? But is there another cognitive bias that provides an even better explanation for Tiger and is even more relevant in the corruption field?[32]

CONVERTING THE RESEARCH TO THE WORLD OF CORRUPTION

There is little in conventional psychological research to clarify how potential coercers and extorters intuitively evaluate their benefits and to what extent they also weigh the adverse consequences of being exposed. However, the experience from hundreds of cases is that bribers consistently ignore downsides or underestimate them. Let's reanalyse the options in example 2 above.

---

31   Around which the world revolves.

32   And that is the fear of failure?

Options: Further Analysis

A salesman has the following options:

Option A is a 30 per cent chance of closing a $1 million contract in a country perceived to be corrupt. This gives an expected value of $300,000 (0.3 × $1,000,000).

Option B is to pay a bribe of $100,000 in a country perceived to be corrupt, resulting in a 100 per cent chance of success: here the expected value is $900,000 ($1 million less the bribe of $100,000).

The salesman has been trained in anti-bribery legislation and knows that what he is considering is a criminal offence for which he could be imprisoned for ten years. He has read about cases in The *Daily Mail*, seen Kenneth Clarke and the SFO Director on television, has formed views on the British criminal justice system, with jails that are too full, and is aware of police and SFO failures. He therefore considers that his chances of being detected are minimal.

How he acts is likely to depend on his reference point:

Reference Point 1: his company is highly successful, with a full order book and he has more than achieved his annual incentive targets.

Reference Point 2: his company is in dire straits and if business does not come in quickly he will be made redundant and factories will be closed.

Most people would agree that the salesman in Reference Point 1 is far less likely to pay a bribe than a colleague at Reference Point 2. This underscores the fact that context is more influential on corruption than country risks. Further, if the poor chap in Reference Point 2 makes a realistic calculation of the adverse consequences, he is likely to come up with a probability in the range of 1:2,500,000 to 1:5,000,000. This is the equal – on an expected value or certainty basis – of around two hours in jail!!

Bribers are unlikely to make such detailed calculations but if they did, the threat of disaster – on an expected value basis – may be a headache but hardly a strong deterrent. The ways in which organisations can create powerful and lasting biases to positively direct instinctive decisions are suggested on page 375 et seq.

Decisions and Risks Associated With Corruption

TYPOLOGY

The analysis that follows is viewed from the position of Company A[33] and does not attempt to explain stratospheric corruption. Decisions can be categorised as follows;

- **Internal decisions (associated with incoming and internal corruption: bribe receipt or extortion)** made by an extorter[34] in or associated with Company A that typically benefit a third party (the entity associated with the coercer).
- **External decisions (associated with outgoing corruption; bribe payment or coercion)** where Company A gains as a result of a perverted decision by a third-party extorter.
- **Remote decisions (associated with competitive corruption)**, which result in adverse consequences for Company A.

The three categories suggested above are to some extent artificial because even perverted external and competitive decisions invariably have an impact on those taken internally. In other words every internal decision has an external partner.

Perverted internal decisions usually result in an organisational loss and potential breaches of Section 2 of the Bribery Act, although corporate liability only arises if a directing mind is involved. External decisions, which prosecutors may subsequently interpret as perverted, are more dangerous from a regulatory point of view. They involve personal breaches of sections 1 and 6, corporate liability if a directing mind participates and absolute corporate liability under Section 7. Thus, external decisions induced by bribe payment – for corporate gain – are potentially more dangerous from a regulatory point of view, especially when they are taken or condoned by senior managers. **Thus the conclusion is that the gravity of financial losses from corruption and regulatory penalties vary inversely.**

Decisions may be further categorised as:

- Binary, when they result in a simple yes or no decision; or graduated when they rank multiple choices;
- Routine, ad hoc or exceptional;
- Discretionary or even arbitrary when made under a specified policy;
- Strategic when they relate to high-level matters and operational for routine matters;
- Supported when based on an expert report or professional opinion;[35] or 'naked' when there is no external or expert back up.

There are two categories of decisions that are often ignored, yet they are really important. The first is internal corruption, where one employee gives an advantage to another to induce his improper performance. The recent LIBOR scandal is an example. Internal corruption can result in substantial financial losses and regulatory breaches, under sections 1, 2 and 7 of the Bribery Act.

---

33 See also Figures 1.3 and 1.4, page 7.

34 Or someone acting on his behalf.

35 And maybe a 'dodgy dossier'.

The second is operational corruption, where blue-collar workers make or accept corrupt decisions. These, again, fall below the regulatory radar yet they can be catastrophic, as in the great green sausage scandal case discussed on page 543.

A perverted decision that leads to improper performance may be made by an individual extorter:

- Within his authority (estimated to account for approximately 50 per cent of corruption cases);
- Above or outside his authority *(for example, by dividing a large transaction into chunks that are within his approval levels; estimated guess of 10 per cent of cases)*;
- Below his normal authority level *(for example, when a senior manager intervenes in small decisions that would normally be approved by his subordinates)*.

Improper performance may also be induced by proxy when an innocent decision-maker is misled or misdirected by the real skuldugger, through:

- An instruction from a supervisor *(for example, 'if you want a pay rise, this is what you must do')*;
- A technical, procedural or other misrepresentation;
- A 'dodgy dossier', including misleading spreadsheets, false reports, surveys, polls and forecasts.

Proxy and committee decisions are especially dangerous because the real skuldugger can avoid responsibility.

DECISIONS BY COMMITTEES

There is a widely held belief that decisions taken by committee are more effective and less likely to be corrupt than those taken by individuals. However, the evidence is counterfactual:

- Decisions by committee can be easily swung by one dominating individual, who is able to avoid accountability.
- Decisions are also influenced by misleading expert and other reports.
- Decisions regress either to the lowest common denominator or to extremities of risk.

This is not to say that committee decisions should be banned forever, merely that their limitations should be recognised and effective procedures along the lines discussed on page 574 et seq put in place.

The Tender Committee

Bill Smith was a member of Company X's Tender Committee. He would routinely approach each of the bidders, claiming he would steer the business their way for 5 per cent of the contract value. Sometimes he would make an effort but more often would remain passive. After a contract had been awarded he would claim his 5 per cent, while explaining to the losers that his colleagues had been paid 10 per cent and that next time they would have to pay him more so that he could 'straighten' his colleagues.

Motivation of Commercial Corruption[36]

INTRODUCTION, SITUATIONAL AND MOTIVATIONAL FACTORS

Corruption, like other forms of crime, occurs when motivation meets opportunity and results in perverted decisions leading to improper performance. Motivation is complex and varies from day to day and from context to context and between a coercer and an extorter. One size does not fit all. Stratospheric skulduggery is in a class of its own and is beyond the scope of this chapter. It is important to recognise that there is no simple or single solution to corruption, except to pay attention to detail and to the context.

Although we probably do not like to accept the fact, no one is or will be or maybe even could possibly be 100 per cent honest all of the time.

The Not So Good Samaritan

In 1973, John Darley and Daniel Batson from Princeton University carried out an experiment to test the effect of situational influences on dispositional performance.[37] The experiment, carried out on a group of theology students, was as follows:

- The students were divided into two groups at random.
- One group was required to research and to deliver a lecture on the parable of the Good Samaritan.
- The other group was required to research and deliver a lecture on employment opportunities for theologians.
- When the groups arrived at the lecture hall to deliver their presentations they were told that the location had changed:
    - one-third of the students were told they had only minutes to get to the new location to deliver the speech (Group A);
    - one-third were told they had limited time (Group B);
    - one-third were told there was no rush (Group C).

---

36   This does not include political corruption or kleptocracy.

37   In simple terms this is a person's inbuilt level of honesty.

- On the route to the lecture hall, Darley and Batson had arranged for an actor to lie, slumped against a wall and apparently in great distress.
- The experiment was to find out how many of the students would stop to give assistance.
- The percentages of those who stopped to help were as follows:

Pressure on Students	Speciality and Front of Mind Subject		
	Good Samaritan	Jobs	ALL
Desperate hurry			10%
Medium rush	53%	23%	45%
Plenty of Time			63%

In some cases the students had to step over the distressed man to get to their destination.

The lesson in the corruption area is that situational influences[38] interact with dispositional integrity[39] and, therefore, performance. This means, among other things, that due diligence-testing on a person's historic performance is of limited value. Secondly, the idea of embedded integrity (often supposedly generated from the good old tone at the top) is helpful but far from determinative.

COMMON MOTIVATIONAL FACTORS

The motivation for corruption in the commercial world differs between the coercer and the extorter and is worth repeating. The coercer's motivation is predominantly to induce an **organisational** benefit from which he or she may gain indirectly through salary increases, bonuses, promotions, share options, etc. It is unusual to find that the coercer's colleagues and supervisors are ignorant of what is going on, although they may claim that this is the case so that they can construct a defence of plausible deniability if the facts come to light. The extorter's motivation is primarily individualistic, for **personal gain** and usually occurs without the knowledge or consent of the organisation with which he or she is associated and includes:

- **Survival**: where the extorter is paid below the subsistence level in the country concerned. *Typically, governments in Less Developed Countries (LDCs) keep wages and salaries deliberately low, knowing full well that they will be supplemented by bribery and fraud;*

Entrepreneurial Talents

The Deputy Finance Minister of an ASEAN country told the authors; 'We know our Customs people cannot survive on what we pay them. We expect them to leverage their entrepreneurial talents'.

---

38 That is, context.

39 Also represented by the psychological bias known as the 'Fundamental Attribution Error'.

- **Greed and Me2**: this is one of the most common motivators of fraud and corruption (see Figure 12.2, page 291);
- **Family Welfare**: this could be viewed as a subset of greed but is distinct and committed by extorters who would never consider taking cash. *Payment of the extorter's medical expenses, home repairs and improvements, and children's school fees, are typical of this genre, as are payments for chores in the home such as painters, cleaners, gardeners (and in one case a butler!);*
- **Special Luxuries**: motivation appears similar to that found in family welfare cases but the bribes relate to luxuries that the extorter could not otherwise afford; *examples in this category include payments for hobbies, sports, visits to lap dancing clubs and sponsorship.*
- **Reciprocity**: is ostensibly just returning favours, but in fact it is endemic and involves closed shops, formal cartels, referral fees, and other skulduggery;[40]
- **Avoiding losses and adverse consequences:** as explained earlier, the psychological drive to avoid or conceal negative outcomes is far more powerful[41] than the drive to exploit opportunities. This includes bribery to cover up bad decisions;[42]
- **Perceived injustice:** these cases are driven by the extorter's belief that he, she or their associated organisation has been unfairly treated;
- **Friendship, nepotism, cronyism and fraternal** and other family and personal relationships;
- **Expected, incited or systemic**: this book suggests that Transparency International's Perception of Corruption Index (CPI) is in fact counter-productive and creates an expectation that 'Bribes'R'Us'. It also results in making false assumptions about contexts in countries perceived to be safe;[43]
- **Corporate psychopaths**: their motivation is discussed later. They make up a significant proportion of grand corruption cases.

In none of the official publications on bribery or corruption is any mention made of the asymmetric nature of motivation as between coercers and extorters, and yet it is critical. Figure 12.2 represents the position that:

- The greater the level of a person's motivation the more likely he is to initiate corruption;
- Corruption is most often driven by extorters;
- Loss avoidance is probably the most important driver for coercers;
- Systemic and incited motivation is very significant.

It is also probable[44] that the shorter the distance on the axis on Figure 12.2 between the motivation of a coercer and an extorter – the stronger the collusive relationship.

---

40 Robert Trivers commented that altruism is more often driven by the likelihood of reciprocation.

41 1.5 to 2.5 times more powerful.

42 The 'sunk cost fallacy'.

43 An example of this is in the recent case where a bank classified Mexico in a relatively low-risk category and therefore did not pay attention to the fact that most of its business was in contexts involving narcotics traffickers.

44 Although there is no research to prove the point.

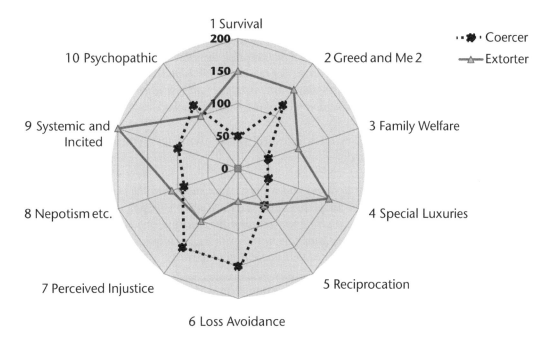

Figure 12.2 Motivation of Extorters and Coercers

There Are Some Unusual Motivations

The Chairman of Satyam Computer services – Ramalingam Raju – which collapsed with losses of over $1 billion, explained that profits and assets had been inflated to avoid the company becoming the victim of a hostile takeover. He and his co-directors had incidentally made hundreds of millions of dollars for themselves, but he grouched that 'every attempt to fill the gap failed. It was like riding a tiger, not knowing how to get off without being eaten'.

Although loss avoidance or money-making may be the dominant motivator for corruption, the true reason – as in the Satyam case – may be more subtle. But there was one point to note before continuing. That is that the excuse given by skulduggers once they are caught is usually quite different – and more publicly acceptable – than the actual motivation.

Professor Kahneman commented:

Except for the very poor, for whom income coincides with survival, the main motivators of money seeking are not necessarily economic. The billionaire looking for the extra billion and indeed for the participant in the experimental economics project looking for the extra dollar, money is a proxy for points on a scale of self-regard and achievement. These rewards and punishments, promises and threats are all in our heads. We carefully keep score of them. They shape our references and motivate our actions [...].

> *As a result, we refuse to cut our losses when doing so would admit failure, we are biased against actions that could lead to regret, and we draw illusory but sharp distinction between omission and commission, not doing and doing, because the sense of responsibility is greater in one than the other. The ultimate currency of rewards or punishments is often emotional, a form of mental self-dealing that inevitably creates conflict of interest when the individual acts as an agent on behalf of an organisation. (*Thinking Fast and Slow*)*

Professor Kahneman also makes an interesting point about loss aversion and what is known as the 'sunk cost fallacy':

> *The escalation of commitment to failing endeavours is a mistake from the perspective of the firm but not necessarily from the perspective of the executive who 'owns' a floundering project. Cancelling the project will leave a permanent stain on the executive's record. Thus personal interests are probably best served by gambling further with the organisation's resources[45] [...]. The manager's objectives are misaligned to the objectives of the firm.*

The above views are probably true for the coercer and the organisation he represents, but less so for an extorter, especially if he is trying to exist on a below subsistence-level income.

A study by the Center for Strategic and International Studies, in a report entitled 'What to Do about Corruption' stated:

The Importance of a Plausible Excuse

People are more likely to be corrupt when they lack mitigating circumstances or can argue against their actions being a clear violation of the law.[46]

The level of corruption is directly related to the extent of bureaucracy in the system.

Control measures, including annual declarations and reviews, which make it difficult for skulduggers to escape through a plausible excuse, are discussed on page 703.

THE ROLE OF CORPORATE PSYCHOPATHS

In the authors' experience a significant percentage of fraudsters, coercers and extorters (including politicians, senior businessmen, academics, researchers and manual workers, etc.)

---

45   Or trying to bribe his way out of trouble.

46   Farha Tarir, 15 October 2010. Available at: http://csis.org/blog/what-do-about-corruption (accessed 13 November 2012).

were institutionalised risk-seekers, suffering from antisocial personality disorders (ASPD), ranging from mild to psychopathic.[47]

Genetic Differences

Marvin Zuckerman is Professor Emeritus at the University of Delaware. His excellent paper, 'Are You a Risk Taker' (*Psychology Today*, 1 November 2000) proposes that risk-takers and sensation-seekers are genetically different from those who are risk-averse. His research indicates that sensation-seeking is around 60 per cent genetic and 40 per cent influenced by environmental factors. Men are normally more extreme risk-takers than women.

Differences In Context

There appears to be two distinct contexts in which risk-seekers and corporate psychopaths wreak havoc on their organisations. The first is when they are directing minds, such as in the cases of Enron or Madoff. The second is when they operate in a lower level unit and are able to detach themselves and their colleagues and subordinates from the company mainstream, by effectively creating a 'company within a company'. The pensions mis-selling cases, Payment Protection Insurance (PPI), etc. are examples of where sales teams severed the ethical connection with the company as a whole.

Professor Robert D. Hare, of the University of British Columbia in Vancouver, Canada, is widely regarded as the leading authority on psychopathy. His diagnostic methodology, published as the Psychopathic Checklist Revised (PCL-R), is relied upon by psychiatrists[48] throughout the world.

PCL-R identifies 20 psychotic characteristics in around 4 per cent of the population, including:

- Deceitful and manipulative
- Egocentric exaggerated sense of self-worth
- Glib and superficial charm
- Impulsive
- Irresponsible
- Lack of empathy and callousness
- Lack of remorse or guilt
- No fear of punishment
- Pathological and blatant lying

---

47 Such behaviour is not limited to people like Hannibal Lecter, the Yorkshire Ripper, Dennis Neilsen and other mass murderers and rapists.

48 Severe warnings that non-psychiatrists should not use the check list.

- Promiscuous sexual behaviour
- Shallow emotions.

Psychopaths are generally considered to be untreatable and are not deterred by the thought of detection or punishment. In fact, they may find the risk exciting and commit crimes simply for that reason. Controlling corporate psychopathic coercers and extorters is a problem, sometimes laughed about, but very serious. It is only ever solved by the principle of 'get rid and quick'.[49]

KEY PERFORMANCE DRIVERS

There are many ways in which key performance drivers, indicators and metrics can be set, ranging from formal business plans, mission statements, forecasts and budgets through to loose understandings. All of them can play a significant and sometimes dominant role in corruption and become the de facto 'tone from the top'.

What Gets Measured Gets Manipulated

The Blair–Brown governments repeated Peter Drucker's wondrous term of 'what gets measured, gets managed'. It became the justification for key performance indicators for every imaginable aspect of human activity, and the quantification of every decision, however perverse.

A more accurate mantra is 'what gets measured, gets massaged', or, more accurately still, 'what gets measured, gets manipulated'. Falsified studies, figures and reports are routinely used as a justification for the most corrupt and perverse decisions and the trouble is that we seldom question them!

The main problem with key performance drivers is not necessarily in their absolute quantum but in the changes (usually unrealistically upwards) they hope to achieve. If they are unrealistic they incite false reporting, fraud and corruption. **But an ever-stronger motivation for skulduggery emerges when it becomes obvious that targets cannot be met and where the far more powerful motivation of avoiding *adverse consequences* comes into play.**

---

49   In one case, a departmental manager decided the best way to get rid of a corporate psychopath was to promote him to Human Resources!!

The Nature of Collusion

ACTIVE AND PASSIVE COLLUSION

Collusion is the agreement between two or more people to commit an illegal act and is an essential element of corruption. Collusion can be regarded as active between people directly participating in the offence and passive when they are on the sidelines, may know what is happening but say nothing.

Active collusion is present in every corruption case and in around 10 per cent facts become known to passive spectators. This low percentage is so because conspirators make every effort to keep their corruption secret. Exceptions appear in coercing organisations, where a small number of people may have to be involved to process and record bribes. This is a serious vulnerability from the coercer's point of view.[50] Within the extorting organisation it is rare to find that his colleagues have any proof that a perverted decision has been taken. This explains why whistleblowing in corruption and other complex fraud cases is relatively rare. It is not because honest people choose not to complain, but simply that they know nothing worth reporting.

A different psychology applies in some blue collar and marketing scams, where active collusion is deliberately maximised so that everyone in the context is compromised and cannot whistle-blow. This is also often the case among FPOs and supervisors in 'dry jobs'.

INITIATORS AND RESPONDERS

It is exceptional for all colluders to be struck simultaneously with the same idea for skulduggery. **Rather, and especially in corruption schemes, there is at least one initiator and one responder.** There may also be a facilitator or facilitators, such as an information broker, a lobbyist and a political or other agent who brings the parties together. Table 12.3, which is no more than an informed guess, indicates that there are variations.

Table 12.3   Roles of Initiators and Responders in Corruption

Category of Corruption	Objective	Role of the Participant and Percentage as the Initiator		
		Extorter	Coercer	Facilitator
Political and stratospheric	Gain	40	40	20
Entirely private sector involving third parties	Gain	50	30	20
	Avoid a loss	25	70	5
Mix of public and private sector	Gain	60	30	20
	Avoid a loss	25	70	5
Internal	Gain	20	75	5
	Avoid a loss	45	45	5
Bribery of FPOs	Gain	20	60	20
	Avoid a loss	70	20	10
TOTAL		355	440	110

---

50   Which emphasises the importance of training back-office staff in how to detect skulduggery.

Although the individual percentages are arguable, there is no doubt that extorters play a much greater part in corruption than is officially recognised and are often at the hub of a multi-spoked wheel (Figure 12.3).

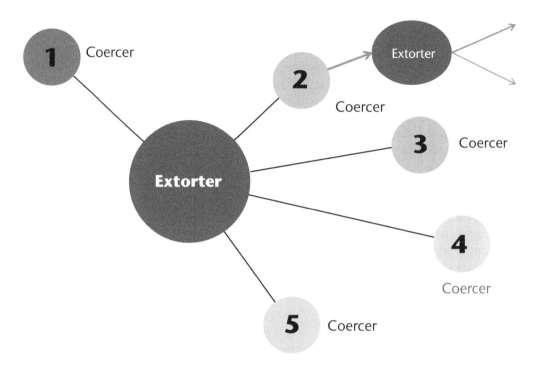

Figure 12.3 Extorters at the Hub of a Wheel

Corruption In The UK Border Agency (UKBA)

In 2011 and 2012 the UKBA was hit by a number of scams where officials extorted or accepted bribes in return for perverted decisions, granting immigrants privileges to which they were not entitled. Most jiggery-pokery was facilitated by 'Immigration Consultants', who were the links between the officials and the end customers. One extorting official was at the centre of a ring of more than ten coercers.

There are two interesting asides to these cases. The first was that the UKBA was criticised for its lack of control. In fact, senior managers should be commended for tackling what were clearly difficult and reputation-damaging crimes. The second point is that most of the villains working for the UKBA were themselves from the same countries (mainly perceived as corrupt) as their ultimate clients. This supports the conclusion that corruption is more context- than country-specific and situational rather than motivational.

Experience suggests that the expectations of potential colluders are significantly influenced by their perception of integrity – or lack of it – in the context concerned. As discussed earlier, the Transparency International Perceptions of Corruption Index is possibly counter-productive because it sets the expectation that Bribes'R'Us.

VERTICAL AND HORIZONTAL COLLUSION

Collusion can take place anywhere, anytime, between anyone. The parties concerned usually believe that their mutual jeopardy ensures that neither will snitch on the other, but in truth it does not. Under pressure the convention is that the coercer will be forsaken by the organisation he represents, he will incriminate his superiors and blame the extorter in a war of all against all. Unless the extorter is a politician or an FPO,[51] he will be dragged into the fight. The bottom line is that collusion is a mug's game except in the stratosphere.

Collusion can take place vertically or horizontally within the same organisation or between different entities, with the latter being by far the most common. Horizontal collusion involves people at more or less the same organisational levels and vertical between people of significantly different status. There are, of course, exceptions such as diagonal collusion between a senior sales director in one organisation who bribes an Accounts Payable junior in another to process invoices more quickly than would otherwise be the case. It is relatively uncommon for collusion to be broached by the junior or less wealthy participant, **but diagonal relationships are always dangerous, whether internal or external**.

THE SHARING OF COLLUSIVE BENEFITS

Seldom are the benefits divided equally between a coercer and an extorter. Typically for every pound given to an extorter, the coercer's organisation will *initially* gain between £5 and £50,000. However as time goes on the extorter usually becomes greedier, demanding that the spoils are shared equally or even distributed in his favour.

Unequal Shares

The buyer responsible for stationery purchases received less than £1,000 from a printer. He then placed orders at excessively high prices and suppressed competitive bids. The overpricing amounted to more than £500,000.

Cases are not uncommon where bribes are simply stolen by the coercer.

---

51   When typically he will walk free.

False Bribery and Sticky Fingers

The Marketing Manager of a major, top class European company made a presentation to the board, urging that he should visit Moscow to see if there was a market for its products. A few weeks later, the manager made a further presentation, supported by colourful overheads, diagrams and projections. There was only one problem, he explained, and that was that a senior Russian official wanted a one-time bribe of $1 million. Being good, honest, trustworthy members of the business community, the board unhesitatingly agreed to pay up.

The manager then explained that the former Soviet Union was short of hard currency and that for the first few years the company would have to keep its prices very low. Shipments went forward and everyone was pleased, presumably on the basis that what it lost on margin was compensated through volume. Then, out of the blue, the company's subsidiaries in India and Pakistan complained that its products were flooding the market at prices with which they could not compete. Investigations established that product destined for the former Soviet Union had been diverted.

The manager was interviewed and readily admitted that he had never been to Moscow in his life; that he had kept the $1 million for himself, had tape recorded the board meeting giving him approval, and coolly asked the board what it intended to do about it. The response, unsurprisingly, was nothing.

Cases like the above are almost the perfect crime because the victim is in no position to complain.

The Importance of Cash

Some politicians and regulators appear to have funny ideas about cash, believing it to be nasty stuff and that people who have it feel compelled to pay in into banks and will therefore be revealed through suspicious activity reporting.

In the real world, fraudsters, crooks, bribers, kleptocrats and even some honest people quite like cash and are more than happy to accept it. Surprising, Eh?

Here are a few facts:

- There is an estimated $1,000 billion in circulation.
- Cash in circulation on Europe rose by 11 per cent per annum between 2002 and 2009, mainly in large denomination notes such as the €500 (known as the 'Bin Laden'). This was so popular with skulduggers it was withdrawn.
- The UK Payments Administration[52] reported that in 2008, spending in the UK was as shown in Table 12.4.

---

52   The UK Payments Administration Ltd. (UKPA) (previously APACS, the Association for Payment Clearing Services).

Table 12.4 Types of Payments

Type of Payment	Volume in Billions	Value in £Billions
Cash	22.6	267
Debit cards	5.4	241
Credit–charge cards	2	139
Direct debits	3.1	935
Direct credits	2.4	3,000
Cheques	1.4	1,429

- £46 billion of counterfeit UK currency is in circulation, of which only £14 million was detected in 2008.

Finally, it is said that that lower socio-economic and less well educated people in the UK use more cash on average as do citizens in LDCs.

Although all of the above shows the importance of cash, it arguably understates the position because it is based only on withdrawals from legitimate sources such as salary payments and ATM withdrawals. Cash in circulation in the red economy (Crime Inc. and drugs cartels) that comes in and out of honest circulation is not included: neither is the massive Hawala economy.

The circulation of large-denomination notes is a good measure of the grey economy and corruption. The fact that it is increasing may be a measure of how successful or otherwise anti-money-laundering regulation has been.

Simple Symptoms of Bribery

On the face of things, the symptoms of bribery *should* be very simple to detect, as summarised in Table 12.5.

Table 12.5 Symptoms of Bribery

Bribe Payer	Bribe Receiver
Normally involves decisions for a corporate benefit	Normally involves a personal gain for corporate disadvantage
Needs to fund bribe payments by: • concealing the payments in accounting records • making payments from off record slush funds or • giving other financial benefits disguised in goods or services provided	No direct impact in its accounts
Needs to explain profits or exceptional third-party decisions	Needs to conceal a perverse decision
	Needs to explain potential losses or performance disadvantages

The problem is that detecting bribes in the records of the coercing organisation – whether directly through its own accounts, or those of its associates, indirectly through goods or services or from off-record slush funds – is like looking for a needle in a haystack, with more than 1,200 possible combinations. On the other hand, detecting perverse decisions in the organisation represented by the bribe extorter is much more straightforward. For this reason:

• Regulators should concentrate equally on the bribe extorter and introduce an equivalent Section 7 offence for organisations – particularly government agencies – that are so poorly controlled they act as magnets to corruption.
• Risk assessment should, where possible, be collaborative and involve coordination with major customers, suppliers and intermediaries in what can be regarded as the extended enterprise.

Under the 'Animal Farm' philosophy (see Foreword) the first suggestion is unlikely to receive much political or regulatory support, but the second is easily achievable.

How Bribes are Paid

There are almost unlimited ways in which corrupt benefits and bribes can be paid and concealed, including those listed in Table 12.6, which are the most common.

Table 12.6 How Bribes are Paid

Benefit	Example and Clarification
Advance purchase discounts	Advance purchase discounts obtained from suppliers and deposited in an off-record bank account or paid directly to the extorter
Advances	Of any type
Aid (especially overseas)	Diversion of overseas development aid
Airline and hotel credit cards	Issued company credit cards
Airline tickets	Purchased for the extorter
Air miles	Transfers of air miles between the coercer and the extorter
Alcohol	Purchased for the extorter
Allocations	Scarce products allocated to the extorter, e.g. Apple Ipods on their launch
Ancillary charges (phantom)	For such things as freight, warehousing or demurrage
Antiques	Purchased for the extorter
Assets	Purchased for the extorter, or company assets sold off to him cheaply
Bad debt write-off	The extorter's debts are written off
Betting and betting accounts	Gambling debt settled by the coercer

Billbacks	False bill back claims from customers are submitted and the credits converted for the benefit of the extorter
Bonuses	In internal corruption, as a way of rewarding consent, or connived
Building works	Typically carried out at the extorter's home
Capital purchases	Bought on the extorter's behalf
Car insurance	Paid on the extorter's behalf
Carbon credits	See page 439
Carbon exchanges	Multiple options of trading and creating phantom profits, as well as making concealed payments through the carbon trading mechanisms
Carbon trading	See page 439
Carbon trading and CERs	
Cars	Cars supplied to the extorter or his family
Cartels	Corrupt agreements to fix prices, etc., or collusive bidding
Cash	Bribes paid in cash
Cash back schemes	The ads said 'Buy a new laptop and get £100 cash back'
Cashier's check	Drawn in favour of the extorter, to a close family member or to settle a third-party debt
Certified cheque	Certified cheques paid to the extorter
Channel support	Additional channel support given to customers in return for benefits diverted to the extorter
Charge backs (see billbacks)	Intercompany transfers used to conceal bribe payment
Casino chips and membership	Paid to an extorter in lieu of cash
Cheques	Paid directly to the extorter or a nominee
Clocks	Expensive gifts typical of corruption
Clothing	Expensive suits and dresses
Club membership	Paid on behalf of the extorter
Commissions	Pseudo-commissions paid to the extorter
Company products	Free of charge goods supplied to the extorter
Company yachts	Free use of luxury facilities
Consultancy contracts	Used to conceal bribe payments
Cosmetic surgery	Provided to the extorter or to an associate (more likely a mistress than a wife!)
Credit and debit cards	Provided to the extorter and paid for by the company
Credit notes	Proceeds from credit notes falsely created to provide the extorter with an advantage
Debt write offs	See 'Bad debt write-off' above
Dematerialised assets	Euroclear, Cedel, spread-betting, etc. accounts and carbon credits
Demurrage	Inflated ancillary charge

Benefit	Example and Clarification
Direct debit	Paid on behalf of the extorter
Discounted goods or services	Supplied to the extorter or an associate
Diverted payments	Payments recorded to third parties diverted to the extorter
Drugs	Supplies of narcotic drugs charged through expenses
Duplicate payments sales	Contrived and refunded to the extorter directly or through a customer
Duplicate payments purchases	Contrived and refunds from suppliers diverted to the extorter
Electronic transfers (diverted)	Genuine payments diverted to the extorter by changing payment providers
Employment	Employment of the extorter's family or promises of future employment (Revolving Doors)
Entertaining	Exceptional entertainment for the extorter or an associate
Equity interests	Free of charge interests in joint ventures, subsidiary companies, etc.
Executive jets	Free use of executive jets
Expense items	Provision of hobby and leisure items for the extorter
Financial advisory services	Provision of free advisory services for the extorter
Foreign exchange	Provision of foreign currency for the extorter
Free goods or services	Provision of free goods and services for the extorter
Furniture	Provided to the extorter's home
Future employment	Promises of
Gambling winnings and losses	Joint accounts with bookmakers, spread betting, etc.
Gift and star catalogues	In lieu of cash
Gift vouchers	Store and other gift vouchers bought for the extorter
Golf gambling	Deliberate losing and conceding 20 foot putts to FPOs, etc.
Goods and services	Free or discounted goods and services
Guarantees	Off-record guarantees provided by the company for the extorter's loans
Hawala	An official Asian system for transmitting funds; essentially a secondary banking system
Health insurance	Free or discounted health services for the extorter or his family
Hedging and derivatives	Creation of funds through false hedging and trading
Hobbies and sports	Provision of free goods and services for the extorter's hobbies, etc.
Holiday villas	Provision of holiday accommodation free of charge
Home improvements	Provision of construction and other services for home improvement
Hospitality	May be corruptive
Incentives	See bonus

Inside information	Provision of inside information, enabling the extorter to make a financial gain
Insurance	Provision of free insurance
International transfers	Payments made and obscured through international transfers
Inventory items	Free issues, including samples
Investments	Purchase of investment options for the extorter
Jewellery	Purchase of jewellery, etc. for the extorter
Joint ventures	Free investment for the extorter in joint ventures
Kitchens	A very common method of bribery in the construction industry
Land	Purchase of land for the extorter or from him at an excessive price
Land options	Allowance of land options to the extorter for future land flipping
Lap dancing clubs	Free nights out with Flossie Flowfinger!!!
Lawyer's client accounts	Payments to the extorter directed through a lawyer's client account
Legal fees	Payment of legal fees on behalf of the extorter
Little luxuries	You name it! But things like personal car registration plates, sexual favours, first class travel are obvious examples.In one case the extorter demanded payment for his full-time butler!
Loans	Loans made to the extorter or a family member
Maintenance charges	Providing maintenance services for houses and cars
Manual cheques	Manually drawn cheques diverted to the extorter
Marketing support schemes	Diversion of marketing incentives, prize awards, etc. to the extorter
Medical expenses	Paid on behalf of the extorter
Mobile telephones	Provided to the extorter and his family
Money purses	Electronic money services paid for on behalf of the extorter
Mortgages	Mortgages negotiated, guaranteed or paid for on behalf of the extorter
Off-book guarantees	Company guarantees given for the extorter's loans and other financial needs
Offset projects	Participation of the extorter in remunerative offset projects
Options	To buy and sell shares and future contacts (of any nature)
OTC share transactions	Creation of dummy profits through fictitious transactions
Overpayments	Refunds of overpayments to customers and suppliers diverted to the extorter
Paintings	Purchased on behalf of the extorter
PayPal and eBay	Goods, services and finance provided through PayPal or eBay
Personal expenses	Extorter's personal expenses reimbursed by the company, possibly through a dummy account
Personal references	False personal references given in respect of the extorter to obtain finance
Phantom transactions	Additional transactions slipped into a sequence
Pre-paid cards	Purchased on behalf of the extorter

Benefit	Example and Clarification
Private jets	Free rides, leasing and vacations
Products	Provided with free-of-charge or discounted products and services
Professional fees	Paid on behalf of the extorter
Promotion	Promoting the extorter to a higher salary level
Protection	See Security and Protection below
Purchase cards	Paid on behalf of the extorter
References and recommendations	Provided for the extorter to obtain third-party advantages
Royalties and licencing fees	Copyright permissions
Sales of scrap goods	Supposedly scrap goods, transfers at discounted rates or free of charge
School Fees	Paid on behalf of the extorter or his family
Security and protection	Provided to the extorter
Sexual favours	Back to Flossie Flowfinger and the Pink Pussy Cat Lap Dancing Club
Share options and warrants	Issued to the extorter or his associates
Share purchase	Dummy share transactions creating fictitious profits for the extorter either directly or through brokers
Shares	Issuing shares to the extorter
Side letters	Off-record commitments
Signing-on bonus	Pseudo-signing on bonus transferred to the extorter
Software licences	Pseudo or inflated
Sponsorship	Supporting an extorter's hobby or those of a close associate
Sports equipment	Supplying free of charge to the extorter
Sports tickets	Free tickets to high-value sporting events
Stamps	Purchased on behalf of the company but diverted to the extorter
Standing orders	Direct payments to the extorter or associate, or diversion of orders
Star catalogues	Personal gifts and rewards provided depending on contracts placed
Stock options	Off-record options provided to the extorter
Store vouchers	Paid for on behalf of the extorter
Subscriptions	Paid by the company. Typically involving golf clubs
Swimming pools	A typical benefit to an extorter in the construction industry
Tax	Tax advice reimbursed by the company or the extorter's tax paid directly or indirectly
Termination bonus	Pseudo-termination bonus transferred to the extorter
Tickets and vouchers	Paid directly from the company
Tolling or split invoicing	See page 316
Trading profits (phantoms)	Dummy transactions entered into to provide the extorter with a gain (e.g. carbon credits)

Transfer pricing	Under and overpricing (see Tolling)
Travel and hotels	Paid directly from the company
Travellers' cheques	Bought on behalf of the extorter and concealed
Uncollected credit notes	Credit notes collected with proceeds diverted to the extorter
Uncollected discounts	Unrecorded discounts diverted to the extorter
University fees	Paid on behalf of the extorter's children
Uninvoiced sales	Free goods or services provided to the extorter or to an associate
Unrecorded Income	Collected off-book and diverted to the extorter in cash
Use of facilities	Office accommodation computers etc. free of charge
Valuations (over- or under-)	Securitisations, collateral etc.
Villa rental and free use	Free use of vacation accommodation
Watches	Provided to the extorter
Write offs	Debts often for goods and services or loans

High-stakes Golf Game

The owner of an international company operating in a country that is widely perceived as corrupt was a keen golfer and every Sunday played a high-stakes match with two senior buyers from his employer's most important customers. He would invariably lose between $3,000 and $5,000 a week, which he figured he would recover from annual dividends.

Disguised Winning

Billy Bung wants to bribe George Grabbit. They both become members of a prestigious London casino. Billy Buys £100,000 worth of chips, gambles for a few minutes, hands the chips over to George, and two hours later George cashes in. What are the chances of this type of corruption being detected?

Bribes may be paid before or after a decision is made and sometimes the timing can be 6 to 12 months apart, so that improper acts and the payments are disassociated.

More astute coercers make sure that there is no separate or distinguishable bribe payment to the extorter, but overpay the organisation he represents and leave it to him to convert the resulting accounting credit internally.

Size of the Bribe

There is no set relationship between the amount of a bribe (or other advantage), the importance of the associated decision and windfall profits or exceptional losses. In some contexts, more or less standard rates of between 10 per cent and 20 per cent are agreed. Despite the fact that most bribes are extorted in the authors' experience, the gains for the coercer are proportionately greater and in the range of five or ten to one.

Money-laundering

Preventing money-laundering (which is simply washing the proceeds of crime and integrating them for legitimate use – but amounting to an estimated $1 trillion a year worldwide) is another noble cause and, according to the regulators, closely associated with bribery. The SFO has emphasised the importance of the mandatory requirement – under the Proceeds of Crime Act and associated regulations – to report suspected money-laundering offences with the clear intention that compliance will automatically result in the self-disclosure of bribery offences. It is a cunning plan.

The fact is that most commercial bribery will not trigger any money-laundering red flags and even fewer Suspicious Activity Reports because there are only two main points of exposure.

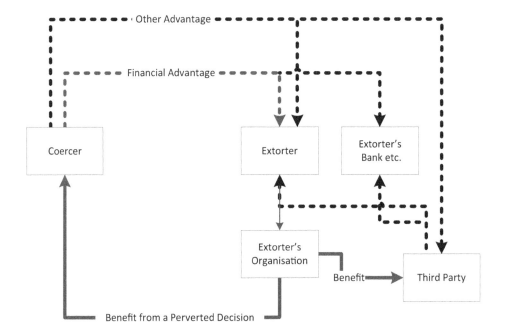

Figure 12.4 Points Where Bribery and Money-laundering Red Flags Collide

Figure 12.4 indicates that in a typical commercial bribery scheme, money-laundering clues appear only at two points: payment by the coercer (1); and receipt by the extorter (2). The most likely reporter of these will be the banks or other institutions concerned.

Typically there will be peripheral clues of money-laundering and/or bribery, such as overspending by the extorter, windfall profits by the coercing organisation, and suspicions, or evidence, of perverted decisions or improper performance.

The position is different with kleptocracy and gross corruption involving political leaders and PEPs, mainly because the amounts are so vast. But even then, recent experience shows that people like Presidents Mubarak, Gadhafi and Mugabe have little difficulty laundering their funds through apparently reputable banks. It is only after they fall from power that all hell breaks loose.

Many money-launderers face the common problems of how to place their criminal proceeds in a legitimate entity (such as a banking or financial system) and to retain control while disassociating themselves from their criminal proceeds (Figure 12.5).

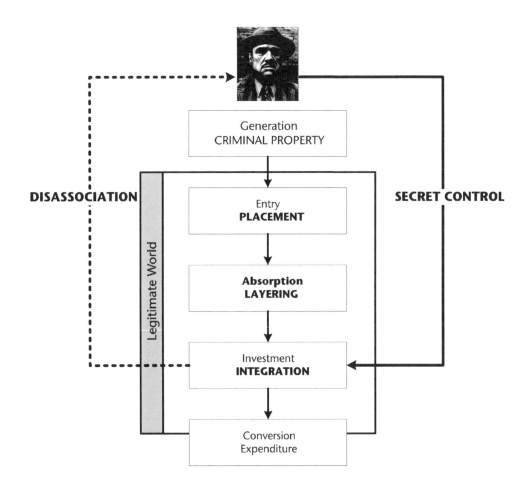

Figure 12.5 Dilemma of Control and Ownership in Money-laundering

The bottom line of the limited connection between money-laundering and bribery – for most commercial organisations – is that they:

- Should include potential money-laundering offences in their corruption risk evaluation (see Chapters 14–15) with heightened scrutiny for any transactions in the Carbon World;
- Ensure due diligence, or know your counterparty controls are proportionate to the risk and, particularly, to consolidate knowledge dispersed in different systems;[53]
- Use continuous monitoring programmes to identify possibly suspicious transactions, tracing them backwards to generation (as shown in Chapters 18–19), of perverted decisions and improper performance;
- Establish a policy[54] on when, how, where and by whom suspicious transactions should be reported;
- Train back office and Treasury employees to remain alert to symptoms of money-laundering (see pages 306–7).

Finally, anti-money-laundering efforts should be put in perspective: the vast majority of Suspicious Activity Reports (SARs) are unjustified and there is no record of any commercial bribery offence being exposed by a SAR (see Chapters 8 and 14–17 on risk-assessing reporting obligations).

Risk-management Technology

Chartis Research[55] estimates that $3.75 billion per annum is spent on risk-management technology: much of it concerned with anti-money-laundering.

Much of the expenditure is wasted on defensive reporting of unjustified suspicions.

How Bribes are Funded

The funding and concealment of bribes can be categorised as shown in Table 12.7.

---

53   For example, a single third party may have accounts set up in trading systems, accounts payable, accounts receivable or in miscellaneous accounts.

54   And decision criteria (see page 572).

55   See website at: http://www.chartis-research.com/ (accessed 23 October 2012).

Table 12.7 Funding and Concealment of Bribes

Initially Paid By	Type	Stage 1 Initial Transfer	Stage 2 Secondary Transfer	Stage 3	Stage 4
Coercer	1	Extorter			
	2	Extorter's Organisation	Extorter		
	3	Nominee	Extorter		
	4	Nominee		Third Party	Extorter
	5	Intermediary	Extorter		
	6	Intermediary		Third Party	Extorter
	7	Supplier	Extorter		
	8	Supplier		Third Party	Extorter
A Customer	9	Coercer	Extorter		
	10			Third Party	Extorter
Cash Pool	11	Extorter			
	12	Third Party or Nominee	Extorter		
Parent or Sub or Owners	13	Extorter			
Guarantee	14	Third Party	Extorter		
Pseudo Trading	15	Coercer	Extorter		
	16	Coercer		Third Party	Extorter

As Table 12.7 shows, the potential sources for bribe-funding are virtually unlimited and certainly not accurately represented by so-called red flags. The starting point is usually to identify who has responsibility (actual for contrived) for budgets (that is 'budget holders') and profit-centre accountability because they are, by far, the most common source of illicit funds. The following paragraphs examine some of the more important ways of funding and concealment.

TYPE 1: COERCER> EXTORTER

Bribes are paid from the coercing company directly to the extorter and may be concealed in accounts payable, expense accounts, journals, or the Nominal Ledger. In some cases the concealment is sophisticated (see the Oil for Food case, page 225) and supported by official-looking contracts involving property sales, options on land purchases, employment and consultancy. In other cases goods and services may be supplied free of charge to the extorter, usually off-invoice, or through an account which is subsequently written off as a bad debt. Payments may be made through any of: carbon registries, phantom over-the-counter (OTC) sales and purchases, or unrecorded shares in projects. There are other possibilities in which a coercing company pays the extorter's tax bills, contributes towards his pension, health plan, insurance, car-running expenses, golf club memberships, etc., etc., etc.!!!!

Sham Consultancy Projects

A senior executive in an oil company was involved in a car accident and his wife telephoned to ask if a colleague could recover some personal effects from his office. In looking for these, the colleague discovered a file of contracts where the company's vendors had for the past five years employed the executive in an advisory capacity. He had been repeatedly passing tendering and other sensitive information to the vendors and had been paid over $1 million for his efforts.

Dangers of Ship To Border

Marketing managers of a leading tobacco company encouraged the view that a sale was a sale, no matter who the customer was or what that customer intended to do with the product. They sold massive quantities of cigarettes to a dealer knowing – or having good reason to believe – that they were to be smuggled into another European country where they would undermine the operations of their legitimate distributor. Bribes and lavish entertaining encouraged their participation.

All went well until the legitimate distributor discovered what was happening. Although he and his family were threatened with violence, he reported the facts to Customs, who arrested members of the smuggling team.

TYPE 2: COERCER> EXTORTER'S ORGANISATION> EXTORTER

This is one of the most effective and safe ways for bribes to be paid. If it is not already (especially given the regulatory emphasis on agents), it is likely to become one of the main methods in future. It can function with a number of variations – depending on the colluder's access to records and authorities – but in a typical procurement process it works as shown in Table 12.8.

Table 12.8   Internal Conversion of Bribes

Action by the coercer, who wants to sell goods or services	Action by the extorter, who has or has contrived a requirement to buy goods or services
Agreement on pricing and the amount of bribe to be paid	
Prepares an invoice for the agreed sales price	Enters it into his organisation's records
Enters the invoice in his company's accounts	Pays in the normal way
Prepares an invoice for the amount of the bribe and enters it into his company's records	Enters the second invoice into his organisation's records
Issues a credit note for the bribe amount but does not enter it into his company's records	Enters the credit note into his organisation's accounts and converts the fictitious accounting credit thereby created by, for example: • entering a payment to the supplier but diverting it for his own benefit • transferring the credit to any accounts payable or accounts receivable subsidiary ledger over which he has control

Internal Conversion

A company wishes to bribe a foreign tax inspector to give a falsely low assessment. A demand is prepared for the agreed amount plus the bribe. This is entered into the official records. An assessment is then made for the agreed amount and the overpayment converted by the corrupt tax inspector (and probably shared with his managers).

In simple terms, including the bribe in the way shown in the examples provides the coercer and the coercing organisation with a plausible excuse if the transaction comes to notice. Cases such as the above show the possibilities of deliberate overcharging, duplicates and unrecorded credit notes in creating slush funds.

TYPE 3: COERCER> NOMINEE> EXTORTER

Bribes are paid from the coercing company to a nominee selected by the extorter and typically include (domestically or overseas):

• His wife, using her maiden name;
• Daughters using their married names;
• Brothers, sisters, father and mothers-in-law;
• Other relations;

- Neighbours, social acquaintances;[56]
- Firms, companies or partnerships in which any of the above, or the extorter, have an interest;
- Solicitors, financial advisers,[57] insurers, brokers, credit card companies.

Abbreviated Names

A senior marketing manager created a fictitious vendor called Beneficial Printing Supplies Ltd. and set up the master file so the cheques were produced to Beneficial. He had already opened a credit card in his own name with Beneficial Bank and used the cheques to pay off credit card debts for himself and those whom he had corrupted.

TYPE 4: COERCER> NOMINEE

This type is very similar to Type 2, except that the nominee further conceals the bribes by washing them through a third party. This, again, may include dummy and genuine companies, relations and friends.

TYPES 5 AND 6: COERCER> INTERMEDIARY> THIRD PARTY> EXTORTER

This type is typical of agency commission payments that are subsequently rerouted to the extorter (Type 4). The bribes are concealed in the coercing company's accounts, supported by credible documentation and in the intermediary's accounts along the lines described in Type 1. In Type 4, the bribes are concealed by further laundering through a third party.

Oil for Fraud

In Oil for Food, as soon as Iraq introduced the additional surcharge, Volvo totally changed its marketing approach and, for the first time, appointed an agent which it empowered to pay the bribes. When the case came to light, the agent wrote to Volvo saying: 'You know very well that during the said period you made and authorised payments to the Iraqi government in fulfilment of your contract obligations, contrary to the UN mandate'.

This was probably not the sort of truth Volvo wanted to hear.

---

56 Especially drinking buddies.

57 These may be avoided because of their Proceeds of Crime Act (POCA) reporting obligations.

TYPE 7: COERCER> SUPPLIER> EXTORTER

In these cases the coercing company overpays a supplier who subsequently routes the bribe to the extorter. The suppliers involved may:

- Be a fictitious vendor or one masquerading as a genuine company or fictitious branch;
- Be a vendor whose account is dormant;
- Be a genuine supplier involved in collusive over-invoicing (especially involving intangibles, freight, demurrage, warehouse charges, etc.);
- Be a genuine supplier or government agency duplicating or falsifying a payment, subsequently converting the incoming refund to the benefit of the extorter – either directly or through a nominee;
- Involve duplicating a payment to a genuine supplier, altering the electronic funds transfer parameters so that the payment is directed to the account of the extorter or a nominee;
- Involve claiming payment and other discounts from a genuine supplier and converting the incoming unrecorded cheque to the benefit of the extorter;
- Require a genuine supplier to pay advance purchase discounts and convert the incoming, unrecorded cheque to the benefit of the extorter.

Mistaken Identity

The extorter set up a company with a name very similar to the coercer's (let's call it ABC Contents Ltd.). When refund cheques were obtained from suppliers they were accepted by the false company's bankers and converted.

A very common method of fraud is to create fictitious payments using the initials of a genuine company or government department.

How Honest?

To test the honesty of its supplier base, a leading company deliberately overpaid 200 of its suppliers, including local authorities and government departments. Some payments were by transfer, some by cheque and others by duplicating Standing Orders. How many disclosed the overpayments? The answer is: just four.

TYPE 8: COERCER> SUPPLIER> THIRD PARTY> EXTORTER

Similar to Type 6 except the bribes are additionally laundered through a third party.

TYPES 9 AND TYPE 10: COERCER> CUSTOMER> THIRD PARTY> EXTORTER

The coercing company under-invoices a customer – in collusion – who pays the balance to the extorter or a nominee.

- Two sales invoices are prepared to a customer in collusion, only one of which is entered into the records. The proceeds from the second invoice are paid to the extorter or a nominee.
- Duplicate invoices are sent to a customer – not in collusion – and if both are paid, a credit note is issued internally, together with a refund which is diverted[58] to the extorter or to a nominee.
- An annual or other discount is recorded for a genuine customer without its knowledge: the refund cheque is directed to the extorter or a nominee.

In Type 9 cases, the payment from the collusive customer is laundered further through a third party.

TYPES 11 AND 12: CASH> THIRD PARTY> EXTORTER

The coercing company has created a cash pool through off-record sales or other means.[59]

Payment is made directly to the extorter and requires no concealment in the accounts. Type 11 involves the routing of the payment through a third party, nominee or intermediary.

How to Create Real Slush Funds

In the late 1990s, the Japanese electronics giant Olympus Corporation was under pressure to maintain its profits and growth records and decided, like many other companies at the time, to speculate in derivatives, credit default swaps, emerging market funds and other high-risk investments. The results were a disaster, but rather than take the hit, the management used the not uncommon scheme of *tobashi*, which involved parking loss-making transactions with third parties, special-purpose vehicles or in other fronts. The idea was that once the market recovered, the deals could be repatriated and entered as neutral or, better still, profit-making. Unfortunately, the market did not recover and Olympus kept the losses off its books, misleading the Tokyo Stock Exchange, bankers and investors in the process. The company lived with the deception for around eight years.

Between 2002 and 2008, Olympus's new management resolved to clear the losses and did so by making acquisitions at grossly inflated prices (up to 5 times turnover and 27 times EBITDA[60]) and through massive consulting and advisory fees routed through special-purpose

---

58   Incoming cheques in relation to amounts which are not recorded as a 'receivable' are as good as cash.

59   It is common for companies, especially those in the extractive industries, to engage in what is called 'tolling', where commodities are invoiced at low prices from the coercing company to an overseas entity or special-purpose vehicle and then reinvoiced to the ultimate customer at the proper price. Tolling can thereby build up substantial cash pools.

60   Earnings Before Interest, Taxes, Depreciation, and Amortization.

entities in the Caribbean allegedly controlled by Hajime Sagawa, an ex-Nomura banker, sometimes described as 'Olympus's fixer'.

However, by 2008, there was still a massive shortfall and Olympus acquired three Japanese companies[61] and Gyrus Group Plc, a reputable British manufacturer of endoscopes and other optical medical equipment. The price for Gyrus was agreed at $2.1 billion, with success fees being negotiated with Axes America LLC and Axam Investments, based in the Cayman Islands. Both were allegedly controlled or influenced by Hajime Sagawa and Akio Nakagawa[62] as fronts for Olympus.

Initially, Axes and Axam agreed a success fee for the acquisition of Gyrus of 1 per cent, but this was renegotiated – supposedly without advice – to include cash and preference shares. Gyrus shares were allotted to Axes–Axam. After the deal had closed, Olympus issued a side letter which gave the allocated preference shares extensive veto rights, dramatically increasing their value. In March 2010, Olympus bought out the Axes–Axam interests in Gyrus for $620 million, making the total success fees more than $687 million (at 31 per cent described as the largest M&A[63] fee ever). Olympus also wrote off between $600 and $721 million from its investment in three Japanese acquisitions (around 93 per cent of the consideration).

KPMG, who was the auditor for both Olympus and Gyrus. resigned as the latter's auditors.[64] KPMG in Japan made the reports it was required to make to the authorities and was replaced by Ernst & Young as Olympus's auditors. It appears that at no stage were any of the accounts of the companies involved qualified.

In March 2011, after the collapse and de-registration of Axam in the Caymans, Olympus booked the success fees. Six months later all hell was let loose when Michael Woodford, a long-serving Olympus executive, resigned after serving just a few months as CEO of Olympus Corporation. It has been suggested that he was selected by the Japanese as a puppet who could be controlled. If this is so, it must rank as one of the least shrewd decisions ever because when he could not get answers internally he reported to the SFO and the Securities and Exchange Commission (SEC).

The case will, no doubt, take years to resolve, but the position at the time of writing is that around $6.5 billion is unaccounted for. How much, if any, was used for self-enrichment by Olympus's and other executives remains unclear, but with that amount of money slushing around it would be too much to expect it was all used to cover up earlier losses. Remember the rule about sticky fingers.

---

61   Now suspected of being fronts for organised crime (Yakuza).

62   Another ex-banker.

63   Mergers and acquisitions.

64   Mainly because it was unhappy about the roles of Axes–Axam.

TYPE 13: ASSOCIATE COMPANY> EXTORTER

A parent, subsidiary, associated company or joint venture of the coercing company, or a director or officer from his or her loan account, pays a bribe directly to the extorter, through a nominee, to a third party or in any of the other ways described above. Depending on the tax situation and the nature of the relationship, the organisation or individual making the payment may back-charge it by debiting an intercompany account.

TYPE 14: OFF-RECORD GUARANTEE> THIRD-PARTY> EXTORTER

This type is entirely off-record and involves the coercing company providing a guarantee (normally unrecorded in its accounts), enabling the extorter or a nominee to obtain loans or a financial benefit from a third party

TYPES 15 AND 16: PSEUDO-TRADING TRANSACTIONS> EXTORTER

The coercing company, directly or through a financial intermediary, enters into pseudo-trading transactions – creating a profit for the intermediary, or a nominee of the third party. In Type 15 cases, the profits are laundered through one or more third parties. Especially dangerous in this type are carbon credit transactions. These are not effectively regulated, nor subject to a Suspicious Activity Report. Transfers can be made through any of the multiple exchanges, through the CDM Registry or elsewhere – and bear in mind that there are hundreds of millions of euros washing around these accounts, much of which are represented by hidden reserves not recorded on any organisation's Balance Sheet.

A Classic Problem of Slush Funds and Tolling

Companies, especially in the former Soviet Union and in countries where there are still exchange control restrictions in place, have developed a system for transacting commodities, known as 'tolling', which normally involves split invoicing and payments to offshore tax havens. Tolling was and, in some cases still is, approved by the Russian, Ukrainian and other governments for processing within their borders commodities (such as oil and metals) obtained from foreign suppliers and after refining selling them on the export markets. Tax and other laws on tolling are complex and subject to political whim.

Essentially, a company (Company A: typically based in the Isle of Man, or the Virgin Islands) delivers raw material to a Russian or Ukrainian processor but retains ownership of it. Company A pays a toll for the raw material to be refined by Company B. The finished product may be sold and exported by A or B to a third party and may be invoiced by both companies, an agent or in a variety of other ways. Company A invoices the end customer for the raw materials (plus a profit) and B for the tolling fee, plus a profit. Such transactions minimise taxes for Company B. They usually appear in the records of the ultimate buyer as split invoices and as such are bound to excite regulators.

Tolling transactions must always be assessed as high risk because they could represent:

- Tax evasion by the processor or by the end buyer (and proceeds of crime);
- Evasion of export or import controls or restrictions on the allocations of scarce products;
- Skimming of profits out of company A behind the backs of institutional shareholders and financiers;
- Fraud by the directors and managers of company A;
- Fraud by the directors or employees of the ultimate buyer;[65]
- Creation of slush funds for use in corrupt schemes or to support local or national politicians by either the exporter or the importer.

There are also cases where split invoicing is explained as legitimate tolling when it does not remotely comply with the principles concerned. On the other hand tolling transactions may be entirely legitimate.

It is very difficult for an honest buyer to confirm which of the above reasons apply and (if it is in the regulated sector for the purposes of the Proceeds of Crime Act, or has appointed a Money-Laundering Reporting Officer or nominated officer) whether it should:

- Seek specific consent from the SFO and the Serious Organised Crime Agency (SOCA) for all tolling transactions;
- Submit SARs on the basis that the transactions may represent the proceeds of crime.

Further, companies in the extractive industries (which are bound by the Dodd–Frank Act) will, in future, be required to fully disclose all tolls.

Based on decision-centric risk assessment (see Chapters 14–16) the critical point to verify is that at no stage were arrangements intended to induce improper performance or, if any of the parties involved are state-controlled, intended to influence an FPO.

Suggested options for maintaining controls over tolling are discussed in Chapter 24.

How Bribes Are Recorded and Concealed

For most bribe payments an audit trail is left in the coercing company's records or in associates' accounts including:

- Accounts Payable and receivable
- Ancillary charges (such as freight, demurrage and exchange differences)
- Associated company records and charge-backs
- Bad debt write-offs
- Bank statement and cash book variances
- Budgetary records
- Carbon Trading, Clean Development Mechanism (CDM) and Exchange Accounts
- Cash Book
- Credit card accounts
- Credit notes

---

65   Who may be the initiators of the tolling arrangements.

- Customer master file (possibly involving changes to payment parameters)
- Debit notes
- Directors' Loan Accounts
- Expense statements
- Fixed asset records
- General Ledger
- Intercompany accounts
- Inventory records
- Joint-venture Accounts
- Journals and vouchers
- Legal records and agreements
- Nominal Ledger
- PayPal and eBay
- Personal Expense Claims
- Project accounts (especially those showing windfall profits)
- Purchase invoices
- Purchase Ledger
- Sales invoices
- Sales Ledger
- Share registers and transfer documents
- Split invoicing and tolling transactions
- Spread sheets
- Statistical records
- Suspense accounts
- Taxation accounts
- Trading, Treasury dealing and other transactional records
- Travelling expenses
- Treasury accounts
- Unallocated cash
- Vendor master file.

The potential for concealment depends on the coercing company's Chart of Accounts, its budgetary and cost centre records and management reports. The ideal accounts are obviously those that are loosely controlled.

In addition, other advantages may be provided to decision-makers entirely off-book. For example, by the owners or directors of a company – wealthy in their own right – from their personal funds or by making luxury personal assets such as executive jets, holiday villas, fishing or shooting estates, corporate golf club memberships available.

There is a final category called in Chapter 7 'advantage schemes', which includes marketing and promotional benefits, channel support, hospitality, gifts, etc., whose provision to third parties may be interpreted as technical violations of the Bribery Act.

Referral Corruption and Reciprocity

It now seems standard practice that participants in a market – having secured revenue for themselves – will then refer the transaction or customer to non-competing businesses in return for a corporate commission or reciprocity.[66] The example of barristers paying referral fees to instructing solicitors is discussed on pages 262 and 319, but the practice is extremely common in other commercial and governmental sectors.

Police Referral Scams

It has been reported that police officers earn up to £1,000 a time, ostensibly for the Police Authority (or personally if they falsify reports), by calling in selected garages to tow away and repair vehicles involved in the UK's 2 million crashes per annum. Large insurance companies also claim commissions by referring accident claims to contingency fee lawyers and car hire firms. This is said to be a £1 billion per annum business that has driven up premiums by around 30 per cent per annum.

Jack Straw, the ex-Justice Secretary referred to this practice as 'this is not a system it's a racket'.

There are two circumstances in which referrals may contravene the Bribery Act. The first involves the corporate commission, where the advantage is intended to induce improper performance and breach the trust between, for example, an insurance company and its customer (see the Law Commission Report page 785 relating to bribery with consent of the principal). The second is far more blatant, where an employee – knowing that his employer has a referral contract with the third party – accepts a personal advantage for making concealed private arrangements.

Professional Firm Referrals

In 2011, Accenture paid $63.7 million in settlement of long-running litigation[67] under the False Claims Act, which alleged that it had received kickbacks from IT suppliers for recommending their products for government contracts on which it had been retained as an independent adviser. Accenture denied liability and said that it had settled to avoid additional time, inconvenience and expense that would come with prolonged litigation. However, the Attorney General's Office took a different view and stated: 'At a time when we are looking for ways to reduce our public spending, it is especially important to ensure that government contractors play by the rules and don't waste precious taxpayer dollars'. IBM, Hewlett Packard, PriceWaterhouseCoopers and Sun Microsystems were also named.

---

66   'Scratch my back'.

67   Which was started in 2004.

Non-financial Corruption

There are many ways that a decision can be improperly influenced other than through bribery. The OECD and others appear to be troubled by family relationships and although it is true that they can be influential, experience suggests that social, leisure and neighbourhood relationships are equally important, involving nepotism, cronyism and tribalism.

Friendly Relationships

The fact that a freight forwarder and a foreign customs officer genuinely like each other and perhaps share the same hobby will have an influence on decisions taken. If the freight forwarder's intention is to rely on their friendship to influence the customs officer, he has technically breached Section 6 of the UK Bribery Act. The wording of the act is ridiculous and could cover cases where a freight forwarder sends a very attractive lady, wearing a low-cut dress and short skirt, to clear goods through customs. Would this influence the officer?

If the same relationship were to exist in the UK there would be no offence because it would be necessary to show that the influence resulted in improper performance.

Many collusive relationships are virtually impossible to detect during due diligence or pre-employment screening but they may subsequently become apparent by careful analysis and mapping of telephone call logs, Christmas card lists, email traffic and hospitality reimbursement. However one red flag that should be emphasised is that described as 'revolving doors', in which a coercing organisation engages a senior official to make introductions to his previous employer or is employed primarily because of his or her inside knowledge.

Internal Corruption[68]

GENERAL

The Bribery Act, unlike previous laws on corruption, does not simply apply to those cases where the coercer and the extorter represent different organisations, but is based on an improper performance model. This means it is quite possible for an employee of an organisation to be guilty of bribing a colleague where his intention is to provoke a perverted decision, probably to deceive a third party. This means that, for example, providing an advantage of any sort to obtain promotion or to avoid disciplinary action could contravene sections 1 and 2 and potentially result in a Section 7 liability.

---

68   If the body corporate is a relevant commercial organisation and the intention is to obtain business for it.

Internal Corruption

Bill Flash is a Sales Manager for company X and to meet his key performance targets needs to close a sale to ABC Ltd. before the end of the month. Colin Cautious, a fairly junior employee in the credit department, has refused to process the order because he suspects that the customer is a Long Firm Fraud. Bill Flash tells him if he passes the order through he will share his commission of £10,000 with him and will also pay for him to join the Pink Pussycat Lap Dancing Club. Colin agrees.

Based on the above, Bill has committed an offence under Section 1 and Colin under Section 2. Because X is a relevant commercial organisation and Bill's intention was to obtain a business advantage for it, Company X is corporately liable under Section 7.

Spiffing

'Spiffing' is a term used when one company gives personal benefits directly to employees of another to take decisions in its favour. Examples include electronic companies that give gift vouchers (or sometimes cash) directly to their customers' employees to push their products ahead of their competitors'. The SFO seems to have the wrong end of the stick on Special Payment Incentives for Fast Sales (SPIFS) and is relaxed about them, provided that the advantaged employee's boss knows and that the benefit is not used to bribe someone else. In fact, SPIFS are an incentive to deceive customers, to whom retail employees owe a duty to perform honestly. They should thus make it clear to customers precisely what the commission arrangements are.

Internal corruption is a serious risk for marketing and sales departments, where employees collude (and gain an advantage from commissions and bonuses) to deceive third parties (see also Chapters 7–8). Cases in the banking sector, where account managers push supposedly brilliant schemes to investors while in their own portfolios short them as rubbish, are likely to contravene sections 1, 2 and 7 of the Bribery Act. Training programmes should specifically address this risk.

INCOMING AND OUTGOING TEAM DEFECTIONS

The improper performance model of the Bribery Act also turns what hitherto has usually been a civil breach into a criminal offence under sections 1, 2 and 7. While employees are free to advance their careers, change jobs or start up their own businesses, they and their associates must make sure that they avoid inducing any breach of the duty of trust and do not get involved in any improper performance.

Team Defections

A bank approaches Tommy Highflyer, the head trader working for a rival, with an offer too good to refuse. They agree to pay him an additional golden handshake of £20,000 for any member of his existing team that defects and joins him. Tommy persuades three traders to decamp and helps them negotiate very attractive packages. In addition he tells them he will split his handshake with them if they are able to convince customer X to transfer his accounts to the new employer.

There is an arguable case that the new employer breaches Section 1 and Section 7, Tommy breaches sections 1 and 2, and the other traders Section 2. If the SFO wants to flex its muscles it could allege that Tommy's breach of Section 2 also involves an equivalent corporate offence because he holds himself out as a director.[69]

Conflicts of Interest

There are many ways in which an agent may hold and conceal an interest which conflicts with his employment. Typical examples include those listed in Table 12.9.

Table 12.9   Possible Conflicts of Interest

Conflicting Activity	Typical Jobs Affected	Possible Result
Hyperactive social commitments, possibly involving the misuse of drugs and alcohol	All	• Poor performance at work • Failure to control subordinates
All-consuming political activity	All, but more usually middle-level managers	• Poor performance • Stretched loyalty
Freelance journalism	All	• Disclosure of sensitive information
Skimming	Top managers	• Interposing their personal interests in transactions involving their employer
Second job	Junior and secretarial employees	• Poor performance and absences
Part-time employment with a supplier or customer	Marketing or procurement staff	• Favours provided for the supplier or customer • Fraud
Part-time employment with a competitor	Marketing and especially salesmen	• Diversion of business • Fraud

---

69   There would be no Section 7 offence as Tommy had no intention to obtain or retain business for the existing employer.

Financial interest in a competing company	Senior Management	• Diversion of business • Fraud
Private consultancy	Professional and technical staff	• Diversion of business • Misuse of resources

In some cases, conflicting interests may be acceptable, providing they are honestly disclosed.

There are additional dangers for companies who do not have a policy on conflicts of interest but rely on Fidelity Insurance as a final safety net against fraud. Most policies require proof that the employee acted with a manifest intent to cause a loss and with the intention of gain for himself or another. The personal gain test excludes salaries, bonuses and similar payments earned in the normal course of employment. Thus if an employee sets up a private company and disguises what are, in fact, bribes, as genuine income for his private company, the insurer can argue the defence that the payments were in the normal course of business and therefore not covered by the policy.

The borderline between conflicting interests and corruption is indistinct. An employee may start off innocently in a small private business, then begin to use his employer's facilities, then approach its suppliers for cheap goods and services. This gives the wrong signal and leads to serious corruption. Conflicts of interest should always be treated seriously and all organisations should specify a policy and require annual declarations of compliance. These points are expanded on page 567.

An Old but Clear Case

Two programmers, working for X Limited, decided it would be okay for them to set up their own consultancy company to offer Y2K solutions. They started off in a small way, but gradually drew other of X's employees into the scheme and spent more and more time, during normal working hours, on their private venture. The pressures became too great and they employed consultants, but processed their invoices through X's accounts payable system. They also used X's computers for testing their private work.

Eventually the bubble burst. The private deal had cost X Limited over £300,000 in lost time and false consulting charges. Worse still, it had delayed its own Y2K efforts by about six months.

Information Broking and Commercial Espionage

Information broking is, as its name implies, the practice of supplying inside information (often stolen), usually to enable an organisation to win contracts. It is a very common practice throughout the world: and not just in LDCs:

A Rare UK Case

In 2007, Michael Hale, aged 58, a senior employee of the Ministry of Defence, was imprisoned for two years for receiving bribes of more than £217,000 for releasing confidential information to Pacific Consolidated Industries, based in California, which enabled it to successfully bid for contracts worth £4.5 million to supply British Armed Forces with gas containers. The information supplied by Mr Hale included his department's budget for purchasing gas equipment, as well as the prices and specifications of previous contracts.

Another Information Broker

In May 2011, Tenaris, SA, a Luxembourg incorporated global supplier of pipeline products and services to the oil and gas industry, entered into a two-year deferred prosecution agreement with the Department of Justice, with a $3.5 million criminal penalty as well as a $5.4 million disgorgement in relation to information broking in Uzbekistan in 2006 and 2007. The US claimed jurisdiction because Tenaris – which had self-disclosed and fully cooperated – had listed its ADS securities on the New York Stock Exchange and processed payments to the information broker through the American banking system.

Tenaris made approximately $5 million in profits based on improperly obtained information on competitors' bids from the state-owned oil company. Bribes were paid from an information broker's commission of 3.5 per cent.

Risks to Confidential Information

A European manufacturer of plastics invented and patented a new process which it believed would revolutionise the industry, and decided to build three new plants incorporating the new technology. Announcements in the trade press attracted the attention of information brokers, and they quickly corrupted a key employee into giving away plans and specifications which they sold to a competitor in Eastern Europe. The manufacturer's advantage was quickly lost.

Ironically in none of the Ministry of Justice or other official guidelines is information broking mentioned, neither is the obvious red flag when an intermediary offers to provide inside information to win contracts.

Advance Fee Frauds

These frauds range from semi-legitimate to indefensibly fraudulent and centre on upfront payment for services or goods that are not delivered. They are often associated with information broking, where corrupt sellers are duped into paying for inside information that is not available, or is falsified.

Trading in Influence and Lobbying

Lobbywatch, an American organisation, reported that between 1998 and 2003 more than $13 *billion!!* was spent on lobbying federal and state politicians and listed the contributions made by the top 250 lobbying firms. Open Secrets Org (the Centre for Responsive Politics) monitored the 2008 election in which President Obama prevailed and noted that political contributions totalled $1,812,960,562. This would seem to be an outrageous waste of money unless the donors were confident of some personal returns: which, of course, they are. There is no such thing as a free lunch.

Successive UK governments have beaten their chests over their enthusiasm for their own intention to deal with political lobbying. Unfortunately the intention was never acted upon and it is estimated that the Westminster lobbying machine collects some £2 billion per annum to influence government and official decisions; and the European Union is even worse!

The Cost of One Meeting

The alleged spontaneous–accidental meeting in Dubai between Liam Fox, then the UK's Defence Minister, and Harvey Boulter a USA defence contractor, apparently resulted from a £10,000 payment to a lobbying firm to arrange the introduction.

Circumvention of the Spirit

In August 2012, allegations surfaced that aides to President Obama had deliberately circumvented White House rules for meetings with lobbyists representing pharmaceutical companies days before health care reforms were being debated in Congress. The spirit of the rules was that all meetings should be recorded.

Mr Jim Messina, who was managing President Obama's re-election campaign, is alleged to have written emails from his personal account stating that he would 'roll' Nancy Pelosi (the Speaker of the House) for the $4 billion needed by the health care program and that he would 'deal' with a reporter who had questioned links between the White House and the pharmaceutical industry.

Jeffrey Smith, one of the President's science advisers, suggested an off-site meeting in a local coffee bar, explaining that this would avoid 'appearing on the White House Visitor Lists [...] which may be not what you would want at this stage'.

These cases demonstrate the extremes that politicians will go to (a) to obtain funding so that they get, or retain, power; and (b) their determination to circumvent rules they have themselves defined.

Revolving Doors

The term 'revolving doors' applies to the placement of someone from a political, governmental, regulatory or competitive entity with the intention of leveraging his or her knowledge, skills or contacts to the benefit of the new employer. Again, it is a very common practice in the UK and includes many senior SFO officers who have left to join law and consulting firms to advise on the Bribery Act and, of course, Anthony Charles Lynton Blair (aka Tony), who is earning money like there is no tomorrow.

Chapter 26 suggests that pre-employment screening processes should ensure that offences of the type described on pages 115 and 326 (revolving doors) are avoided when ex-government officials are recruited or appointed as advisers.

Violence and Blackmail

Although they could hardly be described as financial or other advantages, violence, threats of it and blackmail often feature in corruption cases: sometimes backed by organised crime.

Formula One

The November 2011 case in Germany involving the Formula 1 magnate Bernie Ecclestone threw up some interesting problems, with more to follow. The allegation was that 'Ecc' and trusts with which he is supposedly associated bribed a German manager with tens of millions of pounds to sell out his bank's racing interests. The defence did not deny the payments but said they were to stop the banker from revealing Mr Ecclestone's doubtful affairs to HMRC.

The Bottom Line

The conclusion drawn from the above analysis is that corruption is not quite as simple or as obvious as the OECD and others would like everyone to believe, with its focus on corrupt countries and payments routed through agents. On a rough calculation, there are over 2,000 permutations in which a coercing company can provide undue advantages and conceal them. As a result, audit and monitoring methods, which are discussed in Chapters 18–20, must be wider and deeper than the official guidelines suggest.

On the other hand, everything centres on the improper decisions and performance of the extorter. This confirms that the OECD and others have missed the point by taking such a detached view of so-called passive corruption because it is usually in the **extorter's organisation that the most effective controls can be applied**.

CHAPTER 13 *Examples of High-risk Processes and Contexts*

The Dangers of Red Flags and Profiles

As Homer Simpson, the famous American philosopher, is alleged to have said:[1]

In general, making generalisations is dangerous. Well generally it is.

Everything is bad if you remember it.

Homer's edicts are certainly true of both corruption and corporate fraud because there are so many generalisations based on red flags, profiles, anecdotes and perceptions. Of these, red flags are probably the most misleading and counterproductive. They:

- are often anecdotal, inaccurate or out of date;
- are all given the same weight even though some may have been triggered years ago and are no longer relevant;
- enable potential perpetrators to set up their schemes to avoid triggering a profile;
- encourage regulators to seize upon any flags that a company has not heeded to assert that procedures are inadequate;
- mislead honest people into believing that a transaction is safe because it does not trigger a red flag when in fact it is manifestly dishonest;
- result in due diligence focusing on publicly recorded negative data while ignoring positive attributes;
- are too generic and do not take account of variables in particular industries, organisations and processes;
- are too high-level and do not drill down to specific detail;
- do not take account of the fact that criminal performance changes dramatically to fit the circumstances and therefore tend to be quickly out of date.

To have any value at all red flags must be anticipatory, based on decision-centric risk assessment in the context concerned and cannot be avoided by evasive planning (see pages 224 and 341 et seq).

More meaningful red flags of corruption include:

---

1   Although there is now no trace in his published works.

- A perverted decision leading to improper performance;
- A decision justified by a noble cause such as the Oil for Food programme, private finance initiatives (PFI), international aid, reconstruction and development, privatisation or, now, saving the world from global warming;
- Windfall profits for those favoured with access or being able to flourish in markets that no one else can penetrate;
- A lack of accountability especially between disparate government agencies and the private and public sectors.

The cocktail of a noble cause, and public- and private-sector interactions, is a toxic recipe for corruption.

Nowhere in any of the official guidelines on bribery or any other compliance matter does the term 'green flag' ever appear. The most likely reason for this is that regulators go to lengths to avoid commitment and accountability and parrot what should not be done rather than what should, because it gives them the chance to second-guess.

A strange characteristic of corruption is that organisations disadvantaged by it are unwilling to complain. This apathy is already visible in the Carbon World, where Western companies that have been disadvantaged – and sometimes devastated – by false claims to carbon credits by their competitors, and thus hidden subsidies, have remained silent. As the director of one victim company stated:

Putting Rats on Plates

If we put a rat on their plate, they will put one on ours. We are better off just forgetting it. Besides that, who knows, we may be able to climb on the bandwagon at some point.

For the above reasons this book does not rely on red flags, although the following paragraphs and Chapters 14–15 on Risk Assessment provide background and tools for organisations to identify contexts vulnerable to incoming, internal, outgoing and competitive corruption.

Acquisitions, Joint Ventures and Disposals

For risk-assessment purposes these potentially vulnerable operations can be grouped together because:

- They may incur serious financial losses and regulatory penalties;
- They involve strategic decisions that can be perverted by 'dodgy dossiers' and political and high-level corruption to increase or decrease the value of the transaction or earn outs;
- They are driven by the possibility of windfall profits or loss avoidance;

- Bribes may be paid and concealed[2] by share issuance or options, back-to-back deals;[3] side letters, possibly through front companies in offshore centres;
- Participation may involve derived liabilities[4] for UK participants under Section 7.

The options for fraud and corruption are virtually unlimited and thus acquisitions, joint ventures and disposals must be thoroughly risk-assessed[5] and every important decision leading up to participation and in the new enterprise independently validated.

The Double Whammy of Acquisitions

The Ministry of Justice Guidance, as well as others issued by Transparency International (see Chapters 2–3), emphasise how important it is for the acquiring company to carry out due diligence on the target investment, presumably on the basis that the bigger company is more ethical. In fact, this is not necessarily the case and small acquired companies are at risk by having their senior's unethical practices imposed upon them.[6] For this reason, due diligence should be reciprocal and should also extend to the planned emerging organisation.

A detailed methodology for assessing risks in joint ventures and other collaborative relationships is discussed in Chapter 16 and additional controls in Chapter 32.

Advertising, Marketing and Sales

THE CENTRE OF OUTGOING CORRUPTION?

Marketing and sales are grossly unappreciated skills,[7] especially by people who have never had to sell and who fail to understand that no matter how good a company's products are, its reputation, and policies on compliance, they will all be to no avail unless someone, somewhere, can sell. That said, sales and marketing constitute the greatest risk of outgoing bribery, resulting in breaches of Section 1 and Section 7 of the Act.

Most good marketers have skins as thick as an elephant's: they are determined, resourceful, competitive and do not like control. The most successful are right-hemisphere dominated[8] and are rewarded for overcoming all barriers in the way of a potential transaction.

---

2   As discussed in Chapter 12.

3   Executed after the primary transaction has been completed.

4   Successor liability.

5   Usually in the highest possible band as far as fraud and corruption are concerned.

6   Reciprocal due diligence is especially important for privatisation and PFI transactions.

7   Especially by politicians and regulators.

8   Creative rather than conformist.

Corruption and fraud in marketing (and they can go together, with the salesman sharing in bribes paid by his employer to a buyer) can be viewed in four main categories:

• Gross bribery (outgoing bribery and fraud);
• Frauds in marketing support, advertising and sales promotion (outgoing, internal and incoming bribery and fraud);
• Frauds by professional salesmen (mainly outgoing bribery);
• Referral fees, reciprocation and commission sharing.

The following overview[9] of these categories and Chapters 23 and 29 suggest some ideas for control.

Gross Corruption

History is stained by frauds and corruption in sales and marketing, ranging from British Aerospace to boiler shop scams involving organised criminal gangs and corruption through referral fees. Cases often involve massive bribes to obtain business and should be the main focus of the Bribery Act, rather than tinkering with facilitation payments and hospitality. The problem is that within bribe-paying organisations[10] the marketing and competitive context is endemically corrupt and resistant to control.

Some of the unconventional clues of potential corruption problems within marketing (not red flags!) include:

• A separation from other parts of the organisation – into a fiefdom[11] – deliberately created by senior marketers;
• Repeated small breaches of accounting and other procedures;
• A culture of laddishness and indiscipline involving promiscuity, alcohol, drugs, or expenses abuse;
• Extensive reliance on outside consultants and advisers;
• Unsubstantiated claims of success and false reporting;
• Excessive focus on achieving targets, especially those relating to personal incentives;
• Captive support and accounting teams;
• Unusually close relationships with competitors;
• A repeated unwillingness to deal with poorly performing employees.[12]

Finally, in many cases of grand corruption dealt with by the authors, those paying bribes have shared in them, with the result that their living style (especially on luxuries such as jewellery, watches, cars and houses) has been far beyond that which could be supported by their disclosed remuneration.

---

9   See *Corporate Fraud* III by Michael J. Comer (Gower, Third edition, 1998) for a more detailed examination.

10   That can be government departments as well as companies.

11   Or a company within a company.

12   Often involving generous redundancy packages.

MARKETING SUPPORT

Advertising and marketing campaigns are mounted only after extensive research into the optimum product specification and price, and the nature of the competition. Management relies on the output from this research, usually without ever considering the possibilities that it could be fraudulent and which spill over into bribery offences.

The main risks of fraud (and associated corruption) include those listed in Table 13.1.

Table 13.1 Market Research Frauds

Fraud Committed By	Mechanics and Detail
Employees	Accepting bribes to appoint a Market Research or Corporate Intelligence company or to approve its invoices (incoming and internal bribery)
	Approving the use of unlawful or unethical methods of data collection by researchers
Market researchers	Distorting results to support a vested or conflicting interest ('dodgy dossiers') and sales forecasts that benefit a vendor
	Charging for work not done as specified
Corporate intelligence companies	Using illegal or unethical practices to obtain competitive intelligence
	Charging for work not done
	Falsifying results

Some frauds can involve serious consequences. The case involving British Airways (BA) and Virgin Atlantic, in which it is alleged that agents acting on behalf of BA used dirty tricks, resulted in multi-million dollar legal actions in the USA, which are far from resolved. Even if the allegations are incorrect, the adverse publicity and waste of management time can be substantial.

ADVERTISING AGENCIES

Structure of advertising agencies

Most advertising agencies are honest, but they operate in complex areas, and genuine and not-so-genuine errors can be made. Business for the agencies is highly competitive and only the best survive in the long term. The big agencies are regularly threatened by breakaway groups and have to fight to retain their positions.

Some agencies have associated companies that handle media-buying[13] and production. These sit between the agency and the media supplier, often justified by the claim that this increases efficiency. However, some media-buying subsidiaries are little more than a vehicle to accumulate media-supplier discounts, which are retained as agency profits rather than being passed on to clients. An indication of the scale of retained discounts

---

13   Such as press, radio or TV advertising.

can be estimated from the turnover and profits of the media-buying subsidiaries of the big agencies. They are substantial.

Production may be handled internally by the agency, or passed to an associate company or subcontractor. This structure provides the opportunity for overcharging and duplicate billing, with some of the proceeds being kicked back to employees.

Old Jaguar Case

Roger Fielding, who had been a manager in the technical publications department of Jaguar Cars, was jailed for three years and his colleague Ronald Parker for eighteen months. Three other defendants, including Reynard Platt, the ex-head of the production group in the leading agency – Saatchi and Saatchi – was jailed for two years.

The court was told that Mr Platt acted as the middleman, negotiating contacts with subcontractors for translating Jaguar's handbooks and technical manuals. He farmed out the work to genuine subcontractors but submitted vastly inflated invoices to Jaguar, which Fielding and Parker approved. Fielding, whom it was alleged had pocketed more than £300,000 in bribes, lived in an expensive farmhouse, received free flights and wore Italian suits and spiffy shoes.

A major weakness is that clients take no part in the allocation of production work and whether or not competitive quotations have been properly obtained. The appointment of the agent as well as authorisation of its charges[14] are seriously exposed to incoming and internal bribery, and most agencies are providers of lavish hospitality.

Standard contracts

Standard contracts used by advertising agencies are complex and provide the client with limited opportunities to check their charges. Very few provide the right to audit and when they do, the rights are restricted. Contracts may keep the client in the dark over the situations in which competitive quotes from subcontractors will be sought and the basis on which work will be allocated. It is even more dangerous, however, for a client to retain an agency without a contract.

The basis on which an agency will make its charges can vary substantially. Typically artwork and production, including video and films, will be charged at cost plus an agency commission or a fixed price inclusive of commission.

These prices may be subject to annual or quantity rebates and, more importantly, will be adjusted if the client makes any change to the specifications. For example editors' corrections, even when they are minor, justify an agency exceeding a supposedly fixed price.

---

14   Incoming bribery to approve overcharging.

Media costs for television, radio and newspaper advertising may be based on percentage of expenditure, again subject to adjustment, depending on the amounts spent over the year. The contract of a leading agency stated that its commissions would be in the bands detailed in Table 13.2.

Table 13.2 Agency Commission Rates

Total Media Expenditure by the Client in the Year in £ millions	Commission
less than 5	14.75%
5 to 8	13.0%
8 to 11	11.5%
over 10	9.0%

Keeping track of these varying rates is difficult for the client and errors can be made. In the above example, some agencies will charge commission in each band and others will apply the lowest rate to all bands once expenditure has reached the appropriate limit.

Table 13.3 Commission Calculations

Total Media Expenditure by the Client in the Year in £ millions	Commission	On a £20 million Expenditure	
		Amount due Each band	Amount Due Highest Rate and 9% Throughout
less than 5	14.75%	737,500	
5 to 8	13.0%	390,000	
8 to 11	11.5%	345,000	
over 10	9.0%	900,000	
Totals	—	2,372,000	1,800,00

Also the way some agencies interpret the word 'expenditure' can lead to problems. For example, when a client had reached the 11.5 per cent rate, the agency calculated its commission on invoices as shown in Table 13.4.

Table 13.4 Costs and Expenditure

Element	Calculation Made		Correct interpretation	
	Amount	**Percentage**	**Amount**	**Percentage**
Basic charges shown on the Rate Card of the media supplier	200,000			
Gross cost of media charged to the media-buying subsidiary of the agency	100,000	100%	100,000	100%
Agency discount allowed on the invoice by the media supplier	15,000	15%	15,000	15%
Net expenditure	85,000	85%	85,000	85%
Agency commission	11,500	11.5%	9,775	11.5% on net
Charged to client	96,500	96.5%	94,774	94.7

This resulted in a 15 per cent overcharge. In addition, some media suppliers allow agencies two for one type deals, free space and quantity discounts which are not shown on the face of the invoices. Rarely are these additional discounts passed on to clients and some agencies look upon them as their own:

Media-buying

An agency, which refused to allow its client to audit the records of B, its media-buying subsidiary, stated, 'The nature of media-buying is that it is an art not a science. It will always be dependent on individual negotiations – different rates will be paid by different advertisers at different times. We can also state categorically that no additional discounts are passed to B over and above the normal agency discount'.

It did not admit that the normal agency discount included a further deduction from the newspapers' statements or an allowance of free pages for other clients. The newspapers concerned were prepared to produce copies of their invoices to B but would not allow inspection of their ledgers or statements. Their refusal to assist answered the question, but made quantification of the loss impossible to establish.

Another agency which was found not be passing on discounts to clients responded:

Hidden Discounts

Historically the client has been exceptionally demanding, requiring last-minute changes [...] as a result many jobs run over the estimates of cost [...] while the agency does earn additional discounts from certain external suppliers, these predominantly relate to volume based on total agency expenditure, rather than to specific client expenditure and are mainly linked to payment terms of 30 days.

Because of cases such as the above, it is important that contracts with agencies provide extensive audit rights, including full access to the records of media suppliers, in-house production and purchasing and subcontractors. They should also allow clients to review the competitive bidding and quotation files.

Invoicing and statements

Invoicing by the agencies is usually very complicated and often difficult to track to supporting evidence and especially to job bags, which consist of jumbled quotations, correspondence, journal vouchers and invoices and which frequently seem to have been misfiled or destroyed.

Invoices are submitted for payments in advance, some are based on volume, some fixed price, others cost plus and others a combination. Invoices are frequently cancelled and resubmitted: sections of invoices are credited and others are not. Duplicate invoicing for the same service, but under a different reference, is not unknown. Payments will sometimes be requested on invoices and at other times on statements. Accounting is a minefield for the unwary client and while some agencies admit that it is a shambles, they do nothing to correct it. However, very few errors are found in favour of clients.

MISUSE OF CLIENT LISTS AND SALES LEADS

Some campaigns result in advertisements, with clip-out reply coupons, in magazines and newspapers. These are normally returned to the client – by people interested in the product or service – and each one is a potential sale. Despite their importance, the costs of generating the coupons are seldom controlled:

Security of Mail

A large financial services company regularly placed expensive advertisements in the national press. A female clerk working in the Mail Room intercepted the replies and passed them to her boyfriend, who worked for a small insurance broker. He would call on prospects and persuade them to buy his company's policies. The financial services company could not understand why the response rates from its advertisements were so low and carried out enquiries. When the truth was uncovered, costs of the diverted business were estimated to be in the region of £2 million.

The same sort of diversion is true of telephone calls received in response to national advertising or telemarketing campaigns.

Lists of customers and prospective customers are also attractive to competitors and managers who are considering leaving the company to join a new employer or to start up in business for themselves. Removal or disclosure of these may involve incoming bribery.

ALLOCATION OF SCARCE RESOURCES

Demand for certain products, such as computer memory chips, IPods and pharmaceuticals sometimes exceeds supply and this fact creates an opportunity for sales staff to make windfall profits for their employer or for themselves. They may allocate scarce products to a favoured customer in return for a bribe, or set up their own company as an intermediary between their employer and its customers, raking in a nice return on the premium prices that can be charged.

The ultimate victim of such schemes may be the employer, who obtains less for its products than it should, or honest customers who are deprived of their allocations.

MARKETING SUPPORT SCHEMES

The imagination of marketers, before lunch, is unlimited and over the years there have been a number of good and some very bad schemes to encourage customers to buy products or services. The most commonly used schemes and their potential for fraud are summarised in Table 13.5.

Table 13.5 Marketing Support Frauds

Type of Marketing Scheme	OPPONENTS Type and Mechanics of Fraud	Relative Frequency (100 is very frequent and 0 is never)
COUPON REDEMPTION	**ORGANISED CRIME AND RETAILERS** Discount coupons (for example 10p off a bar of soap when you produce this coupon) are sometimes included in newspaper advertisements. Criminals collect them in bulk and use them to make fraudulent claims against the manufacturer concerned	100
BILLBACKS	**WHOESALERS AND RETAILERS** Major food and drug manufacturers provide special allowances to wholesalers and retailers who place local advertisements for their products. They accept that some of these costs can be billed back to them. The claims may be inflated.	90
ANNUAL DISCOUNTS	**EMPLOYEES OF THE SELLING & BUYING COMPANIES** These are difficult to control. Employees of the company running the scheme may convert cheques due to unsuspecting customers.	20
JUNKETS Overseas conferences Golf trips	**SENIOR MANAGERS** Sometimes expensive trips will be arranged for customers, ostensibly for sales promotion purposes. They can sometimes amount to bribery of customers and often involve padding of expenses and other forms of false accounting. In one recent case, where the company traditionally took its top 20 customers and their wives to luxury holiday resorts, the CEO set up his own travel agency and skimmed off more than $900,000 in a four-year period	100
2 FOR 1	**EMPLOYEES OF THE SELLING AND BUYING COMPANIES** In brewing and other sectors, sales promotions are on the basis of buy one, get one free. These can be abused by people working for the buyer and seller. They often involve tax evasion and false accounting	80

A Case of 'Spiffing'

A major electronics company introduced a scheme under which employees working for its distributors could claim personal commissions for recommending its products in favour of its competitors. Under the Bribery Act 2010 (since the salesmen probably owed a duty of good faith to the customers) the scheme could result in criminal charges.[15]

---

15 Unless the facts were made known to the customers. Such a scheme is known as 'spiffing' (see pages 321 and 337).

Auditors and senior managers would be well advised to exercise the greatest caution over any sales promotion scheme and to determine, in advance, how it might be abused. They should also be carefully monitored.

FREE SAMPLES AND PROMOTIONAL ITEMS

Pharmaceutical companies and others who provide free samples are exposed to a wide range of frauds. Cases where samples have been repacked and sold are not uncommon. Also schemes involving special prizes and gifts, such as free holidays to Miami, are frequently abused by sales staff. Controls over promotional schemes should be reviewed by auditors before being put into operation and checked from time to time thereafter.

UNDER-RECORDED SALES

Throughout the sales and accounts receivable process, there are significant exposures to fraud and incoming and internal bribery. Examples are shown in Table 13.6.

Table 13.6 Suppressed Sales

Risk	Examples and result
OFF-RECORD SALES Goods and services sold off-invoice	• When physical goods are involved, frauds result in an inventory loss
UNDERPRICED SALES Goods and services are sold for prices below those authorised	• These frauds do not involve inventory losses but usually result in an erosion of profit margins
SALES OF SCRAP Raw materials, finished goods, etc., which supposedly fail quality standards or are redundant	• High-quality goods described as scrap • High-quality goods are deliberately damaged so that they can be sold off cheaply • Waste paper, containing confidential material, is sold to paper dealers
INTER-COMPANY SALES	• Sales priced at low inter-company rates are diverted to third parties
STAFF SALES of raw materials and finished goods	• Diverted to third parties • Mis-described
REPLACEMENTS under guarantee and warranty programmes	• Off-record sales are concealed as warrantee replacements
FALSE CREDIT NOTES AND ADJUSTMENTS False credit it given to customers with whom an employee is in collusion	• May result in stock losses and reductions of profit margins

Most of these frauds leave identifiable clues in marketing statistical records and can be detected by the tests described in Chapters 18–20.

PARALLEL TRADING

Every major manufacturer of branded goods is a target for parallel trading. These frauds involve third parties making massive purchases in a country where the prices are the lowest and shipping them to countries where much higher returns can be obtained. The Commissioners of the European Union (EU) believe that such practices encourage free trade and go so far as to make it an offence for a victim to try to intervene. This is all well and good, except that customers in the receiving market often obtain products which do not conform to local standards, or with instruction manuals and warnings they cannot understand. Guarantee cards may have been removed by the parallel traders, so that the source of the product cannot be traced and this removes the end purchaser's rights.

Worse still, the typical parallel trader will bribe salesmen working for the supplier, deal in counterfeits and smuggle products into the importing country to the cost of the revenue and the local authorised distributors. The bottom line is that parallel trading is not simply shrewdness by clever people who exploit loopholes in the pricing arrangements of multinationals. Parallel trading is usually a sign of serious fraud:

The EU Transit International Routier (TIR) Scheme and Cross-border Corruption

Senior marketing managers of some well-known American tobacco companies close their eyes to massive shipments of cigarettes invoiced to Switzerland or Liechtenstein but delivered to Antwerp or Rotterdam and which they know will be smuggled into Spain. Similar schemes run through Cyprus to the Middle East and Albania to Italy. The European Court of Auditors estimate that cigarette-smuggling costs the EU more than $166 million per annum but this is a wildly low estimate.

Marketers employed by the tobacco companies know precisely what goes on, but rationalise their wilful blindness on the grounds that 'a sale is a sale and it's none of our business where the product goes'.

This is a dangerous and short-term view. What would happen if the Spanish Customs took action against the tobacco companies under the FCPA and RICO[16] laws to obtain compensation for the lost revenues, or local distributors who were disadvantaged did the same?

Techniques to detect parallel trading and improper competitive activity are discussed in Chapters 18–20.

---

16   The Foreign Corrupt Practices Act and the Racketeer Influenced and Corrupt Organisations Act (see page 207 et seq).

THE BOTTOM LINE

Cases such as these highlight the importance of enforcing ethical codes in marketing and training salesmen in their application. Also good monitoring controls can be used to detect symptoms of improper activity before they are picked up by regulators and competitors.

Corporate Hospitality

The Law Commissioners seem to have a gruesome preoccupation with the corrupting effects of hospitality at lap-dancing clubs, especially when attendance is – as they say – covert. The Serious Fraud Office (SFO) has stated that hospitality has to be proportionate and reasonable – whatever that means.

With the greatest of respect to the Law Commissioners, the SFO and other regulators, they have no right to say what level of hospitality a company should provide in any marketplace. Most have never had to sell anything in their lives and have not the slightest idea of how difficult it is to obtain business against serious competition (see page 762).

Price-fixing and Cartels

International regulations require that companies in certain industries that compete with each other cannot fix prices nor do anything else that reduces competitiveness. The regulations hit home on the department most resistant to anything that frustrates a sale; this is the Marketing Department.

Given half a chance, marketers at all levels will compare prices with their competitors and some, if they believe they can get away with it, will fix them. This only becomes a problem if the authorities or honest competitors discover the fixing and then the results can involve serious regulatory action and civil suits:

Chemical Cartels and Corruption

In 1995, enforcement authorities, acting for the European Commission, raided the offices of more than 20 chemical companies, after receiving information that they had fixed prices and operated a cartel in 1993 and 1994.

Closely related frauds include:

- transfer pricing manipulation and related party transactions
- creation of a monopolistic position
- anti-competitor frauds.

All of these can involve serious regulatory action.

Agents and Intermediaries

RED FLAGS TO A BULL

Regulators are rightly concerned that many of the disclosed corruption cases involved routeing of bribes to third parties via genuine, shady or fictitious intermediaries, concealed in excessive commission rates or mis-described services. The case involving Volvo and Renault and the Oil for Food Programme is a classic demonstration of when an honest agent was set up by an apparently ethical company as a conduit for bribery.

The greatest dangers are perceived by officialdom to be in emerging and transitional markets. In fact, many intermediaries are major international public companies operating in mature economies.

APPOINTMENT OF AGENTS

The appointment of most agents is commercially justified. They work diligently and honestly on their principal's behalf and cause no compliance or other problems, but this does not necessarily fit with the regulatory view. Besides that-given the regulatory attention to agents-any company wishing to continue paying bribes will find alternative channels of doing so. Thus focusing on agency red flags is akin to hunting for the dodo.

THE OLD RED FLAGS STUFF

For what it's worth the usual red flags[17] involving agents, include:

Introduction of the agent[18]

- recommended by a foreign public official (FPO) or politically exposed person (PEP)
- appointed on the instructions of a government agency (in the case of some Gulf States the government insists that a certain agent is appointed)
- unwilling to have the agency relationship made public
- appears out of the blue with exceptional transactions
- breakaway from an existing agent (such as team defections and start-ups)

Business case

- has little or no expertise or experience in the industry

---

17   Publishers of guidelines seem to collect red flags much like stamps. The more they can accumulate the better.

18   It should be noted that red flags do not carry the same weight or significance and it is therefore important to base appointments on a decision matrix of the type discussed on page 596 et seq.

- offers exceptional windfall profits or the ability to enter a market closed to competitors
- *offers inside information (information-brokering)*
- lacks an office or staff to perform the services
- claims a special relationship with high-value customers or suppliers
- has no physical presence in the country concerned
- unconvincing business case
- unwilling to agree a business plan and budget
- dependent on a small number of customers or suppliers
- unwilling to disclose details of potential customers and suppliers
- unwilling to provide accounting information and routine performance reports

Transactions

- abnormal cash transactions
- transactions that are too good to be true
- insists on over- or under-invoicing (such as tolling[19])
- unwilling to provide details of the proposed transactions or third-party relationships
- repeatedly introduces transactions as urgent or special
- insists that transactions are handled outside the company's normal processes (i.e. director-handling) or routed to a third party
- operates exclusively in a market all with third parties that competitors cannot penetrate
- requires unusual delivery terms (such as ship to border[20])
- works on both sides of the transactions (with a conflicting interest)

Company structure and ownership

- uses shell offshore holding companies or complex ownership structures without a reasonable explanation[21]
- group involves a mixture of private and listed entities
- private company reversed into a public shell
- refuses to disclose details of beneficial owners of the company (without a good reason)
- government equity
- not licensed to conduct business in the country concerned
- unreliable parent or subsidiary companies
- obscure group structure

---

19   A common method with Russian oil and minerals shipments, where goods are sold on paper to front companies in a tax haven (Isle of Man was a favourite) at suppressed prices, from where they are invoiced to end customers. Profits are therefore stripped into the front companies (or 'tolled').

20   Under these arrangements goods are shipped to a duty-free warehouse in an adjacent country for smuggling into the intended market. For example, massive shipments of tobacco were made to Andorra for smuggling into Spain.

21   There are many legitimate reasons why an agent would want to obscure beneficial ownership.

Conflicts of interest

- represents unethical competitors
- works as a principal with the company in an entirely different context through which bribes could be processed

General reputation

- unable to produce satisfactory references
- is subject to credible adverse rumours or press reports
- undisclosed criminal convictions
- bad reputation with local embassies
- bad reputation with local enforcement agencies
- reputation for corruption
- no established track record in the country or sector
- suggests any illegal behaviour

Financial position

- financially unsound and loss-making
- insists on upfront payments
- poor credit history
- excessive borrowing
- adverse bank references
- qualified accounts
- history of failed businesses

Payment method

- demands disproportionate remuneration without justification
- in cash or to a numbered account
- uses multiple bank accounts in different jurisdictions for similar or related transactions
- insists on payment to a third-party account
- payment requested to country different from the agent's base or to a tax haven
- payment demanded in advance
- payment demanded for extraordinary items

Relationships

- covert connections to government employees, FPOs or PEPs
- concealed family, business or relational ties with government official
- links to organised crime
- works extensively through sub-agents
- refuses to nominate a senior employee responsible for liaison on compliance

- insists on communicating with a specific company manager or group (i.e. a single-line communication: see page 410 et seq)

Personnel

- unwilling to provide details
- unqualified or inexperienced

Compliance standards

- unaware of the relevant laws and regulatory standards
- unwilling to confirm adherence to ethical standards
- undefined compliance and ethical policies
- refuses to grant audit rights

Litigation record

- convictions for serious offences or currently under investigation.

None of the above red flags prove that an agent is unreliable or will pay bribes and these days those intent on continuing their corrupt ways will find other methods of corruption. This makes it imperative that companies carry out effective risk assessments and that their due diligence and other processes are anticipatory rather than historical.

WHAT THE BAD GUYS WILL DO

Companies intent on continuing with corruption have a limitless array of possibilities, but malpractice involving agents is likely to include:

- Encouraging agents to become independent third parties and concealing bribes in transfer prices;
- Encouraging the agent to set up associated companies which generate slush funds from contrived or unusual transactions with the principal (or an associate) from which bribes are paid;[22]
- Handling agents through totally independent companies not bound by the UK Bribery Act 2010;
- Colluding with the agent's other principals (who are not bound by the UK laws) and entering into loss-making transactions with them to create slush funds for agent;
- Through over- or under-pricing, creating slush funds with the end customer (which may be a government agency), who subsequently makes internal distributions to the corrupt employees.

---

22 Transactions in the Carbon World are perfect candidates.

All of the above (and a few others not discussed for obvious reasons[23]) are far more difficult to detect and much more relevant than historic red flags (see also page 659 and most importantly, page 422).

THE SENSIBLE FOCUS OF DUE DILIGENCE

Another misconception in the official view is that due diligence should be concentrated on the relationship between the principal and the agent, whereas a decision-centric risk model indicates that it should be between the agent and the ultimate buyer or seller and on the approval and monitoring of specific transactions (see Chapter 19).

Facilitation Extortion

Facilitation payments are typically portrayed as small gratuities or other minor advantages given to lower-level officials to encourage them to simply do the jobs they are paid to do. This is often far from the truth and FPO corruption goes to the highest levels in the countries concerned, and are often related to organised crime, narcotics and people-trafficking. Challenging it can be very dangerous. The following amalgam is based on actual cases and years of experience working inside and outside government departments in Less Developed Countries.

The Nature of Facilitation Payments

Every Customs Officer in Crookedstan who works in what is known as a 'wet job' (which brings him face to face with members of the public or business community from whom bribes can be extorted) is required to produce a certain amount of 'target-value' money (i.e. bribes) every week and to account to his controller, who is usually an elected union representative. If an officer fails to remit less than his target, his colleagues assume he has stolen the value money and he can be beaten up or even killed. For this reason, officers who collect more than their weekly value money hold balances in reserve to compensate for shortfalls in future periods.

Officers working at the airports have targets for each arrival with premiums on flights from the UK, the USA, the UAE and Italy. Some airport officers have their own wholesale and retail business and recruit mules to transport goods on their behalf. The excess baggage charges on some flights are four times the total of all other revenues. But airlines who charge mules for excess baggage are punished when their flights arrive in (or hope to leave) Crookedstan. So most check-in desks for flights to Crookedstan under-weigh excess baggage, with obvious safety implications.

Every Friday morning officers in wet jobs are required to account for the value money they have collected over the previous seven days. They are allowed to keep 30 per cent for themselves, with the balance being remitted to a controller who passes it up the management line to

---

23   An early reviewer of this book asked 'Such as?' Self-evidently so that it does not educate skulduggers in what to do.

other controllers, who allocate set percentages to supervisors in 'dry' jobs (those that have no public contact). The Commissioner gets a share from everyone. He is very wealthy.

Final distributions are made on Friday evenings in a private room at the Presidential Golf Club, where the usual 100 plus attendees are provided with snacks and drinks by the Commissioner. Meetings are followed by parties with male and female hookers.

Also at these meetings aircraft, land and ship arrivals for the coming week are discussed and supervising officers are able to bid to handle the administration, clearance of cargoes, bunkers, etc. Every movement into or out of Crookedstan is open to a bid.

Successful bids are subdivided by supervising officers, passed down the line and added to the weekly value money targets of individual officers. A routine bid for a container ship arriving at Crooked Town River Port is $100,000, although bids can go much higher. Deck cargoes always justify a premium. Junior Officers are keen to work for Supervisors who are good bidders.

Senior Customs Officers also review aircraft and ship manifests to identify high-value containers, especially of computer parts, fashion wear, jewellery and mobile telephones. They sell details to organised criminal groups of vehicle hijackers. This trade is not as well controlled as routine value money and hijacking targets are frequently sold to more than one team by different officers. This has resulted in gun fights and trucks being hijacked two and sometimes three times. Then, of course, there are the serious crimes of collusion with drug- or people-traffickers and money-launderers.

The morale in the Customs Department is high and most officers are wealthy. Many live in houses valued at over $1 million, despite the fact that their official salaries are less than $2,500 p.a. The Commissioner, whose salary is around $15,000 a year, has five wives, twelve children, and lives in a house valued at over $4 million. This year he is Captain of the Presidential Golf Club (joining fee $200,000) and he is the Country Treasurer of Save the Children Fund. He has at least eight cars, including a Ferrari and a Bentley, two Harley-Davidson special edition motorbikes, three chauffeurs and a helicopter. Recently his eldest daughter got married, with a reception said to have cost over $2 million. Over 100 guests were flown first class and all expenses paid for a five-star weekend in xxx.[24] The daughter's presents and gifts were valued at over $5 million.

The Customs Department holds monthly golf competitions. Each player has to bring a prize, which means that no entrant – including guests – leaves empty-handed.

The top (always privately donated) prize is typically a small car or a Harley-Davidson motorbike (which seems to be a much admired possession in Customs circles). At the main annual competition the first prize was a $200,000 motorhome, which was won by the Deputy Finance Minister who is a golfing hacker but a known cheat. The Commissioner was his playing partner and kept his score!

---

24   Naming this would reveal too much.

Customs officers in wet jobs were expert at creating reasons why they were unable to perform their jobs. These were infinitely variable and virtually impossible to predict, including:

- 'incomplete documentation'
- 'insufficient copies of documentation'
- 'wrong colour ink'
- 'spelling mistakes'
- 'official dealing gone away'
- 'unable to access office'
- 'no porter available'
- 'can't find eyeglasses'
- 'bad snake and relaxing container'.[25]

A European citizen appeared at the Immigration Desk at Bentrovia and refused to donate a little gift to the Immigration Officer. After two hours of angry negotiation, he was released to pick up his suitcase at the carousel. There he was stopped by Customs Officers who claimed to have found 2 grams of cocaine in his suitcase. After two years in prison awaiting trial (he faced the death penalty) he was released without charge.

Now, doesn't all of this make you feel good: that if you give an FPO a Homer Simpson mouse mat at Christmas you could go to prison in the UK? Is it so sensible to insist that junior employees in difficult jurisdictions should be required to refuse to comply with facilitation extortion? Facilitation payments are not a white-collar offence: they are often connected to organised crime and heavyweight criminals. This is the real world!

Charitable Donations

Donations to charities are another activity to benefit from the attention of the regulators. Their worry is twofold: first, that bribes will be recorded as donations to charities but diverted for improper purposes.

The second concern is that people connected with a charity and impressed by the donation will be influenced to perform improperly either in relation to the charity or some other organisation with which they are connected. An obvious example is where a government minister or official is also a charity trustee. This is possibly a valid concern, although it will be difficult for a prosecutor to make the connection between a donation and an intention to induce improper performance.

There is a third type of possibility which the regulators have not articulated. These are where, for example, donations are made by suppliers of green technology to an environmental charity to encourage it to conduct dodgy research that supposedly validates their products or services. There is evidence that cases of this type would not be unique.

---

25   An official's entry on a report sheet – implying that it would have been dangerous for the officer to go into the container.

Offset Projects

An extremely interesting article by Shana Marshall, on Jadaliyya.com[26] described offset projects thus:

Offset Scams

Defence offsets are regarded as the holy grail of graft. They are incentive contracts that mainly defence equipment suppliers sign with procuring governments to facilitate weapons sales. They may take the form of investments in the local defence industry or in some major infrastructure or other project. The Gulf States have raised offset projects to become a veritable art form.

Miss Marshall continued that there are currently around $100 billion worth of outstanding offset obligations with even more massive set-asides over the next five years, most of which involve Saudi Arabia and the United Arab Emirates.

Pre-performance Offsets

Pre-performance offsets are those in which companies are required to make investments in the procuring country before invitations to bid for the major projects are placed. Often the performance offsets are committed before the contract is placed and do not necessarily result in success. McDonnell Douglas (Boeing) set up a Berlitz language school in what later became an abortive bid to supply fighter jets to the United Arab Emirates. Newport News (now part of Northrop Grumman) created the Abu Dhabi shipbuilding industry in anticipation of sales of fast patrol boats, but again failed to secure the contract.

The main problems with offset projects are that they obscure the primary procurement decision and can be corruptive in themselves, and involve serious overcharging and non-delivery. For example, an offset housing project may be agreed in the constituency of a corrupt politician to improve his election chances.

Being viewed by the purchaser as effectively a free bonus, offset projects are not usually subject to the same level of due diligence and monitoring.

---

26   Paraphrasing the article at http://www.jadaliyya.com/pages/index/413/the-modernization-of-bribery_the-arms-trade-in-the

Offset Due Diligence

There is no requirement for due diligence regarding offset agreements, no monitoring of the projects themselves and no audits conducted. It is an excellent way for governments to conceal the delivery of public subsidies to their own special-interest groups. Foreign governments as a rule do not want offset costs highlighted or disclosed.

In addition to being opaque and unregulated, offsets also perform many of the same functions as bribes. They allow competing firms to sweeten their bids outside the ordinary channels of price and quality competition and provide officials in the procuring country with opportunities to direct benefits to their domestic political allies.

In the UK planning world it has become commonplace for builders to agree to the construction of council homes as free offsets for permission for commercial developments. There is now massive competition among offset brokers, who provide subtle (and cost-efficient) ways of influencing FPOs through offsets, but will the SFO take any action against them?

Most of the recommended controls are simple and can be introduced with the minimum disruption to normal operations. The fact that preventive controls are maintained at the minimum level to establish prudence (with a corresponding reliance on reactive controls – that give a prompt indication of loss) means that honest employees can operate flexibly. The threat of detection is of no concern to an honest person

Procurement Overcharging

BACKGROUND

Overcharging is at the heart of most purchasing frauds, based on corruption and involving different categories of suppliers.

FICTITIOUS SUPPLIERS

In these cases, often committed by or in collusion with employees, false costs are fed into the accounts payable system. These are sometimes supported by fictitious purchase orders, goods inwards receipts and other corroborative data, although it is quite common to find that the underlying documentation is missing. Thus, when auditing to detect fictitious purchases, the trail should always be from credits in the purchase ledger to corroborative source documentation (see page 529 for profiles of suspect invoices).

INVOLVING GENUINE SUPPLIERS

These frauds may, or may not, involve collusion with employees of the victim company. Vendors may deliberately overcharge to increase their own profitability and succeed because the victim does not check carefully enough. Dangerous areas include partial deliveries, duplicate payments, emergency orders, single-source tenders and excessive charges on changes to specifications.

The American Project On Government Oversight publishes regular statistics – often in conjunction with the Department of Justice – of overcharges on government contracts, which makes chilling reading. Table 13.7 shows just a small selection.

Table 13.7 Examples of Overcharging

Company Name	Contracts Awarded US$ million	Instances of Misconduct	Misconduct Amount $ million
Bechtel	3,936.9	19	378.3
Boeing	19,366.6	42	1,600.5
Deloitte LLP	838.3	11	487.6
FedEx	1,449.2	26	200.7
Hewlett Packard	1,810.2	7	741.1
Honeywell International			703.2
IBM	1,627.9		
Lockheed Martin	$5 billion on labour mischarges		
Merck & Co. Inc.	992.9	12	5,862.7
Royal Dutch Shell	1,038.8	32	1,302.5

Detailed background on the cases usually reveals an alarming pattern of deliberate overcharging by companies who consistently laud their ethical performance. So much for tone at the top.

COMMITTED BY EMPLOYEES OF SUPPLIERS

These cases involve a dishonest employee of a supplier who deliberately overcharges for goods or services provided by his employer for his own benefit. When the victim has paid, a credit note is issued and a refund or internal adjustment prepared. The credit note is converted without the victim's knowledge.

Typical examples are shown in Table 13.8.

Table 13.8 Overcharging by Vendors' Employees

Type of supplier (Examples)	Manipulation by an employee of the supplier	Conversion
Travel agency	Prepares an invoice for an airline ticket in excess of its true cost	Issues a credit note. Applies the credit to the account of an accomplice or converts the outgoing cheque
Credit Card companies Public Utilities	Uses adjustment routines to enter an additional charge on a customer's account or thousands of small charges to thousands of accounts	Applies the credit, again by adjustment entries, to the account of an accomplice
Tax Official	Raises an inflated assessment	Issues a credit note. Applies the credit to an accomplice or converts the outgoing refund
Vehicle tyres Other goods	Invoices for tyres not delivered to the victim. This builds up a surplus in his stocks	The surplus tyres are sold for cash
Advertising agency	Includes a charge from a subcontractor twice	Issues a credit note. Applies the credit to an accomplice or to the subcontractor, or converts the outgoing cheque
Any supplier	Duplicates an invoice	Converted by any of the methods shown above

Duplicate invoices are especially common and when they are discovered, can usually be excused as errors.

WITHOUT THE COLLUSION OF THE SUPPLIER

Invoices from a genuine supplier may be falsely created, duplicated or inflated by an employee of the purchasing company so that the debt outstanding in the victim's ledger is greater than the vendor expects to receive. This credit can be converted by any of the methods described above.

Also included in this category are those cases where an employee of the victim company deliberately overpays a supplier, so that the unrecorded incoming refund payment can be converted.

ORGANISED CRIMINALS

Organised criminals have entered this area. Frauds involving the supply of carbon paper, directories, or non-existent weed-killing chemicals are common place. They usually involve invoices of small value, for goods and services never provided, being sent out to thousands of victims. The loss to the individual is insignificant but a fraud of this type typically returns over $500,000 to the perpetrators. They are quite often backed by organised crime, operating in Holland, Canada or Switzerland.

General Procurement Processes

Although the conventional view is that procurement is exclusively vulnerable to bribe receipt, the reality is that bribes may be paid to vendors to induce improper advantages including, for example, pricing, allocation of scarce products and payment terms.

However, we will focus on the most common risks of incoming bribery – associated with perverted internal decisions, which create slush funds from which bribes can be paid, as follows.

---

1. Budgets

Object of Fraud: *To ensure that inflated costs do not cause a budget to overrun or, if they do, to provide a plausible explanation.*

From a criminal's point of view, the impact of fraud has to be hidden in capital or expense budgets and cost centre records. This may be possible because:

- the cost of fraud has been allowed for in a budget;
- allocated funds are not required;
- the impact can be charged back into the budgets of other departments;
- recoveries and back charges received from other departments can be falsified;
- overruns can be explained by apparently legitimate reasons;
- overruns can be concealed in or transferred to contingency budgets or suspense accounts;
- charges can be forward- or backward-dated into other financial periods;
- or, more usually, because budgetary controls and management reporting are weak.

---

2. Financial Approval Policy

Object of fraud: *To ensure that false or inflated charges will not be detected by honest managers.*

Most organisations set down the authority of managers and employees to commit it to expenditure. This control can be overcome:

- when the cost of the fraud is within the person's authority;
- when an innocent senior person can be deceived or corrupted into giving authority;
- when the signature of an innocent person with authority can be forged without the risk of detection;
- when a person with limited authority can circumvent controls by:

- having the transaction divided into amounts within his own authority or below the level at which competitive bids are required;
- having the goods or services mis-described;
- changing specifications after approval has been given.

Rarely is even a good financial approval policy a barrier to fraud and corruption.

---

3. Perceived Need

Object of fraud: *To establish a need for expenditure when one does not exist and with the object of passing a benefit to a favoured vendor.*

- Obtaining false consulting reports, suggesting that expenditure is justified when it is not;
- Obtaining false internal reports, based on inflated operational requirements or sales forecasts etc.;
- Falsifying investment or disinvestment prospects and potential profits;
- Falsifying requirements for capital expenditure;
- Falsifying reports on the performance of an established and honest vendor to cancel an existing contract and to open the way for a favoured vendor;
- Maliciously damaging equipment: to justify a need to buy spares, replacements and maintenance;
- Determining excessively high re-order levels, contingency stocks and stocks at dispersed locations with the objective of increasing total inventories. *This has a two-way benefit: first it enables a favoured vendor to supply additional goods; and second it provides opportunities for gain when unwanted stocks are sold off. These sales may be handled by the purchasing agent who ordered them;*
- Deliberately wasting or scrapping of production stocks or ancillary materials, such as packaging or finished goods;
- Setting false production formulae and yields to justify excessive purchases of raw materials;
- falsely insisting on health and safety standards, legal or other requirements, or other noble cause advice.

---

4. Requirements Specification

Object of fraud: *Tailoring detailed specifications to match the resources or products of a favoured vendor.*

- Setting conditions that remove the need for competitive tendering. *For example, by processing a large contract as a series of low-value orders;*
- Disguising a new contract as a change of specification to an existing arrangement with a favoured vendor, *thus removing the need for competitive tendering;*
- Informing the favoured vendor to bid artificially low on the promise so that after he has been successful, specifications will be changed to allow him to increase his charges;
- Insisting on false compatibility standards or technical specifications to exclude competitive vendors;
- Setting false operational requirements to favour a selected vendor;
- Setting false batch sizes to suit a favoured vendor. *For example, if economies of scale are achieved in production runs of x quantity and the favoured vendor can produce only in batches of x/2, bids will be solicited in quantities of x/2. The effectively disqualifies the most efficient supplier;*
- Soliciting or assisting the user department with any of the above;
- Setting false company policy to benefit a favoured vendor or to disqualify competitors;
- Releasing advance information to a favoured vendor, so that the specifications can be written in his favour;
- Dividing or changing the user's specifications;
- Setting out oppressive legal or other terms to competing vendors. *For example, imposing unacceptable penalty conditions which the favoured vendor is told to ignore.*

5. Evaluation Criteria

Object of fraud: *To set down criteria for success that will automatically result in selection of the favoured vendor. More usually the criteria are not determined until bids have been received, so that they can then be amended to suit the favoured vendor.*

- Emphasising the known strengths of the favoured vendor and the weaknesses of its competitors. *For example, carbon neutrality;*
- Setting soft costs through which all but the favoured vendor can be disqualified.

6. Selection and Solicitation

Object of fraud: *To ensure that business is passed to the favoured vendor by excluding well qualified competitors. This is one of the most dangerous aspects of procurement and one which is seldom properly controlled. The purchasing agent may have total discretion over who will and will not be invited to tender.*

- Setting down requirements for single sourcing from a favoured vendor. This is especially common in highly technical areas;
- Pre-canvassing: giving inside information to assist the favoured vendor;
- Insisting, without giving a reason, that the favoured vendor is employed;
- Disqualifying qualified vendors, *for example, by falsely claiming that their performance has been unsatisfactory in the past or that they have not worked for the organisation before;*
- Limiting the trawl of suppliers in competition with the favoured vendor to those who are obviously not qualified;
- Removing well qualified vendors from the file to be solicited;
- Allowing the favoured vendor to select his own ring of competitors;
- Releasing false documentation to competing vendors.

---

7. Invitations to Tender

Object of fraud: *To ensure the favoured vendor is successful, by limiting competition.*

- Including fictitious vendors or dummy companies owned by the favoured vendor;
- Restricting invitations to tender to vendors in a closed group;
- Sending invitations to tender to the wrong addresses;
- Providing competing vendors with incorrect plans, translations, specifications, or samples;
- Obtaining unofficial quotations over the telephone and suppressing those which could challenge the favoured vendor;
- Imposing onerous terms or timescales on all but the favoured vendor *(for example, unacceptable penalty clauses or performance standards);*
- Providing incorrect information on the criteria on which the contract will be awarded;
- Imposing impossible performance standards on all but the favoured vendor.

---

8. Bid Evaluation

Object of fraud: *To ensure that the business is awarded to the favoured vendor.*

- Failing to set down the criteria for selection before bids are evaluated. *This allows the goal posts to be moved at any time;*
- Acceptance of an unrealistic low bid from the favoured vendor on the secret understanding that changes to specifications will be issued *(on which excessive profits can be made or losses on the initial bid recovered);*
- Acceptance of a late bid from the favoured vendor;

- Allowing multiple bids from the favoured vendor: *the one which marginally undercuts the competition will be submitted*;
- Disqualification of competitive bids for some esoteric and unjustified reason;
- Subdividing bids to benefit the favoured vendor. *For example, allocating work in small segments, especially when it appears that the favoured vendor will not be accepted overall*;
- Acceptance of a bid from a competing vendor on the condition that the favoured vendor is used as a subcontractor;
- Cancelling the requirement if it is obvious that the favoured vendor will not be successful; *this provides the favoured vendor with a second chance if and when the contract is re-bid*;
- Suggesting that negotiations should be entered into with a shortlist of vendors, especially if it appears that the favoured vendor will not be successful. This enables the negotiations to be steered to benefit the favoured vendor.

9. Beauty Parades and Interviews[27]

Object of fraud: *To discredit competitors of the favoured vendor.*

- Giving all but the favoured vendor insufficient time to prepare for the presentation.
- Steering questions towards the strengths of the favoured vendor and the weaknesses of its competitors;
- Loading the selection panel with sycophants, whose opinions can be influenced;
- Scheduling the main competitor's presentation at a time when its key men are known to be unable to attend.

10. Negotiation

Object of fraud: *To provide a second chance to steer business to the favoured vendor.*

- Agreeing with the favoured vendor that he will reduce his price, or change other conditions, so that he is guaranteed to be successful. *This is usually on the understanding that, after the contract has been awarded, specifications will be changed to the vendor's advantage;*
- Obtaining false, adverse references on the favoured vendor's main competitors;
- Forcing competing vendors to withdraw.

---

27 Although beauty parades are a thing of the past, the term is still used in the procurement field to refer to presentations by shortlisted vendors!

11. Contract Award

Object of fraud: *To release the favoured an, by now successful vendor from penalty and other clauses and to prepare the ground for charges in excess of those agreed.*

- Ignoring normal terms and conditions with the favoured vendor, so that he can escape liability for sub-standard performance;
- Failing to include audit rights in the contract or to issue non-standard terms and conditions which benefit the vendor;
- Losing the contract documentation or supporting correspondence, making it impossible later on to take action against the favoured vendor;
- Agreeing complex schedules of charges; for example, allowing premium labour rates for weekend working, working in bad weather, etc., *which provide the vendor with the opportunity to overcharge*;
- Agreeing to the vendor's recovery of a higher percentage of overheads than is justified for such items as workmen's compensation insurance.

12. Equalisation

Object of fraud: *To give the impression that bidders in second and third place will match the terms of the winner so that supplies are secured from three sources.*[28]

- The fact that a company uses equalisation schemes encourages vendors to collude;
- The winner may agree to supply second- and third- place bidders, who may not even be qualified, with product (with a small discount) which they re-invoice;
- Thus the security objectives of equalisation are nullified.

13. Changes to Specifications

Object of fraud: *To enable the favoured vendor to profit, without further competitive tendering, or to recover from an excessively low and contrived bid. This is one of the most dangerous stages and one which should be closely controlled.*

---

28 An in-vogue approach in Gulf States but potentially very exposed.

- Changing the specifications for quantity, quality, delivery or completion dates, opening the way for unjustified price increases after the contract has been awarded;
- Falsifying health and safety, building, or other regulations that require the specifications to be changed;
- Contriving problems that result in demands from the authorities that specifications have to be changed.

---

14. Other Stages And Accounts Payable

Object of fraud: *To allow the favoured vendor to overcharge.*

- Falsifying the dates of orders to allow the vendor to benefit from price changes in raw materials or labour rates;
- Deliberately over-ordering goods to permit excessive charges; *this may be by the vendor acting alone or in collusion with employees;*
- Allowing the substitution of lower-quality goods;
- Allowing the short delivery of goods;
- Allowing the contractor to prolong work or the hire period of equipment;
- Paying a subcontractor's invoice more than once – *usually there are no checks on the double payment of supporting charges from* **subcontractors**;
- Allowing inventory to run down to crisis levels so that emergency orders, at any price, have to be processed;
- Allowing the vendor to negotiate discounts and spot settlements with subcontractors without passing on the appropriate credit;
- Failing to insist on or to monitor retentions;
- Allowing unjustified extensions to an approved budget;
- Failing to claim credit for goods returned or defective services.

The above are examples of risks that commonly appear in procurement processes and usually involve incoming corruption of user department employees, central purchasing and operational workers in goods inwards, laboratories and quality control.

Typical symptoms of corruption and procurement fraud are listed in Table 13.9.

Look Both Ways

Although procurement is primarily exposed to incoming bribery (see page 349) – resulting in typical annual overcharges of between 2 per cent and 10 per cent – bribe payment and internal corruption should not be overlooked. Bribes may be paid to secure lower prices, preferential terms and monopolistic contracts; sometimes in breach anti-competition laws.

Table 13.9 Signs of Trouble

Where Detectable	Symptom	Possible Dishonest Explanation (Note: there may be honest explanations for all of these symptoms)
In accounts	High prices and excessive costs	Overcharging with or without collusion
	Poor quality	Overcharging with or without collusion
	Physical shortages	Short delivery by drivers
	Excessive and unwanted inventory	Deliberate over-ordering
	Apparent errors	Concealment
	Deviations from approved procedures	Concealment
	Excessive record-keeping by individual (often junior members of staff)	Possibly in the knowledge that corruption is widespread, may keep a private record for his own protection
	Poor or inaccurate record-keeping	Concealment
Personal behaviour of staff *(Conversion symptoms)*	Overspending on houses, cars and luxury items	Signs of conversion
	Frequent unexplained absences from work	Secret meetings with vendors
	Excessive entertaining of and by vendors	Over-friendly relationships with vendors
Within the purchasing office	Dictatorial senior management	A defence mechanism to prevent anyone asking questions
	Pathetically weak or poorly qualified middle managers	Selected deliberately by senior management because they know they will never question their/his actions
	Obvious culture gaps between managers at the top and middle levels and political infighting	Possibly fuelled by senior management to divide and rule.
	High turnover of junior staff	Who cannot condone corruption, but will not report it
	Imposition of artificial barriers and unwarranted specialisation	To create a one-to one relationship with the vendor
	No separation of responsibilities and excessive secrecy	To create a one-to-one relationship with the vendor
	Exceptional or insignificant transactions being handled by senior managers	To provide an advantage to a favoured vendor
	Concentration on irrelevant tasks (Displacement activity)	See stagnation
	Excessive resistance to audit	To deter checks being made

Where Detectable	Symptom	Possible Dishonest Explanation *(Note: there may be honest explanations for all of these symptoms)*
Within the purchasing office	Excessively complicated or bureaucratic procedures	To create the environment for additional bribes
	Unnecessary meetings with vendors	Over-friendly relationships
	No summary of bids or debriefing of vendors after a contract has been placed	Concealment
	Exaggerated claims of savings	To divert attention away from poor performance
	Excessive frequency of low-value orders	To create the opportunities for overcharging
	Excessive changes to specifications	To create the opportunities for overcharging
	Excessive reliance on one or more vendors	Indicating a closed shop or extreme favouritism to the vendor
	Frequent, but unnecessary visits to or by vendors	Over-friendly relationships and meetings to pay over cash
Vendors	Well qualified vendors refusing to tender	Because they know the system is corrupt and that they have no chance of success. However, they will not complain
	Rings of vendors regularly competing against each other with little or no new blood	Closed shop necessary for overcharging
	Vendors being asked to bid for work outside their geographical area or expertise	Extreme favouritism
	Evidence of penetration by organised crime	Overcharging

Purchases may be priced it in a number of different ways, including the following.

Table 13.10 Types of Purchase Contracts

Type of Contract	Effect
Fixed price or lump sum	The vendor agrees to provide goods or services at a set price
Time and Materials	The contract specifies hourly rates for labour and fixed costs for materials supplied. Charges may be supported by time sheets and material records; often signed off by an external adviser (such as an architect, a surveyor or an engineer)
Cost Plus Cost reimbursable	Similar to time and materials, except that the prime contractor is normally allowed to add an uplift to the costs invoiced to him by subcontractors

Of the types of purchase contracts shown in Table 13.10, cost plus-type contracts are usually most exposed to corruption, especially when a single vendor works simultaneously on multiple contracts with mixed terms of payment. For example, advertising agencies usually work for their clients on both cost plus and fixed sum terms. Great care is necessary to ensure that work on the fixed-price element is not charged again on time sheets supporting the cost plus contract.

Frauds in Construction

Despite its importance, the construction industry is riddled with inefficiency, fraud and corruption. It is widely believed that around 20 per cent of all construction costs could be avoided through the elimination of corruption and sharp practice.

Tax frauds, illicit cash and evasion of other regulations are endemic in the industry: relationships in the chain involving architects, structural engineers, designers, contractors, quantity surveyors, town planners and subcontractors are often adversarial, if not completely hostile. And corruption and conflicting interests are ever-present dangers.

Naturally, the client wants to pay as little as possible, whereas constructors want to maximise their profits for their own benefit, to ramp up their market capitalisation, to obtain financing or to mollify shareholders. On the other hand, many good constructors are fighting for survival and have to battle against clients who cynically delay payments as a deliberate ploy to gain a financial advantage. In the worst cases the objective is to force the constructor or subcontractor out of business so that they will not have to be paid at all. In this scenario the unpaid debt is pure profit for the defaulter, but such practices are scandalous and are criminalised offences in Europe.[29]

Unsurprisingly, the culture is one of low trust, in which conflicting interests are more often resolved by sharp practice than by any feeling of fairness. Fraud results in ruin for good people and hardworking companies (Table 13.11), while the crooks usually flourish. In a few years' time, the only successful clients, constructors and subcontractors may be those who are the best at taking advantage of others. It is a daunting prospect.

In mature economies, also, construction fraud costs billions of dollars annually and losses are often associated with bribes, conflicts of interests and blatant overcharging. It is reliably estimated that every business would save up to 20 per cent of its construction costs if fraud and malpractice were eliminated. It is likely that the potential savings are even higher on government projects. And if you agree these are bad, wait until you see what is happening and will get far worse in the Carbon World and offset projects.

Conclusion

Hopefully the above discourse will prompt companies to look beyond the narrow framing of Ministry of Justice Guidance and tackle corruption in all of its forms. In the process, their profits and systems will become more assured.

---

29   In the UK under the Theft Act 1978.

Table 13.11 Victims of Construction Fraud

Problems Against → Caused By ↓	Victims of Construction Fraud and Malpractice					
	CLIENTS Government, Commercial	**DESIGNERS** Architects, Engineers	**LARGE FIRMS** Constructors	**SUB CONTRACTORS** Specialists, Small firms	**FINANCIERS** World Bank, IMF, Banks	**INSURERS** Bond providers, Guarantors, Credit Agencies
	← ← ← ← ←	Non-supportive or adversarial relationships			→ → → → →	
Clients ↑		Unrealistic expectations Lowest price Withheld payments Appointment in return for a bribe			False applications Inadequate collateral Corruption of bank officers	
Designers ↑	Unbuildable designs Conflicting interests Corruption of client's employees	Unfair competition Theft of intellectual capital	Unbuildable designs Conflicting interests	Failure to certify work done Falsified certification in return for hidden payments	Condoning misleading estimates by clients Corruption of bank officers and claims inspectors	
Firms ↑	Overcharging Contrived changes to specifications False arbitration claims Corruption of the client's employees	False allocation of blame for delays and overruns Corruption of employees	Unfair competition CARTELS Information-brokering	Lowest price Withheld payments Forced bankruptcy Soliciting bribes in return for appointment	Inflated claims for work done Falsified stage payments	False claims for compensation
Sub contractors ↑	Overcharging Corruption of employees of the client or prime constructor			Unfair competition Theft of materials and plant		
Financiers ↑	Overcharging Contrived closure of projects	Limited contract	Overcharging Contrived withdrawal of facilities Planned bankruptcies		Fraudulent syndications Falsified prospectus	
Insurers ↑	Overcharging Ineffective policies Hostile claims adjusting					False reinsurance coverage Inter-company litigation to avoid payment

'This is the way we always do risk evaluations in this company'

'Paddy wouldn't listen. He insisted he would be safe because they would know
Ireland was a Demand Side country'

CHAPTER 14 *The Nature of Risk*

Perceptions of Risk

Risk is defined as the possibility that an adverse event will occur sometime in the future and at its core is uncertainty. Risk evaluation is a process that attempts to predict the future and is especially difficult with comparatively low-frequency, covert[1] events for which there are no reliable baseline statistics. It is certainly not a science and questionably not even an art: it is at best a subjective guess.

A person's perception of risk is subject to cognitive bias (see page 278) and in some cases self-interest. It is not surprising, therefore, that there is little unanimity on the scale of fraud and corruption.

An Unappreciated Jest[2]

The authors jestingly stated at a recent conference[3] that a person's 'perception of corruption varies inversely with his rank but directly with intelligence or personal interests'. This was to encourage discussion among the assembled directors and members of the 'Cottage Industry'. Unfortunately, some assumed it was an attack on them, which it was not. But it was a snipe against a pseudo-science.

Many compliance specialists complain that senior managers are not sufficiently interested in controls. The most likely explanation is a misalignment of frames and perception of risks between dedicated members of the 'Cottage Industry' (see Foreword) – who are influenced by an availability cascade – and managers who are not.

Members of the Cottage Industry, including internal compliance, legal and audit specialists are strongly advised not to hyperbolise risks or the omnipotence of regulators. They should also understand that their frames of reference are usually entirely different from the managers they wish to convince. Page 626 describes a subtle bit of reframing that removed the heat from a difficult relationship. Training compliance specialists in interviewing and persuasive skills is worthwhile.

---

1   Such as corruption and fraud.

2   And there is not much of this about in the 'Cottage Industry'.

3   They have never been invited back!

The Availability Cascade

To quote Professor Kahneman:[4] '[an individual's] expectations about the frequency of events are distorted by the prevalence and emotional intensity of the messages to which [he is] exposed.

An availability cascade is a self-sustaining chain of events, which may start from media reports of a relatively minor event and lead up to public panic and large-scale government action. The cycle is sometimes sped along deliberately by "availability entrepreneurs",[5] individuals or organisations who work to ensure a continuous flow of worrying news. The danger is increasingly exaggerated as the media compete for attention-grabbing headlines'.

The case for anti-corruption controls is not advanced when:

- The taxonomy of corruption – such as country risks, supply and demand, active and passive, is mistaken and possibly distorted to throw all obligations on companies in developed countries – who are amenable to integrity – while allowing extorters – who are more often the instigators – to walk away unscathed;
- Risks[6] – and threats that regulators are lurking around every corner – are deliberately exaggerated;
- Regulators refuse to commit themselves to what is acceptable and what is not: lots of red but no green flags;
- There are serious inconsistencies in the laws and guidelines.

Possibly the number one reason why managers do not take anti-bribery stuff seriously is that they suspect they are being gypped.[7] There are two solutions to this. The first is that members of the 'Cottage Industry' – and particularly regulators – should cut back on the rhetoric and reframe problems more accurately. The second and more important one is that best efforts should be made to identify risks accurately. This is the focus of this chapter.

Objectives

The starting point for 'inspirational integrity' and effective control is, as far as possible, to precisely evaluate risks: their what, how, where, who, why? This[8] ensures that controls:

---

4   Kahneman, Daniel, *Thinking Fast and Slow* (Penguin Books, 2011).

5   Such as members of the 'Cottage Industry'.

6   Especially those which are technical and trivial.

7   This could represent a 'reactance bias' – when people do the opposite of what someone else wants them to do, or, less charitably, the 'Dunning–Kruger Effect', under which incompetent people fail to realise they are incompetent because they lack the skill to distinguish between competence and incompetence!!

8   'Assessment' is used in relation to the limited approach recommended for outgoing bribery and 'evaluation' for the recommended method. 'Evaluation' embraces outgoing, incoming, internal and competitive corruption as well as fraud

- Are commensurate with primary and derived risks and capable of reacting quickly to changing conditions;
- Support **entrepreneurial goals** in the most cost-efficient way;
- **Comply with all applicable laws** and best practice.

AND, specifically, in the anti-corruption[9] silo:

- Avoid and recover losses[10] from incoming or internal corruption and fraud;
- Prevent bribes being paid (outgoing corruption), thus averting regulatory penalties, litigation and reputational damage;
- Reduce the impact of corruption by competitors, by developing level playing fields;
- Secure commercial activities in contexts where – under normal circumstances – risks appear impossible[11] to manage. This results in a competitive advantage and opportunities;
- **Protect honest decision-makers from unfounded allegations of misbehavior.**

Risk evaluations should go well beyond the Ministry of Justice Guidance and answer three questions:

1. Where and how is the organisation exposed – or could be exposed – to incoming, internal, outgoing and competitive corruption, fraud, conflicts of interest, related risks and in other silos.
2. Are controls adequate, or are improvements necessary?
3. What evidence would be available to rebut misplaced allegations of regulatory or other transgressions ('rebuttal evaluation')?

Risk evaluations should be supported by detailed testing, data-mining and other analysis (see Chapters 18–20), existing skulduggery brought to an end and past losses recovered.

Overview of Corruption Risks

Corruption risk evaluation can be considered in two categories:

1. **Primary occurrences:**[12] these assess the chances that acts of incoming, outgoing, internal or competitive corruption might occur.
2. **Consequential or derived risks** include, among other things, regulatory penalties, contract nullification and reputational damage.

---

and conflicts of interest.

9   The focus is towards assessing the wider risks of corruption and not simply bribery, as well as FRAUD.

10   Estimated on average at between 2 per cent and 10 per cent of turnover.

11   Resulting in a significant competitive advantage.

12   Or 'predicate offences'.

In theory, consequential losses only arise once a predicate offence has been proven. However, in the corruption silo an allegation – whether founded or not – can result in serious consequential losses and reputational damage.

As a starting point, evaluations should cover the following *primary* risks, summarised in Table 14.1.

Table 14.1   Recommended Coverage of Primary Corruption

Primary Act	Category and Direction	Decision and Improper Performance	Probable Consequences	
			Financial *(Occurrence)*	Bribery Act Offences *(Rebuttal)*
Bribe payment *and technical violations*	Outgoing corruption	External	Gain	Sections 1, 6 or 7
Bribe receipt *and technical violations*	Incoming corruption Internal corruption	Internal	Loss	Section 2
Competitive corruption		Third party (External)	Loss	None
Conflict of interest		Internal	Loss	Fraud Act
Fraud involving payments and slush fund creation		Internal or external	Loss or gain	Fraud Act

From a regulatory point of view bribe payment to induce perverted external decisions, associated with improper performance, is the most serious because it involves absolute corporate liability under Section 7 of the Act. However, incoming, internal and competitive corruption[13] incur the greatest financial losses.

The Ministry of Justice Guidance, the Act itself and associated laws take an extremely wide view of what is regarded as bribery,[14] but there are three distinct aspects, which are listed in Table 14.2.

---

13   And associated frauds.

14   But deftly avoids 'stratospheric corruption': see Chapter 2.

Table 14.2   Differences Between Hard and Technical Offences

Primary Act	Comments
Hard bribery involving the payment of money or another advantage with the intention of inducing improper performance or of influencing an FPO	For these offences there is no ambiguity in the law *Few people would fail to condemn hard bribery*
Technical breaches involving, for example, hospitality, facilitation payments, sponsorship, and charitable donations	The line between legality and illegality is not clearly drawn and is only resolved after the event through prosecutorial discretion. Honest companies may inadvertently overstep the line and find themselves charged with bribery offences. **This is why rebuttal risk evaluation is important**
Accounting Offences (under the Companies Acts) and for USA-registered companies, under the books and records provisions of the FCPA	These are catch-all – usually technical – offences. This justifies a review of accounting systems and back-office procedures

Although there is a vast difference between hard and technical corruption, both should be evaluated. Risk evaluations should be anticipatory but should also expose past and existing offences. They should deal with corruption and fraud and not just bribe payment.

This chapter is written on the basis that most companies already have processes in place for evaluating mainstream enterprise, commercial, regulatory, and operational risks, probably based on ISO 13000-2009 and ISO 31000-2011, the generic standards. It focuses on the corruption silo – fraud (see Chapters 10–13) and for ease of reference repeats some important points mentioned earlier.

Problems with the Ministry of Justice Guidelines

LIMITS OF THE RISK ASSESSMENT

The Ministry of Justice Guidance (see page 92 et seq) correctly emphasises the importance of risk assessment, yet it has very few words on the subject and these are mainly concerned with bribe payment and avoiding liability under Section 7 by developing adequate procedures. It says little about preventing incoming, internal or competitive corruption, related fraud and conflicts of interest. For most companies these are, by far, the biggest problems.

The Guidance is obsessed with technical offences and historic red flags[15] and on countries perceived to be corrupt: it is not anticipatory and, among other things, overlooks the new – mainly unregulated and very vulnerable financial and settlement systems in the Carbon World. The impression given is that the authors of the Guidance have never evaluated a corruption risk in their lives.

---

15   Dodos' footprints.

WHAT IS PROPORTIONATE?

Another misconception in the Guidance is that individual controls (such as due diligence and separation of responsibilities) should be 'proportionate'. This is easier said than done.

There are at least four problems with proportionality;

1. Risks and controls do not correlate on a one-to-one basis, but are loosely associated through a complex matrix, with risks in one column and controls in rows: seldom is a single risk mitigated by a single control.
2. Most individual controls are either on or off and cannot be graduated.
3. Controls are not only necessary to prevent bribery but relaxing them because of proportionality may also create risks in other areas, or even result in problems in other regulatory silos.[16]
4. Applying Draconian preventive controls can be counter-productive by building up bureaucracy, thereby encouraging corruption.

Comparing Like with Like

Can you imagine a jury's reaction if a company was found to be submitting to extortion in Zambia (perceived as high risk), where its controls were demonstrably more relaxed than in its joint venture in Kiribati (which was perceived to be lower risk)? Who can tell the difference between the levels of corruption in the two countries?

Possibly the worst problem with proportionality is that it introduces unnecessary complications and subjective decisions (over which level of control should apply in a particular context) that in the event of failure are open to second-guessing and prosecutorial discretion. Murphy's Law guarantees that the worst violations will take place in countries and contexts perceived as safe.

If this were not enough, savings from relaxing controls are likely to be offset by the confusion and expenses involved in maintaining multiple systems. In short, proportionality – of a single control – as presented by the Ministry of Justice is for the birds, although it can and should be achieved by a combination of risk management techniques and preventive, reactive and reconstructive measures, as discussed in Chapters 21–32.

---

16 For example, 'whistle-blowing lines', although recommended as a more or less mandatory control, are illegal in France and checking in the UK is difficult because of possible conflicts with laws on data protection and discrimination.

THE CART BEFORE THE HORSE

Many companies have responded to the MOJ Guidance, not by evaluating risks – as they are advised to do – but by willy-nilly issuing reams of paper policies, procedures, guidelines, checklists and training modules that hopefully might be judged through the mystic process of prosecutorial discretion as adequate – after the event – to defend a Section 7 charge.

Few organisations have evaluated risks of incoming, internal and competitive corruption, all of which incur losses, penalties under sections 1, 2 and 6 of the Act, and other liabilities. Such losses are worth saving.

The Recommended Approach

This chapter – which is mainly intended for larger organisations – takes a much broader view of risk evaluation and deals with five levels of risk, as well as conflict of interest, fraud and related offences. It first addresses and evaluates:

1. **The primary risk**: incoming, internal, outgoing and competitive corruption.[17]

It also addresses four other important levels of risks that should be evaluated:

2. **Detection failure risk**: assesses the impact of incoming or outgoing corruption not being discovered or being first chanced upon by regulators.
3. **Investigatory risk**: the risks involved in all complex investigations, including legal breaches, disclosure and other problems.
4. **Reporting risk**: evaluates the problems resulting from self-disclosure.
5. **Derivative risk**: evaluates the consequences of any of the above, including reputational damage and derivative litigation.

Figure 14.1 summarises the levels.

There is a sixth level of evaluation – discussed on page 388, Figure 14.9 – which is theoretical: whether or not bribe payment is ever the sensible option. It shows that corruption is a mug's game, unless, of course, you are an idiot, a politician, an academic, a journalist, an aid agency, or a climatologist.

The Prisoner's Dilemma

This is a game theory based on a dilemma where two prisoners are confronted with the decision whether they should incriminate the other to achieve a reduced sentence for themselves (self- interest) or to stay silent (group interest). It demonstrates a conflict between individual and collective rationality and the advantage of decisions against apparent self-interest. In this case both prisoners saying nothing. The same rationale justifies integrity pacts (see page 388 and 741).

---

17   And not just 'bribery'.

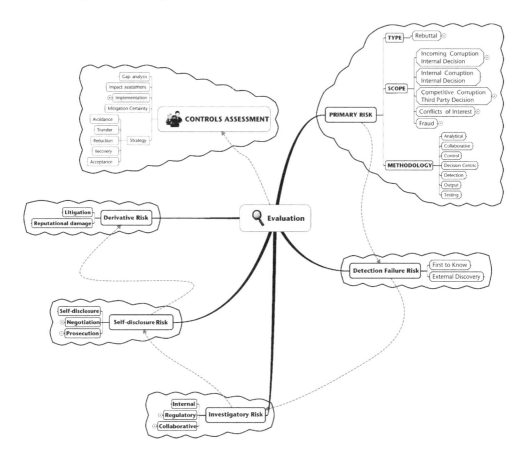

Figure 14.1 Recommended Levels of Risk Evaluation

Being the First to Know

A vital principle of anti-corruption controls (discussed in detail in Chapters 21–32) is that the company should be the first to know through one or more of the channels illustrated in Figure 14.2.

Being the first to know involves intelligence-led, integrated procedures and especially effective incident reporting, business intelligence and continuous monitoring.

Questioning the Statistics

The highly respected Association of Certified Fraud Examiners (ACFE) consistently reports that the majority of frauds are exposed by whistle-blowers. In the authors' experience this is not so, especially for organisations that empower their auditors to use Critical Point Auditing (see page 477) or similar techniques, conduct effective annual appraisals, exit interviews and post relationship meetings with vendors and customers.

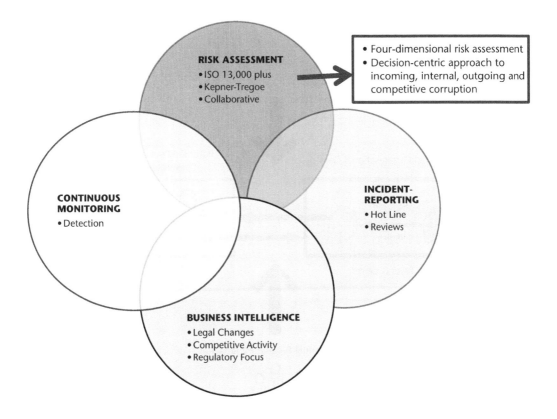

- Four-dimensional risk assessment
- Decision-centric approach to incoming, internal, outgoing and competitive corruption

RISK ASSESSMENT
- ISO 13,000 plus
- Kepner-Tregoe
- Collaborative

CONTINUOUS MONITORING
- Detection

INCIDENT-REPORTING
- Hot Line
- Reviews

BUSINESS INTELLIGENCE
- Legal Changes
- Competitive Activity
- Regulatory Focus

Figure 14.2 The Elements of Being First to Know[18]

Global Evaluation or Decision-centricity

Only a small number of contexts (Figure 14.3) are exposed to risks of serious corruption and fraud. Thus the key is to identify them.

At the very centre of all corruption is an improperly influenced decision: with bribery the influence is usually financial. Despite this, most organisations have no deep understanding of where their important decisions are made or received, whether by their own representatives to favour others *(internal decisions – incoming corruption)* or made by third parties *(external decisions – outgoing corruption)*.

A decision-centric approach can be employed at two levels. The first is as part of comprehensive and collaborative risk evaluation covering the entire Extended Enterprise. The second is specifically targeted at individual jobs,[19] processes, contexts and decisions and can be carried out at any time, used to refresh entity wide reviews or to evaluate the impact of planned operations, personnel, process or regulatory changes. Risk evaluations should be refreshed every two to three years. In the intervening period any significant organisational or operational changes should be monitored and evaluated.

---

18   The Kepner–Tregoe system is described on page 568 et seq.

19   See Job Sensitivity Analysis below (page 393).

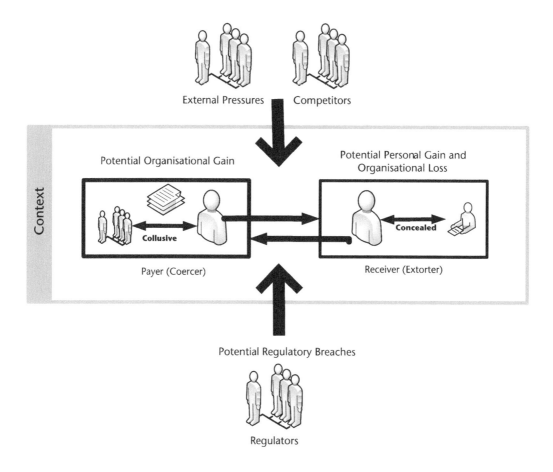

External Pressures   Competitors

Context

Potential Organisational Gain

Potential Personal Gain and
Organisational Loss

Collusive

Concealed

Payer (Coercer)

Receiver (Extorter)

Potential Regulatory Breaches

Regulators

Figure 14.3 The Meaning of a Context

The recommended method drills down to identify vulnerable contexts and then to specific incoming, internal, outgoing and competitive decisions (Figure 14.4).

Risk evaluations should examine the finest detail of specific decisions and then analyse specific transactions to test them.

Leveraging Outliers

The procurement review discussed on page 514 was for an international and highly reputable company whose senior buyers claimed that its procurement systems were perfect. Three weeks later, when the results of specific transactional testing were available, attitudes changed and minds suddenly opened. **The golden rule for auditors and compliance staff, who believe they might be being misled, is to dig into specific detail and to focus on interviews rather than document or procedural reviews. Specific outliers (see page 470) encourage people to start talking.**

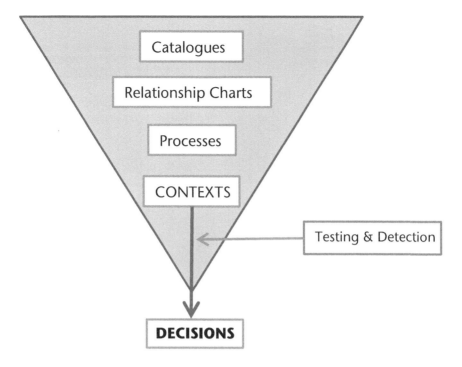

Figure 14.4 Drilling Down to Decisions

Identifying Root Causes of Corruption

Typically, evaluations are based on cataloguing and forecasting risks, possibly generated in brainstorming sessions. The results are then matched against existing controls, gaps identified and improvements made. This process is reasonably effective when those carrying out the analysis understand the risks involved, which is not always the case with fraud and corruption.

The recommended approach, discussed in the following pages, is far more comprehensive and can be compared to a detailed examination of the health of the tree, with the leaves and blossom representing the objectives or output (Figure 14.5, overleaf!!). In the case of bribery this means confirming that output[20] from processes and decisions are sound. The branches can be viewed as discrete contexts and the trunk as the environmental and organisational wide controls. However, risk evaluations should also examine the equivalent of the roots of the tree; such as the key performance drivers, culture, external pressures and personal incentives that ultimately determine the health, stability and growth. And please don't overlook the fact that the anti-bribery oak is not the only tree in the forest. Think about risk evaluating other trees such as the anti-trust holly bush, the class action pine or the prickly pear of global warming and sustainability.

---

20   See Tim Leech, 'Honourably Retire "Internal Controls", Promote "Risk Treatments": It's Time' (The Institute of Internal Auditors, 2012), an excellent paper by a co-founder of the Canadian firm Risk Oversight Inc., who is recognised as a world authority on COSO (the standard supporting Sarbanes–Oxley). He points out the ineffectiveness of 'control-centric' risk evaluation. The paper is available online at: http://riskoversight.ca/wp-content/uploads/2011/03/Risk-Oversight-Honorably-Retiring-Controls-Promoting-Risk-Treatments-July-2012.pdf (accessed 18 November 2012).

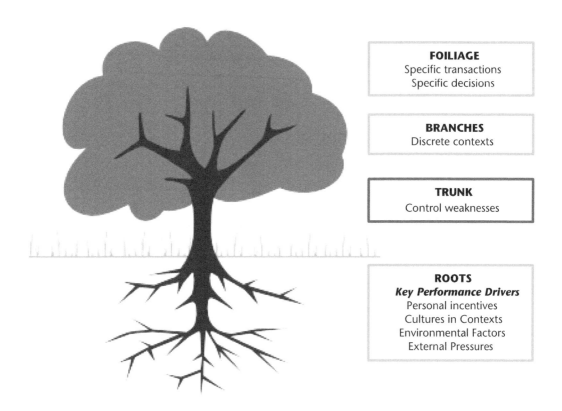

FOILIAGE
Specific transactions
Specific decisions

BRANCHES
Discrete contexts

TRUNK
Control weaknesses

ROOTS
Key Performance Drivers
Personal incentives
Cultures in Contexts
Environmental Factors
External Pressures

Figure 14.5 Roots and Branches

Summary of Differences in Approach

The main differences between the Ministry of Justice approach to risk assessment and the recommended method can be summarised, as follows in Table 14.3.

Table 14.3   Differences Between the Ministry of Justice Guidance and Recommended Method

Ministry of Justice Guidance to Risk Assessment	Suggested Approach to Risk Evaluation
SCOPE	
Limited to bribery and the Bribery Act	Focuses on corruption and all relevant international legislation
GENERIC AND AT A HIGH LEVEL Involves only internal factors	SPECIFIC AND GRANULAR – DRILLING INTO DETAIL Takes into account the two-dimensional nature of corruption and external pressures in the context concerned

Incurs costs	The evaluation should – ideally – be self-financing through hard cash recoveries
Backward-looking	Intelligence-led and specific Anticipatory while taking a balanced view of historical performance. The evaluation is specific to the organisation concerned. Decision-centric
Deals only with the primary risks of outgoing bribery Primarily to defend a Section 7 charge *Plans for the post-mortem on the living patient*	Covers five levels of evaluation, from primary risk to self-disclosure, negotiation and prosecution
	Evaluates the evidence that would be available to rebut mistaken allegations against the company
	Focuses on all aspects of corruption, preventing losses and making recoveries from fraud and corruption
Focuses on technical breaches such as facilitation payments, hospitality, gifts and sponsorship	Focuses on grand corruption
Applies mainly to the company and includes third parties and intermediaries only on the basis that they should not be trusted, leading to adversarial, uncommercial relationships	Applies to the Extended Enterprise, possibly on a collaborative basis involving suppliers, customers and other associates. Encourages supportive relationships
TAXONOMY CORRUPTION	
Based on false conceptions of supply-side bribery, country risks, agents and red flags	Based on practical experience, recognising that both sides of corruption are equally culpable. The focus is specific and analytical, based on key contexts and incoming and outgoing decisions
CONTROLS	
Does not deal in detail with control selection or assess their impact	Specifies procedures for introducing new controls and evaluating their impact (i.e. Impact Assessments)
Assumes the entity-wide tone from the top flows consistently through the organisation	Accepts the reality that each context has its own distinct culture, based on key performance drivers and peer group pressure
Suggests that ambiguity in the Act can be resolved by prosecutorial discretion	Empowers managers to take decisions in real time
METHODOLOGY	
Framed in a negative way and aimed at bribe payment	Branded and widely promoted in a positive, collaborative way
Mainly directed by lawyers from a legal frame	Directed by senior commercial managers with specialist support and legal advice

Ministry of Justice Guidance to Risk Assessment	Suggested Approach to Risk Evaluation
METHODOLOGY	
Managed by checklists and primarily based on desktop reviews and published procedures	Checklists are used only as a final quality and completeness check
	Supported by detailed testing, auditing and external interviews to expose fraudulent transactions
Bases assessments primarily on published policies and procedures	Involves detailed monitoring and analysis, to detect specific transactions and, where possible, make recoveries
Involves high compliance costs and operational overheads	When linked to detailed transactional testing, the entire risk evaluation and control improvement process should be better than self-financing

The result is that evaluations lead to more accurate identification of risks, more cost-effective controls and, in many cases, to hard cash recoveries.

Risk evaluations should normally consist of the stages outline in Figure 14.6.

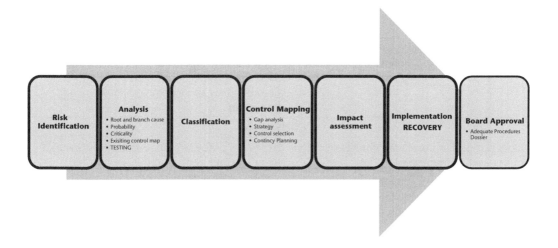

Figure 14.6 Stages in Risk Evaluation

The approach, illustrated in Figure 14.6, involves detailed testing and making recoveries from previous incidents of fraud and corruption.

Risk Defined and Analysed

Simply stated, a risk is the chance of something undesirable happening at some time in the future, and it consists of two elements. The first is probability of occurrence, meaning how often an adverse event is likely to occur on a continuum of impossible to certain. The second is criticality, which is the damage[21] resulting from each occurrence. **For most risks, probability and criticality vary inversely.** Those that occur most frequently usually result in minor consequences, while there is always the possibility of a 'Black Swan': a very rare event which is catastrophic.

This symbiosis is not always true of corruption risks when – because of regulatory and other consequences – a minor infringement may be disastrous,[22] or nearly so. However there is no record of any company failing[23] only because of corruption or regulatory action in relation to it.

Evaluation of Probability

BASIC PRINCIPLES

The first problem with all covert risks is being able to predict probability. The options are shown in Table 14.4.

Table 14.4 Methods of Evaluating Probability

Methods of Evaluating Probability	Comments
Historical and red flags, etc.	For most covert risks, historical and comparative data (such as crime statistics, surveys, perceptions and press reports) is incomplete and unreliable. The approach is also too generic
Comparative (for example, country or sectorial risk)	
Analytical (but subjective)	Specific, based on detailed and brainstormed catalogues of processes, contexts and decisions
Testing and Critical Point Auditing	Aimed to test analytical findings and to uncover existing and past fraudulent and corrupt transactions

Published statistics on fraud and corruption are notoriously unreliable. Therefore alternative methods of estimating probability must be found. The method suggested is eclectic.

In practice, the probability of covert risks is best estimated using brainstorming and Delphi techniques, which result in broad classifications such as very likely (> 80 per cent),

---

21   Which may be financial, regulatory, reputational damage, loss of competitive position, decrease in share prices, etc.

22   This is especially true for repetitive offences, or where warnings have not been heeded.

23   The Enron–Anderson case is cited as an example, but it is not valid.

likely (> 25 per cent) and unlikely (1–24 per cent). **Probabilities must always be linked to a time period and in the case of corruption forecasts over 5 years are realistic.** Thus an estimated probability of 1:50 in a 12-month period can be written as $1:50^1$, which is the equivalent of $1:250^5$, which is the same as $1:50^1$. Often probability estimates are published without specifying the associated timescale and, as such, are meaningless. As Homer Simpson said: 'Everything is a certainty if you can wait long enough'.

THE IMPORTANCE OF BASE-RATE STATISTICS

People overestimate the probability of some low occurrence risk because of what Professor Daniel Kahneman, in his book, *Thinking Fast and Slow*, terms 'availability heuristics'. This is a cognitive bias towards those events which are most easily recalled,[24] most often repeated, and which are emotional or at the front of the mind.[25] In the current climate bribery risks fall into this category because seldom a day goes by when the 'Cottage Industry' does not make a noise.

Professor Kahneman advocates that the distortion caused by availability heuristics can be corrected by referring to base-rate statistics. However, in fraud and corruption there are no reliable statistics.

Infinitesimal Risks

If most companies were to evaluate their risk of prosecution based on Department of Justice, Serious Fraud Office (SFO), Securities and Exchange Commission (SEC) and other sanctions, they would come to the conclusion that the odds are so infinitesimally small that they could be ignored or safely accepted. This would be an unwise conclusion because, as we shall see, the base rate of potentially corrupt decisions is high!

PROBABILITY AND DECISION-CENTRICITY

Basing probabilities of corruption on the recommended decision-centric model results in much more specific, visible and auditable evaluations. Key variables such as:

* The number of internal and external decision-makers involved in the contexts concerned;
* The number of counterparties receiving and making decisions and whether or not they are in the UK or overseas, or in the private or public sectors;
* *The estimated percentage of relationships that could be influenced by soft corruption such as nepotism, friendship, family relationships, etc.;*
* *The estimated percentage of relationships and specific decisions that are influenced by bribe payment (hard bribery);*

---

24   'Recall fluidity'.

25   Like spending a year in jail for giving an FPO $5 not to be injected with an infected needle (see page 125).

- The categories of decisions made or received, segregating those that are routine from others that are contrived or exceptional;
- The total number of decisions taken and received in the context per annum.

These variables can be used to brainstorm probabilities, as is outlined in Table 14.5.

Calculating Potentially Perverted Decisions

Say there are 200 employees working in a purchasing department, all of whom are authorised to make various categories of decisions, such as canvassing potential vendors (estimated at 2,000[26]), appointing them, preparing invitations to tender, placing and processing purchase orders, validating goods received, processing invoices, authorising payments, claiming credits, processing credit notes, etc. A probability map may produce results along the lines of Table 14.5. Columns C, D, E and F show the positions of different categories of decision-makers, separated in the potential liability positions under the Bribery Act.

Table 14.5   Risk-mapping and Decisions-mapping

Type	Factor	Directing Minds	Senior Managers	Employees	Dependent Decisions	
		Section 2 Individual Corporate	Section 2 Individual			
A	B	C	D	E	F	G
INCOMING BRIBERY: bribes paid to a company's representatives to induce an advantage for a third party						
Bribes Received	Number of Decision Types	10	50	40	10	
	Number of decisions per type per annum	100	50	70	20	
	Number of counter-parties	50	100	1,000	200	
	Total decisions per annum	1,000	2,500	2,800	200	
	Number of influenced decisions 10%	**100**	**250**	**280**	**20**	650
	Number of bribed decisions 5%	**50**	**125**	**140**	**10**	325

---

26   Of which 10 per cent would be amenable to soft or hard corruption.

- 650 internal decisions are influenced by soft or technical corruption and 325 by hard bribery, none of which would involve a Section 7 offence by the evaluating company. However, 150 decisions are by directing minds, which could lead to corporate liability under Section 2.

Type	Factor	Directing Minds	Senior Managers	Employees	Dependent Decisions	Section 7 Decisions
		Section 1 Section 6 Individual Corporate	Sections 1 and 6 Individual			
INTERNAL AND OUTGOING BRIBERY: bribes paid by a person to obtain an advantage for the company						
Bribes Paid	Number of decision types	10	50	40	10	80
	Number of decisions per type per annum	100	50	70	20	240
	Number of counter-parties	50	100	1,000	200	
	Total decisions per annum	1,000	2,500	2,800	200	6,500
	Number of influenced decisions 3%[27]	**30**	**75**	**84**	**80[28]**	**279**
	Number of bribed decisions 2%	**20**	**50**	**56**	**40**	**156**

- 279 external decisions involving soft corruption and 156 by hard bribe payment, all of which could involve Section 7 liability. Further, there are estimated to be 50 decisions by directing minds. These could lead to corporate offences under Section 1 and Section 7.

Obviously probability estimates in any model are open to debate, but even if far more conservative estimates are used, the fact is that there are lots of decisions flying around, all of which would be perverted. **The difference between the very high probability of perverted decisions and the small number of regulatory actions is explained mainly by the fact that skulduggery is not detected or, if detected, not recognised as such and reported.**

---

27   A vendor's representative may be corrupted to manipulate prices, discounts, allocations, the quality of goods, delivery dates, etc. However, the number of corrupt decisions is assessed to be less than for incoming procurement bribery.

28   This is estimated at more than 3 per cent to account for blue-collar collusion at goods-received points.

Evaluation of Criticality

The second element of risk is criticality, which is only ever relevant[29] when a probability has hit 100 per cent and the adverse event has materialised. There are no reliable statistics on primary and consequential impacts of corruption and thus evaluations must again be made subjectively. Criticality consists of:

- The primary loss (or gain) from incoming, internal, outgoing or competitive corruption, including the consequential costs of reputational damage;
- The potential regulatory penalties,[30] including fines, disgorgement of profits, debarment from government business, victim compensation and loss of business;
- The derived or consequential costs (such as third-party legal actions and reputational damage).

An analysis of the limited data from cases handled by the Department of Justice, the SEC and the SFO suggests that for cases of bribe payment (outgoing corruption), the sum of the consequential impacts[31] is between one and seven times the intended business advantage.

On this basis bribe payment involves the greatest overall[32] criticality **but only if offences are detected and penalties imposed**. When probabilities of detection are taken into account *(which in most cases is likely to be less than 1:50,000¹)*, bribe payment becomes much less critical, leaving internal, competitive corruption and fraud in joint number one position. Competitive corruption can result in serious long-term financial damage but, of course, no regulatory penalties for the evaluating company.

Prioritising Risk

Theoretically risks should be prioritised so that they can be controlled commensurately. There are two ways of doing this. The first is based on **quantification** of an estimated annual cost (EAC) using the formula

$$EAC = Probability \times Criticality$$

For examples, see Table 14.6.

---

29   Other than for computational purposes.

30   In multiple jurisdictions.

31   Including penalties.

32   That is, losses + penalties + other consequences.

Table 14.6   Calculations of Estimated Annual Cost

Risk	Estimated Probability = P		Estimated Criticality = C	Estimated Annual Cost = P*C
Fire	1 in 5 years	1:5^1	£200,000	£40,000
Robbery	1 in 10 years	1:10^1	£20,000	£2,000
Flood	1 in 20 years	1:20^1	£50,000	£2,500
Mouse eating through a computer cable	Once a year	1:1^1	£400	£400

Table 14.6 implies that it might be more beneficial for the company to install fire equipment than to buy a mouse trap. This is true until a rodent devours a cable and closes down the computer centre for a month.

The same sort of problem arises with quantification of corruption risks. If a company follows the country risk approach and relaxes where it feels safe – such as in the UK or the USA – Murphy's Law will kick in and that is precisely where the disaster will occur. **The lesson is to concentrate on important contexts and decisions, almost regardless of country risk.**

A second method of ranking is the **qualitative**, in which risks are divided into broad categories. For examples, see Table 14.7.

Table 14.7   Classification of Risks

Criticality			Probability *Within a five-year period*		
Classification ⬇⬇⬇⬇⬇		Financial Loss Regulatory Penalties	Very Likely 80% +	Likely 25%+	Unlikely 1–24%
			1	2	3
A	High	> 5% of annual turnover	A1	A2	A3
B	Medium	Limit set depending on the size of the organisation	B1	B2	B3
C	Low		C1	C2	C3

Risks in the shaded cells in Table 14.7 are clearly the most harmful and thus the contexts in which they arise should be given the closest attention while risks in C2, C3 and B3 can probably be safely accepted. Risks can be quantified in broad categories. Too much sophistication is cosmetic and a waste of time.

An eclectic method along the lines of Table 14.8 is preferred by some organisations because it appears to give numerical support for management decisions.

Table 14.8 Estimated Annual Cost Ratios

	Times Per Year		**CRITICALITY** *(Per Occurrence) in Pounds Estimated Annual Cost in Italics*						
			1,000	**10,000**	**100,000**	**1,000,000**	**5,000,000**	**10,000,000**	**20,000,000**
PROBABILITY	100	100	*100,000*	*1,000,000*	*10,000,000*	*100,000,000*			
	50	50	*50,000*	*500,000*	*5,000,000*	*50,000,000*			
	25	25	*25,000*	*250,000*	*2,500,000*	*25,000,000*			
	10	10	*10,000*	*100,000*	*1,000,000*	*10,000,000*			
	5	5	*5,000*	*50,000*	*500,000*	*5,000,000*			
	1	1	*1,000*	*10,000*	*100,000*	*1,000,000*	*5,000,000*	*10,000,000*	*20,000,000*
	1 in 5	0.2000	*200*	*2,000*	*20,000*	*200,000*	*1,000,000*	*2,000,000*	*4,000,000*
	1 in 1o	0.1000	*100*	*1,000*	*10,000*	*100,000*	*500,000*	*1,000,000*	*2,000,000*
	1 in 25	0.0400	*40*	*400*	*4,000*	*40,000*	*200,000*	*400,000*	*800,000*

It is first necessary to assign broad values to criticality, depending on the size of the organisation, the contexts concerned and its risk tolerance. In the example the lowest criticality is £1,000 and the highest £20,000,000. Probabilities of occurrence, ranging from 100 times a year to once in 25 years are entered in the rows, intersecting with criticalities to show EACs. The company may then categorise risks and 'Low' (say with an EAC of under £10,000), Medium (up to £100,000) or 'High' (above £1,000,000). These can then be applied, for example, to set the level of due diligence checking of the supplier or customer base for both financial and compliance purposes.

A Sort of Prisoners' Dilemma

It is technically possible – though not advised – to apply risk-modelling to answer the very important question: '*should we ever consider paying bribes?*'[33]

Table 14.9 sets out a broad estimate of gains and losses from bribe payment based on a simple situation where:

- The business available for division between Company X and its competitors in a foreign private sector market is 200 smackeroos with an expectation that each could win 50 per cent–100 per cent.
- A 10 per cent bribe payment increases the win ratio to 90 per cent.
- The penalties, if discovered, for a UK bribe-paying relevant commercial organisation is seven times the potential gain.
- Law enforcement in the foreign market is ineffective.
- Ratio A/B is a simple calculation of the win–loss ratio of each alternative, with higher being better.

33 This means 'hard bribes', continuing with the Prisoner's Dilemma (see page 373).

The level of bribery in any context normally varies directly with skulduggery by competitors so the position is as follows:

Table 14.9 The Prisoners' Dilemma and Bribery[34]

Alternative Positions	Company X's Position			Competitors' Position		
	Turnover A	Penalties B	A/B	Turnover	Penalties	A/B
Neither pays bribes and the best wins (i.e. X)	200	0[35]	200	0	0	0
Neither pays bribes	100	0	100	100	0	100
Competitors (UK) pay bribes and X does not	20	1	20	180	1400	0.128
Foreign competitors pay bribes and X does not	20	0	20	180	0	**180**
Everyone pay bribes	100	560	0.178	100	560	1.178
Company X pays bribes and competitors do not	180	1,400	0.128	20	0	20
X pulls out of the market	0	0	0	200	0	200

The best option for honest Company X is that neither it nor its competitors pay bribes and it wins the business (200). The worst position is if X pulls out of the market (0) or pays bribes and is caught (0.128). Competitors who are not bound by the UK Act (or, if there are any, any extraterritorial laws in their home country) are in a dominant position because they can bribe with impunity (200). It is overwhelmingly to their advantage if X pulls out of the market, because all of the business comes their way, with serious monopolistic consequences for local citizens.

However, if Company X is *sure* than its chances of being detected by UK or US regulators is less than 1:1200[1] or 1:6,000[5] the picture changes and bribe payment becomes, theoretically, an economically viable option; with emphasis on the *theoretical* nature of the calculation!

The Importance of In-the-Moment Training

The problem really surfaces if salesmen frame an opportunity in purely economic terms and conclude that taking a risk is worthwhile. This emphasises the importance of training outward-facing employees and of creating an attitude of inspiring integrity that applies 'in the moment' to instinctive decisions (see pages 730–32).

---

34 The cost of the 10 per cent bribe is ignored to avoid over-complication.

35 Assumed to be 1, for the sake of making the illustrative calculation.

Risk Management Strategy

There are four main strategies for managing risks, shown in Table 14.10 which may be considered.

Table 14.10 Risk Management Options

Risk Strategy ↓↓↓↓↓ / Criticality →→→→→→	Probability A High			Probability B Medium			Probability C Low			Examples
	1 High	2 Med	3 Low	1 High	2 Med	3 Low	1 High	2 Med	3 Low	
1. Risk Avoidance *Make strategic changes to avoid the risk*	Yes	Yes		Yes	Yes					Transfer operations away from the UK Withdraw from a market
2. Risk Transfer *Transfer risks to a third party*	Try to commit the regulators to decision templates / Involve them in control programmes / Maintain an Adequate Procedures Dossier with Silver Bullets									
3. Risk Reduction *Introduce controls to reduce the probability or criticality of occurrence*	Yes	Yes	Yes	Yes	Yes	Yes	Yes	Yes		Procedures, hardware and technical defences
4. Risk Retention *Tolerate the residual risk* *Prepare contingency plans*	Specify plans for conducting investigations and self-disclosure / Accept residual self-disclosure risks									

Risk Transfer to Regulators

One of the safest methods of mitigating a risk would be to transfer it to the regulators by getting them to agree in advance that a policy, procedure, matrix or control was adequate, or that a transaction or relationship was acceptable. It is abundantly clear that the SFO and other government agencies have no intention of committing themselves in this way, but will reserve judgement to prosecutorial discretion. However, there are ways – by maintaining an Adequate Procedures Dossier – that some risk can be transferred.

Chapters 21–32 set out a menu of controls that reduce the probability and criticality of risks, but they inevitably leave some 'residuals', which have to be accepted: this is a fact of life.

Evaluation Tools and Techniques

BACKGROUND

The following paragraphs discuss the most important tools for evaluating corruption risks. More detailed detection tests (which may be used in addition) are reviewed in Chapters 18–20.

INTERVIEWS

The importance of effective interviewing at every stage in the evaluation cannot be overstated and representatives from all the following groups of people should be interviewed:

Internal Sources

- Owners and directors *(especially concerning their philosophy and values and the advantages they may provide to third parties from their private wealth (see page 318))*
- Employees and ex-employees[36]
- Temporary and agency staff
- Representatives of staff associations and unions.

Associated Sources

- Customers and vendors (possibly as part of a collaborative risk evaluation)
- Ex-vendors
- Lawyers
- External auditors.

External Sources

- Local lawyers in difficult overseas jurisdictions
- Local police and regulators
- Competitors.

---

36   And especially smokers, chauffeurs, personal assistants, porters and messengers.

Foreign Government contacts

- Government agencies (possibly as part of a collaborative risk evaluation)
- Regulatory agencies.

A section of each interview should explore the real world ethical standards, key performance drivers and decisions taken and received in the contexts concerned, progressing upwards and outwards to evaluate the entity as a whole.

Interesting Background

The Institute of Internal Auditors Research Foundation's publication, *Best Practices: Evaluating the Corporate Culture*,[37] is interesting background reading, although it concentrates on compliance with published procedures (that is, box-ticking) rather than probing more deeply into behaviour at a real-world operational level.

Interviews should be polite but probing and based primarily on open questions and narratives.

An Example of Legal Empathy

A top legal team compiled a list of interview questions, including:

- Have you ever been offered a bribe?
- Have you ever paid a bribe?
- Do you make facilitation payments?

Unsurprisingly, the answers from some 100 employees were all 'No'.

A much more productive approach is to get people talking by asking open questions:

- What are the most important decisions you take (and receive)?
- How do you manage them?
- What is your agent in Jakarta like?
  - What is the biggest deal he has brought in?
  - How was he able to secure that?

---

37   Written by James Roth. Available through the Institute's website at: http://www.theiia.org/bookstore/product/best-practices-evaluating-corporate-culture-1469.cfm (accessed 17 November 2012).

- Who is your most effective competitor in Indonesia?
  - Why is he successful?
  - How is your agent able to compete with that?
- What is the best deal you have ever made in Indonesia?

Evaluators should remain on the lookout for subjects who refuse to answer questions, are unwilling to provide detail or who quickly feign anger and attack. Where evaluators have any doubts about the honesty of the interviewee, they should consider asking him to submit a written narrative summarising his position.

CONTROL SELF-ASSESSMENT

Control Self-assessment (CSA) was conceived by Tim Leech[38] and his colleagues at Gulf Resources, Canada, in the 1980s. Most CSA programmes have developed from this model and are normally conducted internally, but there is no reason why they should not be collaborative and involve third parties.

CSA is sometimes called a 'Structured Workshop' and it has been a feature (and very successful) in COSO and Sarbanes–Oxley compliance.

The basic system consists of the stages shown in Table 14.11.

Table 14.11 Stages in a Typical Control Self-assessment Programme

Phase	Action and Comments
Introductory presentation to the division members by the programme leader or facilitator: this is usually an external consultant with extensive practical experience	The object is to gain the commitment of top management to the programme; this is essential
Programme 1 Review of Business Unit 1	• Delegates from the Business Unit concerned are given pre-reading • Each unit arranges a one-day workshop • Delegates determine control objectives, brainstorm risks and controls • They prepare Delphi or similar charts which consolidate the group's views of risks and controls • A draft report is produced • Findings are reviewed by Internal Audit and the Audit Committee • An action plan is prepared • The results are securely retained
Programme 2 to n Reviews of other Business Units	• As above for other departments and divisions

---

38   Tim Leech is still at the leading edge of CSA and can be contacted at Risk Oversight Inc., Canada.

Assessments customarily spread from the bottom to the top of the organisation and involve multiple structured sessions. One of the main advantages of CSA is that it throws responsibility into the business line, confirms ownership, and makes managers and employees think about their responsibilities, discuss them with their colleagues and generate their own solutions. A drawback is that participants may not have a detailed understanding of corruption or the law.

JOB SENSITIVITY ANALYSIS

Job Sensitivity Analysis (JSA) is a risk-evaluation tool that analyses the potential methods of incoming, internal and outgoing corruption and conflicts of interest in individual jobs.

The analysis may be completed by the job-holders themselves, or used as an aide-memoire by evaluators in, or in preparation for interviews. The analysis form may also include psychologically profiled questions[39] to expose the inner thinking or ingrained ethics of the subject.

RISK NARRATIVE

A risk narrative is a detailed textual explanation of a single risk, specifying:

- Precisely what it is (where it arises, how and why);
- What it is not;
- Its probable causes;
- Its extent, impact or significance.

Narratives should drill down into specific contexts and the critical decisions made within them, and how they can be influenced to induce improper performance. Narratives written by the evaluation team should be confirmed by people working in the contexts concerned.

BRAINSTORMING

The *Oxford English Dictionary* defines a brainstorm as 'a spontaneous group discussion to produce ideas and solutions to problems'. The term 'brainstorming' was popularised by Alex Faickney Osborn in 1953 in the book *Applied Imagination*.[40] The technique is ideally suited for evaluating covert risks, especially where historical or comparative data are incomplete or unreliable. The method recommended for corruption risk is to drill down from the catalogues into cross-relational flowcharts, then into specific contexts and finally into decisions.

---

39   For obvious reasons, it would be unwise to include details of such questions here (although further details can be obtained by contacting the authors).

40   Osborn, Alex F., *Applied Imagination; principles and procedures of creative thinking* (New York: Scribner, 1953).

Ideally, brainstorming sessions should be led by an experienced moderator and include all members of the evaluation team supported by a small group of employees from different levels, a fraud specialist and at least one 'pooper'.[41]

Output from the brainstorming session should be incorporated into the Risk Evaluation Database and where necessary probed even more deeply using risk narratives (see page 345 for an example of a narrative on facilitation payments).

---

41   A technical term for a sceptic.

15 *Management and Catalogues*

Overview

The suggested flow for evaluating primary risks of incoming, internal, outgoing and competitive corruption, as well as fraud, can be summarised as shown in Figure 15.1.

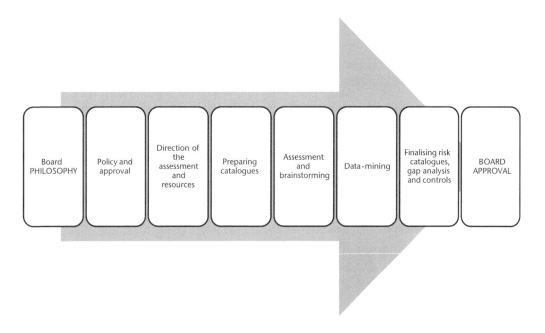

Figure 15.1 Recommended Stages in Risk Evaluation
The stages depicted in Figure 15.1 are examined below in more detail.

Directing the Risk Evaluation

An enterprise-wide risk evaluation should be carried out under the authority of the directors and, ideally, should be completed *before* policies, procedures, standards, guidelines and other documentation are finalised (see Chapters 14–17). Remember, even the Ministry of Justice believes risk assessment is the starting point!

The directors should decide and **RECORD IN BOARD MINUTES:**

- Precisely what the **coverage** of the corruption risk evaluation should be, its objectives and **form of output.** For example, should it include the Extended Enterprise or be restricted to particular internal departments, operations or processes?
- **Whether it should cover incoming, internal, outgoing and competitive corruption and conflicts of interest and related frauds,** or just follow the Ministry of Justice's narrow approach;
- Whether the evaluation should involve **collaboration with associated third** parties and government agencies;
- Whether the evaluation should go **beyond primary risk**s and consider disclosure, investigatory reporting and other related decisions (see Chapter 17).
- Whether the evaluation should be corroborated and reinforced by **data-mining** to identify corrupt and fraudulent transactions and make financial recoveries from them;
- Whether the evaluation should focus on narrow compliance with the **Bribery Act 2010 or include the Foreign Corrupt Practices Act (FCPA)** and other legislation. *(Generally, the requirements of both are similar, but aiming to satisfy the Bribery Act plus the UK Companies Acts on accounting will probably result in more effective control.)*
- What timescale and budget will be allowed.

Consideration should be given to how and what employees and others will be told about the evaluation. Will it be announced as a low-key compliance obligation, kept secret or framed imaginatively and positively as part of an upbeat integrity campaign? Experience shows that the latter approach is preferable.

The next question is whether an amnesty should be offered for employees, suppliers, etc. who admit to previous acts of corruption or fraud; and a special hotline set up offering rewards for information. These are contentious points, but one of the objectives of an evaluation is to get off to a clean start.

Collaborative Risk Evaluation

Even the more sophisticated methods of risk evaluation are one-dimensional to the extent that they examine only factors internal to the organisation concerned. This ignores the fact that corruption involves at least two parties – a coercer and an extorter – and their associated organisations.

To accurately evaluate risks – and especially those of outgoing corruption – it is best to examine all dimensions that combine in distinct contexts, involving all variables, including processes, culture, key performance drivers, controls and concealment possibilities in both organisations, as well as environmental factors and pressures.

Payments to Intermediate Parties

A company maintained a policy of zero tolerance to corruption and prohibited bribes of any kind being paid to foreign public officials (FPOs). An Inspector working in the government's Revenue Department agreed with the company's dodgy tax advisers (without the company's knowledge) to reduce an assessment by $2 million and to share this amount with them. The company, unknowingly, paid in full but the Inspector recorded a refund of $2 million and converted it to his own benefit, Although in a one-dimensional review controls appeared effective, a wider, collaborative evaluation involving the Revenue Department would have uncovered the fraud.

One-dimensional evaluations are akin to a football league manager deciding on the tactics for a match based only on the skills of his own team and ignoring the opponent's strengths and weaknesses, the venue, weather, the referee's foibles and other relevant factors.

Working in collaboration with associated third parties in the Extended Enterprise improves the accuracy of evaluations:

- It enables risks to be more accurately evaluated by taking into account third-party compensatory controls especially in relation to outgoing corruption (see Figures 1.3 and 1.4, page 7).
- It reduces the danger of creating adversarial relationships with agents and other third parties, and is, on the contrary, relationship-building.
- It enables integrity pacts (see pages 655 and 741) to be agreed and reinforces those already in place.
- It creates multiple channels of communication with important third parties, thus making it more likely that collusive arrangements will be prevented or quickly exposed.

Collaborative Risk Evaluation

A collaborative risk evaluation session was, after a great deal of prevarication and negotiation, eventually agreed between a UK company and the Customs Department in a Less Developed Country. The purpose was to evaluate serious delays in cargo clearance linked to facilitation extortion by junior officers.

At the Commissioner's insistence the session – involving 25 of his senior officers – was held in a five-star hotel. At that time the attendees' average salary was probably less than $3,000 a year. Covert surveillance on the hotel's car park and main entrance revealed junior officers arriving in Jaguar saloons, BMWs and on three top-of-the-range Harley-Davidson motorcycles.

Every officer was immaculately dressed, but rather than wearing their official low-quality issued clothing, all had tailor-made uniforms, having replaced the cheap badges and emblems with far more expensive versions.

Amazingly, the session was productive and a protocol agreed for eliminating facilitation payments. The agreement lasted approximately 12 months until the Commissioner was ousted in an unscheduled governmental regime change. Things then reverted to normal and the incoming Commissioner was not prepared to collaborate.

The Pink Pussycat is OK

A collaborative risk evaluation with, for example, an important customer, should result in agreement over the precise criteria on which contracts will be awarded (see Kepner-Tregoe, page 586) and what levels of hospitality can be offered and accepted without causing problems. This makes it far less likely – if not untenable – for regulators to subsequently allege that a decision was corrupted by a night's hospitality at the Pink Pussycat Lap Dancing Club when both sides have aligned their policies.

Invitations to third parties[1] to collaborate in risk evaluations are especially useful when there are suspicions that they might be exposed to corruption by competitors, because it puts all concerned on notice that decisions are under the spotlight. If the third parties agree, decision matrices (see page 568) can be agreed that make it more difficult for competitors to use bribery to induce perverted decisions.

The Evaluation Team

The board should also decide what resources will be used to conduct the evaluation (Table 15.1).

Table 15.1   Resources for Conducting Risk Evaluations

Resource	Comments
INTERNAL ONLY Compliance or Internal Audit	Conducted entirely internally. This has the advantage of being cheaper. However it is unlikely that internal departments have enough real-world knowledge of corruption and fraud to adequately evaluate risks. They are more likely to accept Transparency International's concentration on country risks and red flags and to continue looking for dodos.

---

1   Preferably at a top management level .... See Table 16.4, page 420.

EXTERNAL Specialist Consultants	Specialists may be used but should be carefully selected based on their practical real-world experience (see page 675)
ECLECTIC Project Team	This is possibly the best solution for most large organisations and involves a combination of internal staff (including at least one from marketing), and at least one fraud specialist and a senior solicitor
SELF-ASSESSMENT Line Managers *Control self-assessment* *Automated Risk Packages*	Carried out within a company's divisions and departments as explained below
	Although some off-the-shelf packages claim to assess corruption risks (especially the FCPA), they are insufficiently granular to provide detailed solutions. They are not recommended

The Board of Directors should ensure that skilled resources are used for risk evaluations.

The following pages are based on the assumption that a multidisciplinary evaluation team – probably consisting of no more than five or six members – is formed, led by a **senior commercial manager**. The team should include a sceptic, or 'pooper', and should be assisted by an experienced anticorruption specialist and advice from a top-level solicitor.[2] Ideally, the team should also include (or second) an information technology (IT) technician, for two reasons. The first is that he is qualified to examine the organisation's technical infrastructure and evaluate the effect it has on mitigating risks in other contexts. The second is that technical input may be needed to develop a Risk Evaluation Database (discussed later). **The risk evaluation team should be guided by a senior commercial manager and not by lawyers, consultants or investigators** *(bless!)*.

All members of the team should be fully briefed so that there is no misunderstanding about the evaluation's sensitivity, privileged nature, objectives, budgets and timescales. In many cases short training sessions on the relevant laws[3] and the taxonomy of corruption are worthwhile. Team members should be required to sign nondisclosure agreements.

General Approach to Evaluations

Even the most successful risk evaluations do not start off as things of great beauty, but are rather disorganised ramblings. Anarchy[4] is to be encouraged: primarily because the objective is to throw out the widest net, with no preconceived ideas, using lateral thinking and brainstorming to the maximum extent possible. Order[5] is established by managing the evaluation through a relational database (the Risk Evaluation Database) such as Microsoft Access or FileMaker Pro.[6]

---

2   Who should not 'direct' the evaluation.

3   Especially if the evaluating company is obligated under UK and US laws.

4   This may be one reason why many lawyers and accountants – who are logical and well organised – are not good at risk assessments.

5   And audit trails.

6   Another useful program is Scrivener (for the Apple Mac), which is designed for writing fiction!!... but great for preparing risk narratives. See Literature & Latte at: http://literatureandlatte.com/ (accessed 17 November 2012).

The key template (or schema) in the database is called a Risk Working Sheet. Each one, uniquely and automatically numbered, analyses a specific risk no matter how unlikely it may initially appear to be.

A Risk Evaluation Database should:

- Include details of, and cross references to, all related risks, not just bribery;[7]
- Cross-reference risks to organisational units, processes, policies, specific contexts, decisions and (subsequently to) controls;
- Be able to find and sort by keywords, with hyperlinks to supporting documentation;
- Provide an audit trail for inclusion in the Adequate Procedures Dossier;
- Schedule and record evaluation actions.

It should also be capable of extracting risk and controls, sorted on individual or multiple keys to produce an almost unlimited array of reports.

The Risk Evaluation Database may also include a catalogue of controls, ranging from mitigation strategies through to hardware, technical routines and processes (see page 400). Although it is technically possible to automate the map of risks and controls, human input is always justified.

Checklists, of the type suggested by Transparency International, are not recommended until the final, review stages of an evaluation because they create a narrow box-ticking mentality and precondition the results.[8] It is essential that evaluators think laterally, keep open minds and continuously drill down to identify vulnerable contexts and decisions. This means following trails that are unlikely to be included on any generic checklist.

However:

- Mindmaps (such as *MindManager*[9]) are extremely useful for brainstorming and for project management.
- Evaluators should keep detailed notes,[10] so that all information can be traced back to source.
- Details of risks, controls and recommendations should be updated on the Risk Evaluation Database – as and when they are identified – *and regularly backed up*.

All working papers and electronic files used in the evaluation should be securely[11] retained in the Adequate Procedures Dossier, together with any previous or parallel assessments.

All previous risk assessments, relevant internal and external audit reports and management letters should be retrieved and where appropriate incorporated on Risk Working Sheets.

---

7   For example, export control, money-laundering and cartels.

8   Although they are useful in ensuring that all relevant data is collected.

9   Now rebranded as 'Mindjet'. Available at: http://www.mindjet.com/products/mindmanager (accessed 17 November 2012).

10   Preferably in loose-leaf ring binders with the right-hand pages summarising interviews and other findings with contemporaneous recording of recommendations and follow-up actions on the left-hand pages.

11   Marked 'Confidential and Privileged'.

Defining the Extended Enterprise

BASIC CATALOGUES

Detailed catalogues should be compiled of the most important elements that make up the Extended Enterprise.[12] They should be comprehensive and auditable and entered in the Risk Evaluation Database.

Example

The database can be sorted by company, process, context, asset class, or on other criteria and to produce multiple reports.

Complete and accurate catalogues that define the Extended Enterprise are critical. They provide an auditable framework. For larger organisations the catalogues listed in Figure 15.2 should be considered.

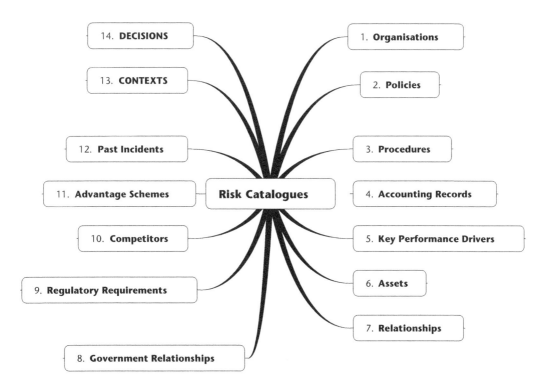

Figure 15.2 Initial Catalogues

---

12   This includes all companies within a group, suppliers, customers, advisers and all others providing services.

Table 15.2 below sets out additional detail. Ideally all supporting documentation should, if possible, be assembled in electronic formats and hyperlinked to the database.

Table 15.2 Recommended Baseline Catalogues

No.	Framework Reference Sub-catalogues	*Answers the Question* Sources of Information (Examples) and Comments
	ORGANISATIONS	
1 ↓	**Companies and entities in the Extended Enterprise (Worldwide)** • Physical locations *(buildings, installations, etc.)* • Parents, associates, joint ventures and subsidiaries • Business lines and divisions • Product groups • Agents and intermediaries • Lobbyists and PR • Advertising agencies • Employees • Stakeholders • ALL OUTSOURCED OPERATIONS	*What are the boundaries of the organisation?* *Is it a relevant commercial organisation?* *Does it carry out any part of its business in the UK?* *Is it listed with the SEC?* *Who are the associated persons?* *Who are the directing minds?* *Who is closely connected?* Annual reports and accounts Audit reports Board Minutes Email logs and address books **Internal telephone directories** Management reports **Organisation charts** **Payroll files** Research reports ('dodgy dossier' production) Share register Telephone call logs
	POLICIES	
2	**Top Management Philosophy and Policies** *(Possibly involving a Concordance (see page 620), benchmarking and linguistic analysis to identify themes, topics and headwords (see page 621))*	*What key policies apply to the anti-corruption programme and fraud prevention?* Board Minutes *(Was philosophy discussed before policies were issued or do they exist only on paper?)* Articles of Association on Directors' Liability Business development plans Compliance (all aspects, not just bribery) Ethics Fidelity and directors' and officers' liability insurance Fraud and security policies *(especially on detection and investigation)* Gifts and hospitality Human Resources OTHER *(How committed are top managers?)*

PROCEDURES (and Legal)	
3	**Procedures and forms (paper and electronic)** • Accounting • ANTI-MONEY-LAUNDERING • **BANK RECONCILIATIONS** • **CARBON WORLD AND CSR INVESTMENTS** • *COMPLIANCE AND CONTROLS* • Human Resources • IT • **MARKETING** • **PAYMENT SYSTEMS** • **PROCUREMENT AND TENDERING** • Referral fees given and received • Standard processes • BLUE COLLAR AND OPERATIONAL DECISION-MAKING	*What are the important procedures throughout the extended enterprise?* *What is the financial significance of each main process?*
		Authority Tables Budgets and cost centre reports Change control Chart of accounts Compliance policies and procedures (all agencies) Credit control Data dictionaries Employee fast-tracking Flow charts FORMS Goods inwards processes Inventory management Job descriptions Management reports Procedure and PROCESS manuals **Procedures on entertainment hospitality and other benefits** Quality control **Salary and incentive schemes** Sample contracts

ACCOUNTING RECORDS	
4	**Accounting records (samples and examples)** Where relevant to: • *Illustrate important decisions* • *Important process stages* • *Potential for concealing bribe payments* • *Potential for creating off-record slush funds* • *Windfall profits* • *Exceptional losses* • *Account opening, closing, and treatment of dormant accounts* • ***Payment and receipts processing (electronic, cash, manual cheques)*** • *Sources of cash income and expenditure* • *Marketing Department records* **Management information systems and reports**	*What are the typical processes and transactions in each context?* *How can bribes be paid and concealed?* *What transactions receive or generate cash?*
		Books of original entry **BUDGETARY AND COST CENTRE RECORDS** Cash transactions Cashiers' cheques Chart of accounts **Company credit cards and purchasing cards** Expenses statements Gateways between related systems Interviews Management reports and information systems Nominal ledger and journal vouchers Pricing and allocations **SALES ACCOUNTING** Statistical records Supplier and customer databases

No.	Framework Reference Sub-catalogues	*Answers the Question* Sources of Information (Examples) and Comments
	KEY PERFORMANCE DRIVERS	
5	**Key performance drivers in the Extended Enterprise** • *External influences (PESTLE: political, economic, social, technological, legal and environmental)* • *Entity level (strategic, tactical long- and short-term, as well as aspirations (such as merger trade sale or IPO)* • *Divisional level* • *Within contexts* • *Strategic plans* • *CSR programmes* • *Offset projects and emissions control* • *Political donations* • ***Present and anticipated government contracts*** • ***Any context in which there are short-term personal or corporate incentives such as earn-outs following an acquisition, or periodic targets***	*What are the key performance drivers throughout the organisation?* **External** Taxation Sectorial red flags **Internal** Decisions within process stages Flow charts Key performance drivers and metrics
	ASSETS	
6	**Assets** • Tangible • Intangible • Intellectual capital **Assets owned by owners, directors and senior managers** *whose provision to third parties may be regarded as technical violations of the Bribery Act. For example:* • *private jets* • *skiing and fishing lodges* • *corporate golf club membership* • *professional league football boxes (excluding Chelsea!)* • *holiday villas* • *luxury cars*	*What are the most important assets?* *How were they procured?* *How are disposals recorded?* Asset register Bank accounts **CASH and cash transactions** Defective goods returned for credit Free-of-charge issues and samples Goods received records Internal stock movements Inventory listings OTHER Proprietary information Quality control (and especially rejection records) Research and development information **Sales of scrap**

RELATIONSHIPS		
7	**Relationships** • Associated persons *(intermediaries, agents etc.)* • Third parties *(customers, suppliers, etc., etc.)* • Government contacts • Politically exposed persons • OUTSOURCED OPERATIONS **See the suggested methodology for categorising third party relationships on page 657**	*What are the most important relationships?* *Why are third parties appointed?* *What laws and regulations apply?* *What due diligence is carried out?* *What monitoring is carried out?* *What contractual rights does the company have?*
		Business ethics policies and codes of conduct Contracts Decision matrices Dormant and duplicate accounts Due diligence procedures Identify third parties and associates required to report under The Proceeds of Crime Act 2002 List of ex-customers List of ex-employees List of ex-vendors and intermediaries Miscellaneous vendors (and expenditure with) **Relationship maps** **REMUNERATION BASIS** Reputation, Internet and other searches **Sales and purchase ledgers** Websites
GOVERNMENT RELATIONSHIPS		
8	**Government Relationships** • As customers and suppliers • As regulators • As FPOs	*Identify all government contacts* ***Identify future government business and potential*** *Identify all FPO relationships*
		Relationship maps Governmental internal policies on gifts and the like
REGULATORY REQUIREMENTS		
9	**Regulatory Requirements** • Laws and enforcement standards in all relevant countries • Rules and regulations relating to FPOs in all relevant countries	*What regulations apply to all members of the extended enterprise?*
		Publications by local law firms Book and CD: Grützner, Thomas, Hommel, Ulf, and Moosmayer, Klaus, *Anti-Bribery Risk Assessment: Systematic Overview of 153 Countries (in German) (Munich: C.H. Beck, 2011).*
		LIITIGATION RISK EVALUATION
	Reporting Requirements under • anti-money-laundering regulations • Proceeds of Crime Act • Listing rules • SEC reporting • D&O or Fidelity insurance • other reporting requirements	*Legal opinion* *Record of reporting* *The high-risk countries based on FATF research are Cuba, Bolivia, Ethiopia, Kenya, Myanmar, Nigeria, São Tomé and Principe, Syria, Turkey and even higher: Iran and The Democratic People's Republic of Korea (North Korea)*
	Optional Reporting • Carbon inventories • Global Reporting Initiative • Sustainability	*Although these are mainly voluntary, they may involve false reporting and internal and external corruption*

No.	Framework Reference Sub-catalogues	Answers the Question Sources of Information (Examples) and Comments
COMPETITORS		
10	**Competitors** **Assessing their compliance obligations** *as, for example:* • *Relevant commercial organisations* • *UK body corporates* • *Closely connected persons*	*Who are the major competitors in all markets?* *Which competitors are not bound by the UK Bribery Act and the FCPA?* *Which conduct any part of their business in the UK?* *Which are the most successful and why?*
		Interviews Bid records Data-mining (see Chapters 18–20)
ADVANTAGE SCHEMES (which could be construed as outgoing bribery)		
11	Public relations and lobbyists	*What advantages are provided by the company that could be viewed as technical breaches of the Act?* *How do these align with advantages the company's own employees are allowed to accept?* *What advantages could be provided by the directors or owners from their personal estates?*
		All other advantage schemes (see page 417) Commissions paid and received Company credit cards Hospitality, gifts, etc., etc. Marketing schemes and free samples Offset projects Referral fees paid and given
PAST INCIDENTS		
12	**Past incidents** • Incident reports • Previous risk analyses • **PREVIOUS REGULATORY BREACHES AND WARNINGS** (It is crucially important to catalogue and analyse these and evaluate the significance they might have when regulators select targets) • **All previous and pending litigation**	*What incidents have occurred in the past?* *Are they relevant to the existing evaluation?* *What regulatory action has been taken in the past?* *How effective are investigation procedures?*
		Audit and investigation reports Disciplinary records (including those still pending) Interviews Management letters
CONTEXTS		
13	**Contexts matrix and key decisions**	**IDENTIFY ALL OUTWARD-FACING JOBS AND KEY DECISIONS**
		What are the critical contexts?
		Risk Evaluation Database extraction

DECISIONS		
14	Drill down to key decisions	*What are the critical decisions?* *Pay special attention to internal corruption involving one employee corrupting another (see pages 6, 27, 260 and 320), especially when the intention is to obtain business, etc., etc. for a relevant commercial organisation*
		Decisions Matrices (see page 568) Dodgy Dossiers Risk Evaluation Database extraction

Compiling accurate catalogues is difficult and time-consuming, but they establish the framework (and audit trail) for drilling down to identify important decisions that are conducive to corruption.

BUSINESS UNITS, PROCESSES AND TRANSACTIONS

Cross-relational matrices of business units and processes along the lines of Table 15.3 should be considered for all sensitive contexts:

Table 15.3 A Simple Cross-reference Matrix of Vendor Approval

Department – Division and Context	Processes: Vendor Approval and Due Diligence						
	Trawl >>	Initial Contact	Initial Selection	Application	Initial Screening	Due Diligence	Account Opening
User Department 1	Yes	Yes	Advice		No		Urgent transactions
User Department 2							
Central Procurement	Sometimes	Sometimes	Yes	Yes	Yes	Yes	Recommend
Accounting	No	No	No	No	No	No	Yes

Table 15.3 highlights three exceptions (in shaded cells) that should be carefully analysed.

Matrices summarise where responsibilities are segregated and how transactions and decisions could be perverted by corruption. Evaluators should pay particular attention to:

- Transactions providing **windfall profits** or involving exceptional losses, unusually good or bad decisions;
- Transactions and contexts generating or receiving **cash** or processing electronic or other payments;
- **Exceptions to standard processes** (in the above example the facility to override controls);

- Decisions approved **above or below the person's authority** (especially if there has been any concealment).

Cross-relational matrices should be prepared (see page 410) for all payment systems showing how transactions are generated, validated and processed: focusing on exceptions to standard systems, short-term and permanent amendments to payment parameters, and the processing of rejected transactions, manual payments and cashiers' cheques. The reason for giving payment systems very close attention is very simple: that is how a lot of bribes are still paid.

Payments are Important and Vulnerable

A cross-relational matrix and reconciliation of the gateway between a front-end procurement and payment processing revealed that account details of a number of miscellaneous suppliers had been temporarily changed to those of an employee and within hours of payments being processed, the account details were returned to their original state.

In addition, evaluators should identify **past errors, discrepancies** and problems and verify their underlying causes, which are often corruption rather than carelessness.

UNUSUAL SOURCES OF INFORMATION

Evaluators should seek out unusual sources of corroborative information such as customer complaints, sales representatives' calls and prospect sheets and disciplinary records, and look for any other information that throws light on the company's culture – in critical contexts – and processes at a working level.

16 *Analysing Vulnerable Contexts*

Identification Clues

The enterprise-wide catalogue should result in high-risk internal and external contexts being identified.[1] These are likely to include those in which:

- Strategic and exceptional decisions are taken;
- Directing minds are actively involved;
- Key performance drivers encourage skulduggery;
- Problems have previously arisen;
- Windfall profits are made or exceptional losses incurred;
- Noble causes are handled, or where they have an effect on decisions;
- The context is effectively a 'company within a company';[2]
- Decisions are delegated to associated persons;
- Decisions are supported by expert reports;[3]
- Decision-makers do not have the specialist knowledge to supervise effectively.

Further profiles have been deliberately omitted to encourage brainstorming in the organisation concerned. But there are two contexts that warrant close attention:

1. Internal corruption (see pages 7, 27, 226 and 260).
2. Blue-collar corruption (see page 260).

Blue-collar Corruption

A junior mechanic working for an airline took bribes from a supplier to accept refurbished and counterfeit spare parts. The corruption only came to light when an aircraft crashed killing 120 people. Van salesmen working for a food company bribed supermarket employees to accept deliveries that were past their sell by date: five customers died from food poisoning.

---

1   That are unlikely to be closely aligned to country risks.

2   Known as a 'cuckoo' because its senior managers deliberately break their upward reporting lines but build close teams below them. Cuckoos are not uncommon in sales, marketing and procurement.

3   That is, 'Dodgy dossiers'.

Both of these can involve serious losses and regulatory breaches, although they are rarely included in risk evaluations and not mentioned at all in the Ministry of Justice Guidance.

Relationship-mapping

It is essential that a potential coercer and a potential extorter establish a dialogue,[4] either directly or via an intermediary such as an agent, an information broker or a colleague. Most corruption involves outward-facing jobs,[5] with collusion initiated in any of the ways shown in Table 16.1.

Table 16.1   Important Dialogues of Corruption

Channel of Communication Between the Coercer and the Extorter or through an Intermediary	Relative Likelihood of a Collusive Agreement in Various Contexts 10 = High 0 = Low					
	At work	Social Events	Meals	Corporate Entertaining	Family Events	Travelling
Face-to-face meeting (when alone together)	7	8	**10**	**10**	5	**10**
Landline telephone conversation	5				7	8
Mobile phone telephone conversation	7	7				
Communication through a social networking site	2	5			5	
Face-to-face meetings (with others present)	2	4	6	6	6	8
Private email	3				3	3
Company email	2					
Correspondence	1					
Communication through a corrupt third party	8	5	5	5	8	8

Table 16.1 suggests that collusive dialogues that initiate corruption are more likely in private face-to-face meetings when alcohol is being consumed, when travelling (especially on aircraft) and through third-party introductions.

---

4   To agree a corruption scheme.

5   Although some 'inward-facing' or 'dry' jobs are also vulnerable to corruption (see page 346).

Evaluators should look for symptoms of potentially corrupt relationships, including:

- Single line or exclusive channels of diagonal communication[6] with a third party;
- The frequency of communication beyond that necessary for a routine commercial relationship in the context concerned;
- Clusters of telephone calls, especially outside normal working hours and on private or mobile phones rather than company handsets;
- Multiple meetings at luxury venues, at weekends and holidays;
- Repeated meetings at which only the coercer and the extorter are present.

These characteristics may be identified from the information sources in Table 16.2.

Table 16.2   Sources of Information

Source of Data	Format/Source	Comment
Company telephone call logs	Electronic	Frequency patterns Out-of-hours calls
Mobile telephone logs and electronic invoices *Provided the company is the subscriber*	Electronic bills	Frequency patterns Out-of-hours calls Contrived relationships (see page 410)
Email archives	Electronic	
Electronic address books (MS Outlook, etc.)	Electronic	
Speed-dialling directories	Electronic	
Email contact addresses	Electronic	
Visitors' car park entry logs	Manual–electronic	
Reception desk entry logs	Manual–electronic	
Representatives' call sheets	Manual–electronic	Frequency patterns
Employee master file	Electronic	Matching of data between files Identifying third parties which are both customers and suppliers
Vendors master file	Electronic	
Customer master file	Electronic	
Miscellaneous sales and purchases	Electronic	
Expense statements	Manual–electronic	See page 532
Personnel files	Manual	Mainly confined to directing minds and senior officers

Flow charts[7] are useful for mapping relationships. All of a sudden the world seems to be full of software and consultants who claim to optimise 'big data'. In the authors' experience, results have fallen well short of the bombast. Companies are advised to all test claims against their own data (and under controlled conditions) before investing.

---

6   See pages 410.

7   Such as Microsoft Visio. Pattern Tracer 2 from I2 (available at http://www.i2group.com (accessed 26 October 2012)) – they can import massive files of telephone call data and prepare relationship maps.

A Real Red Flag

Data-mining identified a supplier with which the client had spent more than £1 million. However, analysis of telephone logs in a relationship map revealed that the supplier had never once been contacted. Subsequent investigations exposed three completely fictitious vendors involving losses of £1.4 million.

Decision-mapping and Evaluation

Through interviews, analysis of procedures and transaction-testing, evaluators should catalogue significant incoming, internal and third-party decisions in potentially vulnerable contexts focusing on:

- The **outcomes** of decisions;
- The **processes** used: their consistency and conformance with policies and validation of the integrity of the parties involved;
- The personal and other biases that could affect outcomes.

The objective is not to generate lashings of paperwork, but simply to evaluate risks based on the principle of 'centricity' and the following categories of decisions.

INTERNAL DECISIONS

When taken corruptly, these typically involve:

- Incoming and internal corruption;
- Bribe receipt by an individual associated with the evaluating organisation;
- A loss to the evaluating organisation;
- A corporate gain by a third party;
- An offence by the individual extorter under Section 2;
- A possible corporate offence under Section 2 if the extorter is a directing mind;
- An extorter is liable for an offence committed entirely overseas if he is a closely connected person (for example, UK citizens);
- Bribery of one employee by another (internal).

EXTERNAL DECISIONS

When given corruptly, these typically involve:

- Outgoing corruption;
- Bribe payment by the evaluating organisation;
- A gain for the evaluating organisation;
- A personal advantage for the third-party extorter;
- A corporate offence for a body corporate if the coercer is a directing mind;

- A corporate offence for a relevant commercial organisation under Section 7 if the extorter's intention was to obtain business or another advantage for it;
- A coercer's liability for offences committed entirely overseas if he is closely connected to the UK; the body corporate is also at risk (under Section 1) if the coercer is a directing mind;
- A relevant commercial organisation's guilt of an offence (under Section 7) committed entirely overseas if the intention of the extorter was to obtain business for it.

THIRD-PARTY DECISIONS

These are taken entirely outside the evaluating organisation by or involving competitors and typically result in:

- A loss of business to the evaluating organisation;
- Theft of proprietary information (for example, in connection with information-broking).

Conflict of interest can be regarded as internal corruption.

SCHEMATIC OF DECISIONS

Figure 16.1 summarises the main considerations that evaluators should explore in interviews, by reviewing procedures and testing transactional data.

Evaluators should also consider what policies, procedures and other evidence would be available to validate decisions and prove their honest intent.[8]

Exposing 'Dodgy Dossiers'

Many perverted decisions are based on what has been termed 'dodgy dossiers', including false accounts, sexed-up consulting reports and deliberately inflated or depressed expert opinions, all of which apparently justify perverted decisions. The authors or originators of such dossiers may have been corrupted by a third party or by the client commissioning them so that he can justify a decision.

'Dodgy dossiers' regularly appear in incoming, internal and outgoing corruption and evaluators should identify all those that were influential in significant loss-making or windfall transactions. Interviews are usually the best starting point.

---

8   Rebuttal evidence.

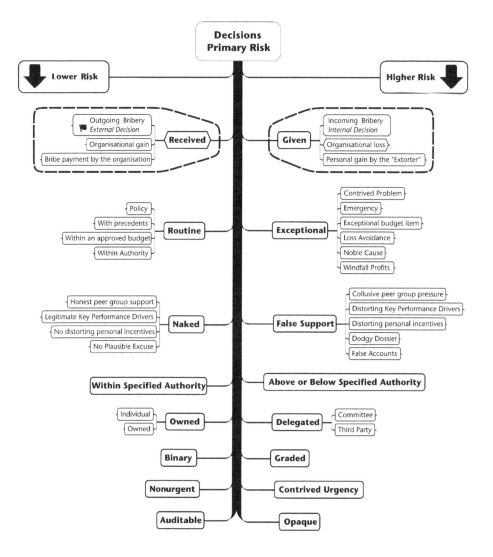

Figure 16.1 Decision Risk Factors Involving Financial Exposures

Research Funding

An interesting liability now arises under the Bribery Act 2010[9] for supposedly independent scientific or academic research organisations who receive funding on the secret understanding that their reports will find in a predetermined direction rather than being independent. If a relevant commercial organisation funds research on this basis it is arguably liable under Section 7 of the Act. This would be a very good thing, especially in the Carbon World.

---

9   Which is based on an 'improper performance', rather than the agent–principal model.

Focusing on Outgoing Corruption

The most risky decisions from a regulatory point of view[10] are those classified as external, taken by third-party extorters to perform improperly.

LEGAL BACKGROUND TO OUTGOING CORRUPTION

The primary occurrence risk of outgoing bribery is simple to evaluate, but the regulatory position is much more complex and varies depending on whether the organisation is classified as a relevant commercial organisation, whether the intention of financial or other advantage offered is to obtain or retain business for it, and/or whether decisions are delegated to associated persons.

For an individual to be found guilty of an offence in the private sector (and in the UK public sector) the coercer must **know** that the outcome he intends (or intended) to induce in itself amounts to improper performance; (or in circumstances[11] that would be regarded by a reasonable person as improper performance).

A much lower standard applies to Section 6, where an offence is committed if the intention is simply to influence a Foreign Public Official (FPO) in the performance of his duties, but only provided the financial or other advantage is aimed at obtaining business or an other advantage in the conduct of business.

Five variables are especially relevant:[12]

1. The identity or position of the third-party decision-maker and whether or not he is a directing mind and/or closely connected with the UK or classified as an FPO.
2. His **authority** under his organisation's procedures for routine and ad hoc decisions.
3. The **precise criteria** on which his organisation expects decisions of the type concerned to be made.
4. His organisation's **internal policies** on hospitality, sponsorship, conflict of interest and the receipt of other personal advantages that in themselves could result in improper performance.
5. Whether these are known to the person representing the evaluating organisation offering or giving them and whether his intention is to induce improper performance or to influence an FPO.

The problem is not so much assessing the risks of hard bribery but of technical violations that could be interpreted with the benefit of prosecutorial discretion as a criminal breach of the Bribery Act 2010.

---

10   Because they involve absolute corporate liability under Section 7.

11   For UK bribery, all of the circumstances can be taken into account. Overseas, local custom and practice are to be disregarded.

12   There are many others that are also important.

DATA AVAILABLE TO EVALUATORS

Evaluators have a limited range of data available. This is represented in the shaded box in Figure 16.2.

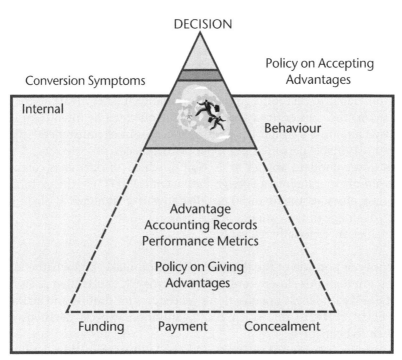

Figure 16.2 Data Available for the Evaluation of Outgoing Bribery

Figure 16.2 indicates that the actual decision process is normally beyond the view of the evaluating organisation.[13] However, the evaluating organisation may be able to obtain:

- The internal policies of third parties which define the personal advantages they are allowed to accept (such as a gifts and hospitality policy);
- The criteria on which they make decisions (possibly decision matrices).

These are discussed below.

---

13   Unless the evaluation is collaborative.

ADVANTAGE SCHEMES

The mechanics of bribe-funding, payment, and concealment were discussed fully in Chapter 12 and relate primarily to hard advantages that are clearly corrupt. Evaluating these is fairly simple. The problem is identifying whether or not marketing and other advantage schemes (see page 336), which are offered without corrupt intent, could be regarded as violations of the Act.

Bribes from Owner's Private Funds

The chief executive of a major corporation owns a luxury holiday home on an Indian Ocean island. From time to time he invites customers and their families to stay as his guests with all expenses paid, flying them out and back on one of his private jets. None of the costs appear in the company's books. The question is whether or not this hospitality would be regarded as a violation of the Act and if so what evidence would be available to fend off a potential prosecution?

Schemes that provide third-party decision-makers – whether individual or corporate – that could be construed as bribery should be carefully evaluated.

Carbon World Example

Some brokers in the Carbon World, who are not regulated, offer Independent Financial Advisers (IFAs) – who are regulated – what most people would regard as excessive if not exorbitant commissions for introducing new clients. This could result in breaches of the Bribery Act.

Evaluators should, therefore, identify and catalogue all schemes – formal and informal – that result in advantages to third-party decision-making individuals or organisations. Preparing this catalogue is easier said than done, but evaluators should consider the information in Table 16.3.

Table 16.3 Possible Sources of Advantages

Advantage Scheme — Excluding hard bribery as described in Chapters 11–13. Italics in the column below indicate corporate and individual advantages	Sponsors	How Detectable (Primary source) Data-mining	Interviews	Accounts Payable	General Ledger	Legal and PR
Accounting adjustments and journal entries	Accounting	☺		☺	☺	
Company cars (allocation or lending)	Corporate	☺		☺	☺	
Gifts	Corporate			☺		
Hospitality and entertainment	Corporate			☺		
Limousines	Corporate			☺		
Personal guarantees	Corporate	☺				
Private jets	Corporate			☺	☺	
Share options	Corporate					☺
Subscriptions	Corporate			☺	☺	
Travel	Corporate			☺		
Use of facilities (sports clubs, etc.)	Corporate	☺				
Extended credit	Credit control			☺		
Loans and mortgages	Finance				☺	
Employment of relatives and revolving doors	HR		☺			
Health insurance and other company benefits	HR			☺		
Fast-tracking of internal colluders	HR					
Internment (of relatives of influential third parties)	HR					
Personal expense accounts	HR			☺		
Sports facilities and clubs	HR					
Advertising support	Marketing				☺	
Billbacks	Marketing				☺	
Cash back schemes	Marketing					
Competitions and prize schemes	Marketing				☺	
Gift vouchers	Marketing			☺	☺	
Two-for-one schemes	Marketing				☺	
Referral fees	Marketing				☺	
Medical facilities	Medical Department			☺	☺	

Directors' boxes at sporting events	Personal funds					☺
Fishing rights	Personal funds					☺
Golf club corporate memberships	Personal funds					☺
Holiday homes (skiing chalets, etc.)	Personal funds					☺
Private yachts	Personal funds					☺
Shooting estates	Personal funds					☺
Prepaid cards and electronic purses	Procurement			☺	☺	
Professional fees	Procurement			☺	☺	
Purchasing cards	Procurement			☺		
Academic bursaries	Public relations					☺
Sponsorship	Public relations	☺				☺
Company credit cards	Purchasing			☺	☺	
Advance discounts	Purchasing			☺	☺	
Commissions (paid and received)	Sales				☺	
Credit notes	Sales				☺	
Discounted goods and services	Sales				☺	
Free samples	Sales				☺	
Retainers	Sales				☺	☺
Staff sales	Sales				☺	
Channel support	Sales and marketing				☺	
Interest rates	Treasury				☺	
Travellers' cheques	Treasury				☺	

The database should be updated with all of the evaluating company's marketing and other advantage schemes and confirm, document and record:

- All applicable policies and accounting records;
- Their primary purpose (and how this can be demonstrated);
- Classes of third parties to whom they are made available;
- Benchmarks against competitive practices;
- Any other evidence that would rebut allegations of impropriety;
- How and where accurate records are kept.

Details should be entered in the Risk Evaluation Database and, in due course, should be the subject of a special report to the directors and legal advisers.

ANALYSING THIRD-PARTY CRITERIA

The second stage of evaluating the possible risks of advantage schemes is to understand the internal procedures of all third parties who might benefit from them. The six main questions are:

- Do the advantages and benefits the evaluating company might make available to third parties contravene their policies?
- What precisely is the purpose and intention of each advantage?
- How can the evaluating company prove that the advantages have no intention to corrupt?
- Should the advantages be discontinued?
- Is there a better way of achieving the objectives?
- Would the evaluating company allow its own employees to receive equivalent advantages?

It is difficult to obtain information for every third party with which the evaluating company deals but the approach summarised in Table 16.4 is recommended:

- Column A means that details of the third party's decision-making processes and policies are obtained during a **collaborative risk evaluation.** *This is the safest solution and virtually guarantees that performance could not be argued as improper.*
- Column B means that the evaluating organisation makes a **specific request** for the answers to questions 6 to 9 above and if possible agrees decision matrices.
- Column C means applying industry or market **benchmarks** as proxies for the third party's specific processes and procedures.
- Column D means **mirroring the evaluation company's own policies** and procedures as though they applied to a specific third party, a category of third parties or to third parties as a whole.

Against the above background, the options in Table 16.4 should be considered.

Table 16.4 Obtaining Decision Criteria on External Decisions

Type of Third Party– *whose representatives could be bribed (Outgoing corruption)*	Risk Level	Basis of Evaluating the Five Factors Options 1= Preferable 2= Next best			
		Collaborate	Specific Request	Industry Benchmark	Mirror Procedures
		A	B	C	D
Foreign government agencies and FPOs with repeated contact involving discretionary decisions	Very High	1	2	2	Not Applicable
Foreign government agencies and FPOs with infrequent contact and routine decisions	Medium		2	1	

Overseas political parties and opposition	FCPA High	1	2	2	
Private companies that could be regarded as 'institutionalities'[14]	FCPA & BA High	1	2	2	2
Inspectors, appraisers and valuers	High	2	1	2	
Private sector companies Routine suppliers, customers, etc.	Medium		2	1	1
Parent, associated and subsidiary companies and internal corruption of group employees	High internal corruption	1			1

In practice the factors for the majority of external decisions will be based on industry standards or mirror procedures.

THE IMPORTANCE OF ACCURATE ACCOUNTING

The third critical factor is to evaluate how potential advantages are accounted for because under the Foreign Corrupt Practices Act (FCPA) and the UK Companies Acts anything but total precision is likely to result in problems.

AON and Willis Cases

AON settled an investigation by the FSA with heavy penalties because its accounting of commissions was less than transparent. The FSA alleged that these funds could have been used to pay bribes, although there was no evidence of this.

Accurate accounting in the context of anticorruption laws means whatever the regulators decide – after the event – that it should mean, but in principle:

- Transactions should be entered accurately into books of original entry and supported by complete and accurate vouchers.
- Expenses should be accurately classified in the nominal ledger, budgetary, cost centres, management reports and reported accurately on tax returns.

The most dangerous accounting aspects result from:

- The mis-recording or mis-classification of payments made by the evaluating company;

---

14   See pages 30 and 432 for a definition of 'institutionality'. This is a very difficult point. Do companies such as SGS, TUV and Den Norske Veritas (which take on the jobs of official Customs departments), become 'FPOs' in all aspects of their business? This question appears to be unresolved, but no doubt – like everything else – can be sorted by 'prosecutorial discretion'.

- Failure to retain accurate and complete supporting evidence.

Although the Ministry of Justice and Transparency International are primarily worried about bribes being paid through intermediaries, going forward this is considered not to be the major risk; if for no other reason than that the subject of red flags has been beaten to death and crooks with any sense will avoid them.

As is explained in Chapters 10–13, bribe payment methods are only limited by the imagination of those involved, but Table 16.5 hazards a guess as to the most likely payments methods that will appear over the next five to ten years and be more sophisticated and less traceable than those of the past. Evaluators should consider the following dirty dozen:

Table 16.5   Anticipated Methods of Hard Bribe Payment

Possible Method of Bribe Payment	Comment and Examples
Carbon World	The Carbon World is a crook's dream for creating off-record slush funds and for paying bribes[15]
Pseudo trading	The creation of false trading gains or losses in lieu of bribe payment
Customers who are also suppliers	Inter-account adjustments, contras or bartering
Overpayment of a third party, leaving the extorter responsible for internal conversion	See page 311
Duplicate payments and price manipulation	
Temporary amendment of banking parameters for legitimate third parties	Payments to the genuine third parties are diverted as bribes
Name confusion	
Payment diversion, for example, dummy branches of reputable and existing customers and suppliers	
Bad debt write-offs and credit notes	Bribes paid by goods or services provided and invoiced, later processed as credits
Suppressed credit notes	
Off-record guarantees	Allowing the extorter to raise external finance in lieu of bribes
Personal funds of directors and senior managers	See page 318

No doubt ingenious corrupters will find alternative methods of bribe payment. The evaluation should try to anticipate these in the specific contexts and processes concerned.

---

15   For example, projects under the Clean Development Mechanism can delay submitting Monitoring Reports (and associated claims to Certified Emission Reductions (CERs)) beyond the close of an accounting period. When CERS are issued they are valued at cost. They can be sold at any value agreed Over-The-Counter (OTC), or transferred to an associated company at any price.

BACK-OFFICE INTERVENTION

The efficiency and independence of a company's back office, including finance and administration, Human Resources and other non-outward-facing functions are critical in deterring and detecting bribe payment. Similarly, strong control over physical inventories – both static and in transit – reduces the chances of both fraud and corruption.

The evaluation team should, therefore, pay close attention to back-office efficiency, update the Risk Evaluation Database accordingly and consider recommending additional training for the employees involved and the possibility of introducing an incentive scheme based on their detection of suspicious transactions.

PERFORMANCE METRICS

Large-scale fraud and corruption inevitably leave an impact in accounting, statistical and performance records. The evaluation team should remain on the lookout for both behavioural and performance clues in every context under review, especially:

- windfall profits
- exceptional losses
- poor decisions
- unexplained exceptions to established policies and procedures.

They should treat each one as a possible indication of corruption and dig into detail until questions are resolved one way or the other.

Even the smallest deviation may be the key to unlocking serious fraud and corruption. When in doubt, the evaluation team should simply pay attention to detail and not be satisfied by the first answer given.

Focusing on Incoming Corruption

PRIMARY EVALUATION OF OCCURRENCE AND REBUTTAL

Incoming corruption, in its simplest form, involves:

- Bribes being demanded or received by an **individual** representing the evaluating organisation with the intention that **he** should perform improperly; this is the conventional view under the old principal–agent laws[16] and still applies civilly;
- Bribes being demanded or received by the evaluating organisation with the intention that **it** should perform improperly.[17]

Option 2 should be carefully risk evaluated because it puts at risk – for prosecution under Section 2 – companies that are paid referral fees, exceptional commissions, or given other

---

16   The Prevention of Corruption Acts and the Anti-terrorism Crime and Security Act 2002 (ATSCA).

17   Under the Act's new model of 'improper performance'.

advantages with the intention that they should perform[18] improperly at a corporate level. It also means that counterparties that provide the advantages with an intention to induce the corporate recipient to perform improperly may also be guilty of bribery under sections 1 and 7.

The conventional view is that incoming bribery is primarily restricted to procurement involving bribes paid by vendors to obtain business. Were this the case, assessing corruption risks would be simple, but the problem is more complicated than that.

Other Exposed Contexts in Procurement

For example, a company may pay bribes to a vendor's employee to obtain price or delivery concessions, extended credit terms, etc. Goods inwards workers may bribe a vendor's delivery driver to drop off additional, uninvoiced, goods or to give full credit for returned goods he knows to be defective.

The most significant impact from incoming corruption is the primary occurrence loss resulting from overcharging for supplies – in terms of quantity or quality – or under-realisation of income, as well as financial manipulation and adverse administrative decisions. These are all discussed on page 352 et seq and are mostly classified as hard bribery. The dominant reason for evaluating risks of incoming corruption are to minimise financial losses. Compliance with the Bribery Act should follow inevitably.

LEGAL BACKGROUND TO INCOMING CORRUPTION

Individuals and body corporates may be liable under Section 2, providing the prosecution can prove beyond reasonable doubt that he or it solicited or accepted a financial or other advantage with the intention of performing improperly. If the offence is committed entirely overseas, the prosecution must show that the individual or corporate extorter had a close connection with the UK.

A body corporate[19] may also be criminally liable under Section 2 if the extorter is a directing mind. There is no Section 7 equivalent corporate offence for incoming bribery. Variations in the legal position described should be considered and entered into the Risk Evaluation Database.

The evaluation of incoming corruption should include both occurrence and rebuttal risks, although the probability of regulatory action against a body corporate are relatively low unless the offence is by a directing mind.

DATA AVAILABLE TO EVALUATORS

Overview

The data available for evaluation is almost the mirror of that for outgoing corruption and is represented in Figure 16.3.

---

18   Or have already improperly performed.

19   Other than a government department that is exempt from liability as a 'Crown Body'.

INCOMING CORRUPTION – INTERNAL DECISION

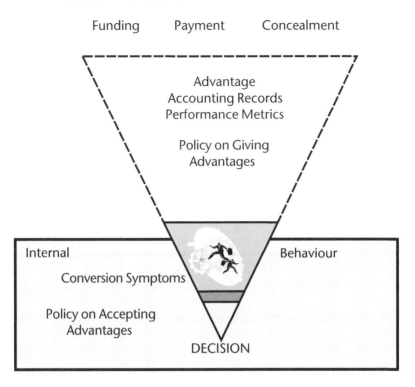

Figure 16.3 Contexts Typically Involved in Incoming Corruption

The shaded rectangle in Figure 16.3 represents the information sources that are available to the evaluating organisation, whereas all accounting and payment records are usually not.

A central feature of incoming corruption is that the financial or other hard advantage given to the individual or corporate extorter does not appear in the accounts of the evaluating company. **This is one reason why collaborative evaluations are more successful, because they allow all dimensions of a context to be considered.**

Evaluators should examine the company's policy on the acceptance of individual and corporate advantages (such as referral fees, commissions, etc.) from third parties, assess them, enter them into the Risk Evaluation Database and in due course provide a summary report for review by the board.

Ideally, the evaluating company's policy on the acceptance of personal advantages should be consistent with the benefits it makes available to third parties.

There are five important internal sources available to evaluators:

1. Evidence of a perverted decision;
2. Behavioural symptoms;
3. Back-office efficiency;
4. Performance metrics;
5. Evidence of conversion in extorter's lifestyle (evidence of conversion).

For individual extorters, evidence that he obtained an advantage in a specific case will be available for confirmation or rebuttal if he and the corporate accused cooperate in defending a specific allegation. The two last sources are discussed below.

EVIDENCE OF CONVERSION

Extorters, like most criminals, enjoy spending their illicit gains. Although they may be careful in shielding their unexplained wealth from their employers and colleagues, this is difficult to do successfully. Thus managers in their day-to-day jobs and members of the evaluation team should remain alert to symptoms of wealth well beyond those normal for the person concerned. A common reaction is to **assume** that he or she has a wealthy relative or some other legitimate explanation. However, experience shows that overlooking such clues allows fraud and corruption to continue much longer than they should.[20]

Focusing On Internal Corruption

People employed in 'dry jobs' (see page 346) become involved in corruption (called 'internal corruption') in three main ways. The first is because an outward-facing coercer (or extorter) does not have the authority to make the decision by himself.[21]

A Simple Example of Internal Corruption

A director[22] of ABC, which is a relevant commercial organisation, anxious to achieve his annual bonus, instructs a junior accountant (inward-facing) to create fictitious sales invoices without the knowledge of the customers concerned and to post the transactions to a suspense account rather than to accounts receivable. The director promises the accountant a significant pay rise at year-end. Because the director's intention is to increase ABC's year-end profits, it is quite possible that the Serious Fraud Office (SFO) – in addition to charging the individuals under sections 1 and 2 of the Act[23] – could also prosecute the company for obtaining a business or an advantage under Section 7.

Internal corruption has not been recognised for the serious problem it is by the Ministry of Justice or by many professional advisers and commercial managers:

---

20 Always suspect the man whose shoes and socks are too fancy: most white-collar crooks have a fetish with their feet. Believe it!

21 Or wishes to obscure his responsibility.

22 A 'directing mind'.

23 As well as under the Fraud Act and with conspiracy.

- It *normally* involves decisions that are initiated by the senior player in an outward-facing job who persuades or commands a subordinate to perform improperly.[24]
- If there is an end party to the decision, such as a customer or supplier, it may be unaware that corruption has taken place.
- The bribe (financial or other advantage) may involve a company-funded bonus, share options, job retention, special privileges or treatment greater than warranted in the circumstances or by the corrupted employee's[25] performance.

A clue to internal corruption is the unjustified promotion or favouritism of any employee, consultant, or adviser, especially when he has special skills or access to sensitive decisions. Internal collusion may be an intermediate step to incoming or outgoing corruption. For example:

Internal Corruption Leading to a Section 7 Charge

The Senior Sales Director[26] of XYZ (a publicly listed company) plans to leave to join a competitor. To get his new job off to a flying start by stealing customers, he persuades his assistant to suppress a number of pending sales orders and bring them with him to join the competitor at an improved salary. The sales director boasts to his new employer, which is a relevant commercial organisation, of what he has done. They pat him on the back and laugh. The Managing Director of XYZ, who is aware of the scam, instructs the internal audit team to take no action. He is simply happy to see the back of the Senior Sales Director.

In this case the Senior Sales Director and the assistant are at risk under sections 1 and 2, XYZ for corporate liability under Section 2, and the new employer under Section 7.

A second channel for internal corruption is where a person in an inward-facing job initiates dialogue with a third party or internally which is not necessary for his normal duties.[27] He then proposes to use his influence to improperly advantage a third party.

---

24 It may also be initiated by a junior employee, although this is less common.

25 In this context 'employee' means contractor, adviser and temporary or agency personnel.

26 A 'directing mind'.

27 Or where a third party establishes contact with him.

Corruption by Junior Employees

A junior engineer was asked to prepare a specification for an invitation to tender for over $5 million worth of equipment. Without his employer's knowledge, he contacted a local supplier and agreed to accept a bribe to tailor the specification so that only their equipment would be suitable. His specification was accepted by the tendering committee and in due course the supplier obtained the contract and paid the bribe.

The third way in which internal bribery takes place is when one employee induces a colleague to perform improperly to obtain an advantage for himself such as a bigger or better company car, medical insurance, temporary leave, promotion, etc. Such cases may result in breaches of Section 1 and Section 2 for the individuals concerned, and for the body corporate if either is a directing mind. If the intent of the bribery is to obtain or retain business, a body corporate may also be liable under Section 7.

Focusing on Joint Ventures and Collaborative Relationships

BACKGROUND

Joint ventures[28] are especially prone to fraud and corruption and detailed evaluation of each one is strongly advised, as is developing a procedure for prospecting new relationships. The following paragraphs set out the criteria for evaluating the three phases of joint ventures and assessing both occurrence and rebuttal risks.

A joint venture may be defined as an agreement between two or more participants to work together towards a common goal. They share a number of characteristics with other forms of collaboration.

All joint ventures should be catalogued and individually entered into the Risk Evaluation Database and analysed and brainstormed in the ways described earlier. The depth of the examination will depend on whether or not the evaluators are able to examine the records and interview personnel employed in the joint venture. Where this is not possible they should consider delegating responsibility to the joint venture's auditors or compliance specialists.

GENERIC RISKS IN JOINT VENTURES

The Ministry of Justice Guidance addresses risks only in the operational phase of joint ventures and concentrates due diligence on the participants when in reality the venture's relationship with end parties is far more important and the development and exit stages most exposed to corruption.

The three phases of a typical joint venture that should be comprehensively risk-evaluated and controlled through life are as represented in Figure 16.4.

---

28 Including agencies and intermediaries.

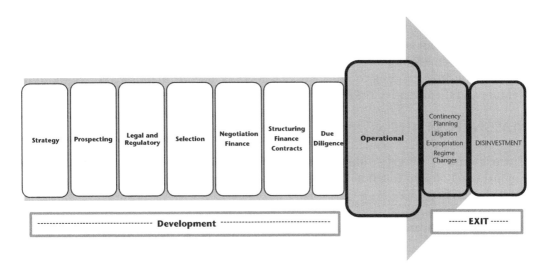

Figure 16.4 Joint Venture Development and Operations

The nature and extent of corruption risks change through the life of the joint venture. Initially it may be between the participants, in the operational stage involving third parties, and on exit a completely different array of risks.

Corruption risks should be viewed as part of a much wider frame and include political, country, financial, environmental and other regulatory factors.

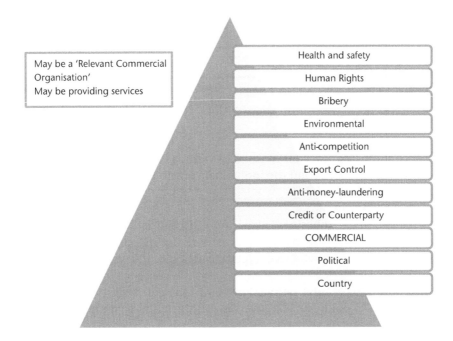

Figure 16.5 Generic Risks in Joint Ventures

Figure 16.5 illustrates the importance of not simply assessing risks in regulatory silos but of taking a much wider approach, to include fraud, cartels, price-fixing, anti-competitive behaviour, theft of intellectual property and money-laundering. The problem is that many long-standing compliance breaches only emerge on termination of the joint venture and the incentive is then to pay bribes to minimise their impact.

REASONS FOR ENTERING INTO JOINT VENTURES

There are many reasons – some good and others problematic or even dishonest – why companies choose to collaborate, including those listed in Table 16.6.

Table 16.6   Reasons for Entering into Joint Ventures

Conventional Reasons for Collaboration	Possibly Problematic Reasons for Collaboration
Enter new markets	Access to political leaders or influential FPOs
Obtain raw materials or production facilities	Pursue a noble cause such as carbon trading
Secure supplies	Obtain windfall profits and honeypots[29]
Comply with foreign government requirements that require appointment of a local partner	Comply with recommendations made by politicians or officials
Access customers or suppliers	Satisfy the personal whims of senior managers
Obtain finance or specialist skills	Me2
Increase capacity	Conceal existing losses
Share risks	Nepotism
Avoid the cost of direct investment	Reciprocate for favours or to avoid losses
Access intellectual capital or know-how	Information-brokering
Make a bigger cake	*Grab a disproportionate share of the other participant's cake*

Experience shows that the most risky joint ventures are those where there is no viable plan to increase revenues beyond the individual contributions of the participants.
Evaluators should examine:

- The initial and updated business plans and justification for the joint venture;
- The objectives of the participants on formation, during operations, and on exit.
- The assets, finance and intellectual capital brought into the venture and their valuation.

They should also check how permissions and licences were obtained and for any indications that FPOs, politicians or government officials were improperly influenced to issue them.

---

29   Like the Oil for Food programme or carbon trading.

TYPES OF JOINT VENTURE ENTITIES

Participation may be into a **new and specially created entity** or into an operation that already exists. The relationship may be planned, opportunistic or mandatory. The collaboration may be horizontal when it involves participants whose businesses traditionally compete against each other; or vertical when participants operate in different levels of a market or stages of a process. Risks vary depending on the options:

Table 16.7 Joint Venture Entry and Structural Risk Factors

RISK LEVEL →	LOWER RISK →→→→→→→→ HIGHER RISK					
	Origination Low Risk (1) > High Risk (20)					
DECISION DRIVER →	Planned *Part of a specified long-term business plan*		Opportunistic *Spontaneous as a short-term reaction to circumstances*		Mandatory *Demanded by external influence Government – Banks*	
ENTITY → ↓	Vertical	Horizontal	Vertical	Horizontal	Vertical	Horizontal
New Formation	5	8	7	11	9	14
Into Existing	7	10	9	12	11	16

Table 16.7 indicates that the most stable joint ventures are those which are planned as part of a long-term corporate strategy, involving vertical integration into a new entity. Risk levels are significantly increased when joint ventures are mandated and involve governmental representatives or are intended to rescue a failing operation.

Joint Ventures Are Risky Businesses

Less than 50 per cent of joint ventures succeed, with around 20 per cent resulting in serious disputes or litigation, especially at the termination phase, when allegations of corruption frequently surface.

Evaluators should resolve the following questions:

- Is the joint venture entity *itself* considered to be a relevant commercial organisation?
- Does the joint venture entity provide services for any relevant commercial organisation and especially the evaluating organisation?
- Was the joint venture planned as part of a specified business strategy or merely as a reaction to short-term opportunities or problems?

- What potentially conflicting interests did (or still do) any of the participants retain?
- What participation in the joint venture is there by governmental institutionalities[30] or FPOs?
- What level of protection is provided to participants – in contracts, memoranda of understanding or formation documents – against corruption and other illegality?
- Are any of the personnel associated with the joint venture closely connected with the UK?

The evaluation should also verify the bona fides of any minority interests, especially if they involve shell entities in tax haven–offshore jurisdictions.[31] **All** risks to joint ventures and international compliance requirements[32] should be evaluated and controlled through all three phases: development; operational; and exit.

REGULATORY POSITION, CONTROL AND LIABILITY

The FCPA holds a participant in a joint venture liable[33] only if it owns more than 50 per cent of the controlling interest. However, in practice control often entails far more than this. History is littered with cases – especially in the BRIC[34] countries – where control has been snatched from Western participants by the issuance of additional or special classes of shares, through disguising true ownership via pyramidal family structures, threats of violence, skimming business to other entities, pricing manipulation and tolling (see pages 316–17).

The Adequate Procedures Dossier should retain all evidence indicating the real-world level of control over joint ventures on a day-to-day basis. It should also include summaries of all control and compliance-related expenditure.

The Bribery Act imposes liability on relevant commercial organisations for associated persons that perform services on its behalf, even when it has only limited control.

The relationship of control and liability in different types of collaborative relationships are summarised in Table 16.8.

---

30 'Institutionality' is a word used in connection with the FCPA to refer to any conceivable agency of a government, including State Owned Enterprises (SOEs).

31 These may be fronts for FPOs and government officials.

32 And not just bribery.

33 But only for FPO corruption and not in the private sector.

34 Brazil, Russia, India and China.

Table 16.8   Risk Ranking of Joint Ventures

All Risks	Type of Relationship or Extension of a Relationship	Degree of Control Scale: 1 (High)– 10 (Low)	Bribery Act Risks Section 7 Scale: 1 (Low)– 10 (High)	Risk Factor Scale: 1 (Low)– 30 (High)
	A	B	C	B * C
High ↓	Joint Venture: Contractual	5	7	35
↓	Joint Venture: Entity	6	5	30
↓	Agencies and other intermediaries	3	7	21
↓	Franchise	3	5	15
↓	Production sharing contracts	3	4	12
↓	Minority financial investment	10	1	10
↓	On consignment shipments	3	3	9
↓	Licensing agreement	3	3	9
↓	Parents	2	4	8
↓	Siblings	2	4	8
↓	Subsidiaries	1	8	8
↓	Strategic relationships with customers	8	1	8
↓	Strategic relationships with suppliers	8	1	8
Low	Pure financial investments	6	1	6

The estimates in Table 16.8 above are arbitrary, but they indicate relative risks.

Contractual joint ventures are normally to be regarded in the highest risk category from a corruption point of view and pure financial investment in the lowest. However, for liability to be created under Section 7 for a UK participant it must be a relevant commercial organisation, the entity must perform services on its behalf and with the intention of obtaining or retaining business for it. Evaluators should also identify closely associated persons – mainly UK nationals working in overseas joint ventures because they are individually bound by the Bribery Act.

The Ministry of Justice has agreed that normal customers and suppliers do not do this.

CORRUPTION RISKS IN JOINT VENTURES

Corruption risks vary throughout the phases of a joint venture involving a variety of different coercers and extorters with inconsistent and sometimes incompatible objectives:

Table 16.9 Parties Involved in Corruption at Stages of the Joint Venture

Phase	Paid by	Financiers	Participant A	Participant B	Venture	FPO	Experts	Inspectors	Unions	Politicians	End parties	Competitors	Crime syndicates	Examples of Decision To Be Perverted to Obtain
							Bribes Paid to Influence Improper Performance by							
Development	**Participant A**	☺		☺	☺	☺	☺	☺	☺	☺	☺		☺	Share allocations
	Participant B	☺	☺		☺	☺	☺	☺	☺	☺	☺		☺	Approvals
	Joint Venture	☺				☺	☺	☺	☺	☺	☺		☺	Licences
	FPOs and officials									☺				Permits
	Experts	☺	☺	☺	☺	☺	☺	☺		☺			☺	Finance
	Inspectors				☺	☺	☺						☺	Land acquisition
	Unions		☺	☺						☺			☺	Political support
	Politicians													Union support
	End parties													Security
	Competitors		☺	☺	☺	☺	☺	☺	☺	☺	☺		☺	
	Financiers		☺	☺			☺	☺		☺			☺	
	Crime syndicates	☺					☺		☺	☺				*Mainly with the objective of grabbing a larger slice of the cake*
Operational	**Joint venture**	☺	☺	☺	☺	☺	☺	☺	☺	☺	☺	☺	☺	New business for the joint venture
	Participant A				☺									
	Participant B				☺									Corruption of and by end parties
	FPOs and Officials				☺		☺	☺	☺	☺				Corruption of FPOs
	Experts				☺									
	Inspectors				☺									*Mainly with the objective of improving the joint venture's performance*
	Unions									☺				
	Politicians													
	End parties				☺									
	Competitors										☺			
	Financiers				☺									
	Crime syndicates								☺					

Terminal		1	2	3	4	5	6	7	8	9	10	11	12	13	Notes
	Joint venture	☺	☺	☺		☺	☺	☺	☺	☺	☺	☺	☺		Improving or deflating exit values
	Participant A	☺	☺	☺	☺	☺	☺	☺	☺	☺	☺	☺	☺		
	Participant B	☺	☺	☺	☺	☺	☺	☺	☺	☺	☺	☺	☺		
	FPOs and officials		☺	☺	☺										Avoiding closure penalties
	Experts														
	Inspectors		☺	☺											
	Unions		☺	☺											Concealing or compromising earlier regulatory violations
	Politicians				☺										
	End parties				☺										
	Competitors											☺			
	Financiers	☺	☺	☺	☺										
	Crime syndicates														

It is not necessary to study Table 16.9 in detail. It is merely included to show the complex relationships involved in corruption in the three phases of typical joint ventures.

The main corruption risks are summarised in Table 16.10, listing the typical characteristics in each of their phases.

Table 16.10 Main Corruption Risks in Joint Venture Phases

Element of Corruption ↓↓↓↓↓	Developmental Phase	Operational Phase	Exit or Termination Phase
Primarily paid to influence →	*Another participant* *Government official* *Competitor*	*Government officials* *End parties (customers and suppliers)* *Bankers*	*Another participant* *Government official* *Regulatory agency*
Purpose (examples) →	*To gain ownership interests or control by a participant or individual* *To overcome restrictions* *Personal benefit*	*To influence end parties* *To obtain taxation, customs or other advantages for the joint venture*	*To avoid penalties, taxes and legal liabilities* *To increase IPO or trade sale values*
Bribe-funding →	**EXTERNAL SOURCES**	**JOINT VENTURE SOURCES**	**JOINT VENTURE SOURCES**
	From funds injection	Price manipulation	Sales proceeds
	Asset flipping *and overvaluation of assets on formation*	Manipulated costs and revenues	Incoming finance
	Allocation of shares	Off-book funds	Asset sales

Element of Corruption ↓↓↓↓↓	Developmental Phase	Operational Phase	Exit or Termination Phase
Bribe Payment →	**DEFERRED OR CURRENT**	**CURRENT**	**CURRENT: DEFERRED**
	Carried interests and options	Cash and profit-skimming	Earn-outs
	Side commitments	Accounts payable	Carried interest
	Buy-back arrangements	Accounts receivable	Cash
Bribe Recording →	Share registers	Cash book	Acquirers' records
	Contacts	Accounts Payable/Receivable	Liquidation disbursements
	External to joint venture	Suspense accounts	Whistle-blower reward payments
Competitive Corruption	*Competitors may intervene at any point in the evolution of joint ventures, by bribing officials to withhold approvals or suborning key employees. Enterprises that conflict with the joint venture may also engage in conventional forms of corruption involving suppliers and customers*		

There are other factors, shown in Table 16.11, that should be considered in evaluating joint venture risks.

Table 16.11 Other Factors to Be Considered in Evaluating Corruption Risks in Joint Ventures

Factor	Examples and Comment	Effect on Risk
Financial stability of participants	Instability or conflicting interests may be a motivation for fraud and corruption	Lower
Potentially conflicting businesses operated by participants, possibly in competition with the joint venture	Revenues may be skimmed from the joint venture to participants' other interests. This is a very common problem	Higher
Limited to a specific project, or:	**More easily controlled and cauterised**	**Lower**
General venture (such as country or regional activity)	**More difficult to control**	**Higher**
Short-term agreement, or:	Limited exposure	Lower
Open-ended or long-term agreement	Limitless exposure	Higher
Level of corruption in the market	**Corruption by competitors may set a market tone**	**Highest**
FPOs or government institutionalities as participant	Section 6 exposures	Highest

Effective corporate governance within the joint venture	Based on how effective procedures are in practice	Lower
Effective management reporting and accounting		Lower
FPO or institutionalities as end parties	Section 6 exposures	Higher
Language and culture	All important documents and contracts should be professionally translated	Higher when different
TI Country Corruption Ranking	Of minor importance	Minor
Cultural incompatibility of participants	Conflicting objectives or cultures tend to increase risks	Higher
Incompatibility of objectives		Higher
Introduction by an FPO or a politician	May lead to corruption, nepotism and other problems, especially under the revolving doors rule	Higher
Joint venture managers bound by the UK Bribery Act or other extraterritorial laws	The extent to which joint venture employees are bound by their home country laws and their operational loyalties	Higher
Presence of organised crime in the context	Considers the risks of internal and organised crime and possible connections to corruption	Higher
Located in a country with weak legal and enforcement processes	Primary risks may be higher, but regulatory risks lower	Variable
Involved in privatisation and PFI	Generally very high risk	Highest
High level of reliance on FPOs	Contact with all FPOs should be catalogued	Highest
Good experience with the partner(s)	This includes all green flags	Lower
Categories of end parties, due diligence on them and the nature of transactions with them	This is possibly the most vital aspect of risk in the operational phase of joint ventures	Variable

A right of veto may result in a UK-participating relevant commercial organisation being held responsible for bribery in a joint venture even when it has no effective control

Although tables 16.5 to 16.12 are admittedly subjective, they are based on extensive practical experience and enable the relative exposure to corruption of joint ventures to be evaluated.[35]

Risks should be evaluated for incoming, internal, outgoing and competitive corruption and controls applied over all joint ventures from the earliest stages through to operation and termination. **Close attention should be paid to relationships between the joint venture and its end parties.**

The final set of risk factors relate to exit strategy or termination of a joint venture. The principle risks are summarised in Table 16.12.

---

35   It will be noted that only limited importance is given to 'perceived' country risks.

Table 16.12 Termination of a Joint Venture

Exit or Termination Path	Category	Nature	Examples
Unspecified or undetermined	1	Unknown	For most joint ventures no exit strategy has been agreed. This is often the cause of serious problems
Planned closure	2	Planned	Optimal course, normally with minimal chances that previous acts of corruption will be exposed Corruption may take place to encourage third parties to overlook or minimise contractual difficulties Corruption of union officials or local authorities to minimise penalties
IPO	3	Planned	Corruption of employees to run down the business or to inflate results to reduce or increase valuations Corruption of third parties to advance or withhold income or expenses to manipulate values
MBO		Planned	
Trade Sale		Planned	
Merger		Planned	Corruption of third-party representatives to take perverse decisions to benefit the joint venture, participants or individuals Corruption of politicians and regulators to approve mergers and acquisitions or to reissue licences
Litigation	4	Forced	Corruption of representatives of opposing parties to minimise the consequences of litigation Corruption of lawyers and members of the judiciary
Liquidation		Forced	Corruption of official receivers and administrators to siphon off assets, to pervert or terminate an investigation Corruption of officials to destroy or hide incriminatory evidence
Expropriation		Forced	Corruption of politicians and officials to avoid expropriation
Regime Change		Forced	Corruption of incoming or outgoing politicians or officials to protect the joint venture or to enable operations to continue Corruption of incoming or outgoing politicians by competitors

Category 2 relates to the discovery of previous acts of corruption during the exit phase. Category 3 relates to performance manipulations to increase or decrease the value of the entity. Category 4 relates to fresh corruption to minimise the consequences of exit.

Many joint ventures face significant contingent liabilities on termination, including potential exposure of earlier corruption offences. Potential exit risks should be evaluated before joint ventures are established or, when this is not possible, while they are in the operational phase.

Focusing on Risks in the Carbon World and Corporate Social Responsibility

Evaluators should pay special attention to decisions taken, expenses incurred in and income derived from the Carbon World or related activities such as Corporate Social Responsibility (CSR) programmes, and especially those listed in Table 16.13.

Table 16.13 Corruption and Other Problems in the Carbon World

Aspect to Be Evaluated	Examples of Illegal Practices
All compliance procedures under Kyoto and the ETS where the evaluating company is classed as a Large Carbon Producer	False accounting and emissions measurement Bribery of or extortion by inspection staff Control of access to national registries and trading platforms
Investments in official or voluntary offset projects	Commercial deception Corruption by project leaders to obtain permissions resulting in vicarious liability for UK participants
Participation in Green Investment Schemes	
Accounting for offsets	False accounting to increase or decrease values Creation of hidden reserves between carbon and official accounts Sales, transfers and assignments of carbon credits as a means of bribe payment
Reconciling carbon accounting with formal accounts	
Pricing of and settlement for carbon credits	
Due diligence on carbon trading counterparties	Corruption to approve investments in suspect projects and transactions
Registration with and dealing through exchanges	Fraud, hacking and phishing: VAT frauds
Payment and income-processing	Use of carbon settlement systems to pay and receive bribes and launder funds
New technology	Theft of intellectual capital Commercial deception
Corporate Social Responsibility programmes	Perverted decisions based on the noble cause Performance metrics (assessment of benefits) Accounts payable

There is every reason to believe that fraud and corruption in the Carbon World will surpass the 2008–2010 banking crisis, make credit default swaps look like the ultimate in security and the Oil for Food programme a beacon of good control. CSR programmes are the poor relation in the Carbon World, but are seriously exposed to corruption and other skulduggery.

Focusing on Competitive Corruption

Evaluations should include a detailed segment concentrating on competitive corruption in every market in which the company participates – particularly in the private sector outside the UK and in all relationships involving government institutionalities.

The evaluation should take account of the regulatory and enforcement standards to which competitors are bound in their **home countries** (Table 16.14).

Table 16.14 Competitors Playing on a Level Field

Competitor Incorporated	WHEN COMPETING						
	In the UK		Overseas				
			Sector		Competitor's Connection to the UK		
	Public	Private	Public	Private	RCO	Services	CCP
Footnote ➔➔➔➔➔➔➔➔➔			*A*	*B*	*C*	*D*	*E*
In the UK	Level	Level	Level	Level	Level	Level	Level
Relevant commercial organisation							
In OECD Convention country	Level	Level	Some	No	Some	Some	No
US company	Level	Level	No	No	Level	Some	No
Local or indigenous	Not applicable		No	No	?	No	No

Table 16.14 indicates that UK companies compete at home on an almost level regulatory playing field. They compete equally overseas in the government sector with US companies, but the greatest inequality is in the private sector of overseas markets, where UK companies are hog-tied and fearful that even routine hospitality or conventional marketing practices will be interpreted as bribery.

The cataloguing suggested in Chapter 15 should result in identification of the company's international competitors and the markets in which they are active. The Risk Evaluation Database should be updated to show which of these are classed as relevant commercial organisations and therefore bound by the UK Bribery Act because they are in the same position as the evaluating company. They may be willing to join in collaborative risk evaluations – especially as far as facilitation extortion is concerned.

Also, if there is any evidence that UK-connected competitors (or their UK-connected senior managers) are involved in skulduggery, suspected corruption should be reported to the SFO and, if appropriate, the US Department of Justice. Regulators should be pressed to take action against corrupt competitors and all correspondence should be filed in the Adequate Procedures Dossier.

There are two other actions that may expose competitive corruption. The first is business intelligence (see pages 670) and routine monitoring of competitors' hospitality and other potentially corrupting practices. The second is to use data-mining techniques to identify contexts and transactions in which businesses has been lost. For example:

The Benefits of Data-mining

Data-mining shows the win–loss ratio of the company's competitive tenders as well as strategic customers won and lost. For example, company X competes with three main international companies, in India, Pakistan and Syria. By analysing its own contract files it is able to produce win–loss statistics as follows in Table 16.15.

Table 16.15 Examples of Data-mining

Competitor Country Base	Country in Which the Competitor Is Active			
	India	Pakistan	Syria	etc.
ABC **France**	Win: Loss 2/10 2 losses: 0 gains	12/12 5:0	0	0
JKL **USA**		Win: Loss 4/9 0:0	2/8 2:0	
XYZ **China**	Win: Loss 1/12 3 losses: 0 gains	0/4 0:2	0/7 0:2	0/3 0:1

Statistics for ABC should put company X on notice that its own personnel or agents may be involved in outward corruption in Pakistan and that XYZ is competing unfairly in all countries.

The exposure to competitive corruption should be risk-evaluated and catalogued. Business intelligence processes should monitor high-risk competitors and especially national companies in overseas markets.

Gap Analysis, Controls and Impact Assessments

Evaluations typically result in hundreds of Risk Working Sheets. They should be analysed, brainstormed and existing controls evaluated on the basis of how they work in practice, from:

- Experience of users;
- Strength of ownership, authority and responsibility;
- Benchmarked against the Sarbanes–Oxley Act (SOX) and other standards;
- Errors and transgressions detected;
- Flexibility (and absence of bureaucracy);
- Cost.

– and to what extent they are justified in the context. All important risks should be assigned to an owner. Where exposures remain, evaluators should consider the hierarchical strategic approach shown in Figure 16.6.

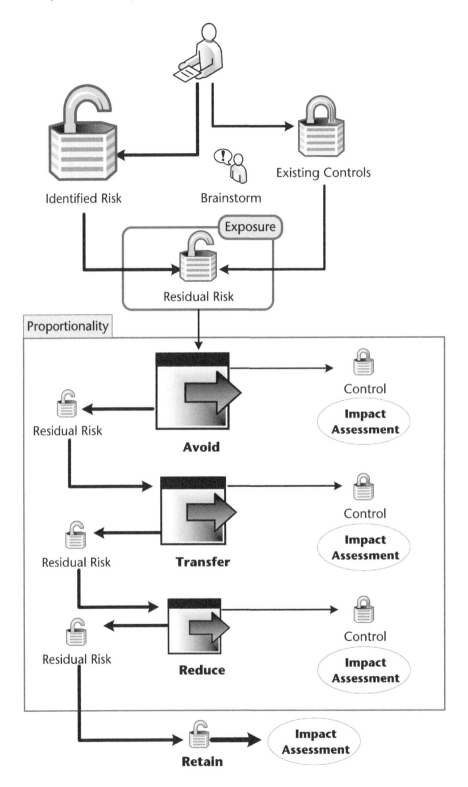

Figure 16.6 Risk Management and Control Options

Providing they have no adverse impact on commercial success, strategic changes should be made to avoid serious technical regulatory risks under the Bribery Act and the FCPA such as:

- Structuring or relocating companies to avoid classification as relevant commercial organisations;
- Disassociating closely connected persons working outside the UK from potential Section 7 liability;
- Converting agency relationships to principal–principal, *thereby removing the associated person problem*;
- Disconnecting from USA and Securities and Exchange Commission regulation;
- Withdrawing from high-risk contexts.

Avoidance of the uncertainty involved in technical violations and prosecutorial discretion may be the safest option.

The second step is to consider risk transfer options, including:

- Committing regulators to adequate procedures and decision templates in such areas as due diligence and decision matrices, if necessary using a double blind approach via third parties unconnected with the evaluating company;
- Maintaining an Adequate Procedures Dossier containing silver bullets;
- Modifying contract terms with important third parties (see page 701) so that they immediately remove all authority if bribes are offered or received;
- Obtaining personal warrantees and undertakings from the directors of third parties providing services;
- Considering additional Fidelity and Directors and Officers Liability Insurance or special policies that will become available to mitigate corruption risks and regulatory penalties.[36]

Risks may be reduced further by improving preventive or reactive controls (see Chapters 21–32), which are implemented by:

- People using hardware or following a specified procedure, *such as approval and authorisation processes and decision matrices*;
- Technical or automated operations, *such as automated fraud detection and monitoring controls*;
- Hardware, *such as access controls and physical barriers*.

In some cases, the team may conclude that controls should be relaxed or removed.

Personal responsibility for controls should, like all risks, be allocated to owners and the Risk Evaluation Database updated accordingly, but only after the evaluation team has impact-assessed all recommendations, including the possibility of:

---

36   But pay close attention to the fine print.

- The creation of new risks in corruption and other contexts;
- The impact of recommended controls on profitability, entrepreneurship, flexibility and morale;
- The cost of introducing and maintaining the controls;
- The consistency of controls in the organisation's various operations and contexts.[37]

Finally, the team should ensure that all evidence necessary, and the processes that generate it, to rebut allegations of skulduggery is securely retained, including the most important Adequate Procedures Dossier.

A brief report[38] should be prepared of the evaluation results for review and approval by the board and its conclusions recorded in minutes. Finally, the team should scrutinise the evaluation process, updating its procedures and retaining them for future use.

---

37 Bearing in mind that any inconsistency may be seized upon by regulators to allege that procedures were inadequate.

38 Marked 'Privileged and Confidential'.

17 *Analysing Secondary Risks*

Evaluating Detection Failure Risk

A second-level evaluation should address the probability that misbehaviour will not be detected by the company or that regulators will be the first to know.

There are an estimated 4.8 million businesses in the UK employing 22.8 million people. The first problem is determining the probability of the evaluating company appearing on the regulatory radar. This depends on a number of factors, including its size, location, whether private or publicly listed, the sector in which it works and geographical locations (see also page 446). The second problem is that most people have no real appreciation of the probability of risk. By way of comparison Table 17.1 sets out some common probabilities for US risks.

Table 17.1 Examples of Common Probabilities in the USA on a One-year Basis

Event	Chance in the Following 12 Months
Having a car stolen	1:100
House catching fire	1:200
Death from heart disease	1:280
Death from cancer	1:500
Killed in a car accident	1:6,000
Murdered	1:10,000
Death through AIDS	1:11,000
Jackpot on state lottery	1:1,000,000
Killed by lightning	1:1,400,000
Killed by a flood or tornado	1:2,000,000
Killed in a hurricane	1:6,000,000
Killed in a commercial aircraft crash	1,10,000,000

So would it be unreasonable,[1] as the Scottish comedian, Billy Connolly, would say, to estimate the probability of a large UK company (10,000 plus employees) coming to the attention of the Serious Fraud Office (SFO) or American regulators involving a serious bribery allegation at 1:50,000 on a yearly basis? Let us take this as a baseline in a hypothetical example. Most people would consider that these odds were so long that the risks of non-disclosure were acceptable.

However, there are 11 main factors that modify this baseline probability:

Table 17.2 Factors Increasing the Risks of Appearing on the Regulatory Radar

Factors Affecting Risk in a 12-month Period	Weight
1. POOR REGULATORY TRACK RECORD Previous investigations by regulatory agencies (especially when they failed) or warnings for infringements	100
2. MANDATORY REPORTING The company's requirement to submit Suspicious Activity Reports under the Proceeds of Crime Act (POCA) or to make disclosures to the SEC, the FSA, or any other regulatory agency	100
3. LITIGATION RISK The possibility of serious litigation as a plaintiff or defendant	50
4. STRUCTURAL CHANGES In or involving the company such as a planned acquisition, disposal, IPO or MBO, or closing of a joint venture (resulting in corrupt transactions being uncovered)	50
5. DISSONANCE AND SERIOUS INTERNAL PROBLEMS Serious discord within the senior management team or the likelihood that internal problems such as management changes, employment tribunal actions, or redundancies will result in allegations and disclosures	30
6. ADVERSE PUBLIC PROFILE The company's adverse media profile and being the target for investigative journalism	40
7. REGIME AND SPONSORHIP CHANGES Leadership changes in overseas countries in which the company has significant investments	20
8. SECTORAL TARGETING AND CONTAGION The likelihood that regulators will target (or have already targeted) the sector in which the company operates	20
9. HEDGE FUNDS The possibility that a hedge fund would commission a private investigation to discredit the organisation and short sell its shares before publicising its findings[2]	50
10. THIRD-PARTY COMPLAINTS The likelihood that competitors – especially in foreign markets – or customers and suppliers will make frivolous or genuine allegations either to the media or to the regulators	10
11. THIRD-PARTY SUSPICIOUS ACTIVITY REPORTING The requirement that any associate, professional adviser or banker is required to report under the anti-money-laundering regulations or POCA	10

1   He said 'There are two problems in the world: overpopulation and not enough food. Would it be so unreasonable, I ask, to eat your neighbour'?

2   And this happens!

The weights in Table 17.2 are admittedly subjective and only time will tell how accurate they might be. But the reality is that if the hypothetical company has a poor regulatory track record, the probability of its name appearing in the Elm Street[3] offices could drop from 1:50,000[1] to 1:500[1]. This is a totally different proposition. If in addition it is a litigious sort of business, the probability drops to 1:100[1], which is as likely as having a car stolen in the USA.

If a company concludes that it is unlikely to come to the attention of the American or British regulators it should still aim to improve its chances of being first to know by:

- Using continuous monitoring programmes to quickly identify potentially corrupt and fraudulent transactions (see page 736);
- Improving its reporting of incidents, procedures and hotlines and paying rewards for corroborated information of fraud or corruption (see page 666);
- Offering an amnesty for all prior or current acts of corruption in or against the company.

High-profile targets should make every effort to stay ahead of the regulators and, having professionally investigated the suspicions and taken all necessary remedial action, decide whether self-disclosure is a viable option in the specific case (see pages 597 and 656 for policy formation on this point).

If a company concludes it is unlikely to appear on the regulatory screens, keeping a low profile and not self-disclosing under any circumstances may be the best option. It may further decide – if it is prepared to play the odds – to create a fund to defend regulatory action.

Evaluating Investigatory Risks

A third level of evaluation should consider the possibility that internal investigations could lead to accusations of:

- Cases being so incompetently handled that – in themselves – they demonstrate inadequate procedures;[4]
- Perverting the course of justice by, for example, destroying evidence or interfering with witnesses;
- Privacy, human rights, data protection, employment and other violations;
- Jeopardising the safety of local staff, especially in dangerous or difficult overseas jurisdictions.

The greatest exposures arise from ignoring the symptoms of corruption and conducting investigations with the sole intention of producing a neutral result, thereby not warranting self-disclosure, or plain incompetence. All are dangerous and are definitely not recommended.

---

3   Where the SFO 'hangs loose'.

4   The mishandling may be deliberate.

Obstruction of Justice

Lauren Stevens, a former lawyer working for GlaxoSmithKline, was charged with obstructing a US Food and Drug Administration investigation by concealing and falsifying documentation relating to alleged off-label marketing of the drug Wellbrutin.

The Maryland District Court ruled that she could not rely on advice given to her by external counsel – the leading law firm of King and Spalding – (under the advice of defence counsel) because it was only applicable to crimes involving specific intent and not to absolute offences.

It is probable that the same interpretation would be applied by British judges.

Evaluating Self-disclosure and Prosecution Risks

INTRODUCTION

There is no obligation under the Bribery Act or the Foreign Corrupt Practices Act (FCPA) to report suspicions of bribery, but the SFO and the Department of Justice (DOJ) have made it clear they will treat (or try to treat) non-disclosure most severely.

The decision to self-disclose, which has been called 'Come to Jesus', or 'to stay silent as in Russian roulette', is discussed on page 158. The supposed arguments in favour of self-disclosure are that it:

- Is ethically the right thing to do (taking the moral high ground) because it publicly acknowledges wrongdoing, encourages remedial action and is a deterrent to others;
- Enables cases to be settled by civil disposal or negotiated settlement, possibly avoiding imprisonment of individuals and protecting the rights of innocent shareholders, employees, suppliers and customers;
- Results in discounted financial penalties for the individuals and companies involved.

However, some people believe that the moral high ground is for companies NOT to weasel their way out of trouble but to take their punishment like any other citizen.[5] The main justification for self-disclosure is that it allows companies to buy their way out of trouble, but it results in one law for the rich and another for the poor. It encourages companies to throw to the wolves associated persons with whom they were in collusion or did not properly control to save their own skins. It leads, in fact, to a perversion of the criminal justice system.

Besides that, self-disclosure comes at a cost with extremely doubtful advantages. The following paragraphs discuss the risks of self-disclosure and how a company's policy might be determined.[6]

---

5   Paradoxically, companies that even hint that they may be amenable to civil disposals mark themselves out as prime targets for regulatory attention.

6   The suggestions are not a substitute for specific legal advice!

MANDATORY REPORTING

Why no requirement to report?

If the government had required persons to self-disclose bribery offences it would have said so in the Act, as is the case with money-laundering, criminal property, terrorism and road traffic offences. By omitting this provision, politicians released government agencies from any obligation to self-disclose incoming corruption, but gave the SFO immense discretional powers to leverage penalties on companies for every minor or technical violation.

Overview of mandatory reporting requirements

One of the first questions a UK company should consider is whether or not it is legally bound to report anything. The position is summarised[7] in Table 17.3.

Table 17.3   Obligations to Report Crimes

Report Required By	Aspect or Purpose of Reporting	Reported to	Dominant Law or Regulation
IN OR INVOLVING THE UK			
UK Listed companies Foreign companies listed in the UK[9] *(around 600!!)*	Impact on shareholders and share price of factors impacting on investors' decisions. Disclosure and transparency rules	Stock Exchange –FSA[8] and Reporting Information Service (RIS)	Listing rules
All UK persons and bodies corporate	Money-laundering defence under Section 338 of POCA when a person knows or suspects	SOCA-UKFIU	POCA 2002
	Suspected terrorist financing		
Firms in the UK Regulated Sector (POCA)	Money-laundering defence under Section 338 when a person has reasonable grounds to know or suspect	SOCA-UKFIU Other authorities	POCA 2002
	Any breach of supervisory authority (e.g. FSA or HMRC) rules, including money-laundering offences	SFA	Financial and Management Services Act (FMSA) 2000, etc.

---

7   In a simplified form.

8   Or, as the FSA says 'anything relating to the firm of which the FSA would reasonably expect notice'.

9   Who may be classified as 'relevant commercial organisations'.

Report Required By	Aspect or Purpose of Reporting	Reported to	Dominant Law or Regulation
IN OR INVOLVING THE USA			
US Incorporated companies Non-US companies who are required to report to the SEC *(around 44 UK companies are so listed and classed as 'Issuers')*	Impact on shareholders Material weaknesses as defined in the Sarbanes–Oxley Act Potential money-laundering and terrorist offences (PATRIOT ACT, etc.)	SEC or Department of Justice	Sarbanes-Oxley Act and COSO Stock Exchange Rules

The reporting requirements shown in Table 17.3 are not uniform. For example, control weaknesses and technical breaches of the rules should be reported by regulated companies to the Financial Services Authority (FSA). The same is more or less true for Issuers in the USA under Sarbanes–Oxley, who are required to report 'material weaknesses'. However, the DOJ has said that even a $5 facilitation payment is 'material' and has to be reported.

In the USA there are other national, local or State laws requiring mandatory disclosure or sectorial reporting such as that planned under the Dodd–Frank Act for the extractive industry. Further, in some jurisdictions if prosecutors feel especially frisky, they could take action for misprision of a felony, aiding, abetting or being an accessory before or after the fact, or conspiracy based only on failure to report.[10]

In the UK, the Proceeds of Crime Act (POCA) mandates reporting by companies and individuals in the regulated sector (see page 190) where they know (or have good reason to believe) that a specific money-laundering offence has been committed. The SFO, the Securities and Exchange Commission (SEC) and the DOJ do not expect reporting of mere suspicions.

It is important to recognise these varying standards. They mean that would be quite proper for a company to report a control defect to the FSA or the SEC without citing a specific money-laundering or bribery offence that failed the knowledge or belief test. In short, in the reporting field, one size does not fit all, although it is likely that once a report has been made to one agency – possibly as a control weakness – it will be referred to others who are interested in specific crimes.

SELF-DISCLOSURE OF BRIBERY

General considerations

Companies should carefully risk-evaluate their approach to self-disclosure; arguments in favour and against are summarised in Table 17.4.[11]

---

10   This is highly unlikely, even in the current regulatory climate.

11   Before finalising their policies (see Chapter 23).

Table 17.4 Evaluation of Risks in Making Self-disclosures

Factors in Favour of a Self-disclosure Policy	Factors Against an Invariable Self-disclosure Policy
DECISIONS ON PRINCIPLE	
The directors believe it is **right in principle** (as a public duty) to follow a policy of invariable self-disclosure. *This is probably the proper approach for organisations that philosophically support the idea that anti-corruption laws are a noble cause, or who believe they cannot live under the cloud of potential detection*	• Top managers who do not buy into the 'noble cause' story are prepared to accept the worry and consequences of non-reporting • Top managers can live with the uncertainty of possible future disclosure
REPORTING OBLIGATIONS AND REGULATORY REGIMES	
The company has a mandatory obligation to report suspected bribery (for example, mandatory reporting to the SEC, the FSA or the UK Stock Exchange) or associated violations under the POCA, or believes for any other reason that the case is likely to come to the attention of regulators anywhere in the world	• There is no obligation to make a disclosure to any regulator of mere suspicion • The case involves a number of different regulatory agencies
FORUM SHOPPING ('REGULATORY ARBITRAGE')	
Companies that fall under a number of regulatory regimes (such as, for example, UK and US laws. or the FSA or OFT) should consider, if self-disclosure is to be made, whether there is any advantage in making the initial report to one rather than another. This is known as 'forum' or 'venue' shopping	• The pattern of cases worldwide suggests that forum shopping can produce some advantages. Mentioning them here would be counterproductive
CHANCES OF REGULATORY DETECTION	
There is a high probability that violations will be detected by regulators	• There is little chance of detection by any third party
NATURE OF THE CASE	
Involves competitive and incoming corruption where regulators can use their extensive powers to assist the company recover	• Outgoing corruption, involving only Section 7 offences or other offences involving a directing mind
The case satisfies the SFO acceptance criteria and thus provides the opportunity of a civil disposal. This only applies if the company would be amenable to a civil disposal	• The case fails the SFO acceptance test and might be handled by another law enforcement agency that does not support civil disposal[12]
The evidence is overwhelming and complies with the SFO's civil disposal test (see page 68)	• The evidence is weak and unlikely to pass the evidential test

---

12   Such as the City of London Overseas Corruption Unit and subject to the company's philosophy on civil disposals.

Factors in Favour of a Self-disclosure Policy	Factors Against an Invariable Self-disclosure Policy
The company made no (or little) financial gain	• Voluntary disclosure would result in serous commercial or other consequences
Successor liability following an acquisition	• Losses may be recovered under pre-acquisition warranties
Potential extradition risks	• The US may apply to have overseas defendants extradited or may use rendition techniques to arrest them when they travel through the country
Co-accused or whistle-blowers are likely to cooperate with the regulators	• There is little chance that details of the case will come into the public domain
There is a potential for recovery under Fidelity or other insurances, or through civil litigation	• There is little chance of insurance for other recoveries
OTHER LATENT SKULDUGGERY	
After disclosure the company has to anticipate that its every nook and cranny will be reviewed, including all of its electronic data, expense claims, correspondence and accounting records. All past cases (that were not reported) will be regurgitated	• It is nothing short of lunatic for a self-disclosure to be made without fully understanding the potential consequences in bribery and all other regulatory areas
PUBLIC INTEREST TEST	
It is clearly not in the public interest to prosecute	• There is no public interest that might mitigate punishment
PENALTY DISCOUNTS	
The SFO has said it will deal sympathetically with self-disclosures except when top management or directors are involved and will work with the corporate concerned towards a civil disposal WHERE A 'SELF-DISCLOSURE' FOLLOWS A MANDATORY REPORT UNDER, FOR EXAMPLE, POCA, IT IS UNLIKELY TO QUALIFY FOR DISCOUNT IN RELATION TO ASSOCIATED OFFENCES	**DISCOUNT** • The discount granted for self-disclosure is likely to be less than the consequential damage resulting from the SFO's insistence on publicity
	• If a case is taken to court, judges will normally indicate the discount they would allow for an early guilty plea, typically in the range of 25% to 35%. Any discount agreed by the regulators is unlikely to be better than this
	PROSECUTION OF INDIVIDUALS • The regulators are likely to insist on prosecuting individuals and require the company to give evidence against them. **There is little evidence that self-disclosure and effective compliance programs make any significant difference to the sanctions imposed (see pages 33 and 34)**
	ADVERSE PUBLICITY • Regulators will seek maximum publicity of a civil disposal, thereby encouraging legal actions by third parties causing serious reputational damage

	NEGOTIATIONS AND DISCLOSURE • During negotiations companies are required to disclose any other suspected offences. Even if the negotiation fails these disclosures can be used against them
	OPPOSITION OF THE COURTS • The discount for self-disclosure may be no greater than would be allowed by a court for an early guilty plea.
	• Negotiated settlements with the SFO require the approval of a court. The judges have been remarkably reluctant to follow the SFO's recommendations
Publicity is unlikely to result in other litigation	• Private or derivative litigation is likely
The SFO will assist the corporate in making appropriate disclosures to other regulatory agencies	• This is a very questionable advantage Problems of disclosure are more acute when multiple jurisdictions are involved
POSITION OF CO-ACCUSED	
Are likely to surrender, possibly as cooperating witnesses	• Will not cooperate with prosecutors • Will be supported by the body corporate or relevant commercial organisation
Are not directing minds	
Are foreign public officials	
DEBARMENT FROM GOVERNMENT CONTRACTS	
The SFO will not normally seek to have companies which make voluntary disclosures debarred from government contracts under the European Procurement Directives and UK laws	This is only of any benefit to companies that do or seek business with government agencies. Publicity may result in counterparties to contracts nullifying them
COSTS AND CONTINUING INVESTIGATIONS	
In theory collaborative investigations should be cheaper and quicker than reacting to an accusatorial case run independently by the SFO or other agency	• The SFO is likely to require further investigations to be carried out after a self-disclosure. It will insist on controlling these, with all costs being paid by the company
	• Even a collaborative investigation with the SFO may disrupt a company for two or three years
	• The SFO may insist on a monitor being appointed, with all costs being borne by the company. This may be costly and intrusive
INABILITY TO TAKE ANY REMEDIAL ACTION	
Unless the case is self-disclosed the company may not be able to take any action (including disciplinary and civil law sanctions) against those involved	• This is an unintended consequence of the Bribery Act

Factors in Favour of a Self-disclosure Policy	Factors Against an Invariable Self-disclosure Policy
If self-disclosure is not made, the company and its managers have to live with the worry that the case may be discovered by regulators. They may therefore be open to blackmail by perpetrators and others involved	• This is a question of risk tolerance
IMPORTANCE OF DETERRENCE	
Individuals and companies guilty of bribery can be punished to the full extent of the law. This creates a deterrent to others and is important for internal purposes	• But this comes at a cost • In any case deterrence – as in the case of BAE – is highly discriminatory
If action is not taken, perpetrators and others may be free to blackmail the company for failing to self-disclose	• This is a very serious risk
ABILITY TO REBUT ALLEGATIONS	
If the evaluation is conducted on the lines recommended, evidence will be identified and retained to rebut mistaken allegations involving the company and individuals	• An Adequate Procedures Dossier (which in fact goes well beyond a Section 7 defence) is critical
RISKS TO THE REGULATORS	
The regulators face serious risks by insisting on prosecution. It is in their interests to reach a negotiated settlement	• The SFO and USA regulators have used expansive interpretation of many terms in the law to their own advantage. It is unlikely that they would wish to have these tested in court
	• The SFO has a conviction rate in contested trials of no better than 50%
	• Jury nullification and jury equity (see page 172)
	• Judicial review
	• Misconduct in public office

The factors that a company considers – based on its individual philosophy and operations – could be incorporated in a Kepner-Tregoe type decision matrix (see pages 568–72) to guide self-disclosure, both at a policy level and in individual cases. Such a matrix should be approved by the board of directors, the audit committee, and legal advisers.[13]

The dilemmas surrounding self-disclosure are illustrated in the following examples.

13   Readers who would like to review an active model matrix should contact info@cobasco.com for a free copy on Excel.

Case 1: FPO Influence Leading to a £25 Million Commercial Contract

You, as a director of a relevant commercial organisation, have discovered that one of your employees has paid a bribe of $5,000 to an FPO to speed up an import licence (for a $10 million commercial contract) to which your company was genuinely entitled. You have to decide whether to self-disclose or not:

Option 1: if you self-disclose the chances of imprisonment for anyone are 0 per cent and the mandatory financial penalty will be 30 per cent lower than the anticipated maximum of £25 million, although the company will almost certainly be subject to further regulatory action, civil litigation and bad publicity. In this case the proceeds of crime could be argued to be the $25 million, making it criminal property and liable to confiscation

Option 2: if you do not self-disclose, the chances of regulators discovering the payments through its own efforts are estimated to be less than 1:10,000; but if they do, the employee may go to prison for up to ten years with a financial penalty on the company exceeding £40 million. with other litigation to follow. Of course, if regulators do not find out, nothing will happen.

Will you self-disclose? Can you and the company live with the risks of discovery?

Case 2: Internal Corruption

The Marketing Director, middle-aged and married with four kids, is seduced (financial or other advantage) by a young, attractive assistant, who induces him to fire the existing representative and appoint (perverted decision = improper performance) her 18-year old brother as the agent in Bentrovia. The Marketing Director also allows the brother increased commissions, favourable allocations and credit terms. After 12 months the previous agent complains and legal advice is to the effect that the assistant has committed a Section 1 offence and the Marketing Director a Section 2 offence, making the company liable under Section 7.

You are the Managing Director. What do you do?

In many cases the advantages of self-disclosure – even in serious cases of outgoing corruption – are at best marginal and self-disclosure should not be an automatic or unconsidered reaction. The following paragraphs discuss the further factors on which policy should be decided.

Attitude towards co-accused

Some people may not appreciate the discussion that follows because it mentions the unmentionable. But here goes. A natural reaction – to save the corporate skin – is for companies to blame employees and associated persons for getting them into trouble, but the reality is not so simple. There are two main considerations in deciding whether or not to support co-accuseds:

- **Integrity and principles**: Is it ethical, for example, for companies to transfer blame to a junior employee for making facilitation payments when senior managers closed their eyes to the obvious or set key performance drivers that could only be achieved by skulduggery?
- **Tactics**: It is obviously to the prosecution's advantage if multiple defendants blame each other and tactically better for defendants to keep their interests aligned: if this is right in principle.

The positions in which co-defendants might be supported are summarised in Table 17.5 and all start from a presumption of innocence.

Table 17.5 Factors Involved in Considering a Joint Defence

Nature of the Underlying Offence			
4= Means the company should probably support co-accuseds in a shared defence 7 = Means probably severing all connections with co-accuseds			
Bribes Paid		Bribes Received	
4	Intended to benefit the company	7	Intended for personal or third-party benefit
4	No breach of good faith	7	Usually a breach of good faith
4	Accurately recorded	7	Unrecorded and off-book
4	Currently employed	4	Reacted to threats of violence
4	Not currently employed	7	Unheeded warnings
4	Associated person (e.g. an intermediary)		
4	Convincing explanation		
7	Invalid or unconvincing explanation		
7	Threatens to damage the company		
4	No money-laundering or other breaches		
4	No other grounds for dismissal		
4	Foolish rather than wilful motivation		
4	Interests aligned with the company		
7	Partly motivated by personal gain		
7	Ignored prior warnings		
4	Successor liability (e.g. post-acquisition)		
4	A joint defence is in the interests of the company	But only if other conditions are met	

Table 17.5 suggests that:

- Decisions should be taken on principle and on a presumption of innocence.
- Any employee or associated person against whom there is convincing evidence of bribe receipt should not be supported.
- Any employee against whom there is convincing evidence of bribe payment involving wilful disregard of procedures, precedents or accounting standards should not be supported.
- In all other cases, the company's inclination should be to offer support and work towards a joint defence. Supporting a co-accused may mean:
  - Paying or guaranteeing their legal fees, at least until after trial;
  - Sharing legal advisers;
  - Delaying disciplinary and other action until the close of the case (and possibly a finding of guilt);
  - Refusing to testify against each other;
  - Negotiating all-inclusive civil disposals.

If a company decides to jettison co-accuseds, it must assume they will testify against it. The effects of this should be assessed before making any self-disclosure.

The bottom line

So the bottom line is whether a company should self-disclose and 'Come to Jesus' or to play Russian roulette. Figure 17.1 summarises the position.

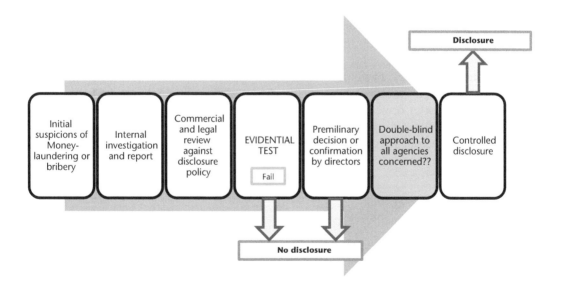

Figure 17.1 Process on Disclosure of Bribery and Money-laundering Offences

An excellent Special Report produced by The Steele Foundation stated in relation to the FCPA states:

> ***Many in the private sector – particularly attorneys at firms that specialise in compliance-related litigation and investigation – voiced scepticism about the wisdom of self-reporting.*** *It is their contention that under a Russian Roulette model, a company's interests may be better served to complete its investigation, take appropriate corrective and disciplinary actions and play the odds that the government will not target the company for investigation.*[14]

Page 451 et seq suggests a possible policy framework for self-disclosure, but like all things, companies must decide what is best, depending on their philosophy and the nature of their business. One size does not fit all.

Conclusions

Risk evaluation, especially for large companies, may appear to be a tedious and costly responsibility, but the good news is that if it is carried out properly it can result in massive savings and recoveries, make the company's controls far more effective and ensure that regulations are observed to the full.

So, just to beat the dead dog[15] to death, the real bottom line is that a thorough and professional risk evaluation results in a company being able to:

- Maintain profitable, flexible, entrepreneurial and enjoyable work environments;
- Have confidence that the decisions it takes will not breach the anti-bribery laws or other regulatory silos;
- Enter difficult markets safely and thereby gain a an advantage over its competitors;
- Make hard cash recoveries that more than cover the costs of controls.

Supporting effective risk evaluation should not be a difficult decision: or should it? Is it best, as the intellectuals working for the Emissions Trading Scheme and the United Nations Framework Convention on Climate Change have said, 'what you don't know, can't hurt you'. How wrong they are! The art is being the first to know what you should have prevented before anyone else does.

---

14 'Steele Special Report: Recent FCPA Cast Overview', available at: http://www.steelefoundation.com/index.php?option=com_content&task=view&id=1052 (accessed 17 November 2012). The Steele Foundation are specialist international due diligence providers.

15 With apologies to Kenneth Mutt. This is an investigator's trait.

'I know you would like to blame the Big Bad Wolf or the Evil Fairy for this,
but the truth is that we should have bribed like our competitors'

V Exposing Corruption

CHAPTER 18 *Introduction and Background*

The Purpose of Detection

In a perfect world, controls would be commensurate with evolving risks, demonstrably cost-effective while balancing entrepreneurship and flexibility against compliance and box-ticking. Unfortunately, this ideal is rarely attainable and most organisations are over- or under controlled: either too lax or too bureaucratic; too risk-tolerant or too cautious. **Detection is both the fine-tuning for controls and the safety net if they come under attack. Detection is an essential contributor to adequate procedures.** This chapter is targeted primarily at detecting bribe payment,[1] although it touches on incoming, internal and competitive corruption and associated frauds: all where there are no existing suspicions.

A Point Worth Repeating

For every coercer there is an extorter. Extortion – which involves perverted decisions and usually excessive personal wealth – is easier to detect. Extorters are the honeypots around which legions of coercers congregate. Reveal one extorter and Pandora's Box opens. This is why the Serious Fraud Office (SFO) should use its powers under Part 5 of the Proceeds of Crime Act to flush out extorters. Companies can do likewise if they collaborate with third parties on risk evaluation and fraud detection (see Chapters 14–17).

Distinguishing between the symptoms of fraud and corruption is difficult and it is usually only after detailed investigations that the distinctions become clear.

---

1   For two reasons. The first is that bribe payment and Section 7 offences are the main current concern; but more importantly, to cover detection of all types of corruption would be unmanageable in one book.

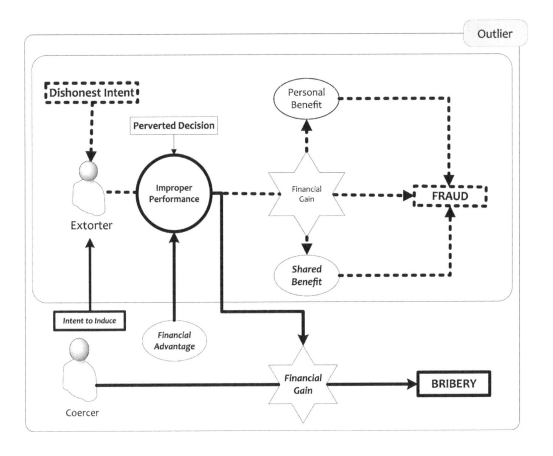

Figure 18.1 Outliers of Fraud and Bribery

Bribery Or Fraud: Does It Matter?

The Director in charge of Central Procurement colludes with a vendor to charge inflated prices for lower-quality goods and to share the proceeds equally. Is this fraud or bribery? Does it matter? A junior buyer notices what is going on, but stays silent when the Director promises to give her a pay rise. Does it matter?

Differences like these do matter because the frauds most likely also breach sections 1, 2 and 7 of the Bribery Act: both companies involved could be corporately liable, banned from all government contracts and face more serious penalties under the Bribery Act than they ever would for fraud.

For reasons illustrated by the above example, this chapter refers simply to 'fraud detection', but includes incoming, internal, outgoing and competitive corruption.

Sticky Fingers

In the vast majority of corruption cases investigated by the authors over the past 40 years, the person responsible for paying bribes took a personal cut. In some, he took the lot (see page 298).

Detection enables organisations to:

- Maximise profits and minimise losses and regulatory exposures by being the first to know to quickly take remedial action and recover losses and costs;
- Establish a meaningful deterrent while relaxing bureaucratic and costly box-ticking controls;
- Help create a climate of honesty in which skulduggery is not tolerated;
- Test and obtain reasonable assurances that controls are effective; and to demonstrate that procedures are adequate;
- Understand – in advance – what other skulduggery might come to light following a self-disclosure of *any* suspected regulatory breaches;
- Use the results to negotiate lower Fidelity, negligence and Directors' and Officers' Liability Insurance.

Despite the obvious benefits of proactive detection, the majority of frauds emerge by accident and are either ignored or compromised through management weakness and ineffective investigations.

Words of Caution

The authors thought long and hard, during intense brainstorming sessions at the Pink Pussycat Lap Dancing Club, before writing anything about detection, mainly because doing so might forewarn crooks of things to avoid.[2] For this reason *precise* details of many Critical Point Audit (CPA) and other tests that have successfully exposed fraud, bribe payment and receipt have been excluded although, hopefully, enough will be said to give a flavour of what can be achieved and to encourage organisations to take proactive steps in the right direction. Detection can pay off because the truth is that when victims and perpetrators are equally well informed, the balance swings in the formers' favour.

Applying the techniques discussed in this chapter is more likely than not (please believe it!) to unmask fraud, corruption, glitches and control weaknesses. Discovery could well result in some difficult decisions, such as whether or not to prosecute or self-disclose to regulators. Effective detection results in many good things but also problems: it is not necessarily a win–win scenario, as Miliband the Banana might say. Thus organisations should not even think of using the tests that follow without first understanding the potentially adverse consequences. THEY WORK!

---

2   Then his colleagues reminded him that no one ever read his books; so where is the problem?

Locked in the Lavatory[3]

A couple of days after attending the authors' seminar on fraud detection (but not investigation) a participant telephoned to say that he had tried out a couple of CPA tests, discovered a cluster of false invoices and had interviewed the Head of Purchasing, who had confessed. The participant, in a state of near panic, pleaded: 'I have locked him in the men's lavatory. What do I do next?'

Legal, ethical and emotional problems routinely surface with fraud detection. The first is over the extent to which an organisation is prepared to face reality – discussed later – and employ effective but controversial techniques such as pretext or undercover investigations that, although legal might not replay well at a Wimmen's Institute Cheese and Wine soirée or the annual Masonic dinner.

Testing Controls and Whistle-blowing Procedures

Contriving to have an anonymous letter – vaguely alleging skulduggery – sent to a manager or intermediary to test reporting procedures may, for many organisations, be a step too far.[4] But the technique is effective. If the letter is reported, it tends to confirm that procedures are adequate and functioning as intended. If not, remedial actions can be taken. Testing in this way also makes it more likely that all information will be reported in future because those who might be tempted into concealment cannot be sure whether or not a trap has been set.

Other problems arise over privacy, human rights, employee relations and, of course, with data protection legislation and communications interception under the Regulation of Investigatory Powers Act (RIPA): all of which are especially relevant to UK government agencies.[5]

---

3 All of the cases discussed in this chapter actually happened, although in some the characteristics have been simplified for illustrative purposes. Where names are mentioned, the cases concerned are already in the public domain. All cases took place before the UK Bribery Act 2010 came into force but they are all relevant to it.

4 In a test conducted by the author for a client some years ago, five agents were overpaid. Only one reported it.

5 For more detail on RIPA and the Human Rights Act, please see *Investigating Corporate Fraud* by Michael J. Comer (and Spot the Dog) (Gower, 2003).

Personal Data Problems

'Whistleblowing lines' can be problematic or even illegal in some less well developed countries, such as France. And, after independence, if someone has the temerity to take a CD containing English personal data to Scotland she might find the Information Commissioner, accompanied by a team of broken-nosed heavies, on her doorstep for a yawn or even dawn raid.

Rupert's Law[6] states that the more controversial a detection technique is, the more likely it is to uncover fraud. This is not the always the case and CPA, in particular, is ethical and effective, and so are interviews.

Obligations for Proactive Detection

There is little in any of the anti-corruption legislation or guidelines that *specifically* requires organisations to actively seek out skulduggery in the ways suggested later; in the Ministry of Justice Guidance and scores of SFO speeches and publications, detection barely rates a mention.

Detection is – sort of – implied in the UK Listing and Financial Services Authority rules, Federal Sentencing Guidelines, Sarbanes–Oxley, and in numerous good-practice publications and auditing standards. There are other equally weighty tomes that absolve, especially auditors, of such disturbing tasks: thus endorsing the fallacy that they are watchdogs and not bloodhounds. **In such confusion it is no wonder that enthusiastic auditors, investigators and others who attempt to detect fraud without any authority end up in trouble.**

A National Strike

An investigator – acting entirely on his own initiative and without ANY authority or even discussion with his supervisors – approached one of his company's customers whom he suspected of receiving stolen products – and offered to pay him if he would covertly tape-record drivers with whom he was in collusion. The customer made a number of highly incriminating recordings but demanded payment far beyond the investigator's authority. When this was not forthcoming, the customer covertly recorded the investigator and sold the tapes to a national newspaper. All hell broke loose and more by luck than judgement a national strike was averted.

---

6   Rupert is a small cuddly Teddy Bear, fond of red jumpers and yellow checked trousers, who does not live in the real world. He speaks in rhyme, believes in the innate goodness of everything and everyone and votes for the Lib Dems.

This chapter recommends carrying out an integrated detection exercise,[7] for the first time, covering the Extended Enterprise. It is possible, of course, to limit testing to distinct processes or contexts, using some or all of the tools discussed but, even then, most of the principles reviewed below apply. Detection is a serious matter.

Policy Decisions

DO MANAGERS REALLY WANT TO KNOW?

A very senior legal colleague (whose integrity and wisdom is normally beyond question) told the authors they were wasting his time writing about fraud and bribery detection because most senior managers in Europe would rather not know. He persisted in saying that the position is different in the USA where the Department of Justice and the Securities and Exchange Commission are all-powerful and exploit the threat of life imprisonment to frighten and gain control. The colleague said:

> What's more, most American firms are, in fact, run by Legal Counsel and managers will not scratch their backsides without first taking legal advice. To protect themselves they may be prepared to invest time and money in detection to make sure their organisations are clean. It is different in Europe: believe me. They do not want to know and there is no way they are going to allow people to poke around trying to uncover fraud.

Because these views did not accord with the authors' – and by applying the false attribution syndrome (see page 472) – they have been ignored. Good investigators often do this! So here goes for three reasons.

1. Even in the worst case the most obdurate managers will see the sense of proactive fraud detection:
    *   before making an acquisition or significant equity investment to make sure they are not inheriting disaster;
    *   before launching an IPO or disposal on the basis that someone else might run a CPA and blow the deal out of the water;
    *   before starting any new venture in the USA,[8] when they may fall, for the first time, under its laws;
    *   before making any sort of self-disclosure to regulators;
    *   before entering into serious litigation following which all records may have to be disclosed;
    *   when either regulators or the media have shown an interest in them, their trading partners or the sectors or countries in which they operate.

2. After board level changes when incoming directors need assurance that they are not walking into trouble.

---

7   Health Check.

8   Or with an American company.

and hopefully, the dominant reason is that:

3. Honest managers will recognise that it is *on principle* overwhelmingly in their organisation's interest – and their own – to minimise losses and regulatory exposures from fraud and corruption. As far as the Bribery Act is concerned some managers may agree it is sensible to get off to a fresh start. This chapter is mainly for them.

HIGH-LEVEL APPROACH

Sensible organisations should specify their policy on detection (and investigation: see page 793 et seq) while recognising eight points:

1. It is overwhelmingly in an organisation's interest to be the first to know.
2. Villains seldom suffer from contrition but rather have to be winkled out like snails from their shells.
3. Dishonesty is contagious.
4. Detection should not be left to chance but should be a routine, specified process as part of adequate procedures.
5. It is in the interests of all honest people and organisations that fraud is prevented and hard-won profits preserved.
6. There is little as debilitating as unfounded suspicions against an honest person or organisation.
7. Testing provides assurance that controls are effective.
8. Detection programmes are supported by honest people but deter and disrupt skulduggers.

If the organisation plans to use CPA techniques, of the type described later, its data protection registration must disclose what information will be analysed. It must also ensure that testing is proportionate and handled, retained and disposed of securely.

Organisations should also make it clear in staff handbooks, on application and other paper and electronic forms that any information provided may be used to obtain legal advice for crime- prevention purposes.[9]

RESOURCES

The directors should nominate the departments or job functions responsible for fraud detection, setting out their authority, including powers to request data, both internally and from third parties, and the tools and techniques that are sanctioned. In larger organisations the directors may empower Internal Audit, Corporate Security, Compliance and Legal, but one senior person should be placed in overall command and *held accountable for fraud detection.*

---

9   Although it is unlikely that routine CPA and other tests would be regarded as privileged.

Who is Responsible?

Something like 65 per cent of senior managers believe their Internal Audit Departments are responsible for fraud detection, yet only 20 per cent are given the authority to do so. It is no wonder, therefore, that most cases are detected by accident and then ineffectively investigated.

TIMING AND SCOPE

Testing to detect fraud may be carried out in the following circumstances (in addition to those discussed earlier):

- To add depth to a risk evaluation (see Chapters 14–17), possibly updated once a year or every other year;
- When misbehaviour is suspected;
- To validate contexts and processes in which unusual decisions have been made, received or minor breaches suspected;
- To monitor changes to organisations and processes;
- On a random basis.

Finally, and this is *most strongly recommended*, a full health check should be carried out before *any* self-disclosure of *any* suspected offence is made to *any* regulatory agency, so that the potential consequences are fully understood and then managed effectively.

Principles of Detection

BASIC SYMPTOMS

Fraud is deviant behaviour and, even when concealed, usually results in symptoms that are outside the norm; these are referred to in this book as 'outliers' or 'deviations' and in the corruption area generically[10] include:

- Perverted incoming, internal, outgoing and competitive decisions;
- Windfall profits or exceptional losses incurred or surprisingly avoided;
- Bribe-funding, payment and concealment;
- Internal conversion of unrecorded incoming funds;
- External conversion of fraud proceeds and slush funds;
- Behavioural and conversion patterns, such as displays of excessive wealth.[11]

---

10   These are high-level outliers. Context-specific outliers are discussed later.

11   Including fancy feet.

Many outliers appear in accounting and other records while others are entirely off-book and may only be apparent from a person's behaviour, lifestyle, attitude or other things in the real world. Thus, while accounting analysis and conventional audits are important they should be supplemented by other techniques some of which, as discussed later, may seem just a little unsophisticated ...

... Such As Fancy Feet

Experienced fraud investigators will confirm that most male fraudsters and bribers have a fetish with their feet. Their shoes and socks (not to mention manicured toenails) are disproportionately spiffy. Detection rule one is: 'Never trust a man with spiffy feet'. There is a similar guide to female skulduggers, which it would be imprudent to mention here.[12]

Fraud detection is not about elegance, sophistication or even glory, such as winning the annual village gardening competition for the biggest marrow, but is entirely concerned with getting results, including confirmation that controls are functioning correctly.

THE DETECTION MINDSET

The aspiring fraud detector should observe a few simple rules:[13]

- Every organisation of over 50 people is currently the victim of fraud and corruption: it is simply a question of scale.
- Systems seldom work as intended.
- Virtually every control can be overcome by collusion.
- Every small act of collusion can be the start of the slippery slope to gross fraud and corruption.
- Major fraud is easier to conceal within large accounts and large organisations; this is why it is critical to drill down into the finest detail.
- Sometimes crooks do the most stupid things. But at the time what they did seemed sensible to them. Thus to detect fraud it is essential to wind the clock back and view things from the villain's position.

Detectors should also:

- Work on the basis that in fraud detection there is no such thing as a coincidence: everything happens for a reason unless proven otherwise: the presumption should be that everything is deliberate;
- Adopt a mindset that fraud can – and will – be detected or conclusively eliminated;

---

12   One is that they are fat and ugly and often suffer from BO.

13   Based on years of making mistakes!

- Not expect fast or easy results: fraud detection is hard work and not for people who insist on 'one pagers';
- Keep an open mind *(but not too open, otherwise brains will fall out)*;
- Pay attention to the finest detail and get (and validate) an explanation for every outlier;
- Never overlook the obvious or seek the most complex explanation. *If it looks like a duck, walks like a duck, waggles its ass like a duck, it is most likely a duck (or a Lib Dem)*;
- Omissions and errors can be as important as false entries.

Another really important rule is that detectors should not arouse senior managers from their slumbers with supposedly brilliant results unless the facts are established with reasonable certainty and independently verified. In other words they should not run ahead of the results. Failure to observe this rule results in TROUBLE, places honest people and organisations under suspicion and discredits existing and future fraud-detection projects.

An Eggsellent Example

Working for the Customs Department in a developing country, the authors discovered that its tariff imposed an ad valorem duty of 20 per cent on eggs imported for eating, while those for hatching were duty-free. It does not take a genius to see the potential for mis-description.

Analysis of import entries showed very few consignments of eating eggs but millions for hatching. In fact, calculations showed that if 50 per cent of the eggs had hatched the country would be overrun by chickens, with no space for humans, golf courses or even lap-dancing clubs. The major egg suppliers were in Georgia in the USA, where premises were raided simultaneously with those of the local importers.

Within minutes of gaining access to the exporters' records it became clear that official figures were hopelessly wrong. Urgent phone calls made to the Customs head office revealed that temporary clerks, who were paid $1 for every five import entries keyed in, had changed a few parameters (to avoid a duplication test) so that a single document would be processed up to 20 times. There was thus nothing eggceptional about the volume of imports.

Another important rule is to avoid what is known as the 'false attribution error'. This means that when a suspicion unfolds, everything supporting it is accepted, while anything contrary is dismissed. Most people incline and reinforce in this way: thereby explaining why some support Chelsea Football Club. **Rather than dismiss any findings that do not fit an existing outlier, they should be treated like gold dust because when they are explained, they will either expose greater and more horrible things or clear the air.**

TYPES OF DETECTION TESTS

There are two sorts of tests. The first is to trawl among the thousands of contexts, relationships, decisions and possibly millions of transactions in which symptoms are concealed to identify outliers that justify further enquiry. Trawling is an initial filter and includes CPA and forensic examination of documents.

The second category is specific or targeted, either because suspicions have emerged from a trawl or because they match an established profile or 'unalterable red flag'.[14] A further division occurs between tests which are conducted openly (such as interviews); in confidence (such as CPA); or covertly, such as undercover, and pretext investigations. For most detection projects, CPA is recommended at an early stage because it provides a high-level overview and focus for interviews and other tests.

Top Management Support

Trying to get time with a top management team to discuss bribery, controls or compliance is difficult. If anyone is lucky enough to get them together in one room, even the most senior and distinguished executives may take comfort in numbers, abandon common sense and sometimes just roll around taking the piss Admittedly there are exceptions, but discussing controls with some management teams is akin to showing a pornographic video to warn of the dangers of tantric sex. It is much easier for listeners to cope with things they do not want to hear by being juvenile. **Unwillingness to face reality is a strong outlier of management incompetence.**

A possible preliminary to an enterprise-wide CPA is first to canvass all directing minds,[15] on their views, attitudes and the contexts in which they consider incoming, internal, outgoing and competitive skulduggery most likely, red flags that concern them, and what they expect from controls. The advantage of a questionnaire is that it pins down responsibility and exposes deeply held attitudes, thereby revealing the true tone from the top. A well-designed questionnaire is very personal and gets managers thinking; and hopefully, if it all goes to plan, confirms their commitment. Thus sensibly completed questionnaires, eventually filed in the Adequate Procedures Dossier, protect good managers. Pillocks hate them.

A typical British reaction to the idea of bothering managers with questionnaires was given by a Risk and Compliance Manager, who said:

> The problem with our directors is that they refuse to read anything that is longer than a one pager and even that may be too much for some. They won't find the time, don't have the attention span or possibly the intellectual bandwidth and at their level they refuse get involved in detail but still won't delegate. Also, you always need to give them a bit of a story or take them on a journey that excites their imagination and a questionnaire will not do that. If you tell them they will go to jail for 20 years there may be a flicker of interest, but most won't believe it.

---

14   See Chapter 13 page 327 for the reality of alterable red flags: which are mainly useless.

15   Who in the context of the Bribery Act are VIPs.

Maybe the Risk Manager was having a bad hair day, simply didn't like the idea and wanted to trash his bosses: we will never know. The alternative and more correct view is that if top managers cannot be bothered, the organisation has little hope. Simply identifying such an appalling tone from the top is a great audit finding, although maybe one that is too career-threatening for most minions to mention!

Revealing Attitude

A director who was very anti-audit and unrelentingly snide was late in submitting his questionnaire (on cartels and the Enterprise Act) and when it did emerge, it was packed with flippant and offensive answers, thereby revealing his true feelings and lack of commitment. The Head of the Audit Committee and Chief Internal Auditor pointed out the error of his ways, line for line, and the significance of flippancy on his personal liabilities. No one would say he was hit by a miraculous flash of divine light but at least a glimmer of hope emerged.

There are three significant principles involved here for the effective fraud detector:

1. Never overplay your hand or exaggerate the risks, but base all arguments on solid facts.
2. If at first you don't succeed in getting top management's support, it's your fault for using the wrong persuasive levers: try a bigger hammer.
3. If you force a person's ass hard enough against the hot pipes (no matter how senior or important he believes himself to be), so that he realises he is personally accountable, sooner or later he will pay attention unless he is a Lib Dem or in HR.

So backgrounded against these three scholarly jewels – of the nature never mentioned by the big accounting and legal firms – consideration should be given to a questionnaire addressed to directing minds and to senior managers in companies targeted for acquisition and in the other circumstances mentioned earlier.

Commitments in Writing

Well-established psychological research shows that when people make their positions and plans public, especially in writing, they are much more likely to follow them through.

The big uncertainty is what to include in the questionnaire, and how to deliver and evaluate it. Should it be:

- A vanilla flavour with simple questions or one that is psychologically probing and includes subtle questions akin to 'When did you stop beating your wife?', or 'Do you still pick your nose?'
- Framed as part of the training programme for directing minds?
- Printed on paper or circulated electronically as a pdf interactive form?[16]

It would not be sensible to go into more detail here and besides that, questionnaires should be tailored for the organisation concerned.[17]

Finally, if a questionnaire is used, it should provide a list of red flags and ask: Have you noticed any of these?

Although the irrelevance of most red flags is a topic that has been beaten to death throughout this book, they warm the cockles of regulators' hearts because a company's failing to react to any one – no matter how silly it is – can be used to demonstrate inadequate procedures. **Getting the red jobbies out in the open is a good thing. They can then be tested during a CPA and either confirmed (usually 0.01 per cent) or shown to be rubbish (usually 99.99 per cent).**

Amnesty and Special Hot Line

Another way to kick off a detection programme and to get off to a fresh start under the Bribery Act is to offer financial rewards for information and an amnesty for all previous skulduggery.

Is It Unbritish?

When the Law Commissioners and politicians were not fretting or more likely salivating about lap-dancing clubs, they addressed both issues and didn't like them. Both were considered 'unBritish', whatever that means. Organisations should decide for themselves.

Experience shows that amnesties reveal very little because skulduggers don't like surrendering without a fight. The main benefit is that amnesties disrupt collusive groups by getting their members to worry that someone else will be first through the door, to claim immunity while pointing fingers at them. Amnesties are both a deterrent and a disrupter.

Offering rewards for information, 'unBritish' though it may be, also disrupts conspiracies and uncovers skulduggery. In the current climate with the Dodd–Frank Act (see page 215) and the SFO Confidential line, any company that fails to offer equivalent

---

16   Further information is available on this from www.info@cobasco.com.

17   However, if anyone gets so far as to read these words of wisdom and is interested in the possibilities, they are invited to contact info@cobasco.com.

incentives is asking for trouble and, rather than being the 'first to know', will be at the end of line. This is not a good thing.

Two important problems with whistle-blowing and rewards are worth repeating here. The first is that not all countries permit them. The second is that if rewards are offered with the intention[18] of inducing a person to breach his obligations of good faith[19] – resulting in improper performance – there could be a violation of the Bribery Act; now wouldn't that be a sad irony?

SFO Confidential May Mean Trouble

It will be very interesting to see how the SFO gets on with its CONFIDENTIAL hot line because it could be interpreted as having the intention to induce breaches of employment contracts amounting to improper performance. Will the SFO prosecute itself or seek a civil disposal? Will it, like HM Revenue and Customs (which apparently paid individuals in offshore havens to disclose confidential information on UK skulduggers), absolve itself on the grounds that everything that results in more tax is okay? Or will it prosecute, as in the case of News International? It may not be nice to mention it, but is there just a tad of 'Animal Farm' déjà vu in all of this?

So what, earnest reader, is the recommended bottom line? It is to offer amnesties and rewards if for no other reason than that it confirms a noble intention and a commitment to maintain adequate procedures. This should play out well before a jury of 12 ordinary folk. For companies unprepared to take such a bold step, an intermediate gambit would be to write to regulators inviting their views. The response, even if there is not one, may be a valuable silver bullet for the Adequate Procedures Dossier (see page 723).

---

18   Deliberately and knowingly (see the House of Lords Case May 2007: De Winter).

19   Such as a contract of employment.

CHAPTER **19** *Critical Point Auditing*

The Basis of the Method

Critical Point Auditing (CPA)[1] is a low-profile technique which *trawls* for the symptoms of fraud, in thousands or millions of – mainly electronic – transactions. It either identifies specific outliers for further investigation, others requiring control improvement, or those (most of them) that demonstrate that controls are functioning as intended.

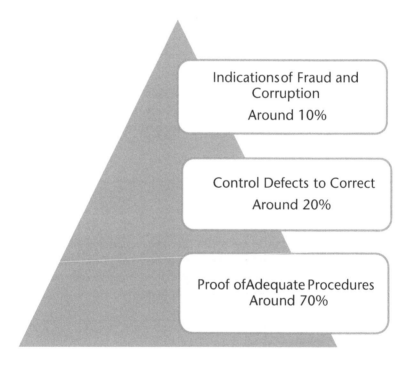

Figure 19.1 Output from a Typical Critical Point Audit

The term 'CPA', as well as the underlying automated methodology, was originated by the authors and Terry Barton, an IT specialist, in 1974,[2] while working for Esso Petroleum Company Limited. Initial tests were run on the company's IBM mainframe, linking

---

1   Which is a posh name for data-mining.

2   If anyone knows of an earlier programme the author would be pleased to refer to it in updated editions of this book.

conventional financial records to marketing and statistical reports, and were successful in uncovering a number of serious, but previously unknown, defalcations.

Some Basic Tests

The first tests were based on bringing together records from disparate systems. For example, matching independent service stations to which Esso had made interest-free loans (recorded in Capital Accounts) to buy automatic car washes with their purchases of washing chemicals and consumables (recorded in Sales). A number of service stations which had accepted funding of £50,000 plus were found never to have bought chemicals. They had kept the cash or bought competitive products.

Also, matching Esso's sales of petrol and diesel to a station's resales on agency credit cards revealed massive discrepancies. One site recorded resales of 400,000 more gallons of diesel on credit than it had bought from Esso. Enquires resulted in the arrest of 19 people for credit card fraud and bribery.

Over the following 38 years, tests have been refined, migrated to standalone platforms and personal computers and now employ neural networks and continuous monitoring. Many large accounting firms have jumped on the bandwagon, but not all have got the message.

Simple But Silly

One accounting firm that claims to be a CPA specialist, recommended that organisations should find out the telephone numbers of call boxes installed in HM Prisons and run these against their vendor master file, the idea being that the test would identify crooked or fictitious vendors – which it has unsurprisingly failed to do.

The CPA tests discussed in this chapter are mainly rules- (or profile) based. Other options derived from complex algorithms or artificial intelligence are also possible and may be used to predict outliers in real time before transactions are concluded. Successful examples include Artificial Intelligence (AI) and algorithmic tests on credit card transactions, telephone calls and money-laundering loan and mortgage applications. All predictive testing requires a large population of genuine and fraudulent transactions. This is rarely the case for bribery and fraud where there are relatively few fraudulent items, meaning that tests have to be primarily reactive and rules-based.

The main problems with CPA, data-mining and similar methodologies are that they:

- Can be time-consuming and expensive;
- Tend to focus more on elegant technological aspects than the utility of the tests;
- Generate false positives, which raise unjustified suspicions.[3]

And even the most penetrating tests seldom prove fraud: they simply expose outliers that have to be resolved through interviews and validation in the real world.

Finally, in the event of regulatory interest, test results may be used against the company to argue that controls were inadequate. For that reason it is better that CPAs are under the privileged umbrella of external legal advisers and that every outlier is resolved and documented.[4]

The Suggested Approach

The approach suggested in this chapter – essentially for an enterprise-wide health check – is based on hundreds of assignments conducted during the past 38 years all over the world, in different sectors and on unique platforms. Tests have identified losses estimated at over £300,000,000, resulting in substantial recoveries and scores of successful civil and criminal actions. Other assignments found nothing wrong, thereby confirming that the organisations' controls were effective. A few, which have fallen into the middle ground, have highlighted previously unidentified operational and control weaknesses that were rectified. Few CPAs could be regarded as failures.

This chapter is not intended to be a technical user's guide to CPA platforms – such as IDEA or ACL – but rather to set out practical techniques and problems involved in fraud detection. Neither is it going to disclose *all* of the 1,000+ proprietary tests that have made the authors a legend in their own snoozetime.

Most of the tests and cases discussed in this chapter are about fraud and bribe receipt (incoming corruption), although there are some on bribe payment. There are four reasons for this bias:

1. Incoming corruption results in the biggest losses,[5] although this fact has been largely ignored by officialdom, mainly because it does not directly result in lots of nice penalties under Section 7.
2. If the regulators are so smart and so confident that they will expose outgoing bribery if it is not self-disclosed, they can develop their own tests. In doing this they might also try and detect incoming and competitive bribery, nail a few politicians, academics, researchers, 'dodgy dossier' writers and civil servants and level the playing field for UK companies trading abroad.
3. There is no desire to tell bribe-paying skulduggers how to avoid detection.
4. Finally, since every act of bribery involves equal but opposite skulduggery, detection of incoming offences is a neat way of dropping bribe payers in trouble with Section 7

---

3   The number of spurious Suspicious Activity Reports (SARS) is the result of false positives.

4   If validation is completed properly CPA results are always silver bullets for the Adequate Procedures Dossier.

5   Although less severe regulatory interest.

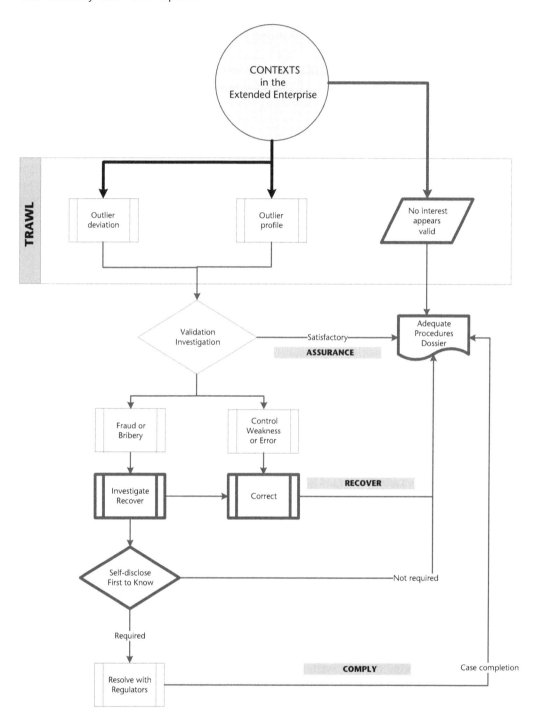

Figure 19.2 Resolution of Outliers

liabilities. This should gain a few Brownie points for the detecting organisation with the Serious Fraud Office (SFO) without itself incurring corporate liability.

The Right and Wrong Approach to CPA

Some, possibly quite a lot of, organisations have bought ACL or IDEA, read the manuals, skipped through the tutorials, downloaded a bit of data, run a few meaningless tests – like checking telephone calls to prisons (see page 478) – found nothing or overreacted to false positives and ended up disappointed, in trouble or more usually both. **CPA *is not for dabblers***. It cannot be done on the cheap or by people who have no real understanding of fraud. For dabblers, Homer Simpson's rule applies: 'Trying hard is the first step to failure'.

It is possible to test specific processes and contexts, but as an opening salvo following the arrival of the Bribery Act, an enterprise-wide project is recommended, if for no other reason than to prove that procedures are adequate.

An Estimate of Costs

A full CPA 'health check' for a UK-based company with 10,000 plus employees, 20,000 vendors, 5,000 customers, a couple of overseas branches and a clutch of intermediaries is likely to take in the order of 200+ man days[6] to complete. If external consultants are retained, fees in the order of £200,000 to £400,000, plus expenses, VAT and one or more fully funded trips to the Pink Pussycat Lap Dancing Club are the norm.

The Reaction

When managers are given this sort of estimate, the not uncommon reaction embraces two four letter words. The first is 'Holy' and the second starts with 'S' and ends with 'T'. And a comment along the lines of 'but we don't have any problems in this company, so the cost would not be justified'.

The authors' usual response (depending on the phase of the Moon) is:

'OK, if you're so sure, we will complete the assignment for nothing and let you have the final report free of charge, providing you allow us to carry out all of the testing we believe necessary. In addition, if we do not find serious fraud, bribery or significant losses, we will donate £10,000 to any charity of your choice – except the Lib Dems. But if we prove skulduggery, our fee will be 50 per cent of the proven losses. The recovery risk is yours'.

---

6   If it's any consolation, the hours actually worked on a CPA are usually at least double those charged because people would not believe testing takes so long. It always seems much easier to those who do not have to do the job.

> 'But', says the manager, 'that is a rip off: 50 per cent?'
>
> 'How come. If you have no problems, you have nothing to lose and everything to gain'.
>
> 'Well, you might be lucky enough to find something'.[7]

Dialogue of this sort is revealing: suggesting that deep down managers do not want to hear about fraud. **If organisations take nothing else from this chapter it is to recognise NOT to get involved in detection without top management support** and to avoid fast and cheap CPAs because they nearly always result in scaremongering with no evidential support and trouble.

Measuring Success

In the fraud context, a CPA's success is usually measured from tangible financial recoveries and this is fair enough, providing the victim is prepared to pursue losses, which is not always the case. When bold decisions are taken, recoveries from CPA far exceed its costs and there are massive control and compliance benefits. Those who fret about the costs of a CPA should appreciate that it is a silver bullet for the Adequate Procedures Dossier, much like an insurance premium only much better.

It may be argued as self-serving to say so, but the greater the expenditure on a CPA, and the more detailed the probing, the better it is for the Adequate Procedures Dossier. But the main justification is that it increases profits and improves and demonstrates effective control.

Well Worth the Effort and Spiffing

A three-week CPA focused on advertising, promotion, marketing and logistics for a medium-sized American food company uncovered $24 million in false marketing support and 'billback' claims that were rationalised by the Sales Manager with what became a career-terminating phrase: 'We suspected that our salesmen, distributors and retailers were abusing the system but my view was that the money ended up somewhere in the channel in a way that must help sales'. His Managing Director did not feel the same way, especially when he found that substantial sums were paid to retail store managers personally to put his company's products in the most prominent display positions and in advertisements on local TV.[8] None of which actually happened.

Recoveries were made and future claims reduced with no discernible impact on sales. The Managing Director reckoned that the CPA added a $100 million to the company's valuation on listing 18 months later.

---

7   TOO TRUE!

8   Known as 'spiffing' (see page 321), which is an offence under the Bribery Act.

The benefits of CPA in the corruption context are much greater than for fraud because, in addition to potential recoveries, controls are tested and validated, decisions confirmed, regulatory breaches prevented and adequate procedures demonstrated. Moreover, CPA provides assurance to directing minds that their personal wellbeing is reasonably protected against breaches of the Bribery Act and other legislation.

The CPA Team

INTERNAL RESOURCES

CPAs should be authorised by the directors and should be run as a team effort involving at least three reasonably warm and enthusiastic hominids:

1. Someone who has a deep practical knowledge of fraud and corruption[9] AND is an expert interviewer and interrogator.
2. An Information Technology (IT) expert who is a regular user of IDEA or ACL.
3. A third person (usually an internal auditor or compliance specialist) who has a good inside knowledge of the organisation concerned.

Ideally, all three should be proficient in the language used in the contexts being tested.[10]

SELECTING CONSULTANTS

Some organisations turn to professional firms – consultants, accountants, software providers and Tarot card readers – to run 'data-mining' projects on their behalf and this is not to be discouraged. First it allows the authors and others like them to keep off state handouts, so that the majority of the UK populace can continue doing so; secondly it is about the only aspect of fraud that lawyers have not hijacked.

The legal profession seems to divide over the benefits of CPA. Some think it is a good idea and support detection initiatives by providing legal advice and the protection of privilege. They are also ready, willing and able to litigate against those responsible for outliers and to give sound advice on compliance. The second group is anti and feels CPA just stirs up trouble. Either way, the decision whether or not to use CPA to provide assurance that controls are effective is for the board to make, not legal advisers.

If an organisation does not have the internal skills to run its *first* CPA effectively it should either forget the idea or turn to a third party for assistance. Selecting the most competent consultants is not easy and there are some around who claim to have the skills and experience they do not possess.[11]

---

9   And ideally owns a dog called Kenneth.

10   For example, there is no point in running a project in Russia in a company whose accounts are in Russian if the team members cannot speak the language.

11   Retaining the organisation's external auditors is not a good idea as they may have conflicting interests not to undermine their audit work.

Thus organisations are advised to:

- Determine their CPA objectives and agree what contexts and processes should be included;
- Prepare a Kepner-Tregoe matrix of needs and wants expected of the consultants;
- Invite – in total confidence – proposals from four or five firms,[12] requiring them to set out their CPA qualifications, experience, track records, a project plan and an estimated budget;
- Ask two or three shortlisted firms to make a 30–60 minute presentation,[13] explaining their approach in detail;
- Pick the best qualified.

Consideration should be given to having consultants retained by and reporting to the organisation's external law firm,[14] rather than directly. Either way the terms of engagement should include a confidentiality agreement and an estimated timetable and budget. Organisations are also advised to nominate one or two of their own employees to work on the project for three reasons. First, it keeps costs down. Second, it makes data collection much easier because insiders should know where to look. Third, and most important, participation in an assignment is excellent training for the employees concerned, making it possible for them to carry out future work unaided.

Types of Systems and Data

SOME REALITIES ABOUT ENTERPRISE RESOURCE PLANNING DATA AND TABLES

CPA tests are usually based on electronic data generated internally and held in database management systems (DBMS) accessed via Enterprise Resource Planning (ERP) modules such as SAP, ORACLE or SAGE. However, when CPA is limited to just ERP data,[15] opportunities for even more effective testing are missed. CPA should extend conventional testing by linking:

- Feeder, satellite, associated and legacy systems (for example, front-end purchasing, dealing, process control and logistics);
- Public databases (credit records, electoral rolls, etc., banned organisations or Financial Action Task Force (FATF) lists);
- Telephone call logs;
- Internet and email logs;
- Manual systems (reception records, car parking logs, goods outward passes, etc.).

These should always be considered for inclusion in a CPA.

---

12 But NOT the external auditors, who may have a conflict of interest.

13 To the decision-makers and in-house or external litigation counsel.

14 To (hopefully) maintain legal professional privilege, which the EU does not afford to in-house counsel.

15 Which is typically the case.

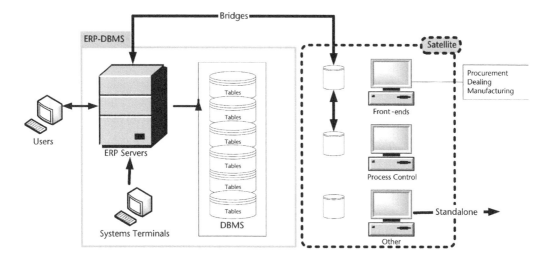

Figure 19.3 ERP, Supporting and Legacy and Satellite Systems

Some of the most successful CPA projects have resulted from merging data from satellite systems, validating reconciliations at gateways between them, concentrating on exceptional transactions, apparent errors or adjustments, misuse of transaction codes, functions and commands.

Not Just a Question of Agents' Commissions

A database of trading counterparties (held on a front-end dealing system) was matched to lists of ERP vendors, intermediaries and customers. This revealed that the owner of one intermediary had never failed to make a profit on personal derivative transactions handled through the principal's trading desk. The suspicion was that these were phantom profits used by the intermediary to bribe end parties in its core business. When questions were asked it cancelled its relationships and refused to cooperate. This was a good result for the Adequate Procedures Dossier.

A few additional points should be made about ERP and DBMS systems and what follows is through the eyes of an amateur cynic[16] rather than an IT guru. The first point is that there is no such thing as a 'standard ERP or DBMS installation'. Each one has variable features, different combinations of modules installed and varying links to legacy and satellite data. Even the language used in what appear to be exactly similar installations is different.

---

16   With lots of practical experience.

Feelings of Superiority

Time after time, people whose data has been requested have picked upon an irrelevant technical point (such as 'it is not a table, but an object: Dummy') to avoid answering a question or to discredit a valid and important point. Fraud detectors should not be fazed by such tactics because they are often no more than a ruse to stop data being examined.

The next point to note is that data is physically held in one or more DBMS, linked together into logical schemas by all sorts of clever stuff, like pointers, indexes, portals, sectors and attributes, so that distinct data subsets (referred to later as 'tables') can be produced for different applications.

Most tables can be viewed as the modern-day equivalent of master files (containing standing data on 'objects',[17] such as vendors, customers or employees), while others are lists of transactions.

Data elements in a DBMS and the way in which they included, defined, linked to satellite and legacy systems and then selected for inclusion in tables, as well as the precise sequence in which they are processed, determines what outliers are created.

Payment Processing

Fields for a third party's Bank Sorting Code, its International Bank Account Number (IBAN) and Society for Worldwide Interbank Financial Telecommunication (SWIFT) identifiers may be in the DBMS but omitted from what is in effect a vendor master file (or 'table').

Vendors' bank account details may be recorded in a procurement front end, in the DBMS itself, linked to various tables, possibly duplicated, sometimes under different names. They may also be included in the bank's proprietary payments system.

Thus the big questions on payment processes are usually:

- Precisely what data element is used to produce final payment instructions?
- What happens if these are incomplete or missing?
- Can critical payment parameters or pointers to them be changed (and quickly changed back after a fraudulent payment has been executed) without leaving a full historical record in the associated table?
- Is the General Ledger updated before or after a payment is finally released?

---

17   Which again is a term not consistently used.

Elements are selected, by the installers or maintainers of a DBMS – ERP, for inclusion in a particular table, but not always connected to each other even through links exist in the DBMS.

Some IT gurus may argue that most if not all of the above are moot points and that their stuff is an all-singing, all-dancing, fully integrated work of pure genius. Experience shows that this is seldom the case and that systems are often held together by Band Aid.

Problems at Systems Gateways

A European electronics manufacturer[18] used a very advanced warehouse robotics and control system for all of its inventory. Orders were transferred in from an associated ERP system,[19] inventory located, picked and despatched. Despatch data was held in storage and at the end of each day transferred to the ERP for invoicing, inventory updating and financial reporting. All seemed great, but the warehouse was suffering significant stock losses. French Private Investigators were called in to keep observation but found nothing.[20]

Then a CPA was commissioned, which established that:

- The delivery notes for customers in collusion with the warehouse manager would be deleted before being transferred to the ERP.[21]
- The customers would not be invoiced and as a result inventory records not adjusted, resulting in stock losses.

As if this scam was not bad enough, a junior operator discovered that the ERP system was configured so that it could only process despatch notes with less than 60 separate product lines. Anything listed on lines 61 upwards would be rejected by the ERP and not invoiced.

The operator colluded with customers (and actually set up his own firm in his father-in-law's name as a customer) to place orders for 60 very low-priced products and another 10 or 20 lines for really expensive stuff. These were despatched but not invoiced and the orders subsequently cancelled. The frequency of cancelled orders was the clue that set the ball rolling.

The bottom line is that few systems operate as planned. There are always exceptions, gateways and glitches through which skulduggery slips which a CPA can uniquely identify.

---

18 In fact, the authors dealt with a very similar case a few years earlier in, of all places, Slough. This came to light because the company's products were flooding local boot sales at ridiculously low prices.

19 Which, it turns out, had not been properly installed.

20 The lesson here is: don't employ French Investigators or English lovers.

21 There was also some clever hanky-panky on adjusting control totals.

DOWNLOADING CRITICAL POINT AUDIT DATA FROM TABLES

When data is provided for CPA it is typically downloaded in separate files based on table data dictionaries rather than by fully analysing the DBMS and selecting precisely what is required and how data can be linked.

Problems with Links

In a CPA review of purchasing, data was downloaded into separate table-based files for internal requisitions, purchase orders, goods received, purchase invoices and payments. Because linking fields were not consistently shown, joining the separate files was a nightmare.

There are a number of problems with downloading CPA data based on tables:

- The data may not be linked;
- A single field in the DBMS may be given different names in table dictionaries: possibly in different formats *(for example, as a character field rather than a date)*;
- Even within a single table, related field formats may be mixed or missing. *For example, some date fields may be 'characters', others 'numeric', others 'date' or 'date and time'. Date formats may be YYYYMMDD or DDMMYYYY. Getting these into a consistent format necessary for a CPA can be difficult and time-consuming (see page 496)*;
- The DBMS *(as well as tables extracted from it)* may contain spare, 'null', 'attribute' and 'global attribute' fields that are not fully defined. They may, however, be critical pointers to other data, operational or transaction codes (see page 513) and should never be overlooked.
- Tables rarely contain a historical record of changes to the data concerned and the identity of the operators making them. All that is typically available is the 'last changed by date' and 'last changed by' data.[22]

In addition to the above, CPA invariably shows that fields that should contain data are blank and that those that should only accept positive numbers are full of negatives (such as negative payments: see page 516).

Missing Data

It is illegal for companies in one Gulf State to trade without being registered with a variety of government agencies. However, analysis of a client's database revealed more than 1,000 unregistered vendors.

---

[22]   This makes it imperative that systems logs or 'mirror files' are available which should show details of every amendment made to the DBMS and by whom.

The above finding was made before the Bribery Act 2010 came into force and, in any case, the client would not have been a relevant commercial organisation. But can you imagine how regulators would view equivalent omissions when assessing adequate procedures?

SECURITY AND SYSTEMS JOURNALS

Every system has super-users who are akin to the mother-in-law insofar as they can do almost whatever they want. Super-users can add, amend or delete data and in some installations there are too many of them and not all are security-aware:

The Danger of Unattended Terminals

A CPA of systems activity logs in an Islamic organisation revealed disproportionate frequencies of alterations to payment parameters between 12.00 and 12.45 when authorised super-users left their terminals connected while attending prayers. Matching data on the flexitime system to computer logs also disclosed activity by super-users when they were not even in the building.

The way security of an ERP is configured, as well as the scope of activity logs maintained, affects the way accountability for outliers can be established.

Systems Logs

A leading utility company paid rent ('wayleaves' or 'easements') for installing its equipment on land owned by thousands of individuals and companies throughout the UK. Rents were negotiated depending on the area of land required for the installation and whether payment was to be quarterly, six monthly or annually, or made by cheque or bank transfer.

When a property containing installed equipment was sold, the owner's name was updated by a dedicated – but fairly junior and largely unsupervised – super-user. He was also responsible for amending all parameters and releasing payments. The master file only retained details of an account's current status and not a history of changes made.

A CPA analysis of amendment frequency in the systems journal showed repeated access to some accounts, clustering over weekends and late at night, including:

- Changes to an account holder's name (repeatedly to what turned out to be friends of the database administrator);

- Altering a three-month payment to an annual amount (ultimately resulting, for example, in a payment being made for say £4,000 rather than the agreed quarterly amount of £1,000).

Large cheques were generated in the names of the administrator's friends and paid away. Immediately afterwards the accounts were reinstated.

The administrator admitted to fraud and implicated a number of people (mainly fellow boozers at the local public house) who had shared the proceeds with him. He and two of his friends were imprisoned and six others fined.

The bottom line lesson from cases such as the above is for detectors to recognise the importance of systems logs and 'mirror' files for pinning down accountability for skulduggery. If they are not maintained (which should be considered as an outlier) the question should be asked: 'why?'

KEYING MANUAL DATA

Important test data can be compiled[23] from keying in data from specialist anti-corruption sources such as the Trace International Compendium, extracts from the excellent blog by the 'FCPA Professor', and Tax Payers Against Fraud (TAF).

A Critical Test Overlooked

The Trace Compendium contains details (including court filings) of virtually all Securities and Exchange Commission (SEC) and Department of Justice (DOJ) enforcement actions and the names of those involved, the nature of the business and specific contracts.

But how many organisations check these names against their supplier and customer databases to make sure that they are not involved? And if the regulators really want to stamp out corruption, why don't they publish comprehensive lists for checking?

Common sense suggests that any organisation that does not make such checks could have trouble proving its procedures were adequate.

---

23   This means entering the data manually into Excel and reading it into IDEA or ACL for matching.

THIRD-PARTY DATA

CPA testing is rarely extended or validated by obtaining data in *electronic form* from third parties such as suppliers, intermediaries, customers and *especially, banks*. This is another opportunity missed.

Electronic Reconciliation of Third-party Data

A CPA analysis identified a number of large customer accounts where the ratio of credit notes to sales invoices was disproportionate. Some of the customers involved agreed to provide electronic files of all transactional data for the previous three years. One reconciliation (in the local currency) was as follows:

Client's Accounts $		Customer's Accounts $	
Sales	2,356,000	Purchases	2,387,432
Credit notes	689,000	Credit Notes	349,900
Receipts	1,667,000	Payments	2,0375,232

What do you make of this in the context of corruption and especially the creation of a $339,100 slush fund, remembering from Chapter 12 that a fraudster's dream is the receipt of unrecorded incoming funds and subsequent internal or external conversion.

Bank Data

Electronic payment data obtained from a company's bankers involving 1,000 transactions revealed 240 made to accounts different from those recorded internally, including over £1,000,000's worth to a vendor that had been disqualified.

There is an obvious risk in requesting data from third parties because it may prompt them into making spurious claims.[24] For this reason, such requests should be considered carefully, legally reviewed and positioned as routine audits.

IDENTIFYING DATA AMENABLE FOR TESTING

Testing should make use of all available internal and external data (and not just bits and pieces from ERP tables) by extracting elements that are relevant, including that shown in Table 19.1.

---

24   Although in the authors' experience, this has never happened.

Table 19.1   Most Critical Point Auditing Exercises Do Not Include Third-party Data

Type of Data	Type and Importance					Examples
	Internal ERP	Internal Other	Manual	Third Party	Public	
Standing	H	H	H	H	H	Vendor, Customer, Materials and other master files
Transactional	H	M	M	H	M	Sales and purchase invoices, credit notes, telephone call logs
Joined, matched and extracted data	VH	H		VH	H	See page 506 for test examples
Codes: transaction, error correction and overrides	H			H		Sales types, product and account codes
Security tables and systems control, including mirror and log files	H			H		Users and privileges
Reconciliations and control totals	H	H	H	H		Gateway reconciliation, error adjustments
Authority tables	VH	H	H	VH		Transaction approval levels

(VH= very high, H=high and M=medium importance.)

Data may be obtained from live and test systems, backup and archives. Every source should be considered.

CPA Platforms and Commands

The most successful CPAs have been based on data downloaded onto standalone *platforms* such as IDEA or ACL, supported by Excel and Active Data,[25] rather than being run on an organisation's own mainframe.

IDEA and ACL originated from the same Canadian source but have evolved separately although they are still very similar. The authors prefer IDEA because it is as least as powerful as ACL and simpler to use for non-technical fat fingers. People who regularly use ACL swear by it, so it all comes down to personal preference. But the two do not mix and it is a case of one or the other.

The advantages of specialist platforms include speed, independence, cost and flexibility. However, their main benefit is that they allow data to be imported from disparate sources, cleaned up, put in a consistent form, related and tested in depth.

---

25   See http://www.informationactive.com (accessed 13 November 2012).

Both platforms can handle unlimited amounts of data and do not alter or corrupt it during processing,[26] although they enable original data to be copied, appended, extracted, sorted and joined, establishing clear audit trails in the process. Their inbuilt integrity, including comprehensive audit trails, is very important if a case comes to court, which should be the assumed possibility in every CPA.

IDEA and ACL provide hundreds of powerful commands, functions, expressions, equations and scripts, enabling data to be manipulated almost without limit. More sophisticated solutions are likely to be beyond the abilities of infrequent users,[27] as is shown in Figure 19.4.

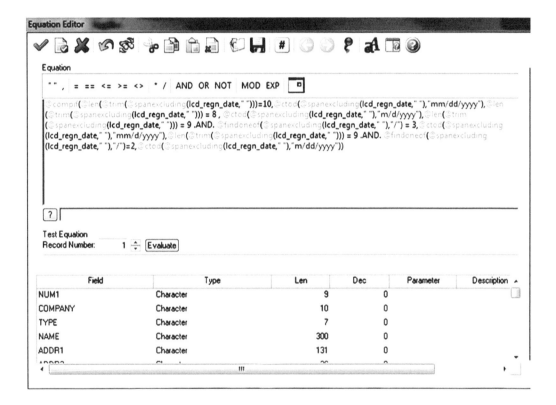

Figure 19.4 Example of an Expression in IDEA

The outcome of the equation shown in Figure 19.4 was that IDEA's 'age' function could be used to identify vendors who were repeatedly paid quicker than the applicable terms. This is a possible sign of corruption. But can you see the potential for further tests that might be even more revealing?

Organisations thinking about using CPA (as well as those who have already tried and failed) are strongly advised to send one or two employees to the IDEA or ACL training courses (basic to advanced) and not penny-pinch by hoping enough can be learned

---

26   Although they have virtually unlimited facilities to extract, merge, reformat, etc. this results in new files without altering the originals. This is much more secure than Excel, where the original data is easy to corrupt.

27   Including the authors.

from the manuals. The investment of time and money is well worthwhile. Further, the suppliers of both IDEA and ACL have technical support desks that for a modest fee will import difficult data, prepare equations and scripts,[28] and deliver files ready for testing.

Data Collection and Initial Processing

GETTING WHAT IS NEEDED

The most critical – although totally underestimated – aspect of CPA is to precisely catalogue what data elements are potentially available, on internal, satellite and external systems, in what format and for what periods. The second difficulty is to get data owners and custodians to hand it over. This is true even when the instruction comes from top management.

Problems Getting Data

Database administrators, systems people, line managers and Human Resources are sometimes more difficult to deal with – when it comes to parting with data – than the Taliban. They simply don't want to cough up.

Cut By 100,000 Transactions

The Finance Director of a leading European company – whose systems were about to undergo a CPA – was concerned about meeting his own incentive targets and instructed the IT manager to remove 100,000 low-value transactions from the sales invoice file.

The third problem is to deeply understand what the data really represents. Inexperienced detectors rush in, full of enthusiasm, give data owners a list of fields they think they need, run a few tests on incomplete data that produce nothing and give up.

UNDERSTANDING THE DATA IN SITU

It is advisable that – before a data request is finalised – time is spent observing how ERP and related systems operate on a daily basis from a user's perspective. This means sitting down with input and other operators noting how data is entered and processed, errors corrected, transactions overridden, and reports and other output produced. Screen prints

---

28   Infrequent users are strongly advised to use these services rather than waste hours, days or weeks struggling with technical complexities.

and other records should be obtained for the observed transactions. This stage is critical to a CPA's success but seldom takes place.

The Importance of Interviewing Skills

Fraud detectors should look upon information-gathering interviews and 'in situ' tests as an opportunity to identify outliers and confront suspected deception with detailed questions and, if necessary, written explanations.

In due course observed transactions should be specifically tested as part of the CPA.

FINALISING DATA REQUESTS

The approach recommended for data collection[29] is – *before indicating that downloads[30] may be required or even that a CPA* contemplated to:

- Define the scope of the intended CPA and agree it with senior managers;
- Identify *all* relevant ERP, related, satellite and independent systems[31] in the contexts to be reviewed, paying special attention to process control and other blue-collar systems that contain electronic data;
- Identify all potentially relevant data fields from DBMS data dictionaries, systems specifications, report formats, screen and report layouts and from other any sources and precisely what they mean;
- Establish what records (such as systems logs) are retained of creation, changes and deletions to standing and transaction files and how gateways are reconciled;
- Finalise a detailed specification of the data needed and the key fields that are used to link them.

Having done this it is important to:

- Put all requests in writing, precisely specifying the field and file formats required – character, numerical or date and time, and the periods concerned,[32] *and discuss the request, and resolve any problems directly, with data owners and custodians;*
- Agree a timetable for delivery of the data: IN WRITING;
- As data is received *(and it will nearly always come in bits and pieces, late, and just before a weekend or a national holiday)* read it on an independent computer, preferably *in the presence of the Taliban's representative;*

---

29   And the advice is written personally: hopefully to make it easier to understand.

30   A word that is a red rag to a bull with some data owners.

31   Including operational, test, backup and archive.

32   Try to ensure that all data relates to a common period.

- Give a receipt,[33] showing precise details of what has been delivered, including counts and control totals: annotate the receipt to show what data is outstanding.

The above points may – to the uninitiated – appear cynical and extreme, but believe them. **If unreliable or incomplete data is provided the CPA exercise will be a waste of time.**

GETTING STARTED

Some would-be fraud detectors worry too much about the CPA process. They want project plans, timetables, budgets, review meetings, seances and visits to the Pink Pussycat Lap Dancing Club to make sure they are on the right track. This is understandable but largely unachievable. **The most successful CPAs start off in near-chaos, progress via lots of free thinking[34] and innovation, and then gradually build up order.**

Another problem is that some senior managers want updating on results – sometimes on a daily basis – which is again understandable, but very dangerous. It is a near certainty that as soon as an outlier is raised as interesting, it will be proven to be insignificant or wrong. Detectors should resist giving out results until all tests have validated.

Importing and Validating Data

Assuming all of the obstacles, real and contrived, have been overcome and the data requested is received, the work begins. The essential first step is to review and understand the significance of every data element and how disparate files can be related, appended or joined, and the order in which these operations should be completed. Time spent at this stage will save a lot of trouble later on.

In more complex cases, it is usually worth making a trial importation of every file and every field (especially apparently irrelevant stuff) into the CPA platform and inspecting the results carefully. Surprises often appear:

Funny Stuff on a Trial Importation

On one trial importation, data appeared randomly in what was supposedly an unused attribute field. This was found to have come from a link to a 'services description' field somewhere else in the DBMS that was not associated with the tables in question. Further analysis showed around £10,000,000 of expenditure on:

- Agency wages
- Advertising
- Cash
- Daily Allowances

---

33   And retain a copy.

34   But like a villain.

- Demand Drafts and gift vouchers
- Donations (including one of £90,000!)
- Court fees and fines
- 'Goods received' notes[35]
- Disability and injury claims and death payments
- Customs duty.[36]

To this day it is not entirely clear[37] how this data suddenly appeared, when it was not in the purchase invoice and payments table data provided. But it did and it was very revealing.

A trial on the lines suggested should confirm the fields needed for final importation and how they can be linked. IDEA produces very valuable statistics summarising the data concerned and their start and end dates, as shown in Figure 19.5.

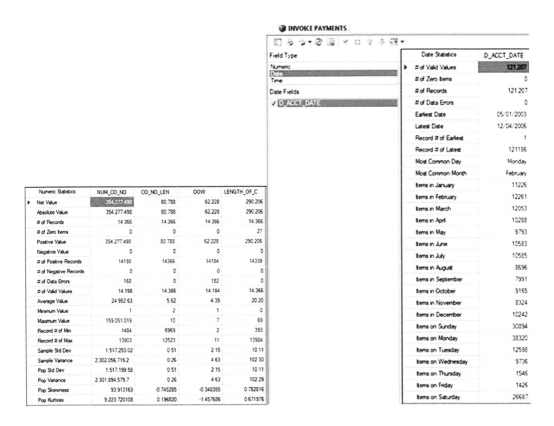

Figure 19.5 Basic Statistical Reports from IDEA

---

35   Actually turned out to be cash purchase with no invoice!

36   Including a bundle of cash payments.

37   The suspicion is that the Finance Director had a sort of private account from which dodgy payments were made. When purchase invoice and payment data were requested for the CPA, data from this account was cleansed.

Detectors are advised to keep *additional* notes of:

- Record counts and control totals (these are important to ensure that data is not lost);
- Joins, appends, extractions, summaries, etc.;
- Start and end dates of all data files (to ensure that comparisons are valid).

As a rule it is better to import any field that might be required for testing, on the basis that adding omitted data later on can be tricky.

Presentation of the Results

GENERAL CONSIDERATIONS

It may seem like putting the cart before the horse, but it is a good idea to plan before starting how CPA results will finally be presented:

- Items for further investigation: *usually around 10 per cent of total outliers*;
- Control improvement recommendations: *usually around 20 per cent of outliers*;
- Confirmation that procedures are adequate: *70 per cent of outliers*.

The factors shown in Table 19.2 should be considered.

Table 19.2　CPA Output

Factor: Consideration	Comment and Recommendation
CONFIDENTIALITY, ETC.	
A CPA report (as well as all supporting and working papers) is potential dynamite and unresolved outliers could be highlighted by regulators to argue that procedures were inadequate	All output and working papers should be protected as strictly confidential and privileged, and released on a strict 'need to know' basis
CHARTS AND SUPPORTING EVIDENCE	
Charts produced by IDEA should be transferred to Excel files	The report modules in IDEA and ACL produce reports that are difficult to read and cannot be easily checked or extended.
All supporting charts should be consistently named, showing their date, author, version number and links to IDEA reports	The naming convention generated by IDEA should be used unaltered on Excel spreadsheets
Consideration should be given to consolidating individual test results in one or more 'focus' lists, which assign personal responsibility for outliers	See below for comments on focus lists
Excel files should be recorded in a table of contents, with hyperlinks to the underlying sheets	This makes it easier for readers to search and cross-reference results

All results should be checked and legally reviewed before release	Output should be accurate and easy to follow
Complex findings should be supported by a fraud narrative and flow charts explaining precisely what is suspected	
All supporting and source documents should be assembled in one or more separate binders, cross referenced and indexed	All output should be supported
COMMENTS, OPINIONS AND RECOMMENDATIONS	
Opinions about an identifiable person or organisation must be supported within the *document concerned* with specific evidential justification	Output must be accurate and accessible See the Supreme Court case of Spiller and another (Appellants) v Joseph and others (Respondents) [2010] UKSC 53
Recommendations should be summarised on charts showing the names of the persons or organisations responsible for implementing them	Thereby pinning down accountability for actions
INDEXING AND ARCHIVING	
The entire report package should be copied in electronic format and fully indexed using Concordance	Concordance allows keyword searching of every data element in them resulting from the analysis
All working papers should be preserved (in paper and electronic form)	A copy should be retained in the Adequate Procedures Dossier
REPORT FORMAT	
The format of output required should be agreed. *Full textual reports take time to write (adding to costs) and are rarely read. However, they are important for the Adequate Procedures Dossier*	The recommended output is: • A brief overview report • PowerPoint slides of each outlier or group showing their significance and further action required supported by detailed spread sheets and IDEA files all consistently named • Investigations plan (see Chapter 34) for the most significant outliers • A separate chart of recommendations summarised by context or process

The 8-foot wide Schedule

The main output from a data-mining exercise was a 20-page schedule. Each one was 5 feet wide and contained 80 columns, all printed in 8 point Courier font. No one could read it.

MORE ON FOCUS LISTS

By following the recommended procedure, spreadsheets will be produced[38] containing individual outliers and the names of:

- Third parties with which the organisation deals;
- Employees and other associated persons;
- Authorisers, users and super-users.

Focus lists summarise names of individuals and companies from separate spreadsheets in league tables, quickly identifying priority interviews and follow-up actions.

Working Example

On individual spreadsheets an outlier may be assigned a **weight** (of 1 = little significance to 100 = very significant) in terms of incoming, outgoing and internal bribery. The extent to which each person or organisation listed fails or passes a test is **scored**, again on a range of 0–100. Scores and weights are multiplied to give a **factor** on a range of 0 = no significance to 1,000 = highly significant.

Various spreaders naming Blair and Brown result in a factor of 700 and zero for Cleggy Enterprises. Blair and Brown is also a customer. The ratio of sales to credit note test results in a factor of 600.

The resulting focus list might look like the one shown in Table 19.3.

Table 19.3   Example of a Focus List

Third Party Name	Vendor No.	Score Transferred from Individual Spreadsheets							Total All
		Procurement Tests			Sales Tests				
		Standing	Negative Trans	Other →	Credit: Sales	Allocations	Other →		
Sheet No →→→→→→→→		P4	P4		S12	S21			
Blair & Brown	2345	700			600	200			1,500
Cleggy Enterprises	4512	0							0
Boris Transport	1298				800	800			1,600

On a typical focus list possibly hundreds of entities would be factored, suggesting priority candidates for interviews and follow-up enquiries

---

38   Usually more than 100.

Similar focus lists can be compiled summarising outliers against employees such as authorisers, super-users, and entry clerks. This is again useful for prioritising interviews and investigations.

Specific Fraud and Corruption Test

GENERAL

The success of any CPA obviously depends on the relevance of the tests applied. Choosing or developing the right ones for the contexts to be examined boils down to a combination of skill, experience, imagination,[39] good luck and persistence.

Testing in the context of corruption is concerned mainly with identifying the outliers discussed in Chapters 10–13, then tracing them – through systems and other logs – to pin down personal accountability.

Stratification Defined[40]

A theory is that skulduggers may divide large corrupt transactions into the minimum number necessary (possibly in round amounts) for all to fall within their authority level. For example, a person with an authority level of £10,000 may accept a bribe for approving a transaction of £90,000 in smaller tranches.

Thus an opening test is to stratify transactions in bands, as illustrated in Table 19.4.

Table 19.4   Example of Stratification

Vendor	Percentage of Purchase Orders In Bands $			
	1–4,999 Band 1	5,000–19,999 Band 2	20,000–99,999 Band 3	100,000+ Band 4
Jones, Bones and Stuff	35	30	3	5
Blair & Brown	2	2	**96**	0
Clegg Intelligent Services	**90**	10	0	0
Banana Brothers Toiletries	5	10	15	70

---

39   Thinking like a villain.

40   Means arranging data in layers, but size, date, etc.

The CPA manual developed[41] by Cobasco Group Ltd. contains over 1,000 tests to weed out fraud and corruption, cross-referenced on a relational database held on Filemaker Pro. When a context or process is selected for examination, FileMaker automatically lists all of the relevant tests, generates a specification of the data fields required, including the recommended sequence of joins,[42] matches, summaries, formulae and equations, suggested report formats, interpretations and recommended validation methods.

For obvious reasons it would be competitively imprudent[43] to disclose all of the manual's proprietary tests, but the following paragraphs give some idea of their scope.

OVERVIEW OF TEST CATEGORIES

Tests can be categorised in two ways. The first is whether they relate to master, transactional or joined data.

Table 19.5 Files Typically Examined

Tests on	Examples	*Illustrative Symptoms of Fraud and Corruption*
Single Master File	Vendor Master	**Missing and duplicated data** *Indicates inadequate due diligence* *Possibly fictitious entities and slush fund creation*
Single Transaction File	Miscellaneous Vendors	**Volume and value with individual vendors** *Suggests inadequate due diligence* *Possibly fictitious entities and slush fund creation* *Quarterly variations*
Joins of Master to Master	Vendor to Agents	**Agents who also trade as principals** *Excessive payments to fund third-party bribes*
Joins of Master to Transaction	Vendor Master to Call Logs	**Large vendors who have never been telephoned** *Slush fund creation*
Joins of Transaction to Transaction	Sales invoices to credit notes	**Ratio of credit notes to sales** *Routing bribe payments through third parties*
Joins and matches of internal, external and third-party data	Sales invoices to electronic purchase ledger data provided by suppliers	**Fictitious credit notes** *Slush fund creation and bribe payment*

---

41 And still a work in progress.

42 Which is very important if time is not to be wasted.

43 That is 'Nuts'.

The second division is whether the test is based on:

- historical or trend analysis
- reasonableness
- proportionality

– and whether or not it conforms to fraud or bribery profile. To a degree the categories overlap and different tests may expose the same outlier. Often a primary (the opening or more direct) test is corroborated by others. The main reason for mentioning the categories at all is to provide readers with a framework for designing their own tests.

Opening tests are usually straightforward, but the art is to become totally immersed in the data and to develop specific ('iterative') tests as results evolve. The best results nearly always come from such iterative testing. This means that detectors should always carefully review results and precisely what they might mean, think like a villain, consider what additional electronic and other data is available and then design further tests accordingly.

Although there are no precise statistics of past CPA successes the authors' best guess is as follows.

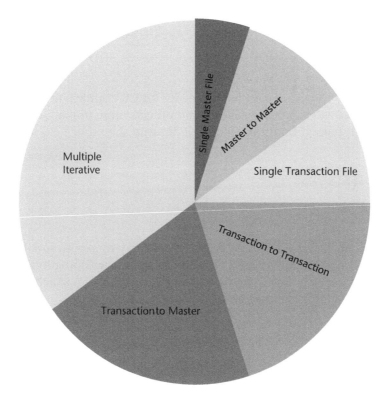

Figure 19.6 Best Guess of the Most Successful Tests

Figure 19.6 suggests that the most significant findings come from iterative tests.

The Zero Payments Problem

An organisation used a front-end package for control of procurement and materials management. Authorised transactions were electronically bridged into an ERP system for payment and account processing. CPA detected a number of reconciliation problems, including possible duplicate payments and transfers to invalid bank accounts. It also exposed over 5,000 payments recorded in the ERP with zero amounts but with valid bank account and other identifiers. Conventional tests do not normally anticipate having to deal with zero payments, so new ideas were necessary.

The explanation given by the IT team (after considerable prevarication) was that the front-end package recorded amounts to four decimal places and, for example, might calculate a part payment as $3,204.4587. The ERP only recognised two decimal places. As a result, they said, payment would be made of $3,204.45 and the residue of $00.0087 transferred back into the front-end package as outstanding. This was automatically reprocessed – as due for payment – on the subsequent run, but again rejected by the ERP and again returned as unpaid. The 5,000 zero amount transactions recycled month after month, potentially producing cheques or payment instructions in a beneficiary's name that had no value. Further iterative tests demonstrated that the explanations were untrue and follow-up enquiries were delegated to the company's external auditors.[44] The results, two years later, are still awaited!

The above case shows the absolute necessity for CPA outliers to be resolved by the initiating team rather than being delegated to others whose primary objectives may be for a quiet life. It follows from this that the CPA team should be held fully accountable for all results.

HIGH-LEVEL TESTS

General

High-level tests of the type described below are unlikely to expose specific outliers, but they point to contexts and processes worthy of further examination and to loosely controlled accounts (LCA), which may involve bribe funding or payment. LCAs are a rich seam in which to mine for skulduggery.

General Ledger

A useful early test is to compare the General Ledger (or trial balances) for the current year with the previous two years and identify changes (for example, new or abandoned

---

44   Who offered to 'resolve' a monster CPA report for two junior employees free of charge, since they did not appear to understand it.

income or expense classifications, discontinued operations) and trends in the value of transactions.

More on Arthur

A company suspected of bribing Arthur (see page 539) agreed to an audit of its records.[45] This revealed that an account for 'Commissions and Freight', which had been used for recording hundreds of thousands of pounds worth of bribes to him and others, had disappeared from the current General Ledger.

The Managing Director of the company admitted that the account had been 'a bit too bloody obvious and our accountants suggested we change it'. He continued: 'If you had a workforce of 300 people to keep employed, especially in this region, you would have no option but to pay bastards like him'. On accounting advice the General Ledger heading used to record bribes had been changed to 'Warrantee Costs': another nicely loose account.

In another European case, the appearance of a new General Ledger heading for 'Loans to Suppliers' uncovered a fraud where, to meet their incentive targets the management team had convinced some vendors to delay invoicing in the fourth quarter. The resulting cash flow impacts on the suppliers' businesses were covered by interest-free loans.

A battery of historical and reasonableness tests may also be conducted on the General Ledger, cost centre and profitability reports, again to narrow down specific contexts and processes justifying detailed testing.

Financial and other ratios

High-level tests on consolidated data, using well established financial and comparative ratios (at a subsidiary, branch or agent level), such as the examples shown in Table 19.6,[46] may also suggest contexts for further testing.

---

45   Rather than be served with a Production Order.

46   The RatioMaster website (at http://ratiomaster.net/ (accessed 13 November 2012)) includes many downloadable spreadsheets for financial analysis that can be adapted for bribery detection.

Table 19.6 Financial and Other Ratios

Name of Test and Numerator	Denominator	Ratio	Possible Outliers of Bribery
Sales Growth Index Sales in Current Year	Sales in Prior Year	Enron was 1.56, indicating impressive growth	Bribe payment
Gross Margin Index Sales in prior year less cost of goods sold/sales in prior year	Sales in current year less cost of goods sold/sales in current year	A ratio of more than 1 means gross margins have deteriorated	
Days Sales Receivable Index Receivables in current year/sales in current year	Receivables in prior year/ sales in prior year		

It is possible that regulators will use similar high-level tests to focus their enquires on companies in targeted sectors. Thus, following the principle of being the first to know, high-level tests are advised and may also be used to analyse published accounts of competitors to uncover third-party corruption.

EXAMPLES OF TESTS ON STANDING DATA AND SIMPLE JOINS

General approach

Under the definitions used in this book, master files hold standing[47] data on customers, suppliers, employees, materials, assets, etc. Satellite and operational systems – such as trading, dealing, logistics, time and attendance, etc. – may also contain important nominal databases.

CPA tests may be run on standing data, on joins with fields from other master files, or from transactional, manual entries or third-party records. It is normally easier (and more productive in the first instance) to run a range of tests on single files of standing data rather than on joins.

Vendor master file example

Simple, one-dimensional tests on vendors' master files may identify:

- Fictitious vendor accounts involved in fraud or used to create slush funds from which bribes can be paid;
- Associated companies, possibly indicating cartels and fraudulent procurement practices;

---

47   In most cases it is far from standing. It does not exist, consists of blank fields, or is frequently altered.

- Conflicting interests by employees and intermediaries;
- Tolling and split invoicing frauds and bribery;
- Trading without the applicable licences and approvals;
- Other perverted decisions (for example, removing discount or retention flags);
- False, fictitious and diverted payments;
- Tax evasion and money-laundering.

Table 19.7 sets out the usual data fields in the vendor's master file and their possible significance.

Table 19.7   Typical Fields in a Vendor Master File

Field(s) and Test	Finding	Notes		Examples of Significance (on Bribery)
		FV	FL	Other
A	**B**	**C**	**D**	**E**
NAME OF VENDOR	Duplicate names *(when stripped of spaces and punctuation)*	✓	30	*Slush find creation Ineffective due diligence*
	No incorporation suffix *(such as 'LTD', 'Inc.', 'S.A.', etc.)*		50	*Easily converted payments*
	Abbreviated name with less than five characters[48] *(such as 'FGO')*		50	
	'Sounds like' an important conglomerate but is not associated *(e.g. IBM Funeral Parlour)*		30	
	Comparing versions of current to past databases to identify new and ceased vendors		30	
VENDOR NUMBER	Duplication and gaps	✓	30	*Inadequate procedures*
ADDRESS	Missing or incomplete	✓	30	
	Common with other vendors, customers or employees		70	*Cartel*
	Key word search such as 'Care of', 'C/o' or 'PO Box'		100	
POST OR ZIP CODE	Missing or invalid post or zip code	✓	80	
	Mismatching post code and area telephone number	✓	100	
REMITTANCE ADDRESS*	Different from 'Address'	✓	100	
	Different from country or currency	✓	100	*Tolling and split invoicing*

---

48   This may enable cheques made payable, for example, to 'ABC' to be altered to 'AB Clarke' and into his account.

Field(s) and Test	Finding	Notes		Examples of Significance (on Bribery)
		FV	FL	Other
A	B	C	D	E
COUNTRY	Summarised for country risk against TI data base		10	*See page 229*
	Different from remittance address	✓	100	*Tolling and split invoicing*
LOCATION (Code)*	Different from country	✓	50	*Tolling and split invoicing*
TELEPHONE NO	Missing, incorrect or incomplete	✓	20	
	Tax Haven (e.g. Isle of Man, Macau, etc.)		80	*Tolling and split invoicing*
	Inconsistent code with post code	✓	100	
	Only a mobile number	✓	80	
	Same telephone and fax number	✓	40	
	Common with other vendors, customers or employees		100	*Collusive bidding*
EMAIL*	Missing or incorrect Suffix not consistent with addresses	✓	20	
HOME PAGE*	Omitted or incorrect Date of registration	✓	20	
OFFICIAL NUMBERS	Missing or incorrect VAT or tax number	✓	100	
	Shared with other vendors or customers		100	
	No tax number		100	
TAX CODE*	Missing	✓	20	
DUNS NUMBER	Missing	✓	10	
CHAMBER OF COMMERCE	Number missing	✓	50	
COUNTRY OF INCORPORATION	Different from address(es)		100	*Tolling Third-party slush fund creation Tax evasion Money-laundering*
REGISTRATION NUMBER	Number missing or incorrect	✓	70	
REGISTRATION DATE*	Recent		30	*No experience*
ORGANSATION TYPE (Code)	Government Institutionality or agent		20	*Possible FCPA liability*

LICENCE DATE	After date of first transaction		100	
	Common with other vendors, customers or employees	✓	100	
CONTACT NAME	Missing	✓	40	
	Common with other vendors, customers, employees or PEPs	✓	100	
	Common with previously failed business	✓	80	
BANK ACCOUNT	No or missing details	✓	100	*Manual cheques and payment diversion*
	Incorrect Sort Code	✓	100	*Payment diversion*
	Shared with other vendors, customers or employees	✓	30	*Collusive bidding Payment diversion*
	Multiple accounts	✓	20	
	No or incorrect IBAN	✓	100	*Payment diversion*
	No or incorrect SWIFT code	✓	100	*External slush fund creation*
	Mismatching IBAN, SWIFT, sort codes	✓	100	
REMITTANCE COUNTRY	Different from address	✓	100	*Tolling Slush fund creation*
REMITTANCE CURRENCY	Inconsistent with address	✓	100	
PAYMENT TYPE (Code)*	Bank Transfer, Cheque, Standing Order, etc.	✓	50	
ACCOUNTS PAYABLE (AP) CONTROL ACCOUNT*	Loosely controlled GL account		50	*Concealment*
AP SUSPENSE ACCOUNT*				
PAY ON RECEIPT*	This usually overrides goods inwards control flags		50	*Bribe receipt for short delivery*
RETENTION CODE*	Shows vendors subject to retentions (see negative payments page 516)		100	*Bribe receipt for favourable treatment*
DISCOUNT CODE	If left blank, quantity and other discounts may not be claimed		50	*Third-party slush fund*
PREPAID DISCOUNT CODE	May allow purchase discounts to be paid in advance		100	*Internal or third party Slush fund creation*
Links and pointers to other fields****	Missing or incorrect Unsecured	✓	100	*Diverted payments Collusive bidding Slush fund creation*
DATE OF ENTRY INTO DBMS	Automatically generated Immediately after incorporation Common with other vendors		20	*Collusive bidding*
ENTERED BY**	Possibly only available from the systems log		100	

Column C indicates that the field is relevant to fictitious vendors; and Column D a focus list weighting factor on a scale of 1–100 (highly significant). Items marked with an asterisk in column A may be in the DBMS, although not downloaded from individual tables. Shaded rows in column A indicate that the reference number concerned contains self-validating check digits (see below).

Missing or inconsistent detail usually indicates ineffective due diligence and poor control, demonstrating that procedures are inadequate.

Other master files

The sort of analysis described above applies to all other master files: again singly and then by relating them to other masters, transactional and third-party data. The tests that can be conducted obviously depend on the data fields downloaded, but the rule is that 'small things matter' and that attention to detail is critical.

Self-validating check digits

Most official reference numbers contain self-validating check digits that can be automatically tested by IDEA. The biggest problem is working out how they are computed.

IBAN Reference Fields

An IBAN reference for a UK account (which is normally the key field for payment processing) consists of 22 characters (4 alphabetic and 16 numeric), such as

GB82WEST12345698765432

The number can be validated as shown in Table 19.8.

Table 19.8 IBAN Check Digits

A	A	A	A	Numeric																	
Country and Bank								Sort Code						Account Number							
G	B	8	2	W	E	S	T	1	2	3	4	5	6	9	8	7	6	5	4	3	2
Move the four initial characters to the end of the string (or ignore)																					
																		G	B	8	2
Replace each letter in the string with 2 digits A=10: B=11: C=12 to Z=35																					
			32	14	28	29	1	2	3	4	5	6	9	8	7	6	5	4	3	2	

Read the number as a decimal integer
3,214,282,912,345,698,765,431
Divide the above by 97
If the division results in a remainder of 1, the IBAN is valid

Another interesting possibility is to compare the first two characters ('GB' in the above example) with the country in which the third party is based and the remittance country and currency. These tests may expose errors,[49] agents and others with offshore accounts in tax havens, and other skulduggery. Country codes of special interest include:

Cyprus	CY	Gibraltar	GI
Liechtenstein	LI	Luxembourg	LU
Monaco	MC	San Marino	SM
Switzerland	CH	Dubai	AE

The Russian Intermediary

A test on IBAN country prefixes revealed that a Russian intermediary's only bank account was in Switzerland. No one had spotted this in what was supposed to have been a comprehensive FCPA due diligence audit!

UK VAT Numbers

Tests can be run to validate UK VAT numbers which, if genuine, contain nine digits, such as:

242188474

Table 19.9 Validating UK VAT Numbers

	Usually Area Specific			Unique Reference				Check Digits	
Number	2	4	2	1	8	8	4	7	4
Multiply	↑ 8	↑ 7	↑ 6	↑ 5	↑ 4	↑ 3	↑ 2		
Product	16	28	12	5	32	24	8		
Add products = 16+28+12+5+32+24 + 8 = 125 and subtract 97 to calculate the check digit = +28 If the result is positive, as in this case, subtract 97 again to get a negative number = 69 Thus the check digit given of 74 is incorrect									

---

49   Possibly poor due diligence.

VAT numbers EU-wide can be individually verified on the EU Taxation and Customs Union site (VIES),[50] although the site is often down!

UK Postcodes[51]

UK postcodes consist of a string of six, seven or eight characters, consisting of two segments separated by a space, as shown in Table 19.10.

Table 19.10 Six Possible Patterns of a Postcode

Outward Segment				SPACE	Inward Segment		
T	N	2	2		3	H	W
Area		District			Sector	Unit	

- There are 124 Area Codes, mostly consisting of 2 letters, resulting in 3,000 outward codes and 27 million full codes.
- The 'unit' is normally specific to between 12 and 15 addresses.
- Large organisations have their own postcodes, for example the HMRC code for VAT is 'BX5'.

The above means that postcodes can be checked by IDEA for format, but are not self-validated. It is possible to download a Comma Separated (CSV) File of the 3,000 outward codes and to automatically calculate the distances between them, although this may be of little use, especially in a general trawl. Cobasco is currently linking post codes to telephone area dialling codes, but whether the output has any value for CPAs remains to be seen.

Other Official Numbers

Other government numbers include:

- UK Companies House Reference Number
- Dun's Number
- UK National Health Numbers
- UK National Insurance Numbers
- UK Passport Numbers
- UK Unique Tax Reference Number
- US Social Security Numbers.

---

50   Available at: http://ec.europa.eu/taxation_customs/vies/ (accessed 13 November 2012).

51   See the excellent website http://www.hexcentral.com/articles/sql-postcodes.htm (accessed 13 November 2012).

All appear to have some sort of self-validating digits that can be used for testing for fictitious entities. Work is progressing on this!

EXAMPLES OF TESTS ON TRANSACTION CODES, ETC.

A separate battery of tests should be run on transaction entry and systems commands that should be reserved for super-users, but in the real world rarely are. The 'forcing code' described below is not untypical of the genre.

The Undocumented Override

A leading international courier and freight forwarder (X Inc.) established a system of advance payment by electronic subscription vouchers that were cheaper for customers than the normal per shipment tariffs. A voucher number could be entered by the shipper or the receiver, or at the sending or receiving depot. Dishonest managers and employees working in France and Italy set up their own rival private business ('a parasite') specialising in cheap heavyweight shipments between the two countries but using X's facilities for doing so.

When a parasite shipment arrived in, say, one of X's French depots, and a subscription voucher was requested, members of the gang would enter what they had discovered was an undocumented override command key 'F15'. This automatically released the consignment for delivery by X Inc. The gang's parasite company then invoiced the shipper at the agreed rate. Losses ran into millions of euros.

The main problem is identifying all of the codes embedded in a system (both documented and undocumented) and the tables in which they appear. Experience suggests the most dangerous include:

- transfers between accounting periods and suspense accounts;
- error correction and adjustment codes;
- interdepartmental transfers or charge backs;
- override codes (for example, allowing goods to be shipped free of charge);
- pricing adjustments;
- reversal codes;
- special payment terms;
- stock adjustments and write-offs.

Often a good clue to dodgy codes are their identification with repeated characters such as '999', 'AAA' or things similar.

514 Bribery and Corruption

Amendments to 'Sector 7'

Vendor accounts in a front-end procurement system and its related DBMS were entered separately and given different reference numbers. When a transaction was approved in the front end for payment, a credit was transferred to the DBMS using a pointer or linking field (called a 'Sector 7 reference'), which was not secure. Even junior operators could alter the pointer so that an invoice approved in the front end for payment to X could be diverted. Systems logs were insufficient to prove whether or not the weakness had been exploited, but controls were improved.

Another test, which IT professionals often say is impossible, but is not, is to test what non-printing characters can be entered into both standing and transactional files.

EXAMPLES OF TESTS ON TRANSACTIONAL DATA AND JOINS

General

Transactional files can be tested singly, although joining them with master files or other transactions is usually far more productive. The following cases illustrate the sorts of testing possible.

Simple joins

Simply joining files that are not normally associated usually produces interesting results.

The Procurement Process

A CPA of a major company's procurement processes (that drilled down behind the front-end system linking data from accounts payable and payments into one file) revealed that:

- 12,800 suppliers out of a total of 14,500 in the vendor master file had never been invited to quote; 200 had been invited only once and 110 invited twice: the trawl of potential vendors was obviously very limited, although this fact was not revealed in standard management reports;
- 135 vendors had duplicate accounts;
- 11, 900 vendors had incomplete or incorrect contact details;
- Of 11,000 unique Requests for Quotations (RFQs) for contracts over $x, 4,400 were awarded on single tenders, yet the rules were that at least three should be obtained;

- Of 36,125 RFQs issued (for around 11,000 unique transactions), 26,394 resulted in no response. The failure rate of 70 per cent is highly indicative of collusive and courtesy bidding;
- Many vendors were repeatedly invited to quote, failed to respond, yet appeared on further bid lists and had successfully obtained business through emergency and other orders that were not competitively bid.

There were other serious problems involving payments to unauthorised bank accounts, changes to bank account details made in the morning but reversed later in the day after payments had been processed, and negative debit notes in place of credit notes.

Can you imagine how the above findings would appear when procedures were being assessed by regulators as adequate or not? And is it preferable that the company should be the first to know of such problems before regulators hit the data?

Historical and trend

Some CPA tests focus on historical data and identifying outlying trends.

Identifying Favoured Vendors

An analysis of purchase invoices, matched against the vendor master, showed the values listed in Table 19.11.

Table 19.11 Trend Analysis

Vendor Name	Value of Transactions		
	2009	2010	2011
Jones and Co. Ltd.	3,000	50,000	2,400,000
ABC	200,000	800,000	0
Global Solar Panels	0	0	3,400,000
Bair & Brown Ltd.	0	0	0
Cleggy Clogs and Shoes S.A.	20,000	20,000	21,000

This analysis should result in questions being asked:

- Why did Jones and Co. Ltd. so suddenly come into favour and is there any pattern in the purchasing agents involved?
- Which vendors, if any, suffered as a result of Jones's success?

- Should ABC be interviewed to establish the reasons for its sudden decline in fortunes?
- The massive new expenditure with Global Solar Panels suggests a major policy decision requiring competitive bids. The processing of these should be reviewed.
- Blair & Brown appears to be a dormant vendor, but a further iterative testing of the RFQ and Purchase Order file shows they were sent invitations to tender on 120 occasions and that in all of them, the successful supplier was Boris Enterprises Ltd. This pattern suggests Blair & Brown were used as courtesy bidders for what were single-source transactions with Boris.
- Cleggy Clogs and Shoes S.A. looks too consistent and too good to be true: such a pattern is common with fictitious vendors, especially when created by junior employees with limited authority.

Historical and trend tests are important, but they are usually more difficult to carry out because they require multiple file importations from previous years involving table layouts that may not be consistent.

Reasonableness

These tests examine the reasonableness of decisions and transactions.

Approval Limits – Again

A comparison of purchase orders and invoices against the Authority Table showed that an unusually high percentage of transactions involving some vendors were approved within 5 per cent of the $250,000 limit requiring formal competitive tendering. Further research established that orders were divided to fall below the limit and filled by single quotes from one vendor on the approval of one employee. This is a typical symptom of corruption.

Negative Payments

Analysis of a purchase invoice payment file identified more than $8 million in 'negative payments'. These were explained as retentions on large infrastructure projects, which was reasonable. However, detailed analysis[52] linking the payments to purchase orders showed that many retentions related to spare parts supplied by small local vendors. When some of these were interviewed, they alleged that clerks responsible for processing payments demanded bribes. If these were not agreed, payments were withheld.

---

52   Iterative testing.

Extending the tests, an even more serious problem emerged. That was that some large suppliers avoided retentions by bribing the same clerks.

A standard opening test is to analyse transaction files for round amounts. That is, for example, sales, purchase invoices or payments, with the last three digits and decimal places as '000.00'. The logic for this, which is not unsound, is that round amounts are more likely to result from guesses, negotiated settlements or fictitious transactions. However, many round amounts may be subject to VAT, and because of this fail the test.

The procedure recommended is to:

- Test for round amounts in the normal way. The transactions identified are unlikely to include VAT but if they purport to do so they are even more suspicious and likely to be contrived *(for example an invoice for £10,212.77 plus £1,787.23 VAT = £12,000 should be carefully examined)*;
- Note the applicable tax rate (say, in the UK 17.5 per cent);
- Calculate a new IDEA field based on the gross amount divided by 1.175;
- If the result is a round amount it should be treated as an outlier.

Detailed enquiries are justified if the net VAT inclusive round amounts cluster immediately below an authority level.

Matching transactions recorded in front-end systems may also expose fraud and corruption.

Reception Records

Visitors to Company A reported to a reception desk where their name, company name, name of person visited, time of entry and time of exit were entered into a standalone computer and a pass (with a photograph) produced. CPA analysis of the computer revealed an abnormally high number of meetings (all between 11.30am and 12.45pm) with three or four vendors, a day or so before Tender Committee deliberations. Subsequent enquiries showed that the meetings were always followed by lavish lunches paid for by the vendors and that the employees entertained never returned to the office afterwards.[53]

Goods Inwards

Similar analysis of goods inwards records disclosed that deliveries from one or two vendors clustered after 5.20pm, only ten minutes before the receiving employees clocked out. The conclusion was that the timing was deliberate to avoid detailed checking of the quality and quantity of goods received.

---

53   Suggesting further discussions at the Pink Pussycat Lap Dancing Club.

Scheduled Times

An agreement with the local trade union specified the 'scheduled hours' for each customer delivery so that work could be allocated fairly and overtime premiums calculated.

The hours were, in fact, far too generous and the union recognised that if drivers repeatedly returned to the depot too early, negotiations of the following year's rates would be adjusted downwards. The local shop steward gave instructions that drivers should 'use up any unexpired time by resting' in a lay-by or a local café so that they did not return before the scheduled arrival time.

Few drivers were happy to do this (mainly so that they could spend time with their mistresses, fishing, playing golf or, in one case, flying his light aircraft) and bribed the security guards to record return times one to four hours later than actual. Comparison of this log with tachometers and times recorded on delivery notes exposed this scam.

Observation was kept by the company's security team and police, resulting in the arrest of 20 drivers and two security guards. When one guard was arrested – and the detectives, as always happens in the movies, said: 'OK Bill. You're nicked, now get your coat on' – he could barely lift it. Its pockets were crammed full of bribes paid in pound coins.

Hypothetical Case for the Bribery Act[54]

To test its exposure to bribery by associated persons, a company merged its vendor and customer master files, summarising values and transactions by country. It then linked this data to telephone call logs by country dialling codes. Partial results were as shown in Table 19.12:

Table 19.12 Indications of Ship to Border Frauds

Country	Transaction Summary US$			Calls	Ratio
	Sales Values	Purchase Values	Total		
	A	B	C	D	C/D
Latvia	4,783,000	300,000	5,083,000	300	16,943
Poland	3,300,000	600,000	3,900,000	290	13,448
Russia	1,453,666	350,000	1,803,666	3,100	581

Table 19.12 suggests that shipments to Poland and Latvia were probably destined for smuggling into Russia in what is known in the parallel trading world as 'ship to border'.

---

54   Based on a successful test for parallel trading and ship-to-border frauds.

The above cases illustrate that bribery (potentially involving Section 7 liability) occurs at all levels in an organisation; and that front-end and satellite data is very important.

Proportional and comparative

Perverted decisions often result in significant outliers involving distorted ratios and patterns.

The Golden Hammer

A retail chain selling home improvement products allowed employees to buy damaged products at between 10 per cent and 50 per cent of the list price. Comparison of branch performance statistics revealed one with an excessively high ratio of staff sales to turnover. Further analysis of the sales transaction file showed that the vast majority of 10 per cent sales involved paint, emulsion and wallpaper, but not in odd cans as might be expected, but for gallons of fully matching colour combinations of gloss and emulsion paint as recommended in good housekeeping magazines.

Employees concerned admitted that they had supplied firms of painters and decorators with products bought under the staff sales scheme. After taking the orders and being paid in cash,[55] they would use what they called the 'golden hammer' to damage cans in the exact combinations required. Their proceeds were shared with the supervisor who, to protect himself, usually took Polaroid photographs of the damaged cans.

No one ever was prosecuted because the Human Resources Manager argued there was nothing in the Staff Handbook to prohibit golden hammering!

Proportional and other tests may uncover internal corruption.

Similar proportional tests on the ratio of credit notes to sales invoices, salesmen's call records to converted sales, highest to lowest prices, inventory turnover ratios and credit periods taken and given, have been successful in uncovering fraud and corruption. Again, iterative rather than standard testing has produced the best results.

---

55   Which they shared with their supervisor.

Internal Corruption (Another Hypothetical)

A test of historical payroll records revealed the following salary progression for Flossy Flowfinger:

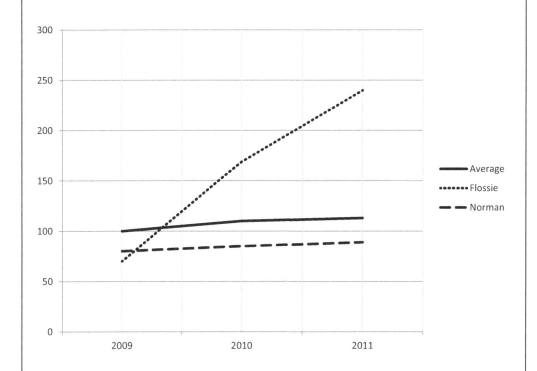

Figure 19.7 The Rise and Rise of Flossie Flowfinger

Maybe Flossie was an exceptional performer, especially in bed with her manager, with whom she was having an affair.

Benford's Law

The background of this 'law' is as follows. In 1938, Frank Benford,[56] a physicist employed by the General Electric Company in the USA, noticed that the pages of logarithmic tables corresponding to the digit '1' were more scruffy and thus more frequently referred to, than the pages for other digits. This set him thinking and he went on to examine more than 20,000 numerical data sets – ranging from the population statistics of towns in the USA to football results – to see if there were any common patterns in the frequency of 1 appearing as the first digit in larger, multi-digit numbers.

---

56   In fact, the law had been discovered by Simon Newcomb, a noted mathematician and astronomer, in 1881.

How Benford's Law Works

For example, in the multi-digit number 123, 1 is counted as the first digit; similarly 4 is counted as the first digit in the number 4,756, 213. The first digit can never be 0 (for example, in the number 0.123 the first digit is 1. In the number 0.06789 the first two digits are 67).

Mr Benford's findings are illustrated in Table 19.13.

Table 19.13 Benford's Law Illustrated

No of Data Sets Sampled	Data Set	Percentage Occurrence of 1–9 as First Digit in Larger Numbers								
		1	2	3	4	5	6	7	8	9
3,259	Population statistics	33.9	20.4	14.2	8.1	7.2	6.2	4.1	3.7	2.2
100	Numbers appearing in newspaper articles	30.0	18.0	12.0	10.0	8.0	6.0	6.0	5.0	5.0
1,800	Molecular weights	26.7	25.2	15.4	10.8	6.7	5.1	4.1	2.8	3.2
308	Numbers in *Reader's Digest* articles	33.4	18.5	12.4	7.5	7.1	6.5	5.5	4.9	4.2
741	Cost data	32.4	18.8	10.1	10.1	9.8	5.5	4.7	5.5	3.1
1,458	American League Statistics	32.7	17.6	12.6	9.8	7.4	6.4	4.9	5.6	3.0
418	Death rates	27.0	18.6	15.7	9.4	6.7	6.5	7.2	4.8	4.1
20,000	AVERAGE	30.6	18.5	12.4	9.4	8.0	6.4	5.1	4.9	4.7
Final Benford's Law Pattern		**30.1**	**17.6**	**12.5**	**9.7**	**7.9**	**6.7**	**5.8**	**5.1**	**4.6**

Thus, according to Benford's Law, in 30.1 per cent of all cases, '1' will appear as the leading digit in larger numbers, whereas '9' would appear in 4.6 per cent of cases.

Benford's Law also covers frequencies of digits in other than first positions and applies to any data set

- that is random: not based on assigned numbers (such as a National Insurance number or tax reference);
- that contains no arbitrarily assigned maximum or minimum value (such as a file of purchase orders applying to an individual employee with a limited authorisation level).

When either of these conditions do not apply, the results may not conform to the law. This is so for most transactional data that is influenced by authority levels and is therefore not random.

Benford's Law has been promoted – especially by accounting firms – as an effective fraud-detection test, although the authors' success in using it has been very limited (to the extent that other tests would have exposed outliers more easily or that it generated false positives). However, trying it on transactional data is very quick and easy using IDEA and is recommended if for no other reason than failing to do so may raise questions about an organisations determination to detect bribery. Besides that, Benford graphs look great in the Adequate Procedures Dossier.

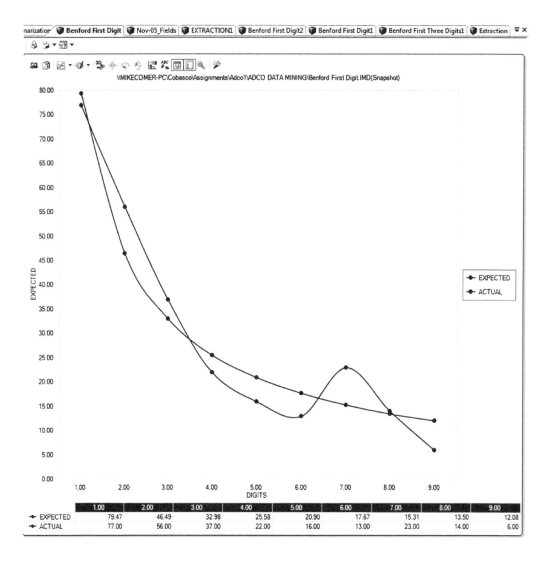

Figure 19.8 A Typical Benford's Law Chart Produced by IDEA

Figure 19.8 suggests that transactions starting with the digit 7 are potential outliers, but what did the test prove? Answer: 'Nothing' but it looks nice.

EXAMPLES OF SPECIAL PROFILE TESTS

Cobasco's CPA manual contains scores of special profile tests for fraud and corruption which are too sensitive to release in a book which could be read by skulduggers, especially if they have nicked it from the local library.

There are two aspects justifying special mention. The first is to list every 'red flag' identified by questionnaires of the type discussed on page 327, or from tarot cards, tea leaves, crystal balls or witchcraft, and to test and resolve every one. The results should be filed in the Adequate Procedures Dossier.

The second is testing for 'financial or other advantages'. These may appear in the variety of forms discussed on page 299 et seq. The following paragraphs deal with advantages provided through payment systems, which probably still account for 60 per cent of bribes paid.

Ask Willy a Silly Question

When Willy Sutton, the notorious bank robber, was asked why he robbed banks, he replied: 'Cause that is where the money is'.

Payments are important in corruption for a similar reason:

- Bribes can be disguised as genuine payments (e.g. fictitious vendors, excessive commissions, emergency expenses, unclaimed credit notes, etc.);
- Payments can be inflated or diverted in return for bribes (e.g. alteration of payment parameters, manual cheques, standing orders or direct debits);
- Overpayments can be authorised in return for bribes (e.g. duplicates, suppressed purchase credit notes, disregarded sales credits notes and claims for returned goods);
- They can be manipulated to create internal slush funds from which bribes can be paid (e.g. recorded payments not made, creating a credit to cash and bank accounts);
- Or to create slush funds with third parties such as intermediaries, customers, suppliers or associated companies from which bribes can be paid.

The possibilities depend on the precise way systems are configured and exceptions to them such as cash or manual payments, standing orders, direct debits and purchase cards.

Manual Payments

Urgent manual payments totalling over £50,000 were requested to settle miscellaneous purchases from 'Beneficial Management Consultants'.[57] When the Marketing Manager completed the cheque requisition form he recorded only 'Beneficial'. He used some cheques to pay off his credit cards with Beneficial Finance and paid others directly into his own account.

Cheques payable to banks, 'cash', 'selves' or 'bearer' are obviously vulnerable, as are standing orders and direct debits.

The way beneficiary names are captured and printed on cheques is also important:

Dangers of Short and Abbreviated Names

In a DBMS the 'Name' field allows for 30 characters. This field is replicated on cheques, again in a 30-character field. If the unused positions are not obliterated on cheques, such as:

Figure 19.9 Secure Cheque-printing

– diversion is simple and will not be reported if the genuine ABC knows nothing of the transaction

Figure 19.10   Insecure Cheque-printing

Companies usually argue that every unused character position is automatically filled, but what happens if in the DBMS the name of ABC is entered followed by 27 keyed-in spaces or non-printing characters? The answer is normally, as in Figure 19.10, the creation of fraud and bribery opportunities.

Even when name fields on cheques are fully completed, how secure is the print? With many laser printers it is possible to use Sellotape to carefully remove the beneficiary's name and type in another. Ballpoint pens are available that can be erased. Again, if the payment is not expected by the supposed beneficiary: BINGO!

---

57   Not the actual name, but gives the idea of what happened.

In the case of electronic transfers, identifying the precise field in the DBMS from which payment parameters are collected is critical because most banks rely almost entirely on the IBAN reference without checking the beneficiary's name or account number.

A Planned Scam

Following a civil search order, the personal computer of a Finance Manager was forensically examined revealing that he had planned a new scam along the following lines:

- He knew the sort code for HMRC VAT was 08-32-00. He planned to open an account at the branch with the sort code 08-23-00 in the name of 'Advance Reserve';[58]
- He would then inflate his employer's VAT return (say from £2,300,000 to £3,300,000) and pay the larger amount to the benefit of 'Advance Reserve';
- A few days later he would transfer £2,300,000 from this account to HMRC at sort code 08-32-00, thereby making himself a cool million.

Would he have got away with it? Who knows. anti-money-laundering experts would say there would be no chance: cynics have seen funnier things happen, especially if a bank employee is involved.

So the recommended bottom line, especially on bribe payment and Section 7 liabilities, is that companies should identify all of the ways that advantages could be provided to third parties, employees and associated persons, as discussed in Chapters 12–13, through accounts payable and receivable, payroll, incentives, inventory, goods and services, owners' funds, marketing and other schemes. Then track the fields in DBMS and satellite systems that are available and design specific CPA tests.

Follow-up and Validation

CPA always results in outliers which rarely, in themselves, amount to evidence of fraud or bribery. Thus the follow-up stage is critical. Every outlier should be brainstormed and fully explained.

---

58   Or something similar.

20 *Manual Tests*

Introduction

Most Critical Point Auditing (CPA) tests involve electronic data, but there are others that are less technical such as forensic examination of:

- purchase invoices
- agents and intermediary files
- personal expenses.

These can be very revealing, especially when the outliers identified are then subject to further CPA.

Hooked on Crime

In the excellent TV documentary – 'Storyville': *Inside Job*[1] – on the banking crisis and the collapse of Lehman Brothers et al., a high-class New York madam said that virtually every Wall Street firm used her 'girls' for themselves and clients at upwards of $2,000 a session. She said she was required to submit false invoices to the firms concerned for consulting or research.

Forensic Examination of Purchase Invoices

The principle involved here is that false or inflated purchase invoices may be frauds in their own right or used to create internal slush funds or surpluses held by third parties from which bribes can be paid.

---

1   Which can be viewed at http://www.bbc.co.uk/iplayer/episode...12_Inside_Job/ or through http://www.insidejobfilm. com (accessed 13 November 2012).

Golf: A Dodgy Game

A fraud consultant with a spare couple of hours – on a wet Monday afternoon with nothing else to do – pulled out 1,000 or so invoices from his client's accounts payable system and began working systematically through them. He discovered a handwritten invoice (No. 1456) from a golf professional for 'Logo'd promotional golf balls' for £5,327 signed off by the Finance Director and approved by the Managing Director. Looking closely at the document, the consultant noticed an impression from invoice 1455. It was on the same date, for the same amount, to the same company, the only difference being that it listed 12 sets of Ping golf clubs, 12 sets of waterproofs and 11 tam-o'-shanter tartan hats. This invoice had never been posted to the client's accounts.

When interviewed, the MD admitted to skulduggery and said that he had bought the clubs to motivate his management team and a couple of key clients.[2] He said it had been the Financial Director's idea to mis-describe the goods. He explained that there were only 11 tam-o'-shanter tartan hats because he already owned two.

The suggested approach for a purchase invoice review is:

1. Determine how and where paid and pending purchase invoices are filed, especially those authorised by directing minds, for joint ventures and for categories of expenditure and contexts highlighted by any CPA test (such as cost-centre overruns, delayed payment, advance or super-prompt payment, or emergency orders).
2. Two or more examiners should arm themselves with portable infrared (IR) and ultraviolet (UV) torches[3] and compile a list of characteristics that will be systematically applied to the examination of 2,000 to 3,000 invoices selected from batches identified from point 1 above. Characteristics may include those identified in Table 20.1.

---

2   He only bought 11 tam-o'-shanter hats because he already had two!!
3   Easily obtainable from Amazon and other Internet suppliers.

Table 20.1   Outliers in Purchase Invoices

Outlier – Characteristic	Comments and Selected Examples
Appearance • Not an original on printed heading such as a photocopy, fax or electronic version (including self-billing) • Watermark • Photocopy with data whited out and then recopied • No logo, or a basic clip art image • Impressions of writing from other documents such as Post It notes (Electro-static data analysis (ESDA)) • Unfolded or unusually clean • Exceptionally dirty • Impressions and indents • Unprofessional layout • Simply looks dodgy or too flash!!	A skuldugger working for a large accounting firm submitted fictitious invoices to one of its clients supposedly from an overseas freight agent. Unfortunately he printed them on paper incorporating his firm's watermark Unfolded documents indicate they were never posted. Too dirty suggest they may have been questioned and carried about for days before being paid
Name of vendor • Abbreviated name (e.g. HMRC Consultants) • Easily confused with a major international but, in fact, unconnected • Containing puffing words such as 'Global' or 'International' when it is clearly anything but	A villain – named Ian Brian Masters – had fictitious payments processed to 'IBM' which he intercepted in the mail room. He then converted 'IBM' to 'IBMasters'. Quickly detected under ultraviolet examination
Trading address and VAT • Post Office Box number • Appears to be a residential address • 'Care of' another company or address • No telephone or fax number or only a mobile number • Same number for telephone and fax • False or missing VAT number for UK vendors	All profiles of fictitious vendors
Description of goods or services and amount • Not described or vague description • Described only by a product code number • Intangible services • Goods on hire or lease • Hotel bills • Goods suitable for personal or domestic use • Round amount immediately below £10,000 (The Proceeds of Crime Act (POCA) threshold) or an internal authority level • Alterations to the amount • Incorrect VAT calculation • Supported by an attached adding machine list or spread sheet	A fraudster annotated invoices with goods described as 'Code ABC 12345' to suggest they were electronic components needed for equipment maintenance. They were in fact colour televisions which he had collected and sold via eBay
Delivery address • Not shown • Blanked out (on photocopies) • Unknown address • Goods collected	

Outlier – Characteristic	Comments and Selected Examples
Other • Classified as a miscellaneous purchase • Paid in cash, standing order, direct debit or manual cheque	*High-value miscellaneous purchases are especially interesting*
Missing vouchers	*These are especially important*

The Financial Controller's Special File

It is far from unusual to discover that missing (supposedly very sensitive) vouchers have been filed away separately in the 'Financial Controller's Special File' or some other similar receptacle. Examination of everything in such files is critical: especially so given that the associated skulduggery is most likely to involve a directing mind.

3. The selected bundles should be divided into two: each examiner takes half, using IR and UV lighting to detect alterations on the backs and fronts of all documents.
4. When a document matching a profile is identified, it should be flagged with a Post-it note or put to one side.
5. The batches should then be switched, re-examined and the results brainstormed.
6. A brief report should be prepared setting out further CPA and other tests on the transactions or entities concerned.

The NATO Scam

A number of leading companies in the UK and USA, including Sony, Philips, Panasonic and EDS, had been solicited by what they believed to be a secret unit of NATO that wished to source optical and other expensive equipment for a Rapid Reaction Task Force to be deployed in Bosnia. To prequalify, the companies were required – by a Colonel Lamar Reid, a fast-talking US soldier – to provide four samples (one for each of NATO's laboratories) for testing to destruction.

The value of the samples requested ran to over $1 million before an astute manager at Sony noticed something amiss with the NATO logo appearing in correspondence and his concerns went into overdrive. This is what he noticed (Figure 20.1).

The logo used:    The correct logo:

Figure 20.1 Fraudulent NATO Logo

Would you have spotted what is wrong with this?

Enquiries commissioned by Sony blew open a scam by a group of Jamaican villains and recovered most of its samples from a video production laboratory in Paris run by a 'Doctor Reed' who, you guessed it, was the same Jamaican as the Colonel.

Other companies were less successful and together lost an estimated $10 million. Colonel Reed, who was more than capable of two-hour long discussions on the finest technical merits of even the most esoteric equipment, turned out to be a London-born Jamaican who had left school at aged 15 with no qualifications. He is, however, a genius and he is now living back in the UK after having allegedly convinced the European authorities he was an undercover CIA agent and should be allowed bail, from which he absconded.

Review of Agents' and Other Files

A small selection of contract and correspondence files kept by the departments and individuals[4] responsible for appointing and managing intermediaries should be examined, focusing on:

- CPA outliers;
- Unusual ratios in the intermediary's publicly filed accounts;
- The identity of and transactions with the intermediary's end parties;
- Missing documentation;
- Unusual or potentially incriminating correspondence;
- Any unusual discretion exercised in the intermediary's favour;
- Potential or actual problems reported by the intermediary and their resolution;
- Transactions with other entities associated with the intermediary's principals.

A brief report should be prepared summarising all outliers and how they were resolved. This should be filed in the Adequate Procedures Dossier.

Testing Personal Expenses

A LITTLE BACKGROUND

Expense claims, company credit and purchase cards[5] and personal items processed through accounts payable are a goldmine for uncovering fraud, corruption and other skulduggery because they:

---

4   As well as Credit Control.

5   Including purchasing cards.

- Identify rogues;
- Are used to pay bribes;
- May involve tax evasion and money-laundering;
- May have serious VAT or other tax implications.

Although there is strong evidence of a close correlation between serious fraudsters, bribers and expense fiddlers, it is not usually the case that small crimes lead to worse. It is rather that people involved in bribery and serious fraud are risk-takers or thrill-seekers who get an extra kick from falsifying expenses.

WHEN TO AUDIT EXPENSE CLAIMS

There are five conditions in which detailed examination of personal expenses are recommended:

1. On a random trawl as part of a CPA programme.[6]
2. When a person is suspected of serious fraud or corruption.
3. As part of the screening process, prior to a person's promotion into a senior or vulnerable position.
4. **Prior to any self-disclosure being made to any regulatory agency.[7]**
5. The fifth and really powerful reason for examining a person's expenses is because you don't like him or want his job.[8]

The starting point for a general trawl is to identify the departments, contexts and individuals with the highest expenses claims, through accounts payable and on company credit and purchasing cards. This provides the focus for specific examinations.

Unless there are exceptional reasons for *not* doing so, the personal expenses of all directing minds should be examined as part of a CPA on the basis that it is better that any problems should be resolved before they emerge after a regulatory dawn raid or tax investigation.

RECOMMENDED TESTING PROCEDURE

The procedure recommended is for detectors to:

1. Obtain the originals of selected expense statements vouchers and print outs for:
- the person concerned
- his immediate subordinates and superiors
  - for at least the previous two years, and log details of missing statements or overlaps in claim periods.
2. Review the employee's personnel file and note:
- his or her birthday, the birthdays of partners, children

---

6   And depending on what data is available electronically.

7   That could involve the person concerned as a witness or a defendant.

8   After contriving an excuse that he was picked out through a random, gobbledegook, BS, regressive statistical analysis.

- date of marriage
- partner's maiden or other names
- details of previous employers.[9]

3. Obtain company and mobile telephone call logs, preferably on a CD or DVD, for the employee and his secretary.

4. Use Excel, FileMaker Pro or Access to set up a database/calendar for the two-year period, showing the fields in Table 20.2.

Table 20.2   Database Fields for Expense Statement Analysis

Field	Comments and Purpose
Date of activity	This must be a proper date field and not character or numeric to allow sorting and ageing tests
Day of the week	Mark weekends and public holidays and dates of personal significance to the employee
Time	From call logs, airline tickets, restaurant bills: hotel check out times, etc. Adjust all times to GMT if international travel is involved
Source and voucher number	Cross reference to source documents
Activity	Nature of expenditure
Paid to	Who was paid
Amount	Numeric
How paid	Credit card, cash, cheque or accounts payable
Currency	This is very important
Third parties named or entertained	These may be employees or third parties
Comments made by the employee	Explanations for expenditure

5. Annotate the calendar with the dates of personal significance to the employee, his manager and immediate subordinates. For example, the date of their wedding anniversaries, wife's and children's birthdays and other sneaky stuff.

6. Examine each voucher carefully. If bundles are stapled together[10] clip them onto separate sheets. Using a UV or IR light, look for:
   - alterations; especially of amounts and dates;
   - incomplete details and missing vouchers;
   - duplicate charges (for example, the same expense claimed on a voucher and a credit card; receipt or in overlapping claim periods);
   - indentations from other writing (ESDA examination);
   - entertaining claimed for third parties;
   - large single expenditures; and check them against accounts payable.[11]

---

9   These names should be run against the vendor and customer master files.

10   A typical profile of a dodgy claim.

11   There is around a 2 per cent duplication on this test.

Funny Old Entertaining

A senior manager claimed £7,300 for entertaining a team of *four overseas clients*[12] to dinner at a top London restaurant and a further £8,000 at an adjoining jewellers which, he noted, were 'presents for xxx's wives'. The expenditure was supported by two photocopied vouchers, both dated 15 May 2010, which the auditors noted was a Saturday and the date of his eldest son's 21st birthday. The times of payment on attached photocopied credit card vouchers had been erased.

The auditor visited the restaurant and discovered that the booking had been made for a table of *six for lunch* and it became abundantly clear from the delicacies eaten that the meal was not for five men. The manager confessed that the meal had been a treat for his son and the 'jewellery' a gold watch to go with it. He agreed to repay and the matter was closed.[13]

---

7. Sort and print out the database (Table 20.3).

Table 20.3 Additional Reports on Expenses

Field	Possible Significance
Dates and days	Look for expenses at weekends and around dates of special personal significance to the employee and his superiors
Paid to	Check against the expenses of subordinates and superiors for duplicate claims and conflicts. Check names against accounts payable files. Test for duplications
Activity, amount and currency	Look for duplications and round amount payments
Third parties named	Check a sample of their expense statements for consistency and duplications. Check the transactions with third parties where entertaining appears excessive
Comments made by the employee	Look for inconsistencies

8. Consider interviewing suspected employees and the authorising signatories to obtain clarification and, if appropriate, information on other, possibly more serious, matters. Run a CPA against other decisions taken by confirmed skulduggers.

---

12   All rather large males with thick necks, broken noses and fancy shoes.

13   What if six months later the manager had been detected paying bribes. Would the writing off of the earlier incident have been regarded as consistent with adequate procedures? You can bet it would not. Moreover, since the initial offence had not been reported to the company's fidelity insurers, there would be no coverage for any further dishonest acts by that employee.

Entertaining the Union

The manager of a distribution depot claimed massive expenses – through his personal statements and Accounts Payable, and sometimes both – for meetings with trade unions, external contractors and others to try to smooth over labour problems, which at that time were common in the industry. He was repeatedly commended for the depot's strike-free record. In the course of a single year he had spent more than £125,000 in a local five-star hotel, supposedly for conference rooms and meals, mainly for meetings with trade union representatives. However analysis showed that the largest expenditure took place on weekends and bank holidays and in some cases when the manager was on vacation overseas.

Investigators interviewed the hotel's internal auditors and after initial prevarication they admitted that the majority of the meetings were fictitious and that the manager had asked for false invoices to cover his purchases of a £20,000 oil painting, crates of top-quality wine, clothing and jewellery, and dinners for his wife and family. The hotel later admitted that it had bought expensive clothing for the manager's wife, adding the costs to its invoices, again mis-described as meetings.

The manager refused to be interviewed,[14] but wrote a letter to his boss admitting false accounting (justifying it as a technicality), but implied that the paintings and fine wines had been bribes for union officials. The company refused to allow the union representatives to be interviewed. The manager went on long-term sick leave before taking a very attractive early retirement package, as did his boss!

The Dangers of Reciprocity

Company X had a hospitality policy of 'reciprocity', which meant that its employees could accept any form of entertainment providing, in the words of the HR manager, 'they could eat, drink or roger it in a single session and within a reasonable period reciprocate with equivalent courtesies'.

The first symptom of corruption manifested in the purchasing department, whose senior members were all grossly overweight, florid, and flatulent and with very fancy shoes. When their expense claims were examined, true enough, they seemed to have reciprocated rather generously. However, closer examination of vouchers revealed that the credit cards used supposedly for reciprocal hospitality were in fact those of the vendors.

The scam was simple and well established to the extent that vendors would pay for all entertainment but would give vouchers for every other 'courtesy' to the bent purchasing agents so that they could claim them on their expenses. They thereby benefited from the double whammy of a tantric session at the Pink Pussy Cat Lap Dancing Club and getting paid for costs they had never incurred. The clever policy of reciprocity had clearly not been 'impact-assessed'.

---

14   Claiming a nervous breakdown.

The point about expenses, illustrated by the cases discussed above, is that some organisations consider investigating them is beyond the pale and 'unBritish'. This foolishness is not sustainable in light of the Bribery Act.

Telephone and Fax Call Log Analysis

The idea that land and mobile telephone call data can be analysed to *detect* fraud is a popular misconception. Extensive practical experience with call log analysis has been at best patchy for the following reasons:

- Usually only the numbers of parties called (outgoing calls) are recorded.
- Some mobile companies refuse to supply call-logging data electronically, even when the company is the subscriber.
- It is difficult and sometimes illegal to try to identify the names of subscribers.
- Any skuldugger who is in anyway surveillance-aware will avoid calls that can be monitored and instead will use personal and unregistered mobiles.

Call log monitoring may be helpful in investigations, especially by law enforcement agencies or when production orders are obtained, but these conditions rarely exist at a detection stage.

That said, outliers may be identified from analysing the organisation's records of INTERNAL incoming and outgoing calls to detect:

- Unusual patterns of internal communication (such as the managing director repeatedly telephoning a junior clerk in sales accounting, which may indicate vertical collusion (see page 297));
- Calls to:
  - Tax haven countries (especially banks, lawyers and company agents);
  - competitors;
  - Head hunters;
  - The Serious Fraud Office (SFO) and other whistle-blowing lines;
  - Thrill-seeking lines such as pornographic and dating sites;
  - Ex-employees and agents.

Analysis may also identify:

- Vendors and customers who are never contacted (called 'orphans');
- A patterns of calls around bid-opening or other critical dates;
- Calls to spread betting companies immediately before financial results are made public or an acquisition announced.

Detectors should not expect any great revelations from call log analysis, but the fact that efforts were made is a useful addition to the Adequate Procedures Dossier.

Electronic Discovery

Every organisation that might be blessed with a dawn raid by the SFO, Her Majesty's Revenue and Customs (HMRC) or any other agency – or becomes involved in any serious litigation – can anticipate being compelled to make full disclosures, including all of its worldwide email traffic and electronic data for the past 5,000 years.

Leveson Enquiry

The Metropolitan Police claimed to be analysing 300 million emails disclosed by News International.

Compulsory disclosure is not a pleasant experience and any attempt to destroy incriminating records even when a regulatory investigation is merely suspected is likely to result in prosecution for conspiracy to pervert the course of justice and other serious offences.

News International

The *Daily Telegraph* reported:

'The chairman of News International was forwarded a chain of emails suggesting that hacking was not restricted to a single rogue reporter. [...] Yesterday, however, it was disclosed that the email was deleted from his account by an IT worker at News International 11 days before Scotland Yard launched Operation Weeting.

[Another] copy of the message was also lost from the email server that held News International emails following a "hardware failure". The deletions meant that the email did not form part of the initial evidence sent by News International to the Metropolitan Police'.[15]

Organisations should consider analysing – on a mock 'electronic discovery' basis[16] and under legal advice – all of the retained data that would emerge following a regulatory raid, with the objective of:

---

15   Mark Hughes, Crime Correspondent, 1 February 2012.

16   Using a firm specialising in electronic discovery and ANALYSIS.

- Detecting and resolving any skulduggery by becoming the first to know;
- Ensuring that employees responsible for writing imprudent correspondence are trained to avoid repetitions;
- Assessing the impact of any potential disclosure, preparing contingency plans in the event of an actual regulatory enquiry and seeking legal advice on what archived records can be safely destroyed.[17]

The results should be discussed with senior managers and legal advisers and records retention policies reviewed.

Review of Past Incidents, Reports and Hot Lines

Details of past incidents of suspected skulduggery and control weaknesses reported in:

- whistle-blowing reports,
- archived anonymous letters,
- internal and external audit reports,
- reports on disciplinary matters,
- customer and supplier complaints,
- liquidations and bankruptcies of customers, suppliers and associated persons, including their end parties,
- claims under fidelity or directors' and officers' liability insurance,
- investigation reports, and
- previous regulatory actions and enforcement notices

– should be extracted for review, to focus CPA testing of the contexts concerned and to ensure that effective remedial steps have been taken.

Great Evidence of Inadequate Procedures

Regulators are unlikely to have much sympathy with organisations which have ignored warnings of control defects through which bribes are subsequently proven to have been paid.

Professional investigators should review reports on the more important cases and explore the possibility that aspects were overlooked. They should also review the investigation processes involved and, where necessary, make recommendations for improvement. Results should be summarised for the Adequate Procedures Dossier.

---

17   This is an entirely different activity when done as part of a routine records retention programme and when there is no regulatory or other action in play or prospect.

Parallel Processing and Reworked Transactions

Under a parallel processing test, a small selection of transactions involving potentially exposed decisions are independently modelled and results compared.

No Smoke Without Fire

An oil company was told it needed to replace two of its fire trucks for which the Fire Chief prepared a detailed specification and internal requisition. In fact, the specification was so detailed that only one vendor should match it. The internal requisition was passed to Central Purchasing and duplicated[18] for parallel processing through what appeared to be a totally independent company.

Central Purchasing, working closely with the Fire Chief, eventually recommended Brand X trucks costing more than $1 million each. However, the parallel process showed that:

- There was no need to replace existing equipment;
- The Fire Chief's specification had been copied – almost word for word – from Brand X's catalogues;
- Brand X was not the best choice. Its trucks were not compatible with existing equipment and were unreliable: ironically they were also prone to self-ignition;
- Far better equipment could be sourced from either of two rival firms for half the cost.

The Fire Chief admitted being retained and paid by Brand X as an 'external adviser' and that he and his mistress[19] had been entertained on a two-week Caribbean cruise at the supplier's expense, but only so he could examine its fire extinguishing system. Oh Yes?

A variation of the test is to select a decision that has already been taken or a transaction that has been completed and rework it with the individuals concerned:

Arthur's case is further discussed on pages 505 and 539, but a postscript: his thespian qualities have to be admired. He faced trial for conspiracy to defraud but gave such powerful evidence that the jury was persuaded and found him not guilty.

Arthur Flying Out of the Window

Arthur – who was without question a psychopathic character[20] – had been recruited to head up a new leasing division (without any pre-employment screening) on a salary package that

---

18 Covertly: without the knowledge of the Fire Chief or others involved.

19 And in fraud and bribery cases there are lots of these, as well as disgruntled lovers.

20 He had a pencil thin moustache and wore Hush Puppies.

was incentivised on the size of the outstanding portfolio (with no account of credit risk or profitability). Within weeks, he approached friends and villains offering leasing facilities of millions of pounds for 10 per cent kickbacks to his wife's company.

If Internal Audit asked him even the simplest question he would fly into a rage, threatening to resign or have them dismissed. Things got so bad that the Managing Director gave instructions that no one was to speak to Arthur – not 'even to say good morning – unless he spoke first'.

Then the bad debts started to roll in. Arthur covered them by making even bigger advances and trousering further bribes in the process. The Group Managing Director intervened and arranged to work with Arthur for a day 'to learn a bit from an expert' by selecting a few transactions and seeing how they were handled.

After 90 minutes Arthur confessed, burst into tears and threatened to jump out of the window and kill himself. The ultra-cool Group Managing Director responded: 'Don't be an ass, Arthur, we are on the ground floor'. Arthur's tears turned to uncontrollable laughter.[21] But he later confessed to receiving £2 million in bribes for approving leases that cost his employer around £70 million.

Created Opportunities and Test Transactions

It is permissible in most countries to provide criminals with opportunities to repeat their crimes. Such techniques must be carefully controlled and proportionate to the potential risks.

Unrecorded Incoming Funds

If the theft of incoming funds is considered a possibility, one or two small bankers' cheques, not recorded as receivables, may be mailed to the organisation. Their subsequent processing can be traced and the accounts through which conversion takes place identified. These can be analysed to identify earlier incidents. If the funds are recorded accurately, it is another silver bullet for the Adequate Procedures Dossier.

Test transactions should be selected carefully and approved by management and a specialist litigation lawyer.

---

21   He was a psychopath (see page 292).

Test Purchasing

A cooperating third party (wearing fancy shoes) may be asked to approach an organisation's Purchasing Department expressing a wish to become an approved vendor. The way in which the application is managed should be monitored.

Testing may involve more elaborate stings, where a professional investigator poses as, for example, a headhunter, an information broker or a lap dancer.[22]

Elaborate Pretexts

The Sales Director of an American company, an unashamed womaniser, was believed to be paying bribes to win contracts in Indonesia. He was expected to attend a conference in Jakarta, flying first class from Chicago via Singapore. Competitors who believed they were losing out retained investigators who put two of their undercovers, posing as father and very attractive daughter, on the same flight. They contrived a flaming argument and the daughter – in tears – moved to sit next to the target. Twelve hours later after multiple glasses of champagne, she had the target's life story, including details of a $2 million villa he had bought for a government purchasing agent in Bali.

Although sting operations can be revealing, they must be carefully controlled under expert legal advice and managed by professionals. They can go horribly wrong, will invariably come to light, and most judges don't like them. If you don't believe this just track some of the recent Department of Justice–FBI stings: and they are the experts!

Site Visits and Inspections

Many frauds escaped detection because the victims never bothered to check in the real world the supposed facts on which they relied:

---

22   In such cases it is preferable to use a female operative!

Bank Loans

Many banks found out after the event that the address of the multinational conglomerate to which they had advanced funds was a camper in a parking lot. A bank loaned £5 million against finished stocks. Had they checked, they would have found that the company's warehouse space had a maximum capacity of £500,000. This is the sort of perverted decision that makes you wonder whether the bank manager was gullible or bent.

Covert visits of premises involved in key transactions or to the homes owned by those exposed to potentially corrupt decisions should be considered.

Corporate Social Responsibility

A CPA revealed what appeared to be excessive expenditure on the company's corporate social responsibility programme and especially on solar panels which covered the roof and side walls of its headquarters building. Investigators covertly drove past the homes of members of the Corporate Social Responsibility (CSR) team and discovered one home (as well as a number of neighbours' houses) bristling with panels and, in one case, a completely useless wind turbine.

The employee concerned admitted that he and his daughter ran an agency for an environmental company (which was the supplier of most of the solar panels) and had received special discounts and commissions for his own and his neighbours' installations. However, his managers were so committed to the environmental cause that they had approved the employee's part-time activities and no action was taken.

Fraud detectors should also consider overt 'walkabouts'[23] in:

- All work areas in which payments are processed, cheque forms stored and bank transmissions prepared and reconciled;
- Areas in which goods are checked in and out;
- Mail rooms;
- Plant, vehicle and building maintenance areas;
- Smoking areas (see page 604).

Detectors are also advised to inspect important operational areas in which control equipment – such as weighbridges, flow metres or distributed process control systems – are located and to examine the equipment for signs of interference, review fault and maintenance records and talk to the operators involved.

---

23   With eyes and ears open.

Concentrated Short Delivery

In a manufacturing process, a very expensive chemical was procured with a 100 per cent concentration and diluted with water to 70 per cent for inputting via a volumetric meter and concentrator as a catalyst. Examination of the device and knowledge of 'O-level chemistry' revealed that the lowest concentration the device could measure was 73 per cent. Thus operators diluted the chemical to 60 per cent,[24] thereby creating a surplus in raw inventory. This was used to conceal the vendor's short delivery of pure chemicals: greatly facilitated by bribing the operators.[25]

Cases such as the above illustrate the importance of testing for blue collar or operational corruption that could result in corporate liability under Section 7 of the Bribery Act.

The Great Green Sausage Scandal

Driver salesmen working for a food company were incentivised for selling product that was near to its sell-by date by offering supermarkets and other customers additional discounts. Most customers preferred product with a shelf life of 14 days or more.

Examination of drivers' incentive claims revealed that some were near-geniuses and able to sell 100 per cent of their short-dated allocations. Then the truth hit home. The rogue drivers had bought date-printing 'guns', so that they could alter sell-by dates on the outer packaging. Then by bribing customers' goods inwards staff to overlook the products' manky appearance, they were able to unload everything.[26]

Interviews

TYPES AND PRINCIPLES

Interviews[27] are an essential part of fraud detection, primarily in the circumstances shown in Table 20.4.

---

24   Which had no discernible effect on the reaction.

25   It turned out that the vendor had supplied the metering equipment free of charge.

26   The above explanation is a simplification of a very extensive scam which resulted in prison sentences for a number of van salesmen and their managers.

27   And just generally 'chatting'.

Table 20.4 Interview Types

Type of Interview	Interview With	Objectives
Information-seeking and intelligence development	Employees Associated Persons Third parties	Understanding how processes operate Test the internal culture Exposing previous incidents
Probing and checking	Contexts in which fraud is suspected	Confirming CPA and other findings Pinning accountability for outliers

Like most things in life,[28] it is much easier to get into trouble than to get out of it. Thus detectors are advised, for potentially important interviews, to:

- Identify the best person or persons to conduct each interview;
- Identify the best place and time to hold the interview and whether or not advance notice should be given. Ideally, sensitive interviews should be held in private on a one-to-one basis and away from work;
- Set objectives and success criteria;
- Check the background of the subject and his or her likely reaction;
- Try to have at least one outlier to discuss;
- Plan the interview's structure and the most important questions;[29]
- Assemble any documentation on CPA or other tests that the subject is required to explain;
- Say nothing that could not be easily defended in the witness box at the Old Bailey;
- Ensure that the subject[30] is not induced to breach his contract of employment or to perform improperly.

The Problems of Notes

One of the main failings of inexperienced interviewers is that they insist on writing copious notes at the time. Usually this is no more than a comfort blanket, but it is a turn off for everyone involved and especially subjects.

Interviewers should fully engage: look, listen, think, analyse and conclude. A few trigger notes are okay, providing a pen does not even touch the paper while the subject is speaking. If necessary, detailed notes can be made – and initialled by the subject – at the end of the interview.

---

28 Especially as you get older.

29 But do not use checklists or written questions until the close of the interview and only then to make sure that all points have been covered.

30 If, for example, working for a competitor.

ROUTINE INFORMATION-SEEKING

There is a massive difference psychologically between expecting a person to come forward to volunteer information and their responding to specific questions. Interviews with ex-employees, ex-vendors and customers are a source of valuable information and should be considered both as part of a detection trawl and for targeted enquiries.

Interviews should begin with open questions such as:

- Tell me all about your job with X.
- What did you like best about working in xx department?
- What were the department's strong points?
- Were there other departments in which you would have preferred to work?
- Each one might be followed with 'Can you tell me more about that?'

Responses to such non-threatening questions will enable the interviewer to assess the subject and how cooperative he might be on more sensitive matters.

If there are any suspicions that the subject is being deceptive, either by holding back relevant information or being deliberately misleading, two approaches are recommended. The first, especially if deliberate deception is suspected, is for the interviewer to play dumb when he already knows the answer,[31] expose the deception and then probe other matters where the answers are not known. The second is to ask for responses to be put in writing or for the interviewer to write detailed notes and ask the subject to sign them.

If the subject appears willing to talk, the interviewer should turn towards specific processes but without mentioning names of people or companies:[32]

- Did you have any concerns about fraud or bribery in Company X?
- What aspects do you think we should look at?

Such questions give the subject the opportunity to raise specific details about processes and suspect ex-colleagues and third parties.

Ideally, the interviewer should identify one or two points that need to be checked so that he has a good reason to contact the subject again. The first meeting with a potential informant is unlikely to produce much intelligence of value. It should be regarded as the first step towards building a relationship.

PROBING AND CHECKING INTERVIEWS

These are generally much more difficult and should only be conducted by experienced interviewers. Readers who have suffered this far with this book may want to apply for a discounted copy of *Deception at Work* by the authors. It may not turn them immediately into expert interviewers, but it is heavy enough to use as an offensive weapon.

---

31   Called, in *Deception at Work* by Michael J. Comer and Timothy E. Stephens (Gower, 2004), 'control questions'.

32   The rule is not to mention a name until it has already been raised by the subject.

Following Up and Investigating

All outliers, however detected, should be documented and pursued to resolution, which will typically include:

- Civil, criminal or disciplinary action;
- Controls improvement;
- Writing off.

Recommended investigation procedures are discussed in Chapter 34.

'I agree with you, Mr Jones. The only chance you have of
proving your innocence of the bribery charges is to bung the Judge'

'I don't care Mr Comer how much you are willing to bung me because
there is no way we can give an advance on this. But you could try Gower Publishing'

VI
Background on Effective Controls

CHAPTER 21 *Introduction on the Nature of Controls*

Politicians and regulators do not run businesses: the remaining parts of this book are for managers/practitioners who do.

The Need for Effective Controls

There are two reasons why companies should be committed to effective controls,[1] if not passionate about them. The first is because it is to everyone's benefit that businesses create wealth and employment and pay taxes, and to do this they have to run profitably. This means controlling and minimising losses and ensuring that commercial objectives – like sustainable profits – are realised. This is by far the most important reason for effective control.

The second reason for controls is that companies must comply with an ever-growing mountain of laws, regulations and rules and, if they fail to do so, they and their employees face severe penalties.

Governmental organisations – which are more usually involved in bribes being paid to their employees to perform improperly (incoming bribery) – should also make sure that controls are effective; firstly so that they discharge their official responsibilities fairly and efficiently; and secondly to protect their managers and employees from personal liabilities.[2] Despite all of the political and regulatory baying about corporates, many international and governmental agencies and departments are hopelessly controlled, wasteful and magnets for corruption. There are no better examples of pathetic control than the United Nations, European Union and, more recently, the Carbon World.

Putting Compliance in Context

Usually the second justification for controls – compliance – dominates commercial objectives and is unsurprisingly seen by those who create wealth in a depressing light and as a burden. The compliance space has been hijacked by negativity, unwarranted risk aversion and fears of legal liability, mainly driven by regulators and lawyers – some on contingency fees – and second-guessed by people who have never had to run a business. Managers with an ounce of experience know that if they make even a minor mistake their

---

1   And not simply 'adequate procedures'.

2   Unlikely as they are to be enforced against them, following the Bribery Act's subtle change in official liability and burdens of proof.

own survival is at risk. Fear can result in corporate cultures driven by uncertainty, in which avoiding criticism is the dominant motivator. Entrepreneurship, flexibility, innovation, profits and job satisfaction go out of the window in the clamour for compliance at all costs. **This is the problem** and if politicians and regulators do not quickly come to their senses, Western companies are doomed to be buried in red tape. But, perhaps, that is what some people want.

Pride and Enjoyment in Effective Controls

An objective of the control style suggested in this book is to create contexts of assured trust and inspired integrity in which employees, agents and others working on the company's behalf are empowered to perform commercially and, within clearly defined entrepreneurial and legal frameworks, to actually enjoy their jobs.[3]

A senior manager recently said:

> *Where is the pleasure in going to work? – I used to love my job. Now with all the red tape and legal liabilities for just scratching your nose, I could not care less. I used to employ 300 people. I will never do that again. I used to generate £100 million a year in revenues and pay around £22 million in tax. I will never do that again. I will just spend the rest of my life on the golf course and when my money runs out I will live off the state.*

There is no reason why managers should be terrified or bound by pedantic and cosmetic restrictions. But politicians, regulators and media commentators must fundamentally change their opinions about business and the nature of trust.

Mr Chomsky

Noam Chomsky, the darling of the Luvvies, is alleged to have said that all businesses are essentially amoral. But to see how connected to the real world was this genuinely distinguished academic, see his interview with Ali G on You Tube!

The University of Essex

Professor Paul Whiteley published a very valuable report in January 2012 which suggested that dishonesty in the UK is on the increase. He also concluded: 'Empirical research suggests that societies in which trust and integrity are strong perform much better on a range of economic and political indicators than societies where they are weak'.[4]

---

3 This is not a misprint!

4 'Are Britons becoming more dishonest' (University of Essex, Department of Government, 25 January 2012). Available at: http://www.essex.ac.uk/government/documents/are_britons_etting_more_dishonest.pdf (accessed 22 November 2012).

If Mr Chomsky's opinion is the starting point, it is little wonder that we are where we are and that there is a massive down on the private sector with senseless rules inflicted by the Nanny State.

'Compliance' is a Negative Word

It is true that there have been serious corporate failures and shocking frauds, but most businesses are run honestly and they – not politicians, regulators, auditors or even lawyers and investigators – create the wealth on which society depends. Compliance, by itself, adds no value, although we all understand that absence of it can be destructive.

'Compliance' is a negative word which implies that someone has to be led by the nose to do something he or she otherwise would not do. This is one reason why the word 'assurance' is preferred by companies that do not need to be led by the nose, that have the confidence to assert their right to manage and do not cower or tremble when deciding whether to scratch their noses or catch a bus.

If Western businesses were to conform to every letter in the anti-corruption and other legislation inflicted on them, they would win few, if any, contracts, especially in the private sector of overseas markets. If they pulled out altogether developing countries would be:

- Forced into the hands of Chinese, Korean, Russian and other nationalities who take no or minimal action to prohibit private sector corruption overseas: in fact it is encouraged, if not state-sponsored;
- Swamped with substandard goods and services at monopolistic prices to fund virtually unlimited bribes to their own national politicians, officials and business people.

The effect of such a unilateral withdrawal would be far more damaging to the deprived citizens than the status quo, and the corrupt extorting elite would remain undisturbed, as is now the case. In fact, skulduggers would welcome Western withdrawal because it removes any effective competition, thus allowing unrestrained pillaging.

Unintended Consequences

Anti-bribery legislation has three unintended but very serious consequences, in addition to those mentioned earlier. First, that if honest companies retreat, Western jobs are lost and tax revenues drop: far more than any benefits from negotiated settlements from alleged regulatory breaches. Members of the tree-hugging community argue that corporate resistance to the Bribery Act is an admission that companies do and have paid bribes. For most, this is not the case, but a reflection of the fact that they cannot run their businesses based on uncertainty over what rules apply to such trivia as proportionate hospitality or facilitation payments, and the hypocrisy of the official guidance, which on one hand says there should be zero tolerance immediately and on the other that companies should try to eliminate them in the longer term. You cannot have a zero tolerance policy that permits tolerance!

Secondly, and perhaps more importantly, Western withdrawal from corrupt markets enables unregulated nations to build long-term strategic relationships with countries that have critical natural resources and to monopolise their supplies.

Thirdly, if any company wishes to dismiss employees for corruption-related fraud (see page 689), to take civil recovery action against dishonest third parties, to claim under fidelity or other insurance, or to establish a deterrent to prevent future violations, it is almost compelled to make a self-disclosure to the Serious Fraud Office (SFO) with the possibility that the SFO will launch Section 7 charges against the company and that regulators and litigants – worldwide – will join in the game. The bottom line of this is that many companies will choose, rather than face this risk, to let fraudsters, bribers and other ne'er-do-wells walk away unpunished. This is a serious unintended consequence of legislation that was ill-considered.

The Opportunity for Effective Control

Part VI suggests ways in which companies can reduce incoming, outgoing and competitive bribery, as well as other types of fraud. **This is the opportunity and it exists today.**

Estimated Average Losses

On average,[5] companies lose 10 per cent per annum of their gross turnover as a result of their employees being corrupted. It follows that their corrupt counterparties, after adding back the bribes paid to individuals, gain an equivalent amount. Corruption is a zero sum game between colluders: although consumers pick up the tab.

Edward De Bono, who originated the term 'lateral thinking', said: 'A problem is something you want to do but can't. An opportunity is something you do not yet know it is your interest to do and can'.

In Part VI of the book we identify the opportunities that companies have for developing effective controls that support entrepreneurship, increases profitability, create enjoyable and fulfilling working environments and comfortably exceed compliance standards. This means reducing losses from incoming, outgoing, internal and competitive bribery and not simply fretting whether a Homer Simpson mouse mat might corrupt a foreign public official or a night out at the Red Pussycat Lap-dancing Club might influence an official's decision to buy a new waste paper basket.

This part of the book is not intended to be an encyclopaedia of every possible control. In fact it assumes that companies already have in place:

---

5   The authors' best guess.

- Effective human resources policies and procedures;
- Comprehensive IT security infrastructures;
- Accounting procedures that comply with international standards.

The discussion is intended to throw light on difficult aspects of control, provoke thought and suggest a few solutions, some of which might be unconventional, but they are based on over 40 years of front-line experience and, what is more, they work far better than adequate procedures. In some cases, the controls suggested (such as audit rights and full-bodied pre-employment screening processes) are at the tougher end of the range and as such inconsistent with the collaborative style recommended in other chapters. This is deliberate because it is easier to tone controls down rather than upwards.

The Nature of Controls

DEFINITIONS AND PRINCIPLES

A control may be defined as a procedure or hardware device,[6] whose *functionality* has been *specified* to assure the performance of something else.

- For example, the requirement for dual signatures on cheques may be a specified control.

Assurance is achieved when a control *functions* to its *specification*.

- For example, when one signatory signs a cheque in blank and leaves it for a colleague to countersign later, functionality is not as specified. The control is not assured and may fail.

Controls should be commensurate to the risk; this means that the starting point should always be risk assessment, which is easier to say than to do. It is examined in Chapter 14.

The relationship between risks and controls is complex and seldom will one control eradicate a single risk. Rather, they relate in a multidimensional matrix where a combination of controls may be necessary to deal with a single risk; or, on the other hand, a single control may be effective against a multitude of risks.

CONCEPT OF THE EXTENDED ENTERPRISE AND ASSOCIATED PERSONS

These days many companies outsource operations to third parties – including intermediaries, suppliers and customers and to others who perform services on their behalf. Such third parties should be regarded as part of the extended enterprise and be fully included in control programmes but not in the contentious way implied in many of the regulatory guidelines.

---

6   Defined later as an element.

Liability under the Bribery Act 2010 extends to third parties (associated persons) when they are performing services on the company's behalf, almost irrespective of the legal connection or ownership position.

What might or might not be classified as an association has not been accurately defined, other than through vague statements by some regulators,[7] that:

- Routine suppliers and subsidiary members of supply chains, as well as customers, will not normally be regarded as associated persons.
- Acts of an overseas subsidiary or foreign parent will only result in a liability under the Act when they are providing services on the UK company's behalf.
- Multinational or joint ventures incorporated overseas will only incur liability for the UK member (despite the fact that it may benefit from dividends and other income) when performing services on the UK's behalf.
- The activities of a UK partner's representative in a multinational or foreign joint venture, established purely by contract, will be assumed to be on its behalf, but the bribe must be for the UK partner's benefit and not simply for the joint venture.

The question of whether any entity is an associated person or performing services on the UK entity's behalf will be determined by the court, taking all the circumstances into account. This means that the safe course is to consider all third parties to be members of the Extended Enterprise and to include them under the integrity programme.

TYPES AND SELECTION OF CONTROLS

Controls may be applied to a specific element – such as an asset, process or human resource – in discrete contexts or in the environment as a whole. Policies on business ethics and technical routines in central computing are examples of environmental controls because they have a wide influence across multiple processes and contexts.

Controls may be mandatory (as standards) or optional (as guidelines); manual or automated, and fall into one or more of the following four categories:

1. **Preventive**: before the event and usually intended to restrict access to an element.[8] *Examples include such things as locks, passwords, separation of responsibilities, physical barriers, and authorisation tables.* Normally preventive controls are costly and if too restrictive lead honest people to believe they are not trusted, to frustration and ultimately disuse. They also lead to bureaucratic systems which encourage corruption. An effective preventive control should reduce at least one risk without creating others: at the same time, it should protect innocent people against unfounded suspicion of misconduct and create a positive, happy environment in which entrepreneurship flourishes. The importance of this second objective is never mentioned in regulatory guidelines.
2. **Reactive, or monitoring**: intended to give a fail-safe indication that a breach of preventive controls has taken or, better still, is about to take place. *Examples include burglar alarms, exception reports and fraud detection programmes.* Reactive controls are

---

7   No doubt to be clarified as time goes on.

8   An element is the something else requiring control.

usually cheap to maintain and do not burden honest people, since the threat of detection is only of concern to those who intend to misbehave. Reactive controls should be focused, automatic, incapable of disablement and carefully integrated into an assured control campaign.

3. **Reconstructive**: these trigger when both preventive and reactive controls have failed. They are intended to minimise the criticality of a loss. *Examples include contingency plans and fidelity insurance.* Reconstructive controls must be available when needed, tested, updated, relevant, simple and understood by the people concerned.

4. **Monitoring and enforcement**: which ensure that controls are maintained, violators are detected and penalised as a deterrent to others, and honest people protected.

Figure 21.1 Control Elements

As shown in Figure 21.1, the overall objective of controls in the commercial environment is to optimise profits and comply with laws and regulations, with the first priority being on prevention flowing through to detection, investigation, disruption and recovery.

The selection and combination of control elements – as shown in Figure 21.2 – has a determinative effect on culture, entrepreneurship spirit and effect.

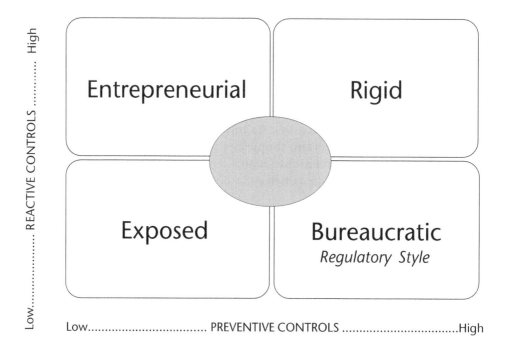

Figure 21.2 Balance of Preventive and Reactive Controls

Regulatory guidelines drive organisations towards reconstructive controls, as in category 3 above, resulting in bureaucratic and uncommercial styles that anticipate failure. Companies should consider using the minimum baseline of preventive controls and rely much more on monitoring and reaction controls, as in Category 2. This positioning is typical of entrepreneurial organisations and is explored in detail later and in Chapter 23.

In the anti-bribery field, as discussed in Chapter 12, there are thousands of ways through which bribes can be paid and concealed, but at the end of each chain they funnel into a perverted decision (or influence) and improper performance. Trying to prevent bribe payment and concealment is difficult, if not impossible. Therefore reactive controls should concentrate on identifying outputs that are indicative of corruption, such as windfall profits, exceptional losses, unwanted inventory, scrapped goods, stock losses, unused capital assets, deviations from normal costs, incomes and margins.

Equally, due diligence[9] (reframed hereafter as the more positive 'integrity validation') should be concentrated on the precise context in which perverted decisions are made.

In the case of agents, potentially corrupt decisions (proxy decisions) are influenced and taken between the agent and the final customer or supplier. This is the context on which due diligence should be concentrated, rather than simply on the agent's appointment.

---

9   Due diligence means checking to prove or disprove the existence of negative or disqualifying criteria. Integrity validation means identifying and validating a candidate's positive attributes, balancing them against any adverse findings.

IMPLEMENTATION OF CONTROLS

Controls may be implemented through:

- People using hardware or following a specified procedure, *such as invoice approval*;
- Technical or automated operations, *such as computer access control*;
- Hardware alone, such as weighbridges or cash registers.

Although, for reasons explained later, the tone from the top is not determinative, it is true that without it, controls will fail. The hierarchy of controls can be represented as follows:

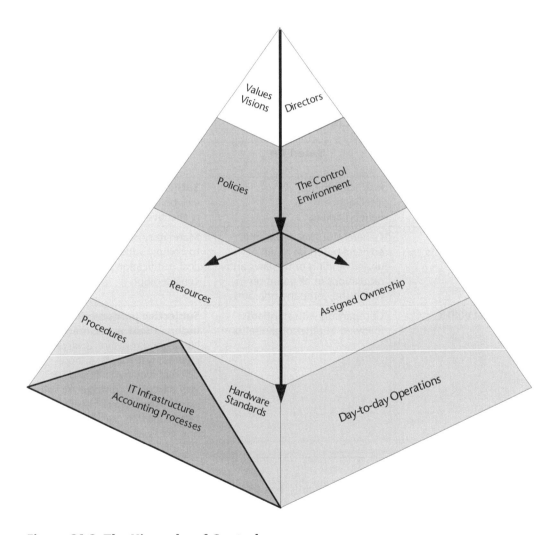

Figure 21.3 The Hierarchy of Controls

Figure 21.3 represents the flow of controls from top management polies down to where it matters at working levels.

The ultimate purpose of controls is to provide assurance at a day in, day out working level. This means:

- Control specification: commensurate with evolving risks;
- Assignment of ownership rights: aligning authority to responsibility;
- Training, mentoring and supervision;
- Effective implementation through procedures, hardware and technical routines;

– and effective monitoring and incident detection, investigation and resolution, leading to assurance.

JUSTIFICATION FOR CONTROLS

In many cases it is not possible to calculate with any degree of certainty whether a control is *cost-effective* or not. Table 21.1 summarises the justification for controls:

Table 21.1 Justification for Controls

Objectives Input:	Based On	Comments
COMMERICIAL SUCCESS	Risk assessment Intelligence Benchmarking	**Subjective judgement** or independent assessment of what is effective and cost-justified
COMPLIANCE Legal requirements	General Counsel or external advisers based on a full understanding of the laws and regulations in all countries in which the company operates	Mandatory requirement to comply with the law: cost-justification is not a consideration
BENCHMARKING	Comparison with standards followed in other organisations	**Subjective judgement or independent assessment**. Not a good measure as varying cultures, systems etc. impose different requirements and it is very difficult to compare like with like. However, if a company falls behind industry standards, this may act to its disadvantage in civil, criminal and regulatory actions

Thus the effectiveness of a control usually has to be judged subjectively on a qualitative basis, recognising that:

- If a control works effectively, that fact may never be known.
- The effectiveness of a control may only become obvious when failure is detected or resists a known attack.

Controls should always be evaluated from the position of a potential opponent, who is at risk if his dishonesty is detected.

- For example, the requirement to make an annual declaration of compliance and to discuss it during a review may be of little concern to an honest person. However, for someone who has broken the rules his or her signature and commitment to what might become a demonstrable untruth has an effect both as a deterrent and on his or her reaction to and during a review.

Thus one of the rules in mapping risks and controls is to think like a villain.

CONTROL GUIDELINES

Nearly every regulatory agency as well as non-governmental organisations and environmental and other charities appear to have no hesitation in issuing guidelines and instructions for compliance with their particular silo of interest. This may be understandable, but it makes it difficult for companies to sort the good from the bad and to consolidate all the requirements in a way that they can be effectively implemented.

In the bribery context, the Ministry of Justice guidelines have six principles, the Federal Sentencing Guidelines have seven, Transparency International has 241 core indicators, the Organisation for Economic Cooperation and Development (OECD) has 12 principles, mainly directed towards foreign bribery, and COSO[10] has hundreds focused on accurately reporting financial results. In July 2009 the SFO issued guidelines in an 'Approach to Dealing with Overseas Corruption',[11] which are quite different from those from the Ministry of Justice. Further, the Bribery Act 2010 does not make it obligatory for companies to self-disclose suspected violations, yet the SFO makes it very clear that if this does not happen, their displeasure is much more likely to result in prosecution.

The problem is that, besides the fact that official guidelines create organisations that are bureaucratic and fearful, the SFO is unwilling to endorse any of them. If regulators are so minded, they can point to any single control or red flag that has not been followed and use it to argue that procedures were inadequate. The bottom line is that companies cannot rely on any of the official guidelines on corruption to help them develop adequate procedures and they cannot rely on adequate procedures to defend other than a charge under Section 7. Companies are being told to work in a climate of unmanageable uncertainty.

---

10   Committee of Sponsoring Organisations – Treadway – used as the model in the Sarbanes–Oxley Act.

11   Which appears to have been withdrawn following the appointment of a new Director.

22 *Control Tools and Misconceptions*

Background

There are hundreds of tools which can be used for control. The following paragraphs explore the most significant in the corporate fraud and corruption context. Chapters 28–32 discuss enhanced controls for anticorruption.

Separation of Responsibilities

The Ministry of Justice (MOJ) guidelines emphasise the importance of separation of responsibilities and the supposed safety of consensus by committees. In reality, functional separation, which is the conventional recommendation, is fragile – another cosmetic – and leads to confused accountability, bureaucracy and a lack of job satisfaction.

There are, in fact, different ways in which responsibilities can – and sometimes – must be separated. Examples are given in Table 22.1.

Table 22.1   Types of Separation

Type of Separation	Separation Between	
	Level 1	Level 2
	Example	Comment
Organisational	Parent company	Subsidiary
Geographical	Head office in London	Remote branch in Jakarta
Functional	End-user Department	Central purchasing
Horizontal versus vertical	Senior manager	Subordinate
Strategic versus tactical	Board-level approval	Lower-level implementation
Date and time	Validity or cut-off dates	
Hardware versus human	Approved at the appropriate level	Implemented automatically
Preventive versus reactive	Line management	Audit or compliance

The most effective forms of separation are usually between stages in high value transactions[1] and between strategy and execution.[2] This should be considered especially in the control of major capital purchases, appointment of intermediaries and government relationships (see Chapters 25 and 32).

Example of Separation

The decision matrix and strategy for selecting intermediaries should be set by the board of directors. Individual appointments can be made at an operational level based on matrix scores.[3]

There is one type of separation that does not get the attention it deserves and that is between the back and front office, especially in banks and trading operations. In Nick Leeson's case[4] lessons learned while he was working in the back office gave him the knowledge – once he was promoted to trader – to run rings around controls.

Ownership and Committees

An essential principle that runs contrary to the separation of responsibilities is that of pinning ownership of a risk or control to an individual or a specific team. This means, among other things, that every asset and every process has a designated owner who has the authority to manage and protect it and bears the responsibility for failure. Ownership establishes personal accountability:

OWNERSHIP + ACCOUNTABILITY = AUTHORITY + RESPONSIBILITY

'Please Turn to Page 252'

Consultants were retained by a major international company to review and improve its IT security. They were told: don't write a big report as our people are too busy to read them; don't try to rush around the world making presentations; and forget about making any sort of gimmicky video. This was a tough brief, but the consultants identified serious problems, mainly caused by a total lack of ownership, with senior managers who had the power and authority to improve controls doing nothing because they knew they could blame their subordinates for any failure.

---

1   Such as payments authorisation.
2   Simply because (as explained in Chapter 12 page 297) horizontal collusion is far more common than vertical.
3   See page 572.
4   And there are plenty of others.

The consultants wrote a very large book, *Information Security Standards*. The first page gave a brief introduction and said: If you want to improve controls over the resources for which you are responsible, please turn to page 2. This contained a checklist with the following introduction:

If you believe everything is fine and you do not need to make any improvements, please turn to page 252.

This page said:

Please complete and sign the following letter addressed to the Managing Director.

The letter said:

I have received the Standards on IT Security and I am totally satisfied that everything is fine and that nothing can go wrong. If it does, I will resign without question and pay back anything that has been lost.

The page also contained a postscript which said: if you won't want to sign this letter, please turn back to page 2. Most people did just that and controls improved.

Senior managers should assign ownership rights and responsibilities through organisation charts, job descriptions, contracts, policies, training, supervision and procedures. Owners may delegate partial custodianship or user rights to others. Delegated responsibilities must be clearly specified preferably through a single managerial reporting line.

Multiple Reporting Lines

Nicholas Leeson, who cost Barings Bank around £800 million, had an administrative reporting line to senior managers in Singapore and a functional line to a Specialist Product Group in London. He was able to succeed in his scam for so long because of a lack of communication, if not rivalry, between his two bosses enabled him to say one thing to one and something totally different thing to the other. No manager had ownership of Mr Leeson's supervision.

The Woolf Report on British Aerospace (BAE), Transparency International, the Organisation for Economic Cooperation and Development (OECD) and especially politicians have an endearing faith in the benefits of committees, possibly brought about by watching too many episodes of the British comedy series, 'Yes, Prime Minister'.

In the fraud and corruption areas, committees are virtually useless: they obscure accountability, can be manipulated by dominant members and are often just plain inefficient.[5]

Need to Know and Need to Go

Access control is a sound principle with the objective of limiting entry to premises, assets, procedures and accounting records to those who have a genuine 'need to go'. The principle can be implemented by hardware such as physical barriers, automated procedures such as passwords, login routines and in other ways.

A similar principle applies to restricting information to people who have a genuine need to know. This obviously applies to such things as the conduct of investigations and personnel matters; but also in the dissemination of procedures, which should be segmented so that skulduggers cannot be sure controls in contexts outside their own might expose them.

The Principle of Raising the Pavement

Controls should be designed to make a potential attacker realise he will be committed to a course of conduct that cannot be plausibly excused. In police terms he puts himself "on offer". This may have a significant deterrent effect, except on psychopaths, who present entirely different problems, discussed later.

Raising the Pavement

If most people were asked to walk on the edge of a kerbstone, along the edge of a pavement, they would have no difficulty doing so. If the pavement were raised 20 feet above the ground, with a sheer drop on one side, the prospect becomes more daunting, even though the probability of falling off is the same as before.

Most people would not commit themselves to walking near the sheer drop (showing a lack of commitment); others would refuse to try; others would try and then fall off. A small number may try and succeed.

This illustrates the point that criticality of failure affects the probability of occurrence.

---

5   The Oil for Food programme contains classic examples of how inefficient and unaccountable committees can be.

Annual Declaration

For five years an employee complied with his company's policy and submitted an annual declaration that he had no private interests that could conflict with his obligations to his employer. When it subsequently emerged that he was effectively the owner of a company supplying industrial gloves and protective clothing to his employer: that he had pre-qualified it as a vendor and approved most of the contracts, the declarations came back to haunt him. They proved his dishonest intent.

Repeated false declarations are also very useful in proving a person's guilty knowledge.

Deterrence

A conventional view is that the fear of detection and punishment is a powerful deterrent against all forms of crime and to an extent this applies to corporate fraud and corruption. However, experience shows that:

- Deterrence is proportional to the perceived probability of detection and less so the severity of punishment: especially the fear of imprisonment;[6]
- But it does not last for long.

Cases are quickly forgotten and many crooks hold the view that they will not get caught; and that if they do they can talk their way out of trouble or blackmail the corporate victim into submission. This is especially true of people with psychopathic tendencies (see pages 290 and 292 et seq) who may even be motivated to commit fraud and corruption simply because of the challenge and excitement or risk.

However, companies should:

- Introduce audit, continuous monitoring and other procedures that increase the probability of detection;
- Empower and hold Internal Audit and Security responsible for fraud detection;
- Investigate all suspicions thoroughly;
- Take the hardest line possible when violations are proven, and even if the action alerts regulators to what they may interpret as a Bribery Act or FCPA violation.

They should also consider publishing the results of investigations in internal communications or, if the company really wants to be effective, hang the withering bodies of skulduggers outside the main gates. However, readers should note that this may contravene the laws of some countries.

---

6   Which, thanks to the MOJ's key performance drivers to cut prison budgets, becomes increasingly unlikely.

Decision Support Procedures and Auditability

MORE BACKGROUND ON DECISIONS

A central theme of this book is that the critical point in all cases of corruption is the integrity of decision-making both in and outside the organisation. This is called '**decision-centricity**'. This is far more important than country risks, red flags and other superficial criteria suggested by the MOJ, especially so since companies cannot function effectively if – as a result of uncertainties created by the laws over what is and what is not a bribe – they become afraid to make decisions and as a result forego genuine commercial opportunities. **However, there is no risk of anyone being charged with a bribery offence if it can be proven that there was no intention to induce a perverted decision and thus improper performance.**[7] So being able to demonstrate the actual or intended decision-drivers is key.

The fact is that very few organisations have identified the contexts and decisions that are most exposed to incoming, internal, outgoing and competitive corruption, the contexts and processes in which they are made, and who makes them, why or when. They have even less understanding of how decisions are made. Chapters 14–17 set out a methodology for identifying high-risk decisions from both a financial and a regulatory point of view and this chapter recommended decision-making and other procedures.

It is important to make a distinction between the processes used to make decisions and their outcomes. Almost all decisions involve uncertainty and a degree of luck and chance, so no one can guarantee the best outcome. But they can be 100 per cent sure that the process used was demonstrably honest. This is what decision-centricity is all about.

DECISION TRAINING AND MENTORING

It is rare for organisations to train their employees and associated persons in decision-making skills in the light (or, more accurately, the murk) of bribery legislation. Even fewer have specified processes that optimise decisions in real time and create evidential trails of integrity. Suggested procedures and enhanced training programmes – which are critical in the context of the Bribery Act – are discussed in Chapters 28 and 29.

RECOMMENDED DECISION-MAKING PROCESSES

Controls must protect honest people and encourage them to take decisions without being worried that their initiative will result in false accusations being made against them. For this reason processes should be specified for making and validating decisions. The recommended model is based on the Kepner–Tregoe (KT) system.[8]

This model should apply to all important internal decisions (Table 22.2). It can also be used to prevent allegations of outgoing corruption by providing an audit trail that an external decision was not perverted by extraneous factors such as hospitality payments or small gifts.

---

7   Or in the case of a foreign public official (FPO), 'influence', whatever that means.

8   There are alternative models (see the Web) but KT has been consistently excellent in repeated assignments and different contexts.

Table 22.2 The Kepner–Tregoe model

Processes Applied to *Examples*	What is Achieved?
Incoming bribery (bribes received) • *Procurement* • *Recruitment* • *Investments* • *Other decisions that could favour third parties*	Provides the methodology for assessing binary (yes or no) and graded decisions Exposes bias by decision-makers Ensures that optimum decisions are taken Assesses the impact of decisions Provides an audit trail Deters and detects corruption
	Decisions are made based on objective criteria Based on needs and wants
Outgoing bribery (bribes paid) • *Marketing* • *Selection of intermediaries* • *Investments* • *Other decisions by third parties*	Reduces the possibility that decisions taken by third parties could be improperly influenced Provides an agreed and transparent basis for making decisions Exposes bias by decision-makers Provides an audit trail Deters and detects corruption Proves that hospitality and other advantages given to third parties were not influential in the decision
	Agreed a criteria with third parties

Defending Spurious Allegations

If regulators allege that the intention was to pervert a third party decision by, for example, hospitality, the matrix can be used to show precisely what criteria were influential. The defence is even more compelling if the third party fully confirms the assessment.

The KT system is built on the principle that there are needs (which are absolute requirements) and wants (which are desirable attributes) in every binary- and multiple-choice decision. Any option that does not satisfy a need should be excluded. The importance of each want is weighted on a scale of 1 (poor) – 100 (excellent) and multiplied by a score reflecting to what extent the attribute is satisfied (again on a scale of 1 to 100). The weighted score of each attribute is multiplied into a total.

Weight × Score = Total for attribute

The revised KT system proposed in this book requires decision-makers to identify positive and negative needs and wants and to calibrate them depending on their relative significance. This may seem no more than common sense but in many aspects of the corruption field – for example, the selection of intermediaries and agents – only the negative attributes are considered. This, as is explained more fully in Chapter 25, does not result in the selection of the best candidate, but merely the one with the least damaging adverse information or red flag in its public record.

A Matter of Luck What Gets Into the Public Record

In the Siemens, Daimler, BAE, Oil for Food and other cases there were hundreds of agents, politicians, customers, suppliers and foreign public officials (FPOs) whose fingers were buried so deep in the cash register of extortion that only the tips of their toes were visible. Have you ever wondered why their prosecutions have never been publicised and neither have their identities?

Have you ever wondered why not one of the regulatory agencies has released the names of such skulduggers in an equivalent of the 'Banned Organisations List'? **Doesn't it make a mockery of the demand for due diligence when such critical information is withheld from public records?** The truth is that an adverse public record is more a matter of luck than integrity.

The following is a simple example, but it demonstrates the recommended process.

Appointing a New Agent

Brightside Industries had been represented in Bentovia for the past three years by Old Agent LLC, which is a small firm with only four employees. It had been reasonably successful but a recently appointed senior Brightside trader – Billy Bent – demanded that the agreement should be cancelled and that Dodgy Deals – which he said was successfully working with a Chinese competitor – should be appointed in its place.

Unbeknown to his colleagues, Mr Bent's enthusiasm was based mainly on the fact that while working for his previous employer he had shared in Dodgy Deals' commissions and was now looking to do the same by introducing it to Brightside. Mr Bent knew that:

- The beneficial owner of Dodgy Deals is a Politically Exposed Person (PEP) although her interest has been deeply concealed by a convoluted arrangement of offshore companies and special entity vehicles.

- Dodgy Deals is paying bribes on behalf of its Chinese client.

- It had been dismissed by Brightside's American competitor for paying bribes and was currently under investigation for corruption.

- Dodgy Deals had no office in Bentovia and no experience in the sector concerned.

- Its main client had given notice of termination.

- It had inadequate financial backing and an appalling credit history.

Mr Bent knew if his recommendation was to be accepted it would be necessary to conceal all of the above and to get his skuldugger's boots on.

Brightside's Head Trader – Sammy Smart – had not been happy and formed a small working group (consisting of himself, Mr Bent and a trader called Norman Nice) to examine five candidates and come to a decision. This did not please Mr Bent and he went immediately on the attack, making false allegations against two of the candidates, which resulted in their immediate disqualification. Mr Smart did not think through the consequences and agreed.

The three remaining candidates submitted application forms. Dodgy Deals lied about its beneficial owner, the current investigation in America and concealed its previous relationship with Billy Bent. The other three other applications were truthful. But:

- Eight years ago Red Herring LLC had been convicted in Bentovia of dumping toxic waste in the Oil Minister's goldfish pond.

- Blue Sky Enterprises Inc., which is incorporated in the Cayman Islands, insisted that its commissions must be paid to a numbered offshore account. (The owner explained and provided documentation to show that the reason for this was to avoid a penal divorce settlement with his ex-wife).

Mr Bent exaggerated these supposed failings and argued that they were disqualifying red flags and that Dodgy Deals should be appointed without further delay, especially following his report that the owner of Old Agent LLC had fallen over a cliff and that the business would be forced to close.

Mr Smart produced a list of criteria he thought might be relevant in selecting the new agent. He asked the other members of the team to complete a chart, showing the needs and wants based on the attributes of Brightside's most successful agents.

Billy Bent had gone ballistic and said they should 'stick to the facts' and that relying on attributes of agents in other countries was 'not appropriate'.

The initial responses of needs and suggesting weights for wants were as shown in Table 22.3.

Table 22.3 Initial Attributes of Needs and Wants

Attribute	Needs and Wants		
	Sammy Smart	Billy Bent	Norman Nice
Totally honest application form and supporting documents	Need	50	Need
Not subject to any criminal or regulatory investigation	Need	50	100
No undisclosed criminal convictions (Company or closely associated persons)	Need	Need	Need
Not included on any banned organisation or sanctions list such as FATF or PEP	Need	50	Need
Strength of the business case and potential income	Need	100	100
Office and track record in Bentovia	100	50	100
No potential conflict of interest (through working with a competitor)	70	20	50
No history of business failures	70	30	100
Services never terminated by a reputable competitor	50	20	100
Matched the attributes of other successful agents	100	0	90

Billy Bent insisted that the division between needs and wants was 'academic mumbo jumbo' and that that they should specify a factor for any criminal conviction during the past 10 years (realising that Red Herring would score badly on this point) and for offshore payments (making the case worse for Blue Sky Enterprises LLC). After much argument the consensus evaluation matrix was agreed as shown in Table 22.4.

Table 22.4 Agreed Evaluation of Needs and Wants

Factor	Final Scoring Needs and Weighting of Wants			
	Smart	Bent	Nice	Agreed
Totally honest application form and supporting documents	Need	50	Need	100
Not subject to a criminal or regulatory investigation	Need	50	100	100
No undisclosed criminal convictions (company or closely associated persons)	Need	Need	Need	100
Not included on any banned organisation or sanctions list, nor a PEP	Need	50	Need	100
Strength of the business case and potential income	100	100	100	100

Office and track record in Bentovia	100	50	100	80
No potential conflict of interest (by working for a competitor)	70	20	50	60
No history of business failures	70	70	100	70
Does not require payment offshore	50	Need	50	70
No criminal convictions in past 10 years	20	Need	50	60

With the benefit of hindsight (although it should have been detected at the time) Billy Bent had manipulated the scoring – especially in the shaded boxes – to make sure that if the adverse data on Dodgy Deals was discovered during a due diligence review, they should still win. The final scoring was as shown in Table 22.5.

Table 22.5 Summary of Scoring

Appraiser	Candidate			
	Dodgy Deals	**Red Herring**	**Blue Sky**	**Variation Low to High**
Sammy Smart	56,480	63,100	59,000	11.72%
Billy Bent	75,600	56,100	53,300	41.83%
Norman Nice	60,800	65,800	63,600	8.22%
Average	64,293	61,667	58,633	9.65%
% High to Low Variation	**33.85%**	**17.29%**	**19.10%**	

It resulted in Dodgy Deals having the highest average score from three appraisers, but before its appointment was made Mr Bent was arrested for corruption with his previous employer.

As the above example shows, corrupt bias may be exposed by:[9]

- Manipulation of the initial needs, wants and scoring criteria (the dishonest participant will usually add or remove attributes to support a perverted decision or to substitute low scoring wants in place of needs);
- Unjustified exclusion of suitable candidates for no or unsubstantiated reasons;
- Massive variations in scoring between the individual appraisers, either in totals or for individual attributes;
- Perverted decisions being highlighted by variations between high and low scores. *In this case Mr Bent's variation was 41.83 per cent against an average of 9.65 per cent and the high to low variation in the score for Dodgy Deals is a dead giveaway.*

---

9   Blank Excel templates for evaluating most types of decisions can be downloaded from www.cobasco.com

DECISIONS BY COMMITTEES

Committee decisions do not eliminate corruption and, on the contrary, are inclined to allow its concealment by obscuring accountability and polarising risks at the extremities.[10] It is only necessary to review the Oil for Food fiasco or President Kennedy's Commission's decision to 'invade' Cuba – to confirm the hopelessness of committees, especially when their rules of engagement require universal consensus, as is the case in the United Nations Framework Convention on Climate Change (UNFCCC) for administering the Clean Development Mechanism (see page 256). Even the distinguished Lord Woolf, in putting together his recommendations to get BAE back on track, was strongly in favour of committees. **With all respect, he was wrong: committees are usually a cop-out by weak people who want to avoid responsibility.**

The old saying sometimes applies:

The Inverse Intelligence of Committees

The intelligence of a committee varies inversely with the number of its members, divided by the square root of the Patchi chocolate biscuits on the conference table, after deducting the vintage of the Château Lafite to be served at lunch.

The Brightside example was effectively a committee decision and illustrated many of the general principles:

- Every committee should include at least one sceptic or 'pooper'.
- Each committee member should be provided with detailed information in advance of meetings and required to write a brief summary of his or HER position[11] with recommendations or to prepare evaluation charts along the lines of the Brightside example. These should be exchanged at the start of the discussion and not before!
- The problem or decision to be made should be accurately framed.
- Junior members should be invited to express their views first.
- Detailed minutes of the meeting[12] – including initial individual submissions and final matrices – should be retained, showing how and by whom votes were cast, and dissenting views.

The selection of members of the committee is also important and for major decisions should include representatives of different sexes[13] with age and experience spreads.

---

10 Evidence shows that people take extreme risk-averse or risk-seeking decisions in committees that they would never take personally.

11 Starting with why a decision is necessary at all.

12 Ideally under an independent Chair.

13 All six.

PEER GROUP REVIEWS

The most difficult decisions to supervise and validate are those taken by technical and specialist staff (including external consultants and lawyers) in aspects beyond their line manager's knowledge. This is dangerous. An effective solution is to have a specialist or technical decision reviewed by a qualified peer group:

Controlling People with More Skills than Managers

Nicholas Leeson was able to bamboozle his managers with a supposedly successful scheme of arbitraging between SIMEX in Singapore and the Osaka Stock Exchange. His explanation was ridiculous, but managers did not want to show their ignorance by asking questions and therefore kept quiet. Had Mr Leeson been asked to present his strategy to traders working as his peers or even subordinates the fraud would have been prevented.

ELECTRONIC CONFIDENTIAL CONFESSIONAL BOX

A feature of most corrupt decisions is their opacity. A person who wishes to establish how and why a decision that might later be questioned was honestly taken, obviously has the option of discussing it with a supervisor or writing memos and file notes. However two or three years later, when the matter is subject to a critical review, supervisors may have moved on, forgotten what was agreed, or refuse to become involved.[14]

One solution is for the company to create a secure website for employees and associated persons to diarise and time-stamp decisions or matters that might later be contentious in a separate and secure electronic archive that one of authors' clients refers to as its 'Electronic Confessional Box'. The Cloud program 'Evernote' – which permits entries to be encrypted – is an excellent platform for both personal and corporate confessional boxes.

In addition, employees might wish to archive meetings with FPOs, details of provided and received hospitality and, in fact, any other matter they consider may be questioned in the future. The electronic confessional box thus protects honest employees. It is also an important component in the continuous monitoring process discussed on page 575.

Competitive Bidding

The principle of competitive bidding is so ingrained in private and public sector procurement that it is taken for granted and yet the control advantages – in practice – are limited and are open to abuse. See Chapters 18–20 for a not exceptional critical point auditing (CPA) review that showed some alarming defects in the competitive bidding process.

---

14   This happens a lot.

This is not to say that competitive bidding is a waste of time, merely that it is not the cure-all it is portrayed to be and needs to be fully risk-assessed.

Approval and Authorisation

Processes that specify that transactions must be authorised at the right level are sound, but they do not always function as specified[15] because:

- Authority tables are incomplete or imprecise;
- People know that signing above their authority level will not be detected or sanctioned;
- Corrupt senior managers impose their will on subordinates and intervene in decisions that should be delegated;
- Transactions are subdivided to fall within an approval level;
- Managers delegate approval unofficially;
- Busy managers do not check underlying documentation before approval;
- People are unwilling to challenge questionable transactions.

The main problem with most authorisation processes is that the initiator is able to change details after approval. This is one aspect where the principle of separating responsibilities is valid and under no circumstances should authorised documents be returned to the originator unless a locked-in copy is retained or a copy duplicated to a third party.

Each organisation has to decide its approach towards authorisation of financial transactions and all other significant decisions throughout the extended enterprise.[16] There are two approaches:

1. Everything is approved unless specified to the contrary.
2. Everything is prohibited unless specified to the contrary.

The choice helps shape the culture of the organisation. The first option, although it involves additional risk, supports a more flexible – job satisfied – culture. The second is typical of bureaucracies.

Whichever option is chosen, supervisors should be trained and encouraged to take a close interest in the transactions or activities they authorise:

Making Controls Fun

A credit-rating agency was concerned that junior employees working in its telephone call centre were far too casual in the way they questioned applicants and approved transactions. It set up a system where operators were told that at least once a day a dummy call would be made by actors who would give false information about their application. Every time a

---

15   They should also clearly state whether levels are inclusive or exclusive of VAT. They should be exclusive.

16   The decisions delegated to intermediaries and other third parties should be specified.

dummy call was detected the operator would score points, providing he or she had been polite. Each month the winner with the most points would receive a £1,000 voucher, with smaller value prizes for second, third and fourth places. The efficiency of the team improved dramatically and morale shot through the roof.

Authority tables should also reinforce the prohibition – set out in procedures, job descriptions and contracts – over the payment and receipt of bribes and gifts, as well as adherence to the company's integrity programme. It is impossible to repeat this prohibition too often. For example, an authority table might state:

Comprehensive Authority Tables

Employees and others retained to perform services for the company are specifically prohibited from offering, giving, etc. any advantage or rewarding any third party with the intention of inducing him or her to perform an official or business function or activity improperly. If they act in contravention of this requirement they will be deemed not to be performing services on the company's behalf and subject to instant dismissal.

To what extent such terms would be upheld by a court in absolving the company of Section 7 responsibility for the actions of an associated person has yet to be tested.

Rotation of Duties

Rotation of duties can be used to break up suspected collusive groups and may be long-term and permanent or applied as a surprise short-term exercise.

Signatures

Signatures are used for identification and authorisation purposes and while they are better than nothing, their control value is limited.

The Weakness of Signatures

Hill Samuel is a leading Merchant Bank, based in the City of London. Various trading departments generate transactions which require settlement. These departments prepared forms authorising payments under the signature of two employees. After authorisation, the forms were sent in the internal mail to the Cables Room, where relatively junior employees compared the signatures against specimens. If the signature on the payment form appeared to match the specimen on visual inspection, the transaction was processed. One day, someone put 13 false payment instructions into the system: these were processed and £100 million paid out. Fortunately, Hill Samuel's reconciliation procedures were such that most of the money was recovered. But it was lucky; most victims are not.

The same sort of scam has been repeated hundreds, if not thousands, of times, and most organisations are vulnerable because they place too much reliance on signatures. A better control – especially on approval forms – is to use secure authentication methods such as check digits, personal identification numbers and biometrics.

Change Control

Procedures should be put in place so that all hardware, personnel and process changes should be risk-assessed and, where necessary, lead to additional or reduced controls.

Business and Counter-intelligence

All companies should have a specified process – with assigned ownership – for developing and disseminating intelligence on all internal and external factors that they consider might affect – either *positively or negatively* – their operations.

Important **sources** of information include:

- The Internet (especially industry blogs and specific sites);
- Publications by professional firms (lawyers, accountants and consultants);
- Liaison with members of the extended enterprise.

Information from all sources should be consolidated and analysed, where necessary supported by further enquiry. Output should be used primarily by business line managers in day-to-day operations and important compliance-related data should be summarised on a short report to be reviewed at board level.

The company might also consider active participation in industry initiatives and other blogs to correct misleading information, to seek or seed ideas and to generally influence the views of the commentariat in its favour.

Tripwires and Created Opportunities

Some frauds are difficult, if not impossible to prevent and consideration should be given to creating a few opportunities which can be closely monitored to detect improper behaviour. For example:

Table 22.6 Possible Tripwires

Areas in which Tests Can Be Set	Examples	Follow-up Action/Results
Goods outwards	Surplus goods may be loaded onto delivery trucks	The vehicle may be followed to identify receivers
Goods inwards	Surplus goods may be delivered	The way in which the surplus is recorded or converted may be audited
Incoming funds	A number of incoming payments (not recorded in accounts receivable) may be sent into the company	These may be monitored. If they are misappropriated, the method of conversion can be used to track previous frauds
Dormant accounts	Accounts payable and receivable	These may be monitored for signs of conversion
Unallocated cash	Small payments are made into the company in a way that their source cannot be traced. They are monitored to see how they are accounted for and whether any attempt is made to convert them	

Care has to be taken not to breach the laws on entrapment. However, it is extremely rare, when created opportunities have been exploited, not to find the same methods of conversion and concealment in earlier cases.

CHAPTER **23** *The Inspiring Integrity Campaign*

Introduction And Background

A DIFFERENT APPROACH

This chapter sets out some important background and then the framework for creating a 'campaign' of inspired integrity that:

- Optimises performance;
- Nurtures entrepreneurial and happy working environments;
- Gives people the confidence to manage and take decisions;
- Ensures that managers are connected and not ambushed with outbreaks of Diamonditis;[1]
- Creates marketing, public relations and other advantages, with integrity as the selling point;
- Surpasses every regulatory requirement.

Inspired integrity can be achieved at a lower cost than a typical 'box-ticking' compliance programme. However and this will be the sticking point, because the proposal requires fundamental reframing and creative thought. The chapter closes by presenting a methodology for benchmarking ~~compliance policies~~[2] integrity campaigns and measuring their effectiveness, and concludes that most fall short of optimal.

The main differences between the usual 'compliance' approach to corruption and the inspired integrity opportunities suggested in this book are summarised in Table 23.1.

---

1   Named after Bob Diamond, who was kept in the dark over the LIBOR scandal.

2   Forget it!

Table 23.1 Different Approaches to Tone from the Top

Consequences of Regulatory Recommendations	Recommended Approach
Focused on compliance	Focused on inspired Integrity
Presented in a legal–compliance frame	Framed as a commercial opportunity
Primarily directed towards complying with UK and US anti-bribery legislation; commercial success is a secondary consideration. This puts the cart before the horse	Focused primarily on realising commercial objectives while complying with all relevant legislation (and not just the Bribery Act 2010)
Framed in a single regulatory silo and mainly to deal with bribe payments to foreign public officials (FPOs)	Inclusive and comprehensive. Attempts to consolidate requirements in all regulatory silos Deals with incoming, outgoing, internal and competitive corruption and fraud
Tone from the top is assumed to apply entity–wide. Honest behaviour is not dispositional	Focused on inspired integrity, especially in risky contexts and the continuous 'capstone' involvement of top management
Assumes that in a nanny state, regulators know best and that decisions can only be judged by prosecutorial discretion or by a court	Managers must assert the right to manage in real time. This makes it imperative that decision processes are sound and auditable
Confrontational and coercive	Inclusive and collaborative
Creation of a fearful, box-ticking bureaucracy in which no one is trusted	Creation of a positive, enjoyable, secure, honest spirit in which employees are encouraged to take decisions
Focused on internal cultures and bribe payment	Concerned with integrity throughout the extended enterprise'
Underestimates the importance of key performance drivers, contexts and decisions	Aligns integrity with key performance drivers

Following the Ministry of Justice Guidance for Commercial Organisations (GCO) (see page 92) will not 'embed' integrity or even be enough to comply with the law. On the contrary, adherence to its six principles can trigger a bureaucratic and risk-averse spiral in which box-ticking compliance becomes an end in itself, regardless of the commercial consequences.

The discussion that follows is mainly for large companies, although most of the principles apply to all organisations that wish to optimise their performance by avoiding losses from corruption, fraud, other skulduggery and compliance breaches.

HEADING OVER A CLIFF

It is obvious that conventional regulatory solutions to prevent skulduggery – fixated on laws – regulations, rules, coercion, zero tolerance, prosecutorial discretion and threats of punishment – do not work, nor are they ever likely to do so.

FSA Hammered

In October 2012, the Treasury Select Committee was more than critical of the Financial Services Authority (FSA)'s incompetence in the collapse of Royal Bank of Scotland, which resulted in a taxpayer's worst case exposure supposedly of £28.2 billion! Words such as 'box-ticking', 'grossly inadequate', 'totally unacceptable' stand out, but even more telling is the criticism that 'it is deeply regrettable that the current rules based activity [is biased] towards technical breaches to the detriment of the most important regulatory failures'.

This is precisely the problem with the Bribery Act 2010: all huff and little puff.

The compliance edifice is based on the notion that businesses are 'essentially amoral' and must be supervised by politicians, regulators, lawyers and others – few of whom have any real world experience – along the path to redemption. This is unrealistic and does not cut the mustard. Compliance is set almost entirely in a legal–regulatory frame, telling people what they should not do, rather than motivating them to do things they should. Compliance is a problem, whereas inspired integrity is an opportunity. Adequate procedures are the minimum required to give the pretence of compliance and only become relevant when things have gone wrong. Assured controls optimise profits, support happy, productive, secure and honest operations. This is our starting point!

WHY DO PEOPLE BEHAVE HONESTLY?

We easily fall into the trap of fixating on how to deter skulduggers and don't analyse why people perform honestly, especially in contexts where they have the opportunity for self-enrichment or other skulduggery. Despite the overwhelming misanthropy of this book, the authors have been amazed how often people do the right thing, even in contexts and countries where perceptions would anticipate the opposite. It is part of our evolutionary heritage to concentrate on dangers, problems and risks while failing to learn from things that go right.

Learning From Risks

If our forebears had stood around learning about organic farming rather than watching out for tigers we would not be here. As Homer Simpson said 'If he was so clever, how come he's dead?'

A central theme of this book is to learn from both negatives and positives, from good outcomes as well as bad. It also proposes that generalised solutions – such as country risks and tone from the top – are not realistic and that situational,[3] as well as dispositional,[4] factors are influential in determining integrity in a given context (see page 651).

What Is Honesty?

The authors are both grandparents to a band of wonderful children and they are both considered – and regard themselves – to be honest. However, if the only[5] way of saving one of their grandchildren's lives were to rip off Gower Publishing,[6] they would have no hesitation in doing so. A similar sort of psychology and rationalisation applies to most cases of fraud and corruption; the only difference being that the threshold of self-justification is far lower.

Experience suggests that the characteristics of honest performance in commercial contexts include:

- Successful and enjoyable working environments, with profits rather than losses;
- Effective and fair (sometimes charismatic or 'transformational') leadership in close proximity;
- Fair compensation;
- Positive encouragement for personal advancement and recognition of good work and ethical performance ('pride in performance');
- An absence of political shenanigans and spin;
- Empowerment and delegated authority with trust;
- Fair and achievable targets;
- Fair treatment when mistakes are made or bad news delivered upwards;
- Commitment to excellence in products and services and pride in performance;
- Hard but consistent and fair punishment for deliberate and repeated violations.

Learning lessons from things that go right – or green flags – is virtually unheard of, because in the compliance space few regulators 'do happy!' or say 'that's fine'.

A BIT OF AMATEUR PSYCHOLOGY

People are more likely to do things that they believe are in their self-interest or which make them feel good about themselves. It does not matter how much a person is told not to do this or not to do that, it is unlikely to make much difference if his inner beliefs are opposed. Although he may superficially comply when under observation (known as the 'Hawthorne Effect') he is likely to revert to instinct as soon as he feels it is safe to do so.

---

3   Context-dependent.

4   'Embedded and certain values'.

5   And this means 'Only'.

6   Hence this book.

For this reason, effective integrity campaigns must confirm or, where necessary, try to mould a person's beliefs to those desired by entering into his consciousness.[7]

In many cases moulding is easier said than done, but two things are clear. The first is that the culture of an entire organisation is not 'embedded' by a letter from top management threatening damnation for giving an FPO an additional Homer Simpson mouse mat. The second is that self-serving hyperbole – of bribery problems and the omnipotence of regulators – is counterproductive to the extent that even those claims that are credible are disbelieved. Thus the integrity moulding and reinforcing process should concentrate on risky contexts, directing minds and positions of 'significant influence'[8] by:

- **Specifying** what is expected in the context; balancing commercial with ethical and other considerations;
- **Not hyperbolising risks** to the point of incredulity;
- **Persuasively communicating** expectations and requirements to individuals, spreading to important contexts and, hopefully, to the organisation as a whole;
- **Continuously motivating**, reinforcing and rewarding good performance;
- **Fairly, consistently and effectively sanctioning** violations.

In the authors' experience there are common and predictable reasons why the above process fails. The most common is the naïve belief that an ethical culture can be 'embedded' by the tone from the top. The second is an appalling communications failure. We will deal with the second and come back to the tonal fallacy later.

EFFECTIVE COMMUNICATION

Most humans believe, or assume, that they are great communicators. In fact many aren't and with the greatest of respect this includes too many politicians, regulators and lawyers,[9] who expect others to accept their frames, without question.

A Communications Breakdown

Time and time again the authors have sat through presentations – predominately by regulators, lawyers and compliance specialists to marketing and other achievement-focused[10] audiences – on the Bribery Act. Most were set in entirely legalistic frames and were unsurprisingly uninspiring, by speakers who were charismatically challenged. And do you know what? The presenters – anchored in their own frames – had not even noticed the audiences' negative body language and that their messages were not getting through.

---

7   See the comments by Garth Peterson convicted in the Morgan Stanley case page 614.
8   An FSA term.
9   But never investigators.
10   Or orientated.

Poor communicators don't recognise the importance of 'frames' (see Chapter 1) and are unable or unwilling to consider how their statements will be taken by others.

The Importance of Framing

There is a story about a Franciscan priest and a Jesuit. The Franciscan decided to see his prefect and ask: 'Father, would it be permitted to smoke while I am praying to the Lord? The answer was a resounding 'No'.

The Jesuit also sought counsel, framing his question somewhat differently: 'Father if in a moment of weakness I smoke, would I be permitted to say a prayer to the Lord?' The answer: 'Yes, of course my son'.

REGULATORY ORIENTATION AND THE REGULATORY FOCUS THEORY

This theory is very important. The 'Regulatory Focus Theory' (RFT[11]) was proposed by E. Tory Higgins, Professor of Psychology at Columbia University and it examines the relationship between a person's motivation (values, beliefs, 'self-regulation' or 'orientation') and their behaviour (performance or 'actions'). Simply stated, it identifies the human priorities of seeking pleasure and positive outcomes (promotion focus: 'Warrior mentality') or avoiding pain and negative outcomes (prevention focus: 'Worrier mentality'). Orientation can be chronic (or long-term) or situational (within a specific context) but it can be influenced by positive or negative stimuli.

RFT is endorsed by the Regulatory Fit Theory, which suggests that a person will be more committed to a behaviour – often instinctively – when a communication:

- Confirms and reinforces his existing beliefs and orientation;
- Makes him 'feel right' about doing what is asked for;
- Gives him a 'positive value'.

Moreover, positive values reinforce or 'intensify' regulatory orientation, whereas someone who is coerced into doing something against his orientation may comply, but without any long-term commitment. A simple example appears overleaf.

---

11   Classified as a 'goal pursuit theory'.

No Smoking and Other Campaigns

Despite considerable spinning to the contrary, 'No Smoking' campaigns – based on doom and gloom – have failed miserably, especially among young people. The same is true of Antisocial Behaviour Orders (ASBOs) and Community Service Orders because they are orientated within the peer groups concerned as 'cool'. They are a badge of honour that generate positive values rather than being a deterrent. It would be much more effective to provide smokers with badges:

Figure 23.1 A Simple Example of Positive Framing that is also 'Sticky'

The same sort of thinking applies in the integrity field and successful persuasion requires alignment of regulatory orientation with message framing or fit, as summarised in Table 23.2.

Table 23.2 Regulatory Focus and Fit

REGULATORY FOCUS (Orientation) of the Individual	Framing or 'Fit' of Communications *Dispositional (Chronic: routed in early childhood) or Situational* THE REGULATORY FIT	
	Promotional *Goals have to be perceived as achievable*	Preventive *Risks have to be perceived as realistic*
PROMOTIONAL: 'The Warrior Class' **Orientation towards achieving positive goals:** 1. *Optimistic* 2. *Achieving opportunities and goals* 3. *Willingness to change* 4. *Prepared to make errors of commission* 5. *Happy after a positive outcome and dejected over failures* 6. *Motivated by transformational leaders* 7. *Unlikely to respond to criticism* 8. *Motivated by success and praise* 9. *More likely to achieve positive goals*	Clever people get the job done without having to pay bribes	The message is unlikely to get through to prevention-focused audiences
	If smart people cannot succeed without paying bribes, they find other, and usually better, opportunities	
	It is much more courageous to pull out of a transaction than to compromise yourself	
	The most important thing to maintain is your integrity	
	People with integrity sleep soundly at night	
	Throughout your career you will achieve more, and gain greater respect by being honest	
	All good managers have to take risks. Don't worry about making a genuine mistake	
PREVENTIVE: 'The Worrier Class' **Orientation towards minimising negative outcomes:** 1. *Vigilant and cautious* 2. *Avoiding mistakes* 3. *Prefers the status quo* 4. *Makes errors of omission* 5. *Experiences relief after positive outcomes and agitation over failures* 6. *Motivated by transactional leaders* 7. *Sensitive to criticism* 8. *Not focused on positive outcomes*	The message is unlikely to get through to promotion focused audiences especially if they are unconvinced about the risks	If you pay bribes you will be caught and go to jail

The reality is that promotion-orientated people are more likely to work in contexts (such as sales, procurement and marketing) that are more vulnerable to bribery, while those in legal, investigatory and compliance jobs are likely to be more preventively inclined. Since the latter write most policies and procedures on integrity, it is critical that they do so in frames most acceptable to the intended audience.

A Quick Self-test

Are you prevention- or promotion-orientated and more anxious about:

- People who drive slowly in front of you?

Or

- People who drive on your back bumper and want to overtake when you know they can't?

The integrity campaign, discussed below, as well as training for both promotion and prevention-orientated audiences (discussed in Chapter 29) must be effectively communicated into the receiving frames. It is not only what is said that is important, but what is heard and listened to.

Tone from the Top

TOP AND OTHER MANAGERS

Every regulatory agency parrots the importance of the tone from the top, usually without thinking what is meant, although the implication is that it applies to the Board of Directors and sprinkles down the organisation to the most junior levels. In truth, directors of large companies have very little contact with most oinks and are as detached as dodos or LibDems. This is so because the main, if not only, communication is through written words, videos or some other distant and impersonal channel of *one-way* communication. In large organisations the definition of 'top management' should include every 'directing mind' and every person who supervises more than 149 people,[12] via more than 4 direct reports. These are the people who influence behaviour the most on a day-to-day basis: much more so than the main board directors. Figure 23.2 represents the relationship between influence and proximity.

---

12   *Blink: The Power of Thinking Without Thinking* by Malcolm Gladwell (Little, Brown, 2005) suggests that a culture can only extend to a maximum of 150 people and that tone is set more through peer group osmosis than by the tone from the top.

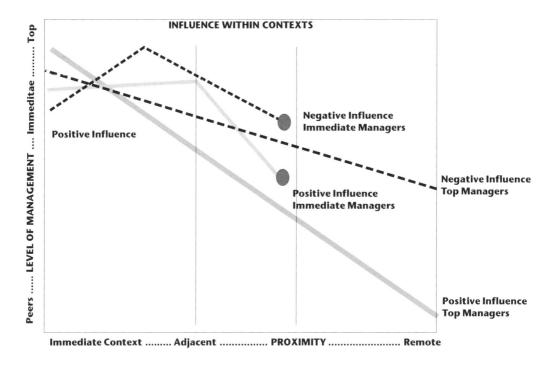

Figure 23.2 The Tone from the Top and Proximity

This figure suggests a number of important points:

- Negative behaviours[13] (such as tax avoidance, 'red top' revelations of the managing director's tantric sadomasochistic sessions with marsupials, other personal or corporate skulduggery by top and proximate managers) has a far more damaging effect than any positive equivalents.[14] Bad news travels fast and is far more potent than good.[15]
- On a day-to-day basis the style and spirit in a person's immediate context prevails and bad examples are the most corrosive, more readily believed and mimicked or used to excuse other misbehaviour. For example: 'If he can avoid tax by claiming he lives in Monaco, why shouldn't I get a little bung for working hard?'.
- The influence (positive or negative) of middle-level managers is usually limited to their immediate contexts.[16]
- A context may be better or worse than its higher-up subordinate or neighbours. The result may be 'companies within a company' which, for reasons discussed in Chapter 12, is especially risky.

---

13   Which are 'tones'.

14   They are known as 'sticky'.

15   These cases – current as this book went to press – of George Osborne's first class rail journey, Mr Davidson and 'plebs', and MPs' continued scamming of housing support, are examples.

16   In Enron there were some excellent and highly ethical departments.

It is also important to recognise that – with third parties – a company develops an image[17] independent of its top managers.

Integrity is a Two-way Street

A company discovered what appeared to be massive overcharging and bribery and retained investigators, who interviewed a number of former vendors. One stated: 'We knew they were being ripped off and even the accounts where the bribes went. In fact we were asked to join in and refused. You ask why we did not report it. The answer is simple. The way they treated us, they can Buzz Off'. Any company that treats third parties unfairly in fact becomes a magnet for their retaliation.

IS TONE THE RIGHT METAPHOR?

There are many definitions of the word 'tone' and most involve a sound, squeak or some sort of racket, with no tangible substance. Tone is ephemeral. The words 'capstone' or 'keystone'[18] are better metaphors in the integrity field because they represent the reality that:

- Top managers are in a pivotal place at the top of a structure and must be an effective presence rather than just a tone or a squeak, a whiff or a whim.
- Top managers' involvement must be obvious and continuous.
- Communication channels must be two-way: top managers must not allow themselves to be isolated or ambushed by bad news.
- Managers must be supported by those below them.[19]

Also the term 'tone from the top' is patronising because it implies that business and political leaders are genetically modified with embedded[20] standards of honesty denied to lesser mortals. Yet the experience is counterfactual, as is discussed in Chapter 23 and is glaringly obvious from the recent banking failures.

Corporate Psychopaths

It is said that there are more psychopaths in British boardrooms and in the Houses of Parliament than in jail.

---

17 Dare it be said 'a perception'?

18 Not quite so good because of its Masonic and Keystone Cops association.

19 This is one reason why letters of representation and annual declarations are important.

20 A dreadful word in the integrity area.

There are two other fallacies. The first is that those at the very top have most to lose if they involve themselves in skulduggery, yet – with a few exceptions like Kenneth Lay, Jeffrey Skilling and some others who are wearing sackcloth and eating porridge – this is not the experience. The fact is that both culpable senior managers and inefficient regulators escape untarnished.

The second is that those at the very top have made it and 'don't do dishonesty'. This may be true in some cases, but for those who have spent their lives plotting their way into the corporate or political stratosphere, sometimes by clambering over the corpses of their competitors, changing beliefs may not be that simple.

Reverting to Type

Hector started work for an international conglomerate as a trainee salesman in Birmingham and over a 30-year career ended up as Chief Executive Officer and Chairman with a salary package in excess of £10 million a year. He admitted to anyone who would listen that he had been 'an absolute bastard … who did everything that was necessary and a lot more besides'. He loved telling stories of his scams and scrapes with the 'Plod'[21] and with other women.

Just before retiring he had a vision and joined a 'happy clappy' religious sect that he claimed had metamorphosed his life. He involved himself and his sixth wife in all sorts of charity work, including weekly visits to a local prison.[22] He tried – without the slightest chance of success – to convert the author, and repeatedly invited him to visit a drug addict who was on remand for stabbing an old lady and her cat. Hector was tearful, saying the prisoner had been 'stitched up' by the police and was a paragon of virtue.

A few weeks later the prison visits came to an abrupt end and the author asked Hector what had happened.

'Well', he said 'that guy turned out to be evil and had bribed the prosecutor to grant him bail on the condition he came to live with me and Hermani – sorry Nancy.[23] Can you believe it? There was no way I was letting him into my home, to steal my candelabra'.

Despite cases such as Hector's, it is likely that those who have arrived at the top are probably less active skulduggers than than those who:

- Are one or two levels below them and who still have continuing aspirations to move and shake;
- Although at senior levels have reached – or passed – their peak;[24]

---

21   The term actually used.

22   Which was outside the UK.

23   He had confused his fifth with his sixth wife.

24   The authors know the feeling.

- Competed for the top job and failed to get it;[25]
- Have personal incentive packages or private-life pressures that motivate misbehavior;
- Consider themselves 'free agents', with no long-term commitment to the company;[26]
- Play golf or line dance.[27]

Finally, and for the avoidance of doubt, there is no suggestion that most top managers are other than situationally honest. The problem is with the regulatory assumption that the embedded DNA of those who have reached the top – whether in their own agencies, trades unions, politics, the media, academia, business or elsewhere – is any different from us oinks.

The Integrity Campaign

OVERVIEW

Many companies have the opportunity[28] to turn compliance into inspired integrity and a compliance problem into opportunities that result in genuine differentiators and commercial advantages. The steps (labeled 'A' to 'H') suggested are summarised in Figure 23.3.

STEP A1: PHILOSOPHY, STRATEGY, VISIONS AND GOALS

Definitions

Philosophy represents the deeply held values of stakeholders. Deontological factors relate to the company's perceived moral obligations within society: teleological relates to outcomes or results. In conventional[29] framing there appears to be tension between moral obligations and the drive to obtain results. This is based on the fallacy that unethical behaviour produces the greatest profits. This is not so: except occasionally in the short term.

Critical discussions

It may seem trite and almost Luvvie-like to suggest that top managers and other stakeholders should take a step back[30] and specify their stance on integrity and compliance and try to resolve any tensions between moral considerations and commercial objectives through questions[31] such as:

---

25 One international company puts these 'failed General Managers' in a separate building to keep them out of harm's way.

26 And are plotting their next career move.

27 Just checking that readers have not dozed off.

28 But don't recognise it.

29 But misplaced.

30 Even an 'away day' and without advisers, lawyers, accountants or consultants.

31 See also the questionnaire suggested on page 473.

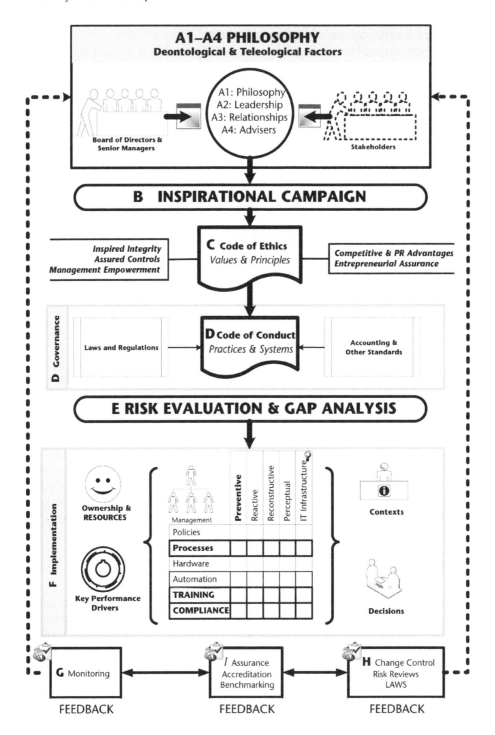

Figure 23.3 The Campaign for Inspired Integrity

Note that 'compliance' comes almost at the bottom of the list. The campaign also recognises that integrity is not 100 per cent dispositional (i.e. embedded) but is more often situational and results from instinctive rather than considered decisions (see page 279 et seq).

- What importance do we attach to integrity?
- Do we regard integrity as a differentiator?
- Do we fully understand the laws and regulations in all aspects of our business?
- What is our vision for the company and our goals?
- What do we stand for: what are our personal and corporate values?
- How good is our reputation: generally and with regulators?
- What have we done (or do we do) that could damage our reputation?
- Are our key performance drivers consistent with our values?
- How good are our communications up and down the line: how would we get to hear of problems before they get out of hand?
- How good and independent are our advisers?
- Do our existing codes embody our values?

Specific questions in the corruption field were discussed earlier but for convenience the most important of them are repeated here:

- Do we embrace the noble cause that supposedly drives the Bribery Act and other laws?
- Do we believe that zero tolerance of such things as hospitality, gifts, sponsorship and facilitation payments is a realistic goal?
- Do we accept the bar lowering, expansive interpretations imposed by regulators or simply follow the laws as they were intended?
- Under what circumstances would we submit to facilitation extortion?
- Do we believe that competitors (particularly those not bound by the Bribery Act) will behave ethically, especially in overseas private sector markets where UK companies are the world exception in facing extraterritorial punishment for technical violations?
- Do we consider it would be better to withdraw from difficult markets rather than face the risk of draconian punishment in the UK for offences that will only be designated as such after the event?
- Can we manage the multiple uncertainties created by the Act and survive?
- If we discovered that we had paid bribes, would we self-disclose?
- Would we be prepared to buy ourselves out of trouble by entering into civil disposals with regulators or do we consider this would be immoral?[32]

Philosophy First: Policy Later

Let's consider the sort of discussions that might take place involving a company which has to comply with both American and British anti-bribery laws.

What should its policy be if it suspects that a manager has paid bribes? Should it carry out an internal investigation to confirm or refute the suspicions? The UK's Serious Fraud Office (SFO) and the US Department of Justice say that it should. The British Financial Services Authority

---

32   Ironically, companies that make it known that they are amenable to negotiation and civil disposals may make it more likely that they will be targeted.

says it should report without delay. So which way should the company turn as a matter of policy?

There is no requirement under the Bribery Act 2010 or any other legislation to report unsubstantiated suspicions. However, regulators have made it clear that if self-disclosure is not made – and in the very unlikely event that they find out for themselves – the company will be given a serious bashing. But if the company self-flagellates and capitulates without question it may be less likely to get prosecuted or mandatorily debarred from government contracts. In the best case the company may even expect a discount on the fines that would otherwise be imposed. UK judges do not like out-of-court settlements and may decide to overturn even the most elaborate and prolonged negotiations with the SFO. There is absolutely no certainty of reaching a settlement and, what's more, during negotiations the company may have been compelled to make other disclosures that make its position far worse.

Self-disclosure[33] will not save directors and employees from jail and discounts negotiated with regulators are usually significantly less than might be expected where a company insists that a case proceeds to trial and then enters an early guilty plea. Besides that, regulators make catastrophic mistakes and end up with failed prosecutions and picking up defence costs. This is another reason why regulators encourage self-disclosure and corporate capitulation. It means they don't have to conduct difficult investigations. Self-disclosure and the inevitable publicity are likely to stimulate third-party litigation, adverse publicity, and serious consequences that far outweigh any discount on fines.

So the next policy question is whether or not a company should self-disclose under any circumstances. If so, would it be prepared to investigate itself under regulatory direction, as it will be required to do?

This means it picks up all of the costs of retaining, external advisers, forensic accountants and, of course, lawyers, and carry all of the investigatory risks. These 'proxy investigations' are dangerous for the companies concerned, although very lucrative for their professional advisers and easy pickings for regulators.

Would the company be willing to waive privilege and provide evidence against individuals, including senior managers who might become co-accused?

There is another important philosophical question. Does the board believe it is ethical for wealthy defendants – in this case themselves – to buy their way out of trouble, when poorer citizens and companies cannot? Does it subscribe to the view that there is one law for the rich and another for the poor?

Does it believe it would be ethical to capitulate and seek civil settlements in a case where it genuinely believes itself to be innocent, in the hope – which is usually forlorn – that it will bring the problem to an end? In other words, that paying up is the cheapest option.

---

33   Please see the detailed analysis in Chapter 17 page 450.

To whom should disclosure be made, and when and how? If the company first reports to US regulators, the SFO may be prevented from taking action because of the British double jeopardy rules. This is why the SFO is so keen to get multinationals to 'Come to Jesus': that is, to its office in Elm Street, London WC1. If the SFO is told first, the company may whacked in both countries, because there are no double jeopardy rules in the USA.

Difficult questions like the above cannot be answered by cutting and pasting from old policies. They need very careful consideration to drive the company's values, but such questions are avoided, possibly on the grounds that it is best not to be too specific. However the facts should be faced; philosophical commitments MUST drive the company's integrity policy; and it is foolish to leave difficult decisions to the heat of the moment.

It is unquestionably much easier to tolerate restrictions when the underlying philosophy is supported and the consequences can be managed.

Supporting the Noble Cause

If you believe in Father Christmas, you will unquestionably support the noble health and safety cause of keeping the chimney clean. If you believe in global warming, you will happily save the planet by not printing out emails from Granny.

Scepticism over the noble cause does not mean that the company should take the law lightly, but the philosophical positioning has two important consequences. The first is that by taking an ultra-safe line[34] on such things as facilitation payments and hospitality, many genuine commercial opportunities will be have to be abandoned. Figure 23.4 attempts to show the position.

If a company rises too near the bar – its actions may be judged after the event and through prosecutorial discretion as illegal. For timorous companies this leads to risk aversion and decision impotency.

Prosecutorial Discretion Creates Uncertainty (Which Crooks Just Love)

Prosecutorial discretion is a ridiculous notion that creates uncertainty. It has two main consequences. The first is that villains can use ambiguity to their own advantage because it equips them with a plausible excuse if their deliberate dishonesty is uncovered. The more significant problem is that honest people will progressively transition to increasing positions of risk aversion, making their organisations uncompetitive and bureaucratic.

---

34   That meets or goes beyond expansive interpretation.

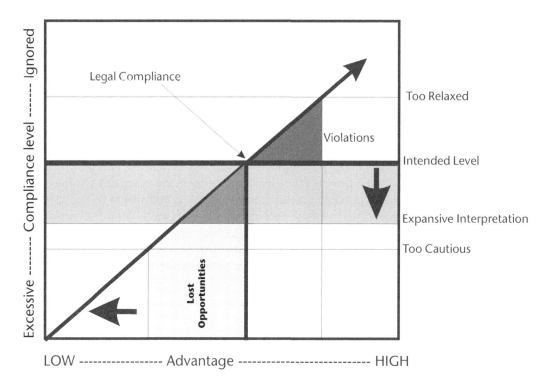

Figure 23.4 The Effect of Ultra-compliance on Commercial Opportunities

The law sets the bar with which companies are required to comply. Regulators have expansively interpreted (known as 'regulatory creep') the legislation so that the bar is lowered to capture trivial and technical offences of bribe payment, thereby opening the doors to easy pickings and negotiated settlements.

Companies may take a blind gamble, go above the bar in the hope that they will not be found out. Others hope to weasel around the fine print: neither approach is recommended.

Aligning shareholder and other expectations

The company's values and visions should be communicated to shareholders, investors, credit-rating agencies, analysts and other influential parties, making it clear that long-term ethical returns on investment are considered more important than spectacular daily, weekly, monthly or quarterly results. The objective, besides transparency, is to reduce short-term pressures on top management to override ethical standards simply to satisfy external and often artificial expectations.

A Good Example

Hermes Pensions Management Limited, which has £36 billion under management, primarily for pension funds, publishes a superb summary of its ten guiding principles and notes: 'If there are some participants in the market who seek to bet on performance over a shorter time period, so be it, but this should not distract company managers from their long term goals'.

As in many aspects of life artificial pressures can be relieved by (a) facing realities and (b) telling the truth.

STEP A2 OTHER IMPORTANT CONSIDERATIONS FOR TOP MANAGERS

Principles

There are many activities within the direct control of top managers that both reflect and determine a company's values. Some are obvious but others, discussed below, may appear trivial. However, in the integrity field small things matter.[35]

Risk evaluation

Managers in every context must have a good understanding of risks and the impact organisational, regulatory and other changes have upon them. See Chapters 14–17.

Strategic and other decisions

There are two types of decisions that should be of concern to top managers. The first are strategic and within their direct control, including:

- Potential acquisitions and disinvestments;
- Procurement or marketing strategies;
- Outsourcing or offshoring operations, especially at a cost to UK jobs;
- Major capital projects and other big decisions;
- Initial public offerings and trade sales;
- Board-level incentive schemes;
- Appointment of board members and departmental heads;
- Downsizing or up-scaling operations;
- Importing management teams from other organisations.

---

35   See Malcolm Gladwell's excellent book *The Tipping Point* (Abacus, 2001) for the importance of paying attention to detail and to small things.

Besides the obvious financial impacts, strategic decisions can have a positive or negative short and long-term effect on a company's morale. Thus an impact analysis should be considered before decisions are made by simply asking one additional question: 'What effect will this have on morale?'

Directors should ensure that all decision *processes* are effective,[36] with the minimum of bureaucracy and delegated appropriately (see pages 241 and 576). In addition, they should try and eliminate decision bottlenecks.

Specifying key performance drivers

Some people seem preoccupied with measuring every conceivable aspect of life against key performance indicators. The usual mantra is 'what gets measured gets managed', but Albert Einstein made a much more telling statement: 'Not everything that can be counted counts, and not everything that counts can be counted'. Too much counting and navel-gazing is for the birds.[37]

Key performance targets and metrics should be specified to ensure that they are likely to achieve the outcomes desired **and** do not motivate skulduggery.

A Bad Incentive

A major manufacturing plant had a superb safety record and was in line for a special award. One day an employee fell from a storage tank and broke his neck. His colleagues quietly smuggled him offsite and dumped him in the road 2 miles away, telling him he had to report that he had been run over by a bus. Unfortunately the man died and the deception came to light.

Although they are normally set out in business plans and formal documents, key performance drivers can sneak into the picture unconsciously, through budgets, forecasts and day-to-day decisions.

It is not necessarily the quantum of key performance drivers that is the problem but rather the increments they impose.

A Real Red Flag

Warning bells should sound when any business unit is found to be falling short of its performance targets. It is a classic red flag of potential fraud and corruption, and difficult to conceal.

---

36   No one can guarantee decision outcomes.

37   OK, so birds don't have navels, but the point is still valid.

Communications and the annual Chatham House scrum down

There is no way that top managers of large organisations have a realistic prospect of knowing everything that takes place below them that could be catastrophic. **That is the hard reality, because bad news is gravitational.** Directors should maintain good communications throughout the Extended Enterprise through participation in newsletters, bulletins, websites, blogs, and even Twitter and Facebook, giving snippets on their work and topics of general interest. From time to time they should just walk around with eyes and ears open and become chatty managers.

 They might also consider an excellent idea from Mark Pyman, Transparency International's defence team leader which he mentioned in a speech to the European Business Ethics Forum on 18 January 2008.[38] In a former life, Mr Pyman was a senior financial officer with Shell in West Africa and therefore had to confront corruption at the heavy end, on a daily basis. He asked his colleagues what he should do when he encountered skulduggery and everyone gave the same answer. Mr Pyman's speech continued:

> [They told me …] you will recognise it when you see it, and you will work out for yourself what you need to do. Is that unhelpful, or what? To find some enlightenment, I registered myself on one of Shell's courses for Finance Directors […]. This two week long course had one four hour session devoted to Shell's business principles and to business ethics. It was mostly rather commonplace, but there was one riveting workshop.
>
> The facilitator asked for a confidential session without feedback to the Shell hierarchy. He then asked each of us to tell a story from recent Shell experience in which we had been confronted by corruption or an ethics problem and to say how we had reacted. The revelations were astonishing to me.
>
> We had everything from extortion threats on the transportation of lubricants to presidential corruption, to corrupt tax officials in Taiwan, even to Shell Chief Executives encouraging their Finance Directors to bend the rules. It was the honesty of this workshop that stayed with me […]. What really will help executives is to hear from their peers inside the company of the problems that they face and the strategies that they adopt […].
>
> Such conversations are hard to have because both the participants and the company fear the potential recriminations of such sensitive revelations. This was a weakness in the Shell program and it wasn't much different five years ago when I left.
>
> Little knowledge is gained in central office about the problems. There was no feedback for improving Shell group training schemes. There was no sharing with other senior executives around the world. Zero tolerance risk turned into a zero learning by the organisation. We were not a learning organisation.

In fact, very few organisations learn from their experiences for precisely the reasons stated by Mr Pyman, but it does not have to be this way.

---

38   A copy of the speech can be downloaded from the European Business Forum website, at: http://europeanbusinessethicsforum.com/Mark_Pyman_speech_2008.pdf (accessed 28 November 2012).

Knowledge Management

Over the past few years, more enlightened companies have appointed knowledge managers, often at board level, to draw out and learn from successful local, commercial practices and tricks of the trade that are not formalised or disseminated. Wouldn't it be a good idea to extend the knowledge brief into the integrity and compliance space?

Top managers might also consider sponsoring an annual scrum down for frontline managers working in vulnerable contexts – perhaps using Chatham House Rules and managed by a professional facilitator – to discuss sensitive corruption and other regulatory issues on a non-attributable basis. Invitations could be extended to agents and other associated persons, especially those who are considered dodgy, who can be made to squirm and may – eventually – get the message.

Small things really do matter

Fixing broken windows
Malcolm Gladwell's great book *The Tipping Point* discusses a number of real-world examples where values and performance were fundamentally changed by what on the surface are trivialities.

Examples of Fixing Broken Windows

The reduction in violent crime in the New York subway started with simple things like making sure platforms were clean and tidy, that staff were polite and well presented. From these small beginnings larger changes took shape and crime was cut dramatically.

There is compelling evidence that even the most obnoxious vandals are unlikely to break the windows of a house which had not already been damaged. But, once one window had been broken, everyone joined in the fun.

In the corporate context – and especially in relation to fraud and corruption – there are many broken windows that have negative effects on integrity, including:

- Bureaucratic procedures and decision bottlnecks;
- Non-accountable committees;
- Weak, inconsistent or unfair managers and especially first-line supervisors;
- Management's refusal to deal with disruption and poor performance;
- Hostility and unfairness towards vendors and third parties (buy low, pay slow);

- Disrespect and unfairness towards customers;
- Empire-building by jobsworths;
- Excessive political correctness.

Promoting Bad Apples

A departmental manager boasted that he had got rid of a troublemaker by promoting him to another department. The effect on the morale of his other subordinates was devastating. He thought it was clever.

Thus every effort should be made to remedy small problems that are detrimental to company spirit.

The importance of first contacts

The impact that externally-facing employees – such as security guards, receptionists and secretaries or drivers – has on visitors and employees is also important. An officious or hostile reception sets the tone for important meetings off on the wrong track, whereas a friendly greeting has the opposite effect. First impressions are very important.

Starting the Day Badly

The Head of Security of a UK company was fixated over car parking and insisted that everyone reverse into bays that were far too small. He installed expensive cctv equipment to ensure that this was done and plastered parking areas with warning signs. If anyone did not comply (including visitors), they would be intercepted by a very officious security guard and told to return to their vehicle and park it properly. A lot of very unhappy people arrived at the reception desk and no doubt their displeasure dominated subsequent discussions. The managing director of an important customer company is said to have returned to his car and was never heard of again.

The same is true of telephone operators. It may be cost-effective to have calls answered by a Dalek that gives 200 menu options before letting the customer speak to a near-human – but it creates a bad impression, hostility and trouble. Even worse is the unbelievably stupidity of companies that send out automated calls to sell their goods or services. Do they ever get any business from them, or do they just annoy potential customers? What impression do they think they create?

Finally, another of the authors' hobby horses is British Telecom, whose call centres are in Bangladesh, India or Outer Mongolia. Again, this might be economic, but for people[39] who

---

39   Who are far from racist.

subscribed to British Telecom – rather than Bangladesh Telecom – incomprehensibility of the operators and the UK job losses are a turn-off, especially when we are all supposed to be pulling together to drag England, Northern Ireland and Wales out of the mess they are in.

Acknowledging smokers

Smokers account for around 25 per cent of a company's workforce and are often Type A[40] personalities and among the most vocal communicators. When they are banished to smoke in the nearest culvert or under a tree they become negative communicators and just moan.

A Small Investigatory Tip

Experienced investigators will confirm that the best place to pick up rumours, scandal and also lashings of the truth about a company is in its smoking area. Besides that, you meet nice people up trees.

Banning smoking during working hours on all company property – including culverts and in holly bushes – is obviously an option, as is not recruiting the puffingly impaired in the first place. But a smoking prohibition leads to higher absentee rates, unwillingness to work overtime and general unhappiness. Having smokers lurking outside the entrance of buildings gives a very bad impression.

For such reasons consideration should be given to designating smoking areas that comply with regulations but which are heated, lighted, have wi-fi and seating, well away from public areas. Smoking zones can then support positive communications. Also, smokers should be encouraged to work a few extra hours a week – to compensate for their time in the smoking area,[41] and most would be happy to comply.

To non-smokers – who mistakenly believe that all of the inflicted want to give up, when in fact most do not – the above suggestions will seem moot points. However to have a quarter of the workforce feeling unhappy is not conducive to a positive company spirit.

Helping with personal problems

Managers should also be trained to be on the lookout for employees who have personal problems – especially when they involve children or family members – and make every effort to help them, including financial support if necessary. The effect of helping one person in trouble may influence scores of others, if not hundreds, and besides that it is the right thing to do.

---

40   Who tend to be opportunistically orientated (see page 586) and high achievers.

41   To remove snide comments that they waste time. A similar rule might also be applied to employees who spend hours on Facebook or surfing the net.

Social media

Twitter, Facebook and other forms – recent equivalents of chats down the pub – can have a good or bad effect on a company's morale and reputation. The best codes of conduct set out the rules on all types of electronic twittering, making it clear what is acceptable and what is not.

Keeping in touch

These days, what with downsizing and early retirement packages, it is rare in some companies to find any employee over 55 years old; with not a grey hair in sight. This may be a good thing in declining markets,[42] because it gives young people a chance. The downside is a loss of experience, continuity and tradition. Companies should consider inviting retirees to join focus groups and to mentor young people.

STEP A3 RELATIONSHIP WITH THE REGULATORS

Regulatory priorities

The SFO has said that anti-corruption controls should be on the agenda of every board meeting to 'demonstrate top management commitment'. The fact is, of course, it does no such thing, but merely enables another box to be ticked.

It is unsurprising that regulators see their own interests in a silo and as the only issue of the day: far outstripping other things such as making profits, surviving, or even other laws and regulations enforced by other agencies that have different frames, agendas and silos. If all regulators adopted the same silo thinking, every board meeting would be consumed with such crucial agenda points as illegal fishing in the Lower River Esk, the sale of grey squirrels, impersonation of traffic wardens or barristers, or entering the hull of the Titanic without permission (see page 236 for the 3,500 new laws introduced under the Blair–Brown regimes).

It goes without saying that directors should be fully committed to all aspects of business integrity, but competing pressures must be prioritised. It is up to the board of directors to decide what is on an agenda, how often topics are discussed and in what depth.

Setting objectives

Directors should decide what sort of relationship they would *like*[43] to establish with regulators and with which ones. But they first need to recognise that they interact from different frames that are inherently misaligned and will remain that way unless the participants agree a common frame – which is unlikely. Thus a degree of tension between those regulating and those being regulated will remain. Managers should think about things from the regulators' frame because relationships are not as one-sided as they might first appear. There is no reason for honest people to cower before any regulatory agency.

---

42   Mainly thanks to risk aversion and over-regulation.

43   In practice they will have little choice.

Risks to the Serious Fraud Office and other agencies

Background

The repeated draconian announcements by the SFO and the US Department of Justice (DOJ) and Securities and Exchange Commission (SEC) have certainly grabbed the attention of businesses worldwide, creating panic in boardrooms and commercial nightmares[44] that heavies will be chasing down their Homer Simpson mouse mat gifts to FPOs, $5 bribes to avoid being injected with an HIV-infected needle,[45] or nights out at the Pink Pussycat Lap Dancing Club as immediate priorities that will lead to their inevitable incarceration. This is not the case and the chance of a normal, decent company arriving on the SFO's radar is as likely as being compacted by a meteoroid.

Absence of long-term political support

To use a common media spin: 'a *friend* of the Prime Minister told us' that the government believes that the Bribery Act goes too far and it does not have its full support.[46] It is already clear that the Ministry of Justice is trying to soften the Act's impact against the SFO's of threats of draconian consequences for everything. There will be only one winner in a dispute between the SFO and political leaders. This means that the SFO cannot afford to make any bad decisions that conflict with the wider agendas of stimulating exports and British jobs; especially after the Tchenguiz debacle (page 835).

The difficulty of proving cases

The SFO has recognised the difficulty of proving corporate liability under sections 1, 2 and 6 of the Act (which is no different from proving a directing mind involvement under the old corruption legislation and UK laws generally) and is expected to pursue these sections only against individuals, prosecuting them and settling with the associated companies under Section 7.

It has already become clear that the civil disposal procedure is riddled with risks for the SFO on the disclosure of information and investigatory process[47] fronts and under Section 6 of the Human Rights Act. Also the ethicality of using permanent and mandatory debarment from government contracts as a negotiating threat will increasingly come under the spotlight from the UK Courts, the Organisation for Economic Cooperation and Development (OECD), the media and business groups.

The bottom line

For the above reasons, and a few others that it is not prudent to mention here,[48] the SFO is not facing an open goal – except its own. You can imagine the headlines (Figure 23.5).

---

44 Nightmares on Elm Street?

45 See Mr Alderman's incredible statements on page 125.

46 Except for a few LibDems, who will support anything that is perverse.

47 See the Tchenguiz case in the UK ('SFO drops multi-million investigation into Robert Tchenguiz', Jonathan Russell, The *Telegraph*, 15 October 2012; available at: http://www.telegraph.co.uk/finance/financial-crime/9609989/SFO-drops-multi-million-investigation-into-Robert-Tchenguiz.html) and the US Department of Justice's hopelessly flawed Africa sting (FCPA Professer's Forum, 23 July 2012; available at: http://www.fcpaprofessor.com/inside-the-africa-sting-trial-anatomy-of-a-failed-prosecution) (both accessed 28 November 2012).

48 But kept in reserve for lovely fee-paying clients who have problems.

A $5 Bribe Results in 200 Job Losses

Robin Blind, Chief Crime Correspondent

Following one of the Serious Fraud Office's first investigations under the Bribery Act 2010, Norman Noggins, 52, of Bolton, was convicted of paying a $5 bribe to a doctor in an Indonesian hospital to prevent his critically ill four year old grandson from being injected with an infected needle. Sentence is awaited.

Peter Robinson, the newly appointed Director of the SFO, said: 'we regard this conviction as a massive success in the fight against international corruption. I had given the clearest warning that offences of this nature would result in draconian penalties, so any sympathy for the defendant is totally misplaced. We are naturally sorry to hear that his grandson died and that as a result of the prosecution, financiers withdrew their support for Noggins's company with the loss of 200 British jobs. These things happen'. Kenneth Clarke, Justice Secretary and Overseas Anti-Bribery Champion, was unavailable for comment, but was in Harrods buying a new pair of grey Hush Puppy zipper boots and a pack of Cuban cigars.

Figure 23.5   A Fictional Press Report

The bottom line is that regulators have to take great care in the way they enforce the law and try to impose severe solutions by coercion.

Setting the relationship

The question is what sort of relationship with the SFO might be possible or even desirable. One approach is for directors to offer full cooperation, thereby creating a one-way submissive deal. Some companies will follow this path – probably unknowingly or based on legal advice. It is a viable option, but it comes at a cost.

But We Are Lawyers

Some 'Cottage Industry'[49] players believe they must build a harmonious relationship with regulatory agencies because failing to do so could mean problems for them and their other clients. This can result in advice being so risk-averse that if clients followed it they would go out of business. One partner in a UK law firm advised a client's board that any agent or supplier that refused to agree full audit rights should not be reappointed. Yet, when his attention was drawn to the fact that his firm was a 'supplier', and was asked if it would agree

---

49   The term 'Cottage Industry' comprises those politicians, regulators, academics, researchers, lawyers, consultants, journalists and even investigators who terrify others by over-emphasising the potential negative consequences and impact of the anti-bribery laws. (See Foreword to this volume.)

to audit rights, he blew a fuse: 'That's stupid', he hollered, 'we are lawyers'. Everyone, except the lawyer, fell about laughing.

No one should expect regulators to grant favours or show compassion simply because they like those being regulated, or to impose unjustified punishment when they believe they have been affronted: although this happens!

Toadying up to Regulators Will Not Work

Some companies believe that toadying up to regulators will be advantageous, and in rare cases this will be true. However, regulators are not fools and the sensible ones resent being patronised. It is worth noting that the biggest seizures of drugs and other contraband take place in the Border Agency's red channel because villains think that by pretending to be honest, they will not be suspected.

The question is: do regulators monitor the 'Cottage Industry' equivalent of their red channel groupies? If they do not: they should.

Positions on the regulatory radar

If a company considers itself to have a high regulatory profile, perhaps because it has a bad track record, operates in one of the so-called high-risk sectors, or extensively in countries that are perceived as corrupt, it may decide that trying to establish chummy relationships with regulators is worth the effort, notwithstanding the 'Red Channel' risks. But for most companies, the best bet is to assert the right to manage – honestly – and keep as far away as possible from courts, regulators and – dare it be said? – lawyers and the 'Cottage Industry' at large, including investigators.

Reacting to warnings

Sometimes regulators will give an indication – ranging from a wink, wink, nudge, nudge or a leak to a formal notification – that a company is heading for trouble. It is by no means clear whether the SFO will do the same,[50] but if it does, the communication should be treated with the utmost respect and delivered to board level without delay.

---

50   It does not give the impression of being a wink, wink, nudge, nudge sort of unit.

STEP A4 SELECTION OF ADVISERS

The directors' philosophical position should influence their choice of professional advisers.

Selecting Lawyers and other Advisers

The SFO has lobbied (some would say leaned on) professional firms to convince their clients that all suspicions of bribery should be self-disclosed without hesitation. Some Cottage Industry firms rely on close relationships with regulators, reciprocate, have revolving doors and rely on business with government agencies. Thus questions should arise over the extent to which a client's interests will prevail.

Companies should also carefully assess the advantages and disadvantages of using UK lawyers, consultants and other firms to advise on worldwide operations, especially when some of their businesses may not be classed as relevant commercial organisations and do not perform services for those that are.

A company should select advisers who understand its philosophical views rather than those who – possibly in what they honestly regard as a noble cause or own interests – invariably fight against them.

I Don't Propose to Tell Them

Solicitors advised their client that it must have a zero tolerance policy on facilitation payments, which the client accepted knowing full well that in some contexts it could not be maintained. Some months later, when the SFO released its 'Six Step Nuanced Approach'[51] – which proposed a much more practical and long-term solution – a partner said he did not intend to say anything to the company's managers because he did not want to 'encourage them'!

None of the above is to suggest that preference should be given to most amenable – or bendable advisers or that potential conflicts actually materialise. In fact the tougher the better, providing they are 100 per cent committed to the interests of their clients and not looking to ingratiate themselves with regulators to advance their own commercial interests.

---

51   See page 125.

STEP B DEVELOPING AND PROMOTING AN INTEGRITY CAMPAIGN

An Integrity Campaign is a stakeholder-driven series of coordinated actions, branded, promoted and marketed with flair and enthusiasm to motivate and maintain inspired integrity in key contexts and – over time and through osmosis – throughout the Extended Enterprise.

The values of stakeholders should be summarised and agreed and – believe it or not for larger organisations – referred to motivational, marketing or public relations professionals (not to lawyers, auditors, compliance gurus or investigators) to outline a campaign[52] that is truly inspirational and includes:

*   A campaign name and logo;
*   A mnemonic (the excellent ADCO website displays the mnemonic 'RIGHT'[53]);
*   A byline (for example 'Inspiring Integrity') and other 'stickies';[54]
*   Communications and training plans including printed material, a website, DVDs, Twitter, Facebook, videos, logon banners, chatlines, and – well – you name it: the more channels of communication the more likely the message is to be fluently recalled.[55]

The content of all existing policies, procedures, guides, codes, legal or compliance requirements and training programmes should be consolidated in one electronic corpus (see page 621 et seq) with topics[56] and orientation reviewed and benchmarked.

Rising Above It All

One Clever Dick said that 'a company's integrity could never rise above that of its top managers', which is demonstrably untrue in some contexts. Far more true is the principle that a code of conduct is unlikely to have any influence over relevant topics which are not included in it.

The corpus (Figure 23.6) should be used by a company's professional advisers, directors and stakeholders to identify what topics are – and should be – addressed in the integrity campaign and most importantly in its code of conduct. The updated corpus should be used to control and coordinate revised policies, procedures, codes and training programmes. The presentation of these should be finalised by marketing and motivational professionals in frames that are most likely to be accepted by the intended audience(s).

---

52   At least equal to the company's best advertising.

53   An acronym from: Respect, Integrity, Good citizenship, Honesty and Trust.

54   These are statements or graphics that are memorable.

55   As an 'availability cascade'.

56   A 'topic' is a subject that is relevant to integrity, compliance and control.

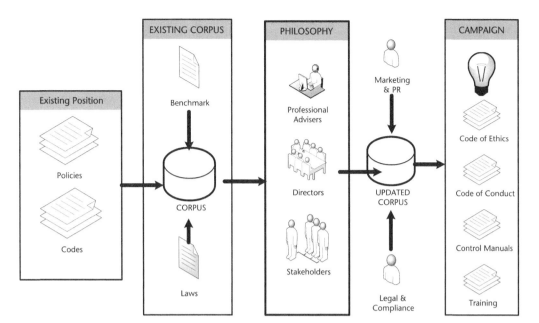

Figure 23.6 From Philosophy to Implementation

Chances are that many readers will assume that the authors – in making the above recommendations about marketing and motivation – overdosed on Phyllosan[57] and lost the plot. Not so, especially in the corruption area, because the fact is that most people who work in contexts in which bribery takes place fall into the promotional 'Regulatory Focus' category and are more likely to respond to upbeat, positively framed messages than to threats of doom and disaster. Even if the idea of a campaign is not accepted, many of the principles discussed above still apply to ethical and related codes which can be classified as shown in Figure 23.7.

The above definitions are used in this book in the absence of universally agreed terms. However, for most companies the starting point (after agreeing deeply held philosophical values) is a Code of Ethics.

Morgan Stanley and Ethisphere

According to the DOJ and members of the Cottage Industry, Morgan Stanley escaped corporate prosecution in the Garth Peterson case (see page 614) because of its absolutely superb compliance program. However, at the material time, Ethisphere (see page 633) gave Morgan's program a D+ rating and commented: 'Annoying, arrogant, NYer attitude with self references to "The Firm" over 70 times in the first six pages. All references for guidance say "call Legal Division". Any ethics department to contact?. Forget about it'.

---

57   A multivitamin and mineral supplement much advertised during the 1950s as a tonic for the over-40s – much like Viagra without the stiffness.

STEP C CODE OF ETHICS

The Code of Ethics is a brief, high-level and inspirational specification of the organisation's values and visions and is unlikely to change much over time. It should emerge from stakeholders' philosophical discussions, rather than – as is often the case – the reverse.

The code should be a *short* statement, ideally branded and promoted as part of the integrity campaign. Although some parts of this book have been critical of Transparency International, it has to be commended for its excellent work with the Defence Industry Initiative.[58]

STEP D BUSINESS CODES OF CONDUCT ET AL.

Definitions

For many organisations the Code of Conduct is the most important document on integrity. It adds depth and detail to the Code of Ethics, usually by setting out specific expectations and examples. It should be supported by Staff Handbooks, training material and a 'help desk'.

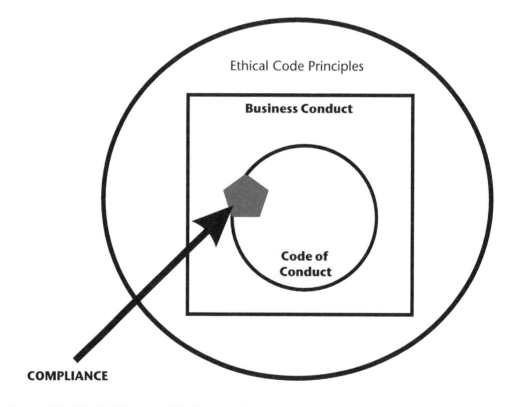

Figure 23.7 Definitions and Relationships

---

58 Comprehensive documentation is available at: http://www.ti-defence.org/ (accessed: 28 November 2012).

In addition:

- **Corporate Governance** is the system through which companies are directed and controlled; it incorporates regulatory, societal and other mechanisms.
- The **Compliance Code** is a rules-based[59] specification primarily designed to mitigate regulatory risks. It must react to changing circumstances and ensure a level of *minimum acceptable* conduct to comply with the law.

No consistent standards

There are no universally accepted standards on what topics business conduct policies should cover. Regulators have avoided committing themselves[60] to what they regard as effective business conduct policies or even adequate procedures. Everything is left to prosecutorial discretion or, in the worst cases, for a jury to decide. This is unworkable because decisions have to be made in real time.

What's the Point?

The Ministry of Justice Guidance (see page 92) contains around 16,000 words, supposedly setting out the principles for adequate procedures, although its authors admitted from the outset that the words were 'not prescriptive' and that it mattered little whether a company followed them or not. A recent report into the UK's compliance with the OECD Convention on bribing foreign public officials stated that the guidance did not have the force of law, was not a safe harbour defence and carried no more authority than an academic text.

An excellent paper by Professor Bruce W. Bean and Emma H. MacGuidwin[61] of the Michigan State University of Law, hammers Section 7 of the UK Bribery Act 2010, describing it as 'egregious' and 'outrageously overreaching'. It concludes that the adequate procedures defence; 'cannot be relied upon', 'stale statements of the intentions of a prior government will provide little protection for the accused' and that '[the Guidance] will be difficult to interpret', and 'utterly fail to show how one can comply with the Act and avoid liability'.

It is notable that very few legal academics support the views of the 'Cottage Industry' and generally agree with Professor Bean's views.

Other regulatory guidelines, press releases and speeches on the Bribery Act 2010 and the Foreign Corrupt Practices Act (FCPA), not to mention related publications, run into

---

59   For example, as set out in the Cadbury Code of 1992, The OECD Principles of Corporate Governance of 2004, the Sarbanes-Oxley Act 2002 and more recently the Dodd-Frank Wall Street Reform and Consumer Protection Act 2010.

60   But see the Morgan Stanley case discussed later.

61   'Expansive Reach – Useless Guidance: An Introduction to the U.K. Bribery Act 2010', 9 April 2010. Available at: http://ssrn.com/abstract=2037200 (accessed 28 November 2012).

millions of words. Few are indexed or cross-referenced. Instructions in different regulatory silos conflict. Often important documents are undated. The bribery world is full of red flags, but devoid of positive advice, so companies have to make up their own minds and their best efforts against a background of ambiguity.

Alleged Good News for the 'Cottage Industry'

If a company comes to attention for alleged breaches of anti-bribery laws, regulators will examine its policies, codes and procedures with a fine toothcomb and – with the benefit of hindsight and prosecutorial discretion – assess the degree of top management commitment and the effectiveness of supporting procedures. Paper policies *should* stand out like a red nose.

In July 2012, some parts of the 'Cottage Industry' went orgasmic over the announcement by the US Department of Justice (DOJ) and SEC that they did not intend to prosecute Morgan Stanley & Co for offences committed by Garth Peterson, one of its Managing Directors, partly on account of its amazingly excellent, superb and outstanding system of internal controls which, 'provided reasonable assurances that its employees were not bribing government officials'.

One 'Cottage Industry' commentator raved that 'the second point to note [...] **is that if it was not clear that a company receives credit for having a best practices compliance program, it is now'.** But does it? Morgan Stanley's current Codes of Conduct and a multitude of 'Global Policies' are generally good, but were not in place when Mr Peterson was active. It would be interesting to see what was around in 2006 that has justified so much tub-thumping.

Garth Peterson, a 43-year old American based in China, is alleged[62] **to have defrauded his employer** of between $2.5 million and $7 million by colluding with Mr Wu Yongchua,[63] the Chairman of Yongye Enterprise Group Limited, a Chinese State Owned Enterprise (SOE). The scam stripped 12 per cent of Morgan's interest in a Shanghai development[64] into Asiasphere Holding Limited, a BVI registered company they misrepresented a subsidiary of the SOE, but which they owned in conjunction with a Canadian lawyer.[65] It is also alleged that Mr Peterson falsified a $2.2 million 'finder's fee' to a Shanghai investor, who then paid over $1.6 million to him.[66]

It is not clear how Mr Peterson's activities came to light, but he was prosecuted by:

- The DOJ: for conspiracy to circumvent internal controls [18 U.S.C § 371. Title 15 United States Code, Sections 78m(b)(5) and 78ff(a)]

---

62   Between October 2004 and December 2007.

63   He does not appear to have been prosecuted.

64   Held by Morgan in a LLC (MSREF IV) and known as 'Project Cavity'.

65   Who, strangely, has not been named but who had worked for Hong Kong law firms (sometimes representing Yongye) and as Chief Legal Officer for an Insurance Company. He also does not appear to have been prosecuted.

66   Of which, supposedly, Mr Peterson gave nearly $700,000 to Mr Wu Yongchua, who had retired as the chairman of the SOE.

- The SEC for violating:
  - Section 30A(g) of the Exchange Act [15 U.S.C §78(dd-1(g)] which prohibits any issuer, etc. to corruptly do any act outside the United States [...] in furtherance of an offer, payment, promise to pay, or authorisation of the payment of any money, or offer, gift or authorisation or the giving of anything of value to a foreign public official [....] In violation of the lawful duty [...] or securing an improper advantage [...] or inducing them to use their influence [...] **in order to assist the issuer in obtaining or retaining business.**
  - Section 13(b)(5) of the Exchange Act [15 U.S.C §78m (b)(5)] which prohibits any person from knowingly circumventing a system of internal accounting controls, or falsifying any book or record.
  - Section 206 of the Advisers Act [15 U.S.C§§ 80b-6(1) and 80b-6(2)] which makes it unlawful for any investment adviser by use of the mails or instrumentalities of interstate commerce [...]. Knowingly, wilfully or recklessly use any device [...] to defraud any client a prospective client or to engage in any transaction [...] that operates as a fraud or deceit upon any client prospective client.

The most likely reason for the disinclination to prosecute Morgan Stanley under the FCPA was simply that there was insufficient evidence to prove bribery and that Mr Peterson's skulduggery was against his employer rather than for it to obtain or retain business.

It is exceptional for the DOJ or the SEC to give details of declined prosecutions and the fact that they did so in this case – while salivating over the excellence of the company's internal control policies – suggests it was little more than a PR exercise to motivate the 'Cottage Industry' to advise clients to self-disclose and to rely on an adequate procedures defence. And the ploy seems to have worked.

The Corruption, Crime and Compliance website[67] noted:

> You have to give the Justice Department credit – they are crafty and can be very politically astute. The Justice Department played a very subtle political game with the Morgan Stanley settlement. You have to give them credit for how they used the case to make a point. DOJ could have prosecuted Morgan Stanley.[68] They could have cited Peterson's actions as evidence of the failure of Morgan Stanley's compliance program. But they did not do so. They wanted to gain political points. DOJ was shrewd and did nothing to undermine its overall FCPA enforcement program.

Other commentators believe the regulators were disingenuous, rather than shrewd, and misrepresented a case they knew they could not successfully prosecute into a misleading signal about best practice. Even then, the SEC and DOJ pointed out that their disinclination was 'case specific' and was not a precedent.

---

67   See: http://corruptioncrimecompliance.com/2012/05/morgan-stanley-did-the-justice-department-rollover.html (accessed 28 November 2012).

68   And would have lost!

The 'Cottage Industry' was far less forthcoming in mentioning that – for the virtually non-existent contested FCPA cases that go before them – American judges rarely follow the regulators' suggested sentences. In this case the DOJ was looking to imprison Mr Peterson for up to five years, but Judge Jack Weinsten would have none of it, believing nine months was quite enough. Few 'Cottage Industry' websites have talked about what – in American terms – was a slap on the wrist.

On Friday, 17 August 2012 – the night before he was sentenced to six months' imprisonment[69] in the New York Federal Court – Garth Peterson was interviewed by Scott Cohn on CNBC's 'Business Day'[70] programme, *Investigations Inc*, and gave a very convincing but less than flattering opinion of Morgan Stanley's ethical policies. He criticised both the DOJ and SEC for pressurising him and his family: in effect coercing him into submission.

The following are direct extracts from that interview:

SCOTT COHN: The U.S. Attorney in the Eastern District of New York said you used a 'Web of deceit to thwart Morgan Stanley's internal controls, despite years of training. Basically, you were held up as a poster-child for enforcement of the Foreign Corrupt Practices Act. What's … what was your reaction to that? What … what's wrong with those statements?

Mr PETERSON: … let's just focus for a minute on the transaction for which I'm being charged. The government hasn't released some important background about that. I made that investment before I joined Morgan Stanley. When I joined, I declared it to Morgan Stanley. Then, Morgan Stanley became familiar with that deal, and decided they wanted to buy in as well. So, I helped them to do that. Then, … … about a year and a half after that … essentially, just to make it very simple, Morgan Stanley forced me out of that deal. And I felt that was unfair …. And so, about a year after that, I found a way to buy back in at the same price that I'd been forced out at. That's still – a wrong action …. But I don't believe that that should be characterised as a, 'web of deceit,' and whatever, to … you know, to take things from Morgan Stanley

SCOTT COHN: So what they're saying is that, as part of that deal, this Chinese government official, right off the bat, got a couple million dollars in paper profits?

Mr PETERSON: You see, it's actually … the details are very complex. **You'd have to ask yourself, at this point, why he's still fine and has no problems.** And the reason is that, actually, he didn't invest as well. He just fronted for me and two other people. So, the Chinese government did its own investigation, and determined I never bribed him. Yeah, I probably shouldn't have, you know, secretly invested. But … I never bribed him, and that's what the Chinese government determined. And that's … the truth, I never bribed anybody.

But it is very, very clear to the government, that actually there was low to zero, FCPA consciousness, not only on my part, but on virtually everyone around me.

69   With a three-year supervision order and a ban from working in the securities industry for life. He was also required to disgorge $250,000 and surrender property interests valued at $3.4 million at a hearing on 24 April 2012.

70   http://video.cnbc.com/gallery/?video=3000109695.

The actions of everyone around me … you know, all the way up to the top … completely showed that people had no consciousness of it (the FCPA) whatsoever … It just wasn't in my head, and it wasn't in other people's head … then you have to ask yourself, if it's obviously not working because people are acting … in ways that show that they have low to zero, FCPA consciousness, then maybe those training programs and emails are not enough

SCOTT COHN: Do you … do you … do you feel like Morgan Stanley threw you overboard?

Mr PETERSON: Yeah. Look, I did things wrong. I deserved to get fired. I never bribed anybody, so it's still a mystery, a little bit why … you know, this whole case is … has been focused on that. Because as I've said, I know what I did. These are the things I did wrong. Morgan Stanley got off scot-free. And I think, you know, I have no … you know, desire for them to be harmed in any way, or you know. So –… it's not that. But what I feel bad about is … the government lying to the – to the public. And – saying that … they had this wonderful compliance … program, when in fact the government knows that it wasn't getting into people's heads. Which is what really matters ….

SCOTT COHN: Right. So, the narrative that's likely to come out of this sentencing is … rogue investment banker in China, pays off public official, the firm that has a robust compliance regime turns him in, Foreign Corrupt Practices Act is there front and center. Big message sent to everybody. I take it, from what we've been talking about, that's not the narrative that you want people to come away with?

Mr PETERSON: That's complete rubbish. It's complete rubbish. I've said, you know, I did things wrong. The one thing wrong in relation to this transaction that … that the government has studied, and finally, is punishing me for. As I say, I made the investment, I was pushed out of it. I bought back in at the same price that I was pushed out of it. There's actually nothing in relation to all of that ever has anything to do with a bribe. But the Department of Justice, particularly, also the SEC, maybe to a lesser extent, are so keen on finding some example that they can get by the scruff of the neck and say, 'See, here? Remember this law? You know, nobody do this again.'

… And so, I totally understand that that's going to be really, really effective. I think now, people really, probably are more aware of the FCPA in … in banking in China. They probably – very much more aware. But they need their – the DOJ needs this example, you know, to hang up like this, and they're getting it at the expense of truth, at the expense of truth. At the expense of truth ….

One, is that – the DOJ, basic ally is rewarding Morgan Stanley for handing me over. So, you know, all this … everything comes onto me. And so, the … government … 'Thank you, for doing this. This is what companies should do, hand 'em over.'

The DOJ clearly, you know, also … it makes their case easier to sit … remember, I'm getting charged for violating internal controls, right? **Well, if those internal controls are … shambles, then it doesn't look quite as good from the DOJ's point of view, as to hold them up as some stellar example of how companies should run themselves.** And then, I'm the rogue over here that kind of … clash, you know, between this beautiful situation here, and this bad guy here. It makes it easier for the DOJ to accomplish what they want ... by bringing out a kind of contrast between me and my employer. Rather than saying ... 'You know, Garth did some things a little bad, and by the way, the .... His .... company was a mess, as well. And they really need to clean themselves up.'[71] (Emphasis added)

The bottom line is that although regulators have avoided committing themselves to the sorts of policies and procedures they would regard as satisfactory, cases like Morgan Stanley & Co. should be regarded as models.[72] The second point is not to automatically accept every word uttered by the 'Cottage Industry'.

Honesty is the ONLY policy

Whatever integrity policies are decided upon, it is essential that they should not be promoted when there is no intention to comply fully. This, incredibly, seems to be the position suggested by a UK solicitor, who insisted on 'zero tolerance', but continued: *'But I am sure you can always find ways around it'*.[73]

BAE's New Policy of Zero Tolerance

Lord Woolf – distinguished as the ex-Lord Chief Justice of the UK and one of the pre-eminent lawyers of his generation – in his British Aerospace (BAE) report commended the company's zero tolerance policy on facilitation payments, while accepting that in the short term they could not be avoided. His Lordship continued that the means [should be] developed to eliminate them completely over time.

So where is the honesty in a zero tolerance policy that promotes tolerance? All this does is pass the responsibility to junior employees at the point of contact with FPOs, exposing them to personal dangers and criminal sanctions. This is an unethical cop-out.

The ultimate question is whether a company has the courage to determine policies on principle and to support employees when they follow them, or is it going to spin with weasel words that have no substance?

---

71   http://www.cnbc.com/id/48648151/.

72   Also, the excellent University of West Virginia website, see:,http://lib.law.virginia.edu/Garrett/prosecution_ agreements/home.suphp (accessed 28 November 2012), contains details of all deferred prosecution agreements, again which commit regulators.

73   He must have been jesting, although his humour genes were not otherwise obvious.

Weaseling Out of Trouble

As Homer Simpson told his wife, Marge: Don't discourage the boy,[74] Marge! Weaseling out of things is important to learn. It's what separates us from the animals! Except the weasel, of course'.

With the Bribery Act, unfortunately, there are far too many weasel words. Companies have the choice – on such things as facilitation payments and hospitality – of facing reality now with policies that regulators may not like (see, for example, the suggested wording on facilitation payments in Chapter 31) or of weaseling. There is no doubt which approach is the most ethical.

Accessibility to policies, codes and procedures

All policies should be supported by a helpline provided through a secure website, which should include procedure manuals and checklists, incident reporting and suggestion schemes, as well as the electronic confessional box (see page 575). Ideally, all compliance and control policies and procedures should be centred on one intranet address and should be comprehensively indexed, cross referenced and dated.

All access should be recorded and logged against the employees' or associated person's names. Exception reports should identify individuals and departments who have never consulted the site and efforts made and recorded to steer them to the path of salvation.

STEPS F TO H IMPLEMENTATION, ETC.

Chapters 21–32 contain recommendations for implementing controls; it is not necessary to repeat them here.

STEP 1: BENCHMARKING CAMPAIGNS AND POLICIES

The SFO has (rightly) said that it will not be impressed by 'paper policies'. In a speech to the Fourth International Symposium on Economic Crime in August 2009, Richard Alderman, the then SFO Director, said:

> *We feel that corporate governance should be more than just a set of systems and controls that have been implemented purely as an exercise in box ticking. Corporates at all levels should examine their processes critically and consider the ethical makeup of their company. Business ethics are the true foundation of good corporate governance and the creation of sustainable businesses.*
>
> *What I emphasise to corporates and advisers though is that we are not looking at this as a box ticking exercise. The culture needs to be set from the top. Members of the corporate need*

---

74   Bart Simpson, Homer's son, who is destined to become an investigator.

to know that the corporate is committed to ethical standards of business and that executives at the most senior levels are role models for ethical business conduct'.[75]

So how can a company benchmark its policies and procedures? Trying to make comparisons manually is a near impossibility. There is no evidence on the Internet that any company has introduced an integrity campaign along the lines suggested in this book, although some have come close and the authors know of at least two of their clients that have very successfully done so.[76] That said, the main generally available benchmarking sources are codes of conduct, and there are many excellent ones around.

Cobasco Group Limited examined the Codes of Conduct (downloaded from the Internet) of 24 companies which were selected to represent a cross-section of commercial sectors bound by both the FCPA and the UK Bribery Act. It also incorporated reports on business principles by Transparency International, the Basic Guide of the UN Global Compact, the GCO, the G3 Sustainability Report, the Index for the Global Reporting Initiative and the Ministry of Justice Guidance for Commercial Organisations.

Plain text versions of the codes were imported into Concordance (Figure 23.8),[77] resulting in a corpus of over 191,000 words.

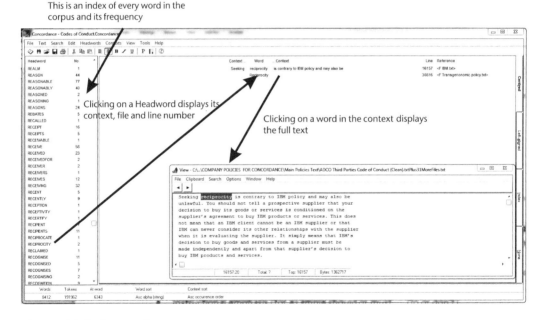

Figure 23.8 Concordance

---

75   Available   at: http://www.sfo.gov.uk/about-us/our-views/director's-speeches/speeches-2009/international-symposium-on-economic-crime.aspx (accessed 28 November 2012).

76   And whose identity cannot be disclosed for confidentiality reasons.

77   Available at: http://www.concordancesoftware.co.uk/ (accessed 28 November 2012).

Indexed headwords words (8,412 of a 191,962 corpus) were categorised into:[78]

- The main topics that should be considered in a code of conduct *(for example, 'bribery', 'fraud', 'facilitation payments', referral fees, reciprocation, lobbying, etc.)*;
- Forensic linguistic analysis to determine the orientation of the code *(for example, possessive and personal pronouns, possessive adjectives, imperatives, verb tense and moods[79])*;
- Instructional emphasis: whether coercive or persuasive *(for example, 'should' or 'must' or 'do' or 'don't')*;
- Specific references to the Bribery Act 2010 and the FCPA.

The corpus identified around 400 integrity-related topics. Subsequently the words in individual codes were then run against the corpus to highlight missing topics, differences in regulatory orientation and to place them in the matrix shown in Figure 23.9.[80]

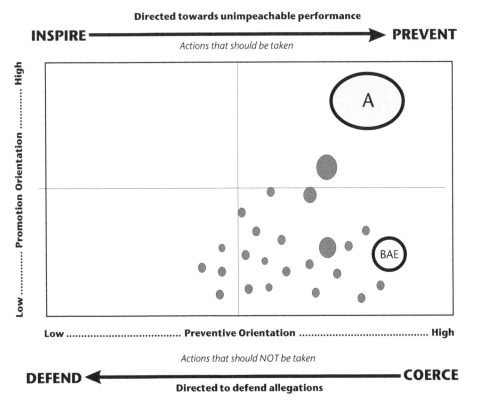

Figure 23.9 Coverage and Regulatory Orientation of Codes of Conduct
The size of the circle represents the topic coverage of the code and the siting its regulatory orientation. The circle marked 'A' lays out what the authors consider to be the optimum for an integrity campaign.

---

78   Among other things.

79   All discussed in Michael J. Comer and Timothy E. Stephens, *Deception at Work* (Gower, 2004).

80   There is likely to be other documentation – not on the Internet – that would change these categories. The matrix does not show to what extent codes are implemented.

Preliminary conclusions are on the codes are as follows:

- Codes vary dramatically in length and topic coverage. The longest is Cisco's with 14,390 words and the shortest Shell's,[81] with 1,496. (Morgan Stanley's current code has around 10,000 words[82]).
- The average length of a code of conduct is around 6,000 words.
- Codes by American companies are 40 per cent longer than their European counterparts. Of the European companies, British Aerospace (BAE) has the longest code, with 12,311 words.
- All are preventively orientated (for example 'don't' rather than 'do' with 'not' appearing 1,047 times and 'allowed', 26).
- All but one are professionally designed and commercially printed. Some companies have more than one code, with inconsistent coverage of topics.
- None includes a summary of the most important laws.
- Only two are indexed and just three include a glossary.
- Only four[83] contain specific references to the Bribery Act and only two discuss 'adequate procedures'.
- None refers to 'country risks' and only four to 'zero tolerance'.
- Only six make any meaningful reference to facilitation payments, except for BAE, which recommends 'zero tolerance' but then allows it.
- Just five talk about hospitality.
- Only one emphasises the importance of decision-making and how genuine mistakes should be corrected.
- Only two refer to reciprocation and none to corporate referral commissions.
- Only three mention cartels and four export controls.
- None discusses 'tax avoidance'.
- Only two deal with 'embezzlement' and the coverage of 'conflicts of interest' is patchy.
- None deals with internal or competitive corruption; and the coverage of incoming bribery is poor or non-existent.
- Some codes do not show their date of issue and none refers to documents that have been superseded. Only five address waivers of the code.

The conclusion is that only four or five would meet Bribery Act standards. Most could be massively improved: the word 'inspire' does not appear anywhere in the corpus, nor does 'happy'!

No Socks

When Sarbanes–Oxley (SOX) is included in the corpus, the omissions and inconsistencies are dreadful.

---

81   But there are obviously additional detailed procedures.

82   But there are some very interesting differences between this and earlier and possible still extant documents.

83   Altegrity, Macmillan, Motorola and Xstrata.

A follow-up test examined the consistency and compatibility of high-level codes and training programmes, procedures, authority tables and sustainability and annual reports (see Figure 23.10).

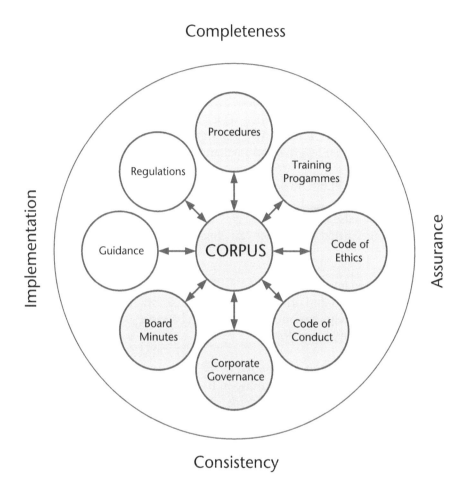

Figure 23.10   The Corpus: Principles and Consistency

Although this analysis was limited to four or five cooperating organisations it identified important topics that were not referred to in training programmes: nearly all of which were set in very narrow legal frames. There was no evidence that companies trained outward-facing employees in how to react when bribes were offered or extorted, or to even discuss blue collar and internal corruption. Further, some sustainability reports contained topics (as well as noble causes and metrics) that are not included in any policy or code.

Public Seminars and Conferences on Bribery

The topics included in what are regarded as the top five international conferences on bribery were run against the corpus, as were guides put out by four leading law firms. Any guesses about their coverage and orientation?

Although there is insufficient publicly available information to be certain, topics covered in pre-acquisition due diligence reviews, reports by corporate monitors and by organisations that certify Bribery Act, FCPA and the Proceeds of Crime Act (POCA) compliance appear to be far less than optimal and, in some cases, even 'adequate'.

MEASURING ETHICAL PERFORMANCE

Continuing with the false credo of 'what gets measured gets managed', the Institute of Business Ethics suggests that companies can check that their ethics policies are working from the number of:

- New policies issued and revised!
- Contacts made by staff and others with compliance and ethics functions;
- Contacts made via helplines or other reporting channels;
- Records of disciplinary infractions;
- Regular surveys of *staff*;
- Internal audit and investigation reports;
- Proportion of staff undertaking training in the year;
- Benchmarking against external standards.

With the greatest of respect to the distinguished Institute of Business Ethics, most of the measurements give absolutely no assurance that integrity is being maintained, especially in high-risk contexts, and its approach reeks of box-ticking.

The Next Stage of Human Evolution

The way things are going, with people choosing to email, Twitter or Facebook each other rather than chat, could result in generations to come being born without ears and vocal cords. The best way to test implementation of integrity campaigns is to speak to people and, more importantly, to listen.[84]

---

84   This is why training senior managers, compliance and audit specialist in conversational skills and interviewing is so important (see Chapter 28).

In 2010, the Institute of Internal Auditors Research Foundation published a manual by James Roth, *Best Practices: Evaluating the Corporate Culture*,[85] which promises much but delivers little of practical value.

The truth is that ethics is an asset that cannot be measured quantitatively although: (a) you will know it when you see it; and (b) here are some possibilities:

- Undercover tests and pretext investigations, along the lines of The *Sunday Times* 'Insight' exposé of defence industry scams,[86] or test purchases and sales;
- Double blind surveys involving suppliers, customers, competitors and ex-employees;
- Focus groups;
- Critical point audits of potentially suspicious transactions and especially windfall profits and exceptional losses (see Chapters 18–20);
- The Managing Director's Annual Scrum down (see page 601);
- Amnesties and payment of rewards for information;
- Control self-assessments in high-risk contexts;
- Analysis of trading and other recorded telephone calls;
- Analysis of email and other archives;
- Sneaky visits to the smoking areas (your own and those of customers and suppliers).

Most of the above may be too near the bone for some organisations[87] and this is fair enough. Others will appreciate that you don't make nice omelettes without breaking a few eggs. As in many areas with integrity, it all comes back to the company's ethical stance on deontological (moral issues) and teological (outcomes) conflicts.

Selling Integrity to OBDURATE Managers

Compliance professionals,[88] auditors and security managers often complain that convincing frontline colleagues – especially those in entrepreneurial roles[89] – that integrity is in everyone's best interests – can be a problem.

A Bad Hair Day

A Compliance Manager was almost in tears when she was accused by the Marketing Director of being a 'vinegary old maid', who had no idea how difficult it was to sell. All she did was ask him to provide further information on a high-risk customer. He was having a bad hair day: she left in tears.

---

85   Available through the Institute of Internal Auditors website, at: http://www.theiia.org/bookstore/product/best-practices-evaluating-corporate-culture-1469.cfm (accessed 28 November 2012).

86   Available at: http://www.thesundaytimes.co.uk/sto/news/insight/article1147765.ece (accessed 28 November 2012).

87   And see contrived anonymous letters, Chapter 18, page 466.

88   Most of these are orientated preventatively.

89   And promotion-orientated.

The Head of Compliance asked for the authors' advice and as a result arranged for a young (and a bit cheeky and very nice) junior member of Compliance to meet with the offender. The junior, who acted as though she were nervous, explained how things were going and then said: 'Mr Jones, can I ask your advice on something that has been worrying me?'. 'Of course', responded the now nurturing parental director[90] Jones: 'Fire ahead: ask me'.

Junior: 'Well it's like this. Someone who works in your department, whom we all respect and like is being really difficult and will not follow the rules. We don't want to make a fuss, but it's putting the company at risk and making our efforts to help impossible. We don't know what to do'.

Marketing Director: 'Who is this?'

Junior: 'I'm sorry to say, it's YOU'.

The Director burst into laughter and from that time on became a different person and a strong supporter of compliance.

Compliance specialists have to accept that they will not win over everyone, so they should concentrate on directing minds, outward-facing employees, budget holders and back office and support staff in risky contexts. If they can succeed with these, most problems will be reduced.

Assigning Ownership Responsibility

PRINCIPLES

Accountability for every process and asset within the Extended Enterprise should be assigned through policies, organisation charts, job descriptions, contracts, authority tables and procedures.

BOARD OF DIRECTORS

The buck stops with directors and top managers of the organisation. In the corruption area they should, as they say on the *X Factor* – 'in no particular order':

- Try to understand the most **significant risks**, laws and regulations, including[91] corruption and bribery throughout the extended enterprise;
- Commit themselves to and 'capstone' an effective and comprehensive integrity campaign that embraces 'decision centricity';
- Empower auditors to detect and investigate fraud and corruption;

90   See Eric Berne's theory of Transactional Analysis.

91   But not limited to.

- Insist on continuous monitoring programmes so that they become the first to know;
- Delegate responsibilities, aligning authority and responsibility;
- Monitor and review progress of all control programmes which hopefully show continuous improvement;
- Ensure that effective action is taken when violations are suspected;
- From time to time review the performance of the board in relation.

Companies should consider appointing a full board member to represent integrity, control and compliance matters and to coordinate the disparate silos in which laws and regulations are issued.

LINE MANAGEMENT RESPONSIBILITIES

Specialist functions such as internal audit, compliance or risk management, work in advisory capacities to set and monitor standards and have responsibilities of their own. But this does not alter the fact that an employee responsible for any task or asset (that is, its 'owner') is also fully accountable for its control. Control goes with the line management turf. This responsibility must be unambiguously assigned through policies, procedures, organisation charts, job descriptions, contracts of employment and budgets, through supervision and audit. It is critical that ownership is assigned for every asset and process in the Extended Enterprise.

THE DIRECTORATE OF INTEGRITY

Larger companies should consider consolidating all control-related interests into one department, represented by a main board director.

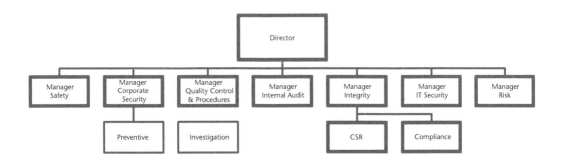

Figure 23.11   Possible Structure of the Directorate of Integrity

The Director should be accountable for the factors summarised in Table 23.3.

Table 23.3 Responsibilities of the Director of Integrity

Responsibilities	Comment
To report to the Managing Director (with an alternative line to the Chairman of the Risk and Assurance Committee)	The director should be positioned to ensure that all aspects of control are considered at board level and before decisions are made. *His or her role is proactive, whereas conventional audit committees usually make their inputs after the event, when it is too late*
To manage the directorate and specify procedures to ensure that line managers comply with integrity and control standards	The director should be the focal point for all aspects of risk and control
To develop and implement strategies, policies and procedures for all aspects of control	
To assess risks to the company and for collating intelligence on them	
To set annual objectives for control	The objective should be to drive continuous improvement; balancing financial performance with integrity
To liaise with their equivalents in associated companies and with important associated persons	The Directorate should develop supporting channels of communication in addition to the usual commercial relationships
To liaise with regulators and law enforcement bodies	The Director should have the status to liaise effectively with regulators. His position goes beyond that recommended by the Federal Sentencing Guidelines, the Ministry of Justice Guidance and the SFO
To initiate audits and investigations	By delegating authority to the managers of the Audit and Security departments.
To monitor the effectiveness of controls	To work with the Audit Committee in accrediting controls

The suggested structure, besides being far more effective, reduces operational costs and should eliminate interdepartmental politics and the silos in which regulations are issued. The company should consider whether the Directorate should be centralised or partly embedded[92] in high risk contexts as is the case with Siemens following its Deferred Prosecution Agreement and enforced monitoring.

THE AUDIT, RISK AND ASSURANCE COMMITTEE

Consideration should be given to extending the role of a typical audit committee to cover all risk, audit and control functions and unify them. The alternative to having multiple committees for audit–compliance–health and safety duplicates work and leads to political infighting and inefficiency. If an organisation is committee-inclined on risks, audit, controls and compliance, the number of committees should be limited to one.

---

92   Overtly or covertly!!

INTERNAL AUDIT

The internal audit department should be headed by a professional, hard-nosed, qualified accountant, supported by a core of dedicated auditors. Salaries and other benefits should take account of limited opportunities for promotion into senior line positions. The remainder of the audit department should be staffed by high flyers on rotational assignments of no less than two years' duration.

The head of internal audit should report to the Director of Integrity or, if there is not such a position, to the Managing Director. Alternative reporting lines to the Chairman and Chairman of the Risk and Assurance Committee should be available, but used only in exceptional circumstances.

The role of Internal Audit should go beyond the most recent guidelines of the Institute of Internal Auditors[93] and should be accountable for the factors summarised in Table 23.4.

Table 23.4 Non-conventional Responsibilities of Internal Audit

Standards and Responsibilities	How Implemented and Comments
To help owners assess risks	Control self-assessment programme and other methods of risk analysis
To provide intelligence on fraud risks	Monitoring all available sources of intelligence
To assist owners specify controls	Control self-assessment, routine and special audits Control manuals Training programmes
To be intimately involved in systems development and the deployment of new technology	Participation in all systems development projects Controls specified at the systems design phase
To develop automated fraud detection programmes	See Chapters 18–20
To carry out audits specifically intended to detect fraud	At least 10 per cent of audit resources should be devoted to fraud detection
To liaise with auditors from the Extended Enterprise	Meetings, conferences and training programmes
To audit major contracts and vendors	Third-party audits under Standard Terms and Conditions of Business Integrity validation reviews
To manage the reporting of incidents programme	
To investigate suspected fraud	
To assist the Compliance and Quality Control managers by including aspects of interest to them in audit programmes	Liaison Shared Internal Control Questionnaires
To develop and run training programmes	See below
To monitor and report on the maintenance of controls by line managers	Control self-assessment Special and routine audits Providing input for annual appraisals by line managers

93   See page 391.

The Institute of Internal Auditors recommends that its members should not engage in risk assessment or designing control systems on the basis that doing so compromises their independence. With the greatest of respect to the IIA this is a luxury that most companies cannot afford and besides that it is nuts. Auditors are control specialists and should be held accountable for all of the tasks set out in Table 23.4 above and should not be permitted to stand back after the war has been fought and taunt the survivors.

MANAGER COMPLIANCE

This position should be filled by a professional compliance specialist with legal, operational and communication skills. It is not purely or even primarily a legal job. He or she should report to the Director of Integrity[94] and should have responsibility and authority for the tasks set out in Table 23.5.

Table 23.5 Responsibilities of the Manager Compliance

Standards and Responsibilities	How Implemented and Comments
To assist owners in assessing all of their compliance obligations. This is especially important for overseas operations and particularly in emerging and transitional economies	Control self-assessment programme Detailed legal reviews and requirements and specifications for compliance, worldwide
To assist owners to develop specified procedures on compliance	These must be integrated with security, audit, quality and environmental topics
To monitor changes in legislation and to update procedures accordingly	It is essential that the effects of changing legislation are incorporated into specified procedures and training courses
To ensure that the Internal Audit department includes compliance testing in special and routine audits	This gives the Compliance department eyes and ears at a working level and makes it proactive
To work with the Internal Audit Department on reported incidents that could have an impact on compliance	This enables Compliance to obtain early warning of potential problems. Links with the Manager of Security provides Compliance with investigative resources
To run training programmes on compliance	These are especially important for senior managers in the extended enterprise
To monitor and report on the maintenance of controls by line managers	Control self-assessment Special and routine audits Providing input for annual appraisals by line managers

Ideally, the Head of Compliance should spend at least six months early in his or her career with the company in a marketing position, preferably overseas, to gain direct

---

94   In a separate department from Legal.

experience. Where this is not possible he or she should be considered for a short-term rotational assignment in a high risk operational environment.

MANAGER CORPORATE SECURITY

In organisations with more than 2,000 employees, a professional security adviser or a small department is justified. This is especially true of companies operating in countries where local law enforcement is inefficient or corrupt.

The Manager Corporate Security should report to the Director of Integrity and should be responsible for the tasks summarised in Table 23.6.

Table 23.6 Responsibilities of the Manager Corporate Security

Standards and Responsibilities	How Implemented and Comments
To assist owners to identify risks	Control self-assessment programme Liaison with law enforcement bodies and security advisers in other organisations Providing intelligence on risks and opponents
To assist in the specification of controls	As part of the control team
To investigate suspected fraud and malpractice, in close cooperation with Audit	This link between Audit and Security is vital in any organisation To assist on third-party audits
To work with the Manager of Internal Audit on automated and other fraud detection programmes	See Table 23.4
To work with and assist Compliance	The Manager of Security should provide investigative support to all other functions in the Directorate of Control
To survey and advise on the physical security of premises and hardware standards	Survey
To develop training programmes for employees in the extended enterprise	Especially on the impact of the criminal law concerning bribery, corruption etc. and the reporting of incidents procedures
To direct electronic countermeasures surveys	Debugging and electronic 'sweeps'
To coordinate the purchase of security hardware and guarding services	Specification of standard products, negotiation of discounts and maintenance contracts
To carry out pre-employment screening programme and integrity validation reviews	See Chapter 25, page 685
To carry out exit interviews	See page 706
To monitor and report on the maintenance of controls by line managers	Control self-assessment Special and routine audits Providing input for annual appraisals by line managers

The manager should have substantial law enforcement experience *as an investigator.*[95] Under no circumstances should he or she have a direct reporting line to Human Resources or the Legal department. The functions should be separated.

GENERAL COUNSEL

The company's General Counsel or Head of Legal should advise on the legality of controls, especially those concerning personnel, data protection and contracts. He should ensure that the Head of Compliance is provided with all necessary professional support. Under normal circumstances the General Counsel should be consulted in investigations, but should not direct them. He or she should be in a separate department from Compliance but with a direct reporting line to the board.

HEAD OF HUMAN RESOURCES

The Head of Human Resources should be the designated owner of the important procedures, described in Chapter 26. He or she should be consulted on major investigations, but should never direct them.[96]

PUBLIC RELATIONS

The person or department responsible for public relations should be intimately involved in the control campaign and should help develop brochures, videos and other material to promote and advertise the ethical and other objectives of the company. He or she should also be involved immediately prior to the start of a major investigation, so media relationships are effectively handled. During an investigation the head of PR should be the company's primary contact with the media.

MARKETING AND SALES DEPARTMENTS

These are critical departments on the bribe payment front and yet they are rarely involved in developing integrity or compliance programmes, but rather have procedures foisted upon them which they do not philosophically support. For this reason:

- Senior representatives should actively participate in developing the integrity campaign or, in its absence, codes of conduct and procedures.
- Audit and compliance representatives should be appointed for short-term assignments in marketing and sales positions and vice versa.

In addition, one or two marketing people should be trained as trainers on integrity topics and, wherever possible, run their own departmental programmes.

---

95   And not just in the Traffic Department.

96   To avoid a fate worse than death!!

COLLABORATIVE RELATIONSHIPS

The Directorate of Integrity should establish good relationships with his nearest equivalents in important associated enterprises, such as subsidiaries, parents, siblings, joint ventures, suppliers and customers.

Certification and Accreditation

BACKGROUND AND CORPORATE SOCIAL RESPONSIBILITY REPORTING

Many companies have their Corporate Social Responsibility (CSR) policies independently certified (including elements relating to anti-bribery) in the belief that doing so has a positive influence on customers, suppliers, agents, investors, other stakeholders, regulators and bankers.

Ethical Outperformance

The Ethisphere Institute claims that companies recognised with its World's Most Ethical Companies (WME) award consistently outperform their peers.[97] But, as we shall see some claims in the CSR field are not always what they seem.

More recently, companies subject to the FCPA and/or UK Bribery Act have sought additional certification of their anti-bribery policies and procedures. The following paragraphs discuss the options, problems and matters to be considered. The World Business Council for Sustainable Development defines CSR as 'business commitment to contribute to the sustainable economic development, working with employees, their families, local community, and society at large to improve their quality of life' including:

- Working conditions including Occupational Health & Safety;
- Environmental resources;
- Human and labour rights;
- Business ethics, supply chain management, fraud and corruption;
- Organisational governance.

The success of CSR programs is difficult to measure and there are at least eight different commonly used methodologies which can be 'cherry picked' to produce the best results, thereby hiding less than optimal performance. The bottom line is that a universal, comprehensive standard is required for assessing CSR programmes and the same is true for anti-bribery, as we shall see later.

---

97   CoreRatings states 'CSR issues rarely have a significant effect on cash flow and earnings but do affect market capitalisation.' See.http://www.unepfi.org/fileadmin/events/2003/roundtable/presentations/oconnor_en.pdf.

Advantages of CSR are difficult if not impossible to quantify and the argument that sustainable companies win a competitive advantage are extremely tenuous, especially in the current economic climate[98] and even more so when the claims made amount to 'greenwash' or are demonstrably untrue.

The Dangers of Greenwash

In November 2012 a highly respected blog[99] reported on a study by Vienna University of Economics and Business Institute working with Middlesex University that around 87 per cent of the 131 companies on the Forbes 250 list that reported[100] sustainability performance misrepresented or concealed the truth.

The authors speculated that the reason for skulduggery varied from a misunderstanding of the protocols involved to deliberate deceit 'in order to achieve a reputation boost, without due consideration of the consequences of being found to making false claims'.

Greenpeace published *The Book on Green Wash*,[101] in 1992 suggesting that the greatest advocates for placing sustainability at the heart of their communications 'were those with the shoddiest green credentials'.

Most CSR reporting is based on internal assessments by the companies concerned.[102] The results appear in impressive 'Sustainability Reports' that are sometimes more of a marketing scam rather than a reflection of deep commitment and progress.

Capacity and Load Example

The CSR reports of some companies misrepresent such things as carbon dioxide emissions or the efficiency of offset mechanisms, like planting eucalyptus trees in Outer Mongolia. They also happily confuse 'capacity' with 'load' for renewable energy projects and especially wind turbines, thereby grossly inflating their green credentials.

If a company misrepresents or exaggerates its CSR successes, it tells you all you need to know about their tone from the top and their supposedly 'embedded values'.

---

98   See the Edleman Trust Barometer http://trust.edelman.com/about-trust/.

99   http://csr-reporting.blogspot.co.uk/2012/11/false-claims-in-sustainability-reports.html.

100   On labour and human rights.

101   http://research.greenpeaceusa.org/?a=view&d=4588.

102   Less than 25 per cent of the UK's largest companies back up their CSR claims by independent third party assurance.

The happenings with CSR certification are likely to be repeated with anti-bribery programmes, especially because the former are purely voluntary, whereas the latter are enforced through the criminal law and are arguably far more important with even greater incentives for skulduggery.

Tall Poppies and Fallen Idols

The question is whether hyperbolising CSR or other ethical excellence stimulates regulatory attention, sets expectations which – if not met – lead to third party litigation and allegations of misrepresentation or fraud. The answer, of course, is simple. If the CSR or integrity campaigns are genuine and effective, extol them: if they are simply box ticking cosmetics, it is probably best to stay schtum.

ANTI-BRIBERY CERTIFICATION (ABC)

Some important points

While ABC may be viewed as part of a wider CSR certification scheme, it is increasingly becoming a freestanding addition simply because companies recognise that UN Global Compact (UNGC) and Global Reporting Initiative (GRI) frameworks and voluntary reporting, self-disclosure approaches fall short of requirements. As a result, freestanding anti-bribery certification schemes are gaining popularity, especially in the light of the UK Bribery Act and the supposed benefits of being able to demonstrate adequate procedures or persuading the Department of Justice and Securities and Exchange Commission into a 'declination' to take no action.

The result is that there are now many anti-bribery frameworks, reporting and certification schemes that overlap with CSR or with each other, seldom converge on assessment criteria and do not even meet the very basic requirements of the Ministry of Justice's Guide for Commercial Organisations or the Federal Sentencing Guidelines, let alone the far more effective standards such as those issued in connection with Sarbanes-Oxley (COSO) or the Financial Services Authority (FSA).One of the supposed benefits of certified ABC programs is that it will persuade prosecutors that it is not in the public interest to prosecute alleged corporate perpetrators. But:

- Of the more than 3,000 organisations that have been pursued by the DOJ or SEC in the past 20 years, only five have been given credit for an effective ethics and compliance programme.[103]
- The OECD Phase III report pointed out the limited benefits of 'adequate procedures' (see pages 133, 218 and 613).

---

103   Sue Reisinger, Corporate Compliance and Criminal Cases: Plan Now or Pay Later, CORPORATE COUNSEL, Jan. 13, 2010 (Citing the United States Sentencing Commission Sentencing Datafile, compiled from FY1991–FY2009) and http://m1.corpedia.com/resource_database/whitepaper-culture-dodd-frank.pdf.

Thus having ABC programs certified simply in the hope that doing so will impress prosecutors may be no more than fool's gold. However, in the unlikely event that a contested corporate case gets into court,[104] certification may convince a jury that procedures were adequate and lead them to acquit. Certification may also help a company that genuinely wishes to develop an effective integrity campaign.

Examples of CSR and ABC certifications

The most widely recognised certification and quasi-certification schemes are as follows.

The UN Global Compact

The UNGC is a voluntary initiative created in 1999 to encourage businesses to adopt socially responsibility and sustainability programmes based on ten principles and various reporting elements on:

- Human Rights
- Labour Standards
- Environment
- Anti-corruption

The Compact claims to have between 7,000 and 8,000 corporate members in around 130 countries although this is difficult to verify, especially when 630 companies were delisted[105] and currently there are believed to be a further 1,469 who have defaulted on the requirement to submit annual Communications on Progress (COPs). COPs are completed by self-assessments which are rarely verified and which in the anti-bribery field are superficial. Members are usually entitled to use the UNGC logo on their promotional material[106] and have other benefits including qualification for government and World Bank contracts and international development financing.[107]

The Global Reporting Initiative 1997

GRI is a non-profit organisation that promotes economic, environmental and social sustainability (including basic features of anti-bribery programmes) through a framework based on AA1000AS to support voluntary reporting for its 5,000 worldwide members. It maintains a data base[108] of company reports[109] and some useful statistics. Members may elect to have their reports independently verified:[110] often by their external accountants.

---

104   In the USA there have only been less than five contested FCPA cases in the past 35 years.

105   In 2008. Delisting is the only sanction including for false reporting.

106   There is no certification.

107   For some overseas governments and banks a potential vendor's support of the UNGC is a prequalification factor.

108   And very useful.

109   Including the Carbon Disclosure Project, UNGC, the OECD's Guidelines for Multi-national enterprises, ISO 2600 on social responsibility and the International Financial Corporation.

110   An estimated 18 per cent of reports are independently verified.

GRI is currently revising frameworks for greenhouse gas emissions and for anti-corruption. However, the anti-corruption standards are superficial and the suggested performance metrics examples of box ticking.

ETHICIntelligence

The company was launched in 2001 by Philippe Montigny, an ex-member of the OECD Secretariat. He was involved in the ministerial negotiations that led to the OECD 'Anti-corruption Convention'.[111] The company is based in Paris and works through representatives (all of whom are respected lawyers and mostly ex-prosecutors) in Europe, Canada, China and the USA and claims to have conducted its first anti-corruption certification in 2006. Its clients include Alstrom, European Aeronautic Defence and Space Company (EADS),[112] Equant LLC, Schneider Electric Egypt and Sofrecom.

Applicants for certification are required to narrate[113] their anti-corruption programmes (based on the ISO 10500-2011: Anti-Bribery Management System, recommendations from the OECD, International Chamber of Commerce, Transparency International, US Federal Sentencing Guidelines, Ministry of Justice Guide for Commercial Organisations, Italian 231 Law Decree and company best practices). Verification is normally carried out by Societe General de Surveillance (SGS) or Den Norske Veritas (DNV) and their reports certified by a ETHICIntelligence Committee.[114]

Benefits of certification[115] are claimed to include:

- increased visibility of anticorruption commitments
- employee support for anticorruption compliance programs
- clear and identifiable standards for anticorruption compliance policies and procedures
- assurance of the quality of an anticorruption program and a benchmark against other company's programmes
- standard target objectives for anticorruption policies
- lower insurance premiums

EthicIntelligence has produced detailed hand book setting out the basis of certification, which is almost entirely in a legal frame.

---

111 Verbatim from the website and an ambitious reframing of the 'OECD Convention of the Prevention of Bribery of Foreign Public Officials in International Business Transactions'.

112 Following detection of the current scandal involving Saudi Arabia.

113 Self-disclose.

114 Comprising of Mr Montigny and his worldwide representatives.

115 Which remains valid for 2 years.

Converging the Ministry of Justice GCO, etc

EI's verification methodology is centred on four categories:

- Information
- Training
- Tools
- Control

And it attempts to align these to the six principles of the GCO and the seven steps in the Federal Sentencing Guidelines and to the Italian Law Decree 231 of June 2001. As such, it is possibly the only methodology that tries to converge multiple standards but it still falls well short of complete alignment.

The company makes is clear that certification does not 'guarantee that an act of corruption has not, is not being or will not be committed within the organisation' or even certify that procedures are adequate.

Ethisphere Institute

The institute describes itself as 'a research based international think tank, dedicated to the creation, advancement and sharing of best practices in business ethics corporate social responsibility, anti-corruption and sustainability'. It is based in Arizona and New York and associated with Corpedia Corporation which is a subsidiary[116] of NYSE Euronext. Corpedia Corporation is a specialist in the fields of corporate governance, risk and compliance (GRC) and provides consulting and training support.

Ethisphere claims to maintain a database of codes of conduct for over 500 of the largest worldwide corporations, which are accessible through a search and benchmarking site. It certifies integrity programs including;

- Anticorruption Programs
- Compliance Leader Verification
- Inside Ethics Certification
- Compliance and Due Diligence Certification

Ethisphere also sponsors the World's Most Ethical Companies (WME) award but has been criticised[117] for potential conflicts of interest with Corpedia, some of whose consulting clients have been awarded WME status.

---

116   Acquired in June 2012.

117   Probably unjustifiably.

BSI 105000-2011

The British Standards Institute (BSI) was established in 1901 as the Engineering Standards Committee and was granted a Royal Charter in the 1930s when it adopted its present name. It operates internationally – often in conjunction with the International Organisation for Standardisation (ISO) and its standards are accepted as among the world's finest.

In November 2011 BSI published the 'Specification for an Anti-bribery Management System' (ABMs); primarily to assist businesses comply with the UK Bribery Act and to help demonstrate that their procedures were adequate. However, BSI 10500 is:

- Very basic; set primarily in a legal frame and limited to the UK;
- Does not easily align with the Ministry of Justice GOC and omits a number of important relevant topics including commissions and contributions, culture, directing minds, dividends, fees, red flags, offsets, licenses, loans, prevention lobbying and self-disclosure.

The specification runs to only 20 pages, costs around £150 and is unlikely bedtime reading. It notes that compliance with the standard:

- 'cannot provide assurance that no bribery has occurred or will take place';
- 'can help establish that an organisation has implemented reasonable and proportionate measures[118] to prevent bribery';
- 'qualification with a British standard cannot confer immunity from legal obligations'.

The normal procedure for companies wishing to be certified – and entitled to use the BSI kite mark – is for their self-assessments to be reviewed by a BSI accredited examiner.

IS ANTI-BRIBERY CERTIFICATION WORTH THE EFFORT?

On the face of it, given the OECD's lack of enthusiasm for an adequate procedures defence and more recently comments by David Green, CB, QC, Director of the SFO as well as the American limitations discussed earlier, it may seem that certification is not worth the effort. However, it may well be justified depending on context and objectives. Companies should consider:

- What are our objectives in seeking certification of our CSR, integrity campaign or anti-bribery policies?
    - To genuinely drive and improve performance;
    - To obtain independent assurance that our procedures are adequate;
    - To construct a defence of adequate procedures;
    - How can we be assured that certification will satisfy our objectives.
- What contexts and processes should be certified?
    - The extended enterprise;
    - High risk contexts;
    - Associated persons, such as agents and other performing services;
    - Pre-acquisition targets;

---

118 Avoiding the term 'adequate procedures'.

- Post-acquisition subsidiaries and affiliates;
- Other;
- CSR in its widest aspects;
- Limited to anti-bribery.
- What standards, laws, regulations and benchmarks should be used for certification?
  - International best practice;
  - UK Bribery Act;
  - FCPA;
  - Both;
  - Sarbanes Oxley, FSA Rule book;
  - Other international laws and standards;
  - Local country laws.
- What level of credibility[119] do we require of the certifying organisation?
  - Fully government backed;[120]
  - Connected to regulators and other members of the cottage industry[121] or;
  - Independent of regulators and other members of the cottage industry;[122]
  - Terms and conditions on confidentiality, conflict of interest and reporting obligations;
  - Professional experience to make practical recommendations for improvement;
  - Its attitude to expansive interpretation of the laws, zero tolerance and self-disclosure.[123]
- What are our criteria for selection the accreditation body company?
  - Needs;
  - Wants;
  - Commercial and regulatory track records;
  - Established, credible and verifiable methodologies based on managerial and psychological techniques rather than being restricted to simply a legal frame;
  - Binding undertakings of confidentiality.
- What level of credibility do require of individual verifiers and certifiers?
  - Established track records as anticorruption specialists;[124]
  - Previously accepted as expert witnesses the jurisdictions that may be involved;
  - Absence of any conflict of interest;
  - Personal and binding undertakings of confidentiality;
- What controls can we apply to make sure self-declarations are accurate?
- What funds and time and we prepared to invest in certification?
- What output do we expect?
  - A draft report for comment and approval prior to final publication;
  - Comprehensive reports with gap analysis and recommendations;[125]
  - Certification to the level of 'adequate procedures';

---

119 Subject to due diligence.

120 As far as possible such as BSI.

121 Confidentiality and problems with revolving doors.

122 After due diligence and see Foreword, page xxiii.

123 For example how will it resolve conflicts between US and UK laws on facilitation payments, offset projects, definitions of an FPO and State Owned Enterprise?

124 Examine and retain biographies.

125 With a summary and implementation plan.

- Unrestricted use of certification logos and publicity material;[126]
- Draft expert witness statements and a contract to appear in legal proceedings if required.

If all of the above points are answered satisfactorily, certification of an integrity campaign – even if it is called 'anti-bribery' is probably worthwhile.

An alternative solution is to validate internally, maintain an Adequate Procedures Dossier and if trouble appears launch a contingency plan to dissuade regulators at the case vetting stage from taking matters further.

Conclusions

If you have got this far: well done and, if you do nothing else, please check out your integrity corpus and get ready to be amazed with the number of regulatory topics that are omitted!

---

126 If the intention is to make the certification public: this may not always be the best option.

24 *Standards, Guidelines, Forms and Basic Training*

Procedures, Standards and Guidelines

OBJECTIVES AND FORMAT

A procedure is a specified and detailed process through which controls are implemented and may either be:

- A standard, which is mandatory;
- A guideline, which is optional and may be followed or ignored at the discretion of the managers or process 'owners' concerned.

Effective control cannot be maintained through guidelines.[1] Especially in organisations that consider themselves to be empowered, there must be a baseline set of mandatory standards. Members of the extended enterprise should be empowered and required to follow and to certify annually that they have done so.

PROCEDURE MANUALS

Procedure manuals should be concisely written in plain language and easy to follow. They must be supported by inspirational leadership, effective training, monitoring and enforcement.

Keep it Simple

In one company, to establish precisely what procedures should be used to appoint an intermediary, it was necessary to refer to 8 separate sets of instructions and 12 forms, few of which were cross-referenced and never indexed. It was no wonder that employees were confused!

---

1   Which may or may not be followed at the users' discretion.

Manuals should be included in the integrity corpus (see page 610) and – so far as sensible – in a modular form, specific to each job, task, context, business unit or element concerned.

Easily Accessible Procedures

Insufficient attention is paid to the ways in which manuals are issued. For example, a typical manual on computer security will be divided into such topics as hardware controls, operating systems controls, programming controls, data input, etc. Thus, a person who wishes to find out what is required of him or her has to work through all of the sections and hope to hit upon the right selection. This has two main disadvantages. The first is that it reveals all controls to everyone, most of whom do not need to know them. This, in itself, is an unnecessary breach of security. The second is that the selection of which controls apply to whom is imprecise and obscures accountability.

Ideally all procedures should be available on a single secure intranet site and comprehensively indexed with access rights segregated according to the requirements of a particular user or group of users. It is a good idea to have important tasks in policies and procedures summarised in simple task-specific check lists, mind maps and flow charts.

All manuals and check lists should be dated to show when they were taken into and removed from use, so that it is possible to prove precisely what instructions applied at any time in the past. Copies should be retained in the Adequate Procedures Dossier.

FORMS

All organisations rely on forms,[2] for recruiting employees, appointing customers or intermediaries, controlling processes, establishing ownership. They are critical to effective control, yet few organisations pay sufficient attention to them.

Forms that provide detail on which important decisions will be based should be supported by a decision matrix (along the lines suggested on page 568) that sets out the needs and wants. This approach enables decisions to be made consistently, without bias, and to demonstrate if they are ever challenged that they were not improperly influenced.

Forms should be designed to ensure that they:

- Give a good impression of the company;
- Present all of the facts needed to make important decisions;
- Ask all relevant questions;
- Deter dishonest applicants;
- Comply with the law, especially the Data Protection Act and the Human Rights Act.

---

2   Defined as: printed or electronic documents which set out questions in a structured way, leaving spaces for the entry of information.

Wherever possible forms should be available online and electronically, with important data captured for monitoring and auditing purposes (see Chapters 18–19).

Important forms used for decision-making should incorporate the principle of raising the pavement through:

- The visual impact of layout and colour, possibly with boxes for official use, indicating that replies will be thoroughly checked;
- Warnings of the consequences of false declarations.

For example, a form to be completed for pre-qualification by potential vendors might state:

> *This form is very important. It will be used to establish the basis of our relationship. We are committed to excellence and integrity and if your application is successful you will become an important member of our team. It is vital there are no surprises. So please take care over the completion of the form; if any information you provide is found to be inaccurate, our relationship will be terminated.*
>
> *If at any time you have any complaints over any aspect of our relationship, please contact our Integrity Directorate on telephone number xxxxx or by email on xxxx.*
>
> *If your application is approved, you will be required to comply with our Code of Conduct, security and other procedures, copies of which are attached. We look forward to working with you.*

Such introductions create a common framework and raise the pavement, making deception less likely and less defensible. Forms may also contain releases under data protection laws:

> *Personal and other information provided on this form will be used for processing your application. It may also be used for the prevention and detection of fraud and for security purposes and may be released to government agencies. If you object to this use, please tick here ….*

The response to such warnings and releases will say a lot about the applicant!

Where appropriate, applicants should be required to warrant the accuracy and completeness of their answers. On a vendor application form this might be along the following lines:

> *I certify that the answers I have given are true, complete and correct. I understand that this form will be used as the basis of any future contract between me and xxx and that any incorrect, incomplete or inaccurate answers will result in my removal for consideration or immediate termination of any contract. I undertake to advise xxx of any material changes in my personal or business circumstances.*
>
> *Signed ………….*

Application and other forms should be carefully designed, considering the principles set out in Table 24.1.

Table 24.1   Elements in Forms Design

Principles to be Considered	Comments and Examples
Understand the significance of the form and the consequences of false declarations, errors and bad judgements that could be made as a result	Identify how key facts will be checked Assess the risks of a false declaration
If the form is to be used as background to making a decision	Associate the form with a decision matrix
State the purpose and importance of the form	Incorporate a polite warning explaining the penalties for providing false information. Wherever possible, design forms so that false declarations become a criminal offence
Emphasise the penalties for false declarations	Raise the pavement (see page 566)
Associate with binding contracts	For example, on job application forms, make it clear that compliance with specified procedures and annual declarations are essential elements of the contract of employment of which the form is part.
Ask probing questions	Too often forms are vague. The greater the detail required, the less likely it is that deception will succeed Consider using open questions (see page 391). These make it more difficult for someone to conceal the truth
Consider possible control features	Sequential numbering Multiple or single copies Duplicate submissions[3] Security printing Colour coding Check digits and process action boxes Covert capture of fingerprints[4] Handwriting samples Profiling or scoring to detect fraudulent answers
Require a closing declaration of accuracy and a signature	This, again, raises the pavement
On copies to be retained internally, summarise associated processes	For example, on internal copies of purchase orders, include an extract from the Authority Manual. This makes it less excusable if someone exceeds his or her authority
Consider incorporating a summary of the terms and conditions of business, especially the right to audit	On purchase orders and invitations to tender; and possibly sales quotations and delivery notes

---

3   The answers on this form can be compared to the original form submitted before the interview.

4   See *Deception at Work* by Comer and Stephens, also published by Gower.

Consider incorporating a summary of the company's ethical procedures and for reporting incidents, the name of the person to which they should reported or the telephone number of the company hotline	Consider including the number of the company hotline and the name of the person to whom incidents should be reported
Show the date of printing	Retain archive copies

The way these principles are incorporated into pre-employment screening and vendor integrity validation are discussed later in this chapter and in Chapter 25.

Training Programmes

GENERAL TRAINING

All employees and associated persons should be adequately trained (under the joint ownership of line managers and the Integrity Directorate[5]) in relevant aspects of the company's integrity programmes through multiple channels,[6] including:

- Board room blog
- Booklets, bulletins and e-mails;
- Business cards and payslips;
- Competitions and awards;
- Computer- based 'live chats';
- Ethics helpline;
- Formal classroom sessions;
- In- house magazines and newspapers;
- Internal ethics blogs;
- Interactive and programmed learning texts;
- Logon screen banners and screensavers;
- Mouse mats;
- On-the-job training;
- Personal coaching and mentoring;[7]
- Posters;
- SMS and mobile phone messages (even Twitter and Facebook in some, depending on the regulatory orientation of the recipient);
- Suggestion schemes;
- Twitter and Facebook;
- Video web casts.[8]

---

5   Not Human Resources.

6   Orientated to match the frames of the recipients (see page 586)

7   Including mentoring hotlines and chat lines.

8   See http://realbizshorts.com/ethics/why/ for excellent short form and funny videos on most aspect of integrity.

In addition, company email templates, forms and other documents should carry a short reference to the company's integrity programme, details of the policy helpline, suggestions scheme, and reporting of incidents channels.

FRAMING AND PRESENTATIONAL STYLE

The style and delivery of all training should be specifically adapted to the orientation (see page 586) of the recipients and should be positive, participative, enjoyable and memorable.

Getting on the Same Wavelength

For example, formal lectures by even the best lawyers on the Bribery Act 2010 and threats of draconian punishment will have little or even negative impact with employees such as traders or salesmen who are usually natural risk-takers and not easily deterred by the threat of punishment.

The precise objectives of all training sessions should be specified and in the integrity field should be aimed at internalising principles rather than simply ticking a box to show that the law has been explained (see page 729 for enhanced training for Compliance and employees engaged in the front line and who could be confronted with bribery).

RETAINED RECORDS

Detailed records of all training programmes should be retained in the employees' or associated persons' file, summarised in annual reports to the board with details archived in the Adequate Procedures Dossier.

More on the Morgan Stanley Declination

Readers who have a few moments to spare might like to track down the interesting and excellent pod cast by Davis Polk and Wardwell LLP who led the Morgan Stanley so-called declination (http://www.davispolk.com/Morgan-Stanleys-FCPA-Declination-and-the-Benefit-of-Effective-Compliance-10-09-2012/)

What is really impressive is the fact that – some seven years after the event – Morgan Stanley was able to present a compelling dossier of its training plans, schedules, actual course material and to convince regulators that it had done everything possible to make sure Mr Peterson complied fully with the FCPA. Unfortunately, the material that existed prior to 2008 – and which so impressed the DOJ, (but not Ethisphere: see page 611) – is no longer publicly available.

---

25 *Due Diligence, Incident Reporting, Contingency Planning and Protection of Information*

Introduction

In the anti-bribery field, due diligence is narrowly framed as a process to check the backgrounds of people and organisations – such as agents and others who perform services – before trust is placed in them: primarily to avoid corporate liability for bribe payment under Section 7 of the Bribery Act 2010 and the Foreign Corrupt Practices Act (FCPA[1]). Incident reporting (or 'whistle blowing'[2]) and contingency plans for investigating suspected bribe payment are also regarded in regulatory circles as mandatory. This chapter tries to put the two processes in an 'Inspired Integrity' frame, suggesting ways that they can generate marketing, reputational and financial advantages while going well beyond compliance. It also discusses contingency planning for investigations and information protection.

Due Diligence

LIMITATIONS

The conventional, but misplaced, justification for due diligence is that a person's history (and essentially his[3] public record) is a reliable indicator of his disposition and how he will perform in the future. In reality this is not so. What is in, or is not in, a person's (or company's) public record is a question of good or bad luck, determined by a complex interaction of dispositional and situational factors.

---

1   Via the standards set out in the Federal Sentencing Guidelines.

2   Which is a term best avoided.

3   Also 'its' when related to companies.

Dual Standards

Tommy Tucker seized the opportunity – over a five year period -to defraud Gullible Games Inc of $400,000 which he wasted on fast women and slow horses before being detected. His managers did not want a scandal and invited him to resign. They further *proposed*, that providing he paid back $20,000 a year, they would give him 'a not unfavourable' reference.

Mr Tucker joined Bonkers Bank (who accepted Gullible's reference) but, as he admitted later, he 'had no option but to help himself to a Bonkers' $500,000 wire transfer to pay off his debts'.

Norman Nutt, stole a single cheque of £20,000 from his employer to pay for an operation on his critically ill daughter. He was prosecuted, given an absolute discharge by a sympathetic judge, but named in local and national newspapers. He was unable to find a new job.

The fact is that a person's record is more often determined by the ethicality of the organisations for which he has worked than his own disposition.

Table 25.1 summarises the interaction of disposition and context on a person's past and behavior (column 1) and the whether or not the truth will emerge through conventional due diligence checking. It also assesses likely future performance (column 2).

Public records – and especially the Internet[4] – are notoriously inaccurate and incomplete. Although they may identify some bad apples, they are not a good foundation for predicting future performance.

Relying on the Internet

The Ministry of Justice guidance recommends, in at least five case studies, using the Internet for due diligence purposes. The Russians condemned Novo Nordisk's due diligence efforts on the grounds that web searches were unreliable (see page 34) and could be influenced by 'black data' or spin. The Russians should know best based on the experience with its oligarchs who commission investigative consultancies – at up to $1 million at a time – to write 'reputational due diligence' reports which portray them in a good light. Unsurprisingly, this sanitised history then appears on the Web.

There is an army of public relations types whose full time job is to scan the deep Internet and make sure that their clients are presented in the best possible light. Most of the information cannot be verified. It just sits there waiting for any mug daft enough to accept it. Conversely, false information can be seeded about competitors or incriminating data redacted or diverted to inaccessible sites. **So rely on the Internet at your peril!**

---

4   Which some organisations rely on for due diligence checking.

Table 25.1   Dispositional and Situational Factors on Public records

Disposition of the Individual in the UK and Developed Countries ↓	Situational Position (Past Contexts)			
	1 **Previous Contexts** *Company Style* **And Result of Due Diligence**		**2** **Future Contexts** **And Likely Performance**	
	Ethical *Inspirational leadership Good Controls Policy to prosecute Gives truthful references*	**Unethical Uncommitted** *Weak-dishonest leadership Poor controls Allows crooks to resign Gives misleading references*	*Highly Ethical*	*Undetermined*
A Dispositonally Honest *20% of the population⁵*	**Good**	Good	Good	*Probably good*
B Undetermined *60% of the population*	**Probably adverse, if exposed** *Like Norman Nutt*	**Not adverse even if exposed.** *Like TommyTucker*	*??*	*??*
C Dispositionally Dishonesty *20% of the population*	**Probably adverse, if exposed**	**Not adverse, even if exposed**	*???*	*??*

The table suggests that due diligence checks on dispositionally honest people (Row A) should give positive results, irrespective of the ethicality of the contexts⁶ in which they have previously worked. At the other end of the scale, the public records of an estimated 20 per cent of people, who are dispositionally dishonest (Row C) and 60 per cent (Row B) that could go either way, are unlikely to be adverse if the organisations for which they have worked are so poorly controlled that skulduggery was not detected or, if it was, kept off the public record.

---

5   Based on the authors' experience and American Fidelity Insurance claims. The percentages for dishonesty by companies is thought not to be significantly different.

6   Or organisations.

Isn't It Strange?

Hundreds of extorters (companies and individuals, including foreign public officials) have been identified as a result of regulatory actions. However, their names have never been publicised or included on any black list. Their history as skulduggers would not be identified by due diligence checking.

Other limitations with due diligence were discussed on page 652 and it is not necessary to repeat them here except to point out some important differences between the conventional processes and those recommended later.

Table 25.2   Due Diligence versus Integrity Validation

Conventional Due Diligence Checks prior to commitment	**Integrity Validation** Integrity Partnering Continuous Monitoring
One time	Initial checking reinforced by training, incident reporting and integrity partnering
Assumes that the company carrying out due diligence is ethically and otherwise superior to the candidate	Framed as a partnership, possibly involving reciprocity on due diligence, audit rights, incident reporting and annual declarations
Based on historic public records (and often irrelevant red flags: see page 570)	Focuses on current and future relationships, transactions and specific decisions as well as historic performance. Identifies positive attributes (green flags) and incorporates them into a decision matrix to identify the best candidate
Only proves that there is no adverse record or red flags	
May create adversarial relationships	Conducted openly with the co-operation of the subject to build partnering relationships
Decisions whether to establish a relationship are taken subjectively on a case by case basis	Decisions are taken against a specified template of weighted and scored criteria. This results in consistency and auditability
Ignoring one red flag could result in regulators arguing that procedures were not adequate. All red flags are given equal weight, irrespective of their timing[7]	Red flags are separated into those which are unavoidable and those which can be manipulated. They are assigned weights (based on their importance and timing) and incorporated into a decision matrix together with green flags
Centred on application forms containing closed questions which provide a template for deceptive answers	Uses application forms with open and attitudinal questions, business plans and other narratives. In all important cases, validation is supported by site visits and interviews by trained compliance staff

---

7   The same importance is attached to an incident that happened ten years ago as one that is much more recent.

Employees responsible for promoting a relationship are often anxious to avoid intervention by compliance because it could offend the applicant	Validation is conducted openly and positively by compliance, providing independence that supports and protects both relationship managers and the applicant. Creates a multiple lines of communications thereby making corruption less likely (see page 297)

Costs of the process suggested – compensated by the ability to recruit the best qualified people and companies – should be no more than the norm.

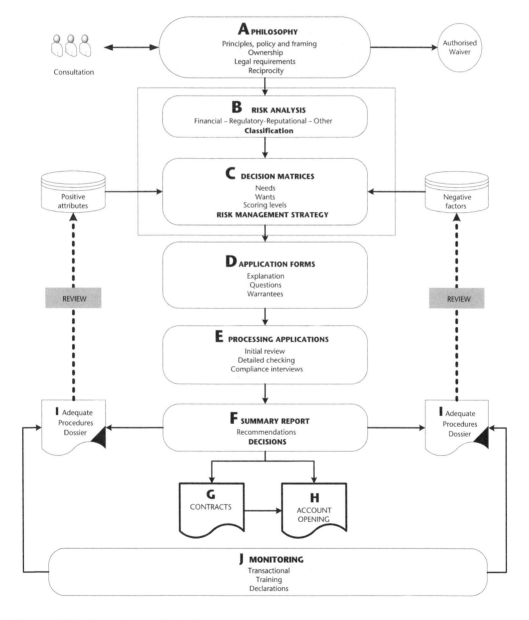

Figure 25.1 Overview of the Process

THE SUGGESTED APPROACH

Process Overview

Due diligence **is unquestionably** a critical control, but not simply for box ticking compliance purposes, as is often the case. Integrity Validation should answer four critical questions:

- Are there *facts* in the candidate's background that should disqualify him, her or it from consideration?[8]
- Will the candidate perform effectively and honestly in the contexts concerned?
- Is the candidate the best choice?
- How can effective and honest performance be assured?

Figure 25.1 summarises the most important elements of the process.

For many organisations, the suggested approach requires a philosophical reappraisal of the way they manage their relationships and particularly whether they consider partnering worthwhile and reciprocity advantageous. But, as for all policies, there should always be the alternative of a waiver – in exceptional cases – at board level.

Integrity Partnerships and Circles

Integrity partnering creates competitive advantages by nurturing relationships with the most effective honest agents, customers, suppliers and joint venture partners (especially in TI's high risk countries such as China, Russia) who resent being treated as criminals simply because of some unsubstantiated perception that their country is corrupt.

The Indonesian Distributor

The director of a medium sized electronic goods distributor in Jakarta told the authors: 'We cannot accept all of the bureaucracy that British and American companies insist on. We are a good, honest company, with nothing to hide and we don't need to be treated like children. I would much rather work with the Chinese, Russians and Canadians who are much more sensible'. He chose to work for a Chinese principal and was very successful.

Features of integrity partnering include the following contributions and benefits as shown in Table 25.3.

---

8   Based on the decision matrix to ensure consistency.

Table 25.3 Contributions and Benefits

Contributions by and *Benefits* to the Sponsor (Principal)	Contribution by and *Benefits* to Third Parties
Agree to what is effectively an integrity pact **Both partners promote integrity as a unique selling point** **'Open book' accounting**	
Assists the third party develop integrity standards, policies and procedures *Helps maintain effective procedures to UK or US standards*	Agrees to maintain mutually supportive integrity and other programmes
Sponsors training programmes for key third party personnel awarding corporate and personal certificates. Maintains consistent standards	*Kudos for the company and individual employees* *Motivates employees and encourages loyalty to the principal*
Maintains multiple channels of communication, especially between Compliance, Audit and Security departments *Quickly learns of problems including competitive corruption*	Improves professional standards for the company and individuals
Makes agency and other relationships transparent[9]	Allowed to advertise the relationship to generate business with other principals, customers and suppliers. *Gains international credibility*
	Obtains preferential prices, payment and credit terms subject to maintaining integrity programmes
	Third parties may be encouraged to nominate sub-agents and end parties to become members of the circle. *This is likely to give them a competitive advantage*

From a control point of view, one of the greatest advantages of integrity partnering is that it opens up channels of communication with different levels in third party organisations, making it much more likely that problems will be brought to the principal's attention.

The UK Manufacturing Company

X plc, a leading UK company was concerned about its agent in the USA and arranged a training session in the Bahamas for their combined compliance and audit teams,[10] with presentations by professional gurus. On the face of it the offer was too good to refuse but that is precisely what the agent's directors did.

---

9   There are always problems when a third party (and especially an agent) demands anonymity.

10   Which had never had any contact up to that point.

Eventually they agreed to attend, providing their team was chaperoned by the Finance Director, who was a bully and universally unpopular.

On the last evening, a junior member of the agent's team took X's Compliance Manager to one side and produced a tape recording of his Finance Director instructing his team to be very careful and under no circumstances to discuss what turned out to be a massive scam.

PHILOSOPHY, PRINCIPLES AND POLICY (STAGE A)

The company should consider – as part of the suggested wider review of its integrity campaign – how it currently handles relationships with third parties and whether partnering and reciprocation would be beneficial.[11] Ownership of integrity validation processes should be assigned to the line managers of the relationships concerned.

Legal, Compliance and Internal Audit should catalogue the laws, regulations and standards that must be maintained (including many items on the decision matrix), communicate them in easy to understand summaries,[12] set classifications and matrices, be available in an advisory capacity, have the authority to carry out audits and investigations, and have a direct reporting line to the board where they oppose a relationship manager's decision **However, relationship risk must be unambiguously owned by line management.**

RISK ANALYSIS (STAGE B)

Basic Classifications

A multi-disciplinary team – led by a senior commercial manager and supported by Legal, Compliance, Human Resources, Accounting, Finance and Internal Audit – should classify[13] all relationships *types* where integrity validation is necessary including:

- Agents and intermediaries;
- Joint ventures (and especially Private Finance Initiative (PFI) projects;
- Professional and other advisers;
- Suppliers and customers (including those classed as 'miscellaneous');
- Wholly and partly owned subsidiaries and affiliates.[14]

Relationships should be classified depending on the following risks:

- Financial (especially credit risks);
- Continuity (especially with strategic suppliers, customers and agents);

---

11   It invariably is for larger companies with their most important third party relationships.

12   The code of conduct of one leading organisation states that 'employees are required to establish what laws apply to them', or words to that effect!!

13   This is usually a one off exercise and not difficult!

14   Especially those performing services.

- Reputational (such as environmental and human rights);
- Regulatory and Legal (including all silos and not just those relating to anti-bribery).

Country risks should also be considered, but on the basis that they are influential rather than determinative. They should be allowed for by adjusting risk thresholds rather than creating additional classifications[15] and should never, in themselves, be the dominant factor.

From the above inputs it is usually simple to compile a spreadsheet of classifications along the lines shown in Table 25.4 based on financial and regulatory risks.

Table 25.4   Classifications

			All Regulatory Risks[16] (R) ↓↓	
			High *Limits should be specified*	**Low** *Limits should be specified*
			Classification Reference Estimated % of Third Party Relationships *Examples*	
Pure Financial Continuity Reputational	**Financial Risk (FR)**	**High** *Limits should be specified* →	**FR1** Probably 10% *Large Agents* *Large customers* **Others performing services**	**F1** Probably 20% *Large suppliers*
		Low *Limits should be specified* →	**R1** Probably 5% *Joint ventures* *Subsidiary companies* *Information brokers* **Others performing services**	**C** Probably 65% *Most customers and suppliers* *Others trading as principals at arm's length*

Matrices of validation levels and processes should be specified for each classification. For example, classification C might involve checking credit references, banned organisations' and politically exposed persons list; possibly outsourced to a specialist agency.[17] Classification FR1 is likely to justify all of the basic checking plus site visits, compliance interviews,[18] detailed analysis of accounts, integrity and other policies, searches of media and other data bases,[19] integrity partnerships and continuous monitoring.

---

15   For example, if the threshold for a financial high risk is $5 million, it should be reduced to say $2 million when the third party operates in a country shown on TI's list in position 70 or below.

16   And not just in the anti-bribery silo.

17   After fully validating the agency in classification R1.

18   See page 648.

19   On the company, shareholders, directors, key employees and end parties.

Allocating Classifications to Existing and New Relationships

Companies should classify existing suppliers,[20] customers and other third parties and verify that they have been properly validated.

Review of Master Files

It is usually possible to tell how effective due diligence has been by examining data (or more often the absence of it) in vendor and supplier master files (see page 507).

A schedule should be prepared – starting with the category FR1 on Table 25.4 – to bring validations for each individual third party relationship up to specification. This was a major task for many companies – following the introduction of the Bribery Act – but it was made much easier by starting with the higher risk relationships: leaving routine customers and suppliers until last.

Simple procedures for opening new accounts (including an authority chart) should be issued to relationship managers, Compliance, Legal and Finance departments (see Table 25.5).

Table 25.5   Ownership and Responsibilities

Departmental Ownership *Examples*	Responsibilities
Relationship Managers *Procurement* *Sales* *Traders*	• **Owning relationship risks** • Classifying third parties(in consultation with Legal and Compliance) • Obtaining application forms and supporting data • Obtaining clarification of points raised by Compliance, Legal or Finance departments • Reporting on performance
Compliance	• Determining classifications and matrices • Liaising with and training relationship managers • Reviewing and validating applications (against decision matrices) • Making recommendations for appointment or rejection • Appealing to the Board where it opposes an appointment • Updating the Adequate Procedures Dossier • Updating decision matrices • Continuously monitoring high risk relationships, liaising with third party compliance teams and holding joint training sessions

---

20   For example from the vendor and customer master files and miscellaneous transactions.

	• Auditing files kept by relationship managers • Reporting problems to relationship managers
Legal	• Preparing contracts subject to prior approval by relationship managers and Compliance • Appealing to the Board where it opposes an appointment • Preserving documentation as vital records
Directors	• Approving waivers to validation processes[21] • Resolving disagreements between relationship managers, Compliance and Legal
Internal Audit	• Using continuous monitoring programs (see page 735) to detect misbehavior and liaising with third party audit teams and holding joint training sessions • Reporting to the Board on the effectiveness of the process

DECISION MATRICES (STAGE C)

A serious defect in most due diligence processes is that the criteria which would result in a candidate's exclusion (because of supposed red flags) are not determined in advance[22] and those in its favour (green flags) not considered at all. Instead decisions are taken on a subjective, case-by-case basis once checks have been completed. This can result in perverse and uncommercial selections which are difficult to audit.

Decision matrices – preferably based on the Kepner Tregoe model (see the example on pages 568–72) – should be prepared for each of the four classifications shown in Table 25.4. They should rank needs[23] and wants[24] and should include both green and red flags for both the corporate entity, its shareholders, directors and key employees.[25] For example when deciding to maintain one or more existing and important relationships the matrix for an agent might be along the following lines shown in Table 25.6.

---

21   For example to accept an urgent transaction with a new customer or supplier before validation can be completed.

22   Standard criteria for employee selection are set out in Chapter 26 and for important intermediaries and agents in Chapter 31.

23   Absolute requirements.

24   Things that are nice to have. Each one is given a weight (positive for a green flag and negative for red) and each candidate scored against it. The result of weight multiplied by score results in a factor. The candidate that meets all of the needs and has the highest factor should normally be preferred.

25   Including its heads of compliance and audit.

Table 25.6 Positive and Negative Attributes

Attribute *For the organisation, directors and other key personnel*	Need *Absolute*	Want *Desirable*		
		Weight 100 = Most Desirable	Score 100 = Best Matches the Want	Factor Weight * Score
GREEN FLAGS (Adds points to the score)				
Exemplary industry knowledge	YES			
Good financial results	→→	80	100	8,000
Responds quickly	→→	50	50	2,500
Other (Listed and scored)	→→			
RED FLAGS (Deducts points from the score)				
Director convicted of tax evasion	→→	-80	30	-2,400
Demands payment offshore	→→	-70	0	0
Rejected previously, possibly by another department	→→	-100	20[26]	-2000
Other (Listed and negatively scored)	→→			
Final Factors				**6,100**

Under the typical regulatory approach the three red flags shown in Table 25.6 might result in the relationship being rejected or terminated. Based on the suggested method, the red flags are classified as wants and recognise the fact that the conviction was 20 years ago,[27] that the offshore payment was required by the third party's bank to pay off a legitimate foreign loan and the previous rejection arose from false information downloaded from the Internet.

The matrices should also specify what future performance by third parties will result in sanctions. For example, an agent who voluntarily discloses that it has been raided by the tax authorities should be treated more leniently than one who conceals it.

Decision matrices may motivate third parties to provide detail to qualify for membership of the Integrity Circle or to make improvements to their own compliance programs to meet the required standard. This is a much more positive framing than is normally the case and is even more so when reciprocation and other features of partnering are offered.[28]

---

26   But updated information shows the reasons for rejection are no longer valid.

27   For a small amount.

28   If a substantial third party does not accept the offer of reciprocation, it may indicate serious defects in its integrity policy and considered a red flag.

APPLICATION FORMS (STAGE D)

Design according to classifications

Good application forms[29] are essential and should be professionally designed[30] in printed and electronic form: ideally incorporating features and graphics from the integrity campaign and setting out the benefits of participating in the integrity circle for both companies and individuals.

They must ask all of the questions[31] needed for the associated classification and decision matrix including:

- Basic that relate to the identification of the candidate and its history and which are required for legal and accounting purposes;[32]
- Personal relating to the biographies of all of directors and officers who will be involved in the proposed relationship;[33]
- Integrity that focus on the applicant's track record, current policies and procedures;
- Transactional and forward looking relating to the proposed business plan and end parties.

Forms should also require details of the company's reporting procedures and boxes for warranties and signatures. For new, important relationships, forms should be supported by a freestyle narrative explaining the third party's business plans, details of its end parties and anticipated revenues.

Reciprocal pack

Where a company subscribes to the philosophy of reciprocation, it should prepare a pack[34] (based on its own application forms) to provide to third parties once their applications have passed through initial screening. Although doing this may seem a burden, it is a powerful good faith gesture and is a positive marketing tool. It also makes it far less likely that third parties can legitimately object to providing detail that they might otherwise be regard as intrusive.

PROCESSING APPLICATIONS (STAGES D, E, F AND G)

Responsibility for getting the appropriate application form completed (with supporting documentation) should be assigned to the relationship managers,[35] validated (against

---

29   Downloadable versions of forms and matrices for agents are available on www.cobasco.com.

30   See pages 646 et seq and marked as confidential and privileged.

31   Obviously application forms for the higher classifications should be more probing and require more supporting evidence.

32   They should incorporate as many government references as possible. This reduces the chances of relationships with false entities being approved.

33   That is not simply the board directors and should include compliance, legal and audit representatives.

34   Detailed and impressive!!

35   Who should countersign it.

the relevant matrix) by Compliance which should make an acceptance or rejection recommendation on the form[36] or in a written report. Where appropriate relationship managers and compliance should sign the decision matrix and jointly instruct the Legal Department to finalise contracts. Original contracts should be and retained in the Legal Department and backed-up as vital records in secure archives. Completed application forms should be filed securely in the Compliance Department.[37]

ACCOUNT OPENING (STAGE H)

Finance Department should be assigned responsibility for opening new accounts based on the joint authority of relationship managers, Compliance and – in more important cases – the Legal Department.[38] It should prepare a monthly report of all new accounts for review by Internal Audit.[39]

UPDATING (STAGE I)

Details of all accepted and rejected applications (or summaries) should be retained by the Compliance Department in the Adequate Procedures Dossier.[40]

Rejected Applications are Important

Every rejected application or refusal to enter into a transaction is a silver bullet[41] in the Adequate Procedures Dossier.

From time to time, compliance should select a few of the rejected applicants and establish how they are currently performing and who with, primarily to test the validity of decision matrices.

The 'O Rings' Failure

The catastrophe that befell the Challenger Space Shuttle on 28th January 1986 was put down to failure of O rings on the booster which on seven previous flights had shown signs of wear: called 'scoring'. Engineers were concerned that scoring was caused by cold weather but their analysis of launch temperatures to failures showed little correlation and was disregarded.

---

36   For low risk classifications.
37   And NOT by relationship managers.
38   In a specified procedure and authority tables.
39   Which should consider monitoring programmes.
40   Files securely in the compliance department.
41   See page 723.

> Then when they examined 23 further successful launches they discovered an irrefutable pattern failure free launches when temperatures were above 65 degrees Fahrenheit.

The significance of reviewing rejections came home loud and clear to Decca Records when they turned down the Beatles with the now famous explanation: 'We don't like their sound, and guitar music is on the way out'. The case reinforces the point that the objective of due diligence is to select the best candidate and not just tick a few boxes that nothing detrimental has come to light.

MONITORING CONTROLS (STAGE J)

Monitoring is an on-going activity that reinforces and refreshes conventional due diligence and should be carried out collaboratively through:

- Annual declarations and reviews;
- Incident reporting;
- Training programmes with prestigious certificates awarded to third parties and individually to their employees (this may also include lapel badges, brooches[42] and plaques);
- Multiple channels of communication;
- Mutual reporting of changes to business relationships, laws, procedures etc.

Self-disclosing Problems

Contracts should encourage third parties to voluntarily report adverse incidents, with the assurance that if they do so they will be assisted and treated compassionately. However, failure to report should result in sanctions and possibly termination of relationships.

In addition, for important and high risk relationships, continuous monitoring programs along the lines of page 735 should be considered.

Integrity Reporting

INTRODUCTION AND OBJECTIVES

Companies should have comprehensive processes for reporting and responding to incidents, including regulatory violations, with the objectives of:

---

42   Which stimulate discussions on integrity

- Being the first to know of fraud, incoming, outgoing and competitive corruption;
- Investigating and establishing the facts of suspected violations as quickly and as accurately as possible;
- Exposing and punishing malpractice;
- Creating a deterrent;
- Disrupting or deterring collusive groups;
- Improving controls.

And most importantly, incident-reporting procedures – involving the steps set out in Figure 25.2 – should protect honest people and organisations against false and malicious allegations:

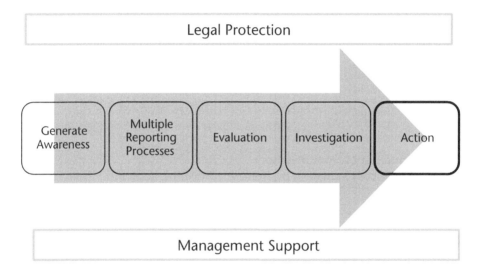

Figure 25.2 Integrated Incident Reporting Procedures

Despite the fact that they are recommended by virtually every regulatory agency, most whistle-blowing lines are ineffective because:

- They fail to recognise the nature and inherent secrecy of criminal collusion and the motivational factors involved (see Chapter 12 page 295);
- The term 'whistle-blower' has negative connotations and being poorly framed discourages people from reporting;
- The perception is that those who report misbehaviour always come out worse off. This is not necessarily the case:

Whistle-blowers Do Not Always Suffer

A relator (whistle-blower) in Florida stands to make the biggest award yet of US$88.4 million after three pharmaceutical firms agreed to pay $421.2 million in settlement of allegations of Medicaid and Medicare fraud. The cases centred on the manipulation of the average wholesale price. Between the start-up of the false claims reward system and 2008 more than US$2 billion has been paid to relators.

The US False Claims Act provides rewards of up to 25 per cent of all penalties and recoveries for information that exposes fraud against the US government. The majority of cases have involved Medicare and Medicaid and overcharging by pharmaceutical companies, all with impeccable business ethics policies – on paper. It is doubtful that the anti-corruption lines will be anywhere near as effective, for reasons explained later.

THE DODD-FRANK WALL STREET REFORM ACT 2010

Traditionally the SEC has paid rewards only for information leading to convictions for insider trading, but from July 2011, Section 922 of the Dodd-Frank Wall Street Reform and Consumer Protection Act[43] permits the agency to pay a bounty of up to 30 per cent of all recoveries, penalties, and disgorgements for a wide range of securities frauds including breaches of both the books and records and internal control provisions of the Foreign Corrupt Practices Act (FCPA). **It should be noted that rewards will not be paid for violations of the FCPA anti-bribery provisions because they are not regarded as 'securities laws'.**[44]

The reporting conditions include:

- The information must be 'original', specific, credible and timely from the relator's independent knowledge or analysis, provided voluntarily and related to a matter previously unknown to the SEC;
- Attorneys, auditors, compliance staff, etc. will not normally qualify for a bounty, except under very limited conditions (see below);
- Relators are encouraged (and expected) to first report internally; if they fail to do so any bounty is likely to be reduced;
- If the company does not respond to an internally reported allegation within 120 days:
  - The relator may report to the SEC without risking any reduction in the bounty;
  - Any other person[45] who becomes aware of the information (even though it is not 'original') may report to the SEC[46] and qualify for a bounty;

---

43 Also includes tough reporting requirements for the extractive industries.

44 Thus the Dodd Frank reward scheme only applies to accounting skulduggery by 'Issuers'. Most people don't understand this.

45 Including compliance officers, auditors, etc.

46 The report may be made anonymously or through a law firm.

- If the report is made by a participant in the offences, any reward paid may be reduced, depending on culpability: rewards cannot be claimed by foreign public officials (FPOs);
- The minimum aggregate recovery must exceed $1 million;
- It is an offence to prohibit reporting to the SEC or to retaliate.

These provisions are expected, by members of the cottage industry, to result in an increase in the number of FCPA cases reported to the Securities and Exchange Commission (and where a UK interest is involved, then passed to the Serious Fraud Office). Other commentators have suggested that Dodd-Frank will result in a war of all against all, with competitors making allegations – some spurious – against each other. This is unlikely to be the case, because experience shows that companies are remarkably reluctant to complain, even about the most crooked behaviour, fearing retaliation; and because their information will be disclosed under the Freedom of Information legislation.

Besides that, the SEC may turn out to be so difficult and mean-spirited over bounty payments that the scheme will fail – much like the US Internal Revenue Service (IRS), which Senator Charles Grassley described as having a 'culture of hostility and intimidation towards whistle-blowers which is hampered by excessive secrecy and continuing hostility towards (them)'.[47] In the four and a half years that the IRS programme has been running, there have been an estimated 4,500 tips but only one pay-out!

Not All Whistle-blowing Lines Work

Patrick Burns of the very successful Taxpayers Against Fraud Group told the press that: 'The IRS is so concerned about the privacy of fraudsters that [...] they're almost unable to operate in the whistle-blower arena'.

As Dodd-Frank is modelled on the IRS enhanced scheme it will be interesting to see how effective it becomes. But the initial cries of success are not supported by the facts. In the first 7 weeks that Dodd-Frank was in operation, only 13 reports of alleged bribery emerged.

Nonetheless, corporate incident reporting systems will come under pressure when associated persons choose to report externally, primarily to claim bounties, possibly supported by lawyers working on contingency fees.[48] For this reason, companies should consider paying rewards for information, despite the fact that the Law Commissioners in the UK regard doing so as 'unBritish'.

---

47 See Michael Hudson, 'IRS red tape, old guard slow whistleblowing on corporate tax cheats' (Center for Public Integrity, 22 June 2011). Available at: http://www.publicintegrity.org/2011/06/22/4979/irs-red-tape-old-guard-slow-whistleblowing-corporate-tax-cheats (accessed 22 November 2012).

48 Known as 'ambulance-chasing'.

OTHER AGENCIES THAT PAY REWARDS

The Office of Fair Trading, HM Revenue and Customs and other UK government agencies pay rewards for information, as do most insurance companies. There no detailed statistics on the total payments and recoveries made, but although they are believed not to be substantial they have little relevance to commercial bribery.

PAYMENT OF REWARDS BY COMPANIES

One objective of incident reporting is to disrupt collusive groups and to get those closest to the most villainous to fragment and turn against each other. Usually this can be achieved only through the payment of rewards, amnesties, first-through-the-door immunity and by supporting participants who are prepared to become cooperating witnesses. These conditions are all bitter pills for some companies to swallow, but unless they do so there is no question that they will fall behind those responding to and claiming financial rewards under Dodd-Frank.

Some potential whistle-blowers do not want to accept rewards, but still need motivation to report. A possible solution is for companies to donate rewards to a local charity such as a children's home.

A Charitable Solution

A bank in a Less Developed Country, which had a reporting line in place for years with very little success, took up the idea of sponsoring a home for sick children and ran a campaign with a picture of the kids, alongside a photograph of a convicted fraudster. The slogan was:

Fraud! Who needs it most?

The campaign was picked up by the press and television with massive publicity. After the first 12 months of operation the bank had recovered over $14 million and had paid nearly $1 million to the home. This had a dramatic impact on the children's lives. All subsequent publicity has been positive.

Other third parties, including:

- Hedge funds (short-selling shares in the company they complain about to the regulators);
- Media;
- Competitors (commercial disruption);
- Ex-employees (revenge).

– are also potential candidates for reporting alleged bribery and other securities violations, with hedge funds at the top of the list.

POLICY DECISIONS

Against the above background, even companies that currently have whistle-blowing lines should carefully review their policy and resolve the questions in Table 25.7.

Table 25.7   Policy Decisions on Incident Reporting

Question	Recommended Answer
Who is the owner of the process?	Corporate Security or Internal Audit
What incidents should be reported?	See below
Will the company pay rewards for information received?	**Yes**. The moral dilemma should be resolved in terms of practicality. If the company wants to be first to know, it has to compete with the Dodd-Frank reward incentive
Will the process apply to everyone, including members of the public, suppliers, customers, etc., or just to employees?	Yes, with details published on the company's website, etc.
Will it apply to people directly involved in the fraud or corruption on the principle of first through the door?	Company philosophy
Is the company prepared to offer an amnesty to those who self-disclose?	
What reporting channels should be used?	Multiple as described below and also through annual reviews, exit interviews and post-termination interviews
Will anonymity be guaranteed?	Yes
What protection will be given to the whistle-blower	In line with the Public Interest Disclosure Act, Sarbanes-Oxley etc.
How will raw information be validated before being passed into the management line with possible adverse implications for honest people against whom false accusations have been made?	Mostly by an external agency and in confidence by Corporate Security
How will allegations be investigated and by whom?	By Corporate Security
Should be process be protected by legal professional privilege?	Determined by local legal advice. May be difficult in the European Union unless the process is handled entirely by external counsel

The key question for most companies is whether in the light of Dodd-Frank they will be prepared to pay for information and, if so, under what conditions? There is one significant danger that is not universally recognised and that is for companies that offer rewards to employees of third parties under conditions could result in breaches their contracts of employment[49] and could possibly contravene the Bribery Act!!

WHAT SHOULD BE REPORTED?

Policy and procedures should clearly specify what incidents should be reported:

- Business intelligence (see Table 25.8);
- Suspected incoming, outgoing and competitive bribery;
- Robberies, burglaries, frauds, hold-ups, etc.;
- Fires, sabotage, actual and threats of violence, and other overt acts;
- Breaches of laws, regulations and compliance standards;
- Unexplained losses;
- Proceeds of Crime Act and money-laundering;
- Suspected unfair competition;
- Demands for facilitation payments;
- Unfair competition.

Some companies' reporting procedures only come into operation when the suspected loss exceeds a certain limit, but such fine tuning is usually ineffective. First, an employee who does not wish to make a report may say later, when it is discovered, that he thought it was below the limit. Second, many large frauds are discovered as a result of minor discrepancies. Third, it is genuinely difficult to calculate the size of a fraud, particularly in its early days. If reporting is delayed until the true picture is known, vital evidence may be lost. The bottom line is that reporting procedures should not impose limits on amounts.

HOW PROCEDURES SHOULD BE PROMOTED

Reporting procedures should be given the highest possible profile as part of the integrity campaign. The term 'whistle-blowing'[50] should be avoided at all costs and substituted by 'integrity reporting' or a similar term with positive connotations.

PROTECTION OF WHISLE-BLOWERS

International laws protect whistle-blowers against any form of retaliation when they:

- Were acting in good faith in relation to a serious matter;
- Believed the information was substantially accurate;
- Believed that the organisation would, or had not, or was unlikely to respond;
- Suspected a miscarriage of justice has occurred or is likely to occur;
- Were concerned about the health and safety of an individual, or that the environment had been, or is likely to be, damaged;
- Reasonably believed that information tending to show any of the above had been, or is likely to be, concealed.

---

49   Much like HM Revenue & Customs paying rewards to Swiss bank employees
50   Which is very negative framing.

If the report is made directly to a third party, rather than first giving the company the opportunity for internal resolution, the whistle-blower must be able to demonstrate that:

- He or she reasonably believed that he or she would be subject to detriment if the matter had been raised internally;
- The disclosure was not made with the intention of personal gain;
- The disclosure was reasonable in all the circumstances.

Under the above circumstances it is illegal for the employer to discriminate against the whistle-blower, but only if he or she is an employee. Company procedures should apply equivalent protection to all whistle-blowers in the Extended Enterprise.

REPORTING CHANNELS

Objectives

Companies should consider specifying multiple reporting channels, some of which may be used anonymously. The objective in each case is to elevate potential problems to senior managers on the basis that they should be first to know. There is a vast difference between a person coming forward to volunteer information and responding to questions. For that reason, so-called whistle-blowing lines must be supplemented by other reporting channels as discussed later.

Internal reporting and business intelligence

A procedure should be specified so that employees and other members of the extended enterprise can report suspicions openly. Such processes typically produce very few reports.

In addition, business intelligence systems– which often expose the first signs corruption – should ensure that the incidents summarised in Table 25.8 are reported.

Table 25.8 Reporting of Incidents from Business Intelligence Processes

Incident or Event to Be Reported	Comments
Potential acquisitions	Pre-acquisition integrity validation often reveals previous acts of corruption which are relevant under the successor liability rule
Potential disinvestments or trade sales of companies	Integrity validation possibly exposing previous acts of corruption
Initial public offerings	

Contract terminations	Disgruntled third parties who may make genuine or frivolous allegations of corruption. In the UK there are 250,000 tribunal actions a year, any one of which could result in genuine or false allegations being made
Dismissal of employees, resignations, and employment tribunal actions	
Civil disputes	
Liquidations and bankruptcies	
Other litigation	
Cancelled contracts, terminated relationships with suppliers, customers, etc. and disputed transactions	Often signs of trouble that lead to litigation and allegations that may involve bribery
Regulatory investigations in the industry sector or in overseas jurisdictions in which the company operates	Regulators will leverage their knowledge and contacts in one case to other companies in the same sector
Regime changes (within a business or involving third parties)	These often result in incoming teams pursuing their predecessors and can be at a political, company or departmental level
Regime changes at a country level	Such as Iraq and the Oil for Food programme
Media monitoring	Routine daily searches of all trade and other media to detect positive and adverse comments on the extended enterprise, concerning its competitors, as well as regulatory action and changes in the law
Internet searches	

Obviously smaller companies do not need sophisticated systems, although they should still monitor both the internal and external environment to detect and quickly react to incidents that could have an impact on both financial and regulatory risk.

Telephone integrity hotline

The most effective hotlines consists of a 24/7/365 multilingual, toll-free, local and international telephone answering service, staffed by professional operators that allow calls to be made anonymously, if necessary. The least effective are run in a single language and connect to a voice-mail or telephone answering machine.

Integrity website

Consideration should also be given to linking the telephone hotline service to an interactive website which may be managed by the company itself or more efficiently[51] by an outside specialist agency. Whistle-blowers who wish to remain anonymous can do so by setting up a Hotmail or proxy account: questions can be posted and follow-up action controlled. Most specialist providers support their services with statistical and analytical reports.

---

51   This is usually the case.

Suggestions scheme

An online paper-based, email, telephone or web-based suggestions scheme should also be considered. Experience shows that people are more willing to report depersonalised control weaknesses[52] than they are to give names and details of associated violations, especially if good ideas are rewarded.

The chairman's annual email

One leading British organisation sponsors an annual email from the chairman to all employees, customers and suppliers. It is an upbeat summary of his company's results and future plans, but contains a closing statement to the effect that

> *if you have any concerns about the ethical conduct of xxx, or suspicions of any improper behaviour, you may report them directly to my office, in total confidence.*

In the first three years of its operation the email was responsible for uncovering frauds amounting to over £4 million.

Other potential reporting channels

Other channels of integrity reporting should be considered, including those set out in Table 25.9.

Table 25.9 Other Sources of Integrity Reporting

Reporting Channels	Comments
Annual appraisals	Self-disclosure
Managing director's blog	Encouraging direct communication with employees and third parties
Compliance and internal audit blog	
Awaydays and social gatherings	
Chairman's lunches	
Exit interviews	Critical intelligence-gathering opportunities
Post-employment interviews	
Vendor and customer open days	Providing open channels of communication with vendors and customers
Vendors' support hotline	
Vendors' debriefing	
Vendors' visits	

---

52   That result in the exposure of skulduggery.

Experience shows that one of the most effective ways of exposing incoming corruption is randomly visiting ex-vendors.[53]

KEY PERFORMANCE INDICATORS FOR INTEGRITY REPORTING

Despite much positive publicity it is surprising how ineffective *basic* whistle-blowing lines are:

- Not one of the multibillion-dollar recoveries under the False Claims Act hotline is believed to have been reported internally;
- None of British Aerospace (BAE)'s competitors or employees reported what turned out to be gross corruption over many years;
- In the Carbon World, legitimate manufacturers who do not benefit from Clean Development Mechanism (CDM) largesse, but who know about dishonest competitive activity, remain silent. In fact, it does not appear that none of the agencies that are responsible for the CDM have a reporting process.

Poor Response

Even after the BAE corruption scandal was resolved and new ethical programmes put in place, its annual report for 2009 shows that it only had 870 enquiries on its ethics line from 106,900 employees worldwide. This is less than 1 per cent! But BAE does not offer financial rewards.

On the other hand, there has been a tenfold increase, between 2004 and 2010, in the number of whistle-blowing cases taken to industrial tribunals, with even more involving allegations of corruption and fraud once a case gets under way. The average payout has been £113,667, with the largest at £3.8 million. This is another indication that money is a significant motivator in reporting malpractice.

Another Blinking Survey

A survey conducted by Cobasco Group Limited in 2009 indicated that conventional whistle-blowing lines produced an average of 10 reports and queries per 1,000 employees per annum.[54] When financial rewards were offered, the level of valid reporting rose by approximately 400 per cent.

---

53   Based on a non-accusatory fact finding survey.

54   Ranging from 4.3 per 1,000 in construction to 18.7 per 1,000 in transportation. *The Business Crimes Bulletin* estimates an average of 7.6 reports per 1,000 employees.

VALIDATION

Information received from any source must be independently validated before being communicated into the management line. This is essential to protect the reputations of honest employees and others against whom spurious or malicious allegations are made.

Reports should be assessed along the lines of the matrix presented in Table 25.10.

Table 25.10 Assessment of Incident Reports

Source of Information		Content of Information		
		Credible 1	Undetermined 2	Unlikely 3
Reliable	A	Priority action	Priority	Validate
Unknown	B	Priority	Consider	Ignore
Unreliable	C	Validate	Ignore	Ignore

Any report classified better than B2 should be analysed and fully investigated. Normally, anything below B3 can be disregarded, although indexed and filed for statistical and archiving purposes.

INVESTIGATION

Integrity reporting processes should be supported by professional investigative and legal resources and contingency plans (see Chapter 34 and pages 483, 609 and 675).

ONWARD REPORTING

The procedure should also specify how, by whom and under what circumstances incidents and suspected regulatory breaches will be reported to the authorities and especially to anti-corruption and anti-money laundering regulators.[55]

Companies covered by Fidelity Insurance are usually required to advise their insurer as soon as practicable or within 30 days of discovery of a loss. This does not mean they have to rush to report before carrying out an internal investigation and generally companies should set their own objectives for each case before making *any* external reports. However, if companies do not advise their Fidelity Underwriters of dishonesty involving employees (whether prosecuted or not), their coverage will be invalidated.

ANNUAL SUMMARIES

Every year a summary of all incidents reported should be circulated to senior managers and to members of the Risk and Assurance Committee. Consideration should be given

---

55   But only if the organisation is in the regulated sector or has appointed a Money Laundering Reporting Officer.

as to whether or not to include depersonalised statistics in the company's Annual Report and Accounts.

Contingency Planning for Incidents

INTRODUCTION

Companies should prepare for the time when they *might* be confronted with suspicions of serious corruption and fraud or a raid by regulators **in any country in which they operate** or to which employees travel. Plans are especially important for Less Developed Countries, where defendants can be imprisoned for years before trial and where the safety of investigation and legal teams, as well as witnesses, may be threatened by organised crime and corrupt state agencies.

If policy decisions are left until the heat of the moment, mistakes will be made. **The fact is that the majority of fraud and corruption investigations are irreparably compromised within 24 hours of discovery**. Risks of failure can be significantly reduced if companies retain professional investigative and legal advice before the disaster strikes, to be available on a 24/7/365 basis anywhere in the world.

INVESTIGATIVE RESOURCES

The need for additional resources

If there is an in-company professional investigative capability, so much to the good, but additional support should be considered – especially for:

- Cases in foreign jurisdictions;
- External investigations involving competitors, customers, suppliers, and third parties;
- Cases involving organised crime;
- Undercover and pretext investigations;
- Computer forensics;
- Interviewing external witnesses and suspects;
- Asset-tracing.

Normally such retentions should be free of charge, with fees and expenses charged on hours worked on a case-by-case basis.

Selecting investigators

Before approaching any firm, the company should make sure it is prepared to actually engage investigators and is not simply wasting time and money and going through a pointless exercise; this happens. A number of firms should be canvassed – in the jurisdictions potentially concerned – based on past experience, personal recommendations and Internet searches.

Brochures and other publicity material should be carefully analysed to identify the firms' specialities and track records, and a shortlist of three or four firms prepared. Selection criteria (on a Kepner-Tregoe basis) should be agreed with needs and wants.

Those selected for interview should be required to enter into confidentiality agreements, under which even preliminary discussions cannot be disclosed. The firms should be presented with an actual or hypothetical case[56] and invited to prepare a fraud theory, an investigation plan, and estimated budget; and to provide references from at least three clients.

The submissions should be carefully reviewed and potentially suitable candidates asked to make presentations, when they should be questioned about their plans, tools and techniques to be used, their understanding of the law, language skills and any other factors that may be relevant to a long-term relationship. They should also be asked to nominate two or three individual investigators to work with the company. The backgrounds of these investigators should be carefully checked and they should be personally interviewed before a decision is made on a final appointment.[57]

The references of the preferred firm (or firms) should be carefully verified, and if satisfactory, letters of engagement or contracts agreed. The retained investigator(s) should be introduced to the senior management team and to the company's external legal advisers, ready to go.

Selecting legal advisers

Companies should consider retaining nominated lawyers from one or two firms of – hard-nosed, blood-drinking firms[58] – that put the client's interests ahead of maintaining their own relationships with the regulators and are prepared, if necessary, to take an adversarial position.

Potential Conflicts of Interest

There are four potentially worrying – and not always publicly disclosed – relationship issues. The first is the practice of some law firms to negotiate what are effectively commissions for referring cases to counsel or other advisers.[59] This may result in selections that are not in a client's best interest.

The second arises from the pressure applied by some regulators on law firms and accountants (as fellow professionals) to advise clients to invariably self-disclose and cooperate in investigations. Because of this, there may be a conflict between what is in their own best interest in maintaining cordial relationships with regulators and what is best for their clients. There is no evidence, or even suggestion, that professional firms have behaved other than

---

56   Possibly one that has been completed.

57   It cannot be emphasised strongly enough how important nominated individuals and personal relationships are, because standards, even in the bigger firms, vary significantly.

58   The fact that a lawyer works for a big firm does not mean he is a bloodsucker.

59   Some investigation firms do the same.

impeccably, but potential conflicts should be discussed and, where necessary, assurances sought.

The third consideration is the revolving door relationship between regulatory agencies and law firms and the positive and negative factors that result from what the brilliant FCPA Professor, Mike Koehler, describes as a 'cottage industry and the bribery racket.'[60]

The fourth is the practice of some law firms to nurture close relationships with the SFO and other agencies by providing free-of-charge training for their officials.

Selection of the law firm should be made on a Kepner-Tregoe basis with nominated individuals being available to react anywhere in the world at short notice,[61] again on a 24/7/365 basis.

RECOGNISING THE REALITIES

Companies should recognise that there is sometimes a natural antipathy between lawyers and investigators, usually caused by the fact that the former are always in the wrong.[62] Although such tensions may be disturbing to those involved, it is essential if the client is to get the best legal advice and the best investigative support (see Chapter 25 and page 675 et seq). It is essential that the firms do not have fixed reciprocal arrangements, referral fees or are so entwined that a civil partnership is on the cards.

INTERNAL INVESTIGATORY PROCEDURES

The company should specify – again in advance – its procedures for conducting investigations including:

- Designation of investigative responsibilities (that is: who will investigate?);
- Registration under the Data Protection Act of all computer and structured manual systems – that might be used in investigations for data-mining, etc.;
- The company's right to monitor communications on its internal telephone and computer systems (under the Regulation of Investigatory Powers Act);
- The requirement of employees, intermediaries and third parties to cooperate fully in investigations: their rights to representation and appeal;
- Approval of investigation tools and techniques that are acceptable to the company and allowed in all of the countries in which it operates;
- Records retention policies (for example, organisation charts, procedure manuals, telephone call records, expense statements, and staff list for at least five years);

---

60   Mr Koehler's blog, available at: http://www.fcpaprofessor.com (accessed 22 November, 2012), is recommended as a primary source on the FCPA and the Bribery Act 2010.

61   Probably not the same firm as provides compliance advice and maybe a different firm for parts of the organisation that are not relevant commercial organisations with 'Chinese walls' in between.

62   Intended joke!!!

- The allocation and control of budgets necessary to conduct major investigations;
- The decision processes, procedures and authorities for reporting suspected cases to regulators and particularly the SFO in relation to the Bribery Act and to all relevant agencies concerned with money-laundering and the proceeds of crime.

The basics of investigatory procedures should be available to all employees and associated third parties (possibly as part of a fraud policy or staff handbook) and, where appropriate, extracts included in contracts and job descriptions (see page 700).

Tapping Internal Telephones

A sensitive issue is whether a company would be prepared to monitor its internal telephone and email traffic in cases of serious fraud as (in the UK) it is allowed to do, providing a user's rights to privacy at work have been explained and the technique is proportionate to the seriousness of the offence. Some managers would never contemplate intercepting communications, whatever the circumstances, and this is understandable. The question should be resolved before the heat of the moment.

Larger companies, operating in high-risk sectors or countries, should consider developing a 'Dawn Raid Manual' (see page 846) in anticipation of an SFO Section 2 order, search warrant, civil freezing, or search orders.

MEDIA RELATIONS

By the time the subpoena lands on the company secretary's desk, or an article appears in the *Financial Times* it is too late for anything other than a quick trip to the pub and reacting as events unfold. Even unsubstantiated allegations of corruption can have a devastating effect.

Cyclone at SciClone

The US company SciClone received notice of a SEC investigation. Within a week, its stock dropped over 31 per cent and five law firms announced that they were investigating the company for potential securities laws violation.

Companies are advised to prepare simple press releases on its integrity policies to issue immediately the first signs of a potential allegation appears and to manage media relationships carefully thereafter, working closely with the managerial, investigative and legal teams (see Chapters 34–5).

Protection of Information

Procedures should be specified, for the Extended Enterprise, for classifying all information according to its sensitivity, assigning ownership, rights and processing standards. Recommended classifications are shown in Table 25.11.

Table 25.11 Information Classifications

Classification	Applies to
SECRET	Information which, if disclosed, could lead to serious financial loss, adverse publicity or disruption. Information classified as SECRET requires the highest level of protection
PROPRIETARY	Technical or commercial information restricted for internal use and not generally available to third parties
PRIVATE	Personal information relating to employees

Each classification should set down who is authorised to access the information and the protective measures necessary for use, copying transmission, storage, destruction, etc. In addition, companies should introduce procedures for identifying and retaining vital records.

The security of most companies would improve dramatically if they would simply:

- Establish a clean desk policy, requiring papers to be locked away when premises are unoccupied overnight;
- Provide all employees with one secure container to lock away sensitive papers;
- Provide sufficient numbers of shredding machines, especially adjacent to photocopiers;
- Make sure that waste paper, microfilm negatives, computer printouts and carbons are disposed of securely *(both at work and at home)*;
- Specify standards for the protection of PCs and laptops;
- Secure remote printers and fax machines.

In addition, board and conference rooms should be secured and important meetings outside company premises carefully risk-assessed. Employees should be trained:

- Not to leave briefcases containing sensitive information with airlines, baggage desks, or porters;
- Frequently change passwords to mobile phone voice messaging, SMS and to personal computers;[63]
- Not to discuss sensitive business matters on aircraft, trains, in chauffeur-driven cars or in restaurants or – far worse still – in Twitter or other social media;
- Not to leave sensitive papers in hotel rooms;
- Not to write supposedly humorous emails and correspondence that will end up in company archives, later to be interpreted as incriminating.

---

63   As demonstrated by The *News of the World* hacking case.

They should also remain alert to the possibilities that competitors and others might target their homes to collect trash or conduct surveillance.

Eavesdropping equipment can be detected by physical searches or by electronic sweeps. Although there are many devices on the market which are supposed to detect bugs, their value is limited and they would be unlikely to reveal anything but the most amateur equipment. It is dangerous to rely on them.

Sensitive areas, such as boardrooms and the offices, homes and cars of senior executives should be checked at least every three months and more regularly during periods when the company faces increased risks:

- During hostile takeovers;
- During and after regulatory investigations;
- When there are known information leaks;
- When the company is subject to adverse media interest;
- Prior to important meetings on strategy or research and development.

In most cases, companies are advised to use specialist consultants to check out premises, telephone and data lines, but they must be selected with the greatest care and their backgrounds and professional expertise should be confirmed.

Counter-surveillance specialists should be required to sign confidentiality agreements and standard contracts. Under no circumstances should consultants carrying out this very sensitive work be left unsupervised. They should be required to submit a detailed report after each survey.

26 Contractual Controls and Personnel Procedures

Contractual Controls

Contracts with senior managers, suppliers, customers, agents and other members of the Extended Enterprise are important building blocks in a control programme and establish the company's legal rights. Wherever possible they should be positively framed and provide realistic reciprocal rights based on expert legal advice, possibly incorporating some of the following ideas.

WARRANTIES

Facts or representations on which the company will rely should be included in a warranty section.

Example

In contracts of employment or those with any significant intermediary, accuracy of the original application form and subsequent annual declarations should be warranted. Thus any false declarations should allow the company to immediately terminate the relationship, without penalty.

For agents and other important intermediaries, consideration should be given to requiring their individual directors and officers to personally warrant that the information provided is accurate and that they will comply with integrity standards, reporting of incidents, annual declarations and other important control requirements.

COMPLIANCE WITH CONTROLS

All counterparties should be provided with a copy of the company's integrity policies and possibly a small handbook, a 'Third Party Code of Conduct'. Contracts with intermediaries, vendors, customers and other members of the Extended Enterprise should bind them to the company's integrity standards and to comply with all relevant laws.[1] Contracts should also incorporate the agreement (of all important third parties) to make annual declarations of compliance and to provide corroborative documentation and audit access when required. **Failure to comply should empower the company to terminate contracts with immediate effect and to withhold all outstanding payments with terms possibly along the following lines:**

Immediate Cancellation of Authority

Employees and others retained to perform services for the company are specifically prohibited from offering, giving, etc. any advantage or rewarding any third party with the intention of inducing him or her to perform an official or business function or activity improperly. If they act in contravention of this requirement they will be deemed not to be performing services on the company's behalf and will be subject to instant dismissal.

ANNUAL DECLARATIONS: BASIC AND OF NET WORTH

Consideration should be given to requiring (preferably on a reciprocal basis) key members of the Extended Enterprise to submit annual declarations, or letters of representation, certifying that they have complied with all applicable laws and with the company's integrity policies and procedures.

THE RIGHT TO AUDIT

Consideration should also be given to negotiating audit rights with high-risk intermediaries, agents and vendors, especially those retained on a cost plus or time and materials basis, including advertising agencies, consultancies, mailing houses, telesales and software developers. The rights to audit might include:

- Unrestricted acccss to all relevant books and records, including those of associated companies, parents and subsidiaries;
- All files relating to competitive bids obtained on the company's behalf and all delegated purchasing;
- Invoices from suppliers, accounts and other data on which the above depend;
- Correspondence and contracts relating to subcontractors;
- Access to any relevant computer system, including permission to download data;
- Office space in which to carry out the audit, copying and other facilities;
- Technical assistance and all other facilities necessary to carry out the audit;

---

1   Possibly backed by personal guarantees.

- An undertaking that managers and employees will attend interviews and answer questions;
- An undertaking that if overpayments are detected, these will be returned with interest: additionally the vendor will reimburse the costs of the audit.

Contracts might also require third parties to obtain similar rights to audit the records of their subcontractors,[2] and to retain records for a minimum of five years.

The clauses should be carefully drawn before contracts are finalised at a time when the third party may be more cooperative. Consideration should also be given to summarising audit clauses on purchase orders, invitations to tender and on other forms.

RETENTIONS AND DEPOSITS

Standard terms and conditions, where appropriate, may require a deposit or advance payment from customers or allow for retentions on purchase contracts. Alternatively vendors – especially those involved in construction, offset projects or IT development – should be required to enter into bank guarantees or performance bonds.[3]

INDEMNITIES

Where appropriate, third parties should indemnify the company against losses, the results of its negligence and breaches of regulations. Consideration should be given to seeking personal indemnities from the directors and officers of high-risk third parties.

ALTERNATIVE DISPUTE RESOLUTION

Wherever possible, contracts should specify that disputes will be resolved by arbitration or through an alternative dispute resolution (ADR) procedure. This provision is especially important on insurance policies and on contracts with third parties based in countries where legal systems are inefficient or corrupt.

STANDARD CONTRACTS SUBMITTED BY THIRD PARTIES

Companies should take great care before acceding to standard contracts proposed by third parties including insurance policies, leasing and consultancy contracts.

In the Carbon World standard contracts have resulted in serious problems for primary sellers of Certified Emission Reductions because they do not allow for substitutions when a project does not deliver the reductions anticipated. A number of very expensive legal fights are currently under way.

---

2   Especially time sheets and travel expenses.

3   It is estimated that over $25 billion worth of offset projects are still to be completed.

Standard Contracts

Standard contracts proffered by third parties, such as advertising agencies, give very limited rights of audit. They may only provide very limited rights of audit on such things as media costs, in-house production, inter-group charges, or other information on which their charges can be assessed. The usual argument is that such data is confidential since it identifies or relates to other clients. In such cases, the clauses should be amended to permit a full audit by independent specialists.

STANDARD TERMS AND CONDITIONS OF BUSINESS

Companies should consider incorporating details of its integrity programmes – and especially requirements to comply with the Bribery Act 2010 – in its general terms and conditions of business incorporated on purchase orders, delivery notes and invoices. The wording might also include the conditions of automatic cancellation in the event of bribes being offered or solicited by any associated person.

SUMMARY OF PROVISIONS

The principles described above should be considered for contracts with third parties, as shown in Table 26.1.

Table 26.1   Contracts with Third Parties

Principle	Contracts with				
	Employees	**Vendors**	**JV Partners**	**Bankers**	**Insurers**
Integration	Linked to job application forms, job descriptions	Linked to purchase orders and standard terms and conditions of business	Included in main commercial contracts	Included in main commercial contracts	Included in contracts with brokers and in policy documents
Principles repeated	On expense statements	On purchase orders	On purchase orders, sales invoices and remittance advices		

Warranties	Warranting the accuracy of job applications and annual declarations	Warranting information given for integrity validation screening	Warranting information given for integrity validation screening	Warranting information given for integrity validation screening	Warranting information given for integrity validation screening
Certificate of Compliance	To comply with controls and to cooperate in investigations To report suspected violations To report changing circumstances				
Annual declarations	As members of the extended enterprise			Limited declarations	
Audit clauses	Tied to the policy in investigations	Full audit access to relevant records, etc.			
Retentions and advance payments	Personal bonding, but only in very high-risk cases	Standard terms	Very important in countries where the legal system is corrupt or inefficient		
Indemnities	Against dishonest and ultra vires acts	Against negligence, dishonesty and breaches of regulations		Against fraudulent EFTS and other payments	
Arbitration and ADR	Standard provision in all contacts				

When contracts are negotiated on a case by case basis they should be approved by specialist lawyers.

Personnel Policies and Procedures

INTRODUCTION AND OBJECTIVES

Fair, open and efficient personnel procedures have a major effect on a company's resistance to fraud and corruption. There are a number of important procedures that should be owned by Human Resources departments.

PRE-EMPLOYMENT SCREENING

The objective of selection is to ensure that the best candidate is chosen: not simply the one with the least adverse public history.[4] Accurate figures are not available to show the true rates of criminal recidivism, although in the white collar crime area they are

---

4   See page 570.

extremely high and the tendency is for crooks to go from one company to another inflicting further damage. This does not imply that people who have been previously convicted of a criminal offence should not be employed. But a company has the right to evaluate its risks and an obligation to existing employees to provide a safe and fulfilling working environment.

The job applicant who falsifies his educational qualifications or job experience is dangerous and cannot be trusted. 'Degree mills' offer unqualified people apparently genuine qualifications on payment of a fee. There are more than 500 such providers of spurious educational qualifications in Britain and an estimated 4,000 worldwide.[5]

Degree Mills

Some offer a BA for as little as £28 and a PhD for £56 and for £100 one enterprising college will bestow the title of Professor Emeritus. The scale of charges at one of Britain's leading degree mills, Sussex College of Technology, is a little higher: a BA costs £80, an MA can be acquired for £98 and a PhD for £155.

In addition, a simple desktop publishing system can produce impressive, but totally false, educational and other certificates.

Because of such dangers, all organisations should specify procedures for checking the backgrounds of potential employees and for screening existing employees, prior to promotion or transfer into sensitive positions, especially those involving high-risk overseas assignments. Also, for sensitive jobs, a procedure for annual screening should be considered.

Predictors of success and dishonesty

The process suggested here is to prepare in advance of final selection a simple matrix of factors that will assist in an accurate and graded evaluation of a candidate's positive and negative attributes.

The positive factors can be identified:

- By noting the prerequisites (no more than five or six) for success in the position concerned;
- By carefully preparing a list of questions that will identify the positive traits and how they might be scored.

5   A definitive report by an authority on Diploma Mills, John Bear, *Bonus Report: Diploma Mills of the World* was published in 1982 (Mendocino Book Company, Ukiah, CA). *Diploma Mills: the billion-dollar industry that has sold over a million fake diplomas* (Allen Ezell and John Bear, Amherst, N.Y.: Prometheus Books, 2012), which gives links to lists of fake (and bad) diploma schools.

There are usually warning signs in a candidate's background that may indicate a disposition towards dishonesty and these are listed in Table 26.2.

Table 26.2 Factors Indicating Future Problems

Warning sign Indicating the Likelihood of Future Dishonesty	How it can be Identified	Score 100 = most significant
Undisclosed previous dishonesty	Detailed application form and checking	100
False data on an employment application form or given during recruitment process	Effective interviewing	100
Refusal to answer questions	Effective interviewing	100
Unexplained wealth or assets	Detailed application form and checking	100
Criminal or psychopathic personality	Professional psychological analysis	99
Unexplained gaps in employment	Detailed application form and checking	90
Serious drug or alcohol abuse	Medical examination	90
History of bad debts	Detailed application form and checking	70
Serious marital or family problems	Detailed application form and checking	60
Regular expenditure in excess of incomeor other serious financial problems	Detailed application form and checking	50
Disclosed previous dishonesty	Detailed application form and checking	20

Most of these warning signs can be uncovered by basic pre-employment screening procedures and through effective interviewing.

Management policy

Pre-employment screening should never be carried out other than under the full authority of the board of directors and should be based on the considerations listed in Table 26.3.

Table 26.3 Considerations in a Screening Programme

Consideration	Comments
What job positions should be included in the programme?	Should it apply to all employees? Should it apply to agents and advisers? Should it apply to temporary employees? Should it apply to staff employed by contractors, such as security guards and cleaners?
When should checks be made?	Prior to employment Annual reviews for sensitive positions Prior to promotion or transfer
What areas should be checked?	See below
Do Fidelity Insurance policies require background checks to be made?	This is a condition on some policies If so, details of the checks made should be permanently retained
What are the legal implications?	What questions are prohibited under law? What are the different requirements in the countries in which the company operates?
How can data be confirmed?	Through external specialists or in-house
Who will administer the programme?	Personnel department? Security? Compliance or internal audit?
Are the costs acceptable?	Bearing in mind that the average employee will remain on the payroll for ten years and earn over $200,000, and could involve the company in fines as high as $290,000,000, is spending even $5,000 on checking employee backgrounds excessive?

Company policy and decision matrices should be based on the answers to these questions and should be incorporated in the appropriate procedure manuals, included in an employee handbook and in training programmes, and possibly summarised on job application forms. The procedure should be given a high and transparent profile.

Legal positions

Laws governing privacy and access to government information vary from country to country and extreme care should be taken to confirm the legality of questions and the methods through which answers can be confirmed.

The law also imposes serious obligations on the job applicant. If he attempts to obtain employment by deception he is at risk of criminal prosecution and, in the UK, imprisonment. If the deception is not discovered until later, his employment may be terminated. This fact should be made clear on application forms and during the interview process.

Unfortunately, previous employers owe no obligation to future employers and are not compelled to give a reference, or even tell the truth. This is a very bad situation for the international business community. Often employers will do anything to avoid giving a derogatory reference in the mistaken belief that it could expose them to an action for defamation. In fact, there is little danger if the reference is true and, even when it is incorrect, it will normally be privileged providing it is not malicious.

Application forms and decision matrix

A clear, comprehensive and well-structured application form is essential. In some cases, companies have two forms. One is completed in advance of the preliminary interview and a second, and possibly shorter version, under supervision in the second interview. The answers given should be compared and the candidate questioned about any discrepancies.

Subject to legal advice in the country concerned, application forms should contain some words of warning. Many applicants do not realise the serious criminal implications of false declarations and it is in everyone's interests that this position is clarified. Also, warnings raise the danger level for dishonest candidates and may deter them.

A possible form of wording is set out below:

> *Thank you for your interest in ABC Limited. It is a very special company; we care very much about our employees, customers and suppliers and we intend to maintain the very highest standards. If you join us, we are sure that you will agree with our philosophy and with our objectives.*
>
> *Because we intend to maintain these high standards, coupled with close and friendly team work, we must have absolute honesty in all of our dealings. There can be no secrets between members of our team and no surprises. For this reason, we urge you to complete the form fully and accurately. Take your time and if you have any questions or problems, please ask us. Do not put down information unless you are sure it is correct.*
>
> *The fact that something may have happened in your past that you now regret need not rule out your employment with us. Neither will the fact that you have potentially conflicting interests providing they are openly disclosed. But we do need to know where we stand and to be absolutely honest with each other.*
>
> *If you start to work with us, we will need to see your birth certificate ..., etc.*
>
> *Good luck; we hope to have you working with us.*

The form should also refer to or summarise the company's integrity policies or refer the candidate to a handbook which he should be given as early in the recruitment process as possible. The candidate must not be ambushed with conflicts of interest and other policies the day he or she is due to start work.

The closing certificate, signed by the applicant, should be along the following lines:

> *I certify that the above replies are true, complete and correct. I know that it is a criminal offence to attempt to obtain employment by deception and that any misrepresentation of a material fact will be cause for cancellation of consideration, or dismissal. I have been provided with [the company's] policy on security and I agreed to abide by it. I understand that if employed, I will be subject to a probationary period of 3 months.*

The form should be signed and dated.

Job application forms should also contain clauses giving the candidate's permission for checks to be made with previous employers, bankers, credit bureaux, schools, universities, etc. They should also include a release to third parties, permitting them to provide information. The exact wording of these releases should be drafted by specialist employment lawyers in the jurisdictions concerned.

Some companies – especially in the USA – have an additional page titled 'Special Concerns On Background Checking', which is prefaced by:

> *I have the following concerns or comments about potentially negative information that may be revealed during verification of this application for employment. I understand that I do not have to provide any personal information that is not relevant and I have been told that if I have any questions about what is relevant or not relevant I should ask. I have no questions or reservations on this point. My questions or comments about potentially negative references or information are: ...*

For most countries, declarations of this type are unnecessary. However, it is critical to check the legality of any proposed system with local employment lawyers.

Where allowed by local laws, job applications should be structured so that they become part of the candidate's contract if he or she is employed. Wording should make it clear that false information on the application will be regarded as a breach of contract and will result in immediate dismissal, without compensation. The form may also contain an undertaking that the candidate, if employed, will observe the company's security, investigatory, compliance and related policies and will provide annual declarations of compliance.

Application forms should be designed and laid out with care. For each question, the person designing the application form should satisfy himself on the following points.

- Is the question necessary to identify the applicant?
- Is the question necessary to assess his qualifications, suitability, experience, honesty or reliability?
- Is the question legal? Has the company the right to ask it in the country or State concerned?
- Will the information be used and is it capable of being checked?

Most application forms consist entirely of closed questions, often requiring simple yes and no answers which are easy to falsify. Sometimes it is more meaningful to include a number of open questions, leaving space for free-style answers. For example questions such as:

- Why do people trust you?
- Under what circumstances would you believe dishonesty is justified?
- How would you react if we discovered that you have not told the whole truth on this application form?

– can provide a good insight into the candidate's honesty.[6]

---

6   See *Deception at Work* by Comer and Stephens.

A genuine applicant should not resent completing a detailed form. People who have something to hide may show more reluctance and fail to pursue their interest, perhaps alleging that the forms intrude upon their privacy or civil liberties.

Intrusive Forms

A company which uses forms of the type recommended was concerned because around 10 per cent of candidates failed to pursue their applications. The Personnel Director argued that the forms were intrusive. The backgrounds of the candidates who had withdrawn their applications were checked and in every case they had either provided false information or had derogatory histories that would have caused their rejection.

Experience shows that a detailed form, with appropriate polite warnings and releases deters only unsuitable applicants.

The questions most frequently asked on employment forms are listed in Table 26.4, together with **the likely decisions based on replies to background checks**. Because of possible allegations of discrimination, the legality of questions shown in **BLOCK CAPITALS** should be checked with local lawyers to make sure they are permissable.

Table 26.4   Questions Frequently Asked[7]

% of Forms Asking the Question	Information Requested	Finding and Action Taken As a Result (Decision Matrix)		
		Finding	Management positions	Other
	Identification:			
100	Full name	False	Reject	Reject
17	Previous name	False	Reject	Reject
50	Maiden name	False	Reject	Reject
100	SEX	False	Reject	Reject
74	DATE OF BIRTH	False	Reject	Reject
33	PLACE OF BIRTH	False	Reject	Reject
15	CITIZENSHIP	False	Reject	Reject
2	Passport number	False	Explain	Explain
22	Social Security or National Insurance	False	Confront	Confront

---

7   Subject to checking their legality in the jurisdictions concerned.

% of Forms Asking the Question	Information Requested	Finding and Action Taken As a Result (Decision Matrix)		
		Finding	Management positions	Other
11	PHYSICAL DESCRIPTION	False	Confront	Confront
9	ENCLOSE CURRENT PHOTOGRAPH	Wrong person	Reject	Reject
100	Current address	False	Reject	Reject
40	Years at address	False	Reject	Reject
15	Previous addresses	False	Reject	Reject
37	Home telephone number	False	Reject	Reject
26	Person to contact in an emergency	Does not exist	Reject	Reject
	Education:			
20	Names of schools attended	False	Reject	Reject
20	Dates of attendance	False	Confront	Confront
20	Names of university attended	False or Degree Mill	Reject	Reject
20	Dates of attendance	False	Confront	Confront
100	Qualifications obtained	False	Reject	Reject
30	Name of teacher	False	Reject	Confront
Findings	Unexplained gaps in schooling	Findings	Reject	Reject
Findings	Record of violence or insubordination	Findings	Reject	Reject
Findings	Record of stealing or lying	Findings	Reject	Reject
Findings	Record of serious drug abuse/ dealing	Findings	Reject	Reject
Findings	Record of truancy	Findings	Reject	Reject
	Financial Information:			
15	Total family income	False	Reject	Reject
15	Regular monthly outgoings	False	Reject	Reject
15	Name and address of banker	False	Reject	Reject
7	Credit cards held	False	Reject	Reject
Findings	Excess of outgoings over salary offered	Findings	Reject	Reject
Findings	Bad credit record	Findings	Reject	Reject
	Miscellaneous Information:			
Findings	Disclosed serious criminal convictions • In last 5 years • Earlier • Minor juvenile offences	Disclosed	Reject Consider Accept	Consider Consider Accept

	Undisclosed criminal convictions	Discovered	Reject	Reject
	Personal and Family:			
20	Personal referees	False or derogatory	Confront	Confront
24	Membership of clubs and associations	False	Reject	Reject
40	Membership of trade union	False	Reject	Reject
20	Details of driving licence and endorsement	False	Reject	Reject
0	Directorships and private business interests	False	Reject	Reject
39	Marital status	False	Reject	Reject
20	Number of children	False	Reject	Reject
15	Names of children	False	Confront	Confront
17	Dates and places of children's births	False	Explain	Explain
15	Number of dependants	False	Explain	Explain
9	Date and place of marriage	False	Reject	Reject
7	Wife's maiden name	False	Reject	Reject
11	Wife's date of birth	False	Explain	Explain
4	Details of previous marriages	False	Reject	Reject
4	Names and addresses of parents	False	Reject	Reject
Findings	• Unstable family – criminal background	Findings	Confront	Explain
	• Criminal associates	Findings	Confront	Explain
	Housing:			
17	Owned or rented	False	Reject	Reject
7	Name and address of landlord	False	Reject	Confront
	Employment History:			
43	Name and address of present employer	False	Reject	Reject
24	Years with this employer	False	Reject	Reject
61	Work responsibilities	False	Reject	Reject
31	Salary record	False	Reject	Reject
Findings	Non-competition agreement • Disclosed • Undisclosed		Accept Reject	Accept Reject
10	Name of company referee	False or derogatory	Reject	Reject

% of Forms Asking the Question	Information Requested	Finding and Action Taken As a Result (Decision Matrix)		
		Finding	Management positions	Other
20	Reasons for leaving previous employers: • resignation • redundancy • dismissal	False	Reject	Reject
Findings	• Job-hopping	Findings	Reject	Confront
Findings	• Unexplained gaps in employment	Findings	Confront	Confront
Findings	• Unsatisfactory performance	Findings	Confront	Confront
Findings	• Dishonesty/subversion/ violence	Findings	Reject	Reject
	Health:			
20	Physical disabilities	Concealed	Reject	Reject
11	Name and address of doctor	False	Reject	Reject
Findings	• Undisclosed condition affecting the person's ability to do the job (e.g. drugs)	Findings	Reject	Reject

The decision whether to accept or reject an application should be determined – as a specified standard in advance – possibly on the scale shown in Table 26.5.

Table 26.5   Findings and Results

Answer	Finding as a Result of Checks		
	Honest replies	Ambiguous Replies	False Replies
Positive attribute	Accept	Explain or confront	Reject
Derogatory attribute	Consider	Confront or reject	Reject

The scale between acceptance and rejection is as shown in Table 26.6.

Table 26.6   Decisions to Hire or Reject

Decision	Explanation
Accept	Honest replies and acceptable background
Consider	Generally acceptable: honest replies
Explain	Some problems with background or replies but more likely to accept than reject
Confront	Some serious problems, but the candidate may be able to provide a satisfactory explanation
Reject	Unacceptable background or dishonest replies

Generally any dishonest replies on an application form should result in rejection as they demonstrate that the candidate is prepared to deceive the employer from the very start.

Method of checking

Consideration should be given, at the policy formation stage, as to how details shown on application forms can be verified. The most common methods, their advantages and disadvantages are summarised in Table 26.7.

Table 26.7   Methods of Checking Application Forms

Method	Disadvantages	Ratings 10 = most efficient 0 = least efficient		
		Effect	Cost	Speed
Written references	• Do not check in depth • Easily forged	3	10	5
Telephone references	• Do not check in depth • Caution by the referee • Possible to forge (by giving the phone number of a friend)	5	7	7
Interviews by Personnel	• Superficial on security issues • Easily deceived	5	3	5
Interviews by experienced personnel officers and/or security	• None: usually excellent results	10	4	8
Polygraph examination	• Not legal in some countries • Doubtful accuracy	9	8	6

Method	Disadvantages	Ratings 10 = most efficient 0 = least efficient		
		Effect	Cost	Speed
Psychological testing	• Excellent at predicting future dishonesty	10	1	3
Handwriting analysis Handwriting examined by a graphologist	• Subjective • Questionable accuracy	4	7	5
Weighted score cards Candidate completes tick boxes on forms: replies scored based on profiles	• Questionable accuracy	4	9	9
Positive vetting Detailed background checking and probing interviews	• Confrontational	10	10	3

In most cases, where the job concerned is sensitive or important, organisations would be well advised to pass responsibility for background checking to a specialist pre-employment screening agency.[8]

The initial interview

A distinct portion of the initial interview should be devoted to screening and introduced by specifically stating its purpose. The candidate should also be given a summary of the company's integrity policies conflicts of interest and pre-employment screening, and the significance of these should be discussed. The candidate should be given an application form, or a blank duplicate if one has already been submitted, and should be told that his background will be thoroughly checked. The criminal nature of false declarations should be discussed.

The candidate should be asked to complete the application form in full and return it as soon as possible. He should be told that if his name is added to the shortlist, he will be required to produce originals of birth and marriage certificates, driving licence, passport and educational and professional qualifications, as well as a current photograph. *This requirement should be checked with local lawyers, as in some jurisdictions these items cannot be requested until employment has commenced.*

8   Many firms advertise on the World Wide Web.

Drugs testing

Candidates[9] might be required as part of their medical examination to be tested for the use of narcotic drugs[10] and alcohol abuse. There are three reasons for this. The first is that narcotics users and alcoholics are more frequently absent from work than their drug- and alcohol-free colleagues. Secondly, their decisions can be adversely affected by narcotic drugs and alcohol. Thirdly, the cost of drugs usually puts addicts under severe financial strain and this can be a motivation for fraud.

The clearance interview

If results of these checks contradict any detail given on the application form, the candidate may be asked to attend a further interview and asked to explain any discrepancies. This should be after any medical examination.

External verification

If the candidate appears suitable, the application form and all supporting detail should be checked,[11] as set out in Table 26.8.

Table 26.8 Checking Details

Reference Source	Areas to Check and Questions
The applicant's passport Produced at the interview or in jurisdictions where this is not allowed, on starting employment	• Name, place and date of birth • Citizenship • Names of spouse and children *(notify in an emergency)* • Physical description
The applicant's Birth Certificate Produced at the interview	• Name, place and date of birth • Names and addresses of father and mother
The applicant's Marriage Certificate Produced at the interview	• Names, place and date of birth • Name of spouse and any previous names • Addresses
The applicant's Driving Licence	• Name, place and date of birth • Addresses • Endorsements and convictions
Educational and other certificates Produced at the interview	• Name • Schools attended and dates • Qualifications obtained
Housing or rating list	• Ownership and value of house • Confirm address and dates of residency

9   Especially for high level positions.

10   Not including nicotine!

11   Again, legal advice should be obtained on the legality of the aspects which can be checked.

Reference Source	Areas to Check and Questions
Schools and universities	• Confirm dates of attendance and qualifications obtained • Confirm attendance and disciplinary record • CHECK THE STATUS OF THE COLLEGE: is it bona fide?
Previous employers	• Names and addresses • Obtain a copy of the employment application form • Confirm employment dates, positions held, salary and reasons for termination • Confirm work responsibilities • Check eligibility for re-employment • Check restrictive covenants on employment • If possible, speak to the applicant's immediate supervisor
Bankers	• Confirm financial standing
Credit agencies (if allowed)	• Check financial history
County Courts	• Check bad debt record
Roll of electors	• Check residency • Identify neighbours • Speak to immediate neighbours
Telephone directory	• Confirm residency • Check for businesses registered at the address
List of directors	• Check for present and past directorships

The external agency should provide a brief report summarising its findings.

The sign-off

Based on these external checks and interviews a brief clearance report should be submitted to Human Resources or the line manager, who will take the decision to hire or reject the candidate. Copies of the clearance report should be retained in a confidential security file and in the personal file for the applicant. These documents could be vital if at some point in the future the candidate becomes the cause of a Fidelity Insurance claim. Details of all rejected applications should be noted in the Adequate Procedures Dossier.

Justification for rejection

Some candidates whose applications are rejected immediately start actions for discrimination: in fact some crooks apply for jobs solely with the intent of extorting money from the potential employer. The risks of actual and frivolous actions are reduced when the company has prepared a list, possibly weighted along the lines of Table 26.8 above, which it applies to all decisions.

This is a much better approach than taking decisions on a subjective basis, which can lead to inequality of treatment.

The details or summaries of all rejected applications should be retained in the Adequate Procedures Dossier.

The offer letter

The offer letter, which should be in more or less a standard form approved by lawyers, should make employment conditional on any outstanding references, medical examinations, the production of a birth certificate and other documents, on the candidate's acceptance of a contract of employment, and on satisfactory completion of a probationary period. The candidate should be asked to sign and return a copy of this letter, acknowledging acceptance of the conditions.

Probationary periods

All employees should be required to serve a three-month probationary period. During this time their performance should be carefully monitored. At the end of the period, candidates' security clearances should be reviewed. This is the final safety net.

Comments on the system

The system outlined may seem tedious and pedantic, but it is more than justified against the risks of employing crooks and liars. The cost, whether through an outside agency or internally, is minute, bearing in mind the possible consequences.

EMPLOYMENT OF TEMPORARY STAFF

Specified procedures should ensure that temporary and part-time staff, especially contract programmers and secretaries, are not employed in sensitive jobs, unless their backgrounds have been checked. One of the most common ways in which competitive intelligence is obtained is by infiltration of the target company by opponents. Wherever possible, short-term vacancies in sensitive positions should be filled by rotating trusted employees, so that temporary staff take over the least sensitive jobs.

In addition, the background of the agency through which temporary staff are obtained should be carefully checked and it should be required to sign a contract agreeing to comply with the company's integrity and other policies. The agency should be required to produce a copy of the job application form and the results of its own checking into the background of the candidate. It should also provide references from other companies for whom the person has worked on a temporary basis.

The temporary employee should be briefed on the company's policies on integrity conflicts of interest, etc. and asked to sign the appropriate declarations. Performance should be carefully monitored and, as a general rule, access privileges should be limited to those absolutely necessary.

At the end of the assignment, the line manager concerned should require the temporary employee to sign a Termination Agreement. He or she should also prepare a brief appraisal, stating whether the person concerned is suitable for future work.

REMUNERATION AND INCENTIVES

Highly geared bonus schemes can be an encouragement for employees to falsify results. The case of Barings is a good example of the blindness that can affect even honest people when they share a common goal of maximising their incentives. Ideally a percentage of all salary packages should be in deferred earnings conditional on ethical performance.

JOB DESCRIPTIONS

All job descriptions should show the requirement to comply with security procedures. For example:

> *The [job title] is responsible for maintaining control over all aspects of his or her work and for compliance with company's integrity, Codes of Conduct and other policies, copies of which have been provided. Non-compliance will be subject to disciplinary action including immediate termination of employment.*
>
> *Specifically the employee is required to:*

- *comply with all laws and regulations, on which he has been fully briefed;*
- *provide an annual declaration of compliance and to provide such further information as may reasonably be required;*
- *not to engage in any activity that might conflict with his or her work for the company;*
- *report incidents of suspected fraud or malpractice and not to any external agency without first giving the company 120 days' notice[12] of this intention;*
- *cooperate and assist in investigations when requested to do so and to answer questions posed by management;*
- *refrain from discussing sensitive company matters with third parties.*

This simple statement should ensure that responsibility for controls is confirmed by line managers and that penalties are imposed for non-compliance.

Wherever possible, job descriptions should be written so that they support or are in lieu of legally binding contracts of employment. Where employees are issued with job descriptions in addition to their contracts of employment, the terms should be compatible with each other and also with staff handbooks.

Job descriptions should make it clear that employees and associated third parties have a direct obligation to report their suspicions, and failing action within 120 days, have the right to report to the external auditors and other external agencies. It should also be made clear that any employee who makes an external report other than in the above circumstances may be liable to summary dismissal.

---

12   To comply with the Dodd Frank Act, But note that in the USA (and for issuers) it is illegal to prohibit a person reporting to the Securities and Exchange Commission.

Finally, job descriptions should state:

Employees are specifically prohibited from offering, giving, etc. any advantage or rewarding any third party with the intention of inducing him or her to perform an official or business function or activity improperly. If they act in contravention of this undertaking they are be deemed not to be performing services on the company's behalf and their contracts will immediately be terminated.

This term should also be incorporated in authority tables (see pages 576–7).

CONTRACTS OF EMPLOYMENT AND AGREEMENTS

Contracts with employees in the Extended Enterprise should contain specific reference to the requirement to comply with controls and include undertakings to:

- Comply fully with all policies on integrity fair reporting and accounting, the environment, and corporate social responsibility;
- Report changes in personal financial or domestic circumstances without delay;
- Report suspicions of fraud or corruption internally;[13]
- Answer questions and provide information when reasonably required to do so;
- Provide annual declarations of compliance and letters of representation;
- Comply with other legal agreements;
- Submit any disputes to arbitration or a procedure for Alternative Dispute Resolution.

Contracts of this nature serve a preventive purpose and are extremely valuable in legal proceedings taken as a result of an employee's dishonesty.

In some countries[14] it is permissible for the employer to monitor telephone calls, emails and Internet activity made from company equipment on company premises. In jurisdictions where employees must give their consent, or at least be advised of the possibilities, consideration should be given to including the following clause in secrecy or search agreements:[15]

Employees are permitted to use telephones and other equipment for occasional non-business purposes. Nevertheless, the employee has no right of privacy as to any information or file maintained in or on it or transmitted or stored on the company's computer or telecommunications systems, voice mail, email ....

Employees are allowed to use personal computers on company premises, to download, process and upload data and programs on the basis that they will secure such data or programs and will permit inspection by the company at any time.

Employees using encryption or other security packages on company or their own computers for company work, must register the keys or other devices with the IT manager and permit inspection at any time. If the key or other security feature has not been previously registered, the

---

13   With failure resulting in disciplinary action.

14   Always check with local litigation lawyers.

15   An subject to specialist and local legal advice.

employee will immediately make it available on request by [state name and contact details].
Failure to comply will result in disciplinary action.

Any item on company premises or in any vehicle or craft owned by the company is subject
to search for security purposes at any time. Personal information provided by employees and
others may be used for data-matching and other fraud prevention and investigation purposes.

The applicant accepts that any data provided on the form or at any time during his
employment may be used at any time for the purpose of preventing and detecting fraud and
may be released to other organisations involved and to public authorities.

Wording such as this may prevent problems in investigations generally and especially
when an employee's calls have been intercepted and used against him to prove dishonesty.
As with other possibly controversial policies, it is always best to be open and high profile.
This is consistent with the organisation's goals of being an exemplary corporate citizen
and a very hard target.

ROTATIONAL ASSIGNMENTS

The chances of fragmenting collusive groups are improved when short-term rotational
or exchange assignments are made into high-risk contexts – for example, by transferring
for a three to six-month assignment a member of compliance into marketing and vice
versa. There is an additional benefit that a person in an advisory role gains a better
understanding of operational roles and problems.

GIFTS DECLARATION

The case in the UK involving the prolonged subsidised stay at Champney's Health Club by
Sir Paul Stephenson, the Metropolitan Police Commissioner, and his wife was presented
as kosher because he had made a declaration in **his** Gifts Register.[16] At no stage does it
appear that Sir Paul made any public claim that he had obtained any prior approval.
This is the problem with relying purely on after-the-event declarations – it is difficult
to distinguish between honest behaviour and quickly covering up when skulduggery is
about to be disclosed. Therefore, companies should consider a process for pre-approval or
transparent pre-declarations in the electronic confessional box (see page 575).

EXPENSE STATEMENTS

Companies should consider adopting a completely different frame for expense statements,
turning them from basic accounting records into powerful tools to prevent and detect
corruption, as well as to protect honest employees against unfounded suspicions.

Wherever possible expense statements should:

- Be pre-printed with brief extracts of the company's integrity policies and a reminder
  of the consequences of false declarations;
- Have sufficient space to enter all important detail;
- Be submitted electronically and supported by printed versions signed by the claimant;

---

16   Nothing has been said about where or by whom this register was maintained, or when the gift was declared.

- Be submitted in strict monthly intervals with no gaps or overlaps;
- Zero amount claims should be required;
- Vouchers should be scanned electronically,[17] but where this is not possible, those over a certain amount should be glued, unfolded, on to separate A4 backing sheets to make them easily checkable; an alternative is to have all vouchers electronically scanned;
- Details of all hospitality and gifts given and received, expenses paid on behalf of third parties, together with the names and job positions of the people entertained, the place and nature of the entertainment and the reasons for it should be entered on a detailed supplement to the form. This page effectively plays the role of a gifts declaration book;
- Claims should be authorised electronically by a supervisor; if authorization is by signature, they must not be returned to the claimant after approval (see page 576).

Consideration should also be given to having a closing certificate certifying that the claim is accurate and that none of the expenditure was intended to influence a foreign public official or other third party in their jobs.

Detailed monthly summaries of expense statements – with emphasis on hospitality given and received – should be reviewed by senior management and from time to time by the board of directors.

ANNUAL DECLARATIONS AND APPRAISALS

A procedure requiring annual declarations by key employees in the **Extended Enterprise** and letters of representation from managers is an important control tool and should include the points set out in Table 26.9.

Table 26.9 Annual Declarations and Appraisals

Aspect of the Declaration	Consequences
That they understand the **significance of their declaration** and that their continued employment is conditional on their compliance with the integrity and related policies	This is important
That they have **reviewed risks** in the operations for which they are accountable and are satisfied with the controls in place	This statement pins employees to the responsibility for control self-assessment programmes
That they have fully **complied** with their integrity and control responsibilities	This enhances the profile of the control programme It makes all employees accountable for their control responsibilities It denies them the opportunity of a plausible excuse if dishonesty is discovered

---

17   An excellent way of using this is with scanners such as Neat Desk. Scanned vouchers are converted to readable PDFs and can be used in fraud detection and continuous monitoring programmes (see Chapter 19).

Aspect of the Declaration	Consequences
That they are not aware of any **breaches in control,** compliance breaches, improper practices or weaknesses which have not been reported	This makes it more difficult for an employee, after his services have been terminated, to make wild allegations about improper practices in the company
That they have reported (n) **incidents** in the year	This is a cross-check. If an employee chooses not to report an incident he may always claim that the form has been lost. This annual declaration denies him such an opportunity
That there has been **no change** in their personal or financial circumstances affecting their declarations on conflicts of interest	This updates and reinforces previous declarations
That they have **received no income** other than that from their employer	This should be a specific declaration. When there is any doubt, the employee should be asked to produce his tax return
That they have not **received any gifts** or benefits other than those (n) disclosed on expense statements	This is a cross-check. If an employee chooses not to report a benefit he may always claim that the form has been lost. This annual declaration denies him such an opportunity
That they have not **given any benefits** to any third party with whom the company does business, other than those declared on their expense statements	This also is a final cross-check on the accuracy of declarations made throughout the year

Contracts of employment should include an undertaking to report all of the usual types of conflicts of interest and significant changes to their circumstances such as:

- Arrests, summonses and appearances in court;
- Actions taken for debt or bankruptcy;
- Treatment or counselling for drugs or alcohol abuse.

Or any offer or request that he should perform improperly.

For especially vulnerable positions – such as overseas country managers – some companies require an annual detailed declaration of net worth, income expenditure, etc. Although this may seem to be overly intrusive, the requirement is effective both as a deterrent and an investigative aid if problems are suspected. An alternative is to require managers in senior positions to provide copies of their personal tax declarations.

Appraisal interviews held to support the above declarations also contribute to effective control. Experience shows that there is a vast difference between expecting an employee to volunteer information and to reveal it in response to specific questions. Many routine appraisal interviews have resulted in serious frauds being exposed.

A short file note should be prepared after each interview and placed in the employee's personnel file. If the subject has given information that justifies follow-up action, the employee should be kept informed of the results.

On a more positive front consideration should be given (see page 474) to inviting employees to write down and obtain their commitment to integrity programmes and their objectives and plans.[18] In this way the culture of contexts can be positively influenced, thereby changing the tone from below.

DISCIPLINARY PROCEDURES

Line managers in conjunction with their professional advisers should compile a list (decision matrix) of misbehaviour that will result in disciplinary action. This should be checked by lawyers specialising in employment law. Details should be incorporated in the appropriate personnel manuals and training programmes and should reduce the number of claims that are made for unfair dismissal, simply because the process is so transparent.

TERMINATION PROCEDURES

Procedures should be specified for dealing with employees whose services are being terminated and these procedures should include the points given in Table 26.10.

Table 26.10 Termination Procedures

Procedure	Comment
The employee should be interviewed by someone other than his normal line manager as part of a formal **EXIT interview** process	In addition to other matters, the employee should be asked about controls and areas he would recommend for improvement A note should be prepared, copied to the Risk and Assurance Directorate and placed in the file of the employee concerned
The employee should sign a **termination agreement** acknowledging that all company property has been returned and that he or she is not aware of any control weaknesses or policy breaches which have not been reported	Where the employee had access to sensitive information, the name of his future employer should be established. The employee should be reminded (and a note made of this fact) that he is prohibited from disclosing classified information This declaration makes it less likely that false allegations can sustained in the future
All keys, identification cards, access codes, passwords etc. allocated to the employee should be **returned or cancelled**	Personnel department should install a system for automatically notifying Central IT, etc.

In most cases, employees whose service is being terminated should not be required to work out their period of notice. Specifically employees who are dismissed should be politely escorted from the premises after collecting – under supervision – any personal effects. In some cases, it is advisable to negotiate a post-termination agreement to the

---

18   Experience shows that written commitments are more likely to be honoured.

effect that the employee has no outstanding claims against the company and is not aware of any control breaches that have not been reported.[19]

EXIT AND PRE-TRANSFER INTERVIEWS

Companies should have a specified procedure for conducting interviews (exit interviews) with employees whose services are being terminated, through retirement, resignation or on transfer to another location.

The employee's personnel file and audit reports for the area in which he or she has worked should be reviewed and any points relating to control issues noted. Interviews should be conducted as soon as it is known that an employee is leaving and by someone senior to the employee, other than his line manager. At least one hour should be allowed for each interview.

The control objectives of exit interviews are to:

- Obtain information on risks and control weaknesses;
- Leave the ex-employee with a better impression of the organisation by showing that it is interested in hearing his or her views;
- Keep communication channels open for the future;
- Minimise the risk that the ex-employee can raise false allegations in the future.

Interviews should be:

- friendly, positive and non-accusatory;
- focus on weaknesses in processes and not on personalities;
- based on seeking recommendations for control and work improvements.

Under no circumstances should the interviewer give the impression that the objective is to cause trouble for anyone but simply to identify recommendations for improvement.

It is imperative that any concerns raised by a subject are treated in confidence and checked thoroughly. If appropriate, three or four months later he or she can be contacted again to clarify points and to enquire how the new job is progressing. These follow-up calls have generally produced the most valuable information.

POST-EMPLOYMENT INTERVIEWS

Consideration should be given to introducing a process to interview ex-employees and associated persons 6 to 12 months after their leaving the organisation.

---

19   Such an agreement may make it impossible for an ex-employee to contrive a claim under the False Claims Act (see pages 23, 665 and 673).

27 *Accounting Procedures, Fidelity and Other Insurance*

Accounting Standards

This chapter is written on the assumption that most companies already have compliant accounting and reporting systems in place, but the majority of American prosecutions under the Foreign Corrupt Practices Act (FCPA) have been for failure to keep proper accounting records or to maintain effective internal controls. There have been one or two notable prosecutions in the UK for similar accounting failures under the Companies Acts.

In the corruption area it is critical that financial and other advantages, payments and receipts that could be regarded as corruptive are recorded accurately on accounts of first instance, such as expense statements, invoices, credit notes and day books. It is also important that transactions that could result in the creation of slush funds – especially in 'Accounts Payable' and 'Accounts Receivable' – are controlled, monitored and reported on an exception basis (see Chapter 19).

The opening, closing and reactivation of accounts for suppliers and customers, as well as changes to payment and other master files, should be carefully controlled, with changes reported on an exception basis. Page 662, which deals with continuous monitoring of transactions, provides more details of accounting exceptions that are symptomatic of bribe payment and receipt.

Fidelity, Directors' and Officers' Liability Insurance

INTRODUCTION AND OBJECTIVES

Fidelity Insurance policies – which potentially provide cover for incoming corruption and possibly some legal and other liabilities of outgoing corruption – are only of any real value to an insured company or other organisation (the 'Insured') if claims are paid, but seldom is settlement made without difficulty and dispute.

> ## What is a Valid Claim?
>
> A leading London underwriter stated that Lloyds has never been known to reject a valid claim, but the question is: who decides what's valid? What is valid in the eyes of an 'Insured' may be totally unjustified when viewed by insurance company. The opposite is often true. Sounds a bit like prosecutorial discretion.

It is difficult for any company that has not filed a large claim to accept that the friendly relationships it has with its insurance company and broker could turn sour. But good relationships can deteriorate, particularly when subject to raw financial pressure and an insured company or other organisation should always anticipate that a large claim will only be settled with difficulty.

THE QUESTION

The question that must inevitably arise is whether or not Fidelity Insurance is justified or even fair value for money. In many cases, the answer must be in the negative. Insurance is not a cure-all, sometimes not even a safety net, but more often a placebo. The decision to purchase fraud insurance should always be based on a clear understanding of the risks in the company concerned and the coverage afforded by the policies available.

Many people within a company **should** take an interest in fraud insurance and controls generally. Too often, senior managers do not know if they have coverage and, if they do, what it costs or what it protects them against. Auditors seldom evaluate the operations of the insurance department or the cost justification for selecting policies, appointing brokers or making claims and recoveries.

Frequently insurance is relegated to a corporate backwater, free from senior management direction or independent audit. This is a dangerous situation; insurance is important, expensive and a potential time bomb and demands high-level attention.

STANDARD FORMS AND COVERAGE

Often companies purchase policies on standard forms which they know do not cover their exposures, simply because nothing else appears to be available and on the basis that it is thought better to have something, rather than nothing at all. In internal corporate politics, the fact that a manager has purchased insurance may be defended as prudent: the fact that the claim is not paid and that premiums have been wasted may escape criticism. Having insurance appears prudent and it covers exposures of the rear end, political kind, but appearances can be deceiving.

Standard policies are often prepared by the interested insurance companies working together in committee. In the USA the Surety Association of America acts as the coordinating body; in the UK, the Bankers Blanket Bond Sub-Committee serves a similar purpose.

Insurance companies in some parts of the world use very limited standard form policies. In Asia, for example, the so-called Blanket Bond usually covers only employee infidelity and then on a very limited basis with penal methods of claims settlement. Where there is no local competition, or where Insureds are unsophisticated, cover may be limited to the minimum acceptable, while premiums are set to the maximum tolerable. Brokers are often reluctant to compete for the same business and have been known to warn clients that to shop around between insurance companies would be to their disadvantage. This is a fallacy.

RETENTION OF BROKERS

An 'Insurance Requirements' document, which can be prepared as a result of a Control Self-assessment programme (see page 392), should be submitted to one or more qualified brokers who are asked to tender for the business.

The broker should request a number of competitive quotations from various insurance companies. The coverage afforded and the reputation of the insurance companies for claims settlement, as well as their financial stability, should be carefully evaluated. The best policy is seldom the cheapest. The proposals should be carefully evaluated against the Insurance Requirements document.

Companies on the shortlist should be asked to provide details:

- Of the last three major claims they have settled;
- Of outstanding claims and the reasons why they are in dispute;
- The names of three satisfied clients.

The chances are that there will be a reluctance to provide this information; the brokers may even argue that the request is unreasonable. Companies faced with such a response have their answer and should look elsewhere. **The one thing worse than having no insurance is incurring the cost of expensive policies that never pay up.**

The appointment of the broker should be in writing and it should be made clear that it acts as an agent for the insurance company and not for the company requiring insurance. This precaution may minimise problems when a claim is made and can open up a line of recovery if the broker acts negligently.

PROPOSAL FORMS

Extreme care should be taken in completing all application or proposal forms. If any question is not clear, it should be clarified in writing and then answered in as much detail as possible. Particular attention should be paid to any material fact which the insurance company may argue over when a claim is made.

On applications for Directors' and Officers' Liability (D&O) Insurance, all directors and officers should be asked in writing to declare whether they are aware of any current problems which could give rise to a claim. Pending litigation against the company should be analysed to determine whether it is likely to be extended to include directors and officers, personally. If so, full details must be disclosed.

Each proposal should be checked by a senior director and preferably also by experienced lawyers. A complete copy should be retained, together with any correspondence and file notes of meetings.

NEGOTIATING COVER

Principles

An Insured, or a potential Insured, should always be prepared to negotiate with their insurance company for special terms and conditions, so that coverage is exactly tailored to their particular needs. Wherever possible, Fidelity, D&O and Computer Crime policies should be placed with one insurer. If different insurers are used, the dangers are that they will all fight each other when a claim is made, with none being prepared to pay up.

Insuring clauses

Insurance policies are difficult to understand fully, but generally what is given by the insuring clauses is taken away by the exclusions, warrantees and general provisions. There are scores of good reasons why an insurer can deny a claim and coverage is not what it seems.

For example, on a typical policy, see Table 27.1.

Table 27.1   Examples of Coverage and Exclusions

Examples of What Appears to be Covered	Examples of Exclusions, Counter- arguments and Reasons for Non-payment
Dishonesty by an employee	• Even though the employee caused a massive loss, he did not **intend** to do so • The loss was not **caused** by the employee's dishonesty • Management knew that the employee had been **previously dishonest** (e.g. he had told a lie about some innocuous matter), did not report it and thus from that date onwards, the employee was not insured • The employee did not **gain personally**. Even in cases of massive dishonesty, false accounting, etc., such as Barings, if all the employee gained was a £1 million bonus, that does not qualify as personal gain
Forgery	• The fraudulent wire transfer instruction came directly to the Insured's computer and was not therefore received in writing • An employee of an overseas bank sent a forged EFTS instruction; coverage of the receiving bank was denied on the grounds that the instruction was not false as to origin nor intercepted in transit

It is not possible to list all of the ways in which claims can be denied: those described above are typical. It would also be nice to know precisely what legal actions current D&O policies actually cover especially in relation to the Bribery Act.

Limits

The limit of the policy is the maximum that the insurer will pay out for one claim or for an aggregate of claims in the policy period. Most policies specify a deductible amount, which is the lower layer of the loss that will be accepted by the company. Generally, Insureds should seek to obtain the highest limits with high deductibles. It is a mistake to try to insure against small losses. It is also important to decide whether policies should be bought centrally or by individual companies in a group. As a rule, group policies are more cost-effective.

Arbitration

In some countries, such as the USA, each party to litigation bears its own costs. This may encourage spurious litigation. To overcome these dangers, the Insured should seek to incorporate a clause in all policies agreeing that all disputes will be referred to arbitration. As an alternative, special terms may be incorporated, so that in disputed cases the losing litigant will bear all of the legal costs.

Policy amendments and riders

Technically an insurance company may be in breach of contract when it arbitrarily issues any amendment ('rider') after the terms of a policy have been agreed. If the Insured passively accepts the amendment it may become binding, although the Insured always has the right to give notice of cancellation and to obtain a refund of the unexpired premium.

In practice, riders normally become effective when issued by the insurance company and it is vitally important that these are evaluated and controlled by the Insured. The Insured should seek agreement that a rider only becomes effective when it is acknowledged in writing. This provision should minimise the danger that an insurance company may produce an amendment – of which the Insured has no knowledge – to deny a claim.

Details of all applicable riders should be endorsed on the face of the policy, showing their effective dates, and should be filed securely with the policy.

PORTFOLIO SECURITY

All documents relating to each policy should be carefully assembled. If the documentation appears to be incomplete, the broker should be asked to obtain copies from the insurance company. The Insured should maintain a full set of all policy documents, proposals, riders and correspondence, all of which should be filed securely.

MAINTENANCE

The Insured should set up a system through which any changes which have to be notified to the insurance company are brought to the attention of the insurance specialist and then promptly reported in writing. It is also important to make sure that all applicable riders are endorsed on the face of the policy with their effective date. From time to time, the endorsements in force should be confirmed with the carrier.

TERMINATION AND RENEWALS

The Insured should make a careful note of the date that each policy falls due for renewal. At least three months ahead of these dates, the broker should be asked to seek competitive quotations and to consider the advisability of extending the period for discovery.

On all loss sustained policies, a full fraud or negligence audit should be considered prior to the termination date so that claims can be submitted within the policy term. Similar efforts should be made if it appears that the company might be taken over by the state or regulatory authorities. Whenever appropriate, an initial notice of a potential claim should be given to the insurance company prior to the expiry or termination of the policy or government takeover. Even though it may not be perfected, state or regulatory agencies may be able to complete the claim and in so doing mitigate any actions they might otherwise consider against the directors and officers.

No one understood how Basil was always a step ahead

'It turned out our procedures were not adequate'

PART VII

Additional Anti-bribery Controls

28 *Introduction, Principles and Policies*

The Real Problems

The main problems for honest companies is that the anti-bribery laws create uncertainty, such as:

- **Inability to compete in the overseas private** sector against local competitors and companies from countries which have no extraterritorial legislation equivalent to the UK Bribery Act 2010;[1]
- **Inability to operate in foreign markets** by following a zero tolerance policy on facilitation payments;
- **Financial losses from competitive and political corruption** (at international, national and local levels);
- **Alleged technical breaches of the Bribery Act 2010** (judged with the benefit of hindsight and prosecutorial discretion) relating to such things as hospitality, sponsorship and offset projects;
- **Bribery of its own employees** (incoming bribery) involving serious financial losses.

Although the financial and regulatory impacts of corruption are impossible to quantify accurately, **any large multinational that loses less than 10 per cent of gross turnover from incoming bribery and fraud is doing well**.[2] It should count itself especially blessed if it is able to operate, especially in foreign markets, without exposing itself to draconian regulatory threats for technical breaches of the laws.

Not Just a Legal Problem and Adequate Procedures

Dealing with corruption is not primarily a legal problem but much more a human, operational, managerial, motivational concern with obvious financial and potential regulatory consequences. Neither is it just a case of preparing a defence of adequate procedures. Fixating on compliance simply to construct a case to prove adequate procedures is akin to carrying out an autopsy on a living patient.

---

1   This means every major exporting country.

2   Authors' estimate.

Companies that merely tick boxes to comply with the Bribery Act and the Ministry of Justice Guidance (see page 92) are likely to incur substantial costs and restrictions with few commercial benefits. They will also create mistrusting or even adversarial relationships with employees and important third parties such as agents, intermediaries, customers and suppliers. Worse still, they will miss significant opportunities to increase their profitability by preventing unfair competition and incoming and internal corruption: as a result the British economy will suffer, leading to job losses, tax increases and reductions in public services.

The controls recommended in this book go well beyond mere compliance with the Bribery Act and are based on a campaign of 'inspiring integrity'.

Some of the views expressed in this book will unquestionably incur the chafe of politicians, regulators, Transparency International, the Organisation for Economic Cooperation and Development and members of the 'Cottage Industry'.[3] However, if they result in people thinking afresh rather than reacting, knee jerk fashion, to the draconian legislation and throwing UK Plc down the drain, they will have served a useful purpose.

The Height of Idiocy

A major UK bank, which had been a subject of regulatory action, took the decision to close all accounts of business and private clients in Kenya, on the grounds that the country was perceived to be unacceptably corrupt. One account, closed on one month's notice, was for a farmer – who had joint English and Kenyan nationality – who had been with the bank for more than 20 years. When he asked his relationship managers for advice on how to transfer to a different bank, they declined to answer on the grounds that it would be a 'breach of the anti-money-laundering regulations'. And the bank extols its integrity policies!

Seeking Advice from the Serious Fraud Office

In January 2011, Sir Richard Lambert, the outgoing head of the Confederation of British Industries, commented that the Bribery Act puts UK jobs and growth at risk and that its lack of clarity would hamper hard-pressed honest firms. He added 'it's just not good enough to say that this can be resolved in the courts'.

Sir Richard was absolutely right, especially given the SFO's unwillingness to follow the American example and issue 'opinion letters', supposedly because it would be inundated with requests. Perversely, the SFO has consistently urged corporates[4] to come through

---

3   Because they go against the normal flow on such things as country risks and tone from the top.

4   However, David Green, CB, QC is less keen to consult: stating that 'it is not the serious champagne office' with a sign that states 'free advice not given here'. In this, he is absolutely right. The SFO is a prosecutorial agency and not a corruption counselling service.

their open doors to discuss problems, which would seem to be far more time-consuming and burdensome than writing the occasional 'opinion letter'. What is going on?

Come Into My Parlour Said The Spider

On 13 January 2011, following an industry webcast, Mr Vivian Robertson, QC, the SFO's then General Counsel[5] was asked:

> If a company goes to the SFO to get guidance on how to comply with the Act, does that company run the risk that it will subsequently be the subject of an investigation–prosecution based on the company's potential questions regarding its risk areas?

Mr Robinson responded: 'We can't exclude that as a possibility, but the more likely approach would be to ask the company to conduct an internal enquiry[6] and then provide a report to the SFO concerning the specific matter at issue. The SFO would then decide how to proceed based on that report'. (Bruce Carton, *Compliance Week*, 20 January 2011)[7]

This response strongly suggests that any approach to the SFO for clarification should be on a double blind basis to avoid the 'come into my parlour said the spider to the fly' risk. This suggestion is discussed later.

The Rights and Obligations of Management

Companies that genuinely believe that the ambiguity and uncertainty created by the current legislation cannot be managed by self-flagellation and capitulating to the whims of regulators (with all decisions being exposed to prosecutorial discretion, possibly years after the event) will hopefully find the recommendations in this book useful. The principle is that companies have the right to manage their own affairs and this is especially so when regulators doggedly refuse to define the rules of engagement.

Not Just in Less Developed Countries

It is also important to emphasise yet again that contrary to the views of Transparency International and the OECD, corruption is as corrosive in sophisticated, developed countries as it is in those conventionally perceived as crooked. The difference, in countries such as the UK,

---

5   He has since revolved out into the private sector.

6   Note no suggestion that advice would be forthcoming.

7   'Q&A with the SFO's Vivian Robinson on the Impact of the UK Bribery Act on U.S. Companies', available at: http://www.complianceweek.com/qa-with-the-sfos-vivian-robinson-on-the-impact-of-the-uk-bribery-act-on-us-companies/article/194657/ (accessed 22 November 2012).

the USA, France, Germany, etc. is that corruption is far more subtle, frequently motivated by supposed noble causes, political skulduggery, by almost imperceptible influences, supported by questionable academic and other research – 'dodgy dossiers' – and deeply concealed. Because of this, corruption in developed countries is much more dangerous and difficult to expose, but there is no political will to deal with it.

A second point to note is that in many countries perceived to be the most corrupt, the majority of bribes are paid (not, as the OECD would have us believe, by Western companies) but by local businesses and citizens.[8] It is not simply the white man's handshake.

Additional Controls

Additional anti-corruption controls discussed in this chapter are based on making every reasonable effort to optimise profits by reducing the impact of primary and consequential costs of incoming, internal, outgoing and commercial corruption and of being the first to know. They are dominated by commercial objectives that comply with the law rather than the alternative of compliance at all costs. The balance, discussed in Chapter 1, is critical.

---

8   See, for example, the excellent Indian site http://www.ipaidabribe.com (accessed 22 November 2012).

29 *Additional Anti-corruption Strategies*

Background

There are a number of controls in addition to those discussed in Chapters 21–8 that work against incoming and outgoing corruption. These are discussed below. They have two objectives:

- To empower honest people to work effectively;
- To minimise the risks of corruption, losses through fraud and comply with regulations.

Usually the second objective dominates the first, but this is not the way it should be. Thus the controls discussed later and in Chapters 30–33 are all about maintaining inspired integrity and effective (and not just adequate) controls.

Keeping Up To Date With the Law

Someone – possibly in Legal or Compliance – should be responsible for ensuring that changes to the laws in all of the countries in which the company operates are identified and their impact considered. Similarly, responsibility should be assigned for monitoring regulatory actions (for example, from the website of Trace International,[1] anti-bribery blogs,[2] and the annual reports by the leading law firms) to note any prevailing regulatory fixation in the sectors or countries in which the company operates. The names of the companies and individuals subject to regulatory action (these will mainly be bribe payers although sometimes extorters are identified) should be checked against the company's customer, supplier and other personal databases. What action is taken[3] will depend on the circumstances, but the fact that such checks are made should be entered into the Adequate Procedures Dossier.

---

1   See http://www.traceinternational.org/ (accessed November 2012).

2   Especially the excellent FPCA Professor website (a blog on the Foreign Corrupt Practices Act, available at: http://www.fcpaprofessor.com/)

3   For example, the SFO might be asked for its opinion!

Maintaining the Adequate Procedures Dossier

A MORE THAN JUSTIFIED APPROACH

Effective controls cannot be measured by box-ticking or by the number of policies and procedures issued (see page 624), training courses held, or other false metrics: it is immediately apparent and obvious that this is so. However, because all of the uncertainties inherent in the Act may only be resolved in court, companies should ensure that they continually build up a compelling case that in the worst eventuality, they can rely on to convince a jury that allegations are unfounded or that if an offence took place it was in spite of overwhelming procedures. **An Adequate Procedures Dossier is central to this principle** (see page 723).

The idea of such a dossier may be controversial and likely to incur the disapproval of the regulators on the grounds that it creates an adversarial relationship when all they are seeking is to be helpful and engaging with 'corporates'. However, if the Serious Fraud Office (SFO)'s positioning could ever be regarded as helpful this is far from obvious, with threats of draconian punishment for esoteric breaches which they only intend to clarify with the benefit of hindsight.

The Alderman's Needle Example

A haunting memory is the example given by Mr Alderman, the SFO Director, to the effect that if a foreign hospital was about give an injection it would be unlikely to prosecute a UK citizen who paid a small bribe for a new needle – rather than an infected one – to be used. He also announced that any company that did not maintain a zero tolerance policy on facilitation payments could not claim to have adequate procedures.

CONTENTS OF THE DOSSIER AND WHEN IT SHOULD BE USED

An Adequate Procedures Dossier should archive all of a company's risk evaluation schedules, policies, procedures, details of training programmes, and any other relevant material to prove it used its best endeavours to comply with the Act and other legislation.

To An Extent Cost-Related

It will be considerably more difficult for the regulators to sustain the case that procedures were not adequate when the company can demonstrate it has invested, for example, £2 million a year on additional controls.

The main objective of the dossier, besides establishing an audit trail of good intentions, is to produce an overwhelming case that (in the worst eventuality) convinces[4] regulators – at the earliest possible stage in the process illustrated in Figure 29.1 – that prosecution for an esoteric breach of the laws is not justified or likely to succeed, and is not in the public interest.

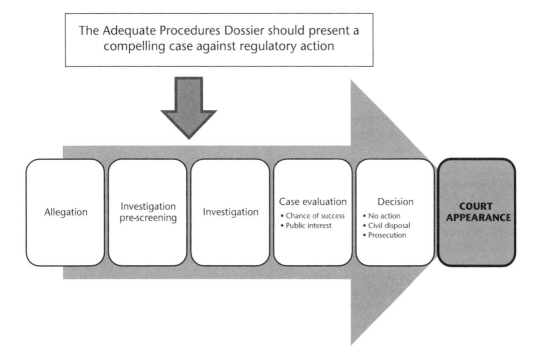

Figure 29.1 The Adequate Procedures Dossier

Waiting to make defensive or mitigation arguments until a case gets to court is far too late because reputational damage will already have been done. The Adequate Procedures Dossier should be influential before the case evaluation phase shown in Figure 29.1. The dossier should be maintained preferably by the Legal Department, ideally in an electronic and searchable database.

THE SILVER BULLETS

All the company's positive actions as well as prevarication and other unrealistic opinions of and actions by the regulators should be valued as Silver Bullets,[5] and they include those listed in Table 29.1.

---

4   Or perhaps embarrasses.

5   A Silver Bullet comes from folklore and is supposed to be the only thing that is effective in killing werewolves, witches and other monsters.

Table 29.1 More on the Adequate Procedures Dossier

Evidence of: [– including]	Possible Persuasive Effect
The company's efforts to comply, including: • Board minutes • Policies and procedures • Enforcement and operation of procedures • Results and successes • Costs of compliance • Risk evaluation schedules • Benchmarks and external reviews • Legal opinions **Publicly available publications by its legal, accounting and other advisers** • Investigation results • Disciplinary and other actions	Convincing the regulators that procedures were adequate
All relevant correspondence and Minutes of meetings with any governmental agency	Especially with British embassies in relation to FPO and competitive corruption
Refusal to compete in a market, with a third party or in a specific transaction because it was impossible to do so honestly, and relationships and transactions rejected as a result of integrity validation checking	Such decisions should be recorded in Board Minutes and, if appropriate, communicated to the regulators with a request for assistance
Permissions given by the regulators In the unlikely event that they will agree to such things as decision matrices (see page 568)	**All declined business should be meticulously recorded**
Transparent disclosures to the regulators • Business plans • Appointment of agents • Decision matrices (see page 568) • Complaints of unfair competition • Alleged corruption by third parties	Evidence showing that the regulators were wilfully unhelpful. This may have very little effect if a prosecution reaches court, but may be highly influential before that point, especially in cases given maximum exposure to other government departments and media
Disciplinary, contract termination and other action taken as a result of integrity concerns	Including those which did not result in bribery offences being proven
Integrity validation and monitoring controls resulting in a refusal to enter into business relationships or to terminate existing services	

Unhelpful responses by the regulators	Even if the regulators decline to respond to communications, the correspondence should still be filed as a Silver Bullet. In fact the less responsive the regulators, the better
• Refusal to respond • Ambiguous or uncommitted response • Unrealistic response • Threatening response • **Failure to investigate competitive bribery**	
Dramatic, emotional or inconsistent public pronouncements by the regulators (see page 722)	Especially press statements, websites and TV interviews Seminars and conferences
Publications by the company's legal advisers and accountants	See below
Benchmark Surveys	
Responses that conflict with other government policies	For example, policies and procedures announced by the Department of Business Innovation and Skills or the Ministry of Justice

Internal investigative reports backed up by extracts from the Adequate Procedures Dossier[6] should be easily available to convince the SFO and other regulatory agencies that they are:

- Unlikely to succeed with a prosecution;
- That a prosecution or civil disposal is not in in the public interest;
- Enforcement action is not in the regulator's interest nor in the interest of the UK government.

Hopefully, for most companies it will never be necessary to use the dossier, but it is an essential defence and fully justified because of the uncertainties created by the Act.

ADVICE OF COUNSEL DEFENCE

Advice of counsel defence[7] is not normally relevant for strict liability offences such as those under Section 7. Nevertheless, proof that legal advice was followed may convince the SFO at its case-screening stages that prosecution is not warranted.

Sections 1, 2 and 6 are specific intent crimes and following legal advice (for example, on what does or does not amount to improper performance) may be a valid defence in – and prior to – court, provided:

- All relevant facts were disclosed to counsel;
- There was no reason to believe that the advice was erroneous;
- The advice was followed in good faith.

---

6   If a case is to be self-disclosed it should not simply be a 'case for the prosecution' but a balanced summary including all defensive evidence and mitigation.

7   Meaning that the defendant followed the legal advice he was given. Cripes!

Using such a defence will call for careful consideration as it will usually mean that legal professional privilege (see page 804) has to be waived and this may not be the ideal course, especially if other aspects of counsel's advice were not followed.

REBUTTING THE ADEQUATE PROCEDURES DEFENCE

For a prosecution to succeed, regulators have to prove – beyond reasonable doubt – that financial or other advantages were in the offing with the intention of inducing improper performance or, in the case of foreign public officials (FPOs), 'influence'. This is much easier said than done.

To defend a Section 7 corporate offence, the company must show – on a balance of probabilities – that adequate procedures were in place and that offences took place despite these. Although the Law Commissioners were less than enthusiastic about pushing the burden of proof from the prosecution to the defence, with possible repercussions under Section 6 of the Human Rights Act, this is how the law now stands, but only to Section 7 offences.

One of the easiest ways that the prosecution can rebut an adequate procedures defence is to show that the company did not have or did not follow its own written policies or procedures, or applied them inconsistently (see page 717), or ignored red flags. This makes it imperative that:

- Policies and procedures are clearly defined and function effectively as specified with the absolute minimum of exceptions;
- Redundant procedures are withdrawn and archived so the control position at any time in the past can be reconstructed.

Policies and procedures should also be updated with changes in the law, operational conditions, organisation charts, authority levels and business objectives.

BENCHMARKED HOSPITALITY, ETC.

Regulators give the impression of having a ghoulish preoccupation with hospitality payments, and the Law Commissioner with lap-dancing clubs who commented;

Excessive Hospitality

Even in the private sector context, rare though this will be, the provision of hospitality may be of such a nature or extent that it amounts to an inducement to employees or agents or potential contractors to breach an expectation that they will act in good faith or impartially. In such circumstances the provision and acceptance of hospitality can amount to bribery.

An example might involve covert entertainment of a potential contractor's employees at a lap-dancing club, where the company providing the entertainment intends the employee to feel obliged to favour the company in case the nature of the **entertainment they received comes to the attention of their employer.**

Companies should consider commissioning independent benchmark surveys of levels of hospitality in a given market by international competitors. These should be used to validate the company's policy on corporate hospitality and retained in the Adequate Procedures Dossier. It might also be worthwhile carrying out occasional surveys involving people who have been entertained, as well as their managers, to pinpoint what, if any, influence it had on their decisions.

THE REASONABLE PERSON PANEL

The measurement of improper performance in the Bribery Act 2010 is based on a breach of good faith and impartiality, but is ultimately determined in foreign climes by a test based on what a reasonable person in the United Kingdom would expect in relation to the performance of the type of function or activity concerned, while disregarding any local custom or practice.

Companies should consider constituting a group of 12 randomly selected citizens on a Reasonable Person Panel (RPP) to review its policies, from time to time, on such things as hospitality, gifts and on incoming and outgoing decision matrices, and to retain the results in the Adequate Procedures Dossier. Obviously, the panel's opinions would not be binding on a jury but they may be influential.[8]

Accurate Recording of Advantages Given and Received

The majority of American enforcement actions for corruption has centred on violation of the accounting provisions in relation to hospitality, gifts, sponsorship and provided travel, mainly because:

* Documents of original entry such as vouchers, expense statements and Accounts Payable records were unspecific or incomplete;
* Consolidation of transactions into management reports and final accounts failed to identify the nature and extent of the expenditure;
* Payments were recorded against unapproved or mis-described budgetary headings or cost centre reports.

Recent Cases in the USA

Recent cases in the USA, where regulators have expansively interpreted the level of detail necessary to comply with the FCPA's books and records provisions, imply that for facilitation payments, vouchers of original entry should say something along the lines of:

'A facilitation payment extorted by officer number XXX, on [date] at [place] from [name of the associated person] to resolve a problem with an import entry which he had contrived and in respect of which our failure to capitulate would have involved financial losses of $5 million'.

---

8   For more details on RPPs, readers are invited to contact the authors on info@cobasco.com.

> The voucher should be entered in the General Ledger under a specific heading such as 'Facilitation Extortion by Government Agencies', not tax deducted and shown separately in the company's Profit and Loss Account. The company should also consider creating a reserve account for the notional income tax for which the corrupt officer would be liable.

When an ex-regulator was asked about the above wording he smiled and said: 'I think it should be sufficient, but don't hold me to it because there will always be exceptions'.

The UK Bribery Act contains no equivalent accounting provisions, although various Companies Acts compensate for this apparent legislative oversight. Thus companies are advised to capture data accurately on any expenditure that could be regarded as providing a personal advantage to the representative of a third party, especially if he or she works for a government agency.

Accurate Self-reporting and Internal Corruption

Increasingly companies are required – or volunteer – to make self-appraisals and reports on noble causes and such schemes as the Global Reporting Initiative, carbon inventories and footprints, not all of which have a direct financial impact. However, experience shows that there is more than a modicum of skulduggery and 'dodgy dossier'-ing with such reporting, collusion and offering of advantages to internal colleagues and external validators to collude. All of these have potential consequences under sections 1, 2 and 7 of the Bribery Act and should be identified as part of the risk evaluation process, carefully controlled and audited.

Enhanced Integrity (Anti-corruption) Training

ESSENTIAL REFRAMING

This book recommends a much more collaborative approach to controls throughout the extended enterprise. In the training field this means providing programmes for important agents and others that perform services on the company's behalf: resulting in their certification – corporately and individually – of an 'Integrity Circle'. This provides the following advantages:

- It ensures that important players in the extended enterprise are fully engaged in the integrity campaign;[9]
- It establishes multiple channels of communication (see page 655) with associated persons, making it more likely that skulduggery will be exposed and establishes relationships between the company's compliance and audit departments with their opposite numbers;

---

9   And are made aware of their legal obligations.

- Training can be viewed as part of a monitoring process.[10]

Programmes should be pitched at a high professional level and orientated to the regulatory fit of the audiences.[11] **Successful completion of each programme should be recognised with a certificate[12] for individual attendees and their employing companies.**[13]

Enhanced training should be introduced for people in positions – throughout the extended enterprise – listed in Table 29.2.[14]

Table 29.2 Suggested Enhanced Training

Category	Directing Minds[15]	Outward-facing Staff	Support Staff *Back Office*	Third Parties
Examples of Positions ➜➜	*Directors Senior Officers Country Managers Compliance Money-laundering Reporting Officers*	*Sales Traders Purchasing Manual Workers*	*Accounting IT (Managerial) Internal Audit Back Office Payments*	*Intermediaries Agents Major Suppliers Distributors Service Providers*
Overview of legislation in all relevant jurisdictions focused on outgoing, incoming, INTERNAL and competitive bribery	General Training Policies and procedures Electronic Confessional Box Integrity validation procedures Reporting of incidents			
Maintenance of the Adequate Procedures Dossier	Yes			Possibly
Public Interest Disclosure Act and protection of whistle-blowers	Yes	Yes	Yes	Yes
Anti-money-laundering controls	Yes	Possibly	Essential	Possibly
Relationships with bankers and other service providers in the AML regulated sector	Yes	No	Possibly	Possibly
Cartels and price-fixing	Essential	Yes	Yes	Yes

10   See page 736.

11   See page 586.

12   Perhaps a lapel badge, plaque or shield and no question a team photograph with Vince Cable (or another 'celeb').

13   Which hopefully will be displayed when they return to work.

14   This matrix should be adjusted to suit the organisation and contexts concerned.

15   And closely connected employees in risky overseas positions and in foreign joint ventures.

Category	Directing Minds	Outward-facing Staff	Support Staff *Back Office*	Third Parties
Contingency planning and investigations procedures	Essential	No	No	Reporting of Incidents
Handling and reporting initial suspicions of corruption	Essential	Not necessary	Yes	Yes
Relationships with FPOs	Yes	Essential	Not necessary	Yes
Decision Support processes	**Essential**	**Yes**	**Not necessary**	**Yes**
Audit of personal expense claims	Possibly	Possibly	Essential	Possibly
Detecting symptoms of corruption and fraud	Yes	Possibly	Essential	No
Continuous Monitoring Programme	Overview	Possibly	Essential	No
Reacting to requests for or offers of bribes (Verbal judo and Tongue Fu), blackmail and threats of violence	Essential	Essential	Yes	Possibly
Aligning front office, back office and control frames	Yes	Yes	Yes	Yes
Poaching of competitive skilled teams (see pages 321–2) and team defections	Yes	Yes	Yes Human Resources	Possibly

The enhanced integrity training should be much more focused than suggested by the Ministry of Justice, concentrating on vulnerable contexts with meaningful, professional and enjoyable content: expertly delivered.

Irrelevant Training

One leading company boasts that it has trained 92 per cent of its approximately 14,000 employees in anti-corruption measures, thereby ticking yet another compliance box. However, deeper analysis shows that the training lasted 45 minutes and was mainly about facilitation payments. What is the point, for example, in training 200 young call centre telephone operators, based in London, on this subject when they are never likely to come into contact with an FPO or even travel overseas: except on their annual holiday to Benidorm?

Four critical aspects of training not covered by the box-ticking approach are discussed below.

FOCUSING ON INTERNAL AND BLUE COLLAR CORRUPTION

The basic training for every employee should alert them to the fact that it is a criminal offence under the Act to give any advantage[16] to ANOTHER EMPLOYEE with the intention of inducing his or her improper performance.

Corruption and by blue collar workers (see page 260) is not usually included in training programmes but, for most companies the risks are high and can involve breaches of all sections of the Bribery Act including unlucky seven. Consideration should be given to closing this gap.

TRAINING FOR OUTWARD FACING EMPLOYEES

Corruption normally takes place in a closed, secretive one-to-one context (see pages 279 and 410) and is broached in a vague sort of way, like 'I need a drink out of this' to test the reaction and groom the counterparty. This is a critical point and the instinctive reaction will determine whether collusion takes place or not. At such points, corruption can be stopped dead in its tracks.

The Official Reaction

Transparency International and its followers recommend that the reaction should be along the following lines:

'Good God, don't you realise I'm British! Our company has a zero tolerance to bribery and under the UK Bribery Act we could both go to prison'.

If the groomer persists, he should be reported to his boss; and if that fails to law enforcement.

To describe the above as 'prudish' would be an understatement because it totally ignores the relational dynamics in the context and the objectives of an honest participant. It frames grooming as a dire problem, thus the solution is doomed to failure with the business lost and the relationship destroyed.

The Personal Frame of Grooming

Being asked to pay a bribe should be reframed as extremely good news. It tells you that the transaction concerned is 'doable'. But the attempted grooming is also an insult because, in effect, the extorter reveals that he believes you are a 'dodgy geezer' who would be willing to pay bribes. This is a bigger affront that his saying you have a big nose, smelly feet or look like Nick Clegg.

---

16   Including an amorous grope in the filing room.

So, what are the objectives for an honest person who is being asked to pay a bribe. **The first thing – with 100 per cent certainty – is not to pay unless facility extortion is unavoidable.** The solution is to use 'Verbal Judo' and 'Tongue Fu' techniques (VJTF),[17] have some fun, and:

- Successfully close the transaction;
- Build a relationship in which future business is probable, if not assured;
- Expose competitive corruption involving the same extorter and in the best possible taste, steer him onto the path of salvation and then beat the corrupt competitor to a pulp.

Even if it were possible to explain the power of VJTF techniques in writing, to do so for the ridiculously modest price of this book would be unwise (see page 760). Besides that it would give too much away to potential bribers.[18]

'Verbal Judo' and 'Tongue Fu'

As one student said: 'This is a new tool for me. I used to worry about being asked for a bribe. Now I look forward to it and the challenge of making the pests squirm and completing the transaction honestly. Once I have succeeded, his ass is mine for life'.

The first principle is not to refuse immediately or enter into a prudish dialogue but to move into a shared frame with the skuldugger and, having done that, turn him.

Avoiding Confrontation

Winston Churchill was at a banquet when he saw a VIP pocket a very expensive salt cellar just as he was about to leave. Winston knew if the theft came to light there could be a diplomatic crisis and besides that it was not in his nature to sit passively by and let crooks escape. He put another salt cellar in his own pocket, walked towards the VIP, sidled up to him and said, very confidentially: 'I think we have been spotted. We had better put them back'. The VIP complied immediately and a diplomatic scandal was averted.

Training in the suggested techniques should be considered for every outward-facing employee and is far more relevant that turgid discourses on the finer points of the Bribery Act.

---

17   These are training programmes run by the authors.

18   Details are available via info@cobasco.com.

The message to get across is that really smart people do not need to pay bribes.

The second message is on the reverse side of 'Verbal Judo' training is intended to warn outward facing colleagues that if they are offered or asked for a bribe, the groomer may be an FBI Agent or SFO sleuth out to trap him.

Oh, I Do That All the Time

Investigators, posing as headhunters,[19] approached the Senior Vice President of a company that was suspected of competing improperly with their clients. After an initial meeting in his home country, he was told he was on a short list and was invited to London to meet the 'directors'. He returned home believing the job was his. A few weeks later he was seen again and told that there was some bad news: 'You were by far the best candidate, but we have to be honest and tell you that our client sails a bit close to the wind and bribes some of its biggest customers. We got the impression you were a real straight shooter and would not be interested'.

'Hell', he replied 'I do that all of the time'. He then went on to explain in excruciating detail how and to whom he paid bribes and boasted that he would bring their business with him'.

The object of the reverse VJKF training is to get the message across – in a worrying sort of way – to potential bribe payers and receivers that:

- Bribery is stupid: as Forrest Gump's mum said 'Stupid is as stupid does'.
- **You never know whether the person you plan to bribe or suggests bribing you is an undercover cop or a journalist.**
- Even if you have known the person for years and have bribed him before, you can never be sure that he has not been 'turned' and is working for regulators to trap you.

Besides all of this anxiety raising stuff, the company itself may use covert techniques to confirm the integrity of outward facing employees.

SPECIAL TRAINING FOR COMPLIANCE, LEGAL AND AUDIT TEAMS

All members of Compliance, Legal and Internal Audit should be trained in conversation management, persuasion, interviewing and, if all this good stuff fails, in interrogation and mile forms of torture: primarily with the objective of getting them away from books and records and into the real world and chatting to humans and humanoids. There are many good courses about but unquestionably the best are those run by the authors on VJKF, cognitive and other forms of interviewing and interrogation. The only possible

---

19   And advised by a leading law firm.

drawback is that participants must take up cigarettes, cigars or better still pipes so that they can optimise their results by empathetic visits to smoking areas.[20]

Anti-Money-Laundering Controls

ADDITIONAL MEASURES

The close[21] connection between the Proceeds of Crime Act (POCA), money-laundering regulations and the Bribery Act is important and is discussed in detail on pages 187. Organisations should include money-laundering and the POCA in their bribery risk evaluations (see Chapters 14–17) and ensure that controls are effective. The Financial Services Authority and HM Revenue and Customs (both supervisory authorities for the regulated sector) have published excellent guidelines on money-laundering which establish effective baseline controls.

Companies should also consider:

- Enhanced training on anti-money laundering controls for key (especially in the back office) employees, whether or not they are in the regulated sector (see page 190 et seq);
- Continuous monitoring of payments and receipts to identify suspicious transactions[22] (see page 190 et seq);
- Their policy on submissions of Suspicious Activity Reports (SARS) and other anti-money-laundering reports;
- Whether, even if they are in the non-regulated sector, they should nominate a senior employee to coordinate all anti-money-laundering activities (i.e. a Nominated Officer).[23]

Finally, it is clearly in the interest of all honest companies that they minimise the risk that third parties[24] will regard transactions as justifying suspicious activity reporting. As explained in Chapter 8, well over 90 per cent of SARs are unnecessary and simply create problems. The best way for a company to avoid misunderstanding and misreporting is to define its own reporting procedures (see page 450) and to keep bankers and other members of the regulated sector fully informed about transactions that could be misinterpreted as red flags. This is a relationship task for the Nominated Officer and senior Treasury managers.

---

20   See pages 604, 625 and 734.

21   And dangerously time-wasting.

22   Many anti-money-laundering detection packages are available. However, most produce far too many false positives and raise unjustified suspicions.

23   This is a tricky decision that will depend on the extent of a non-regulated company's degree of contact with the regulated sector. The Ministry of Justice Guidance does not address this decision, but generally the advantages of such an appointment outweigh the disadvantages, show good intent and go beyond adequate procedures.

24   Especially those in the regulated sector.

APPLYING FOR CONSENT

The reporting procedure under Section 338 of the Serious Organised Crime Agency (SOCA) allows anyone to apply for the consent of a constable or a Customs or SOCA officer to proceed with a transaction where there is any suspicion of a money-laundering offence. Applications can be made online,[25] or faxed to 020 7238 8286, preferably using the standard form:

- SOCA must respond within seven days with permission or state its reasons for refusal.
- If a response is not made within eight days,[26] the transaction may be completed.
- If consent is refused the authorities have a further 31 days (the moratorium period) to take further action, including a restraining order. If nothing is heard within the 31 days, the transaction may be finalised.

Given that the SFO has made clear that it will not give any prior opinion comfort for potentially corrupt transactions, the SOCA consent procedure may be an alternative solution: at least in some cases.

Number of Suspicious Activity Reports

Between October 2009 and September 2010, SOCA received 14,334 applications for consent of which 1,709 (9.95 per cent) were (at least initially) refused. This suggests a false alarm rate of around 90 per cent. Detailed analysis of consent applications (as a percentage of all SARs submitted by sector) indicates that bookmakers, bureaux de change and banks were by far the most trigger-happy[27] and that solicitors and pension providers were the least likely to submit a full report.

The above figures suggest that a few large banks engage in what is referred to as 'defensive reporting' of anything that could be mildly suspicious. In their own self-interest they create problems for honest clients.

Continuous Monitoring

Companies should consider introducing automated processes for continuously monitoring transactions that could be indicative of incoming, outgoing or competitive corruption, producing brief exception reports for internal audit and ultimately senior management to follow up (Figure 29.2). Auditware Systems Limited is a company that provides software and supporting consultancy platforms services that enables transactions to be

---

25   To SOCA.

26   Allowing SOCA an additional day.

27   That is, submitting a full report rather than applying for consent.

drawn from collating and analysing data from disparate datasets.[28] ACL also sells similar software, analysed, filtered and displayed on a dashboard for further investigation.

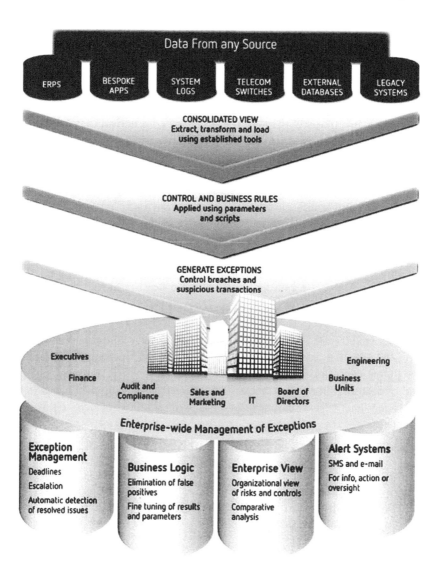

Figure 29.2 Elements of Continuous Monitoring
Figure reproduced with permission of Auditware Systems Limited.

Software can be configured to provide a prompt alert, for example, of transactions that are typical of bribe concealment,[29] the creation of slush funds in the accounts of

---

28   Available at: www.auditware.co.uk (accessed 22 November 2012).

29   For obvious reasons, these are not included in this book. Anyone who would like further details is invited to contact info@cobasco.com.

intermediaries, customers or suppliers, and deviations which are symptomatic of perverse decisions (see pages 314 and 316).

Reports and follow-ups resulting from continuous monitoring should be filed in the Adequate Procedures Dossier.

Reporting to Insurers

There is a possibility – albeit remote – that some acts of corruption[30] are covered by Fidelity or Directors' and Officers' Liability Insurance, in which case underwriters expect to be notified as soon as practicable 'on discovery of circumstances that could lead to a claim'. Any delay is likely to result in a claim being denied.

Therefore companies are advised to check with their brokers and underwriters what coverage there might be for outgoing corruption and, if applicable, agree reporting conditions and timetables as a matter of policy.

Joining Trade and Other Associations

Larger companies should consider joining anti-corruption groups such as TRACE International for three reasons:

1. Some produce very useful publications and training programmes.
2. Membership does no harm and helps demonstrate the company's commitment to compliance: it ticks another box and the DOJ and SFO both like the idea.
3. In some international markets association members may work together in Integrity Pacts or join forces to persuade developing countries to enforce their laws and eliminate facilitation payments.

A list of organisations and associations involved in anticorruption efforts can be found on the Internet.[31]

Pre-emptive Investigations and Trial Run

Companies should consider a limited pre-emptive investigation by external investigators and lawyers simulating those that could be expected if the SFO or Department of Justice were to serve a Section 2 order or subpoena. Obviously great care has to be taken to ensure that records are not destroyed or anything else done that could later result in an allegation of perverting the course of justice.

---

30   Most policies provide technical coverage of the losses resulting from incoming bribery.

31   The United Nations Campaign 'Act Against Corruption Today' provides links to regional and international organisations. Available at: at www.unodc.org/yournocounts/en/resources/index.html (accessed 22 November 2012).

Electronic Data Recovery

It is especially important to understand what problems would be revealed by a forensic analysis of the company's electronic and other archives, including traffic rejected and trapped in email filters.

Experience in other areas shows that exercises of this nature are extremely beneficial and result in improved awareness, highlight possible vulnerabilities and lead to improved controls. Details should be carefully documented and the results retained in the Adequate Procedures Dossier.

External Reporting and Reviews

Companies should consider providing short synopses of their integrity, audit compliance and other relevant programmes in annual reports, again phrased and branded positively.

Statement in Annual Reports

Transparency International recommends that companies should include a statement in their annual reports setting out details of any disciplinary or other action taken in relation to bribe payment or receipt to demonstrate their commitment to compliance and to deter future breaches. This course is not recommended.

The report by Lord Woolf into British Aerospace (BAE) recommends that companies should commission and *publish* an independent external audit on ethical business conduct and the management of reputational risk once every three years. This is generally a good idea but again calls for careful positioning and wording.

30 *More on High Risk Aspects*

Introduction

This chapter sets out additional notes on four aspects that are especially exposed to corruption:

* Competitive
* Procurement
* Entering new markets and competitive bidding
* Internal corruption.

Corruption by Competitors

COMMENTS ON RISKS

There are many ways and places in which a company can suffer from unfair or illegal behaviour by its competitors (which includes companies in the same line of business, its own employees with conflicting business interests, information brokers, organised crime, and opportunists) but the main risks of bribery[1] include:

* Shared customers, suppliers, intermediaries, politicians, research or licencing bodies and FPOs;
* Of contractors or sub-contactors;
* Of other competitive firms to bid high,[2] low or to refuse to compete;
* Cartels.

However – for most companies – the main problems involve competition in the both the private and public sectors worldwide. Transparency International publishes the Bribe Payers Index[3] which supposedly ranks the countries in which the most prolific bribe paying[4] companies are headquartered, with Russia, China, Mexico and Indonesia at the bottom. Although the Index makes interesting reading it does not align with the authors'

---

1   Involving inducements to perform or not to perform.

2   Usually referred to as 'courtesy bidding'.

3   http://bpi.transparency.org/bpi2011/in_detail/

4   But only relates to public sector bribery.

experience[5] which puts American, Canadian, French, German and Australian companies in the dog house, especially in – what for them is – the overseas private sector.

UNFAIR COMPETITION IN THE UK

Companies operating entirely in the United Kingdom should not drop their guard one notch, because corruption involving subtleties such as reciprocation, nepotism and revolving doors are the norm and if they believe that the police, the Serious Fraud Office (SFO) or other regulatory agencies have any intention of creating a level playing field they are best advised to forget it. It simply is not going to happen.

This is not to say that victims should not insist that regulatory action is taken. When nothing happens, that fact should be fully documented as a Silver Bullet and retained in the Adequate Procedures Dossier.

OPERATIONS IN THE OVERSEAS PRIVATE AND PUBLIC SECTORS

The problem with the Bribery Act 2010 really hits home in the private and public sectors of overseas markets. This not because an honest company would wish to pay bribes but merely because of the uncertainty created by the Act over such things as hospitality, gifts and sponsorship, which are traditional and essential features of developing business relationships in many cultures. Uncertainty results in risk-aversion and lack of competitiveness. It is a dark cloud hanging over the heads of honest British business people.

A further unfairness arises because companies from countries that do not have extraterritorial laws[6] can develop business – by effectively paying bribes – in the private and public sectors, usually in the knowledge that local law enforcement is non-existent.

AN OVERVIEW OF SEVEN OPTIONS

How competitive corruption can be dealt with depends on the timing that suspicions are first aroused. If they are entirely historical (that is after the chicken has already fled the coop), the chances of successful intervention are lower than if action can be taken before business has been lost. Options are also defined by the country in which skulduggery takes place, the regulatory obligations of the competitor, whether it is a private or public company, the standing of its professional advisers and external directors.

Depending on the above, honest companies have seven options:

1. To convince competitors (both local and international) to enter into integrity pacts for a specific market or project.
2. To make every effort to develop business on equal terms and hope for the best.
3. To take strategic risk-avoidance measures.
4. To ignore the Bribery Act completely and bribe a little better than their international competitors.

---

5   Or with the World Bank's.

6   And not one matches the severity of the UK Bribery Act 2010.

5. To take an assertive, intelligence-led approach to exposing crooked competitors, disrupt their business and teach them a lesson they will never forget.
6. To report the case to regulators and hope that they will take action.
7. The final option is to pull out of the market concerned and wait … and wait.

Option 1: Integrity pacts

The idea of negotiating integrity pacts was proposed by Transparency International over 20 years ago and was aimed primarily at major works being contracted in the public sector. A pact involves a binding agreement between everyone concerned to refrain from corruption, overcharging and collusion. Undertakings may be reinforced by financial bonds and personal guarantees of directors and officers.

The advantages include:[7]

- **Companies** can abstain from bribing, more or less safe in the knowledge that:
  - their competitors have provided assurances to do the same, and
  - government procurement, privatisation or licensing agencies will follow transparent procedures and undertake to prevent corruption, including extortion, by their officials;
- **Governments** can reduce the high cost and distorting impact of corruption on public procurement, privatisation or licensing in their programmes, which will lead to a more hospitable investment climate and public support;
- **Citizens** can more easily monitor public decision-making and their government's activities.

Although widespread successes have been claimed for integrity pacts, the truth is that international and local competitors – who are not bound by the UK Bribery Act and whose ethical standards to say the least are flexible – have absolutely no reason to subscribe because it surrenders all of the advantages they have.

Nevertheless it may be possible for UK companies to persuade the ultimate customer – possibly a government or international aid agency – that an integrity pact should apply to a particular project or transaction. All efforts in this direction (which may include a request for support from the British Embassy, the SFO, the Department for Business Innovation and Skills (BIS), the Ministry of Justice, etc.) should be included in the Adequate Procedures Dossier on the basis that every time officialdom declines to help, another Silver Bullet is loaded. There will be lots of Silver Bullets.

Option 2: Hope for the best

The second alternative is for companies to do their best in the markets concerned and hope they strike it lucky by meeting potential clients that do not extort bribes. This sometimes

---

7   Detailed procedures are available at: http://www.transparency.org/global_priorities/public_contracting/integrity_ pacts (accessed 22 November 2012). A specimen pact is available at Appendix C to the excellent publication 'Business Ethics. A Manual for Managing a Responsible Business Enterprise in Emerging Market Economies' US Department of Commerce on http://ita.doc.gov/goodgovernance/business_ethics/manual.asp.

happens and are known as 'islands of integrity'. The SFO has suggested it would be available to assist British companies that face unfair competition in overseas markets by putting pressure on local governments and law enforcement agencies. Whether this promise will be honoured remains to be seen, although all requests for assistance should, again, be documented as Silver Bullets in the Adequate Procedures Dossier.

Option 3: Strategic avoidance

When the integrity pact offer fails and if the market is important and depends on sensible levels of hospitality or normal marketing promotion,[8] UK companies should consider structural changes, the incorporation of distinct non-UK entities run by non-UK nationals that neither perform services nor are closely connected with the UK. The approach is no different from tax avoidance schemes; only in this case the intention is to legitimately reduce the inequalities and uncertainties created by the UK Bribery Act.

The strategy demands *international* legal advice[9] of the highest calibre and careful execution, but in most cases it will be the only option short of pulling out of some markets altogether. This is the reality, and it results entirely from the internationally unique but hare-brained philosophy of successive British governments which on one hand urge for export led growth and on the other make it impossible to achieve.

Option 4: Ignore the Bribery Act

The fifth alternative is mentioned purely for the sake of completeness and is not a recommended option.

Option 5: Detect, disrupt and make life miserable

This option is probably the most realistic solution, but it calls for more than a little chutzpa and professional intelligence- and investigative-led[10] commitment – and the confidence to enter into battle. For obvious reasons, it would not be sensible to give further details here.[11]

Option 6: Report the case to regulators

Every case of suspected corruption by a competitor should be reported – at the appropriate time – to the SFO and the local British Embassy. The correspondence, as well as any replies, should be filed in the Adequate Procedures Dossier as Silver Bullets. However, companies should expect no more than a token response.

---

8   That could be second guessed with prosecutorial indiscretion as 'bribery'.

9   From the earliest possible stages.

10 Within the law and with full legal support.

11 But see the case at pages 541 and 733.

Option 7: Withdrawing from a market

The reality is that, in most cases, the only viable option for British companies is to pull out of the export markets concerned and suffer the financial and UK employment and tax consequences. However, before a final decision is made in this direction, all of the concerned UK government departments (and especially the SFO and Ministry of Justice) should be consulted and their opinions sought. Their responses should filed as Silver Bullets in the Adequate Procedures Dossier.

BASICS IN FOR ALL OPTIONS

The first steps recommended for all of the above options are:

- When suspicions are first aroused keep them confidential, do not panic or rush into action;
- Try to establish the facts: if necessary by hiring local, professional investigators;
- Write a detailed narrative setting out; the suspicions and evidence to back them up, an investigations plan,[12] the objectives, the estimated losses, possible offences committed and jurisdictions concerned and finally an assessment of the impact that pursuing the option might have.

The narrative should identify the individuals involved in the suspected skulduggery. The investigations plan should focus on them rather than on just the organisations they represent. **The rule is to 'make it personal' and focus on individuals.**

Procurement Problems

THE SCALE OF THE SKULDUGGERY

In most companies there will be only a small number of contexts in which decisions taken could be perverted by bribery but procurement is one and typically incurs annual losses amounting to between 5 and 10 per cent of throughput.

REVIEWING PROCUREMENT STRATEGY

Companies are advised to reconsider their purchasing strategy and to carefully assess the benefits of competitive bidding. Often, it is no more than a placebo and an invitation for manipulation. The alternatives, including partnering with strategic vendors, open book accounting and other collaborative agreements, should be carefully considered.

The most careful consideration should be given to specifying the selection criteria[13] of competing vendors and products. For example, should selection be based on lowest price alone, on other attributes, on a spot cost basis, or on through-life costs?

---

12   And whether the primary target should be the competitor of the shared client or supplier

13   Especially the significance given in selection criteria to a vendor's compliance with Corporate Social Responsibility and emissions reduction programmes. These should normally be scored as low-priority wants.

Through-life Costs

For example, in deciding what type of laser printer to buy, the lowest spot cost is barely relevant. Much more important is the anticipated cost per copy through the life of the equipment, including replacement cartridges and servicing.

Also, extreme care should be taken over the issue of credit cards and company purchasing cards, which experience shows are widely misused in fraud and corruption.

VULNERABLE DECISIONS IN CONTEXTS AND PROCESSES

Corruption of purchasing agents and others who could make perverted decisions on behalf of the company to the benefit of third parties should be identified as a result of the risk evaluation discussed in Chapter 14–17. Important procurement decisions will be taken at various stages, as summarised in Table 30.1.

Table 30.1 Examples of Controls in Procurement Processes

Procurement Stage		Examples of Specific Controls
Stage	Detail	
	Purchasing strategy	Ensure that key performance metrics do not encourage dishonesty and false reporting Take care over noble cause criteria (carbon neutral, etc.)
	Budgets	Decisions to allocate budgets and control of overruns Interdepartmental charge-backs Company cross-charging
	Exceptions	Control of exceptions and specially handled transactions
8	Specified procedures and authorities	Setting authority levels, competitive quotation and formal tender levels Division of amounts below approval thresholds
10	Key performance metrics	Claims of savings, etc. by purchasing department should be independently validated
14	Selection and prequalification of vendors	Canvass the widest selection of vendors possibly through an Internet portal
15	Entry into the commercial register (vendor master file)	Ensure details of potential vendors are accurately entered Try to minimise the number of transactions processed through miscellaneous vendors
16	Vendor's response and expression of interest	Ensure responses are not suppressed

17	Entry of payment details – Standard Settlement Instructions (SSI)	Carefully control the recording of vendors' bank account details
19	Incident reporting	Encourage vendors to report through a hotline or special portal
20	Creation of a need for goods or services	Establish procedures for documenting the requirements for goods and services, including external consultancy reports ('dodgy dossiers') Setting excessively high reorder levels or stocking points
21	Initial specification	Ensure specifications are not manipulated to unfairly favour a particular vendor
22	Determination of evaluation criteria	This is a critical control, based on the Kepner-Tregoe approach on needs and wants
23	Invitation to tender	Ensure invitations are not subdivided to avoid the requirement for competitive tendering and that selection is inclusive
24	Tender receipt	Establish procedures to ensure that tenders received are held securely until the bid opening date
25	Tender opening	Establish procedures to ensure that tenders cannot be substituted after receipt
26	Technical evaluation	Ensure the technical evaluation is independent and on a graduated basis, again based on needs and wants
27	Commercial evaluation	This should take place independently after tenders have passed the technical approval
28	Award strategy and equalisation	Final evaluation should again be conducted on the Kepner-Tregoe basis, with rankings allocated for technical and commercial strengths on a through-life basis
29	Negotiation	Care should be taken to ensure that negotiations with shortlisted vendors do not effectively allow rebidding
30	Debriefing vendors	This is a critical stage: all vendors, successful and unsuccessful, should be invited to participate
31	Contract preparation	See Chapter 26
32	Contract administration	A nominated person should have ownership as contract administrator
32a	Equalisation	In some cases, to spread the supplier risks, companies will allocate the major portion of a contract to the successful bidder and smaller portions to others providing they will reduce their costs or make other amendments to their conditions. This is a very dangerous stage and allocations can be fraudulently manipulated outside the normal procurement controls
33	Goods inwards receipt	These are critical stages when even the best procurement processes can be defeated, often by low-level collusion. Control over goods received and internal distribution is vital
34	Inventory management	
35	Internal distribution	
36	Returns of defective goods	

Procurement Stage		Examples of Specific Controls
Stage	Detail	
37	Low-value miscellaneous purchase orders and miscellaneous purchases	These are normally exceptions to standard systems and should be carefully controlled
39	Invoice receipt	These accounts payable processing stages are exposed to fraudulent manipulation and should be carefully controlled
40	Invoice validation	
41	Processing of credit notes	
42	Payment authorisation	
44	Payment processing	Special care should be taken over amendments to the bank accounts recorded for vendors and payment processes, especially by EFTS and manually prepared cheques
45	Funds management	
46	Bank payment instructions	
48	Payment variations	Temporary alteration to payment parameters: accounts, currencies, etc.
49	Changes to specifications	Changes to specifications are a conventional way of bypassing competitive bidding procedures. They should be fully justified and carefully controlled and recorded

There are normally four main contexts in which corrupt procurement decisions may be taken:

1. **At board level**: for example, determining procurement strategies and the value over which competitive tenders will be sought.
2. In **end user departments**: needs are created, initial specifications drawn, technical evaluations prepared, goods received, internal distributions quality-controlled, and refunds managed.
3. **Central purchasing**: potential vendors are solicited, screened and appointed.
4. **Finance and accounting:** payments are processed and funds managed.

Controls should focus on decisions taken within these contexts using the most flexible and cost-effective options discussed in Chapter 21–32. In addition procurement processes should be continuously monitored (see page 735) to detect deviations and transactions that are symptomatic of fraud or corruption.

SOME ADDITIONAL IDEAS

There are some characteristics of procurement fraud which should be additionally considered. The first is that the base of vendors may be artificially restricted so that those who pay bribes are not faced with effective competition. A possible solution is for the company to open an Internet portal inviting potential vendors to express their interest against a list of the goods and services typically procured and the price ranges.

Also a more detailed Intranet – secured for employees only – should be considered, capable of listing payments by supplier and postcode, as well as detailed pricing information on products and services.[14]

Problems of the Private Finance Initiative

It has been reported that under the Private Finance Initiative (PFI) some hospitals are paying £350 for a single light bulb to be fitted in a standard socket. The threat that such ridiculous expenditure will be exposed to everyone working in the company is a possible deterrent.

Obviously the benefits of transparency and inviting monitoring by employees has to be balanced against confidentiality.

SUPPLIER AND EX-SUPPLIER AUDITS

Consideration should be given to surprise quality control or other vendor audits, whether or not agreed in contracts or terms and conditions of business. Also, occasional surveys involving ex-vendors can be used to test an organisation's integrity programme and uncover problems.[15]

OUTGOING BRIBERY RELATED TO PROCUREMENT

Procurement also involves bribes being paid to influence external decisions.[16] For example, bribing a supplier for lower prices, allocation of scarce products, etc. These should be risk-evaluated (see Chapter 14–17) and effective controls and training put in place.

Entering New Markets

DRIVEN BY ENTHUSIASM

A new market may be chosen, for example, in terms of geographical region, through a new product line or method of distribution, through acquisitions, joint ventures or agency arrangements. Such activities are usually driven by top-level enthusiasm, are under time pressures and supposedly against competitors (real or imagined) who are anxious to step into the opportunity. It should be noted that these pressures – which are often contrived – are a classic symptoms of commercial scams.

---

14   The Brazilian Government runs such a scheme, which is also open to members of the public. It is said to have resulted in substantial savings.

15   Experience shows that such surveys and visits are highly effective in uncovering fraud and corruption.

16   Outgoing bribery.

Because of such cases, companies should take great care in deciding whether or not to enter a new market. Risks should be accurately evaluated and impacts assessed. Integrity validation and final approval should be taken by individuals other than those in the department, or managers driving the investment.

Dangers of Regime Changes

One of the biggest dangers for dishonest companies investing and corrupting in foreign countries is the possibility of a regime change. What might appear to be a safe, corrupt relationship with even the most established leaders can quickly turn catastrophic – as the Oil for Food programme demonstrates.

INDEPENDENT MARKETING ANALYSIS

Companies that are active in markets where international competitors (not bound by the Act) are believed to pay bribes or entertain excessively should consider commissioning a report by local or regional expert marketing consultants, preferably with good connections to government and law enforcement.[17] The results should be discussed with embassy and government representatives and, if appropriate, with the SFO and the Department of Justice (subject to the conditions discussed on pages 457). The results should be used to set the company's marketing strategy and then retained in the Adequate Procedures Dossier.

BIDDING FOR IMPORTANT CONTRACTS

Companies should carefully consider the justification for competitively bidding for new business, especially in overseas markets and against competitors who are not bound by laws equivalent to the UK Bribery Act.

The main risks (besides the normal political, trade and credit risk) include:

* Wasting time on hopeless cases and becoming cannon fodder[18] for rigged bids;
* Winning loss-making business;
* Advance fee and information-brokering frauds;
* Winning and then being accused of corruption;
* False allegations of corruption.

Every effort should be made – before time is wasted – to ensure that the invitation to tender is genuine; that the list of potential vendors is such that there is a chance of

---

17   After appropriate due diligence etc., etc.

18   This applies to cases in which a corrupt representative of a procuring third party invites tenders from companies that cannot compete with his favoured supplier. They are invited to quote to make up the numbers.

success; and that the selection criteria are not weighted in favour of noble causes that are impossible to prove quantitatively.[19]

If the chances are reasonable, the company should consider the possibilities of:

- Agreeing an integrity pact with all the parties involved;
- Insisting that details of all vendors being solicited are made available, together with detailed specifications and evaluation criteria;
- Requesting a detailed briefing at a pre-bid conference involving all of the potential vendors;
- Prohibiting the use of information brokers and offset projects;
- Applying the highest levels of security to the preparation of the bid, possibly to the point of developing a number of alternatives and alternative pricing, with a final decision on which to submit being taken at the last minute;
- Supplying details of its hospitality and integrity programmes to the customer and competitors;
- Disclosing the details of agents, if any are being used;
- Closely monitoring for unfair competitive activity.

In addition, the company should consider trying to persuade the customer to require performance bonds from all bidders and personal guarantees from the directors that might trigger their engagement in unfair practices.

Internal Corruption

Internal corruption is the forgotten orphan in the Bribery Act and Ministry of Justice Guidance (see pages 7 and 260) but as discussed on pages 275 it is very common in both private sector and governmental organisations and can lead to serious losses and regulatory penalties. The essence of internal corruption is that one employee bribes a colleague to make or condone a perverted decision; it does not matter whether the beneficiary is internal or a third party.

All of the controls discussed in this chapter concerning incoming and outgoing corruption are relevant, and possibly the only additional measure that is necessary is to include internal corruption in policy documents, staff handbooks, training programmes and to feature it in annual declarations and appraisals.

---

19   Especially contracts with the European Union, where evaluation criteria attach undue importance to noble causes.

31 *Facilitation Payments, Gifts and Third-party Agents*

Facilitation Payments

BACKGROUND

Just for the avoidance of doubt, as lawyers would say, facilitation payments are small (and sometimes not so small), ad hoc (and not always so ad hoc) payments of other advantages (usually, but not necessarily, made to foreign public officials (FPOs)) to encourage or reward them to perform their duties as required or, more often, to remove artificial barriers they have deliberately contrived to extort bribes.

Although the definition of an FPO is clear (Bribery Act 2010 Section 6 (5) and (6)), the Serious Fraud Office (SFO) is likely to widen the interpretation to include organisations with even the smallest governmental involvement.[1]

Instrumentalities of Government and State-owned Enterprises

The US regulators have argued that the following made companies into instrumentalities[2] (in the sense of 'subsidiary branches') of governments whose employees might therefore be classed as FPOs, where:

- Some board appointments were made by governments;
- Companies acted for the government;
- Government officials sat on board or senior management meetings;
- Oversight was by government agencies;
- Government approved major company expenditure or operational decisions;
- Government had shareholdings.

These interpretations go far beyond the original intentions of the Foreign Corrupt Practices Act (FCPA), but none has been tested in court.

---

1   As is the case with the Securities and Exchange Commission (SEC) and the Department of Justice in the USA.

2   A semi-official term in connection with the FCPA meaning an entity that is controlled by a government and some or all of its employees are classified as Foreign Public Officials. For example it could be argued that many British banks are instrumentalities of the UK government.

Under Section 6 of the Bribery Act the prosecution must prove that the intent of the advantage was merely to influence the FPO to obtain or retain business or an advantage in the conduct of business. Although the Ministry of Justice Guidance[3] makes it clear that this section of the Act relates only to public procurement, it is likely that the UK regulators will copy their American counterparts and expansively interpret the law.

The first thing to realise is that facilitation payments are not white collar or minor crimes. As discussed on page 756, they are often associated with high-level political corruption and organised crime to the extent that if an FPO (in a 'wet job'; i.e. working in a position where he or she comes face to face with someone from whom he can extort bribes) fails to collect at the rate demanded by their superiors and colleagues they may be injured or killed.

Company employees and agents are also in danger if they object too strongly to extorsive demands from FPOs (see page 345). The responsibility for resisting extortion should not be informally delegated to a junior employee at the point of contact and under a zero tolerance policy which is not intended. This is immoral if not wicked. The second point is that refusing to concede to FPO extortion is not going to make the slightest difference to grand corruption. It is worth noting that since 2002, when the Anti-terrorism Crime and Security Act 2002 (ATSCA) criminalised facilitation payments, there has not been a single prosecution in the UK.[4] Not only that in none of the actions taken against companies is there ever any mention of the corrupt FPOs being prosecuted or even named and shamed. The chances are that they remained in their jobs and free to make demands from new victims.

MIXED SIGNALS

International laws on facilitation payments are confused. They are permitted, under the Foreign Corrupt Practices Act, by Canada, New Zealand, Australia and the laws of most signatories to the Organisation of Economic Cooperation and Development (OECD) Convention on Combating Bribery[5] of Foreign Public Officials in International Business Transactions and are permitted, tolerated or not enforced by most Less Developed Countries.

The UK Civil Service Code

British civil servants are bound by the Civil Service Code,[6] which was presented to Parliament pursuant to Section 5 (5) of the Constitutional Reform and Government Act 2010.

Civil servants must not (among other things):

---

3   There are two sets of Guidance: the main publication ('Bribery Act 2010: Guidance about commercial organisations preventing bribery') and a Quick Start Guide for small companies. Both available at: http://www.justice.gov.uk/legislation/bribery (accessed 7 November 2012). See discussion and analysis of the Ministry of Justice Guidance on page 92.

4   Although the Bribery Act 2010 makes prosecution much easier and its scope more extensive.

5   Not on combating corruption.

6   Issued in November 2010.

- Misuse their official position, for example by using information to further a private interest or those of others;
- Accept gifts or hospitality or receive other benefits from anyone which might reasonably be seen to compromise their personal judgement or integrity.

Thus British civil servants are permitted to accept gifts and hospitality and other benefits which may influence them – providing they do not compromise their integrity[7] – whereas the Bribery Act applies the much lower standard of influence to foreigners.

LIMITED OPTIONS

UK companies have only limited ways in which they can react to demands for facilitation payments. These are summarised in Table 31.1.

Table 31.1   Options for Facilitation Payments

Policy on Facilitation Payments	Intended in Practice	Comments
Zero tolerance *No exceptions*	Zero tolerance: • No payments under any conditions anywhere in the world	Fully compliant with the most draconian interpretation of the Act, but in many countries the business will fail or have to withdraw This will have an adverse effect in the UK and on the welfare of foreign employees The vacuum will be filled by Chinese, Korean, Russian, Australian, New Zealand, Canadian, American and nationals of other countries Withdrawal will not make the slightest difference to gross corruption, nor will it reform corrupt FPOs
Zero tolerance *As per Lord Woolf and British Aerospace (BAE)*	• Payments will be made when there is no alternative, although in the longer term efforts will be made to eliminate them	Will probably incur the displeasure of the SFO and may lead to prosecution if more than an isolated incident is exposed. It puts an unacceptable burden on employees based in the country concerned **More importantly, it is simply not ethical**
Zero tolerance *Never intended*	• Ignore the policy and pay whenever and wherever payment is needed	This will unquestionably incur the wrath of the SFO and if discovered probably lead to prosecution

---

7   Tantamount to improper performance.

Policy on Facilitation Payments	Intended in Practice	Comments
Honest policy	• Every effort will be made at a governmental and official level to eliminate extortion by FPOs • Every effort will be made to plan operations to avoid exposure to extortion demands • Payment will never be volunteered • Payment will only be conceded where there is a significant and quantifiable business impact • Receipts will always be issued and recorded fully in the company's accounts • Reports will be made to senior management summarising every facilitation payment, to whom it was made and why it was necessary	Unlikely to win SFO's Company of the Year Award but it is the most honest and pragmatic solution to a long-term problem It takes the burden off junior employees most often exposed to extortive demands It is transparent and realistic
No policy	Do nothing except pay when necessary	
Any of the above	• Employees claim to have made facilitation payments but keep them for themselves	A very common problem that can be dealt with by the type of controls discussed in Chapter 21–27

The Bribery Act, Ministry of Justice Guidance and SFO advice to prosecutors have created a confused situation where companies are damned if they do and damned if they don't.

However, Richard Alderman, in his latter days as Director of the SFO, was far more helpful. He stated:[8]

---

8 'Managing corruption risk in the real world', speech to Salans, 7 April 2011. Available at: http://www.sfo.gov.uk/about-us/our-views/director's-speeches/speeches-2011/salans---bribery-act-2010.aspx (accessed 22 November 2012). For a summary of the SFO's guidance on facilitation payments, see http://www.thebriberyact.com/facilitation-payments/ (accessed 22 November 2012).

Leading to the Six Step Nuanced Approach

'I do not expect facilitation payments to end the moment the Bribery Act comes into force. What I do expect though is for corporates who do not yet have a zero tolerance approach to these payments, to commit themselves to such an approach and to work on how to eliminate these payments over a period of time.

'I have also said that these corporates **should come and talk to the SFO** about these issues so that we **can understand that their commitment is real**. This also gives the corporate the opportunity to talk to us about the problems that they face in carrying on business in the areas in which they trade. It is important for us to know this in order to discuss with the corporate what is a sensible process'.[9] (Emphasis added)

In continuation he suggested a six-step (nuanced) approach:[10]

When considering the activities of a company which continues to make small facilitation payments after 1 July 2011, the SFO will be looking to see:

1. *whether the company has a clear issued policy regarding such payments,*
2. *whether written guidance is available to relevant employees as to the procedure they should follow when asked to make such payments,*
3. *whether such procedures are being followed by employees,*
4. *if there is evidence that all such payments are being recorded by the company,*
5. *if there is evidence that proper action (collective or otherwise) is being taken to inform the appropriate authorities in the countries concerned that such payments are being demanded,*
6. *whether the company is taking what practical steps it can to curtail the making of such payments.*

If the answers to these questions are satisfactory then the corporate should be shielded from **prosecution**. *(Emphasis added)*[11]

These comments and suggestions were helpful but did not guarantee that compliance with them would avoid a whacking civil disposal. Thus companies should consider going a few steps further to ensure that they are not only shielded from prosecution but also from other regulatory action. All steps taken should be recorded in the Adequate Procedures Dossier. **It should be noted that David Green, CB, QC who replaced Mr Alderman as SFO Director seems to have changed the rules (see pages 67, 69–70, 80 and 140) and it is therefore possible that the six steps have nuanced down the drain.** However, even if this is so, it does not alter the suggestions that follow.

---

9   This sounds like an invitation that could be politely declined.

10   To Pinsent Masons, a UK solicitor. Available at: http://thebriberyact.com/2011/06/09/exclusive-facilitation-payments-after-july-1st-a-six-step-solution/ (accessed 22 November 2012).

11   But not from being punished through a civil disposal.

THE RECOMMENDED APPROACH

Quantifying the problem

Companies are advised to examine all the countries and circumstances in which historically, facilitation payments have been and are currently being extorted. This research should involve a full and frank exchange with agents and intermediaries and ideally should be conducted in collaboration with UK competitors operating in the markets concerned.

The research should be summarised for each FPO department within each country along the lines shown in Table 31.2.

Table 31.2 Catalogue of Facilitation Payments Example of Bentrovia

Country	Response
Country	Bentrovia
Research conducted for years	2005–2009
The agency from which payments were demanded	Customs
Ministry responsible	Revenue and Customs
The position of the FPO making demands	(1) Junior officer (2) Supervisor (3) Collector
The circumstances in which the demand was made	Face to face when agents present Customs Entries
The supposed reason for making the demand	Import documentation supposedly not completed properly. However in all cases the problems were artificial and exaggerated
The amount of the demand	Normally around $100 per shipment normally around $500 per shipment normally around $1,000 per shipment
What decisions did the payment influence?	Motivated the Customs officer to do the job he was supposed to do. Did not involve discretion. The problems with documentation were contrived
Were any competitors disadvantaged by the payment?	It is difficult to see how the SFO's concerns on this point are relevant (see below)
What action is taken by international competitors who are not bound by the Bribery Act?	Benchmark solutions and performance by American, Australian, Canadian and New Zealand companies operating in the market

The consequences of not conceding to the demand	Typically adverse decisions involve the delay of cargo discharge with a value in excess of $6 million a time. Delays can involve serious breaches of contractual terms with customers, demurrage and port charges of $30,000 a day, chartering penalties of up to $200,000 a day and in the case of perishable cargos a loss of $6 million plus after a delay of seven or more days
	Agent resisted payment and later that day his house was robbed, his wife and daughter raped
	Closing down operation in Bentrovia. Loss of 100 local jobs and 40 in the UK Business vacuum will be filled by Zen Wa Industries and other Chinese and Korean competitors
Possible avoidance measures	Hold additional stocks Include force majeure terms in commercial contracts
Extortive Payment v At risk	Approximately $2,000 to avoid loss of $8 million
Extortive Total v At risk	$300,000 per annum v $200 million
Percentage on value	0.15%
The way in which payments were recorded	By agents as a line addition to invoices
The total amount of facilitation payments made per annum	$300,000
Alternative solutions possible?	None Reported to the Minister Finance with no action Reported to the British Embassy in Trade Commission with no action Discussed with local Member of Parliament with no action Five letters to the Department of Trade and Industry with no action

The research should also include a summary of the applicable local civil[12] and criminal laws on corruption, the enforcement standards, the key performance drivers and metrics[13] of each government department involved and its management structure.

The Official View

Politicians and regulators claim that when a company is known not to submit, demands for facilitation payments stop. **However, the authors' experience is in entirely the opposite direction and when one of their clients followed the official line they were victimised**: not only by the department concerned but by a number of other agencies. One employee was threatened that if his employer 'does not lighten up, some of your colleagues coming through the airport might find a few ounces of cocaine in their bags'.

---

12   There might be some chance under civil laws, but companies should not hold their breath.

13   For example, some customs departments have a target to clear importations within 48 hours of arrival.

Top-level meetings

Companies should meet and correspond with the British Embassies in the countries concerned, the Department for Business Innovation and Skills (BIS) and any other UK government agency that might be prepared to listen and ask for their solutions.

Meetings with the overseas governments

Experience shows that complaints to overseas government ministries and politicians about their corrupt FPOs are invariably unproductive. Promises may be made but nothing happens and extortion continues as before. In fact complaints may make problem much worse.

An alternative, suggested in pages 391–6, is to adopt a completely different frame for approaching the ultimate political and other supervisors of corrupt FPOs. It is based on a collaborative risk assessment, seeking official advice and support in developing the company's own procedures. This non-critical, non-accusatory frame may produce results, although again the chances of success are fairly low.

Staff training to avoid problems

Employees who come face to face with FPOs should be given special briefings on 'Verbal Judo' and also trained to:

- Try to avoid situations where they meet FPOs on a one-to-one basis;
- Avoid exposing junior employees to risky situations;
- Always give the impression that they expect honest performance; that is, forget any perceptions that corruption is inevitable;
- Deal on a friendly but entirely professional basis;
- Watch for signs of 'grooming' and pretend not to have heard or steer the dialogue away to the weather or, better still, Nick Clegg.

Finally, it is imperative that the documentation (such as applications for licences or Custom Entries) submitted to an FPO is 100 per cent accurate, making it very difficult for the official to raise objections or contrive a problem.

Other out-of-the-box solutions

A number of solutions have been suggested:

- Paying the extortion fee with pseudo hundred dollar bills bearing the words 'this $100 was paid to an FPO as a bribe and is not worth the paper it is written on'.[14]

---

14   These notes should be issued only by employees who can run very fast and who have good life cover.

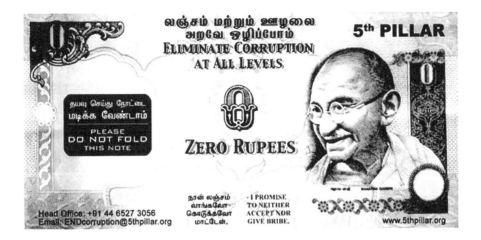

Figure 31.1 Zero Rupee Note. India's 5th Pillar has provided 1.3 million notes since 2007

- Paying, and demanding an official receipt;
- Agreeing with the appropriate ministry that no individual facilitation payments will be made, but an equivalent contribution will be donated to the departmental pension fund for widows and orphans or to a local children's home.

A final alternative, which may just work without exposing junior employees to retaliation, is to issue employees who have to face corrupt FPOs with a pre-printed receipt book, each one with four copies in the local language, marked:

- Copy 1:Copy for the Official
- Copy 2: Company's Copy
- Copy 3: Ministry Copy
- Copy 4: Press File.

The layout – which should be very official-looking – might be along the lines of Figure 31.2.

Far From a Joke

It is worth repeating that facilitation payments are often the tip of an organised crime iceberg, meaning that resistance can be dangerous. 'Zero tolerance' policies that are not intended (see page 618) or cannot be maintained, put a burden on junior staff at the point of contact with FPOs. This is one of the most unethical and improper outcomes of box ticking compliance.

PLEASE READ CAREFULLY – COPY FOR THE OFFICIAL

Under the UK Bribery Act, and (local laws) it is a criminal offence, imprisonable in the UK, for the bearer of this receipt to provide any advantage to a foreign public official with the intent to influence him or her in the performance of his duties.

The foreign public official may be extradited to the UK and also be imprisoned there.

Receipt for Payment
YOU ARE A FOREIGN PUBLIC OFFICIAL

Date, place and time	
Name of Official and Badge Number	
Department	
Nature of Problem	
Reason for Payment	
Amount of Payment	
Method of payment	
Decision Required	
Signed by official	**FINGERPRINT HERE**
Signed by company representative	

Figure 31.2 Possible Receipt with the Fingerprint of a Foreign Public Official

If an FPO demands a bribe, the employee's response (under the 'Verbal Judo' – 'Tongue Fu' approach[15]) might be super-cooperative and very friendly:

Employee: Yes of course. Absolutely right. How much?
FPO: Er, how about $100?
Employee: Are you sure that is enough?
FPO: Ok. Make it $200.
Employee: Fine, **WE** WILL just make out the receipt (Now a shared problem and not accusatory).
FPO: What receipt?
Employee: We have a policy. Must get a receipt. Don't worry I will fill it out (Produces receipt book with a flourish).
FPO: I don't want a receipt. No. No receipt.
Employee: Must do. What is your name? (Starts writing the receipt … very willingly. FPO suspects the employee is working some sort of scam).

It is not possible to say what the outcome might be,[16] but it might just work.

---

15   Training programmes run by the authors.

16   Never been tried.

Annual summaries

An annual summary of all facilitation payments and efforts made to eradicate them – by country and department – should be reviewed by the board of directors and, if appropriate, discussed with the British embassies involved with the objective of applying further pressure to government ministers in the countries concerned. Ideally, the summaries will show progress!

Possible policy wording on facilitation payments

Some of the above suggestions admittedly border on flippant, but it is difficult to take the government's foolishness too seriously when so much is at stake for British exports, jobs, taxes and social programmes.

A possible policy wording (in the Integrity Policy) is as follows:

Facilitation payments are relatively small benefits given – usually in cash – to foreign public officials to encourage them to do the jobs they are supposed to do anyway. Such payments are condoned by the governments for which the officials work, which knowingly pay less than survival wages on the unwritten understanding that the deficiency will be made up through extortion. The practice is well known to the British Government, the OECD and other regulatory agencies. If extortive demands are not conceded, the consequences for the companies and individuals concerned can be very serious.

The OECD Convention on Combatting Bribery of Foreign Public Officials in International Business Transactions does not prohibit facilitation payments but urges companies to try to eliminate them over time. It also recognises that support is required from all governments, especially those in which the FPOs work.

Company A's position is clear and over time it will make every reasonable effort – providing support is forthcoming from its international partners, competitors, politicians, the UN, the OECD and governments – to eliminate facilitation payments entirely.

This policy will be reviewed in 24 months.

A has a zero tolerance policy towards corruption under which employees and associated persons are prohibited from offering any financial or other advantage to foreign public officials or to others acting on their behalf which could reasonably be seen to influence the performance of their official functions.

However, if a financial or other advantage is demanded by a foreign public official or by anyone acting on his or her behalf, it may be given subject to the following conditions:

- *The demand relates to a routine matter that the official is required to perform;*
- *Payment does not induce the FPO to perform an official function improperly;*
- *Not submitting to the demand could result in serious financial or other consequences for the company, its employees and associated persons;*
- *The payment is accurately recorded.*

*A detailed record of the advantage demanded (whether or not it was given) must be made and entered accurately **into a separate account in the Nominal Ledger** as a non-tax deductible expense. The policy should be brought to the attention of all employees and associated persons who come into contact with FPOs and to the company's accounting teams.*

The above policy accords with both the SFO's Six Step Approach,[17] the recommendations made by Lord Woolf – the ex-Chief Justice of England and Wales in his report for BAE – the Organisation for Economic Cooperation and Development (OECD) and Transparency International (TI) and, although there is no guarantee that a civil disposal will not be suggested, it should avoid jail.

HOSPITALITY, GIFTS, CHARITABLE PAYMENTS, ETC.

Background

Regulators worldwide have obsessed over the question of corporate hospitality which, from a regulatory frame, may be considered corrupt. From a commercial perspective hospitality may be essential to promote a company's products and services and to build relationships, but the SFO's posturing makes UK companies uncertain, risk-averse and therefore uncompetitive. The good news is that for the SFO's view to prevail it must prove beyond reasonable doubt an intention – for private sector operations – to induce improper performance. In practice this will be almost impossible if the decision-centric approach recommended in this book is followed (see page 568).

Regulators are neither qualified nor empowered to dictate to commercial managers what level of hospitality – based on a financial limit, choice or nature of the venue – is acceptable in a given context. What is reasonable and effective hospitality can only be decided by commercial managers based on what competitors, who are not bound by the peculiarities of UK Bribery Act, do in the markets concerned.

Focus on Trivia

It is clearly ridiculous, for example, to expect British companies to compete against Chinese businesses, which routinely put on expensive events for business contacts, when all they are allowed to do is give away mouse mats at Christmas.

When the Law Commission reviewed the Bribery Bill, the wording then in place required the advantage, whether hospitality or something else, to be the *primary* reason for inducing improper performance. The word 'primary' was dropped by government lawyers, who apparently intended that lunch involving a £200 bottle of Chateau Neuf would invariably be corrupt.

---

17   Which may be a dead duck. See pages 67, 70 and 80.

Fortunately, it will be left to a jury to decide whether the hospitality was intended to induce improper performance or to influence an FPO. The amount involved is not determinative, despite regulatory inference. It is one case where size should not matter.

Consistent policies

Some companies make it difficult for themselves by having totally different standards for hospitality that can be received by their own employees and the benefits it gives to others.

> ### Consistent Standards
>
> As one manager said, 'if we let our salesmen use the techniques they do with customers to entertain our purchasing department, all hell would break out. We have one standard for salesmen and a completely different one for buyers'.

Policies on gifts and entertaining given and received should be consistent for two reasons. The first is that this is the inevitable outcome when ethics are driven on principle. The second is to demonstrate (if ever the contrary is alleged) that hospitality was not influential in obtaining a business advantage.

Good and bad hospitality

As usual the SFO reserves its right to exercise prosecutorial discretion over what might or might not be excessive hospitality, but common sense suggests it cannot be based simply on cost. The list of points below set out a 'best-guess' matrix of what might demonstrate honest intention:

- Included in a marketing strategy, approved by the directors with the objective of establishing or building relationships with third parties or to promote the company's products or services;
- Conforms with the company's hospitality policy for its own employees (i.e. reciprocity or equivalence);
- Transparent and openly disclosed to potential recipients and third parties;
- Costs (which may be high) are comparable to competitive hospitality or the significance of the event;
- Not directly associated with a specific business decision.

If a company genuinely believes it is beneficial for building a long-term relationship to take potential customers to the Pink Pussycat Lap Dancing Club then it should do so, providing the intention is not to induce improper performance.[18] Regulators are free to infer whatever they want: they do not determine society's moral conscience. However, great care must be exercised in entertaining FPOs.

Benchmarking and reasonable persons test

Companies whose business in overseas markets is significant should consider commissioning an independent survey of the levels[19] of hospitality by international competitors, thereby establishing a baseline for the Adequate Procedures Dossier.

Mr Blair's Gifts

When Anthony Charles Lynton Blair left Downing Street he took many of the gifts he had been given as Prime Minister with him, including a £100,000 guitar from Bono, another expensive instrument from Bryan Adams, and another from Fender, the US manufacturer,[20] nine watches from Mr Berlusconi, earthen pots from an ancient site in Israel, an ornamental jewel-encrusted dagger,[21] necklaces, bracelets and a lot of other stuff. It's no wonder he had a bad back transporting all of that stuff on easyJet.

This by no means alleges that Mr Blair's gifts were improper but only emphasises that what is proportionate depends, in part, on the status of the recipient.

Promotional plans, budgets and cost centre reporting

Detailed budgets should be prepared at the Extended Enterprise level down to individual departments and contexts for all hospitality-related expenditure, gifts, charitable donations and free samples and sponsorship. The purpose of each expenditure should be evaluated and recorded, together with impact assessments in terms of benefits and potentially adverse consequences. The plan should be approved by the directors with expenditure subject to continuous monitoring and cost benefit analysis.

Policy on hospitality

Whatever policy document is issued it should be generally available as part of the company's integrity programme, branded and positive. For example:

---

18   Excluding Flossie Flowfinger ... who can perform improperly.

19   Including the nature and frequency.

20   If he had all of these guitars and sang to them it is no wonder that his neighbours in No. 11 did not like him.

21   Used once on the occupant of No. 11.

More Than Just Working Together

We are committed to maintaining enjoyable and rewarding relationships with suppliers, customers, agents and third parties and to support charities and other worthy causes. We encourage employees and third parties to enjoy working with us and to build long-term, mutually beneficial relationships.

We take pride in delivering outstanding quality products and services and treating everyone with understanding and respect.

To support this spirit we allocate a substantial annual budget for hospitality, special events, entertaining, gifts, sponsorship and charities.

This year we will be sending out invitations for business associates to join us at:

- The Open Golf Championship
- Wimbledon
- Twickenham
- Dinner with David Beckham and Posh Spice
- A gala night at the Pink Pussycat Lap Dancing Club with a special performance by Flossie Flowfinger.

Our hospitality is offered without obligation. We don't expect any favours from anyone in return: just a closer understanding of what we do and how well we do it. In the unlikely event that your policies prohibit such cooperation please let us know.

We also encourage our employees to enjoy social and business hospitality sponsored by others. We trust our employees and know they will take business decisions impartially and in our best interests.

The bottom line is that deciding what is reasonable or not in the circumstances is a management and not a regulatory decision.

Summarising and management reporting

The Woolf report for BAE recommends that a central register, by individual country, should be compiled and monitored on expenditure on gifts,[22] hospitality, sponsorship, free samples, etc., overall to each customer. This is a good idea, providing it does not lead to a mountain of unnecessary paperwork.

---

22   There is an excellent program for collecting such information available at: http://www.accuitysolutions.com (accessed 22 November 2012).

RELATIONSHIPS WITH AGENTS AND INTERMEDIARIES

Red bull to a flag

Regulators blow a gasket every time the words 'agent', 'joint venture' or 'intermediary' appear. This is not wholly unsurprising given the role they have historically played in the less sophisticated, but far too common, bribery schemes. What TI and other promoters of red flags overlook is that bribers intent on continuing in their cunning ways will make sure they don't trigger known profiles. For this reason it is much more likely that only honest companies will continue to use agents and then do so properly.[23]

The second problem is that many reputable foreign agents have absolutely no interest in the UK Bribery Act, possibly have never even heard of Mr Alderman, let alone recognise his photograph standing on the roof of the Elm Street building, and are reluctant to contort themselves in the way British companies want. If compliance standards – which they may regard as irrelevant – are demanded, some good potential agents may decide to represent companies from other countries with less draconian regulations. Achieving compliance by both domestic and overseas agents is more a matter of persuasion and partnering than brute force. The idea of 'integrity circles' discussed on page 728 is highly relevant to developing mutually supportive relationships with agents.

The third problem is that it is not the agent's appointment that should be of primary concern. Much more important from a Section 7 of the UK Bribery Act point of view are the decisions it is empowered to make and the end parties with which it deals; especially if they are FPOs.

The importance of agents

Not all agents are shady one-man bands – with fancy shoes and pencil thin moustaches – operating in countries perceived to be corrupt and retained only so that they can pay bribes. Agents provide important and sometimes vital services to, among other things:

- Develop business opportunities in new regions without the expense of hiring or relocating employees;
- Expand presence within a region or country on a temporary basis;
- Assist with the logistics of importing and exporting goods;
- Provide legal, administrative or accounting services.

In some countries – and the United Arab Emirates is an important example – governments demand appointment of local agents and will often nominate who they must be. This is a reflection of local culture and not usually of corruption.

---

23   Of course, it is possible that the cleverest corrupters will continue to use agents on the basis of the double bluff.

Official Introductions

TI and the OECD fly the red flag when a potential agent is introduced or recommended by a government official. In many cases the flag is meaningless if not counter-productive. It is one thing, and positive, if the official makes the recommendation openly, in writing and will support it within his own department; and entirely another if it is covert and personal. It is yet another thing when under its local laws a government department insists on a particular agent being appointed.

Another important reality is that it is difficult to find effective agents in many markets where competition to secure their services is extreme. If British companies are prevented from taking a sensible approach, agents will look elsewhere.

Policy and visibility of agents

Companies should consider whether it should publish their policy on appointing agents, listing them and the territories in which they operate. Similarly in contracts with end customers or suppliers consideration should be given to voluntarily disclosing the participation of an agent.[24]

The approach suggested in this book is that agents should be advertised and motivated as part of the extended enterprise and integrity circle: they should be allowed to promote their relationship and participation in an integrity circle to impress other customers and suppliers.

Agents' relationships with politicians and government officials

Following regulatory guidelines would normally result in any agent that has any sort of family relationship with a political leader or government official being rejected or dismissed. This is so because it creates an inference of corruption, when in fact the position may be entirely innocent and beneficial to all concerned. Who is to say that a family connection is inherently more corrupt than any other shared interest, such as freemasonry, a love of golf, tantric sex or stamp collecting?

Thus the scheme of integrity validation recommended takes a much more pragmatic approach but drills into detail to ensure that whatever the relationship is, it does not result in decisions being perverted by a financial or other advantage, the influence of an FPO, or improper performance.

---

24   These conditions may be incorporated into a wider policy on the retention and operations of intermediaries.

Applications, integrity validation and the business case

Criteria for selecting,[25] retaining and renewing agreements with agents should, ideally, be set out – in advance – on a decision matrix, which should be extended to include details of potential end customers, suppliers[26] and transactions.

Limited Value of Due Diligence

Although regulatory guidelines beat due diligence on the appointment of agents to near death, it is only part of the problem because if corruption is to happen it will take place downstream between the agent and the end customer or supplier. Based on the decision-centric approach recommended in Chapter 23, validation should extend to cover all parties in and decisions taken throughout the entire stream.

Before appointing any agent, directors should consider and fully document the business case based on a SWOT analysis and risk assessment. The decision matrix should first evaluate the candidates' positive attributes and then make adjustments for any adverse factors.

Picking the Best or the Least Worst?

Nobbly Nuts Ltd. was considering appointing an agent in Bentrovia and had three candidates. Company A had an excellent reputation, but worked for a number of competitors and had a conviction ten years ago for tax evasion. Company B was even better commercially but had been recommended by a government employee. Company C was worse than harebrained but run by a Lay Preacher.

Company A refused to grant audit rights; Company B would do so but only on a reciprocal basis; but Company C was prepared to open up everything and to swear on the Bible that it would stick to every word of the Bribery Act. Because Company A and B ticked the red flag boxes they were rejected. Was this the most sensible commercial decision?

---

25   Or disqualifying.

26   End parties.

The moral of this sad tale is that conventional due diligence seldom picks the best candidate: it merely identifies the one with the least red flags or negative entries in public records.

Integrity validation of agents should be built around an affirmative, partnering and reciprocal process (see Chapter 25, page 652) and sensible application forms, rather than intrusive (but box ticking) questioning about beneficial ownership[27] and dogged insistence on one-way audit rights.

Affirmative Due Diligence

Brightside Enterprises Ltd., a potential agent, responds on a detailed application form that its beneficial ownership is established through two offshore companies in Panama, ultimately owned by Wilfred Smith, a Canadian national and banker. Mr Smith certifies that this is correct. Checks in Panama confirm that Mr Smith has a majority interest but that two other companies – one registered in Macau and the other in Niue – have a 49 per cent interest. The structure is clearly tax advantageous: to someone.

The beneficial owner of the Macau and Niue companies is a Canadian lawyer – John Jones – and he certifies that this is the case.

On the basis of these checks Brightside Enterprises Ltd. ticks all of the boxes and is appointed. However the two Canadians are acting under side letters and represent President Bunga Wonga of Bentazia. Brightside negotiates multi-million dollar contracts with the Ministry of Works in Bentazia.

There are two important points to note from this example. **The first is that confirming beneficial ownership[28] – when someone wishes to conceal it – is virtually impossible.** It appears to be a sensible control but, in fact, is worthless. The most painless solution is to ask agents to provide a notarised Beneficial Ownership Certificate that either affirms that no politically exposed person (PEP), government employee, etc. has any ownership interest or specifically names him, her or it. But in every case the reality is that there is no way of corroborating the response.[29]

The second point is that integrity validation should be focused on the real priorities:

- The positive attributes of the potential agent and its business case;[30]
- Its end customers or suppliers;
- Individual transactions, where, how and by whom important decisions are taken.

---

27 Unless mandated in the specific sector by Anti-Money-Laundering or other regulations.

28 An assumption is that beneficial ownership is concealed only to hide skulduggery when in fact there are scores of genuine reasons for doing so.

29 But another box is ticked.

30 Or the green flags.

Integrity validation should be completed preferably before the first transaction takes place, although there may be occasions when a commercial opportunity is so urgent that checking has to be completed subsequently. Copies of all checks made and their results should be included in the file for the agent, consolidated in the Adequate Procedures Dossier and summarised in routine reports to directors.

The Importance of Documenting Rejections

It is especially important to document – in the Adequate Procedures Dossier – all cases in which a candidate has been rejected through failure to pass the integrity validation process. These are Silver Bullets.

Building partnering relationships

The principal reason for appointing agents is commercial and relationships should be collaborative and friendly, assisted by:

- Affirmative and reciprocal integrity validation;
- Helping the agent establish effective integrity validation procedures for end customers and suppliers;
- Joint risk evaluations;
- Joint training programmes, which award company and personal certificates;
- Permitting (if not encouraging) the agent to advertise its connection with the company;
- Reciprocal annual declarations of compliance;
- Open books auditing offered on a reciprocal basis;
- Shared reporting of incidents and unfair competition procedures;
- Suggestion schemes.

Overall, an agent should be brought into the extended enterprise as an important partner and not simply treated as an unreliable oink. The programme for agents should be positively branded – with names such as 'Continuous Care' or 'Integrity Circles' that reinforce the partnering relationship. Wherever possible, multiple communication channels should be maintained (see page 410 for the dangers of single channels) at both a commercial and compliance level, although from a commercial point of view one senior employee should be designated as the owner of each agency relationship (see Chapter 22 on the importance of ownership).

In many companies, the relationship with an agent is maintained by one person or a small team and this is understandable. However, sometimes the relationship may become too proprietorial to the point that, for example, Compliance and Audit are not allowed to even contact the agent on routine matters. This is a mistake and an invitation to fraud and skulduggery.

The Dangers of Single-channel Relationships

The essence of most corruption is a one-to-one or single-channel relationship between the coercer and extorter. Risks are reduced and the chances of detection enhanced when there are multiple communication channels between the organisations involved.

Contracts with agents

Relevant commercial organisations may be liable for bribery by associated persons who perform services on their behalf. This ambiguous phrase is clarified in the Ministry of Justice's Explanatory Notes to show such liability that Section 7 of the Bribery Act relates to the actual activities being undertaken at the time and not simply the general nature of the relationship.

Thus companies should consider incorporating the following type of condition into

Contract Terms

Intermediaries are specifically prohibited from offering, giving etc. any advantage or rewarding any third party with the intention of inducing him or her to perform an official or business function or activity improperly. If they act in contravention of this undertaking they are be deemed not to be performing services on the company's behalf and contracts are immediately terminated.

contracts with intermediaries:

Whether such terms would be binding – to demonstrate that the agent was not performing services on the company's behalf when it engaged in malpractice – will be decided on a case-by-case basis, but it may be a useful Silver Bullet if a prosecution is launched.

Contracts should be agreed with all agents (for a maximum term of two years, when they are renegotiated and subject to refreshed integrity validation) to include the normal agency clauses but also, if possible, to commit them to:

- Comply with all appropriate laws and regulations;
- Conduct integrity validation on their end customers and suppliers;
- Nominate a senior employee to liaise on compliance and audit matters;
- Not to contract with subcontractors without the principal's written permission;
- Report any suspected compliance breaches without delay;
- Fully cooperate in investigations;
- Make annual declarations and appraisals;
- Report any changes in circumstances, without delay.

Consideration should be given to requiring personal guarantees from the agent's principals and directors, or performance bonds.

Remuneration of agents

Although they may not like the idea, neither TI, the OECD, the Ministry of Justice nor the SFO has any legal, moral or other right to poke their noses into the remuneration of agents: this is entirely a commercial decision properly made by the company concerned depending on all of the circumstances. Similarly, whether or not to standardise rates between different agencies is entirely a management decision, as are the mechanics of payment.

The problem is that if the regulators believe the remuneration is too generous or paid indirectly they are likely to infer skulduggery

---

Uncommercial Ideas

One of the regulatory guidelines suggests that an agent's commission should be on a sliding scale that declines as revenues increase. The idea is that it will result in the agent having less money to pay bribes, but that is unadulterated nonsense and uncommercial.[31]

A record of all of the influential factors that determine an agent's remuneration should be prepared, approved by the directors and be subject to continuous monitoring along the lines suggested in Chapters 18–20. The driving force in setting remuneration should be to achieve the best possible commercial results and if this means increasing commission rates for higher revenues, regulators can infer whatever they like.

Prohibited Behaviour

Christopher Hitchins said something along the lines that no one ever prohibited behaviour he would not wish to participate in himself. How true!

Agents should be required to nominate one or more bank accounts[32] into which their remuneration is paid. Bank references should be obtained and any change to payment instructions properly authorised, accurately recorded and approved by senior

---

31   It makes you wonder what planet these guys inhabit. If commission rates are reduced as success increases, even honest agents will switch the excess to other principals who are not so foolish.

32   Unless there are exceptional reasons, in their own name (or the company's name).

management. Under no circumstances should payment be made other than to authorised bank accounts.

Granting of audit rights

Much has been said about the importance of requiring agents to grant rights of audit (see pages 607 and 652). These can be an effective control, but more often they are a cosmetic and when the time comes to invoke them permission is withdrawn, usually on the advice of a local lawyer or for some other spurious reason. Besides that, if the company wanting rights of audit is not prepared to reciprocate, it puts the relationship on a bad footing, which is counter-productive. Thus the bottom line is that companies should think carefully before making audit rights with agents a deal-breaker and if they are to offer reciprocal facilities.

Continuing care and monitoring of agents

The Ministry of Justice Guidance suggest that the performance of agents should be monitored, but gives scant information on how this should be done. Again, the word 'monitoring' has a negative connotation, implying that agents are inherently unreliable.

Relationships with agents should be supportive through a programme of Continuing Care, including:

- **Training and ongoing advice**, embracing codes of conduct, training sessions, websites and quarterly bulletins to actively promote the programme;
- A reporting of incidents programme *(involving employees, associated third parties and members of the public)*, including a 24/7/365 telephone hotline and website with …
- … Reporting requirements to cover breaches of any integrity or control programme, fraud, theft, etc., **including suspected violations by competitors and foreign public officials**.[33]
- Annual declarations by and interviews with risk-assessed end parties[34] and employees;
- Exit interviews for senior agency employees;
- **Careful monitoring of key performance indicators and targets**;
- A suggestion scheme open to employees and third parties *(again with consideration being given to payment of financial rewards)*;
- Unannounced integrity reviews and audits;
- Collaborative meetings on integrity matters with third parties.

The above should be supported by a system of continuous monitoring to automatically identify potentially deviant transactions (see page 736).

All relevant documentation under the Continuing Care programme should be retained in the Adequate Procedures Dossier.

Employees who have contact with agents should prepare brief file notes of any significant matters that arise, such as new principals represented, new business plans

---

33   Consideration should be given to the payment of rewards for information leading to proof.

34   The agents' customers, suppliers, etc.

or any other development that could influence the relationship.[35] Routine monitoring should quickly uncover adverse information concerning the agent, its beneficial owners or directing minds. Any adverse information should be taken seriously, but on the principle of innocent until proven guilty, and with a view to protecting the business relationship:

- Problems should be fully investigated by Compliance, Audit or Security (and not by the person or team managing the relationship);[36]
- A detailed report should be prepared and considered by the appropriate level of management (for example, whether to suspend the relationship until court proceedings are completed or to carry on as normal).

The work of agents and others involved in collaborative relationships should be automatically monitored by data-mining and other processes.

Renewal and termination of agreement with agents

Many companies had agents in place before the Bribery Act came into force, whose integrity was not validated to the necessary standard. A reasonable timetable should be taken to correct this position on a risk-assessed, priority basis (see classifications page 657).

Similarly, integrity validation should be refreshed before contracts are renewed or extended, again using a system based on a decision matrix but refined to acknowledge good past performance which should be given a high positive score.

---

35   In banks, these are usually called 'Call Sheets' and they are very useful.

36   Which protects that individual or team against allegations of collusion or conflicting interests.

CHAPTER 32 *Joint Ventures, Acquisitions and Initial Public Offerings*

Joint Ventures

A DIFFERENT APPROACH

The Ministry of Justice Guidance[1] takes a very superficial view of joint ventures and differs from the approach recommended in this book in the ways summarised in Table 32.1.

Table 32.1 Differences Between the Official Approach and the Recommended Approach

Relating to Collaborative Relationships	
Ministry of Justice, OECD and TI Focus	**Recommended Focus**
Based on perceived country and sectorial risks suggesting there are demand and supply sides to bribery	Considers that perceived country risks are influential but not determinative
	Risk assessment is more granular and specific, based on contexts and decision-centricity
Limited to the Bribery Act 2010	Takes account of US legislation, including the Foreign Corrupt Practices Act (FCPA) and the Dodd–Frank Wall Street Reform Act
	Considers offences under the Fraud and Companies Acts
	Considers fraud risks and assesses their relationship to bribery offences
Framed as a legal problem	Framed as a managerial, operational and motivational challenge with legal input
	Emphasises the importance of consistent standards across all joint ventures
Assumes joint ventures will be primarily in Less Developed Countries	Considers joint ventures in all countries, including the USA and the UK

---

1   There are two sets of Guidance: the main publication ('Bribery Act 2010: Guidance about commercial organisations preventing bribery') and a Quick Start Guide for small companies. Both are available at: http://www.justice.gov.uk/legislation/bribery (accessed 7 November 2012).

Relating to Collaborative Relationships	
Ministry of Justice, OECD and TI Focus	**Recommended Focus**
Concerned primarily with bribes paid (outgoing bribery) and demonstrating adequate procedures (which relate only to Section 7)	Covers incoming, outgoing and competitive bribery, conflict of interest and fraud
	Recognises the limited application of adequate procedures and incorporates special provisions to avoid corporate liability under sections 1, 2 and 6
Claims that the Bribery Act assists UK companies in international markets	Considers that the Act creates serious disadvantages in international markets for UK-based companies
Ambiguities are to be resolved after the event through prosecutorial discretion	Considers that the Act creates almost unmanageable uncertainty. Does not accept that a business can be managed when the line is drawn only after the event
Emphasises the criticality of self-disclosure and negotiated settlements with the SFO	Takes a pragmatic approach to self-disclosure and recognises the risk involved
Due diligence is focused on red flags concerning joint venture participants	Establishes an integrated methodology for due diligence on all phases of joint ventures, with additional focus on end parties, specific transaction types and decisions
Prioritises compliance, putting commercial considerations into second place. The suggestions may result in adversarial relationships with other participants	Prioritises commercial goals but fully supported by compliance. Mutually supportive relationships with participants

STRATEGY FOR MANAGING UNCERTAINTY IN JOINT VENTURES

One of the most serious uncertainties in the Bribery Act is the extent to which UK companies may be criminally liable for the behaviour of their partners in joint ventures, including collaborative enterprises with parent, subsidiary and sibling companies. This chapter specifically addresses joint venture risks and recommends the following approach:

- **Risk Assessment**
  - All existing and planned joint ventures should be **comprehensively risk-assessed**[2] **and managed on a through-life basis** – meaning from identifying a prospective relationship through to operation and termination.[3]
  - **All decisions** leading to, during, and resulting from the termination of joint ventures that are potentially exposed to corruption should be catalogued and risk-assessed.
  - Wherever possible **criteria for evaluating decisions** should be specified in advance in weighted and scored matrices, thereby minimising the dangers of perversion and providing a visible audit trail.

---

2   Not just for anti-bribery risks.

3   The termination of joint ventures often results in the uncovering of bribery and other compliance breaches.

- **Controls should be specified** for all existing and proposed joint ventures, commensurate with their *specific* through-life risks.
- **All compliance requirements should be assessed** based on an eclectic selection of British and American regulations and should be **maintained at a level beyond best practice**.
- **Risk Avoidance**
  - Wherever possible **joint venture entities[4] should be structured to avoid classification under the UK Bribery Act as relevant commercial organisations**. This means that no part of their business should be carried out in the UK, thereby avoiding the uncertainties inherent in Section 7 – the absolute corporate liability offence.
  - From a risk management point of view, **each joint venture should be limited to a specific, self-contained project** – so that if necessary it can be cauterised.
  - Wherever commercially feasible, a company's **participation or investments in** joint ventures should be through entities that have no close connection with the UK.
  - Where joint ventures also involve participation by foreign government instrumentalities, they **should be structured to avoid liability under the FCPA**.
  - UK companies that transact business with joint ventures in which other group **companies participate should do so on an arm's length commercial (supplier or customer) basis.[5]**
  - Wherever possible, managers and employees with close connections to the UK **should NOT be appointed to joint venture positions**, especially those in which they could be regarded as directing minds.
  - **Relationships between parent company, subsidiaries, affiliates and siblings** should be structured and maintained to avoid Section 7 liabilities.
- **Risk Reduction**
  - Companies should make every effort to **maintain their high standards of compliance in all joint ventures, even** where they do not have control, and should set up non-intrusive monitoring processes on the basis that they should be the first to know of suspected compliance violations and other problems.
  - **Due diligence procedures should be based on decision matrices** and, for joint ventures, **extend to significant end parties** – meaning customers, suppliers, agents and others associated with the joint venture.[6]
  - **Contracts and memoranda of understanding should specify compliance requirements**, including immediate and automatic termination of all authority if illegal and ultra vires acts are committed in or by the joint venture or its participants.
  - **Personal contracts with the directing minds and closely connected persons employed in joint ventures** should reinforce corporate-level undertakings.

---

4   This means the distinct legal structure through which the joint venture is operated.

5   And avoid being regarded as providing services and liability under Section 7.

6   This standard goes far beyond that recommended by the Ministry of Justice.

- Senior managers in joint ventures should be required to submit annual declarations of compliance.
- Whether or not a UK participant has management control of a joint venture, one of its senior employees should be empowered with the necessary authorities and responsibilities for all aspects of governance and should have **an unrestricted liaison channel with the company's Compliance Department**.
- Company employees who are responsible for developing or participating in joint ventures should be **provided with additional training and direct lines of communication** to their company's Compliance Department.
- **Contingency Planning**
    - Detailed plans should be prepared for terminating or exiting from all joint ventures.

The recommendations may be mistakenly interpreted as encouraging companies into non-compliance. This is not the case. The suggestions are a prudent and proportionate response to the unmanageable uncertainty created by the UK Bribery Act and are no different from legitimate tax planning. However, managers should decide – based on a combination of legal and commercial advice – whether a risk avoidance strategy is consistent with their approach towards compliance.

SPECIFIED CONTROLS AND CONSISTENCY

All of the controls discussed in Chapters 21–32 are relevant to joint ventures but it is critical that they are consistently applied in the three phases:

1. Development.
2. Operation.
3. Termination or exit.

On 9 February 2011 when questioned about a speech he had just made to industry representatives, Richard Alderman, Director of the Serious Fraud Office (SFO), said:

Relaxation for Existing Joint Ventures

'We will have to make a distinction between new and existing [joint ventures] [...] For existing [joint ventures] we are sympathetic to them being tied into these very complicated arrangements. If they have done everything they can we will be satisfied with that'.[7]

---

7   'Bribery Act: SFO to be "sympathetic" towards joint ventures in corrupt countries' (Richard Tyler, *The Telegraph*, 9 February 2011). Richard Alderman's speech, 'The Bribery Act 2010 – The SFO's approach and international compliance', made at the law firm McGrigor's in Aberdeen, is available at: http://www.sfo.gov.uk/about-us/our-views/director's-speeches/speeches-2011/the-bribery-act-2010---the-sfo's-approach-and-international-compliance.aspx (accessed 22 November 2012).

Mr Alderman continued that for new joint-venture agreements it would be necessary to build in auditing and transparency provisions. The suggestion here is that companies should go much further and that all existing joint ventures should be thoroughly risk-assessed and, effectively controlled.

Acquisitions, Initial Public Offerings and Similar Transactions

THE CONVENTIONAL ONE-DIMENSIONAL APPROACH

So far the biggest problem with acquisitions has been for companies which have inherited problems under the successor liability rules and whose integrity validation checks are subsequently proven to be inadequate.[8]

Transparency International Guidance

Transparency International (TI) published in 2012 what could best be described as an interesting draft report,[9] 'Guidance for Anti-bribery Due Diligence in Mergers, Acquisitions and Investments',[10] which it modestly suggests is best practice. But it does not mention a single word about the target company carrying out any checks on its parent-to-be or investor who, for all it knows, could be a Mafia front! And it puts bribe payment in an exclusive silo when, in fact, pre-acquisition due diligence should be all-inclusive.

Regulators urge acquiring companies to disclose skulduggery discovered in their targets' accounts under the 'Come to Jesus' principle. In a speech in October 2011 in Washington DC, Mr Alderman, the SFO Director, said:

The SFO's Position

'Some time ago we said publicly in the SFO that we were prepared to assist corporations that were in the process of carrying out a merger or acquisition and discovered problems during the course of due diligence. We made this willingness clear about two years ago although I have to say that there was little take up at that stage. That seems to be changing now. I have been struck in recent months by the fact that a number of corporations have been to see us about some sensitive potential acquisitions where they are identifying some real issues about corruption.

---

8   Usually SEC actions for violations of the FCPA Accounting Provisions.

9   Circulated for consultation in October 2011 – on bribery, not corruption.

10   Available to be downloaded at: http://www.transparency.org.uk/our-work/publications (accessed 22 November 2012).

> [...]
>
> 'What we do is to talk to the corporation and its advisors about what they are finding and what they propose to do about it if the acquisition takes place. It is quite clear to me as a result of the discussions that a negative response from the SFO is sufficiently important to put the acquisition in jeopardy. On the other hand, a positive view from us on the basis of what the corporation intends to do could enable the acquisition to go ahead'.[11]

Pre-acquisition FCPA due diligence is a lucrative revenue stream for lawyers, accountants and other professional advisers, who are nearly always retained by the acquirer. Yet the company to be acquired is also exposed to financial loss or regulatory penalties if it associates without carrying out the necessary checks.

CORRUPTION IN THE ACQUISITION PROCESS

The other problem is corruption in the acquisition process itself, where shareholders in either entity may be bribed to support the acquisition, to agree a price above or below that justified – possibly based on a 'dodgy dossier', accounting or other report – or to agree a carried interest for a concealed beneficial owner, a foreign public official (FPO) or a politically exposed person (PEP).

THE BOTTOM LINE

For the reasons explained about pre-acquisition, diligence should be holistic: covering the past performance[12] of **acquirer and acquiree**, the integrity of the acquisition process itself and forward looking into the proposed new venture. Due diligence should not be limited to compliance with anti-bribery laws but should include validation of the business case and all other regulatory and taxation aspects – of both parties and the emerging entity.

Validation should be based on an agreed risk evaluation[13] and decision matrix, setting out the factors that could be deal breakers. The Memorandum of Understanding (as well as equivalent and supporting documentation) should contain anti-corruption and other compliance affirmations by both parties[14] and if the USA is involved should ensure that public declarations conform to the March 2011 ruling by the Securities and Exchange Commission (SEC) in the Titan case.[15] Documentation should also include an agreement

---

11 'The changing landscape and its impact on global enterprise', speech at the Anti-Corruption Summit 2011. Available at: http://www.sfo.gov.uk/about-us/our-views/director's-speeches/speeches-2011/anti-corruption-summit-2011,-washington-dc.aspx (accessed 22 November 2012).

12 Going back at least three years.

13 Along the lines of page 568.

14 Including personal warranties.

15 Basically involving actionable liability for false declarations of compliance. See the full report in Trace International's Compendium, available at:http://www.traceinternational.org/Knowledge/Compendium.html (accessed November 2012).

on how and by whom suspected violations will be investigated and, if appropriate, reported to the authorities.

GETTING READY FOR AN INITIAL PUBLIC OFFERING OR TRADE SALE

Another problem, which has not been fully recognised, arises for smaller companies that may wish – in the future – to seek a Stock Exchange listing or trade sale. For them any act of corruption is likely to be a poison pill that results in reduced consideration, possibly prosecution of their directors and other adverse consequences. For this reason even small companies should take extreme care over all aspects of compliance and should go well beyond the reduced procedures suggested by the Ministry of Justice Guidance.

33 *Some Other Problem Areas*

Offset Projects

Surprisingly, offset projects[1] cause the Serious Fraud Office (SFO) little angst,[2] yet they are often hopelessly vulnerable to both political corruption and commercial bribery and potentially far more corruptive than facilitation payments or hospitality. The essence of offsets is that in major projects rival bidders offer additional schemes and benefits as part of an overall package.

Politically Beneficial Offsets

In the recent FIFA scandal at least one of the representatives was revealed to have wanted, in return for his vote, an athletics stadium built in his home town.

The problem with all offsets is:

- They can amount to political corruption when they benefit a decision-maker's local constituency and effectively buy him or her votes;
- The decision-maker or company in which he or she has an interest may provide and gain revenues from the offset;
- They complicate and obscure the primary procurement decision.

---

1   Offset projects are simply giveaways associated with a major contract: mostly in the defence industry.

2   It does not even include them as a required policy area: incredible!

Many Offset Projects Have Never Been Delivered

Estimates[3] suggest that something like $25 billion worth of offset projects were agreed as incentives in primary procurement decisions and yet up to ten years later have never been delivered. The possibility is, therefore, that the contractors concerned had been given unrecorded permission to exaggerate the worth of their offsets on the understanding that they would never have to be delivered.

Companies should think very carefully before offering offsets or agreeing to participate in them, especially in the overseas public sector, and when they do so, they should ensure that decisions are fully documented and effective controls put in place. Equally, they should take the greatest care when considering the appointment of offset brokers.

Political Contributions

The SFO has made it clear that it expects companies to have a policy in a number of areas discussed in earlier chapters of this book and, in addition, on political contributions and lobbying (see page 325). The approach recommended in this book is very simple and that is to give the mongrels nothing until they clean up their own acts. But this may not be advice companies wish to follow because the thought of an inside track to political leaders seems so attractive.

An alternative approach to the above is to decide at board level what the real objectives of lobbying are: whether it is directed at an elected representative; indirectly through a public relations or similar firm; or via a revolving door, and to:

- Carry out and document a detailed SWOT (Strengths, Weaknesses, Opportunities and Threats) analysis, coupled with a Risk Assessment relating to the countries and representatives concerned (remembering – incredibly – that it is permissible under the Organisation for Economic Cooperation and Development (OECD) Convention to make contributions to political parties and opposition politicians). Further, because of the UK's failure to incorporate the Convention into its laws, it is also acceptable for companies and other organisations to lobby to their heart's content.
- Obtain a detailed specification (before coming to a final agreement) on precisely what the beneficiary will deliver (if anything).
- Carry out a detailed integrity validation on the representative or party concerned, paying particular attention to conflicting interests and unhealthy associations.
- Brief the representatives or political party concerned on the company's ethical policies and disclosure requirements and the need for annual declarations of compliance.
- Subject to the above, lobbyist fees and payments should be recorded accurately and summarised in annual reports and accounts.

---

3   See reference to the paper by Shana Marshall, page 384.

- The recipients should prepare monthly, detailed reports of the efforts they have made, the work they have done, expenses incurred,[4] and results obtained on the company's behalf.[5]

If there is any doubt, the company should consider an off-record discussion with the SFO, but the bottom line is that donations must not be made with the intention of inducing improper performance.

Revolving Doors

The term 'revolving doors' applies to the recruitment of someone from a governmental, regulatory or competitive entity with the intention of leveraging his or her knowledge, skills or contacts. The greatest danger, from a Bribery Act perspective, arises from the recruitment of foreign public officials (FPOs) – or Politically Exposed Persons (PEPs) – into the private sector, especially when the intention is to use his or her influence to obtain a business advantage.

Revolving Out of the SFO But Still In the 'Cottage Industry'

Senior members of the SFO and Lord Goldsmith, the former Attorney General, have recently joined leading UK law firms to work in the anti-corruption teams.

The Law Commissioners gave the following example of how liability under the revolving doors rules may be applied:

A Revolving Example

R has recently retired from an influential position in the civil service. He or she is approached by P who is seeking a lucrative contract with a Government department. P pays R a large sum of money to provide confidential information to P about the bidding processes.

In this example, a prosecution should not fail at the outset simply because R is not currently engaged in a profession or performing a public function. The transaction between P and R clearly relates to past conduct of a public or professional kind.

---

4   Usually at Table 1 at Langhan's in Piccadilly, the Ivy or the Waldorf Grill in Basingstoke.

5   Normally this can be written on the back of a postage stamp.

Routine pre-employment screening (see Chapter 26) should ensure that potential conflicts of interest with a candidate's prior employment are identified. In addition, the recruitment of senior politicians or government officials should be approved at board level and minuted. As with all decisions the impact should also be assessed.

Revolving Doors Appointments

Although the view is generally held that people employed through a revolving door add value, this is not always the case. Experience shows that successors may want little to do with their previous colleagues or in the worst case seek to punish them. Revolving Doors appointments can sometimes be counterproductive.

Notwithstanding the above, business intelligence processes should identify potentially conflicting revolving doors appointments by competitors and monitor developments carefully. Where appropriate report should be made to the regulators as Silver Bullets for the Adequate Procedures Dossier.

Controlling Tolling

For reasons explained on pages 314–16, tolling is an extremely risky business and wherever possible should be most carefully controlled. The fact that pricing of tolled transactions appears to be in line with market rates is no assurance that there has been no improper performance by any of the parties involved.

Where tolling transactions are justified,[6] the following additional controls should be considered:

- Negotiations should be confirmed in writing at a principal-to-principal level involving all of the parties invoiced and should not delegated.
- Wherever possible, transactions should be structured so that payments are made only to the contracted counterparty (avoiding all payments to offshore entities and special purpose vehicles).
- The precise justification for split invoicing should be documented and the legitimacy in all jurisdictions confirmed in writing.
- Enhanced integrity validation should be carried out on all the parties concerned (including proof of beneficial ownership[7]) and, where appropriate, personal indemnities sought.
- Transactions should be accurately recorded.
- Where extractive commodities and issuers are concerned the additional conditions of the Dodd–Frank Act should be fully observed.

---

6   Or, in some cases, the only way that commodities can be bought.

7   Which is of very limited value.

Even with all of the above controls fully in place, there is only limited assurance that tolling transactions will comply with all laws in the jurisdictions affected. An option is to seek an 'opinion letter' in advance from the SFO (although it is unlikely to be met with much enthusiasm) or the US regulators.

Payments Control

When Willy Sutton, the notorious American bank robber, was asked why he robbed banks, his answer was simple: 'Cause that's where the money is'. Life would be much simpler if controlling outgoing bribery was simply a matter of ensuring that all payments were bona fide. This is not the case because, as discussed in Chapter 12, financial or other advantages can be funded, provided and concealed in hundreds of different ways, many of which do not involve conventional payments.

Notwithstanding this, companies should carefully control all of their disbursement processes, including cash, manual and automated cheques, certified or bankers' cheques, standing orders, wire transfers, intercompany accounting and charge-backs.[8]

Although separation of responsibilities is generally a fragile control (see page 563), it is worthwhile in most payments contexts between:

- The opening and maintenance of accounts (including removing dormant and duplicate accounts);
- Entry and updating of payment parameters (for example, bank account details of the vendors);
- User departments and central IT;
- Operational and test systems;
- Primary systems and backup;
- Routine transaction processing (for example, accounts payable, expenses and payroll);
- Reconciliation of gateways between associated systems (for example, between front and procurement systems and payments processing);
- Adjustments and error correction;
- Treasury management;
- Bank and account reconciliations.

Logging and mirror recording should be fully enabled and important reconciliation or scratch files retained for at least three years. Wherever possible voice or fax-initiated bank transfers should be avoided and external transactions (for example, between a company and its banks) encrypted or otherwise electronically authenticated.

Preventive controls should be reinforced by continuous monitoring or automated fraud detection testing to identify potentially deviant transactions, including bribe payment.

8   Which should be fully catalogued and risk-evaluated (see Chapters 14–17).

Marketing and Promotional Schemes

Companies should consider stipulating policies and decision-centric procedures on other potential exposures under the Bribery Act 2010, including:

- Provision of free samples;
- Marketing support schemes (such as cash back for equipment purchases);
- Educational visit for potential customers, suppliers and FPOs such as sponsored site visits, training and conferences;
- Relationships with routine customers and suppliers.

Again, the spirit and wording should be positive and based primarily on commercial objectives that are compliant with all relevant laws (see page 417).

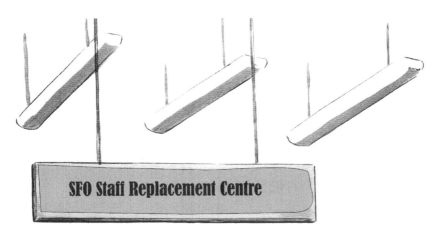

'To be frank, Miss Jones, I like the idea of night work and dawn raids'

PART VIII

Internal and Regulatory Investigations

34 *Background and Strategy to Internal Investigations*

Coverage and Reasons for Investigating

This chapter is intended as a guide for senior managers of organisations and their advisers who need to conduct *internal investigations* into fraud or incoming, internal, outgoing and competitive corruption.[1] Chapter 36 extends the subject to adversarial investigations initiated by a regulatory agency or run collaboratively with one (proxy investigations), possibly after a self-disclosure has been made. Although most of the discussion applies to all regulatory agencies, the Serious Fraud Office (SFO) has been singled out, because for UK companies it is the lead agency.

A Word of Caution

The approach is based on over 40 years' experience of successfully conducting complex and difficult cases in the real world, by working with regulators and defending regulatory actions.

Bigging It Up

A client telephoned the authors late at night, saying his company had been raided by HM Customs and Excise Investigation Branch, its premises searched, directors cautioned and told that penalties and arrears of £10 million plus were imminent. A parallel, pre-emptive investigation, reporting to the company's solicitors, established that a simple tariff misclassification – rather than dishonesty – had resulted in underpayments of duty and VAT of no more than £40,000. The case was settled for £50,000.

This chapter is not a substitute for specific legal advice and it may be disputed, especially by some members of the 'Cottage Industry', thus serving its purpose. It is intended to be helpful and stimulate thought, particularly on what is best for companies

---

1   They are all referred to as 'fraud investigations'.

and individuals when confronted with suspicions of bribery. It, and page 594 et seq, pose questions that are often thought best left unanswered such as:

- Should self-disclosure and civil disposals ever be considered on the grounds that they are unethical and a corruption of criminal justice principles?
- Under what circumstances should a particular case be disclosed to the SFO?
- Should a company that self-discloses be prepared to, in effect, investigate itself in a proxy investigation, *which is fraught with conflict, and evidential and procedural dangers*?
- What support should be given to individuals charged jointly with a company?
- What terms should be negotiated with regulators, possibly on a double-blind approach, before a formal disclosure is made?

Most that follows is directed towards serious suspicions and allegations that could result in significant financial, reputational and other harm. Minor breaches may also be investigated in the ways discussed, but with less formality. **In every case, suspicions should be professionally assessed and, where justified, expertly investigated and then resolved.**

Another Problem With Regulatory Silos

The Financial Services Authority (FSA) would like regulated companies to report suspicions immediately without conducting any internal investigation, whereas the SFO, the Department of Justice and the Securities and Exchange Commission (SEC) goes the opposite way.

The Importance of Being the First to Know

The sooner the company learns that it is suspected of paying or receiving bribes or is involved in any other potential regulatory breach, the better. It is better still if it is able to *anticipate* that an allegation is about to be made (see page 846). **Being the 'first to know' puts the company in control.** When suspected skulduggery is first discovered by a third party – and especially a regulatory agency – control is removed, forcing reactive rather than proactive responses. This is always bad news.

The Importance of Planning Ahead

There are a number of important policies, procedures and arrangements (see Chapters 23–5) which should be put in place long before they are needed for a specific investigation,[2] including answers to the following questions:

---

2   Anywhere in the world where the company operates, has associated persons, or visits.

- How and by whom will all initial suspicions be evaluated?
- Who will direct and conduct investigations?
- What investigatory tools, techniques and procedures are acceptable to the company?
- What reporting and self-disclosure requirements must be complied with?

Any organisation that has not prepared along these lines in advance is likely to make possibly catastrophic mistakes in the heat of the moment. This, too, is very bad news.

Why Most Investigations Fail

Most fraud and corruption victims:

- Fail to prove guilt *conclusively* or to clear allegations *conclusively*, thereby leaving the company and others accused in limbo: this is a wholly unsatisfactory outcome;
- Are put on the defence by counter-attacks from those suspected or challenged by spurious litigation often brought by opportunistic plaintiffs or lawyers on contingency fees;
- Do not get **any** money back; *not a single penny*;
- Waste money on unproductive legal, investigative and accountancy fees.

The common reasons for failures are that victims:

- Did not take suspicions seriously when they first appeared;
- Tried to sweep the symptoms under the carpet;
- Reported the case to the police and waited for years for any action;
- Took disciplinary or other action before the facts had been established and, as a result, were put on the defensive *(usually with no evidence to justify the action already taken, leaving them naked!!)*;
- Alerted the suspects, allowing them to destroy evidence, silence witnesses, prepare excuses and to counter-attack;
- Rushed in too quickly, but then let the investigation drag on;
- Had unrealistic expectations over the possible outcome, costs and timetable of complex cases;
- Conducted an inefficient or illegal investigation, resulting in the exclusion of evidence at trial;
- Steered the investigation to achieve the results it wanted (for example, ignoring compelling evidence of corruption).

The Mistake of Taking Action Too Early

Some badly advised organisations suspend employees and contractors immediately suspicions are aroused. This is usually a dreadful mistake. Firstly, it removes any incentive the accuseds might have to cooperate, mainly because it assumes their guilt. Secondly, it alerts others involved, enabling them to counter-attack. Thirdly, it invariably results in the suspended party threatening or taking legal action for unfair dismissal or other harm. For these reasons, companies are advised to delay disciplinary or remedial action until the First Step (see below) has been taken.

Overarching all of the above and the dominant reason for failure is the fact that companies turn to unqualified advisers, consultants, investigators and, dare it be said, lawyers.

Bouffant Hair, Bow Tie and Plain Wrong

A UK company suspected that its Property Services Manager was taking bribes and extorting free-of-charge services from his employer's contractors to maintain his extensive but concealed private property portfolio. A meeting was held in the company's headquarters with senior managers, investigators, in-house lawyers and the senior partner of retained external solicitors.[3]

The meeting started on time, with no sign of the partner. He arrived some 40 minutes late, entered the room with a flourish: he was tall, sporting an exaggeratedly bouffant hairstyle – that could have been a wig – a red bow tie with matching braces and fancy shoes. His assistant was straight from page 3 of The *Sun*.

The partner, being a lawyer, quickly took command and when the author suggested that the company should consider applying for a civil search order, he said that: 'under a recent review conducted by Lord Woolf they were no longer available' and continued: 'but you should forgive Michael's ignorance because he is not a lawyer'.

Rather than challenge this eminent lawyer in public, he was politely invited to pop out for a quick chat, which he did, and his error was pointed out to him. 'Oh' he said 'I have to admit I was not really sure about it. I see, Woolf just changed the name. Leave it to me, old boy!'

On returning to the meeting, again with a swagger, the partner said: 'I have advised Michael and I think I have found a way around **his** problem. Given this, I think a civil search order would be a good idea'.

---

3   Not one of the leading firms and a property specialist with no knowledge of litigation. In fact the appointment of his firm was shrouded in mystery.

Admittedly this is just one case and most lawyers are far better informed. But can you imagine what the result might have been had his advice not been challenged?[4]

Mr Bouffant is a good example of advisers working beyond their competences and, believe it or not, even investigators do it. The reality is that very few lawyers are good street-level detectives, although there are rare exceptions. It is one thing dealing with people in court or Counsel's Chambers, when the facts have been sorted, and quite another in real life. Equally, few investigators are qualified to give legal advice.

The point is that a team of specialists is needed for complex investigations, with each discipline playing its part under the command of a senior, independent line manager (see page 823).

The Objectives of Internal Investigations

Once suspicions have been aroused, they must be resolved because there is a three-way obligation:

1. To the company, its honest employees, shareholders and others.
2. To those accused.
3. To comply with regulations.

There is little more debilitating for an organisation than to live with unresolved suspicions that one of its employees or associates is a crook. It also makes life impossible for those wrongly suspected and their honest colleagues. It is critical that investigations resolve suspicions conclusively: one way or the other.

Thus the objectives of *internal* investigations are to:

- Establish the complete facts *of the worst case* within the law, using the most effective, legally permissible, ethical and proportionate tools and techniques;
- Produce overwhelming evidence that:
  - totally clears innocent people wrongly suspected (including the company);
  - gives crooks no room to manoeuvre, leading to their full cooperation and financial and other recovery;
  - avoids contested proceedings in court and minimises legal and other expenses;
- Prevent repetition;
- Create a deterrent to others; this usually means criminally prosecuting, taking disciplinary and recovery action;
- Minimise disruption to the business and protect the company's reputation;
- Improve controls;
- Uncover other cases.

But usually the most immediate objective is for the company to recover and minimise its losses and costs. **There is a strong arguable case that any company that has no policy, specified procedures or skilled resources for conducting investigations cannot have adequate procedures.**

---

4   The order was granted and £2 million recovered.

Essential Components of Successful Investigations

There are five vital components of most successful investigations:

1. A compulsive objective to find the facts before taking remedial action.
2. Effective, independent commercial **management** control, based on clear objectives, policies and budgets.
3. Skilled investigative and legal resources.
4. An effective Investigations Plan, including the precise tools and techniques to be used, and realistic timetables and budgets.
5. Legal protection, confidentiality and security of all actions and findings.

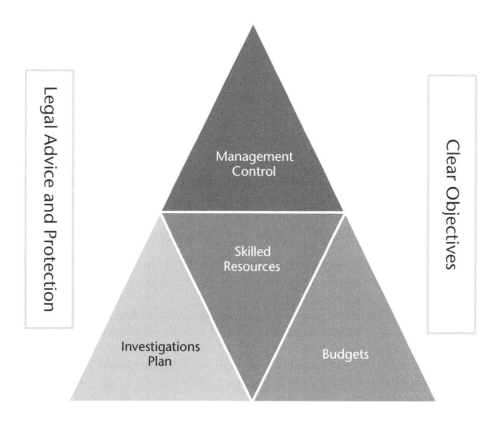

Figure 34.1 The Vital Components of Successful Investigations

The components illustrated in Figure 34.1 are discussed later and they must be brought together in a detailed Investigations Plan, approved by the company's senior managers and legal advisers.

Pre-approval of Investigatory Tools and Techniques

In most investigations it is necessary to break through an imaginary yet difficult barrier between merely going through the motions,[5] and getting to the deep truth. **The difference between failure and success is often a hair's breadth.** Breaking through requires a flash of inspiration, a bit of luck and extremely hard work; and it normally takes place at what is described in this book as the FIRST STEP. This is a pivotal point and the one at which suspects first come to realise that they are under investigation. The FIRST STEP must be an ambush.

The breakthrough *(aimed at proving guilt or innocence conclusively)* usually involves one or more of:

- The suspects being caught in the act of committing offences for which they can provide no plausible excuse (known in the trade as pants down–hands up);
- Simultaneous interviews in which admissions and confessions are obtained;
- Execution of civil search and freezing orders ('a dawn raid');
- A Section 2 Criminal Justice Act (CJA) Order issued by the SFO;
- Criminal search warrants executed by a law enforcement agency.

Some companies may consider the idea of a pre-emptive FIRST STEP overly aggressive or disproportionate, but everything that follows is within the law and the suggested approach is usually the only way to prove innocence or guilt, conclusively. However, companies should specify the resources, tools, techniques and investigatory procedures – well in advance of their being needed – that accord with the law and their own ethical beliefs. They should not be too squeamish, because proving fraud is seldom easy.

Problems of Counter-attacks

Investigations are controversial and emotional. Each one is different, suspects and witnesses react unpredictably and there is always the risk that one mistake will jeopardise everything and cause adverse publicity and long-lasting problems. In many cases, criminals counter-attack and make threats that cool the victim's enthusiasm for pursuing its rights.

Another common feature is that junior employees who pay or receive bribes have a strong incentive to blame their supervisors to minimise their own culpability. It is also in the regulators' interest to encourage defendants to accuse each other and it is one of the reasons why companies are treated differently from individuals.

---

5   More box-ticking.

Companies Pay Up While People Get Porridge

From a regulatory perspective negotiating a civil settlement with a company makes good sense. First, companies have the money and resources to mount a powerful contested defence and so are opponents for regulators to avoid. Companies can take negotiating decisions on a purely financial cost-benefit basis and quickly recover from even multi-million pound penalties. On the other hand, few individuals – especially if their associated organisation jettisons them – have the resources to support massive legal bills and are therefore much more vulnerable to enforcement arbitrage.

Fragmentation tactics are often aided and abetted by companies themselves, whose knee-jerk reaction is to abandon individuals accused of corporate-level skulduggery to save their own skins. This can have disastrous consequences.

The Domino Effect

The domino effect was clearly demonstrated in the case of Enron, where junior employees were turned against their superiors, ultimately leading to the downfall of Jeff Skilling and Kenneth Lay, the two senior officers. Watergate is another good example of the power of falling dominos.

We will return to the important point of how companies should treat co-accuseds later.

Strategic Approach to Allegations

This chapter deals with internal investigations up to the point when they will, or will not, be self-disclosed to the authorities. It should be noted that many acts of bribery could be prosecuted[6] as fraud or money-laundering, because the offences overlap and are sometimes indistinguishable.

Is it Fraud or Bribery?

Bill Bunger, a salesman for Evil Boys Limited, and Gordon Grabbit, a buyer for Silly Billy Toys, collude to make lots of money for themselves. Gordon Grabbit signs Goods Received notes for £500,000's worth of toys that were not delivered but were instead sold for cash by

---

Billy Bunger to market stallholders. They share the proceeds of £400,000 equally and have a happy time.

The question is, which offences prevail? Did Billy Bunger bribe Gordon Grabbit, or are they primarily guilty of offences under the Fraud Act, or of conspiracy?

Is there any difference if the share-out is as shown in Table 34.1?

Table 34.1   Relationships Between Bribery and Fraud

Billy Bunger Gets	Gordon Grabbit Gets
£1,000	£399,000
£100,000	£300,000
£200,000	£200,000
£300,000	£100,000
£399,000	£1,000

Table 34.1 suggests that the smaller the proportion of gains to the corrupt decision-maker (in the example, Gordon Grabbit) the more likely the primary offence is bribery rather than fraud.[7]

There is little doubt that regulators will try to classify overlapping cases as bribery simply to bring them into their own domain. But do the facts actually support this? Internal investigations should concentrate on establishing the facts, how they might be interpreted. What charges, technical defences or negotiations that might result should be left until much later.

In some fraud–corruption cases, unless the company is prepared to:

•   allow the perpetrators escape ***all*** criminal and civil sanctions;

or to:

•   take no contested disciplinary or contractual action;

it must either:

•   self-disclose the case to the SFO (on the basis that it will find out from any remedial action actually taken);

or:

- accept the risk that if the SFO discovers what has gone on, it will try to take draconian action.

This sort of dilemma – when **_fraudsters_** are in effect able to extort immunity – is an unfortunate consequence of the Bribery Act.

Brief Legal Background in the UK

INTRODUCTION

The civil and criminal laws on fraud and corruption are more than slightly complex, subject to change and judicial interpretation, and well beyond the scope of this book.[8] However, there are some basic points that managers should note when entering the unsafe world of fraud investigations.

STANDARDS OF PROOF FOR REGULATORS

Different standards apply as an investigation unfolds:

- **The first stage** is whether there is evidence of a reportable offence, because there is nothing in any law or regulation that requires anyone to self-disclose mere suspicions. The evidence must have substance.
- **The second stage** is whether a case meets the SFO's acceptance criteria (see page 67). If it does not it will be abandoned or referred to another agency that is unlikely to have – or want – powers to negotiate a civil disposal.
- **At the third stage** UK prosecutors must apply the Full Code Test (see page 140) in deciding whether to lay criminal charges:
  - Is the evidence sufficient to result in a reasonable prospect of conviction?
  - Is prosecution in the public interest?
    If both of these conditions are not met, prosecution should, in theory, be abandoned, but here is the rub: civil disposal introduces an intermediate level where the evidence is not strong enough to satisfy the test but enough to justify negotiations.
- **Then to the fourth stage**: to succeed with a criminal complaint, the prosecution must prove – to the satisfaction of a jury – all of the elements of the offence and the accused's responsibility beyond reasonable doubt. This is an extremely high standard.

Civil cases must be proven on a balance of probability which is obviously a lower standard, but still sometimes difficult to meet. The different civil and criminal law standards mean that it is quite feasible that evidence from an internal investigation is sufficient to support civil action against a fraudster but not enough to pass the Full Code Test for a bribery offence.

---

8   And the authors' knowledge.

LIBEL AND SLANDER

Libel is an untrue defamatory statement in a permanent form: usually in writing. Slander is oral libel and is governed by similar rules. Anything which is true is unlikely to be judged as defamation.

People who are the subject of an investigation sometimes threaten to take civil action claiming that they have been defamed. In most cases, this is no more than a ploy to throw an investigation off course.

Defamation

An accusation made directly to a suspect to the effect that the interviewer believes him responsible for dishonesty is unlikely to be slanderous. Similarly, an unproved, or even incorrect, allegation to a potential witness will not normally be actionable. However, an unproved and untrue defamatory statement, for example, that someone is a thief, made in public or to a person who does not have a common business interest, may be actionable.

In proceedings for libel or slander, the claimant must establish that the words used about him were *untrue,* defamatory and lowered his estimation in the minds of right-thinking people (i.e. not readers of The *Guardian*).

So Bad it Didn't Matter

Interestingly, in the fight between Neil Hamilton and Mohamed Al Fayed, it was argued that neither could be defamed, as their reputations were already in tatters. This is an interesting concept, but not one that companies should rely upon.

The claimant has to prove that the statement was made to at least one person[9] and that it caused him some quantifiable damage. There is a vast difference between threatening to take action for alleged defamation and succeeding. Besides that, during the ensuing discovery and legal processes, the claimant may be compelled to produce records that destroy his case and provide evidence of other transgressions. Threatening action for libel or slander is easy but it can be a very unwise tactic for skulduggers. They would be well advised to follow the dictum:

Before you litigate, dig two graves.

---

9   Other than the defendant's wife and – these days, presumably – his or her 'civil partner'.

There are two defences to actions for defamation:

1. Justification

The burden of proof is on the defendant to show that the statement was substantially true. *For example, in the British case of The Observer v Redgrave the general article was substantiated although some words could not be justified. The court determined that libel had not been committed.* Thus if a defendant can prove that the allegations were substantially true, he will not be penalised.

2. Legal Professional Privilege

Communication between a lawyer for advice (in contemplation of legal proceedings) and his client is normally absolutely privileged (see below).

Only in exceptional circumstances could the victim of fraud, or someone working on its behalf, be successfully prosecuted for slander or libel. However, the rule is to handle all investigations confidentially and to avoid making wild allegations whatever the circumstances.

MORE ON PRIVILEGE

The principle is[10] that in both criminal and civil proceedings, certain material is classified as privileged and does not normally have to be disclosed to the opposing party, including regulators. This may be important, for example, in protecting the results of an internal investigation from disclosure. On the other hand there are also many cases where it is beneficial to release privileged information.

Bad Lawyering

An investigation report set out overwhelming evidence that a senior American bank manager had accepted bribes in return for approving multi-million dollar loans on commercial properties that did not exist. The Bank's fidelity claim was disputed by insurers on orphic grounds and depositions were ordered. The Bank's lawyers argued for four days that its investigator's reports were privileged and refused to release them. They also objected to almost every question: again on the grounds of privilege.

Over a relaxed team dinner on the fourth night of depositions, the leading lawyer congratulated himself on 'holding those bastards at bay' over the privileged reports and was obviously not displeased that his firm was clocking up fees at the rate of $3,000 an hour. He asked the

---

10   The rules have recently become much more complicated. For example communications between in-house counsel and managers are privileged under UK law but not in European Union cases.

investigator what he thought, but was visibly shaken over the response that the whole affair was nonsense and that rather than damage the bank's case, releasing the report would assist it. 'Oh', said the lawyer, 'I haven't really read it word for word'.

A few days later the report was handed over and the case took a dramatic turn for the better.

Communications subject to legal professional privilege normally include:

- All communications between a client (or his agent) and his solicitor (or his agent), to obtain legal advice or in contemplation of legal proceedings;
- Without prejudice correspondence;
- Internal reports prepared by a Special Task Force specifically created to investigate an important matter with a view to legal proceedings or to obtain legal advice;
- Communications between employees and others who have a common business interest. For example, internal reports, staff appraisals and personal references are usually protected under this rule.
- Also, an accusation made about a suspected crime to the police with a view to detecting an offender is privileged (In the UK see Kine v Sewell 1838).

Privilege may be lost:

- When the communication forms part of a criminal or civil fraud scheme or its planning;
- Publication is excessive or malicious;
- When information that would otherwise be privileged is obtained illegally (see the cases of Dubai Aluminium and Memory Corporation v Sidhu (1999)).

The European courts have ruled that communications between managers and in-house lawyers are not privileged,[11] but those with external counsel are! Privilege can only be waived by the party entitled to its protection, including boards of directors, liquidators and trustees in bankruptcy.

RIGHTS AGAINST SELF-INCRIMINATION

In theory, everyone in the UK has a fundamental right against self-incrimination and is not required to answer questions or reveal self-incriminatory evidence, but there are exceptions:

- If the police execute a search warrant, any document or other material recovered can be produced in evidence, although the accused is under no obligation to explain it;

---

11   Although they are privileged under UK law.

- Under the Police and Criminal Evidence Act (PACE), when officials or company representatives 'charged with the investigation of offences'[12] reach the point in an interview where they conclude they have reasonable grounds for suspecting that an offence has been committed, they must caution the subject with the following:

Words of a UK Caution

You do not have to say anything. But it may harm your defence if you do not mention when questioned something which you later rely on in court. Anything you do say may be given in evidence. Failure to comply with this requirement is likely to render all further interview evidence inadmissible.

- Under the Criminal Justice and Public Order Act 1994, if a person – when questioned by a public authority (such as the police or the SFO, or cautioned by a company-retained investigator) – fails to mention any fact relied on in his defence, the court may draw such inferences as appear proper.

False Alibis

If a robber claims that he is innocent and at the time of the alleged offence was at ballet classes, he is required before trial to produce details of the witnesses and other evidence he plans to call to support his alibi. The object of this is to prevent the prosecution being ambushed at the last minute by a specious defence.

- The services of employees and third parties may be terminated immediately if they fail to comply with contractual terms that require them to cooperate in investigations (subject to compliance with PACE).

Everyone is required to answer every question honestly and to produce every record requested in response to a Section 2 CJA 1987 Order, whether or not it is self-incriminatory. The Court will not admit oral evidence thus obtained unless it is to rebut the defendant's untruthful statements subsequently given under oath. The prosecution can, however use all evidence to launch other, unrelated, charges.

Defendants in civil cases (and especially in response to a civil search order) have no general right against self-incrimination, although some will protest on the grounds

---

12   This is not restricted to professional investigators. Courts decide on a case-by-case basis whether a caution should have been administered or not.

that disclosure could result in criminal prosecution or interfere with their human rights. Specific legal advice should be obtained on a case-by-case basis.

DISCLOSURE OF EVIDENCE AND OTHER MATERIAL

In civil cases

In civil cases, the parties normally go through a stage of 'discovery', when any evidence, or any other material that could be relevant, has to be disclosed to the opposing side. *For example, the defendant might be compelled to disclose all of his assets or documentation which establishes his responsibility for wrongful acts.* The claimant also has to disclose any evidence which could conceivably assist the defendant. This aspect has to be carefully handled.

Disclosure in Civil Cases

When a civil Search Order is executed, any material which the defendant argues is privileged is usually retained by the supervising solicitors, who may refer disputes to the judge. In short, the self-incrimination argument should not be an issue. However, evidence recovered in civil proceedings is not normally admissible in criminal courts, but there are exceptions, the most notable being when the accused gives permission.

Under Section 7 of the Civil Procedure Act 1997(2) a civil court can grant an order (Search Order, or the artiste previously known as Anton Piller) authorising a person 'to enter on any land or in any building in the possession of a party to the proceedings to detain or take custody of any relevant property or evidence'.

These are extremely powerful orders, often used as a FIRST STEP and issued on the basis of an application without notice, heard in camera,[13] and executed by the plaintiff's solicitors and investigators, accompanied by independent supervising solicitors in what is usually a dawn raid. A defendant's failure to comply – and provide the evidence ordered or property specified – amounts to contempt of court.

Applications for search orders must be supported by affidavit evidence giving full and frank disclosure of all matters that the court should take into account and setting out fully the reasons for – and against – the application, including the probability that evidence would disappear if the order were not granted.

A supervising solicitor, who must be present when the order is served and represents the court, is obliged to explain its terms to the respondent. Once the search order has been executed, the supervising solicitor must file a report with the court and provide a copy to the respondent.

---

13   By a Judge in Chambers without the plaintiff's knowledge.

In criminal cases

Prosecutors are required to disclose, to the accused's representatives before trial, all of the material they have, including that which is not part of the case or which assists the defence.

Problems of Civil Disposals

This poses a problem for the SFO over both timing and extent when it wants, for example, to prosecute individuals but to conclude a civil disposal with their associated companies. If the disclosure is not fairly handled, defendants may have a valid claim for an unfair trial under the Human Rights Act.

The disclosure obligations make it imperative that all evidence (whether important or not) collected during an *internal investigation* is catalogued and preserved so that at the appropriate time, the company's legal advisers can decide what has to be disclosed. It should be noted that many criminal and civil prosecutions fail because of technical problems with disclosure. It is very important and sometimes critical.

PERVERTING THE COURSE OF JUSTICE

Perverting the Course of Justice is a serious crime and may arise from any action – in addition to statutory crimes such as perjury, fraud or witness interference – that is designed to warp decisions of a court or tribunal. The maximum sentence on indictment in the UK is 24 months' imprisonment *per incident*. Perjury and witness intimidation can result in imprisonment for life!

Perjury Act

Section 1(1) of the Perjury Act 1911 makes it a criminal offence when a lawfully sworn witness or interpreter in judicial proceedings wilfully makes a statement which he knows to be false or does not believe to be true and which is material to the proceedings. It should be noted that a perjury conviction cannot rely solely on the evidence of one witness but must be corroborated. A witness who swears in court something which he believes to be untrue, even if it later emerges to be true after all, is still guilty of perjury.

Thus companies conducting internal investigations must be careful to ensure that:

- Evidence is not destroyed or fabricated;
- Witnesses are not intimidated or coerced;
- False evidence is not produced.

And that no other action is taken (or not taken) that could be convincingly argued as perverting the course of justice. Risks are reduced, if not eliminated, when investigations are conducted under a specified policy, to an agreed Investigations Plan, by professional investigators supported by experienced litigation lawyers.[14]

Legal representatives and solicitors must not allow a client to deliberately mislead the police or other investigating authorities. If they suspect this is the case, they must advise the client accordingly or quietly withdraw. It is unethical for a legal adviser to assist any client he knows is lying.

Internal reports that incorrectly conclude that an act of bribery has not been committed (or are deliberately contrived to that effect) could, in the extreme, be argued as a perversion of the course of justice. For this reason, alone, all investigative reports into alleged serious frauds and corruption should be reviewed by independent Queen's Counsel[15] before a decision is taken whether or not to self-disclose.

Disclosures do not have to be made to any regulatory agency or any other external party until the facts of the case have been established and this must always be the first priority.

ILLEGALLY AND UNLAWFULLY OBTAINED EVIDENCE

The Investigations Plan should ensure that evidence is obtained legally.

Hewlett-Packard

In an investigation into alleged boardroom leaks, Hewlett-Packard admitted that its retained investigators had improperly accessed telephone call logs by pretexting, spied on other board members and their families, collected trash and attempted to install hacking software on the laptop of a journalist. The scandal led to a federal investigation, a Congressional enquiry and the resignation of H-P's board members, including the Chief Ethics Officer.

Illegal[16] collection of evidence in the UK normally involves one of more breaches of the Acts listed in Table 34.2.

---

14   Not Mr Bouffant.

15   With the written opinion filed in the 'Adequate Procedures Dossier'.

16   'Illegal' means 'against the law': 'Unlawful' means there is no law specifically approving an action.

Table 34.2 Unlawful–Illegal Investigative Techniques

Relevant Statute	Offence	Types of Evidence
Data Protection Act 1998	Obtaining or disclosing personal data from a computer system	Hacking Telephone call records, credit cards and banking details
Theft Act 1968	Obtaining property by deception	Trash searches (when the material concerned is not returned to the trash bins after analysis)
Regulation of Investigative Powers Act	Interception of communications	Including internal communications when the business practices provision of RIPA are not observed
Computer Misuse Act 1990	Unlawful access to computer systems	Hacking, decoy and Trojan programs
Protection of Harassment Act 1997	Trespass, nuisance inducing a breach of contract	Surveillance Pretext investigations
Bribery Act 2010	Bribery	To obtain information by inducing improper performance by its custodian

In addition investigators must take care that they do not incite witnesses to breach their contracts with their employers by, for example, getting them to disclose confidential material, especially when they receive a financial or other advantage for doing so.[17]

Illegally or improperly obtained evidence is normally admissible in both civil and criminal proceedings in the UK,[18] although censure of the party exhibiting it is likely. A detailed and legally approved Investigations Plan should eliminate such risks.

PRIVATE PROSECUTIONS

Under the Prosecution of Offences Act 1985 Section 6(1) a private criminal prosecution can be started by anyone and if it succeeds, costs may be recovered from police funds. Police authorities do not like coughing up, but it should be noted that private prosecutions are not permitted under the Bribery Act.[19]

Individuals and companies should carefully consider the advisability of launching a private prosecution, but the option may be valid in cases of competitive bribery–fraud where the SFO shows disinterest.

A private prosecution is commenced with an application (laying of information) to a magistrate to issue a summons or a warrant[20] for the arrest of the accused. Magistrates are required to comply unless there are compelling reasons for refusal. Thereafter, the case

---

17   Which may be a breach of the Bribery Act 2010 and could result when whistle-blowers are paid for informing.

18   But this may not be so in the USA.

19   But an almost identical offence under Section 4 of the Fraud Act can be privately prosecuted.

20   The legislation is being changed so that the permission of the Director of Public Prosecutions will be required before an arrest warrant is issued.

will continue through the normal process. It may be adopted by the Crown Prosecution Service, pursued to the full extent of the law, or abandoned.

HUMAN RIGHTS ACT

Human Rights legislation is (or was intended to be) to protect citizens against intervention by the State and includes the right to a fair trial, privacy, and enjoyment of assets, among other things. Public Authorities, including the police and SFO have to follow very strict guidelines on the way they conduct investigations to make sure they comply with a vast array of complex procedures on such things as interception of communications, surveillance, interviews, undercover and pretexts, disclosure and the use of confidential informants.

All courts have to take Human Rights legislation into account and they are inclined to expansively interpret it, resulting in cases being dismissed for what to ordinary folk appears to be a minor technical breach. The other side of the coin is that Public Authorities are authorised to use a battery of powerful weapons in the fight against crime.

A potentially serious problem arises under the self-disclosure regime and the idea that companies should be invited to investigate themselves. Firstly, by acting as proxies of the SFO, they and their advisers arguably become public authorities, with all of the obligations and restrictions but few of the benefits. Secondly, any technical or procedural misjudgments may result in disaster. Thirdly, the incentive for companies to shift blame for corporate skulduggery may compromise the rights to a fair trial of the individuals concerned.

KPMG and Employee Rights

In the case of United States versus Stein, 16 employees of KPMG were indicted for tax fraud. KPMG cooperated fully in the investigation and told the employees that if they did not cooperate individually with the regulators they would cut off all legal support. The employees appealed but eventually did as instructed, made admissions to regulators but later claimed that the compulsion imposed was a violation of their 5th Amendment protection against self-incrimination. Further, they contended that the government had deprived them of their right to a fair trial by holding a gun to KPMG's head. The court chastised prosecutors over their pressure tactics and subsequently dismissed thirteen of the indictments.

The bottom line of the self-disclosure and self-investigation regime is that it shifts the massive investigatory risks, costs and liabilities from regulators to the accused company. It also presupposes that the resulting evidence will not be judged on the Full Code Test but by much lower standards (see page 140). It is little wonder that the SFO likes self-disclosures.

RIGHT TO A FAIR TRIAL

The Universal Declaration of Human Rights, the US Constitution, the European Convention on Human Rights and the UK Human Rights Act, among others, all enshrine the principle that everyone is entitled 'in full equality to a fair and public hearing [...] in the determination of [...] any criminal charge against him'.[21] To what extent basic rights apply to body corporates is less clear but a working assumption is that they do not.

A fair trial – as well as all investigations leading to it – must adhere to a number of important protections and if it does not is likely to fail. The protections most relevant in the context of the Bribery Act include:

- A presumption of innocence;
- Rights against self-incrimination;
- No retrospective application of the law;
- A prohibition of double jeopardy.

A prosecution may also be impeded or quashed because of:

- Contempt of court;
- Witness intimidation;
- Non-disclosure of evidence;
- Adverse public prejudicial comments by a public authority:[22] for alleging that the accused is obviously guilty;
- Coerced confessions.

In addition, public authorities, such as the police, the SFO and other agencies, as well as private firms and citizens working on their behalf,[23] are required to adhere to a complex matrix of regulations designed to protect citizens against state interference. These include investigative techniques such as surveillance, use of informants, communications interception, undercover investigations and searches. One procedural mistake and it's curtains.

The system of self-disclosure, proxy investigations and civil settlements, used by the American authorities and much admired by the SFO, is baited with traps in which they could fall, resulting in trials being held as unfair. We will return to this point later.

---

21   http://www.echr.coe.int/ECHR/EN/Header/Basic+Texts/The+Convention+and+additional+protocols/The+European+Convention+on+Human+Rights/.

22   Or possibly in the media.

23   And this is a serious danger in 'Proxy Investigations': see later.

35 *Key Elements and Case-handling*

Introduction

A number of important elements[1] must be proven beyond reasonable doubt in criminal cases and on a balance of probabilities under civil law. These are described below, mainly as they apply to fraud and corruption.

Proof of Intent or Guilty Knowledge

Proof of responsibility of intent, guilty knowledge, or mens rea, which involves the highest degree of fault (see pages 98–9) may be proved by:

- Admissions and confessions by the accused;
- Failure to volunteer the truth when initially questioned, or inconsistent and demonstrably untruthful answers;
- Inference, being the outcome of a deliberate act or repeated transgressions;
- Circumstances surrounding the crime and deviations from accepted procedures;
- Falsified or destroyed records;
- Physical evidence, photographs and films;
- Opinion of expert witness.

Usually the best method of establishing guilty knowledge is through admissions made by the suspects during interviews, through demonstrable lies or from statements of witnesses. Success in this area depends on effective interviewing.

It is important to note that, in bribery cases, the intent of the coercer is entirely separate from that of the extorter. Thus it is conceivable, even in apparently simple collusive agreements, for the coercer to be convicted under Section 1 of the Bribery Act and for the extorter to be acquitted under Section 2, and vice versa.

Proof of Personal Gain or an Advantage

Proving that fraudsters gained from their dishonesty is always persuasive and may result from:

---

1   In basic terms.

- Admissions made by the suspects;
- Analysis of the suspect's bank accounts, credit cards, cash books and other records;
- Analysis of bank accounts of suppliers, customers and third parties showing payments to the perpetrator or to a party nominated by him;
- Analysis of records kept by the perpetrator;
- Personal expenditure in excess of known and declared income;
- Statements of witnesses, especially expert testimony;
- Observation records;
- Extrapolations of known facts.

It is also essential in fraud cases to show that the loss was caused by the fraudster's actions (causation) and was not merely consequential. The offer of, request for, etc., a financial or other advantage has to be proven in bribery cases, but it does not matter whether or not any actual value was transferred.

Proof of Loss and Business or Other Advantage

Proof of loss (or intended loss) is vital in fraud cases and may be established by the methods shown in Table 35.1.

Table 35.1   Proof of Loss

How Proof is Established	Examples
Admissions by the suspect or his accomplices on the amount they have stolen	• The admissions may be presented to a court by the person who interviewed the suspect or by the suspects themselves
Documentary evidence Schedules	• Sales by a receiver of stolen goods or sales in excess of his legitimate purchases • Analysis of bank statements • Analysis of stock or other losses
By surveillance	• The results of surveillance or observation may be summarised on schedules, produced by a witness
Expert testimony	• An expert may give an opinion on the amount lost or defrauded

Loss computations must be fair and capable of scrutiny, but the victim is entitled to maximise its recoveries (see page 183 et seq for bribery cases).

Regulators usually calculate the benefits companies make from bribery with a messianic zeal unseen outside the Pink Pussycat Lap Dancing Club, using accounting techniques that sometimes defy gravity. **There is little to be gained by discussing the detail here of regulatory accounting other than to say that before making any self-disclosure, companies should pin down the intended approach in the specific case (see page 183 et seq).**

Causation

Causation connects intent and with an outcome (for example, that obtaining or retaining business can be linked to improper performance) and is a significant element in most fraud cases. However, offences under the Bribery Act do not require a causal link to be proven between an advantage offered, given, etc., and improper performance. It is only necessary to prove that the payer's intention was to induce improper performance or to influence a foreign public official (FPO). It does not matter whether or not the intended outcome was completed, but the coercer must know that what he intended was improper.

Proving the Essential Ingredients of Corruption Offences

OVERVIEW

Proving corruption cases beyond reasonable doubt is not easy and usually involves the following considerations[2] for bribe payment and receipt summarised in Table 35.2.

Table 35.2   Considerations in Bribery Offences

Element of the Offence	Questions and Comments
APPLICABILITY OF THE BRIBERY ACT	
Venue of the alleged offence	• What part of the Act was committed in the UK? • If wholly outside the UK, was bribery committed by a closely connected person (sections 1 and 2) or by anybody performing services for a relevant commercial organisation (Section 7)?
Status of the person accused	• A UK citizen or one normally resident in the UK? • A body corporate? • A relevant commercial organisation? • A closely associated person?
ASSOCIATION AND RESPONSIBILITY	
By an associated person	• What precisely is the nature of the association? • Was the person actually 'associated' at the time and bribing in that capacity? • What other interests does the 'associated person' have that may have caused him to offer an advantage?
Acting specifically on the company's behalf in the transaction concerned	• What precisely was the authority of the 'associated person' in the specific context concerned? • Is there anything, for example, in his contract of employment that proves he was not acting on the company's behalf at the time?

---

2   The overlapping of points is unavoidable.

Element of the Offence	Questions and Comments
COUNTERPARTY	
Was the recipient an FPO/PEP?	• Did the bribe payer know the extorter's status as an FPO? • Will he or his organisation be a cooperating witness?
OFFER, ETC., AND NATURE OF ADVANTAGE	
Offer, acceptance, request, etc.	• What factual evidence is there of this? • What alternative explanations are there?
Financial or other advantage	• What precisely was the advantage offered, etc.? • Was the advantage a bribe or a share in illicit profits? • How was it authorised? • How was it recorded? • Was it overt or covert? • Would acceptance of the advantage have been an offence in itself? • How does it benchmark in the context concerned?
Approved in the written law	• Was the recipient permitted to accept the advantage under the applicable written laws?
Causal link	• What is the link between the advantage and improper performance? • How can the two be related?
INTENTION	
Intent to induce	• What precisely was the intention of providing *or receiving* the advantage? • For what other reasons could such an advantage have been given? • What advantages, if any, were given in the past?
Evidence of guilty knowledge	• What evidence is there?
Was a directing mind involved, gave consent or connived?	• Which is likely to result in corporate liability
IMPROPER PERFORMANCE	
Of a relevant function or activity	• Does the function performed fall under the Bribery Act?
Was improper performance completed?	• This is not a defence to a section 1 or 2 but may be taken into account by a jury
Improper performance *The bribe payer must know that the performance he intended to induce was improper (the receiver does not need to have the same level of knowledge)*	• What precisely was the improper performance expected to achieve and how precisely did it differ from alternatives taken in good faith, etc.? • Did the bribe payer realise the performance he was supposedly trying to induce was improper? • Did he know that the acceptance of the advantage itself constitutes improper performance? • What alternative decisions could have been made? • What historical performance or precedents are available? • What policy decisions apply? • How would an expert witness regard the performance? • What was the financial or other impact of the alleged improper performance?

	• How does this differ from a decision taken in good faith? • How was the decision approved and recorded internally? • Was it in accordance with established procedures and precedents? • Did it result in adverse financial performance outside the normal limits of similar transactions? • If the decision were to be reprocessed, would the outcome be any different?
Decision criteria	• What precisely were the decision criteria used in the alleged improper performance? • How precisely do they differ from a decision taken in good faith? • How precisely do they differ from any precedents, benchmarks or previous transactions?
Receiving the advantage itself amounts to improper performance	• Did the 'associated person' know whether or not providing the advantage in itself amounted to improper performance? • Did he have understanding of the recipient's internal policies?
Written Law	• What written laws apply?
OBTAIN OR RETAIN A BUSINESS ADVANTAGE (Sections 6 and 7)	
To obtain or retain a business advantage in the conduct of business	• What precisely is the alleged business advantage? • How should the benefits be calculated?[3]
OTHER IMPORTANT FACTORS	
Previous offences	• Is the current case part of a continuing pattern?
Authority sought	• Was the decision declared in advance and transparent?
Motivation of the informant and improper actions by him or her	• What genuine or improper reasons could have motivated the decision?
Dominant offence: fraud or corruption	• Which is most relevant, based on the evidence?
Accounting violations and other offences (Companies Acts) and conspiracy	• What alternative or additional crimes may be involved?
Breaches of local laws and local regulatory action	

The Investigations Plan (see page 825) should focus on proving or disproving the above elements plus any others that arise as the case moves forward. The following paragraphs comment on some of the more important and contentious points in Table 35.2.

---

3   Pay very close attention to this.

PROOF OF IMPROPER PERFORMANCE

The prosecution must prove beyond reasonable doubt that the person offering the advantage knew that the performance he intended to induce would have been improper because:

a) acceptance of the advantage in itself would amount to improper performance;

or

b) the performance he intended to induce was taken from a position of trust and would be:
    – contrary to what a reasonable person in the UK would expect in relation to the type of function or activity concerned,
    – not in good faith,
    – not impartial.

Improper performance is the inevitable result of a perverted decision such as:

* One taken outside the decision-maker's authority;
* Non-compliant with procedures or precedents;
* Contrived or unnecessary;
* Concealed or misreported;
* Based on false evaluation criteria or invalid research or other input (a 'dodgy dossier').

Proving that a decision was not, in fact, actioned may seem irrelevant because it is only the intention that matters. But proof that nothing improper actually occurred (or could not have occurred) may influence a jury.

PROOF OF CONSENT OR CONNIVANCE

Investigations should also focus on whether *incoming, internal or outgoing bribery* was with the active participation of a senior manager or a directing mind. If so, the company could be corporately liable under sections 1, 2 or 6 of the Bribery Act. Once corporate liability has been established, any other senior officer who consents or connives is also guilty of an offence under the same section. None of these offences are mitigated or excused by adequate procedures. However, individuals cannot be guilty of consent or connivance in a Section 7 offence.

Consent or connivance has to be more than mere negligence:

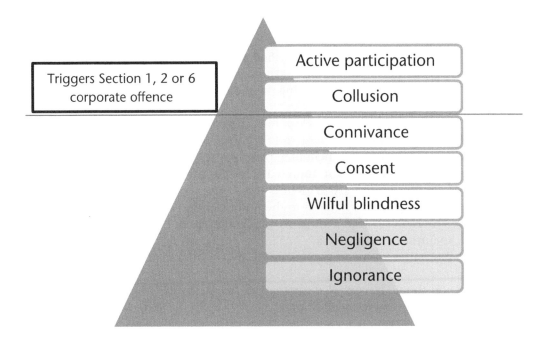

Figure 35.1 Hierarchy of Senior Management Involvement

Figure 35.1 represents the position that active participation by a directing mind is required to prove a corporate offence under sections 1, 2 and 6 of the Bribery Act 2010. Under sections 1 and 2 proof that the purpose was to obtain or retain business is not necessary, although it is under Section 6. Once corporate liability has been established, any other directing mind that connives or consents in the offence is also guilty under sections 1, 2, or 6.

The Investigations Plan should therefore thoroughly test for the involvement of directing minds both as participants and after the event. Cases involving them – that will result in corporate liability – are more serious than Section 7 charges, do not require the objective of obtaining or retaining business and are not mitigated by adequate procedures.

Handling the Specific Case

INTRODUCTION

In the first few hours after suspicion has been aroused, victims rush in blindly and make mistakes from which they never recover. Through disbelief, they try to seek more information, perhaps hoping that their suspicions are unfounded, or press too hard or too soon and alert the criminals too early. The result is that the initiative is lost, evidence destroyed, funds disbursed and, in some cases, the culprits forewarned and able to counter-attack, or disappear.

Every allegation has to be taken seriously, carefully assessed and, if necessary, elevated to senior management and on the basis that actions they take, or do not take, may be subject to examination in excruciating detail by regulators, a court or a tribunal.

INITIAL RECORDING AND ASSESSMENT

Procedures and resources should be specified to centrally record and professionally evaluate every allegation or suspicion of skulduggery. The unit or persons[4] responsible should as a minimum and without alerting the subjects:

- Make a permanent record of the allegation–suspicion;
- Assess the credibility of the content and the source (see page 674);
- Check all internal records, including personnel files and accounts, if necessary running a limited Critical Point Audit (CPA; see Chapters 18–20);
- If it is not already obvious, try to identify the source of the information;[5]
- A short report should be addressed to the Audit Committee (with a file copy for the Adequate Procedures Dossier) with a recommendation to:
  - take no further action;
  - refer the matter for investigation and to advise senior managers.

An annual report should be compiled summarising all incidents. This should be reviewed by the directors and noted in Board Minutes.

The remaining discussion assumes that the initial evaluation has identified a serious case that could result in serious fraud–bribery-related offences.

HANDLING THE INITIAL INVESTIGATION AS A TRUSTEE

A safe and fair way to deal with internal investigations – for organisations that might subsequently consider self-disclosing them – is to regard themselves as trustees of the regulators, especially in respect of individuals who may subsequently become defendants. This is prudent because mistakes made during a pre-disclosure investigation could compromise a case if it gets to court.

So is this the Answer?

One seminar delegate, on hearing the above, asked 'Well, isn't that the way to go? Mess up the internal investigation and make sure the regulators never recover from a poison pill?' **This is not advised!!**

The fact is that it is almost impossible to decide how serious initial suspicions or allegations might be and whether they involve fraud, bribery or both. The safe bet is not to worry about the distinctions, to assume the case is probably much worse than it first appears and to concentrate on establishing the truth.

---

4   Ideally a team consisting of Legal, Compliance, Internal Audit and one professional investigator.

5   This is especially important for anonymous letters.

SENIOR MANAGEMENT RESPONSIBILITIES

Immediate priorities

There are five things directors should do immediately credible and serious suspicions come to their attention. They must ensure that:

1. Suspicions are treated seriously and assumed to be true.
2. Suspicions are handled securely and confidentially and preferably under the protection of legal privilege.
3. No external or remedial action is taken until the facts have been established.
4. Authority for the investigation is delegated to skilled resources under the command of a senior, independent line manager.
5. They monitor all important cases and ensure they are resolved.

Failure in any of the above usually leads to problems.

Delegating authority

Experience shows that delegating command (and worse still the day-to-day running) of an investigation to a committee results in disaster. It is far better for the board to authorise an individual director (not in legal, compliance, corporate security or Human Resources) – independent of all contexts that might be investigated – to take command of a specialist team.

The main reasons for this are;

- Investigations should be professionally managed in the same way as any other major project. Lawyers, investigators, forensic accountants, all lovable though they undoubtedly are, are seldom good managers;
- All decisions must be taken in a commercial context based on what is best for the organisation and all of its stakeholders;
- Budgets and costs must be controlled;
- The senior line manager should be empowered to make quick decisions and to control the tension that there MUST be between legal and investigative specialists (see below page 677).

Delegation of authority to conduct potentially serious investigations should be recorded in Board Minutes, setting out:

- The objectives of the investigation(s);
- The covert and other techniques that are approved;
- Legal and investigative budgets;
- Guidelines for the retention of legal, investigatory and other resources;
- Reporting format and frequencies.

Reporting Frequencies

It is both understandable and proper that senior managers should be updated as an investigation moves forward, but a sensible balance must be struck. In one case, the investigative–legal team was required to make a formal presentation to a special committee of the board every morning. The result was that around 20 per cent of the team's time was spent investigating and 80 per cent preparing PowerPoint presentations.

No matter how enthusiastic they may be, or how many detective books they have read, directing minds should not attempt to conduct investigations themselves, or allow them to be conducted by their partners, wives, or even mistresses or lovers.

INVESTIGATIONS TEAM RESOURCES

Structure and roles

For complex or difficult cases a project team or Special Task Force should be appointed (under the command of an independent line manager, as suggested above) containing *more than sufficient skills* and experience to complete the investigation quickly and professionally. The recommended team structure is as shown in Figure 35.2.

The **Documents Coordinator** should ensure that all evidence is catalogued, showing where and when it was found and by whom, so that the chain of evidence can be proven. He should maintain a detailed diary of the fraud or bribery case and the investigation. There must be a complete record of every enquiry made and every piece of evidence collected. This record may be critical if subsequently an internal investigation is handed over to regulators. He should also keep a record of all investigatory, legal and other costs for the Adequate Procedures Dossier.

The **Investigator** should be given the prime responsibility for being difficult, developing fraud theories, investigations plans, identifying informants, interviewing suspects and witnesses and for other tasks of an investigative nature. Under no circumstances should he command the case.

The **Lawyer** – *ideally a specialist in criminal and civil frauds* – should guide other members of the team on legal matters generally and review the evidence as it unfolds. He should not be put in command of the investigation, nor should he become involved in interviews with witnesses and suspects.[6]

The **accountant and a computer technologist** should be locked in a dark room to review records, accounts and computer files, looking for symptoms of concealment and deviations from normal procedures and for other actions listed in the Investigations Plan. And please remember, few forensic accountants qualify as investigators, primarily because they lack the street-level charm that is abundantly obvious with the real thing.

---

6   See pages 609 and 823 for suggestions on selecting lawyers.

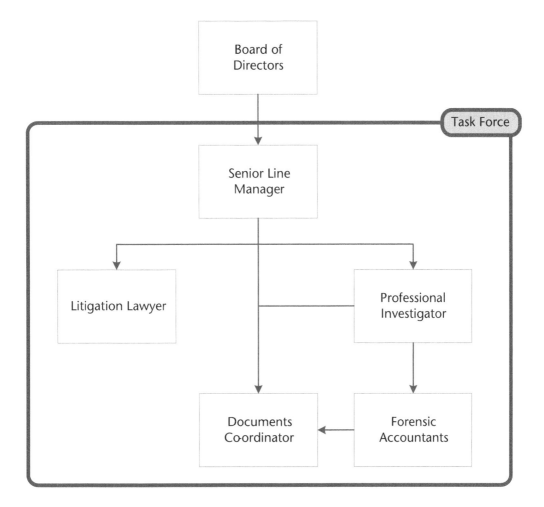

Figure 35.2 The Project Team or Special Task Force

Tension is a Good Thing

Tension between lawyers and investigators is what is known in the trade as a Tom Jones: meaning it is not unusual. Tension is usually a good sign because it means both are trying their hardest. Normally investigators push while lawyers pull. Teams without tension seldom get a case off the ground.

Selecting lawyers, investigators and other external resources

Most complex cases will justify the retention of external support and choices should be made carefully on a Kepner–Tregoe basis to avoid people like Mr Bouffant (see page 568).

THE FRAUD THEORY

The investigations team should consider the exact mechanics of the suspected skulduggery and write down everything that is known: the who, why, where, when, what and how. They should also list the who not, why not, where not, when not, what not and how not on the basis that things that did not happen but should have done are as important as deliberate acts.

The fraud theory is much like a jigsaw puzzle and at the start of an investigation the team will only have a few pieces and are unlikely to see the complete picture. As more pieces are collected they should be fitted into the puzzle. Investigators should keep an open mind. Pieces that do not fit are usually great clues to discovering brilliant new evidence: they should never be dismissed lightly.

The Missing Piece

Investigators were retained by the Central Bank of a South American country to examine the evidence following the arrest and incarceration of two of its junior telex operators on a $20 million wire fraud. The case against them was powerful: three fraudulent telexes appeared to have been sent from machines under their control and they were the only people on duty at the time. The police were confident of securing a conviction.

The Investigators asked to see the bills from the telephone company charging for the fraudulent telexes, but when they eventually appeared there was no mention of the three incriminating messages. Not only that, but the bills showed that after 12.11pm on the day in question, the bank had not been charged for a single telex when in fact it had sent over 200.

A computer log of the country's incoming and outgoing telexes was reviewed and this revealed that after 12.11pm not a single telex had been sent or received by hundreds of subscribers. This was an impossibility and the sort of deviation that cries out for investigation.

Subsequent investigations proved that the fraud had been committed in the central exchange by masquerading a test machine as the bank's. This connection had resulted in the exchange's logging system being inadvertently disabled until 00.00 hours the following day. The bank's employees were released and operators in the central exchange successfully prosecuted.

Explaining the one piece that did not fit broke the case open.

Similarly, evidence of any – even minor – dishonesty helps swing the initiative in the company's favour and is particularly important when suspects are interviewed.

The Expenses What Did It

A senior marketing manager was suspected of large-scale fraud, although evidence was neither clear nor convincing. However, the Investigators discovered that, for the previous five years, he had falsified his expense statements. When they interviewed him, they made it clear that, whatever happened, he would be dismissed and prosecuted for the expenses fraud. Against this background the manager believed he had nothing to lose by admitting the more serious offences and he did so and offered to make full restitution. Although he was still prosecuted, the victim company supported his pleas in mitigation.

So the bottom line of all investigations is that small things and attention to the finest details matter.

THE INVESTIGATIONS PLAN

Principles

An Investigations Plan should be prepared to align with the Fraud Theory and should be a step-by-step series of actions[7] leading from the starting position to a conclusive resolution of the case. The Investigations Plan and the Fraud Theory should be updated in parallel as a case moves forward.

Establish and maintain privilege

Every effort should be made to ensure that internal investigations are protected by legal professional privilege, with all reports and correspondence incorporating a caveat along the following lines:

> *This communication has been prepared for legal advice and in contemplation of legal proceedings.*

This, hopefully, will prevent the release of the information to any third party without permission, but it is always worth double checking that a proposed battle over privilege is really worth fighting (see page 804).

---

7   Involving only techniques that have been approved.

Secure critical records

Immediately suspicions are aroused, the company should suspend its routine records destruction programme and make sure that everything that could be relevant is preserved, including:[8]

- Cancelled cheques and cheque stubs;
- All electronic data and emails;
- Computer systems logs;
- Access control logs;
- Correspondence files;
- Expenses statements and vouchers;
- Purchase invoice originals and goods inward records;
- Telephone call and computer access logs;
- Trader and other voice archives (including voice-mail).

If some or all of these cannot be secured without alerting the suspects, collection should delayed until the FIRST STEP.

Identify potential witnesses

Investigators should consider what evidence might be obtained from witnesses and how they might be persuaded or compelled to help. For example:

- By simply asking for cooperation (but after the FIRST STEP);
- In lieu of civil or criminal actions being brought against them;
- In lieu of dismissal or termination of a business relationship;
- In lieu of payment of arrears or damages;
- In response to a summons Section 2 Order or witness order.

Any proposed payment or grant of immunity to witnesses should always be specifically approved by the team's legal advisers. The danger is that inducing a witness to breach his contract of employment could be regarded as bribery.

Consider covert techniques

The team should consider what covert techniques might help in breaking through the imaginary barrier referred to earlier, including:

- Interception and covert recording of company telephone lines;
- Installing covert telephone logging equipment, to record the details of calls made and received;
- Installing covert monitors on computer systems and data lines;
- Intercepting company mail *(including email)*;

---

8   And recorded so that at the appropriate time they can be reviewed for self-disclosure.

- Installing video or audio recorders and automatic number plate recognition equipment;
- Using pretext or undercover investigations;
- Searching the suspect's work area or office;
- Searching or freezing the suspect's PC and covertly copying his fixed and removable media.

It is critical that only approved techniques are used and that they are proportionate to the seriousness of the offences suspected.

Problems of Covert Techniques

In February 2012 the US Government filed a motion in the US District Court to dismiss with prejudice all cases against multiple defendants in what is known as the Shot Show Sting by an FBI and Department of Justice undercover team. The farcical case demonstrated just how easy it is to foul up with undercover and sting operations, even when arguably the best teams in the world are involved.

In proxy investigations the company's lawyers and investigators need to remain alert to all of the procedural requirements imposed on public authorities and if they fail to do so, there will be trouble.

Planning the first step and finalising the plan

The team should plan the FIRST STEP carefully so that it seizes the initiative from skulduggers while providing the foundation for clearing innocent people and organisations of suspicion.

There are usually six critical aspects:

1. Maintaining a detailed chronology of the skulduggery.
2. Effective interviewing of witnesses and suspects based on the domino principle (see pages 800 and 837).
3. Analysis of documents.
4. Forensic accounting.
5. Electronic – and especially email – discovery.
6. Forensic analysis of computers.

The Investigations Plan should be finalised, showing the actions to be taken, by whom, and the realistic timescale set. In complex cases, creating a database on Microsoft Access or FileMaker Pro is recommended,[9] because it enables activities to be efficiently scheduled

---

9   Details are available from info@cobasco.com.

and tracked, automatically creates a chronology, tracks exhibits and statements and establishes an audit trail. The plan should be subject to a final legal and managerial review.

TAKING THE FIRST STEP AND FOLLOW-UP

Normally, the FIRST STEP should be taken early in the morning and early in the week through simultaneous actions. The results should be analysed at the end of the first day or the following morning and further work completed in line with the Investigations Plan. The team should ensure that:

- All aspects of the investigation are progressed as quickly as possible, aiming for overwhelming proof;
- The Fraud Theory and Investigations Plan are constantly updated as new facts emerge;
- Civil actions to discover evidence and freeze assets are considered;
- Detailed file notes or reports (copied to the Documents Coordinator) are prepared on every significant meeting, interview or action and the database updated.

Delay is always to the advantage of skulduggers, if for no other reason than that should an investigation drag on, the company will lose interest.

THE FINAL REPORT

As soon as possible, one or more reports should be prepared, marked as privileged and addressed to the company's lawyers with the primary objective of obtaining legal advice, pursuing recoveries and deciding whether remedial action and self-disclosure are necessary. The report must be professionally written, indexed, supported by copies of all exhibits, statements and detailed schedules. It is critical that opinions are supported by facts and that the report is written on the assumption that its every word can be justified from the witness box in the Old Bailey (see Chapter 37).

INDEPENDENT REVIEW OF THE EVIDENCE

In serious cases, where there is any evidence of a bribery or money-laundering offence or any mandatory disclosure requirement, the report should be reviewed by a specialist litigation lawyer (and preferably a Queen's Counsel) who was not involved in the investigation, giving his or her written opinion on whether or not the evidence passes the Full Code Test and whether or not any report has to be made.

If the answer to both questions is in the negative, there is no reason to self-disclose, but remedial[10] and disciplinary actions should be taken and the results recorded in the Adequate Procedures Dossier.

If the answer is in the affirmative, it is important that – before making any self-disclosure – the company:

---

10   Especially control improvements.

- Conducts a **CPA analysis** of all contexts and processes that might be relevant in a regulatory investigation;
- Carries out a high-level review of evidence – electronic and archived – that might be subject to disclosure;
- Reviews specific decisions, personal expenses and other matters that might compromise a directing mind;
- Carefully assesses other consequences of self-disclosure, including loss of business or damage to important business relationships and risks to employees and others based overseas **and, most importantly, tries to agree supposed losses with victims (see page 183);**
- Identifies potential victims, quantifies losses, claims and litigation;
- Consults directing minds working in the contexts concerned.

It is a bad mistake to self-disclose – even the most mundane case – without first fully assessing all of the potential consequences. A further briefing document should be prepared for the directors by their legal advisers and commercial managers setting out the arguments for and against self-disclosure *of the particular case.*

DECIDING NOT TO SELF-DISCLOSE

Even when the advice is that a bribery case might pass the Full Code Test, it may still be advisable not to self-disclose, especially if the violation is technical or trivial and appropriate remedial and disciplinary action has been, or will be, taken.

Self-disclosing to the Regulators

BACKGROUND

The reaction of most honest managers when they are confronted with a potential Bribery Act or other violation is to cooperate fully, confess and get the matter behind them as quickly as possible on the basis of 'Come to Jesus' and to avoid the time and costs of litigation. This decision should not be left to the heat of the moment, but should have been risk-evaluated and resolved as a policy decision along the lines discussed on pages 450–51. Even when policy has been specified, the facts of a particular case may dictate that it is treated exceptionally after all impacts have been assessed.

In short, it is imperative that all of the potential adverse consequences of self-disclosure be fully evaluated and that the current suspected misbehaviour is not seen in isolation. Almost equally, the company should consider the effect that prompt non-disclosure might have on its Fidelity and Directors' and Officers' Liability Insurance.

SETTING THE TERMS OF SELF-DISCLOSURE

Companies should consider precisely what their objectives are for self-disclosure. The principles are discussed in Chapter 17.

Once and For All

The Serious Fraud Office (SFO) has implied that companies that do not self-disclose are forever committed to a path of concealment and can never, ever report in the future. This is not so if the case is based on unsubstantiated suspicion with independent professional advice to that effect, fully documented and filed in the Adequate Procedures Dossier. Similarly, there is nothing to be gained for a company that genuinely believes that civil disposals are unethical to self-disclose if it can take effective remedial measures internally.

The company should carefully consider[11] what guarantees it would require as a condition of self-disclosing *alleged bribery offences*,[12] including:

- The regulators will not seek a 'civil disposal' or any other sanction unless the case fully passes the Full Code Test;
- Where such a standard is disputed, the facts will be assessed by an independent Queen's Counsel, whose decision shall be binding;
- The case will be handled in the strictest confidence and no identifying details will be publicised without a written agreement;
- All transactions and incidents that took place before July 2011, when the Bribery Act 2010 came into force, will not be investigated unless they are directly relevant to the current case;
- The company would not be willing to carry out a 'Proxy Investigation';
- All negotiated settlements must include individuals;
- Computation of alleged gains (criminal proceeds) will be assessed by a firm of independent accountants;
- Any order for repatriation of proceeds to a foreign country will be pro-rated according to the complicity of the nationals involved and in such cases the SFO will make every effort to ensure extorters are prosecuted in their home country;
- No effort will be made to pursue the company for alleged breaches of Section 2 of the Bribery Act 2010;[13]
- If a settlement cannot be reached, all information disclosed in the negotiation process will be disregarded.

It is highly unlikely that regulators will agree to the above 'wish list' but that does not mean it is not worth formulating.

---

11   BEFORE MAKING ANY SELF-DISCLOSURE.

12   The risk is for companies that are committed to the integrity of trying to eliminate bribery (by self-disclosing) is that the emphasis is switched to a civil disposal of technical Proceeds of Crime Act (POCA) violations with absolutely no action being taken against extorters. The net effect is at best zero and more likely an encouragement to others. This has been the result of most civil disposals, so far.

13   Where committed by a directing mind and on the basis that it is the loser.

APPOINT A HIGH-POWERED TEAM

The company should appoint a high-powered team consisting of a professional negotiator, the company's legal advisers, possibly a specialist Queen's Counsel, maybe even investigators, to finalise the reporting strategy. If both American and British regulators are potentially involved, even more care is necessary (see pages 146 and 211) over how, when and to whom disclosures might be made. If the company is regulated by the Financial Services Authority (FSA) it should decide whether the report will be addressed to that authority or to the SFO or to both.

DOUBLE BLIND INITIAL APPROACH

An initial approach should be made to a single agency in a face-to-face meeting by a professional negotiator accompanied by specialist lawyers,[14] none of whom have a traceable connection to the company, its directors or individual suspects. The company's name should not be disclosed, nor should details be revealed that could lead to its identification. The objective of this meeting (or meetings) is to outline the case anonymously and to seek the regulators' reaction to the 'wish list'. Full details of the approach and the reaction should be filed in the Adequate Procedures Dossier: whatever the outcome.

PREPARING A BALANCED CASE

If the double blind conditions are agreed,[15] a file should be presented to the selected regulators, based on the company's final internal report, supported by:

- Proof of adequate procedures;
- Any management changes that have been made;
- Control improvements that have been implemented and a summary of costs;
- Other mitigating factors, including extracts from the Adequate Procedures Dossier;
- Detailed calculations of supposed 'but for the bribe' profits (see page 183) and supposed losses;
- Has assembled its arguments in favour of a declination.

Finally, companies should never forget that regulators have as much to lose from a contested prosecution as defendants. Losses can be humiliating and bad for the CV when revolving through the regulatory–private sector door and along the Yellow Brick Road.

The excellent podcast by Davis Polk (see page 648) explains that it advanced Morgan Stanley's interest with the DOJ down three channels. The first was to handle the investigation into Mr Peterson's activities professionally and to check other areas for similar problems: the second was to document the compliance program in place at the material time and the third was to employ its advocacy skills against prosecution. This is very sound advice but there is a fourth channel. It is to make sure that the profits (if any) from bribery are accurately quantified (see page 183) and, if possible agreed with the alleged victim.

---

14   Possibly from a different country.

15   Which, it has to be said, will be unlikely.

36 *Regulatory Investigations*

Introduction

This chapter discusses collaborative (or proxy) and adversarial investigations involving the Serious Fraud Office (SFO) or other regulatory agencies. In essence, a proxy investigation is most likely to result from a self-disclosure,[1] whereas if a case is initiated by regulators it is classed as adversarial.

The background and possible approaches to both proxy and adversarial investigations, discussed below, are based on the assumption that, one way or another, the case is already in the hands of the SFO or other regulators. **Again, readers are cautioned that the discussion that follows is not a substitute for specific professional advice**, especially because some of the views expressed are so anti-Luvvie and the points covered so controversial that few people want to discuss them. So be it: wrinklies rush in where angels fear to tread and if this book gets people thinking – even if they do not agree – it will have served its purpose.

Common Background to Regulatory Investigations

EFFECTIVE AGENCIES

The sporadically satirical magazine *Private Eye* calls the SFO the 'Serious Farce Office', suggesting that it is useless. In truth, the agency carries out a difficult job reasonably well. Despite all the recent defections of senior officers through revolving doors, it is staffed by qualified lawyers, accountants and professional investigators. The agency has extensive powers, including compulsory disclosure and search and communications interception (see below). It should never be underestimated and neither should the US Department of Justice, or Securities and Exchange Commission (SEC), or any other regulator for that matter. They are serious critters who are best avoided.

However, there are two worrying concerns. The first is that the revolving door, Yellow Brick Road[2] highway tempts officials from regulatory agencies straight into the private sector, which encourages massive exaggeration of the importance of the Bribery Act, empire-building, and terrifying the amenable. As Ali G, the Prime Minister of West Staines Massiv, would say, they 'big it up'. The reality is that the more regulators hyperbolise the laws the more likely it is that they will create very lucrative employment opportunities

---

1   Note that it is possible to self-disclose and insist the SFO conducts the investigation with all of the attendant investigatory risks.

2   Investigators are well known for mixing metaphors.

for themselves in the private sector. As the excellent FPCA Professor says,[3] the cosy relationship between regulatory agencies and private sector specialists is a 'Cottage Industry' but, in reality, it is more like a gentlemen's club. But there is an important point to note and that is that the 'free agent' career path of some regulators is damaged if they make mistakes or get into deep water with courts.

Empire-building

An ex-Department of Justice lawyer, now in private practice, said that career progression in his old department depended on dreaming up expansive interpretations of the Foreign Corrupt Practices Act (FCPA) to empire-build the department and the powers of the lawyers working in it. The greater the fear generated, the more attractive their ex-employees became to private sector law firms.

The second concern is that the SFO shares the financial penalties. This again could be a motivator for exaggeration and the abandonment of the Full Code Test, resulting in creative framing of settlement agreements that avoid the word corruption, thereby enabling skulduggers to evade automatic and permanent debarment from government contracts. The result is a criminal justice system that is driven more by money than principle.

THE SFO'S TECHNIQUES AND TOOLS

Background

Richard Alderman, the ex-SFO Director, announced that the agency intends to use the full powers allowed under the Regulation of Investigatory Powers Act (RIPA) to investigate bribery cases, even when the most likely outcome is a civil settlement rather than a serious crime. The American SEC, Department of Justice and FBI have recently employed – in bribery cases – covert and aggressive techniques previously reserved for organised crime, narcotics and terrorism.[4] It is therefore important to examine what the most important of these tools and techniques are.

Orders under Section 2 Criminal Justice Act 1987

These enable the SFO to demand the production of any document and the answering of any question from any suspect or witness allegedly involved in skulduggery; and in cases of suspected overseas corruption to do so at a 'pre-investigation' stage. This means

---

3   A blog on the Foreign Corrupt Practices Act, available at: http://www.fcpaprofessor.com/ (accessed November 2012).

4   But have usually failed.

Section 2 orders can be used on fishing expeditions. This was never their intention and is no protection against self-incrimination. The orders are a dream weapon for regulators; yet they still moan that they don't have sufficient tools!

However, Section 2 orders and search warrants are not without danger for regulators: any misuse of privileged information, failure to make complete or truthful applications or full disclosures of both used and unused material can lead to disaster.

Iceland Fiasco – The Tchenguiz Case

The SFO had obtained search warrants alleging that Mr Vincent Tchenguiz, an Icelandic businessman, had provided Icelandic banks with false valuations for a property portfolio used to secure funding and had failed to disclose that many of the properties were already mortgaged. Mr Tchenguiz challenged the warrant.

In February 2012, Mr Alderman, the SFO's Director, had to eat dollops of humble pie, admitting that:

- The SFO had inadvertently miscast[5] information when obtaining the search warrants, exculpating that its caseworkers were extremely busy ... and had failed to identify and verify documents in their possession that contradicted the case against Mr Tchenguiz;
- The warrants were wrong and the SFO would be explaining to the courts what it did and why; ultimately it will be up to the judges to form a view;
- Mr T is claiming £100 million in damages.

The bottom line is that handling complex cases is always difficult, more so when they are pursued with a messianic zeal for a noble cause, or being bigged up for whatever purpose.

International cooperation and production orders

The SFO has extensive international powers that effectively mean that any record – including bank accounts, company formation records, powers of attorney, and other skulduggerish information can be obtained almost *anywhere in the world*. The SFO also has persuasive powers to motivate witnesses based overseas to fully cooperate in its investigations.

---

5   Luvvie-speak for a total cock-up.

Communications interception

Certain public authorities, including the intelligence agencies (MI5 and MI6), the police forces, HM Revenue and Customs, the Serious Organised Crime Agency and other enforcement agencies, including the SFO and the Information Commissioner's Office, are approved by Parliament to acquire and monitor voice and data communications in real time.

Detailed procedures are published by the Home Office in a Code of Practice which is available on the Internet and specifies:

- Warrants must be individually approved by the Secretary of State, but may cover multiple telephone lines, computer systems or mailing addresses;
- The Secretary of State must be satisfied that interception is 'necessary and proportionate' and in the interests of national security, for the purpose of preventing or detecting serious crime, or safeguarding the economic well-being of the United Kingdom;
- Information obtained from communications interception is not admissible in court, nor is it disclosed to the parties being investigated;
- Information obtained from communications interception must be destroyed immediately it is no longer required;
- All interceptions are regulated by the Interception of Communications Commissioner.

The Commissioner's last report was published in July 2010 and reveals that in the year ended December 2009 1,514 communications interception warrants were granted. The report does not say how many individual subscribers were involved,[6] identify the agencies making the applications, nor the results. It is likely that most warrants were obtained for terrorist and drug offences, rather than bribery, although that emphasis may change, given the revenue-enhancing benefits of civil disposals.

Call and Internet traffic data

In addition to real-time monitoring, authorised agencies *(including many local authorities which investigate such major crimes as Granny Smith's putting recyclable waste in the wrong bin)* are able to obtain land and mobile telephone call data showing the who, when and where of a communication, although not the content. The authorities are required to comply with the provisions of the RIPA and Codes of Practice. Applications are regulated by the Interception of Communications Commissioner, whose report for the year ended 31 December 2009 revealed that 525,130 requests were granted. Again, the number of individual subscribers involved is not disclosed.

Burgle and Bug

Part 3 Section 6 of the Police Act 1997 allows a Chief Constable (or his equivalent in other law enforcement agencies, which includes the SFO Director) to authorise covert entry

---

6   On warrants involving multiple targets.

into any premises, vehicles, boats or aircraft in the UK to search and plant eavesdropping or visual monitoring equipment providing such techniques are proportionate to the offences suspected. Operations are regulated by the Surveillance Commissioner. There is some question over how many B&B exercises take place annually, but it is suspected to be quite a lot.

Surveillance

Covert surveillance is also covered by the RIPA and may be authorised by a senior police officer as a proportionate technique. Surveillance includes observation or recording from static positions, vehicle and personal tracking, remote viewing via CCTV, trash searches and lip-reading.

Covert Human Intelligence and cooperating witnesses

Law enforcement agencies traditionally develop informants (politely referred to as 'Covert Human Intelligence Sources' (CHIS) and rudely as 'super-grasses') who may be paid or unpaid, or granted immunity and witness protection. Their involvement should be officially registered by the agency concerned.

The SFO, like any good investigator, works on the 'domino theory' to identify skulduggers low in a hierarchy to be turned to give evidence against their superiors. Many are very dodgy geezers and their participation in investigations must be made known to the defence, although this does not always happen. The unrevealed involvement of a CHIS should always be probed by the defence, because it is a potential case destroyer, as HM Revenue and Customs has found to its cost.

Electronic discovery and data-mining

All modern regulatory agencies have advanced technology that enables them to download, analyse and search massive datasets to quickly identify specific documents and to chart complex relationships.

Computer and other forensics

Current technology enables deleted files to be recovered from computers, tape recorders, mobile telephones, pagers, satellite navigation devices and other electronic equipment. Mobile telephone operators may be served with Section 2 orders to require them to deliver up data that enables either real-time or historic tracking of mobile telephones.

Access to official and other databases

The SFO has access to many official and other databases, including Suspicious Activity Reports (SARs), credit card and banking transactions, criminal and tax records, all of which should be disclosed at the relevant time to defendants. This does not always happen.

Civil disposals and negotiated settlements

Although these are technically not investigative tools, they are possibly the most powerful weapons in a regulator's armoury and have been a fact of life in the USA for decades. The SFO, Attorney General and Solicitor General all seem hell bent on importing and legitimising them into in the UK, claiming that they represent best practice and the moral high ground. They do not; rather, they are a perversion of the entire criminal justice system.

The USA: A Model Not To Be Admired

The US model of negotiated settlements is predicated on a criminal justice system that routinely imposes sentences ranging from 25 years to life imprisonment for white-collar crimes. These truly draconian sentences are mitigated if a defendant prostrates before prosecutors by admitting guilt at an early stage. Penalties can be mitigated even further if he becomes a cooperative witness and implicates others.

In the Enron case, Andrew Fastow, who pleaded guilty, was sentenced to six years' imprisonment, while his colleague, Jeff Skilling, who was found guilty after a contested trial on less serious charges, was sentenced to 24 years. The same sort of disparity appears in WorldCom and other cases.

In the USA guilty pleas are entered in:

- 95 per cent of fraud cases;
- 98 per cent of cases of embezzlement, forgery and counterfeiting;
- 96 per cent of bribery cases;
- 88 per cent of cases of money-laundering, racketeering and extortion.

These amazing rates might be because:

- Prosecutors only proceed with overwhelming cases. *But since prosecutors do not state what percentage of investigations are jettisoned at the initial vetting stage, we will never know*;
- US Prosecutors are godlike in their efficiency: this is unlikely;
- People capitulate even when they know the evidence against them is weak (or non-existent) to avoid life imprisonment or massive legal costs.

In the UK, penalties are less severe and thus the temptation for the innocent and semi-innocent to knee jerk into capitulation is far less.

Interesting Syntax

A consultation paper by the Attorney General (See 'The Introduction of a Plea Negotiation Framework': April 2008) stated that: 'at present only 66 per cent of criminal defendants in England and Wales plead guilty before trial, with 10 per cent of the remainder (assumed to compute as 3.4 per cent of the total) waiting until the first day of trial'.

There are three words in this statement that are especially revealing. The first two are 'at present', implying that things are due to change for the worse. The second is 'only', suggesting that regulators expect more than 66 per cent of citizens to hold up their hands before trial.

But please note that if these figures are correct they suggest that only 15 per cent of people charged with fraud and related offences are convicted following a contested trial. Again these statistics exclude all cases rejected at the vetting stage.

THE BOTTOM LINE

It should be clear from the above that the SFO and other agencies should be treated with respect. However, fear of a regulatory investigation should not intimidate individuals or companies into weakly capitulating just to avoid legal costs or for a quiet life, or to bribe their way out of trouble. It is one thing for a prosecutor to make up his or her mind that there is evidence to blag a settlement and quite another to convince a jury of this fact.

The Justice Department and the SEC (and, more recently, the SFO) have succeeded in negotiating settlements based on what are expansive interpretations of the legislation and particularly the definition of a foreign public official (FPO) and what constitutes obtaining or retaining business. Many interpretations have never been tested in court and there are powerful reasons for believing that regulators would rather not risk doing so. Even if they succeed, avoiding other problems is not easy.

Prosecutorial Discretion – No; Disaster – Yes

The US Department of Justice charged Lindsey Manufacturing, two senior officers and its Mexican agents of bribing Nester Morino, an employee of Comisión Federal de Electricidad (CFE) with a US$1.8 million yacht, a $300,000 Ferrari Spider and clearance of $170,000 worth of American Express charges, as well as a remittance of $600,000 to one of his relatives. The skulduggery started in 1997 and ended in March 2009 when ABB Limited, the Swiss electrical giant, voluntarily disclosed that its employees may have bribed CFE representatives. CFE had awarded contracts worth $81 million to ABB and $19 million to Lindsey.

The evidence against Lindsey appeared clear cut and was enhanced by the high rates of commission (30 per cent amounting to US$5.33 million) paid to the Mexican agents. However, the defence launched a vigorous argument against the Department of Justice's interpretation (which had never previously been challenged in adversarial litigation) that CFE was an instrument of government, arguing that Mr Morino was not a 'foreign public official' under the FCPA definition. US District Judge A. Howard Matz ruled that the jury would be allowed to decide the issue on the facts.

In May 2011 the jury found all the defendants guilty; the defence immediately appealed, alleging misconduct by the prosecution. In December 2011, Judge Matz dismissed all charges against all defendants with prejudice,[7] on the grounds of prosecutorial misconduct, stating:

'In this Court's experience, almost all of the prosecutors [....] for this district display admirable professionalism, integrity and fairness. So it is with deep regret that this Court is compelled to find that the government team allowed a key FBI agent to testify untruths before the grand jury, inserted material falsehoods into affidavits submitted to magistrate judges in support of applications for search warrants and seizure warrants, improperly reviewed email communication between one Defendant and her lawyer, recklessly failed to comply with the discovery obligations, posed questions to certain witnesses in violation of the Court's rulings, engaged in questionable behaviour during closing arguments and even made misrepresentations to the Court.'[8]

It is noteworthy that few of the websites run by regulators ever mention their failures, and there are enough of them. **Concealment of failures gives the impression that regulators are more effective than they truly are.**

The frightening statements made by some regulators about their draconian powers, including their intention to intercept communications and use other heavyweight investigative techniques, may come back to haunt them in cross examination in a contested trial.

Alderman's Needle

It was not clever for the SFO to make the bombastic statement that a person who pays $5 to a foreign hospital in order not to be jabbed with an infected needle (Alderman's Needle) might be prosecuted, when it is inconceivable that a jury faced with such a case would reach a finding of guilt, or a judge impose other than an absolute discharge. If the SFO carries through with some of its draconian threats to prosecute trivial cases it will fall flat on its face, lose all credibility and public, commercial and political support.

---

7   Meaning that they cannot be prosecuted again for the same alleged offences.

8   http://www.fcpaprofessor.com/milestone-erased-judge-matz-dismisses-lindsey-convictions-says-that-dr-lindsey-and-mr-lee-were-put-through-a-severe-ordeal-and-that-lindsey-manufacturing-a-small-once-highly-respected-ente.

The bottom line is that both individuals and companies against which bribery allegations are made, as well as regulators themselves, have much to lose by forcing a case to a contested trial or by trying to impose an unjustified and resisted civil disposal. Companies should remember this when negotiating with regulators!

Collaborative or Proxy Investigations

BACKGROUND AND PRINCIPLES

The scheme is that companies that self-disclose will be treated sympathetically and invited to appoint lawyers and other sleuths to investigate themselves. Self-disclosure is framed in a positive light and as a model of cooperation, but it is a disaster waiting to happen.

PriceSlaugherhouseCoopers

In criminal justice terms it is little different to having the Yorkshire Ripper engage PriceSlaughterhouseCoopers to investigate his mass murders with a view to negotiating a civil disposal.

Self-disclosure and proxy investigations are morally questionable, but companies will continue to accept them hoping to score Brownie Points with the regulators, while believing they can control the investigation's outcome. On both counts they are wrong because if self-investigation is not a temptation for skulduggery, nothing is.

News International

In the News International case investigating solicitors failed to disclose thousands of incriminating emails, claiming they were damaged beyond repair, only to find when challenged that this was not so. In the same case, the Metropolitan Police was called upon to investigate itself and the initial result was a lemon.

The procedure also encourages companies who were widely aware of what was going on to jettison co-accuseds – such as past and present directors, employees and agents – to save their own skins. This is highly unethical and results from coercive disposals rather than, as portrayed, civil jobbies. However, since some companies will accept proxy investigations, something should be said about them.

INVESTIGATIONS PLAN

Objectives

The objectives of a proxy investigation should be to establish the truth, including defensive and exculpatory evidence. The investigation should not simply be a one-sided dirt-digging pillage against submissive defendants. Planning should be along the lines suggested in Chapter 34, but with additional care applied to interviews and covert investigative techniques: both of which are fraught with more than the usual dangers.

The problem of proxy interviews

Interviews, held as part of a proxy investigation, are problematic for two reasons, besides their ethicality and inherent difficulty. The first is that company-retained lawyers and consultants must administer cautions as soon as they have grounds for suspecting that a subject has committed an offence (see page 806). If they fail to do so, the resulting interview evidence is likely to be ruled inadmissible in a criminal trial.

A Word of Caution

In a very large fraud–corruption case, in which the police were already involved, the company's solicitors, who were aiming for civil recovery, instructed the author to interview the principal skuldugger. The police were consulted and agreed, but asked that he be cautioned at the appropriate time, so that the interview would also be admissible in criminal proceedings. The lawyers disagreed and instructed the author not to administer a caution, warning 'If you do, and he clams up, your ass is grass.'[9]

The police consented to the interview being held without a caution. In a nine-hour session, the skuldugger confessed to everything suspected and to lots more and afterwards drove the author and a colleague back to the railway station, inviting them to join him and his mistress for a Chinese dinner! The offer was politely refused.

Six months later when interviewed by the police, the skuldugger refused to say a word, but the Crown Prosecution Service decided to call the author at the criminal trial, notwithstanding the fact that everyone knew the evidence was unlikely to be admitted.

Immediately the author was called into the witness box all hell broke loose and following a defence objection the jury was excused. For 90 minutes – which seemed like a lifetime – the author's ass was kicked for not administering a caution, without a word of support from the solicitors or prosecution. The inevitable happened and the interview evidence was, quite rightly, excluded but softened somewhat by the Judge's commendation of the

---

9   Verbatim from a lawyer with whom the author had worked extensively and was also a good friend.

author's skills and honesty. As a postscript, that confirms that justice works in odd ways, this must be the only trial ever in which a witness, who technically never appeared, was commended for his evidence.

The purpose of mentioning this case[10] is to emphasise that cautioning is tricky and investigators may be damned if they do and damned if they don't. Proxy investigations, therefore, make it much more difficult for companies to recovers losses, civilly because administering a caution may close the door on everything. Table 36.1 summarises the problem:

Table 36.1   Caution

Caution Administered?	Effect on Criminal Proceedings	Effect on Civil Proceedings
Yes: subject cautioned	Evidence is likely to be admissible or subject refuses to answer	Subject refuses to answer questions Recovery compromised
No: subject not cautioned	Subject answers (and maybe confesses) but the evidence is likely to be inadmissible	Subject answers question Recovery assisted

Table 36.1 indicates that administering a caution damages the chances of making civil recoveries.

The second point, which is particularly important when action might also be taken in the USA, is that lawyers must give witnesses and potential defendants what is known as the 'Upjohn Warning', along the following lines:

The Upjohn Warning to be Given Prior to Interviews

I am a lawyer from the xx Corporation which I exclusively represent. I do not and cannot represent you personally. This interview is to gather facts to provide advice to the Corporation in contemplation of legal proceedings. Your communications are protected by the attorney–client privilege but I must tell you that this applies solely to the Corporation and not to you. This means that the Corporation alone may decide to waive privilege and disclose our discussion to third parties including law enforcement and regulatory agencies. The Corporation alone may decide whether or not to waive this privilege at its sole discretion without notifying you further.

To proceed with this discussion you must agree that it will be kept in confidence and that with the exception of reporting to your own attorney you may not disclose the substance or

---

10   Besides the author bigging it up.

content with any third party including other employees or anyone outside the company. You may of course discuss the facts of what happened but not reveal details of this discussion. Do you have any questions?

Although the Upjohn warning is fair, for most subjects it is a turn off, especially when supplemented by a caution.

An Imaginary Case

X Ltd. was raided by the SFO. The company self-disclosed and agreed to run a proxy investigation during which its lawyers and investigators interviewed Douggie Skuller the Export Sales Manager. He said he wanted to help X; and asked if the interview was confidential. He was assured that it was.

Two months later, X Ltd. negotiated a settlement with the SFO – in return for an agreement that nothing would be done to interfere with its lucrative government contracts under the mandatory debarment rules.[11] It then released details of its interviews with Douggie Skuller and others who were charged under the Bribery Act. Do you believe Douggie received a fair trial?

Possibilities such as this confirm the folly of proxy investigations.

AGREED REPORT

An agreed report should be prepared at the end of the investigation. Companies should insist that the resulting evidence satisfies the full code test *for a bribery offence* before even thinking of negotiating a settlement. Finally, as Forrest Gump would say 'That's all I have to say about THAT!'

Adversarial Investigations

HOW THE REGULATORS FIND OUT

Very few cases, whether in the UK or the USA, have been detected by regulators, with the vast majority resulting from self-disclosures and then mainly connected to the Oil for

---

11   Which, as in the Siemens case, are a joke.

Food programme which was a sitting duck. This can be updated from the excellent website of Trace International's Compendium.[12]

INVESTIGATIONS BY OVERSEAS AGENCIES

It is possible, although unlikely,[13] that an overseas regulatory agency will be the first to detect alleged bribery. Most of these have neither the ability nor the intention to reach a 'civil disposal' and some are hopelessly corrupt. In such cases priority should be given to the personal safety of all involved (see page 347 to see what can happen with facilitation payments). A trend is appearing of lazy regulators in foreign jurisdiction monitoring the Statement of Facts in DPAs and using them for a local whammy. This is another reason why companies should consider self-disclosure very carefully.

INVESTIGATION PROCESSES

Overall flow

Adversarial investigations normally commence with a FIRST STEP initiated by regulators without notice, possibly as some form of dawn raid. Figure 36.1 depicts the usual investigation sequence.

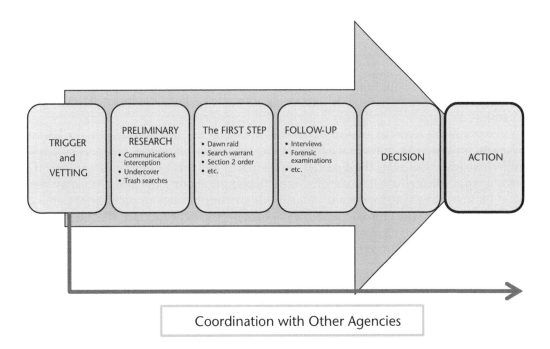

Figure 36.1 The Normal Flow of Adversarial Investigations

---

12   Available at: http://www.traceinternational.org/Knowledge/Compendium.html (accessed November 2012).

13   Except in the USA.

The first time a target becomes aware of regulatory interest is through a dramatic FIRST STEP such as a dawn raid, the service of a Section 2 order, a search warrant or an arrest. However, clues may appear before that, including:

- Preliminary Research and fact-finding by regulators:
  - Unexpected VAT or tax inspections;
  - Unusual calls by repairmen for telephone exchanges, computer servers, etc.;
  - Apparent burglaries and break-ins to offices, cars and homes;[14]
  - Unusual patterns of computer or voice-mail access;
  - Lost or stolen PCs;
  - Vehicle thefts and thefts from vehicles;
  - Removal of waste paper and trash (from offices and homes);
  - Lurking strangers around homes or offices;
  - Contrived anonymous letters and hot line reports (to test the company's reaction);
- Probing by an informant or turned employee or other inside witness:
  - Unusual downloads of computer data and email files;
  - Unusual amounts of photocopying, especially outside normal working hours.

Companies should not be paranoid about any of the above or worry that regulators might break the law, but unusual incidents should be considered possible advance notice of adversarial interest.

Reacting to the dawn raid

A dawn raid or any equivalent as a FIRST STEP is traumatic for everyone concerned, especially if there has been no contingency planning along the lines suggested in Chapters 25 and 34.

A dawn raid is likely to involve simultaneous raids at multiple locations in the UK and overseas, private and commercial addresses, freezing orders, Production Orders on banks, interviews with witnesses, third parties and suspects, and lots of other nasty things. It is possible that the media will learn of – or be tipped off about – the raid. This may seem good PR from the regulator's point of view, but any impropriety or prejudicial publicity may be a breach of the Official Secrets Act or damage the right to a fair trial. Either could lead to dismissal of all charges. Thus companies should not be alarmed over the presence of the media at the FIRST STEP, but rather view it as a potential 'silver bullet' to be used later.

Resistance to a pre-emptive strike is likely to be ineffective and generally, it is much better to accept the inevitable:

- A short suspension of operations should be requested to allow the company's lawyers to attend. In the meantime company representatives should not tip off other people or hide or destroy evidence;

---

14   More likely by the press or private investigators than the SFO.

- In the meantime the officials[15] should be politely asked to produce evidence of their identification and asked to explain their powers to search, seize and interview;
- If the raid is accompanied by the media,[16] photographs or video evidence should be collected, together with car registration numbers and other identifying details;
- Company representatives should not antagonise or argue with officials, nor should they make any comment or statement until legally advised to do so;
- If CCTV or audio recording equipment is available it should be activated (openly);
- Regulators and their associates should not be allowed free access to the company's premises, but should be accompanied at all times;[17]
- Obtain a detailed receipt for every document and other items seized.[18]

Legal representatives should examine the orders as well as any supporting evidence and if they are satisfied permit the search or other action to continue with the objective of having it completed as quickly and amicably as possible. All employees and others involved in the FIRST STEP should prepare confidential and privileged file notes covering everything they can remember about the raid and cataloguing any improper behaviour by regulators[19] or media on the basis that ultimately the defence may depend both on factual and rebuttal evidence and procedural transgressions.

Impact assessment

The company should try to establish whether the FIRST STEP is part of a pre-investigation, a fishing expedition, or a far more serious venture, and try to assess:

- The likely strengths and weaknesses of the prosecution case;
- Possible defensive strategies;
- All of the potential adverse consequences and especially any other alleged skulduggery that might emerge, especially if co-accuseds are likely to throw themselves on the mercy of regulators;
- The likely follow-up actions and timescales, including intervention by other regulators, possibly in other countries.

The board of directors – under specialist legal advice – should decide what position it intends to take over the investigation, whether conciliatory or disputatious. The latter option is normally the safest opening gambit, if for no other reason than it is consistent with innocence. Besides that, people accused of crimes have every right to put the prosecution to the most severe test both on facts and process. Prosecution should not be a one-sided fight.

---

15   As well as accompanying advisers.

16   As in the Tchenguiz case.

17   Except in the loo.

18   This may take hours, but DO NOT RELENT. GET A DETAILED RECEIPT.

19   More silver bullets.

In the nicest possible way, the company[20] should press for disclosure at every stage in the investigation and remain on the lookout for procedural mistakes, weaknesses in the prosecution case and technical defences that could be used later on.

Nominating representatives

If the action is evaluated as serious – and not just a bit of fly-fishing – the company should retain a top Queen's Counsel specialising in fraud. Regulators should be advised of his appointment. Consideration should also be given to appointing public relations advisers and a professional negotiator.

Negotiations

A common misconception is that a company's legal advisers are best qualified to negotiate with regulators, but experience shows this is seldom the case. It is better to nominate a team, which should include one or more senior litigation specialists but is always led by a senior commercial manager and, ideally, a professional negotiator.

The company should also nominate a senior, board-level manager (who is detached from the contexts being investigated) as the focal point for all communications with the regulators, normally through outside Counsel. Other managers and employees should be instructed to refer all official communications to him. The manager should delegate day-to-day control of documentation to a responsible, and preferably legally qualified, junior. A diary of all events relating to the investigation should be centrally maintained, including copies of all evidence delivered to and received from the regulators.

Follow-up investigations

Almost inevitably regulators will want to interview company employees and associated persons and obtain documentation and other evidence, possibly under a Section 2 order. Companies should comply but should not self-flagellate. Potential witnesses and defendants may be guided on how to respond, possibly involving a dry run with company lawyers and investigators, but with care to avoid accusations of perverting the course of justice. Some insightful notes at the end of this chapter on giving evidence may also be helpful (or they may not to readers who worry). Subjects required for interview should be accompanied by an experienced litigation lawyer (and not just some acned junior with scruffy shoes on high fees: pay for and expect the best).

There is nothing to stop a subject insisting on tape recording his interviews with regulators and this is recommended in complex cases or interviews under caution. In all

---

20 Normally through its lawyers.

cases a detailed record should be prepared of every interview, request for documents or any other potentially significant investigatory step.

Parallel investigations plan

Companies should not wait inactively for regulators to complete their deliberations but should launch a parallel investigation, so that at each stage it is as well as, or preferably better, informed than them. Regulators should be advised that a parallel investigation is taking place with a view to obtaining advice. The Investigations Plan should be along the lines suggested in Chapter 34, focusing on the factual case, defence and rebuttal evidence, procedural and other mistakes and on following up any points emerging from interviews with regulators. It should also involve forensic accountants to quantify alleged profits and losses and estimates of the likely scale of confiscation and recovery orders (see page 183).

The company should also consider its obligations to report to its auditors, insurers or any other regulatory agencies.

Final report

A final report covering all aspects of the parallel investigation should be prepared. It should be reviewed by Queen's Counsel with a written opinion on the likelihood that a prosecution would succeed, based on the facts and procedural abidance. This may be used to guide strategy along the lines indicated in Table 36.2.

Table 36.2 Options

Strength of Evidence	Against	
	Individuals	**Directing Minds Leading to Corporate Liability**
1 Overwhelming with little chance of acquittal **DEAD IN THE WATER**	Consider whether it is ethically correct and tactically advantageous to separate their interests ➔➔	Advise the individuals concerned and concentrate on the company's defence
	If not ➔➔	Wait for charges to be laid. Review and consider entering into negotiations covering all defendants, or entering a plea of guilty before the opening of the case in Court. This can result in discounted sentences equal to or better than a civil disposal

Strength of Evidence	Against	
	Individuals	**Directing Minds Leading to Corporate Liability**
2 Reasonable prospect of conviction *i.e. the case would pass the dual test* **A FIGHTING CHANCE**	Consider whether it is ethically correct and tactically advantageous to separate their interests ➔➔	Advise the individuals concerned and concentrate on the company's defence
	If not ➔➔	Wait for charges to be laid. Review and consider entering into negotiations covering all defendants or entering a plea of guilty before the opening of the case in Court. This can result in discounted sentences equal to or better than a civil disposal
3 Less than a reasonable prospect	Do nothing, but wait for the regulators to make the first move Show total confidence in allowing the case to go for trial	
4 Non-existent		

Obviously, the fact that advice falls into rows 1 or 2 should not only be treated in confidence but, on the contrary, should be compensated by a display of utter self-assurance. This is not always easy and is the justification for employing a professional negotiator.

Not a Hope

In a negotiation with an insurance company over a large contested fidelity claim a company's Risk Manager opened up with: 'I know we don't have a chance but ...'

No doubt regulators will have also obtained advice, but one thing potential defendants may have noticed is that their own legal advisers always seem more timorous than the opponent's. They also seem less intelligent and have unspiffy shoes. The irony is that opponents probably feel the same way. So even if the company's advice is that it is dead in the water or without a hope in hell, etc., which is gloomy stuff, it is unlikely that the regulators will be equally as confident. In any case, in all negotiations it is usually better to let opponents make the running and for a potential defendant not to appear anxious. This calls for more than a little chutzpah, a poker face, and powerful negotiating skills.

There are two likely outcomes from this position. The first is negotiating with a regulatory agency and the second is having to appear in court if negotiations fail. These are both very serious matters.

That's Nearly All Folks

Negotiating is an art form and not a legal or investigatory skill. Persuading regulators is little different from dealing with the Taliban or the mother-in-law on a bad beard day and companies should not delegate responsibility for what are essential financial negotiations[1] to a lawyer no matter how clever he or she is. Negotiation is a specialist skill and a very high level and independent professional should be seconded to a small team supported by a senior manager and a litigation specialist. Just to repeat: it is absolutely not recommended that negotiations be left to internal or external lawyers or, even worse, to any investigator.

Giving away too much detail here on strategies and tactics that have been successful in negotiating with regulators would be injudicious so: THAT'S ALL FOLKS! Except to say that plans should be made for appearing in court, which is a daunting prospect.

Attending Court and Giving Evidence

BACKGROUND

The day may come when you are called into court or before a tribunal to give evidence either as a witness or a defendant. Although this is a terrifying prospect, your ordeal can be made easier if you heed the following warnings. These are written in a very personal way simply because, when you most need them, everything will be extremely personal. The advice is written primarily for members of the male sex, because women are far too smart to get entangled with Courts unless they are solicitors, barristers or judges; in which case they can more than look after themselves and need no encouragement.

Giving evidence is a good example of the saying: 'what goes round comes round' and you just have to accept the reality when it is your turn in the barrel. If you have done your job professionally and honestly, the experience in court will be nauseating but tolerable. If you have been unprofessional, dishonest or unfair, this is the time when your backside is going to get severely tattooed and it serves you right. We trust you will not be in this position, but if you have any 'little problems' it is essential that you tell your legal advisers what they are before the case starts. This is the time to be really honest. But remember if you admit to your lawyers that you are guilty, they cannot normally argue

---

1   Negotiations on settlements and DPAs is – at the end of the day – mainly horse trading.

your innocence. They can leverage mitigating factors and technical mistakes, or even claim that you are mad or terminally ill but they still cannot say you are innocent when you have admitted you are guilty.

PREPARING THE CASE AND STATEMENTS

You should take the greatest possible care when drafting your statement, affidavit, proof of evidence, quantification or other schedules and should not get carried away with literary licence, enthusiasm or emotion in the heat of the moment. The words may look good and powerful when you write them, but when they are read out in court it is entirely a different matter and it is worse still when you are cross-examined. Remember that you may have to justify every single word and syllable – under hostile cross examination – so be factual and certain. If you have any doubts, tell your legal advisers and DO IT NOW! If you are a defendant you do not have to give evidence on your own behalf, but juries are not stupid and if you claim the Fifth Amendment they will usually assume the Sixth, which is that you are as guilty as hell and were unable to take the heat.

CHECK YOUR PAPERS

Always prepare for court carefully; know your statement, proof of evidence or affidavit, backwards forwards and inside out and the exhibits to which they refer. Understand every scribbled note, every entry and deletion on every exhibit and have a TRUTHFUL answer for it. Double check all schedules, calculations and the conclusions you have drawn and on which you might be required to comment during your evidence. If you believe that a source of information should be protected,[2] or if you have some other problem, tell your lawyers. You must also make sure that you tell your lawyers about every piece of evidence, intelligence or rumour, so that he or she can decide what has to be disclosed to the opposing side. If you do not make a full and proper disclosure, you could lose your case on this point alone.

Also, although you may discuss your evidence with your colleagues, to refresh your memory and avoid mistakes, you must not improperly influence them and not try to get them to say things they do not remember or do not know to be true. Similarly, you must not be improperly influenced by other witnesses, your partner, boss, lover, psychiatrist or even one of your mistresses. Just tell the truth and your chances of survival jump off the scale. Lie and you are in deep trouble.

Double check your notes and other records that you may be allowed to refer to in the witness box to refresh your memory; make sure you can read and understand them. Try to remember when you wrote them and do not lie that they were contemporaneous when they were written that morning on your way to court. Check with your lawyers precisely what papers you are allowed to take into the witness box but never take anything that is not needed or slightly dodgy, like *Playboy*, *Sadism Now!*, the *Racing Post* or the latest Women's' Institute magazine.

Anticipate that your notes and other papers will be taken from you while you are in the witness box and scrutinised by opposing Counsel and possibly by a forensic document examiner acting on his behalf. This makes it imperative that they do not

2   Such as your mistress or lover.

contain embarrassing things such as details of your Swiss bank accounts, or notes of your insider trading. Never back date documents or claim they were prepared earlier or later than they were: different inks or typefaces glow like Rudolph's nose and document examiners can date things precisely. Do not say you have never seen a document when you have, because fingerprinting will prove your lie. Look very carefully at the documents you may have to hand over for impressions made on them from other documents. ESDA examinations can retrieve the slightest indentations on documents written five or six sheets above those being questioned. Now if that is not worrying enough, worry a bit more, because forensic examiners can pick up DNA from just about any surface including those from a single touch or a transfer from one surface to another.

GET IT IN YOUR DIARY

Make sure you have multiple reminders – in your diary, Filofax, PDA or iPad and on the back of the fridge door – of the date and time you are required to attend court. If you forget to appear and instead scamper off to the lap dancing club with your local MP, or go to have your nails polished you will be in very serious trouble and may be punished for contempt of court. AND DO NOT BE LATE!!!

THINK ABOUT THE QUESTIONS

Think, if you were the opposing party, how YOU and your evidence might be attacked. Consider the questions you might be asked and discuss them with your colleagues and, if he or she is willing, with your lawyer, but never with your wife or mother in law, because they will go like Exocet missiles to the weak points which will unsettle you. If there are holes in your evidence, or if you have made mistakes, be prepared to admit them and apologise, if necessary. It is much better to make an open and remorseful admission than to have the truth painfully dragged out of you in cross examination. You may get your backside kicked but that is nothing compared to a perjury or contempt of court charge and once you start to fib or prevaricate you are at the top of a very slippery slope.

CHECK OUT THE COURT

Familiarise yourself with the court, how to get there and how long the journey takes even when you have to stop every ten minutes for anxious lavatorial breaks. If you have not given evidence before, sit in on another case[3] for a couple of hours before your big day. Watch and get the hang of things. It is pretty awesome; lawyers are very clever and courts are nasty places, to be avoided at all costs: if you can and you can't.

---

3   You cannot attend one in which you might be called as a witness and if you are a defendant you will not be able to avoid every painful moment.

ON THE DAY

Appearance

On the day you are required to give evidence or appear as a defendant, arrive at court really early and make sure you dress sensibly. Your wife or partner may tell you that you look amazing in your yellow waistcoat, pink braces, Gucci sunglasses and Hush Puppies, but it is doubtful that the court will appreciate their sartorial elegance. Wear loose clothing and comfortable shoes, just in case you have to make a dash for it. Also wear clothing that – unlike Tony Blair's – does not show excessive sweating and whatever you do, do not go to the Taj Mahal for a vindaloo the night before, get plastered or engage in tantric sex. Like fierce hunting dogs, lawyers smell fear and seeing signs of your terror or exhaustion will just make matters worse.

If you wear dentures, a glass eye or a hair piece, make sure they are firmly affixed. It will not help your credibility if in the heat of the moment an appendage becomes detached and the judge and jury (but, obviously, not the barristers) have to rummage around the floor of the court trying to find it.

If you are a member of the Surbiton Train Spotters' Club, or the Cheam Lady Gardeners' Magic Circle – no matter how proud you might be of such a rare distinction - do not wear the lapel badge, tie or cap. This is not impressive. All you will achieve is to mark yourself out as plonker and thus damage your credibility before you even open your mouth. If you must have facial hair, make sure you do not look like a member of the Taliban and if you have a pencil thin moustache, please shave it off. Only ballroom dancing instructors or car salesmen have these. Same if you have one of those silly beards that you have to sculpt every morning with the precision of a brain surgeon.

If you have tattoos try and cover them up. Obviously this is a bit tricky for the graphic of your gerbil which you had burned into your forehead on a boozy night out in Slough or a ring through your nose or tongue. But on arms, legs, boobs, and bums concealment of an idiotic past is strongly recommended. Finally, look at your shoes. Really astute observers[4] pay close attention to a man's shoes and if yours are woven crocodile and ostrich scrotum with pink tassels and high heels, everyone will know you are dodgy. Women's' shoes don't count in the same way, but ladies should think carefully about wearing twelve inch high Jimmy Choo stilettos for two reasons. The first is that they can set stuck in the pavement: making them late or unable to move in court. But more importantly, if a witness appears a lot taller than the lawyers they will immediately resent it, especially if they are vertically challenged as many are.

Waiting to be called

You can guarantee you will be kept waiting outside the court, possibly for hours if not days. Do not worry about this because it is all part of the softening up process. Do not read sensitive papers in public areas and be careful with your mobile telephone, Blackberry, iPad or laptop. Do not engage strangers in casual conversation because the delightful blond – who says her name is Flossie Flowfinger – sitting next to you in the waiting room,

---

4 Who have attended the authors' seminars.

who tells you she finds fat, old, grey haired men an aphrodisiac, could be a plant for the opposing side to get you into a compromising position. Believe it or not, this sometimes happens and what you tell her may be used against you when you are later impaled in the witness box. There is a similar rule for lady witnesses; the guy chatting you up in the waiting room is more likely to be a spy for the opposition than George Clooney[5] even if he does have a cup of Nespresso coffee in his hand.

So take care: do not discuss your evidence or the case, generally, with anyone else waiting around the court and especially with a witness who has not completed giving evidence and not been released. A little paranoia does no harm and waiting about makes matters worse. This is the time to have a nap, read this book or *The Guardian*.

While you are waiting you will see barristers, solicitors, and even ordinary homo sapiens and Neanderthals walking around, clutching papers and looking either very happy or very anxious, but note that they all walk very quickly, using short jerky steps giving the impression that their legs are stuck together at the knees. And they all have scruffy shoes.

Although lawyers are very clever, some do have human inclinations, but do not be misled by their emblems – such as wigs, gowns, or a battered face. Wigs are a historical relic meant to increase your anxiety, as is the layout of the court. If you do not believe how important venue and emblems are in increasing anxiety, you are about to find out. Courts are nasty places, full of testosterone and very aggressive men and women. They are best avoided: but you can't.

Entering the court with élan

You will have to wait outside the court – for hours if not days - until your name is called. When this happens your legs will buckle and your past flash before your eyes, so much so that you will wish you had heeded your mother's advice and, like your uncle Alf, become a butcher or followed your Auntie Nora into a convent: but it's too late.

Make sure you pick up all of your belongings – TURN OFF YOUR MOBILE TELEPHONE – and walk into court nice and slowly; do not panic but look around and – if your head will accept the command – upwards. Take your time and grab some deep breaths. Wait to be spoken to and do not start off with a cheery 'Good morning, judge. I like your wig' or with some flippant remark to the opposing party like 'Guilty bastard'. Neither will go down well.

Also if you are a Freemason, do not be tempted to give any secret gesticulation to members of the jury, the judge or anyone else. This will not be appreciated, especially if you outrank them. Stand still and wait until you are spoken to and take a few deep breaths, without overtly panting or gasping.

Giving your evidence in chief

You will be asked to give your name and take an Oath or to make some other form of incantation, depending on your beliefs. But this is not the time to get into a philosophical

---

5   So ladies, please wear your glasses.

debate about religion and it is best to accept the book given to you, even if it is a Rastafarian creed. Repeat the Oath very carefully and remember that first impressions count and that within seconds the judge, jury and counsel will have unconsciously categorised your emblems and formed an opinion of you. If you get off to a bad start, or anyone senses any weakness, your backside will get kicked even harder and more often: that's a promise. Never forget that animals only attack when they believe the prey is weaker than they are. You are now in the jungle and you are about to be marinated ready for lunch.

There is not much you can do about your name, but it does have an effect on the way you are perceived, especially by the jury, which is made up of ordinary folk – too gullible or too honest to avoid their noble duty. If your name is Peregrine Anstruther Tarquin Jocelyn Maltravers-Blythe, you might want to abbreviate it a bit. You may have noticed that in days gone by people with double barrelled names were all from the upper classes. Today commoners, and even football players, have them so maybe you want to say your name is Perry Blythe and leave the gory detail to the imagination

On the other hand if your name is Richard Head, you should avoid abbreviating your first name, even though your wife says she likes it a lot. If, 60 years ago, you served in the Catering Corps of the armed forces and reached a commissioned rank, do not say you are Major Jones or Field Brigadier Nonkins. Neither is the court interested that you were once a Boy Scout or even a Brownie.

Do not lie about your qualifications or experience. If you are an estate agent, try to find an alternative title such as property consultant or real estate specialist; juries like such words because they remind them of the National Health Service and that nice Mr Jones, the specialist consultant at Balham Hospital, who operated on their ingrowing toenail. Consultant is a great word, except to those who have to pay their fees.

Similarly do not append your academic qualifications to the end of your name, such as Dick Head, BA, MA PhD and five GCE O levels, including Scripture. Unquestionably, you and your mum are proud of your achievements, but most people won't give a hoot and will regard your claims to academic excellence as irrelevant trade puffing. This is especially so if they can't read or write as is the case with more than a few jurors.

In court, you must appear ordinary

In normal circumstances you should be led through your evidence by counsel representing your side, but do not be thrown if, as soon as you enter the witness box and have got your breath back, his opposite number jumps up and makes an objection. This is usually because his case is hopeless and his only chance is to argue some esoteric legal point to have your evidence excluded.

In criminal cases, the judge may ask the jury to leave while such fine legal objection is being considered. Do not worry and just stand there, look around the court, and answer any questions you are asked. This is the time for you to watch the lawyers closely and you will discover that many are more nervous than you. In fact the only person who is really cool is the judge.

If all goes well and under normal circumstances, you will then be asked questions by counsel representing your side. This is called your evidence in chief. Your counsel should be friendly, or superficially so, and he may even smile from time to time, nod his head and give you positive non-verbal feedback. Do not relax, because if things go wrong, he will drop you like a hot potato.

Remember, lawyers are very clever and you are only in their world because they get paid for beating you to a pulp. Even if they are friendly towards you and in the breaks call you by your first name, do not expect an invitation to join them for a night of fun at the Pink Pussycat Lap Dancing Club. Within minutes of the case ending they will not even recognise you, let alone speak to you. If a scapegoat has to be found, lawyers close ranks and will turn on you or some other poor mortal. It does not matter who the scapegoat is, how old, or how innocent; his only qualification is that he must not be a fellow barrister.

Direct all of your answers to the judge and try and establish eye contact with him and members of the jury from time to time, but do not glare or wink or look shifty. Keep your answers simple and truthful. Most honest witnesses genuinely want to assist the court and thus volunteer things they believe could be helpful. Do not do this or try to be clever and on no account make any comment that could remotely make any of the lawyers look foolish, because they are all excessively vengeful and never wrong. Just answer the questions you have been asked, preferably with a binary yes, sir, no, sir or no judge. If the judge is a lady (which is normally very good news) it is best to address her as 'judge' or 'Ma'am' and definitely not as 'Missus' or 'Luv'. Remember, lawyers do not necessarily want to hear the truth but they do expect their questions answered and to be shown unlimited respect.[6]

If – at any point – you are not certain of a fact, ask the judge if you can refresh your memory from your papers. Under no circumstances should you guess or try and crack a joke. Humour, especially, will backfire on you, although you must always laugh at the judge's jokes. Before you get into court you might want to rehearse laughing at stuff that is not funny as well as bursting into tears and practicing how to faint and fall to the floor gracefully, without hurting yourself.

Counsel for the other side may continue to jump up and down and make objections to your evidence. This is a good sign, unless he has a gerbil in his underpants or in his or her knickers in which case it means nothing. In the very unlikely event that opposing counsel has a spontaneous attack of humour, you may laugh, but it is much better to look puzzled or, better still, burst into tears. This should throw him off course. If it all comes on top, you might want to feint a heart attack or fit.

It is definitely to your advantage if you are a little deaf and can legitimately claim that you have not heard a question. Having a question repeated three or four times will give you time to think. But do not claim poor hearing only when nasty questions are being asked: this is a dead give-away. If you are going to feign being deaf, at least be consistent.

When you have finished your evidence in chief, wait in the witness box and whatever you do, do not look smug because the ambush is just around the corner. Never forget that lawyers are clever and the older they are the more clever they become.

Cross-examination

The big problem comes with cross-examination by the prosecution (if you are a defendant) or by opposing counsel, otherwise. If there are a lot of defendants, each one will have his own barrister, who will attack you and all will try to out-do his colleagues in terms of nastiness. If the opposing barrister appears to be female, take even more care. It is one of life's great truths that opposing lawyers always appear bigger, better, cleverer and more

---

6   But they won't show you any!

determined than yours, but do not worry. Revert to the neuro-linguistic picture of them without their clothes on.

Opposing counsel will ask you lots of dreadful questions, try to trip you up, catch you out and make you appear an incompetent idiot or much worse. Remember this is his job and he will be doing his best, but it's no worse than being grilled by your wife or mother-in-law when you forgot to buy the tomatoes you were asked to get from Asda. Just remain calm and do not take it personally and remember when you get home your dog will still love you. Tell the truth and if you have made a mistake admit it and, if necessary, apologise. Lawyers are not used to apologies and your candor will impress them if only for the microseconds before they kick your backside.

Do not argue the case or matters of law – you are not an advocate – appear impartial and concede points genuinely in favour of the opposing party whom, deep down, you know is a loathsome lowlife who pulls the legs off spiders and picks his nose. Just stick to the facts, remain emotionally detached and never look at the opponent because, if you do, he will have a face like thunder and this could unsettle you.

Occasionally, counsel will make mistakes and if this happens do not laugh because if you do he will get you later. Lawyers are very clever and have long memories. As ordinary folk we are in the firing line and if any human wants an easy life he should become a lawyer or politician or, if clever enough, a judge: now that is a really good job. True the judges' pay is not great but the perks, like unrestricted ability to kick ass and having your jokes laughed at all the time more than compensate.

Finally, remember that courts are the lawyers' hunting ground and that witnesses are their next meal. Lawyers always win, whatever the outcome. But every dog has its day and that's why this book has been just a little bit rude to them.

Witnesses are to lawyers what plankton is to whales

Re-examination

When the opposing barrister eventually sits down, you may be re-examined by counsel for your side. You can tell how badly you have been damaged in the cross-examination by the number of questions he asks and the way he avoids eye contact. If there are lots of questions, you can assume you have not been impressive. Do not worry: that's life, and lawyers are very clever.

Finally, you may be asked questions by the judge. These are the most important. Take care as judges are cleverer than anyone else and they have unlimited power to kick ass. Simply tell the truth.

Breaks in the case

You can almost guarantee that you will not complete your evidence in one session and will have to worry through a lunch, overnight or during some other adjournment. George Carman, QC – perhaps the leading advocate and cross-examiner of his generation – used to love this, if not contrive it. He used to say it will give the witness time to worry and he was right.

Do not speak to anyone during breaks in your evidence. Politely ignore and avoid eye contact with members of the jury and the defendant if you happen to bump into them in the pub, bingo hall, lapdancing club or Lodge. Just pretend you haven't seen them and get out of their space as quickly as you can. If you ask them questions or make any comment to them about the case, you could be in real trouble for contempt of court: so say nothing.

During longer breaks – however tempting it might appear – do not console yourself by a prolonged session in the pub. Keep off the juice overnight and arrive at court the next day nice, fresh and preferably celibate: imagine you are a Premier League footballer the night before a big match.[7] Tell your spouse you have a migraine and get a good night's sleep; if that's at all possible. Think about your evidence, the drift of the opposition's case and the questions you might be asked the following day. If you have made mistakes, tell your legal advisers and be prepared to admit them in the witness box.

Leaving the witness box

Do not attempt to leave the witness box until the judge says you can and before moving off, make sure you can still ambulate your legs. The Judge may or may not thank you, depending on how well you have performed. Pick up your stuff, look confident and walk slowly away, taking care not to fall over or faint. If it is possible, sit down at the back of the court and wait until the next adjournment.

Most witnesses rush from court immediately after completing their evidence and this is a big, big mistake because in kingdom Animalia – which is where you are – this is interpreted as a desertion of territory and a cowardly flight response. So hang around for a while and look cool. If you were a dog this is when you would pee against the jury box to claim your territorial rights: but avoid doing this because it could give a bad impression.

The opponent's evidence

At some stage evidence will be called for the other side, including witnesses, experts, other defendants and even the malodorous villain may be shameless enough to take the stand. Last time you saw him he was six foot nine tall, with muscles like Popeye, a dark Benidorm tan, a pencil thin moustache, and oozing with jewellery and fancy feet. In court he will present himself as a fragile old gentleman, possibly terminally ill, in whose mouth butter would never melt, so do not be taken by surprise. This is justice at work.

If you have the time, sit in court while opposing evidence is being given, but do not glare at the witnesses even though they may be telling dreadful lies and poking holes in your brilliant evidence. From time to time you can shake your head in disagreement, put your hand over your mouth, or affect a sickly smirk, but do not overdo the acting and do not let the judge catch you doing it. Just sit back and wait, because your counsel will be able to cross examine the opponents and this is where the fun _should_ start although it is usually the case that the opposing barrister seems much more effective than yours, who never asks the right questions and is far too wishy-washy. But that's life and he is

---

7   Not a good example!

probably being much more effective than you realise. Anyway, that's what he will tell his wife when he returns home to Battersea.

If you discover that any of the witnesses are telling lies, try to get a message to your counsel, but do not bob up and down like a kangaroo. Chances are, in any case, counsel will ignore you. Lawyers, like waiters in posh restaurants, are trained to be deaf and blind when it suits their purpose.

The summing up

Eventually, at the close of the case and submissions, the judge will sum up the evidence and this will reveal just how clever he really is. You may have thought he was an old buffer who was asleep for most of the time, but now you will discover he has a mind as sharp as a razor and the recall of an elephant. Keep your eye on the jury during the summing up but again do not nod, wink or make Masonic signs. Just watch, try and look really confident and nod when the judge makes a point in your favour and he may make some.

It always seems to be the case, whichever side you support, that the judge's summing up is against you. Do not worry because it is much like watching the England football team where the detail is far worse than the result.

The deliberations

When the judge has finished, he will send the members of the jury out to consider the evidence and the court will adjourn to wait for the result. This is a bad time for everyone, so just relax. Many jurors who have boring lives will see their noble calling as a chance to stay overnight in a fancy hotel, all expenses paid, while they deliberate. This is especially likely if one or more of the jurists has tantric desires involving one or more of his or her colleagues because it is a great excuse for a serious amount of rogering, at the state's expense. Do not worry about this: it is life and with any luck one-day you might serve on a jury and your turn will come.

After what will appear a lifetime's wait, the court will reconvene and the jury will shuffle in. It's strange, but jury members always look sheepish and have their heads down, especially after a boozy night's deliberating in a luxury hotel. When the verdict is announced, grip your seat really hard and do not leap in the air and shout, but just accept the verdict and remember you are a participant in British justice at its very best and it will make you proud that you pay our taxes.

If subsequently you happen to bump into a member of the jury, do not ask him anything about the case or the nights in the expensive hotel. Just acknowledge him and walk away because what happened in the jury room is secret: what happened in the hotel is even more secret, so do not even think about it.

Post-script

Chances are that at the end of it all, you will leave court, feeling drained and with acutely hurt feelings because unfair allegations have been made against you and the fact that the case did not go the way you *just know* it should have gone. Even when you have carried out your work honestly, professionally and to the best of your ability, you will still feel drained.

Exceptionally, you might get commended by the judge. Do not wallow in false pride because commendations are but temporary aberrations in the miserable lives of witnesses: especially investigators.

You might wonder whether the whole episode and especially the torment in court was worthwhile. The answer is overwhelmingly affirmative, because someone has to take a stand against skulduggers. Besides that if there were no witnesses, there would be no lawyers and then where would we be? It doesn't bear thinking about: innit?

Index

Page numbers in **bold** refer to figures and tables. BA in subheadings means Bribery Act.

For Product Safety Concerns and Information please contact our
EU representative GPSR@taylorandfrancis.com Taylor & Francis
Verlag GmbH, Kaufingerstraße 24, 80331 München, Germany